Johor

The **ISEAS – Yusof Ishak Institute** (formerly Institute of Southeast Asian Studies) was established as an autonomous organization in 1968. It is a regional centre dedicated to the study of socio-political, security and economic trends and developments in Southeast Asia and its wider geostrategic and economic environment. The Institute's research programmes are the Regional Economic Studies (RES, including ASEAN and APEC), Regional Strategic and Political Studies (RSPS), and Regional Social and Cultural Studies (RSCS). The Institute is also home to the ASEAN Studies Centre (ASC), the Singapore APEC Study Centre and the Temasek History Research Centre (THRC).

ISEAS Publishing, an established academic press, has issued more than 2,000 books and journals. It is the largest scholarly publisher of research about Southeast Asia from within the region. ISEAS Publishing works with many other academic and trade publishers and distributors to disseminate important research and analyses from and about Southeast Asia to the rest of the world.

The SIJORI Series

Johor

Abode of Development?

Edited By
Francis E. Hutchinson
&
Serina Rahman

ISEAS YUSOF ISHAK INSTITUTE

First published in Singapore in 2020 by
ISEAS Publishing
30 Heng Mui Keng Terrace
Singapore 119614
E-mail: publish@iseas.edu.sg
Website: <http://bookshop.iseas.edu.sg>

ISEAS Library Cataloguing-in-Publication Data

Names: Hutchinson, Francis E., editor. | Serina Rahman, editor.
Title: Johor : Abode of Development? / editors: Francis E. Hutchinson and Serina Rahman.
Description: Singapore : ISEAS – Yusof Ishak Institute, 2020. | Volume 2 of a trilogy on 'Floating frontiers'. | Includes bibliographical references.
Identifiers: ISBN 9789814881272 (paperback) | ISBN 9789814881289 (pdf)
Subjects: LCSH: Economic development—Malaysia—Johor. | Johor—Malaysia—Politics and government. | Johor—Malaysia—Social conditions.
Classification: LCC HC445.5 Z7J61

Typeset by Superskill Graphics Pte Ltd

CONTENTS

LIST OF MAPS

LIST OF TABLES AND APPENDIXES

LIST OF FIGURES

FOREWORD

In 2016, when ISEAS published the book, *The SIJORI Cross-Border Region: Transnational Politics, Economics, and Culture,* co-edited by Francis Hutchinson and Terence Chong, Malaysia was on the cusp of major political change. The ruling Barisan Nasional (BN) coalition secured a parliamentary majority in the 2013 general election, but lost the popular vote. This book, the second in a series of three, began in 2016 and took three years to complete, by which time the Pakatan Harapan (PH) coalition had ousted the incumbent to become the ruling party. Johor, Peninsular Malaysia's southernmost state, also fell to PH, which secured thirty-six out of fifty-six seats in the state parliament.

Johor enjoys a central place in the SIJORI region. Over the last two decades, it has seen significant political and economic developments. Its economic and social interactions with Singapore and proximity to the Riau Islands have contributed to its stellar growth. The state's population grew from 2.7 million in 1990 to 3.7 million in 2017. These factors facilitated Johor's industrialization drive as well as economic diversification, and altered its politics, society and environment. The establishment of Iskandar Malaysia in 2006 further accelerated these developments.

Today, the close economic and people-to-people relations between Johor and Singapore continue to flourish. Both are connected to each other by cross-border networks in sectors such as electrical and electronics, oil and gas, logistics, as well as agriculture. In Iskandar Malaysia, health and education services are new elements of this co-operation. In the near future, the proposed rapid transit system to link Johor and Singapore will further enhance interactions between them. The growing importance of their interactions saw Singapore establishing a consulate in Johor in November 2009.

Francis Hutchinson and Serina Rahman, the co-editors of this book, have assembled a team of twenty collaborators. Their collective work will contribute to a better understanding of the key transformations that have taken place in Johor since its embrace of export-oriented industrialization in 1990, and the different influences to which the state has been exposed as a result of its position within the Malaysian Federation and the SIJORI Cross-Border Region.

Tan Chin Tiong
Senior Advisor, ISEAS – Yusof Ishak Institute

ACKNOWLEDGEMENTS

The idea for this project came from the Deputy Director of ISEAS – Yusof Ishak Institute in 2013, Ooi Kee Beng, who put forward the idea of studying Southeast Asia's "Floating Frontiers". Focusing on border regions between Indonesia, Malaysia, the Philippines, and Singapore, the emphasis was, rather than on land borders, to be on connections between countries across the sea. Seen from a historical perspective, this is consistent with Southeast Asia's precolonial maritime focus, which was characterized by intense linkages. Consequently, the three sites of this project were: the Singapore and Johor Straits; the Sulawesi Sea; and the Andaman Sea.

This led to the work on the first volume of this trilogy, *the SIJORI Cross-Border Region: Transnational Politics, Economics, and Culture*, which looked at the interaction between Singapore, the Malaysian state of Johor, and the Riau Islands in Indonesia. Following the publication of this volume, the then Director of the ISEAS – Yusof Ishak Institute, Mr Tan suggested building on this work with two stand-alone projects on Johor and the Riau Islands.

As with the first volume, we have collaborated with the ETH Zurich to cartographically depict important interactions. In-depth conceptual and empirical discussions with Hans Hortig and Karoline Kostka were extremely fruitful and their work on the collection of maps has provided a valuable complement to much of the conceptual work contained in this volume.

Heartfelt thanks go to Benjamin Hu and Pearlyn Pang for developing the maps used and referred to in the various chapters. Ng Kok Kiong and Rahilah Yusuf of the Publications Unit helped finalize and publish this volume in record time. We are also grateful to the Royal Geographical Society for letting us include Harry Lake's 1893 map of Johor which was published in the 1894 volume of the *Geographical Journal*.

This project was supported by the ISEAS – Yusof Ishak Institute, under the support of then Director Tan Chin Tiong and now under Mr Choi Shing Kwok. We would like to convey our appreciation to them. We also thank Ooi Kee Beng for developing the Floating Frontiers concept.

We would also like to express our gratitude to the contributors to this volume for their extensive work on their chapters.

Francis E. Hutchinson and Serina Rahman

PROLOGUE

This book has been three eventful years in the making. As we began to gather the stories, data and information that make up the pages of this publication, Malaysia was still under Barisan Nasional (BN) rule and under the leadership of Najib Razak. As our chapters began to take shape, the 14th General Elections captured everyone's attention, and some research findings were released to the public to share our perspectives. Then, the unthinkable at the time happened—BN was voted out and Pakatan Harapan (PH) took over the reins in Putrajaya, with Mahathir Mohamad once again Prime Minister at the age of ninety-two.

As Malaysia's people and myriad observers ran the gamut of emotions, expectations and critical reflection, we worked to amend our content to meet the changes of the day. Where possible, the writers tweaked content to include the unprecedented changes that were afoot and include projections of where the new regime might take the nation. The book was then sent to publication in 2019.

Just as the manuscript was going through the necessary processes of copyediting, proofreading and typesetting, however, political commotion erupted once again in Malaysia's halls of power. In what still remains a somewhat confusing turn of events, an attempted coup took place, Mahathir Mohamad resigned as Prime Minister, his own party, Parti Pribumi Bersatu Malaysia (PPBM or BERSATU) split into two, and the faction led by Muhyiddin Yassin pulled out of the PH coalition. The country was effectively without a government for eight days as various individuals sought an audience with the King for approval to regain or retain power. On 1 March 2020, Muhyiddin Yassin was sworn in as Malaysia's 8th Prime Minister, leading a loose coalition of previously ousted parties under the banner of Perikatan Nasional.

Following this, the COVID-19 pandemic effectively ground the world to a halt. At the time of writing this prologue, Malaysian borders are closed, barring selected export of goods to Singapore and highly controlled returns of Malaysians working, studying or living overseas. The nation is on its 64th day of various permutations and phases of Movement Control Orders (MCO), and many in Singapore (where this book is being published) are also working from home.

Even as Malaysia's political story continues to unfold and the world comes to grips with a "new norm", the content of this book remains relevant. Nothing that happens in Malaysia today can be properly understood without its context, and this publication seeks to provide that. From an understanding of the evolution of myriad political parties and royal involvement in politics and society, to more functional developments in economy and business, this book continues to provide unique insight into how Johor ticks—and beyond that, how it may then relate to its immediate neighbours.

While the new government seems to be more of BN and a little bit of PH, and there is a possibility of more political turbulence to come at the highest echelons of power, for the most part, the civil service and the nation continue to run, albeit within the constraints of COVID-19 restrictions. Even as there is turmoil (or fanfare) at the surface, long-term structural issues remain. This book becomes all the more relevant now as a comparative tome with which to benchmark and trace developments as they come. It has taken a while to come to fruition, but we hope that its content is worth the wait.

Francis E. Hutchinson and Serina Rahman

CONTRIBUTORS

Nicholas Chan is a PhD student with the Department of Politics and International Studies, University of Cambridge. His research interests include religion and politics, governance, and Southeast Asian state and society. He has published with the journal *Critical Studies on Terrorism* and has written for portals such as *New Mandala* and *Middle East Institute*.

Jeamme Chia is studying for a Master of Environmental Management degree at the Yale University School of Forestry and Environmental Studies. Her previous work was on the intersection of political economy, geography, and development, including research on electoral outcomes in rural FELDA settlements and mobility access, and using geo-spatial and political economic techniques to analyse rural agribusiness sectors in Southeast Asia. She is interested in the impacts of climate change and geography on tropical natural resources, specifically water, food, and agricultural systems in developing countries.

Goh Hong Ching is a senior lecturer at the Department of Urban and Regional Planning, Faculty of Built Environment, Universiti Malaya. She holds a doctoral degree in Geography from Bonn University, a Bachelor's degree in urban and regional planning and a MSc degree in tourism planning from Universiti Teknologi Malaysia. She is a corporate member of the Malaysia Institute of Planners and a member of the Global Young Academy. Her research interests include tourism governance, natural resource governance, planning and impact management, sustainable development of cities and urbanization.

Hans Hortig studied landscape architecture at the Technical University Berlin, the ETH Zurich and the School of Design, Mysore. In 2013, he joined the Architecture of Territory project under Professor Topalovic at the Future Cities Laboratory, Singapore and at the ETH Zurich where he taught design and research studios, organized lecture series and guided numerous student works. Since 2015, he has been running the cartographic studio *maps&more* with Karoline Kostka and recently started his PhD research on processes of extended urbanization in Southeast Asian palm oil plantation landscapes.

Francis E. Hutchinson is a Senior Fellow and Coordinator of the Malaysia Studies at the ISEAS – Yusof Ishak Institute and the Managing Editor of the *Journal of Southeast Asian Economies*. His research interests include: local economic development, industrialization, innovation, federalism and decentralization. He is the author of *Mirror Images in Different Frames? Johor, the Riau Islands, and Competition for Investment from Singapore* (ISEAS, 2015); and co-editor of the *SIJORI Cross-Border Region: Transnational Politics, Economics, and Culture* (ISEAS, 2016).

Khor Yu Leng is Research Head at Khor Reports – Segi Enam Advisors Pte Ltd. She is an Oxford University and LSE-trained political economist. Ms Khor is a consultant with a Southeast Asian focus on transport, commodities and regional development economics; combining big data, geospatial and social media analytics plus deep-dive market intelligence. Her commentaries are featured in regional and international media outlets, including *Bloomberg*, *Channel NewsAsia* and the *South China Morning Post*.

Karoline Kostka studied landscape planning and architecture at TU Berlin, the ETH Zurich and the School of Design, Mysore and graduated in 2013 in Landscape Architecture and Open Space Planning. From 2013 to 2015, Karoline worked as a researcher at the ETH Future Cities Laboratory in Singapore. Currently, she teaches design and research studios at the ETH Zurich, Architecture and Territorial Planning with Professor Topalovic. Since 2015, she has been running the cartographic studio *maps&more* with Hans Hortig. Their work has been published and exhibited in Villa Renata Basel (2017), Landesmuseum Zurich (2019) and Kunstmuseum Luzern (2019).

Lee Hock Guan is a former Senior Fellow with the Regional Social and Cultural Studies Programme at the ISEAS – Yusof Ishak Institute, Singapore.

Lim Chee Han is a scientifically trained policy researcher and holds a PhD in Infection Biology from Hannover Medical School, Germany, a Master's degree in Immunology and a Bachelor's degree in Biotechnology from Imperial College London. Chee Han has diverse interests in socio-political issues, including health economics, public health, sustainable development and social equality. Formerly a Senior Analyst at the Penang Institute in Malaysia, in 2018 he co-founded the NGO Agora Society, which aims to strengthen participatory democracy, defend human rights, and promote good governance.

Guanie Lim is Research Fellow at the Nanyang Centre for Public Administration, Nanyang Technological University, Singapore. His main research interests are public policy, value chain analysis, and the Belt and Road Initiative in Southeast Asia.

Guanie is also interested in broader political economic issues within Asia, especially those of China, Vietnam, and Malaysia. He is currently working on his monograph, which details the development of key Southeast Asian economies.

Vandana Prakash Nair is a former Research Officer with the Regional Strategic and Political Studies (RSPS) Programme at the ISEAS – Yusof Ishak Institute, Singapore. She holds a Master's degree from the John Hopkins School of Advanced International Studies and a Bachelor of Arts degree from George Washington University. She is currently with the Geneva-based International Trade Centre. Her research interests are primarily in international political economy; trade and development; and Southeast Asian politics and history.

Keng Khoon Ng is a lecturer and research associate at the department of Architecture, UCSI University Kuala Lumpur. He has an interdisciplinary PhD in architecture and urban studies from the Department of Architecture, School of Design and Environment, National University of Singapore. He has a Bachelor's degree in Architecture from Universiti Teknologi Malaysia, and a Master's degree from Oxford Brookes University specializing in architectural redevelopment and urban regeneration. Keng Khoon's research interests focus on architecture, urban planning and critical urban studies in Southeast Asian cities.

Meghann Ormond is Associate Professor in Cultural Geography at Wageningen University in the Netherlands. Her research offers insight into how shifting visions and practices of citizenship and belonging transform travel, health and social care practices. She is the author of *Neoliberal Governance and International Medical Travel in Malaysia* (Routledge, 2013) and more than thirty-five articles and chapters on transnational mobility, health and care.

Geoffrey K. Pakiam is Fellow at the ISEAS – Yusof Ishak Institute, Singapore. In April 2018, he received his PhD in History from SOAS, University of London. His most recent publication was the Malaysia country overview chapter for the 2019 edition of *Southeast Asian Affairs*. His research draws on histories of commodities, migration, environment, food, farming, and health, with special attention to the Malay Peninsula. Amongst other things, he is working on his first monograph, a history of smallholder farming and environmental change in Johor, one of the world's leading agricultural frontiers since the nineteenth century.

Serina Rahman studies rural and coastal community attitudes and behaviour with regards to politics, natural habitat use and urbanization. A Visiting Fellow at the ISEAS – Yusof Ishak Institute, Singapore, her practice is in community empowerment for marine ecosystem preservation. Serina obtained her PhD in Science from Universiti Teknologi MARA, in collaboration with the Faculty of Education at Universiti Malaya. She has a Master in Applied Linguistics degree from the University of Wales, Cardiff. Serina is Malaysia's Citizen Science Ambassador for Citizen Science Asia and an Iskandar Malaysia Social Hero Award Winner for Environmental Protection (2014).

Javier Revilla Diez holds a Professorial Chair in Human Geography at the Institute of Geography and is associated with the Global South Study Center at the University of Cologne. He has research interests in the regional outcomes of participating in global production networks, regional impacts of transformation processes induced by political and structural change, and impacts of natural risks on people, firms, and regions. He has published in *World Development, Regional Studies, Environment and Planning A, International Regional Science Review,* and *Papers in Regional Science,* among others.

Norshahril Saat is Senior Fellow at the ISEAS – Yusof Ishak Institute, Singapore. In 2018, he published *The State, Ulama, and Islam in Malaysia and Indonesia* (Amsterdam University Press), *Tradition and Islamic Learning: Singapore Students in the Al-Azhar University* (ISEAS), and edited *Islam in Southeast Asia: Negotiating Modernity* (ISEAS). Norshahril's articles have recently been published in journals such as *Asian Journal of Social Science, Contemporary Islam: Dynamics of Muslim Life, Review of Indonesian and Malaysian Affairs,* and *Studia Islamika.*

Chang-Da Wan is the Deputy Director and a senior lecturer at the National Higher Education Research Institute, Universiti Sains Malaysia. He earned his doctorate from the University of Oxford in the field of higher education and was trained as an economist at the University of Malaya and National University of Singapore. His main research interest is higher education policy, specifically in Malaysia, Southeast Asia and other developing systems and regions. Chang-Da is also an EXCO of the Malaysian Society for Higher Education Policy and Research Development (PenDaPaT).

Wan Saiful Wan Jan is Visiting Senior Fellow at the ISEAS – Yusof Ishak Institute, Singapore. Prior to that, he was Chief Executive Officer at the Institute for Democracy and Economic Affairs (IDEAS), Malaysia. He contested in Malaysia's 14th General Elections for the parliamentary constituency of Pendang, Kedah, but did not win. Subsequently, he was appointed as Special Adviser to the Malaysian Minister of Education, Chairman of the National Higher Education Fund Corporation, and Board Member of the Tunku Abdul Rahman Foundation. He is also a member of Parti Pribumi Bersatu Malaysia's Supreme Council.

Benedict Weerasena is an economist attached to Bait Al-Amanah (House of Trust), a Malaysian political think-tank, where he analyses economic development policies. Benedict previously worked with the National Higher Education Research Institute (IPPTN), researching on university autonomy and shadow education. His research interests include development economics, public finance, behavioural economics, international political economy and education policy. Benedict is a recipient of the Conference of Rulers' Royal Education Award Malaysia.

ABBREVIATIONS

AKIM	Angkatan Keadilan Insan Malaysia
ARA	Amsterdam-Rotterdam-Antwerp
BN	Barisan Nasional
BOR	Bed Occupancy Rate
cbm	cubic metre
CBR	Cross-Border Region
CDP	Comprehensive Development Programme
CGPV	Country Garden Pacificview Sdn Bhd
CIQ	Customs, Immigration and Quarantine
CNY	Chinese yuan
CSR	Corporate Social Responsibility
DAP	Democratic Action Party
DEIA	Department of Environment Impact Assessment
DHPP	Dewan Himpunan Penyokong PAS
DOE	Department of Environment
E&E	Electrical and Electronics
EDB	Economic Development Bureau
EIA	Environmental Impact Assessment
EISB	EduCity Iskandar Sdn Bhd
EPF	Employees Provident Fund
EPP	Entry Point Project
EPU	Economic Planning Unit
ETP	Economic Transformation Program
FCL	Future Cities Laboratory
FDI	foreign direct investment
FELDA	Federal Land Development Authority
FIREBS	Finance, Insurance, Real Estate and Business Services
FPTP	first-past-the-post
FW	foreign workers
GDP	gross domestic product

GE-12	Malaysian 12th General Elections
GE-13	Malaysian 13th General Elections
GE-14	Malaysian 14th General Elections
GLC	government-linked corporations
GNP	gross national product
GRDP	gross regional domestic product
HMI	Health Management International
HSR	High Speed Rail
ICT	Information Communication Technology
IHH	IHH Healthcare Bhd
IIB	Iskandar Investment Bhd
IIBD	Ibrahim International Business District
IJN	Institut Jantung Negara; National Heart Institute
IM	Iskandar Malaysia
IMP	Independence of Malaya Party
IRDA	Iskandar Regional Development Authority
ITA	Investment Tax Allowance
IWC	Integrated Wellness Capital
IWCB	Iskandar Waterfront City Berhad
JB	Johor Bahru
JCI	Joint Commission International
JPDC	Johor Petroleum Development Corporation
JPO	Johor Premier Outlet
KIM	Kawan Iskandar Malaysia
KNB	Khazanah Nasional Bhd
KPJ	Kumpulan Perubatan Johor Sdn Bhd
KPRJ	Kumpulan Prasarana Rakyat Johor
LNG	liquid nitrogen gas
LOHAS	Lifestyles of Health and Sustainability
MARA	Majlis Amanah Rakyat
MCA	Malaysian Chinese Association
MDIS	Kolej MDIS Malaysia
MFA	Ministry of Foreign Affairs
MHLG	Ministry of Housing and Local Government
MHTC	Malaysia Healthcare Travel Council
MIC	Malaysian Indian Congress
MICE	Meetings, Incentives, Conferences and Events
MIDA	Malaysian Industrial Development Authority
MIM	Medini Iskandar Malaysia Sdn Bhd
MM2H	Malaysia My Second Home
MMHE	Malaysia Marine and Heavy Engineering
MMU	Multimedia University
MNC	Multinational Corporation
MNE	Multinational Enterprises

MOTAC	Ministry of Tourism and Culture
MP	Member of Parliament
MRT	Mass Rapid Transit
MSQH	Malaysia Society for Quality in Healthcare
NEP	National Ecotourism Plan
NEP	New Economic Policy
NGO	non-governmental organization
NHP	National Housing Policy
NKEA	National Key Economic Areas
NMIT	Netherlands Maritime Institute of Technology
NPP	National Physical Plan
NSC	Nalanda-Sriwijaya Centre
NTU	Nanyang Technological University
NUMed	Newcastle University Medicine
NUS	National University of Singapore
O&G	oil and gas
PAHFSB	Private Aged Healthcare Facilities and Services Bill
PAS	Parti Islam Se-Malaysia
PasMA	Persatuan Ummah Sejahtera Malaysia
PDT	Pengerang Deepwater Terminal
PH	Pakatan Harapan
PHFSA	Private Healthcare Facilities and Services Act
PIC	Productivity and Innovation Credit Scheme
PIDP	Pengerang Integrated Development Programme
PIPC	Pengerang Integrated Petroleum Complex
PIV	Pulau Indah Ventures
PKR	Parti Keadilan Rakyat
PLKS	Pas Lawatan Kerja Sementara
PMED	Penang Centre of Medical Tourism
PMIP	Pengerang Maritime Industrial Park
PMO	Prime Minister's Office
PPBM	Parti Pribumi Bersatu Malaysia
PR	Pakatan Rakyat
PR1MA	Perumahan Rakyat 1 Malaysia Act
PTPTN	National Higher Education Fund Corporation
R&D	Research and Development
RAPID	Refinery and Petrochemical Integrated Development
REHDA	Real Estate and Housing Developers' Association Malaysia
RM	Malaysian ringgit
RMMJ	Rumah Mampu Milik Johor
ROI	Return On Investment
RSH	Regency Specialist Hospital
RTS	Rapid Transit System
RUI	Raffles University Iskandar

SEZ	Special Economic Zone
SIJORI	Singapore-Johor-Riau Islands
SKM	Skills Certificate
SLA	State Legislative Assembly
SME	Small and Medium Enterprise
TCM	Traditional Chinese Medicine
ULCC	Ultra Large Crude Carriers
UM	University of Malaysia
UMNO	United Malays National Organization
UMS	Unfederated Malay States
UORM	University of Reading Malaysia
UPEN	Unit Perancang Ekonomi Negeri
US$	United States dollar
USMC	University of Southampton Malaysia Campus
UTM	Universiti Teknologi Malaysia
VLCC	Very Large Crude Carriers
WWF	World Wildlife Fund for Nature

Introduction

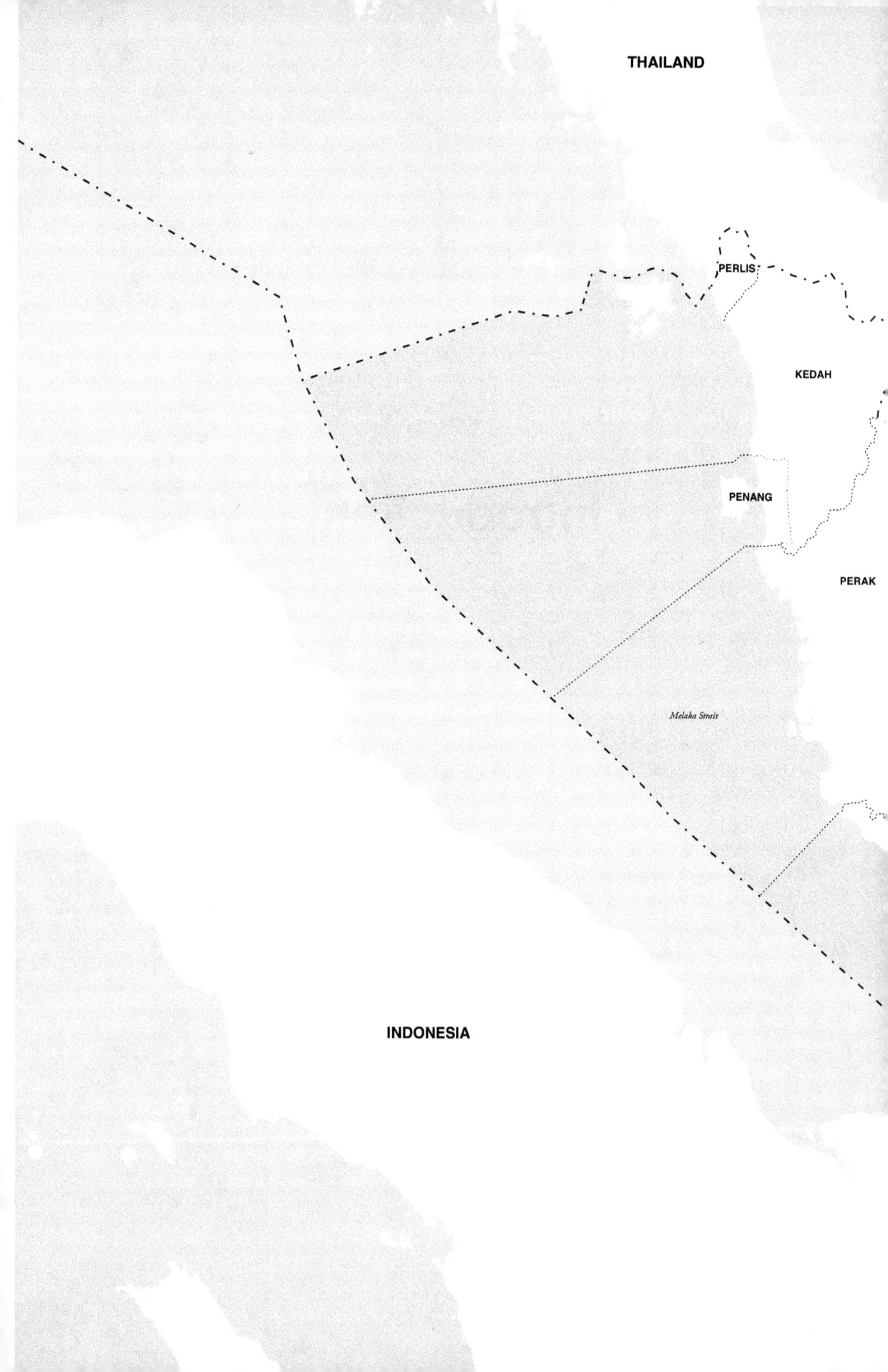

THAILAND

PERLIS

KEDAH

PENANG

PERAK

Melaka Strait

INDONESIA

MAP 1.1
MALAYSIA AND JOHOR

—·—·— National Border
·········· State Border
Pu Administrative Capital

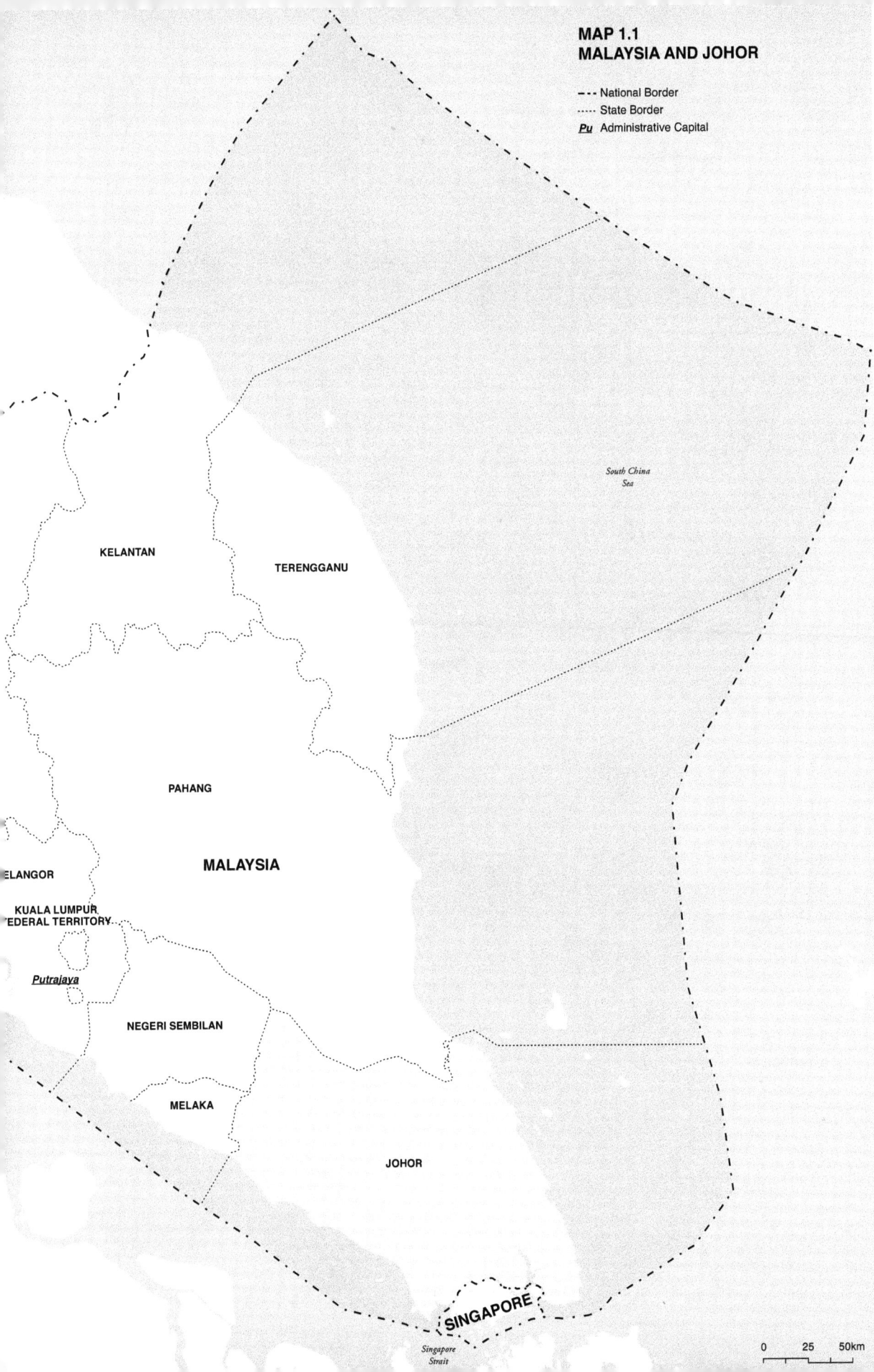

*South China
Sea*

KELANTAN

TERENGGANU

PAHANG

MALAYSIA

ELANGOR

KUALA LUMPUR
EDERAL TERRITORY

Putrajaya

NEGERI SEMBILAN

MELAKA

JOHOR

SINGAPORE

*Singapore
Strait*

0   25   50km

1

SITUATING JOHOR

Francis E. Hutchinson

INTRODUCTION

In the southwestern corner of Johor, Malaysia's southernmost state—a new administrative capital has shot up. Nestled amid African oil palms and pockets of red earth where the trees have been peeled away, lies Kota Iskandar. Comprising the state parliament, the offices of the Chief Minister, as well as state and federal government agencies, these buildings bring together elements of Moorish-Andalusian and traditional Malay architecture. Close by and connected via large, but rather empty, boulevards are facilities—many partly owned by Malaysia's sovereign wealth fund Khazanah—such as private hospital complexes, high-tech industrial parks, and university campuses, all expectantly open for business.

A little further south, four islands are being reclaimed in the Johor Strait, the body of water which separates Peninsular Malaysia from Singapore. Backed by a large private Chinese real estate developer and the Sultan of Johor, the Forest City project is slated to house high-end apartments and a hotel, as well as a private hospital and international school catering to an estimated 700,000 residents. The marketing centre on the first completed island receives busloads of prospective buyers from China that are attended to by Mandarin-speaking sales staff. Barges carrying sand and gravel for the reclamation work constantly ply the Strait—encroaching on traditional fishing grounds and disrupting the livelihoods of nearby coastal communities.

Further east along Johor's coastline lies Johor Bahru, the state's economic capital, which is being extensively remodelled. Led by the state government, the revitalization encompasses restoring the historic centre, uncovering and beautifying a formerly submerged river, and building ambitious mixed-use developments. Work is also underway to connect down-town Johor Bahru to Singapore via a rapid transit system, in order to ease the daily commute of the estimated 300,000 people crossing to the city-state to work. When completed, Johor Bahru's urban core will be transformed, sparking interest in potential opportunities as well as unease about rising costs among residents.

Even further along Johor's coast towards the South China Sea, a 20,000 acre project, the Pengerang Integrated Petroleum Complex (PIPC), is being developed. Led by Malaysia's state-owned oil giant, Petronas, this sprawling compound will house an oil refinery, petrochemical plants, liquefied natural gas import and regasification facilities, as well as a deep-water port. Substantial stretches of coastline were cleared and five villages relocated to make this possible. The incoming labour force for the project has increased demand for local services in the area but also driven up rental prices.

THE FRUITS OF ECONOMIC DEVELOPMENT

Johor is, clearly, undergoing deep and far-reaching change. Much of this is economic, as the state has enjoyed solid and consistent growth in recent decades. In 1990, per capita income stood at US$3,740 and had reached US$5,080 in constant dollars by 2012 (Toh and Bo 2016).[1] Recent estimates have Johor's GDP per capita at US$8,590 in current terms, double the upper-middle-income threshold of US$3,956, as defined by the World Bank.[2]

This expansion has been driven by a far-reaching structural transformation. In 1990, agriculture, industry, and services accounted for 29, 32, and 39 per cent of Johor's GDP, respectively. Following a decline in commodity prices, the state embarked on an ambitious industrialization drive. By 2005, agriculture constituted a mere 13 per cent of GDP, with industry generating 43 per cent and services 39 per cent, respectively (Toh and Bo 2016).

This, however, marked the industrial sector's apex as, after this, Johor's economy gravitated towards services. In 2012, while agriculture continued to account for 13 per cent of GDP, industry had fallen to 38 per cent and the service sector accounted for almost half of the state's economy. Looking forward, Johor's income level is projected to reach US$10,000 per inhabitant by 2030 and the structural transformation process is expected to continue, with industry generating roughly a quarter of GDP and services more than 60 per cent in that year (Toh and Bo 2016).

While economies transition towards services as they grow and mature, this process nonetheless causes disruption as established sectors, many in traditional areas of manufacturing, fade away and displace thousands of workers. Furthermore, while new sectors do emerge, not all will survive. In addition, many of these activities will generate only a few jobs, and a substantial proportion will not map onto locally available skill-sets.

The forces of creation and destruction can be seen at work in Johor. In the 1990s, the state established its reputation as a manufacturing hub for the electrical and electronics sector. However, over the last fifteen years, the sector's capabilities have stagnated, with little locally based innovative capabilities, limited automation and upgrading, and almost no autonomy within the affiliates of multinational corporations located there. This, in turn, has generated frustration among policymakers, who are seeking to deepen capabilities and catalyse higher value-added activities in the local economy (van Grunsven and Hutchinson 2016).

At present, the state's sunrise industrial sector is oil and gas, with multibillion dollar investments from Petronas, a government-linked corporation, as well as a range of supporting companies in PIPC. And, even more than the industrial sector, attention is focused on services, particularly areas such as tourism, education, and health. Despite their relative newness, these activities have been able to capitalize on Johor's factor endowments and geographic location. These fledgling sectors have been supported by Khazanah through strategic investments and provision of specialized infrastructure, both for their potential to diversify the state's economic base as well as generate skill-intensive jobs.

Yet, there have also been constants in this process. In spite of an initial dip in the 1990s, agriculture continues to generate a substantial proportion of Johor's GDP. However, the sector is evolving as it shifts away from labour-intensive to more sophisticated and large-scale production. The nature of what is farmed is also changing and becoming more specialized, implying disruption for smaller and more traditionally focused producers.

Much of this transition is driven by long-term policies regarding trade, human resources, and innovation. However, these processes can also be shaped by shorter-term measures such as modifying incentives and making strategic investments in new areas. In this sense, the Johor state government, the Malaysian federal government, and their government-linked corporations are influential players in the local context.

Beyond opportunities and costs, rapid and sustained economic growth also generates other changes. As argued by Huntington in his seminal *Political Order in Changing Societies*, societies do not simultaneously evolve economically, politically, and socially. Rather, these aspects can, and do, develop at different speeds and according to distinct logics. Indeed, rapid changes in one facet of a society can generate disruption in others. For example, high rates of economic growth can generate political and social turmoil, as traditional relationships and institutions are undercut. Conversely, dysfunctional political or social institutions can impede or retard economic growth.

Echoing Huntington, Johor's political structures are in flux. In May 2018, the erstwhile ruling coalition, Barisan Nasional (BN), was roundly defeated nationally as well as in the state. The former ruling coalition had been in power at both levels since 1955, when the first elections were held under the aegis of the British.[3] Over the ensuing five decades, BN secured crushing majorities at the parliamentary and state levels in Johor.

Yet, in the 2008 general election, this political compact began to come undone, as opposition candidates began to make inroads, first in urban and then semi-urban areas. This process deepened in 2013, when the opposition coalition won the popular vote but could not secure a parliamentary majority. In 2018, BN was routed, as the reformulated opposition grouping, Pakatan Harapan, retained its existing holdings and made substantial gains in UMNO's rural heartland. Johor exemplified this process, with Pakatan Harapan securing thirty-six out of fifty-six seats in the state parliament (Hutchinson 2018).

This result was unexpected, given the coalition's unblemished electoral performance, strong economic track record, and "developmentalist" campaign platform. In particular, the 2018 result goes against: the "performance legitimacy" hypothesis, which holds that voters acquiesce to relinquishing political freedoms in return for consistent economic growth (Stubbs 2001); as well as the "economic voter" hypothesis, which contends that citizens prioritise the overall performance of the economy and their material welfare most of all in casting their vote (Monroe 1979).

Rather, part of the explanation for this political upheaval lies in the ensuing societal changes that have occurred in the wake of Johor and Malaysia's economic transformation. This includes higher rates of urbanization and literacy, more sophisticated methods of information gathering, and evolving priorities that have come to include aspects such as the quality of governance. These structural changes were alluded to in Loh and Saravanamuttu's work on new politics in Malaysia (2003), and have made Johor and many parts of Malaysia less fertile terrain for BN.

Beyond changes in the state's political environment, Johor's social context has also changed in important ways—not least the size and composition of its population. In 1990, the state's population was 2.1 million and, by 2017, had reached 3.7 million—constituting an increase of 75 per cent in less than three decades. This expansion has been due to natural population increase, but an important additional driver has been migration from other parts of Malaysia as well as other countries. In 2017, a recorded 356,000 non-Malaysians were residing in the state (DOS 2017, p. 35). This does not include a substantial fraction of the estimated 4.6 million undocumented foreigners living and working in Malaysia (*Bernama*, 11 November 2014).

Always at the intersection of trade routes in the region, Johor is now even more cosmopolitan. With greater movements of people, traditional institutions come under pressure in the face of new mores, customs, and religious practices. In addition, inflows of people, investment, and urban development can drive up prices for basic necessities and housing. A survey conducted by ISEAS in 2017 revealed considerable consternation among Johoreans over inflation and housing affordability (Chong et al. 2017).

Greater numbers of people, regardless of their provenance, also place stress on the environment. Once water-abundant, Johor is now having to reconcile demands from multiple sources for this precious resource (Ewing and Hangzo 2016). This is further compounded by large-scale projects such as those in Forest City and Pengerang which entail significant costs in the form of affected natural habitats, pollution, and displaced communities.

Thus, taking the rapid growth launched by Johor's turn towards industrialization in the late 1980s as a point of departure, this book studies how its economy has developed and diversified, before turning to assess the political, social, and environmental effects of this economic transformation.

While internal dynamics are important, Johor does not exist in a vacuum. It is not an independent nation, but rather a constituent part of the Federation of Malaysia. Thus, while it enjoys a degree of autonomy on certain matters such as land management, investment promotion, as well as religion and custom, decisions regarding education, trade, and macroeconomic policy are decided at the national level. Furthermore, Johor occupies a very specific geographic location, situated as it is at the southern tip of Peninsular Malaysia, bordering Singapore and close to several Indonesian provinces.

Consequently, while agency in the form of policy frameworks, investment decisions, and local context has played a role in the changes seen in Johor, they have also been shaped by national dynamics and decrees as well as spillover effects from the state's neighbours. To this end, the next section will situate Johor within its Malaysian context. The subsequent one will place it within the SIJORI Cross-Border Region, comprised of Johor, Singapore, and the Indonesian province of the Riau Islands. The final section will then set out the aims and structure of the book, relating its questions and themes to existing literature in the process.

JOHOR IN MALAYSIA

Johor is located in the southern part of the Malaysian peninsula, abutting Singapore to the south and three Malaysian states—Malacca, Negri Sembilan, and Pahang—to the north. It is a geographically large state, spanning some 19,200 square kilometres, and has a number of urban centres, as well as a vast rural hinterland in its middle and along its eastern seaboard. Nonetheless, 72 per cent of Johor's inhabitants live in urban areas, roughly in line with the national average—making for a well-connected and literate electorate (DOS 2010).

With 3.7 million inhabitants, Johor has the country's third largest population, after Selangor and Sabah. Of its 3.3 million citizens, 60 per cent are Malay, 33 per cent are Chinese and 7 per cent are Indian (DOS 2017, p. 35). The remainder is comprised of foreign residents, including Indonesian, Nepali, and Myanmar nationals, among others (Weerasena, this volume).

The state's urbanized and ethnically diverse composition is a product of its colonial experience, geography, and deep enmeshment in Malaysia's political life.

As with other parts of the Malayan peninsula, Johor came under British control. However, because British expansion occurred over a long time period, from the late eighteenth century to the early twentieth century, and took a variety of forms, it gave rise to three different types of governing structures. This included: the Straits Settlements in Singapore, Penang, and Malacca, which the British colonized first and were geared to trade; the Federated States of Selangor, Perak, Negri Sembilan, and Pahang, which the British colonized later, and which were centred on mining; and the Unfederated Malay States (UMS) including Johor and the four northern territories of Perlis, Kedah, Kelantan, and Terengganu, which they colonized last and whose economies were based on agriculture. Unlike the first two categories, the UMS retained more features of independent political entities, receiving fewer British advisers and civil servants (Emerson 1937; Gullick 1992).

Johor's unique identity was further due to its lineage of entrepreneurial traditional rulers who proved very apt at cultivating British favour, particularly to cement their contestable claims over the sultanate's territory. Yet, they were also able to generate substantial amounts of revenue and maintain a maximum degree of autonomy. Consequently, the sultanate had its own bureaucracy, the Johor Civil Service (JCS), which retained top positions within the government, including senior positions such as those of the chief minister, state secretary, and state financial officer. Relative to other sultanates, Johor also retained control over more government departments and was able to enshrine vestiges of independence in agreements with the British, such as the right to dismiss unwanted colonial administrators and retaining preference for Malays from Johor in the public service (Trocki 2007; Zainah 2011).[4]

Johor's vast swathes of flat fertile land also played a defining role in its identity. The felling of rubber wood and cultivation of pepper and gambier drew people into the territory's interior from the 1830s (Trocki 2007). After 1900, the sultanate began to cultivate and export rubber, whose profitability translated into considerable levels of state revenue, which enabled social services to be expanded. By the end of the 1930s, Johor's per capita spending on health and education rivalled that of the Straits Settlements, and it had the largest education system of the Unfederated Malay States (Statistics Department 1939, pp. 143–44). The commodity-based economy also changed the demographic composition of the territory—away from a Malay-majority to a more diverse population, drawing in immigrants from China, India, Java and Sumatra. After the Second World War, Johor had the second largest population in Malaya following Perak, and also had one of its largest Chinese communities (del Tufo 1947).

Upon their return following the end of the Second World War, the British sought to fuse the various settlements and sultanates into one entity, called the Malayan Union. This initiative sought to drastically reduce the role of the Sultans, transfer sovereignty of the various territories to the British Crown, and extended very liberal citizenship requirements to those living in Malaya at that time. This measure stoked Malay nationalism and helped consolidate a pan-Malay identity (Noordin Sopiee 1974; Amoroso 2014).

In this context, Johor came into her own, as her cadres of senior civil servants, literate population, and location between Singapore and the Federated Malay States made the territory a seedbed of political activity. A number of influential local Malay political organizations were established by members of the JCS, most of which then joined UMNO when the party was founded in Johor Bahru in 1946 (Hutchinson 2015b, pp. 145–48).

Consequently, Johor supplied a disproportionate number of the party's leaders, who, in turn, negotiated with the British and governed Malaya upon her independence. Notable leaders from the sultanate included: Onn Jaafar, founder of

UMNO; Hussein Onn, the third prime minister; Ismail Abdul Rahman, the second deputy prime minister; as well as Mohamad Noah bin Omar, the first speaker of the house. Delegates from Johor also dominated the Supreme Council, the party's prime decision-making body, and headed the party's Youth and Women's wing for the first two decades. Johor-based politicians also supplied three out of the ten members of Malaya's first cabinet (Hutchinson 2015b, p. 127).

However, while Johor supplied many senior leaders to the fledgling country, the territory itself was subsumed into greater Malaya. Thus, in 1948, Johor was included as a signatory to the Federation of Malaya agreement. In so doing, the sultanate became a state government within the federation and transferred many aspects of sovereignty, such as responsibilities for defence, trade, and foreign affairs to its central counterpart. This process was taken further at independence in 1957, when Johor also relinquished the delivery of education and health services, retaining responsibilities for issues such as local government, natural resources, land management, as well as religion and custom (Shafruddin 1987, pp. 132–33).

Furthermore, despite Johor's over-representation within UMNO, leaders from the state were unable to influence national party decisions unduly. This is because during the 1950s and 1960s, the party underwent an internal reform process that prevented large states with large grassroots organizations such as Johor from dominating it. The power of state branches was broken through decentralizing key decisions to lower levels of the party's machinery, as well as centralizing the choice of national and state-level candidates at its apex (Azeem Fazwan 2011).

Beyond UMNO, the Malaysian Chinese Association (MCA) has a deep association with the state. The demographic weight of the territory's Chinese community has meant that almost every leader in the party has either hailed from Johor or led the state branch of the party during his career (Lee and Chan, this volume).

Beyond its close ties with UMNO and MCA, Johor's diverse ethnic make-up mapped well onto the consociational model that BN developed in the run-up to independence. Under this framework, UMNO, MCA, and the Malaysian Indian Congress joined to form the Alliance to compete in municipal, state, and national elections held under the stewardship of the British. This "grand coalition" proved very effective, as the grouping was able to pool candidates to contest in a maximum number of seats and usually match candidates with the prevailing ethnicity in each constituency. In addition, members of other communities were still comfortable voting for the coalition, as they knew that their interests were represented within the grouping (Horowitz 1993, p. 33).

Given Johor's diverse make-up, this grand coalition model worked in the state and delivered consistent victories. This was further boosted by the successful roll-out of the Federal Land Development Authority (FELDA) in the state, which enabled vast numbers of poor, rural Malays to receive land, credit, and training to begin producing oil palm and generate higher incomes. At the state level, UMNO leaders were closely associated with the programme through selecting beneficiaries. In addition, prominent Johorean politicians such as Musa Hitam took senior leadership positions in FELDA (Bahrin and Lee, 1988, p. 3). Indeed, from 1959 until 2013, levels of popular support for BN in Johor were consistently 10 percentage points higher than the national average (Hutchinson 2018, p. 12).

The importance of Johor at the national level has been magnified over time by parliamentary redelineation exercises, which have favoured the state's rural, Malay-majority hinterland. Consequently, despite its population being substantially smaller than Selangor's, Johor has twenty-six parliamentary seats as opposed to the bigger state's twenty-four seats. Indeed, Johor's parliamentary constituencies are second only to Sarawak, whose vast rural areas have been carved into thirty-one constituencies.

These factors have made the state one of the country's most important political battlefields, with non-BN parties targeting Johor. The Democratic Action Party (DAP), Pakatan Harapan's oldest component party, has long been active in the state's Chinese-majority areas, winning its first parliamentary seat in 1978 (NTSP 1990). The Islamic party, PAS, has also sought to establish a presence, fielding candidates for the state parliament in every election since 1959. In 2013, the previous opposition grouping, Pakatan Rakyat, made a concerted effort to target Johor, through fielding high-profile candidates such as Lim Kit Siang and Salahuddin Ayub in competitive seats. And, in 2018, new Malay-majority parties such as Parti Amanah Negara and Parti Pribumi Bersatu Malaysia also sought to make inroads in the state's rural constituencies (Wan Saiful, this volume).

Beyond the various political parties and elected office-holders, Johor retains its traditional ruler, the Sultan. Under Malaysia's constitutional arrangements, while executive power at the state level lies with the Chief Minister, the Sultan has responsibility for religion and Malay culture. In addition, his symbolic importance means that his power and influence extends beyond this. In particular, the Sultan enjoys particularly close ties to the Johor Civil Service that pre-date independence. In certain circumstances, the Johor ruler is able to argue positions based on historical precedent, referring to the territory's pre-independence period when the sultans enjoyed a considerably expanded remit. Thus, the Sultan has weighed in on a variety of state-level and national issues, from education to transport links between Singapore and Johor (Hutchinson and Nair 2016; *New Straits Times*, 8 August 2017).

In addition to its enmeshment within Malaysia's political life, Johor is also an important composite part of the country's economy. The state has the fourth largest GDP, following Selangor, the Kuala Lumpur Federal Territory, and Sarawak. Its per capita income is somewhat below the national average, at RM34,360 in 2017 versus RM41,093 (Ministry of Economic Affairs 2018, A-6). Yet, despite this, Johor has a diversified economy and ranks among the top three states in terms of the contribution of its agriculture, manufacturing, and service sectors to the national GDP (Bait-al-Amanah 2017, p. 14).

With regard to agriculture, Johor is a very important producer of oil palm, generating the most output in West Malaysia and trailing only Sabah and Sarawak at the national level. The state is also a very important producer of chicken, fruits, vegetables, freshwater aquaculture, as well as ornamental plants and cut flowers (Pakiam, this volume).

Johor also has a tradition of manufacturing, dating back to its successful drive to diversify its economy following a collapse in commodity prices in the mid-1980s. Over the course of the 1990s, the state cemented its reputation as a major hub for Malaysia's electrical and electronics (E&E) industry. While the E&E sector's growth has flattened out of late, Johor has a substantial presence of petroleum and petrochemical producers, as well as chemical and plastics makers. The state regularly figures amongst Malaysia's top destinations for manufacturing FDI, and has the largest concentration of SMEs outside the Klang Valley (Bait-al-Amanah 2017, p. 41).

In the early 2000s, Johor began to promote its services sector in a more concerted fashion. In 2006, the state, in conjunction with the federal government, rolled out the Iskandar Malaysia (IM) region.[5] This 2,200 square kilometre swathe of land in southern Johor is one of the country's five economic corridors, which are large-scale regional development initiatives to catalyse growth and new industries outside the Klang Valley. The main emphasis of IM has been to develop a range of new sectors, from logistics to finance and from education to creative industries. While existing manufacturing activities are incorporated into the area's strategic plan, additional incentives are reserved for new service activities (Khor 2011). To date, Iskandar Malaysia is the country's most successful corridor, having attracted RM41.8 billion and generated 32,000 jobs, in both cases double the second most successful such initiative, the East Coast Economic Region (Ministry of Economic Affairs 2018, pp. 7–11).[6]

A significant part of Johor's economic development has been due to local-level agency and autonomy, as the state was not a federal government priority up until the mid-2000s. Following independence, the national government attention focused on Malaya's rural, northern states, which received higher levels of development expenditure, as compared to the more urbanized and developed states such as Selangor, Penang, and Johor. From the 1970s onwards, this focus on rural areas was complemented by emphasis on Greater Kuala Lumpur, with the aim of creating a world-class urban centre (Hutchinson 2017).

Furthermore, relative to other state governments on the peninsula, Johor retains important vestiges of autonomy. Unlike many other state governments, it has retained its own civil service and civil service commission. Johor also has its own economic planning office, investment promotion and liaison arm, as well as a bevy of state-owned corporations (Hutchinson 2012). Consequently, up until the establishment of Iskandar Malaysia, many of Johor's key economic decisions and priorities were the result of autonomously developed plans and initiatives, including investments by the state government's corporate arm, JCorp (UPEN Johor 1989; RMA Perunding Bersatu 1996; PKENJ 1991).

While BN was in power at the national and state level from independence until 2018, differing priorities at different points in time have given rise to disagreements between the two levels of government. For example, during the 1990s, federal–state friction emerged due to Johor's desire to maximize investment through enacting education, training, and marketing initiatives. Despite their potential to attract greater flows of investment, federal leaders took a dim view of such autonomy. Regardless of Malaysia's federal system of government, internal UMNO procedures by the party's national leadership were used to replace the Chief Minister of Johor (Hutchinson 2015a).

Conversely, Johor has resisted federal policies perceived to go against its interests, as seen with the establishment of the Iskandar Malaysia region. In its incipience, the corridor was exclusively a federal initiative. Consequently, feasibility studies were carried out by Khazanah, the central government-owned sovereign wealth fund, with little involvement from Johor agencies. Furthermore, the corridor's planning processes duplicated the state government's, and the remit of the agency entrusted with managing Iskandar Malaysia overlapped with an existing state government organization. Iskandar Malaysia also entailed a shift in economic weight from Johor's east to the west, wrong-footing the state government's plans for a new state capital. And, the entry of central government-linked corporations effectively ended the monopoly the state government enjoyed on the sale of industrial land (Hutchinson 2015c).

Leveraging its constitutionally stipulated mandate over land planning and permission, the state government implicitly threatened a slow-down of investment permits and approvals and also deployed its Chief Minister to lobby federal authorities. The end result was that Iskandar Malaysia is now jointly chaired by the Prime Minister and Chief Minister of Johor. Beyond this, the Chief Minister has an effective veto over the head of Iskandar Malaysia's regulatory agency, IRDA, and state government officials are also seconded to the entity to ensure adequate information flows (Hutchinson 2015c).

Consequently, Johor is a central part of Malaysia's political and economic make-up. However, while the state is enmeshed in the country's political life and there has been policy and party congruence at the national and local level over the past six decades, Johor's degree of autonomy within the Malaysian federation is not uncontested.

JOHOR AS PART OF SIJORI

While linkages with Malaysia are certainly a key part of Johor's identity, it also has deep connections with other territories. In the 1990s, the SIJORI Growth Triangle, comprising Singapore, Johor, and the Riau Islands was used by authorities in the city-state, Malaysia, and Indonesia to market the three territories as a destination offering complementary attributes and differing cost structures in close proximity. However, the connections between these entities are rooted much deeper in history.

From the early 1700s until 1824, the areas along the Johor River and its close connections with the Riau Archipelago constituted at the heart of the Johor-Riau kingdom. The kingdom was, in fact, a sultanate, the predominant political entity in archipelagic Southeast Asia at the time. In contrast to Western conceptions of a nation-state with a fixed population and borders, these were more fluid entities.

Wealth and power flowed from attracting and retaining a large population as well as controlling and taxing trade along maritime routes and waterways (Milner 2011).

This sultanate was in a strategic location, at the crossroads of two important maritime trading routes—the first running east and west, linking India and China; and the second north and south, connecting Java and the islands east of it with the South China Sea. The precise borders of the Johor-Riau kingdom waxed and waned with time but, at its apex, encompassed what are now: the states of Johor and Pahang in Malaysia; Singapore; and part of the Sumatran coast as well as the Riau Archipelago in Indonesia (Wee 2016, p. 246). During this period, the capital city moved back and forth between Johor and Bintan, one of the islands in the Riau Archipelago (Carruthers 2018, pp. 22–25).

This same strategic location attracted other interests. Following the end of the Napoleonic Wars, the Dutch sought to reassert their control over trade routes through Southeast Asia from their bases in Batavia and Malacca. For their part, the British sought to contain Dutch influence and secure control over trade routes to China. They thus aimed to establish a trading post at the bottom of the Straits of Malacca. Singapore, because of its location, was seen as particularly desirable (Andaya and Andaya 2017, p. 124).

In order to secure control of the island, Stamford Raffles, an agent of the East India Company, capitalized on a succession dispute within the Johor-Riau Kingdom. The sultanship had been passed from the previous sultan, Mahmud, to his younger son, Abdul Rahman, bypassing the eldest son, Hussein. In addition, while the territory of what is today Singapore and Johor was within the sultan's realm, his control over this territory was nominal. In reality, he had ceded power to the Temenggong, the holder of a hereditary chieftainship who had territorial rights to the waterways around Singapore, the northern part of the Riau Archipelago, and part of the Johor coastline (Trocki 2007).

In 1819, the British negotiated a treaty with the sultan's elder son, Hussein, and the Temenggong, Abdul Rahman. In return for allowing them to establish a port on the island and forgoing the right to sign treaties with, or allow settlements from, other powers, the British recognized Hussein as the Sultan of Johor and agreed to pay him and the Temenggong yearly pensions. While this treaty entailed effective shared rule between the three parties, two subsequent treaties signed between the British, Sultan, and Temenggong dispossessed the latter two of their control over Singapore in return for a financial settlement (Allen, Stockwell, and Wright 1981, pp. 35–41).

The Dutch sought ineffectually to limit the increasing influence of the British, and the latter's claims to Singapore were settled by the Anglo-Dutch Treaty of 1824. This established Dutch and British control to the west and east of the Malacca Straits, respectively. Regarding the Riau-Lingga archipelago, the Dutch retained Riau, and British control over Singapore was recognized (Allen, Stockwell, and Wright 1981, p. 287).

The partitioning of the Johor-Riau kingdom also split the Temenggong's realm in two, and left him dependent on the British for revenue and legitimacy. However, while he and the Sultan had given up any claims to Singapore, the Dutch had relinquished control of Johor in 1824—meaning that this territory was unclaimed. While Temenggong Abdul Rahman could lay claim to the territory of Johor, he was—in theory—a subject of the Sultan and subordinate to him.

This was not to prove a barrier to Abdul Rahman and his son Ibrahim—who, over the next sixty years, strove to establish their claim to Johor. This was done by: courting British favour; tapping the territory for revenue where possible; and seeking to displace the Sultan and his descendants as the hereditary rulers.

In the 1840s, Ibrahim established the nucleus of the Johor government in Singapore. It first consisted of members of Ibrahim's retinue, who administered taxation revenue generated from pepper and gambier cultivation in Johor. In 1855, the Treaty of Johore was signed between Ibrahim and the British, which recognized him (and not Sultan Hussein) as the ruler of Johor. Following this, the development of the fledgling administrative apparatus began to grow faster. Various offices were opened up in Johor and, in 1866, Ibrahim moved his administration from Singapore to the newly founded capital of Johor Bahru (Trocki 2007, p. 116).

A subsequent agreement, the Anglo-Johore Treaty of 1885, recognized Ibrahim and his descendants as the legitimate rulers of Johor. However, this accord coincided with an increase in British interests in Malaya, and consequently, Ibrahim had to accede to: yield the conduct of foreign relations to the British; commit to not award concessions to foreign interests; and accept Britain's right to appoint an Adviser if thought necessary (Allen, Stockwell, and Wright 1981, p. 70).

Due to Johor's central location between Singapore and the Federated Malay States, British pressure over the Sultan increased towards the end of the century. This interest was heightened by plans to integrate the western coast via railroad, as well as the long-term potential of the territory for rubber cultivation (Thio 1967, p. 8).

British control over Johor was formally recognized by a series of amendments to the 1885 Treaty, and a British Adviser was appointed to the territory in 1914. With this, Johor was drawn into the administrative apparatus that linked Malaya's three Straits Settlements, four Federated Malay States, and four other Unfederated Malay States. Substantial responsibilities pertaining to immigration, labour, police, and the military were yielded to British civil servants posted in Singapore and, to a lesser extent, Kuala Lumpur. That said, the Sultan and his senior civil servants were able to maintain a substantial degree of autonomy over other matters of administration (Hutchinson 2015b, pp. 132–33).

Within this context, many aspects of what were to become bilateral issues between Singapore and Malaysia were actually established between the Johor government and the British colonial administration. For example, after the First World War, the Federated Malay States proposed linking their railway system to Johor's, to enable direct freight services to Singapore. Initial plans put forward by the British were for the connection across the Strait of Johor to be reserved for train traffic only. The Sultan of Johor proposed that the link cater to vehicles and pedestrians, and eventually contributed two-thirds of the costs of the Causeway, which was eventually completed in 1923 (National Archives of Malaysia/Singapore 2011, p. 58).

The interconnections of Singapore and Johor's water systems was also established during this period. In 1927, Sultan Ibrahim signed the first water agreement between Johor and the Singapore municipality. Singapore bore the cost of building two reservoirs in Johor and constructing the connecting pipes. This agreement, in turn, formed the basis for the 1961 and 1962 water agreements between the two entities (Tortajada and Pobre 2011).

In 1928, as per the wishes of Sultan Ibrahim, the British administration signed an agreement delimiting the boundary between Johor and Singapore as well as the territorial waters of each (Straits Settlements and Johore Territorial Waters (Agreement) Act). Without this agreement, all of the Johor Strait and areas along Johor's southern coast would have remained under British and eventually Singaporean control (Lee 1980).

After the Second World War, the Malayan Union brought the Federated Malay States, the Unfederated Malay States, as well as Penang and Malacca into one governing entity. Singapore, for its part, was retained under British control. This was further concretized by the establishment of the Federation of Malaya in 1948. Singapore and Johor were brought together again from 1963 to 1965, when the city was included with Sabah and Sarawak in the expanded Malaysian Federation (Noordin Sopiee 1974).

Following Singapore's departure from Malaysia in 1965, the city-state and Johor maintained close linkages. However, in an attempt to boost its manufacturing base and develop its own logistics sector, particularly Port Klang, Malaysia imposed tariff barriers and customs controls (Rimmer and Dick 2009, pp. 100–2). This was taken further in the 1970s, when Johor port was built in order to capture some of the freight from Malaysia shipped out through Singapore (Fong 1984).

Yet, in the mid-1980s, Johor began to rebuild its connections with Singapore. As part of its drive to diversify away from commodity exports and develop its manufacturing sector to generate jobs and modernize, it turned to Singapore as a source of capital and technology (UPENJ 1989). The Johor state government was very proactive at liberating land for manufacturing, and opening up a network of industrial parks in attractive locations. Conversely, Singapore was in the midst of its own economic restructuring, and in order to deal with an appreciating currency and increasing land and labour costs, it wanted to offshore lower value-added operations to proximate locations (Hutchinson 2015c).

In late 1989, then Deputy Prime Minister, Goh Chok Tong, put forward the idea of the Growth Triangle. In its incipience, this initiative was restricted to Johor, Singapore, and the island of Batam in the Riau Archipelago. In June 1990, the idea was supported by President Soeharto of Indonesia, and Prime Minister Mahathir of Malaysia, and its scope expanded to include the whole of Riau Province. In 1994, a memorandum of understanding was signed by the Singapore, Malaysian, and Indonesian governments (Phelps 2004, p. 348). The Growth Triangle was used to market the three territories as a "single investment destination" offering: a high level of connectivity; different cost structures; and a significant degree of political capital.

At the national level, Malaysia proceeded to liberalize its investment regulations, and its Malaysian Industrial Development Authority (MIDA) worked extensively with Singapore's Economic Development Bureau (EDB) to foster tourism and cross-border production. The two countries also began negotiations on a range of issues such as water, free services and the sale of land from Malaysia to Singapore that provided a good context for deepening business links (EAAU 1995, p. 30; Ooi 2009, p. 45).

Over the course of the 1990s, Singapore-based multinationals and Singaporean firms were encouraged to relocate labour-intensive functions to Johor as well as Batam, whilst keeping their capital- and skill-intensive functions in the city-state. The effects of the turn towards manufacturing as well as concerted marketing of the state had a substantial effect. During the 1980s, Johor drew in an annual average of US$210 million in FDI. For the 1990–97 period, this climbed above US$800 per annum (Hutchinson 2015c, pp. 61–62).

By its nature, the Growth Triangle construct was one that had Johor occupying the land- and labour-intensive production spaces. This caused some frustration in the state, which after a time sought to apply a more selective approach to inward investment, and also sought to push Johor towards higher-value activities, even if it meant a more explicitly competitive approach to Singapore (*Straits Times*, 16 October 1997).

However, in the late 1990s, the Growth Triangle faded from view for several reasons. First, the governments of Indonesia and Malaysia had requests for other states to be included in the Growth Triangle. Thus, in 1997, Malaysia added three more states and Indonesia four more provinces, which diluted the initiative's attractiveness. Second, the severity of the Asian Financial Crisis undermined collective attempts to attract investment. And, finally, bilateral relations between the three nations went into flux, as Malaysia and Indonesia's political systems came under pressure following their economic contraction (Hutchinson 2015c).

Nonetheless, while the trilateral approach to marketing and investment promotion fell by the wayside, the liberalization measures in Malaysia and Johor's concerted attempt to promote industrialization resulted in a proliferation of cross-border production linkages that have continued until the present. Beyond the electrical and electronics sector, deep networks connect Singapore and Johor in areas such as oil and gas, logistics, as well as aquaculture (van Grunsven and Hutchinson 2016; Breul and Revilla Diez 2018; Lim 2016; Gasco 2016).

Over the past decade, further economic linkages between Johor and Singapore have been promoted by Iskandar Malaysia. Much more focused on services than the previous development framework, the region's Comprehensive Development Plan seeks to integrate southern Johor into Singapore's transport networks. While certain priority sectors such as food processing do not overlap with areas that the city-state focuses on, and others such as E&E and oil and gas articulate with other areas in a complementary fashion, aspects of the CDP do imply a more competitive relationship with Singapore (Khazanah Nasional 2006; Hutchinson 2012).

At present, Singapore obtains 40 per cent of its water, the bulk of its fresh fish, and a substantial proportion of its vegetables from Johor. In addition, much of its manufacturing sector depends on the estimated 300,000 Malaysians who travel to the city-state on a daily basis (*Straits Times*, 28 October 2018). And, Johor is itself a gateway to Malaysia for flows of people and goods to Singapore. Looking forward, these links look set to deepen, with a planned rapid transit system linking Johor and Singapore and, potentially a high-speed rail link between Kuala Lumpur and Singapore, with three stops in Johor (Hutchinson 2016a).

Notwithstanding the far-reaching and frequent interactions between Johor and Singapore, there are also connections between the Malaysian state and the Riau Islands. These interactions are primarily linguistic and cultural. The Malay spoken in both locations is very similar, with many inhabitants in the Indonesian province taking pride in speaking—not Indonesian—but rather Malay. This legacy is linked directly to the Johor-Riau kingdom. There are flows of people from Johor to the island of Bintan, which contains the graves of its sultans. Furthermore, Raja Ali Haji, one of the foremost scholars of Malay history and culture, who is credited with codifying the Malay language, also lived in the Riau Islands and is buried there (Carruthers 2018). Consequently, for many Johoreans, the Riau Islands are the site of "real" Malay culture.

In addition, as the economies of Johor and the Riau Islands have grown and become more sophisticated, the possibilities for trade and people flows have increased. Recent policy frameworks have promoted a complementarity of sorts, as Johor has sought to develop its services sector, and the Riau Islands is focusing on industrial activities and tourism. Thus, Riau Islanders are increasingly looking to the Malaysian state as a destination for healthcare services and higher education, and Johoreans travel to resorts in their southern neighbour. Moreover, as the populations of Johor and the Riau Islands grow and become more urbanized and affluent, these linkages look to increase in size and complexity (Hutchinson 2016b).

Consequently, Johor also occupies a central place within the SIJORI region. However, as with its position within Malaysia itself, this is open to contestation, as Johor attempts to maximize the benefits accruing to it within the constraints of this construct.

THE AIMS AND STRUCTURE OF THE BOOK

This book is the second in a series of three that looks at Singapore, Johor, and the Riau Islands Province. The first volume, the *SIJORI Cross-Border Region: Transnational Politics, Economics, and Culture* was published in 2016. The book was the product of a three-year research project which brought together a core of researchers based at the ISEAS – Yusof Ishak Institute as well as a selected group of collaborators to look at interactions between Singapore, Johor, and the Riau Islands.

The project's theoretical approach was informed by the Cross-Border Region (CBR) literature, which defines these territories as a "unit that comprises contiguous subnational units from two or more nation-states" (Perkmann and Sum 2002, p. 1).

Primarily applied to North America and Europe, well-known CBRs include Oregon-Washington-British Columbia spanning the United States and Canada's

Pacific Northwest; and the Basque country, which brings together four provinces in Spain and three in France (Sparke 2000; Garcia-Alvarez and Trillo-Santamaria 2013). A subset of the literature looks at the dynamics between capital cities in small nations and contiguous provinces of larger countries, such as Luxembourg and the surrounding areas of France, Belgium, and Germany, as well as Liechtenstein and Switzerland and Austria (Sohn, Reitel, and Walther 2009; OECD 2011).

According to the literature, CBRs have emerged as a part of the rescaling of economic, political, and social processes that began in the 1980s, as the primacy of the nation-state has declined, but no other, clearer alternative for concentrating power has emerged. There are a variety of economic and non-economic drivers behind the emergence of CBRs. They include: metropolitan spillover; the revitalization of a pre-existing economic territory; historical and cultural links between constituent territories; differing cost structures; policy frameworks enacted by national or subnational governments to attract investment, reduce internal income inequalities, or attract funds; cross-border initiatives taken by communities; or measures taken by supra-national entities or organizations (Jessop 2002).

This approach was preferred to the traditional Growth Triangle approach, which: centres exclusively on economic issues; treats borders uniquely as an impediment to business; ignores the power relations between the constituent members; and does not have clearly defined boundaries. Conversely, when applied to SIJORI, the Cross-Border Region: clearly specifies the three territories of Singapore, Johor, and the Riau Islands as the unit of analysis; is open to analysing non-economic dynamics; can be used to analyse power dynamics between the constituent territories; and does not assume away the importance of the border. Indeed, the border is a key aspect of the entity's identity. To quote the first book, the Cross-Border Region is "simultaneously a whole as well as a number of constituent parts that are divided, yet bound together, by its borders" (Hutchinson and Chong 2016, p. 19).

The project and the resulting book had two guiding questions:

- How have the component territories, namely Singapore, Johor, and the Riau Islands evolved over the past twenty-five years as a result of deeper interactions?
- What will the territories look like in the medium term, if some of the trends witnessed continue?

The analysis was structured around three dates: 1990, which coincided with the launching of the Growth Triangle; 2013/14, which was when data collection for the project began; and 2030, which was taken as the analytical end-point.

The project used Brunet-Jailly's framework for the analysis of borders and their surrounding regions (2005). The axes of the framework included: the policy frameworks of governments to influence cross-border dynamics and their effects; the political context of borderland communities; the evolving culture of communities in border areas; and market forces and trade flows. The book's eighteen chapters were grouped into four sections, mirroring these four themes.

Due to its primacy in political and economic terms, Singapore loomed large in the *SIJORI Cross-Border Region* book. This present book—and the following volume on the Riau Islands—aim to complement this initial focus by focussing specifically on the non-core aspects of the CBR.

Consequently, these two volumes are motivated by the same guiding questions, namely:

- What have been the political, social, and environmental impacts on these territories of the rapid economic development set in motion since the early 1990s?
- What can be said about the future of the manufacture for export model, as well as the policy frameworks being put in place to diversify their economies?
- How are these two territories evolving in response to these developments within their respective countries on one hand, and the SIJORI CBR on the other?

While analysis on the SIJORI CBR may tend to be overly shaped by Singapore's influence, so, too, work on Malaysia and Indonesia can focus too much on the Klang Valley and Java, respectively. Consequently, these two tomes also seek to redress the geographic imbalance in the study of these two countries by deepening our knowledge of two physically remote, but potentially vital territories.

The Johor project and its Riau Islands Province equivalent ran concurrently for three years, from 2016 until 2018. As with the *SIJORI Cross-Border Region* project, staff from ISEAS constituted the core of the team, which was then complemented by a group of invited researchers from other organizations. For the Johor project, the majority of additional researchers were based in Malaysia. The bulk of fieldwork was carried out in 2017 and early 2018, before Malaysia's 14th General Elections. While the elections are of seismic importance for the country, the emphasis in this volume is retrospective, focusing on the broad sweep of events from 1990 until the present.

Following this introduction, the book will be comprised of three sections. The first will focus on Johor's economy through analysing key sectors, including: agriculture and palm oil; sunrise manufacturing activities such as oil and gas; as well as new service activities, such as healthcare, tourism, and education.

The second section of the book will focus on the state's political context. This involves analysing: the reasons for BN's long-running success; the development of Chinese-based political parties, in particular the Malaysian Chinese Association; the emergence and consolidation of Malay-majority parties such as Parti Pribumi Bersatu Malaysia and Parti Amanah Negara; and the role of the Sultan of Johor.

The third section will explore key social and environmental issues that have emerged in the state as a result of Johor's economic growth model, such as: a larger and more diverse workforce; the impact of new religious influences; urban development patterns; as well as the environmental implications of large-scale projects under construction and the ensuing policy response, if any.

The final section of the book will conclude, bringing together the themes raised in the chapters and relating them to the central questions posed above. From there, it will then set out areas for further research.

As with the first SIJORI volume, ISEAS researchers worked with Hans Hortig and Karoline Kostka from the Professorial Chair of Territory and Urban Planning of ETH Zurich to develop a series of bespoke maps to accompany the various chapters. These are grouped and placed at the beginning of each section of the book. In addition, two ISEAS-based GIS specialists, Pearlyn Pang and Benjamin Hu, developed the maps used within the chapters themselves. Consequently, as much as an empirical and theoretical exercise in deepening our knowledge of Johor, this is a cartographic endeavour to pinpoint and analyse relationships within the state and with its neighbouring territories.

Notes

1. 2005 constant US dollar and 2005 exchange rate.
2. http://blogs.worldbank.org/opendata/new-country-classifications-income-level-2017-2018 (accessed 2 November 2018).
3. Founded as the Alliance, this grouping changed its name to Barisan Nasional (National Front) in 1971.
4. For further information on the Sultanate of Johor, consult Trocki (2007) and Hutchinson (2015).
5. This area has been referred to as the South Johor Economic Region and the Iskandar Malaysia Region. Iskandar Malaysia is its current, official, title.
6. One northern-eastern district of Johor, Mersing, is included in the East Coast Economic Region (Map 2.2, this volume).

References

Allen, J. de V, A.J. Stockwell, and L.R. Wright. 1981. *A Collection of Treaties and Other Documents Affecting the States of Malaysia, 1761–1963*, vol. I. London: Oceana Publications, Inc.

Amoroso, D.J. 2014. *Traditionalism and the Ascendancy of the Malay Ruling Class in Colonial Malaya*. Singapore: NUS Press.

Andaya, Barbara Watson, and Leonard Y. Andaya. 2017. *A History of Malaysia*. 3rd ed. Basingstoke: Palgrave Macmillan.

Azeem Fazwan Ahmad Farouk. 2011. "Culture and Politics: An Analysis of United Malays National Organisation (UMNO) 1946–1999". Sudostasien Working Papers No. 46. Berlin: Institut fur Asien- und Afrikawissenschaften, Humboldt University.

Bahrin, Tunku Shamsul and Lee Boon Thong. 1988. *FELDA: 3 Decades of Evolution*. Kuala Lumpur: FELDA.

Bait-Al-Amanah. 2017. *Johor Development Report 2016*. Kuala Lumpur: Bait-Al-Amanah.

Breul, M., and J. Revilla Diez. 2018. "An Intermediate Step to Resource Peripheries: The Strategic Coupling of Gateway Cities in the Upstream Oil and Gas GPN". *Geoforum* 92: 9–17.

Brunet-Jailly, Emmanuel. 2005. "Theorizing Borders: An Interdisciplinary Perspective". *Geopolitics* 10: 633–49.

Carruthers, A.M. 2018. *Living on the Edge: Being Malay (and Bugis) in the Riau Islands*. Trends in Southeast Asia, no. 12/2018. Singapore: ISEAS – Yusof Ishak Institute.

Chong, Terence, Lee Hock Guan, Norshahril Saat, and Serina Rahman. 2017. *The 2017 Johor Survey: Selected Findings*. Trends in Southeast Asia, no. 20/2017. Singapore: ISEAS – Yusof Ishak Institute.

del Tufo, M.V. 1947. *Malaya Comprising the Federation of Malay and the Colony of Singapore: A Report of the 1947 Census of Population*. London: Crown Agents for the Colonies.

DOS. *Current Population Estimates*. Putrajaya: Department of Statistics, 2017.

———. *Demographic Characteristics*. Putrajaya: Department of Statistics, 2010.

EAAU. 1995. *Growth Triangles of South East Asia*. Canberra: Department of Foreign Affairs and Trade, East Asia Analytical Unit.

Emerson, R. 1937. *Malaysia: A Study in Direct and Indirect Rule*. New York: Macmillan.

Ewing, J.J., and P.K.K. Hangzo. 2016. "Development in Johor and Singapore's Water Access: Challenges and Opportunities". In *The SIJORI Cross-Border Region: Transnational Politics, Economics, and Culture*, edited by F.E. Hutchinson and T. Chong. Singapore: ISEAS – Yusof Ishak Institute.

Fong Chan Onn. 1984. "Johore Port: Its Role in the Growth of South Peninsular Malaysia". *Developing Economies* 23, no. 2: 185–204.

García-Álvarez, J., and J.M. Trillo-Santamaría. 2013. "Between Regional Spaces and Spaces of Regionalism: Cross-Border Region Building in the Spanish 'State of the Autonomies'". *Regional Studies* 47, no. 1: 104–15.

Gasco, A. 2016. "The Airport and the Territory: Transnational Flows in the Singapore-Johor-Riau Cross-Border Region". In *The SIJORI Cross-Border Region: Transnational Politics, Economics, and Culture*, edited by F.E. Hutchinson and T. Chong. Singapore: ISEAS – Yusof Ishak Institute.

Gullick, J.M. 1992. *Rulers and Residents: Influence and Power in the Malay States, 1870–1920*. Singapore: Oxford University Press.

Horowitz, Donald. 1993. "Democracy in Divided Societies". *Journal of Democracy* 4 no. 4: 18–38.

Huntington, Samuel P. 2006. *Political Order in Changing Societies*. New Haven and London: Yale University Press.

Hutchinson, Francis E. 2012. "Johor and its Electronics Sector: One Priority among Many?". ISEAS Working Paper no. 1. Singapore: Institute of Southeast Asian Studies.

———. 2015a. "Centre-State Relations and Intra-party Dynamics in Malaysia: UMNO and the State of Johor". *Asian Journal of Political Science* 23, no. 2.

———. 2015b. "Malaysia's Independence Leaders and the Legacies of State Formation under British Rule". *Journal of the Royal Asiatic Society*, Series 3, vol. 25, no. 1: 123–51.

———. 2015c. *Mirror Images in Different Frames? Johor, the Riau Islands, and Competition for Investment from Singapore*. Singapore: Institute of Southeast Asian Studies.

———. 2016. "The KL-Singapore High-Speed Rail: Costs, Contracts, and Complications". *ISEAS Perspectives* no. 7/2016. Singapore: ISEAS – Yusof Ishak Institute.

———. 2017. "Evolving Paradigms in Malaysian Regional Development Policy". *Journal of Southeast Asian Economies* 34, no. 3: 462–87.

———. 2018. *GE-14 in Johor: The Fall of the Fortress?* Trends in Southeast Asia, no. 3/2018. Singapore: ISEAS – Yusof Ishak Institute.

——— and Terence Chong, eds. 2016. *The SIJORI Cross-Border Region: Transnational Politics, Economics, and Culture*. Singapore: ISEAS – Yusof Ishak Institute.

——— and Vandana Prakash Nair. 2016. *The Johor Sultanate: Rise or Re-emergence?* Trends in Southeast Asia, no. 6/2016. Singapore: ISEAS – Yusof Ishak Institute.

Jessop, B. 2002. "The Political Economy of Scale". In *Globalization, Regionalization, and Cross-border Regions*, edited by M. Perkmann and N. Sum. Basingstoke: Palgrave Macmillan.

Khazanah Nasional. 2006. *Comprehensive Development Plan for South Johor Economic Region, 2006–2025*. Kuala Lumpur: Khazanah Nasional,

Khor Yu Leng. 2011. "Iskandar Malaysia: Policy, Progress, and Bottlenecks". RSIS Malaysia Programme, Malaysia Update, September 2011. Singapore: Nanyang Technological University.

Lee Yong Leng. 1980. *The Razor's Edge: Boundaries and Boundary Dispute in Southeast Asia*. Singapore: Institute of Southeast Asian Studies.

"Letters of Declaration, 1914 Johore Treaty". 1981. In *A Collection of Treaties and Other Documents Affecting the States of Malaysia, 1761–1963*, edited by J. de V. Allen, A.J. Stockwell, and L.R. Wright, London: Oceana Publications.

Lim, G. 2016. "The Role of Ethnic Chinese Business Networks in the Regionalization Strategy of Singaporean Fish Farming Firms". In *The SIJORI Cross-Border Region: Transnational Politics, Economics, and Culture*, edited by F.E. Hutchinson and T. Chong. Singapore: ISEAS – Yusof Ishak Institute.

Loh, Francis and Johan Saravanamuttu. 2003. *New Politics in Malaysia*. Singapore: Institute of Southeast Asian Studies.

MIER. 1997. *Johor Industrial Master Plan Study*. Kuala Lumpur: Malaysian Institute for Economic Research.

Milner, Anthony. 2011. *The Malays*. Oxford: Wiley-Blackwell.

Ministry of Economic Affairs. 2018. Mid-Term Review of the Eleventh Malaysia Plan: 2016–2020. Kuala Lumpur: National Printing Office.

Mohanlall, Premilla and Majella Gomes. 2009. *The Making of Kota Iskandar: Johor State New Administrative Centre*. Nusajaya: Cahaya Jauhar.

Monroe, Kristen R. 1979. "Econometric Analyses of Electoral Behavior: A Critical Review". *Political Behaviour* 1 no. 2: 137–73.

National Archives of Malaysia/Singapore. 2011. The Causeway. Kuala Lumpur/Singapore: National Archives of Malaysia/Singapore.

Noordin Sopiee. 1974. *From Malayan Union to Singapore Separation: Political Unification in the Malaysia Region, 1945–1965*. Kuala Lumpur: Penerbit Universiti Malaya.

NTSP Research and Information Services. 1990. *Elections in Malaysia: Facts and Figures*. Kuala Lumpur: Balai Berita.

OECD. 2011. *OECD Territorial Reviews: Switzerland 2011*. Paris: OECD Publishing.

Ooi, K.G. 2009. "Politics Divided: Malaysia-Singapore Relations". In *Across the Causeway: A Multi-Dimensional Study of Malaysia-Singapore Relations*, edited by T. Shiraishi. Singapore: Institute of Southeast Asian Studies.

Perkmann, Markus, and Sum Ngai-Ling. 2002. "Globalization, Regionalization and Cross-border Regions: Scales, Discourses and Governance". In *Globalization, Regionalization, and Cross-border Regions*, edited by Markus Perkmann and Ngai-Ling Sum. Basingstoke: Palgrave Macmillan.

PKENJ. 1991. *Memori Sambutan Ulang Tahun ke-20 PKENJ*. Johor Bahru: Perbadanan Kemajuan Ekonomi Negeri Johor.

Phelps, N.A. 2004. "Triangular Diplomacy Writ Small: The Political Economy of the Indonesia-Malaysia-Singapore Growth Triangle". *Pacific Review* 17, no. 3: 341–68.

Rimmer, P.J., and H. Dick. 2009. *The City in Southeast Asia: Patterns, Processes, and Policy*. Singapore: National University of Singapore Press.

RMA Perunding Bersatu. 2006. "Background Industrial Surveys for SJER Development Master Plan Study". Subang Jaya: RMA Perunding Bersatu.

Shafruddin, B.H. 1987. *The Federal Factor in the Government and Politics of Peninsular Malaysia.* Singapore: Oxford University Press.

Sohn, C., B. Reitel, and O. Walther. 2009. "Cross-Border Metropolitan Integration in Europe: The Case of Luxembourg, Basel, and Geneva". *Environment and Planning C: Government and Policy* 27: 922–39.

Sparke, M. 2000. "Excavating the Future in Cascadia: Geoeconomics and the Imagined Geographies of a Cross-Border Region". *BC Studies: The British Columbian Quarterly* 127: 5–44.

Statistics Department of the SS and FMS, Singapore. 1939. *Malayan Year Book 1939.* Singapore: Government Printing Office.

Stubbs, Richard. 2001. "Performance Legitimacy and Soft Authoritarianism". In *Democracy, Human Rights and Civil Society in Southeast Asia,* edited by Amitav Acharya, B. Michael Frolic, and Richard Stubbs. Toronto: Joint Centre for Asia Pacific Studies.

Thio, Eunice. 1967. "British Policy Towards Johore: From Advice to Control". *JMBRAS* 40, no. 1: 1–41.

Toh M.H., and J. Bo. 2016. "The SIJORI Cross-Border Region as an Economic Entity in 1990 and 2012, and Perspectives for 2030". In *The SIJORI Cross-Border Region: Transnational Politics, Economics, and Culture,* edited by F.E. Hutchinson and T. Chong. Singapore: ISEAS – Yusof Ishak Institute.

Tortajada, Cecilia, and Kimberly Pobre. 2011. "The Singapore-Malaysia Water Relationship: An Analysis of the Media Perspectives". *Hydrological Sciences Journal* 56, no. 4: 597–614.

Trocki, Carl A. 2007. *Prince of Pirates: The Temenggongs and the Development of Johor and Singapore, 1784–1885.* Singapore: NUS Press.

UPENJ. 1989. *Pelan Ekonomi Negeri Johor, 1990–2005.* Johor Bahru: State Government of Johor Darul Ta'zim, Economic Planning Unit.

van Grunsven L. and F.E. Hutchinson. 2016. "The Evolution of the Electronics Industry in Johor (Malaysia): Strategic Coupling, Adaptiveness, Adaptation, and the Role of Agency". *Geoforum* 74 (August): 74–87

Wee, Vivienne. 2016. "The Significance of Riau in SIJORI". In *The SIJORI Cross-Border Region: Transnational Politics, Economics, and Culture,* edited by F.E. Hutchinson and T. Chong. Singapore: ISEAS – Yusof Ishak Institute.

Zainah Anwar. 2011. *Legacy of Honour.* Petaling Jaya: Yayasan Mohamed Noah.

Periodicals

Bernama
New Straits Times
Straits Times

I
Economics

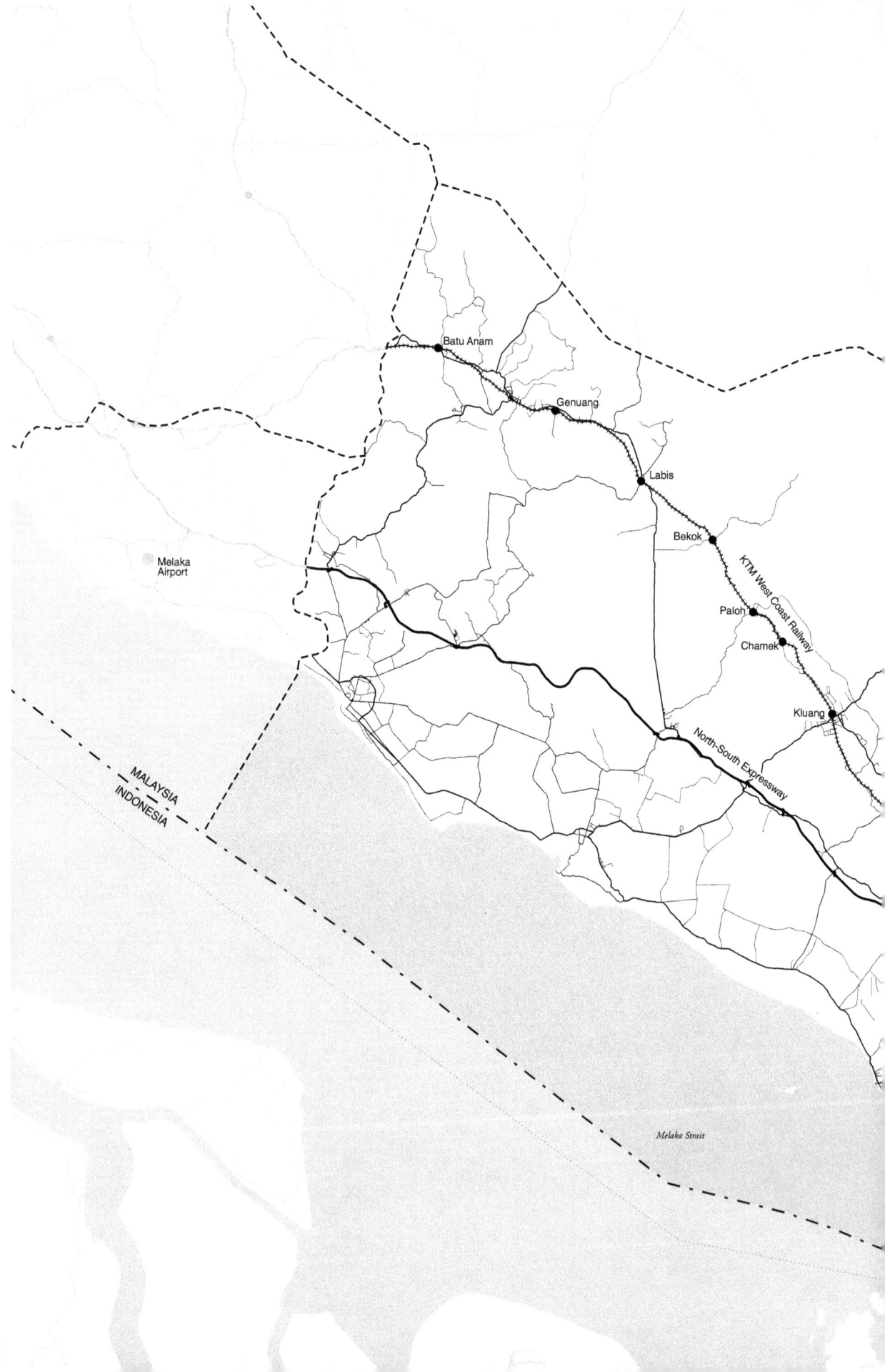

MAP 2.1
MOBILITY AND TRANSPORT

● International Airport
━━ Expressway
── Road Network
• Ferry Terminal
---- Ferry Connection
● Railway Station
╫╫ Railway Network

Tioman
Airport

Mersing

Tanjung
Leman

South China
Sea

ayang

Senai
Airport

Kulai

JB Larkin

Stulang
Laut

JB Sentral

Puteri
Harbour

Woodlands

Tanjung
Belungkor

Tanjung
Pengelih

Changi
Airport

Singapore
Strait

up

SINGAPORE

0   10   20km

Segamat II

Tangkak

Muar

Kluang

Ayer Hitam

ISK
(FU

Batu Pahat

Simpan
Rengga

MALAYSIA

INDONESIA

Melaka Strait

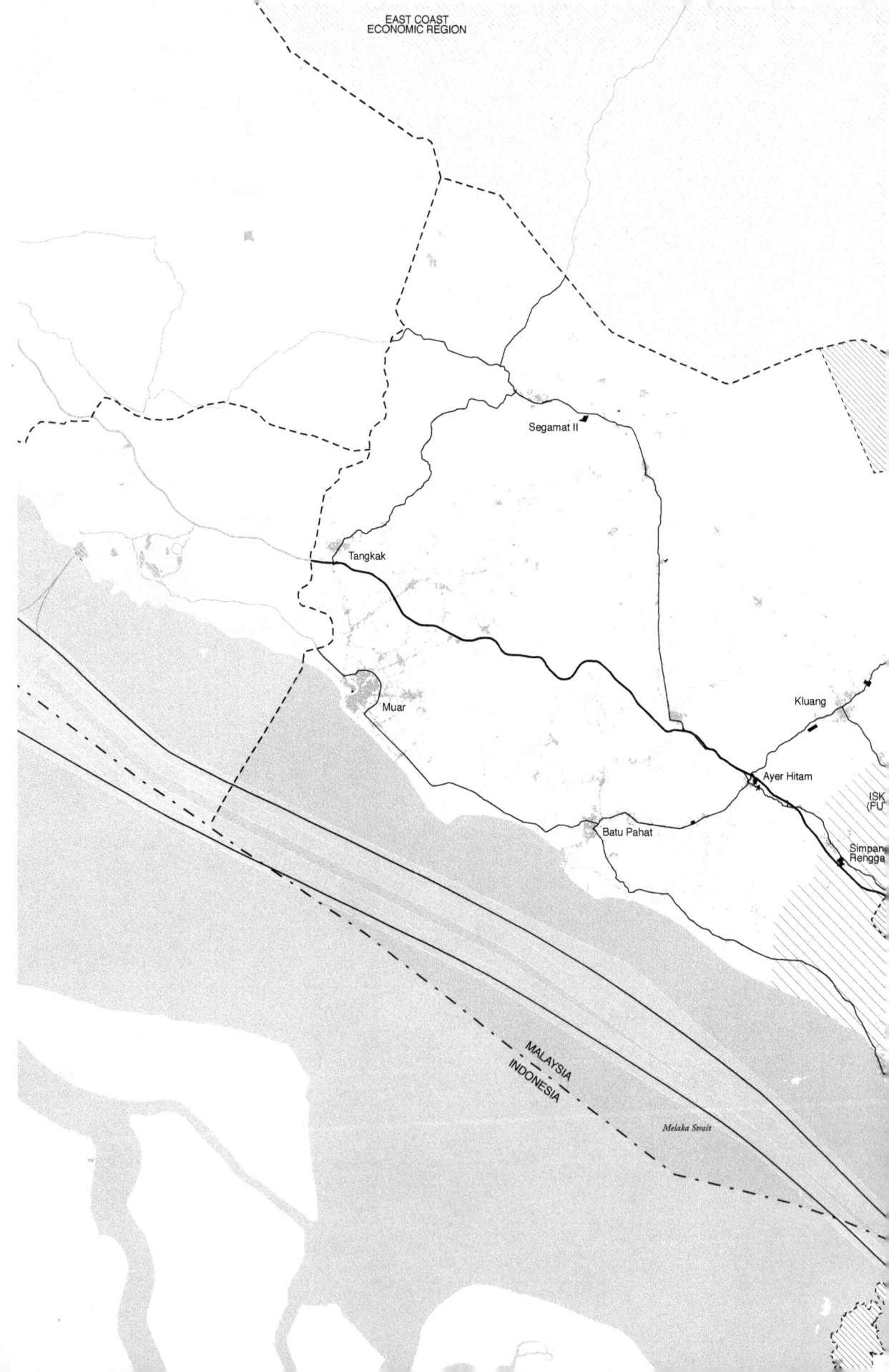

MAP 2.2
INDUSTRIES AND TRADE REGIMES

Special Economic Zone
Free Trade Zone
Industries and Logistics
○ Cyber City or Cyber Centre

Mersing

EAST COAST
ECONOMIC REGION

*South China
Sea*

AYSIA
SION)

ISKANDAR
MALAYSIA

Kota Tinggi

Senai

Stulang
Laut

Gelang
Patah

Menara
Cyberport

Tanjung
Langsat

Pasir
Gudang

anjung
elepas

Pengerang

*Singapore
Strait*

SINGAPORE

0   10   20km

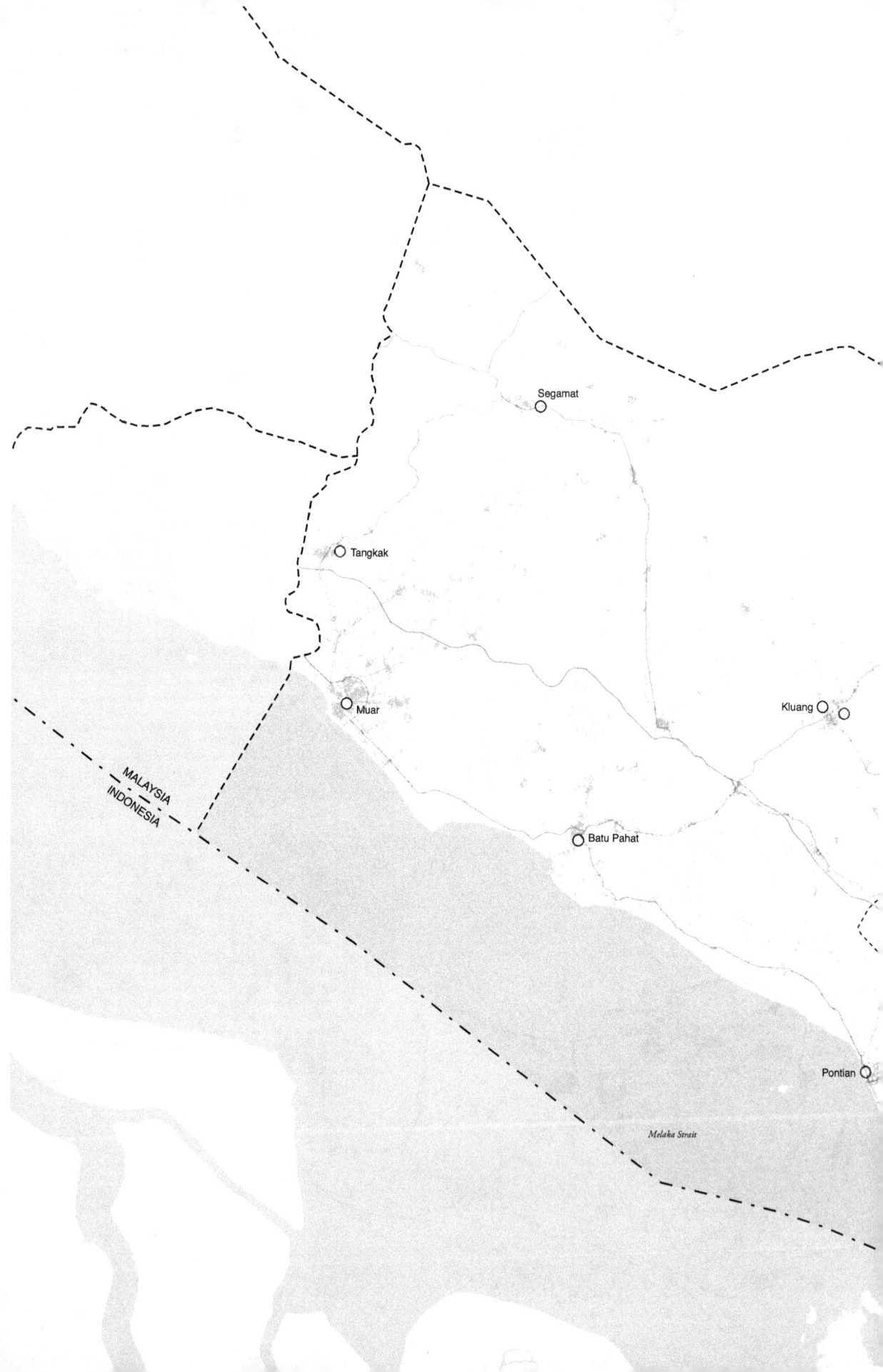

MAP 2.3
HEALTHCARE FACILITIES

○ Regional Specialist Hospital
● Private Healthcare Institution in ISKANDAR
⌷ ISKANDAR Special Economic Zone

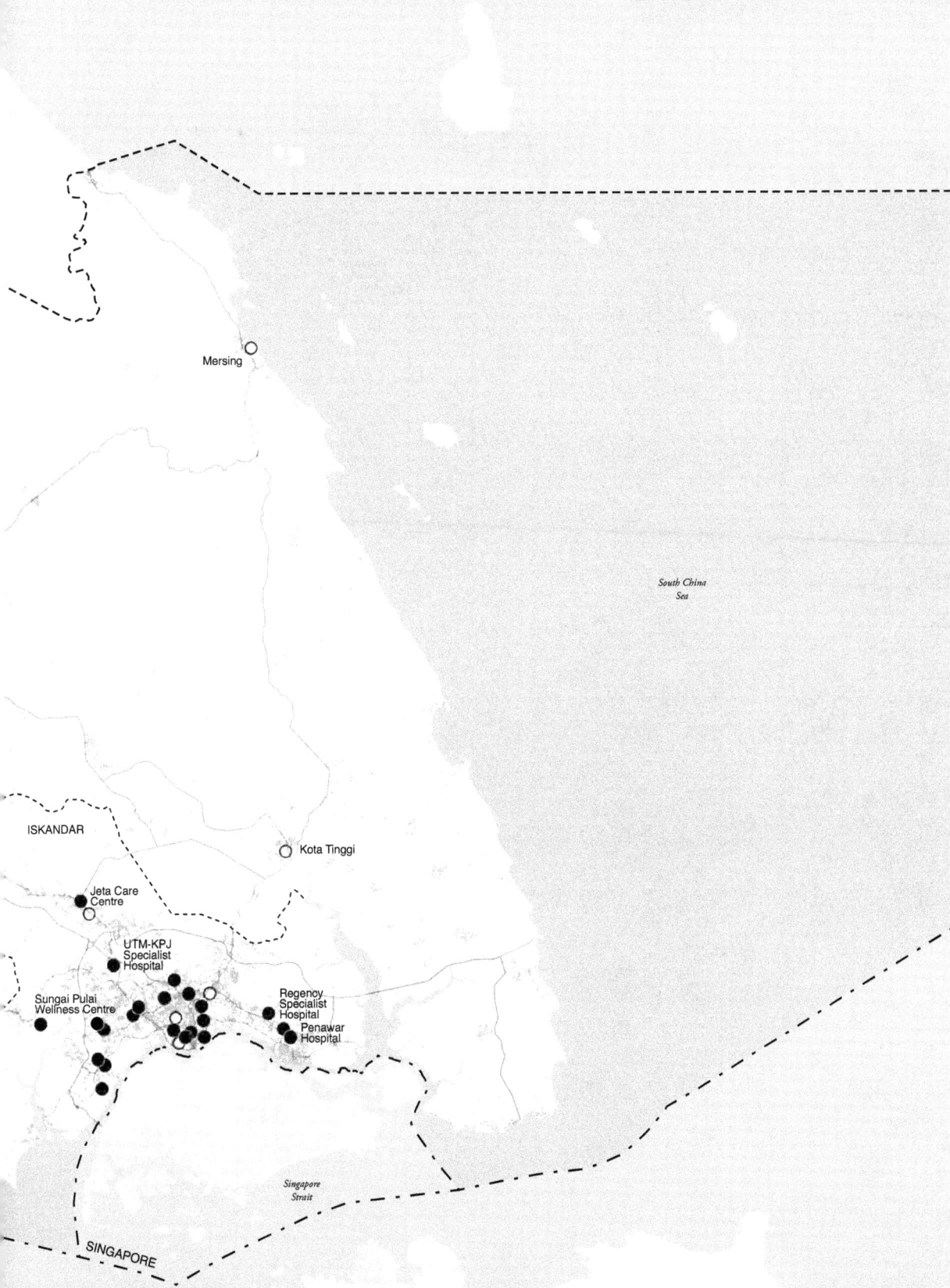

Mersing

South China
Sea

ISKANDAR

Kota Tinggi

Jeta Care
Centre

UTM-KPJ
Specialist
Hospital

Sungai Pulai
Wellness Centre

Regency
Specialist
Hospital
Penawar
Hospital

Singapore
Strait

SINGAPORE

0   10   20km

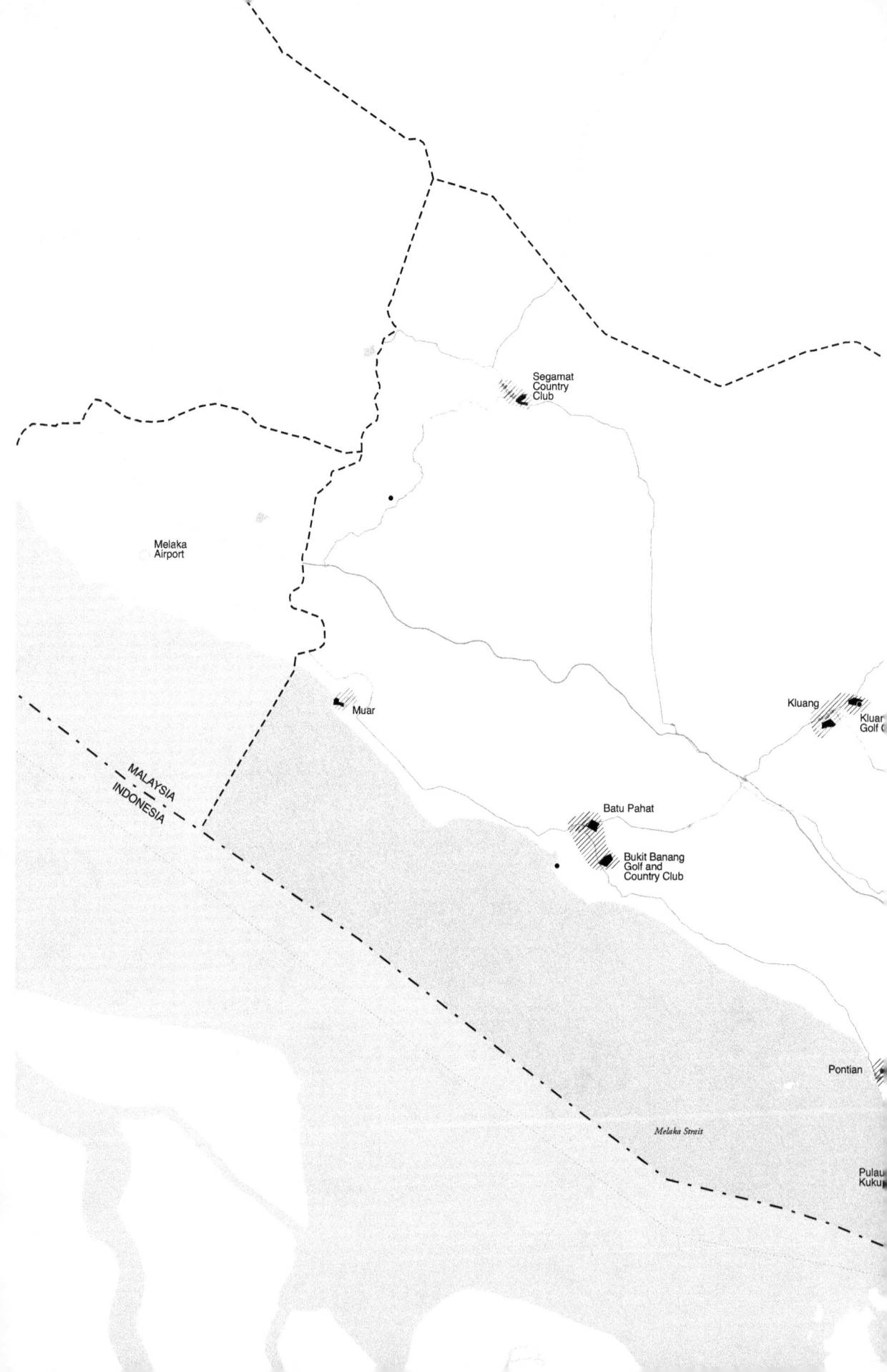

Segamat
Country
Club

Melaka
Airport

Muar

Kluang

Kluar
Golf (

Batu Pahat

Bukit Banang
Golf and
Country Club

MALAYSIA

INDONESIA

Pontian

Melaka Strait

Pulau
Kuku

MAP 2.4
TOURISM

Legend:
- Hotel
- ● Resort in Johor State
- ■ Golf Course
- ▨ Tourism Cluster
- ◯ International Airport
- ---- Ferry Connection
- ○ Ferry Terminal

Tioman Airport

Seribuat Archipelago

Pulau Rawa

Pulau Babi Besar

Pulau Aur

Mersing

Pulau Tinggi

Pulau Sibu

Tanjung Leman
Tunjuk Laut Beach Resort

South China Sea

Sea Horizon Resort

Mahkota Bay

Kota Tinggi Waterfalls Resort

Senai Airport

Kota Tinggi

Palm Golf Resort

Jova Golf Resort

Lotus Desaru Beach Resort

Desaru Beach

Desaru Holiday Chalet seaview

Starhill Golf and Resort

Pulai Springs Golf Resort

The Els Club Golf Resort

The Westin Desaru Coast Resort

Tanjung Puteri Golf Resort

Forest City Golf Resort

Sebana Cove Golf Resort

Poresia Golf Country Club

Changi Airport

Tanah Merah

Harbour-front

Singapore Strait

SINGAPORE

Batam Center

Sekupang

Banda Bintan Telani

0   10   20km

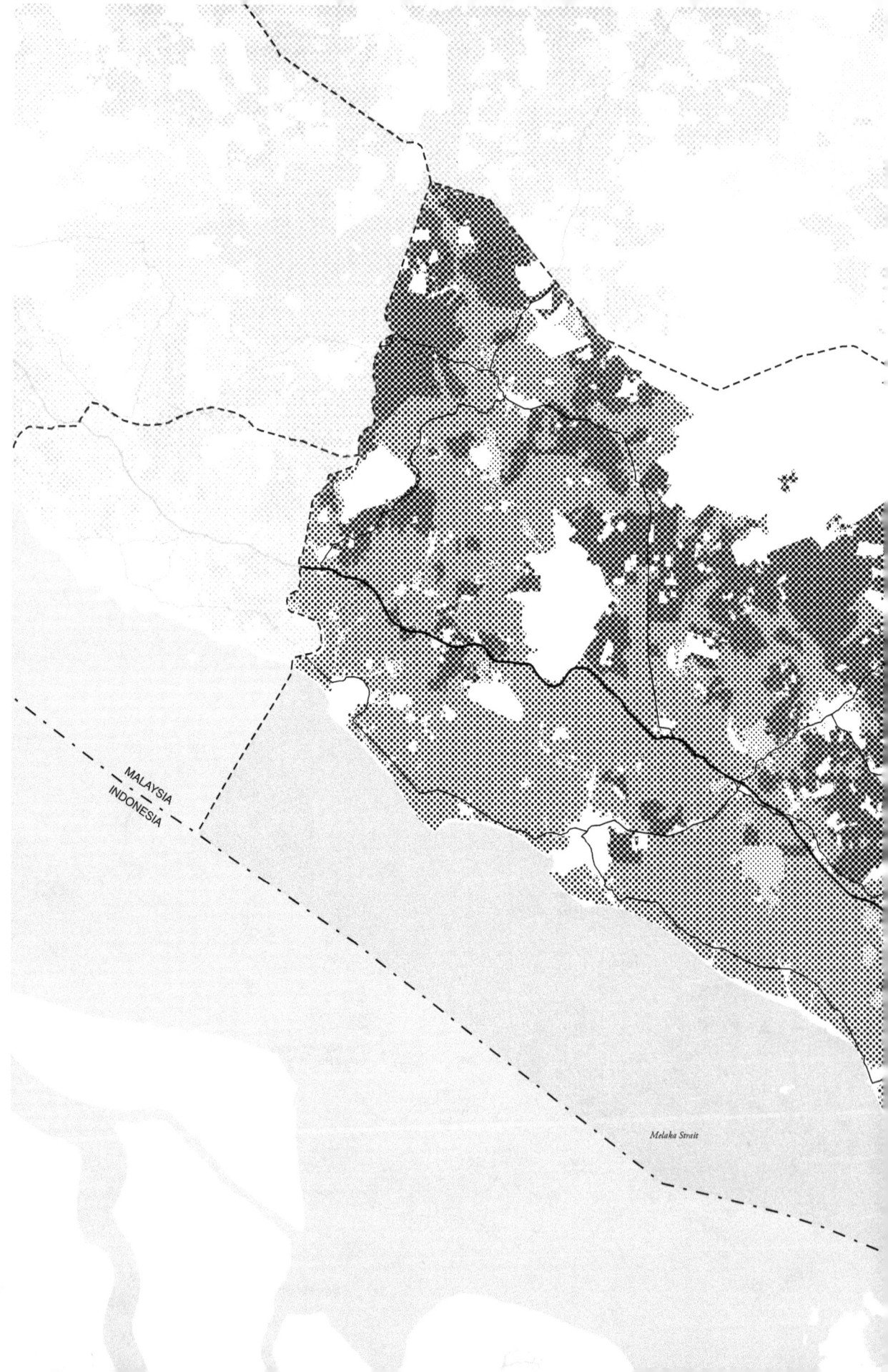

Melaka Strait

MAP 2.5
LAND UNDER CULTIVATION

- ▨ Large Industrial Plantations
  (Oil Palm and Rubber)
- ▧ Medium- and Small-sized Plantations
  (Oil Palm and Rubber)
- ▫ Other Agriculture

*South China
Sea*

SINGAPORE

*Singapore
Strait*

0   10   20km

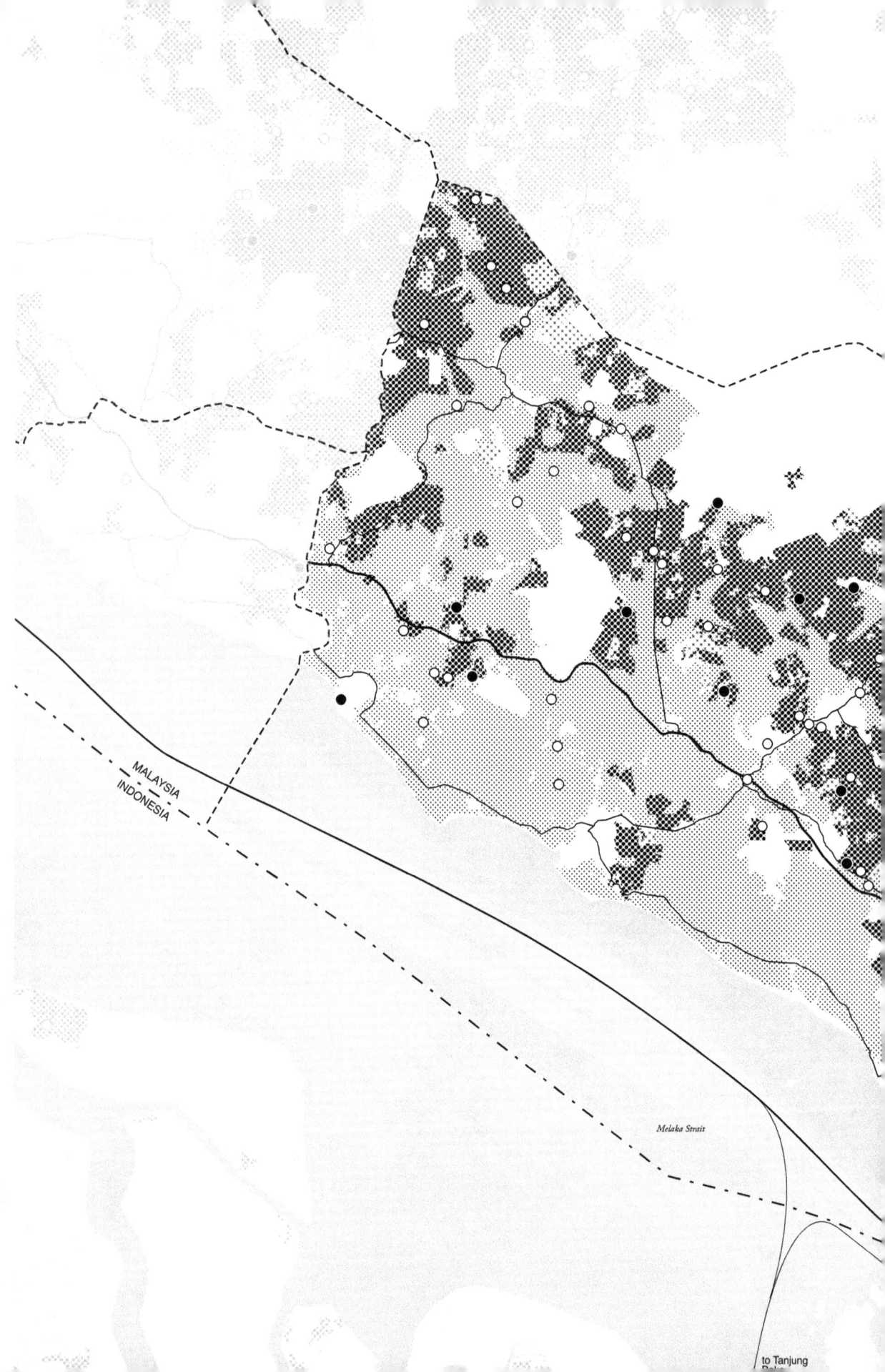

MALAYSIA

INDONESIA

Melaka Strait

to Tanjung

MAP 2.6
PALM OIL TERRITORIES

○ Palm Oil Mill
● Palm Oil Mill, RSPO Certified
 (Roundtable on Sustainable Palm Oil)
— Main Export Routes
■ Main Export Hub
▨ Oil Palm Plantations
░ Mixed Plantations, Predominantly Oil Palm
░ Clearings and Very Young Plantations

South China Sea

Johor
Biofuel Hub

Singapore Strait

SINGAPORE

Batu Ampar

0   10   20km

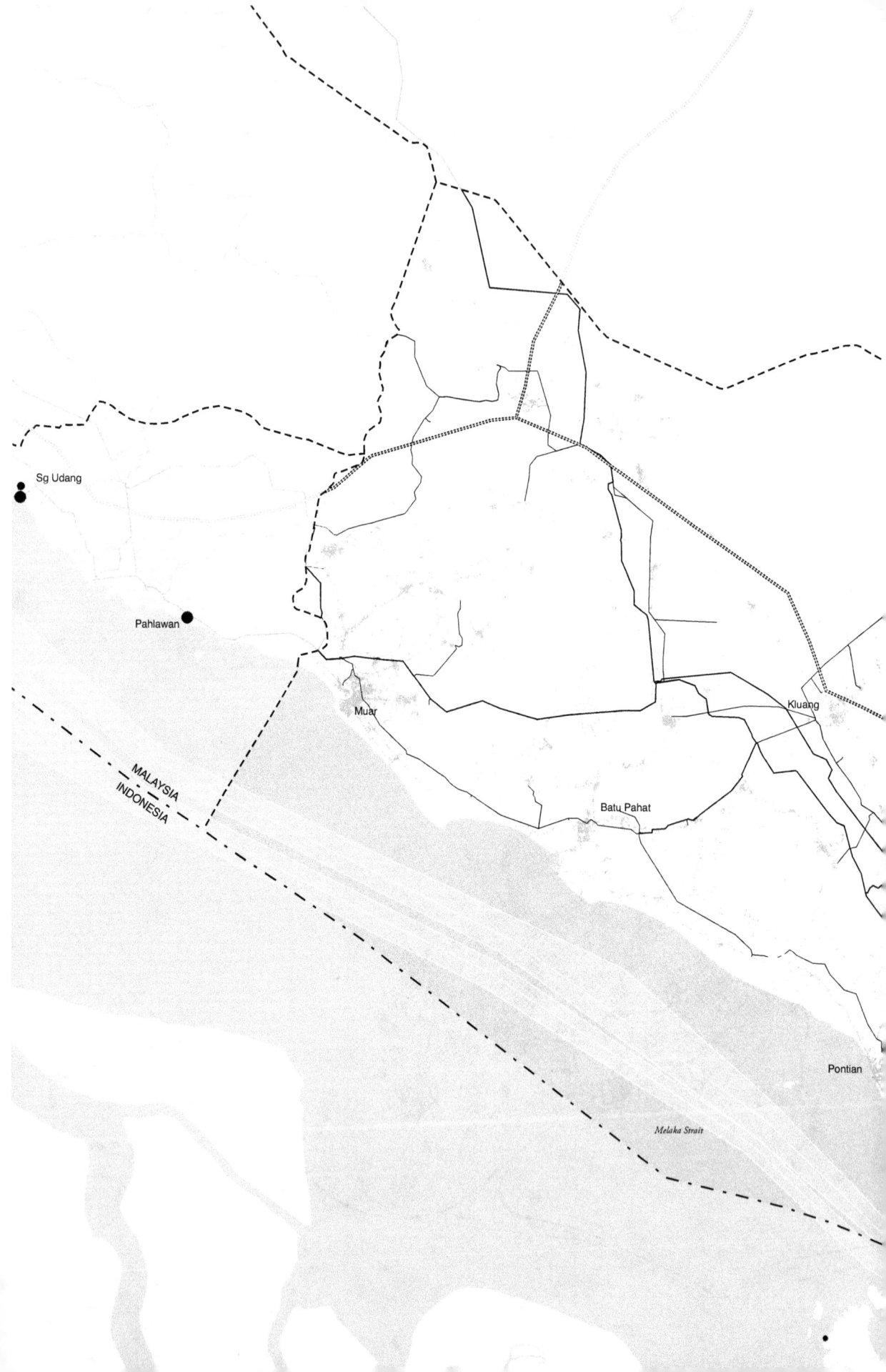

Sg Udang

Pahlawan

Muar

MALAYSIA
—·—
INDONESIA

Batu Pahat

Kluang

Melaka Strait

Pontian

MAP 2.7
OIL AND GAS NETWORKS

● Power Plant
● Refinery
● Storage and Terminal
○ Manufacturing
— Electricity Grid
▪ ▪ Pipeline

Endau

Mersing

South China Sea

Kota Tinggi

Senai

Sultan Iskandar Power Plant

Tanjung Langsat

Tanjung Pelepas

Teluk Ramunia

Tanjung Bin Power Plant

Tuas

Pengerang Cogeneration Plant

Jurong

Bukom

Singapore Strait

SINGAPORE

0   10   20km

MAP 2.8
PENGERANG
OIL AND GAS COMPLEX

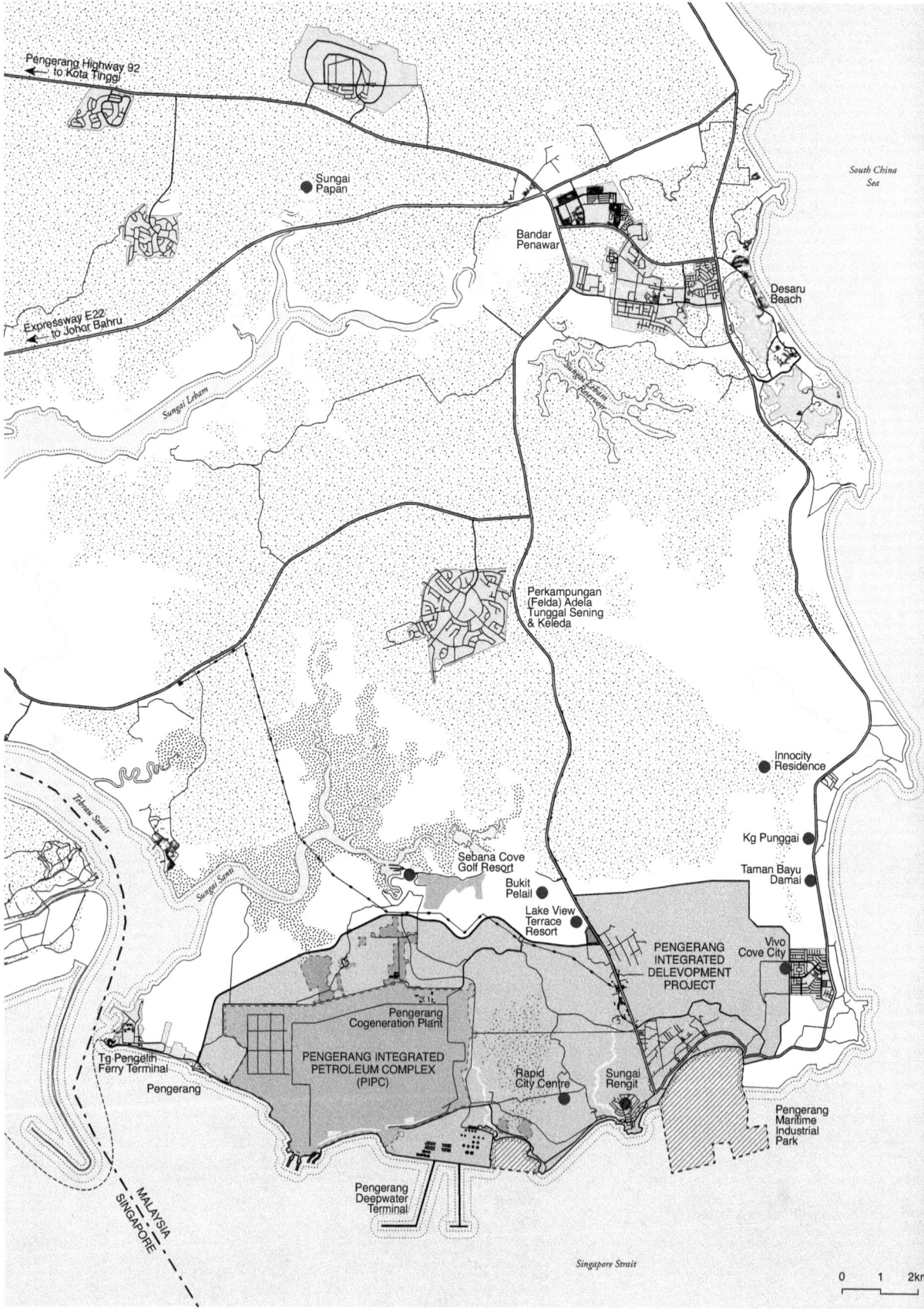

Pengerang Highway 92
to Kota Tinggi

South China
Sea

Sungai
Papan

Bandar
Penawar

Desaru
Beach

Expressway E22
to Johor Bahru

Sungai Lebam

Perkampungan
(Felda) Adela
Tunggal Sening
& Keleda

Innocity
Residence

Kg Punggai

Taman Bayu
Damai

Sebana Cove
Golf Resort

Bukit
Pelail

Lake View
Terrace
Resort

PENGERANG
INTEGRATED
DELEVOPMENT
PROJECT

Vivo
Cove City

Pengerang
Cogeneration Plant

Tg Pengelih
Ferry Terminal

PENGERANG INTEGRATED
PETROLEUM COMPLEX
(PIPC)

Pengerang

Rapid
City Centre

Sungai
Rengit

Pengerang
Maritime
Industrial
Park

MALAYSIA
SINGAPORE

Pengerang
Deepwater
Terminal

Singapore Strait

0   1   2km

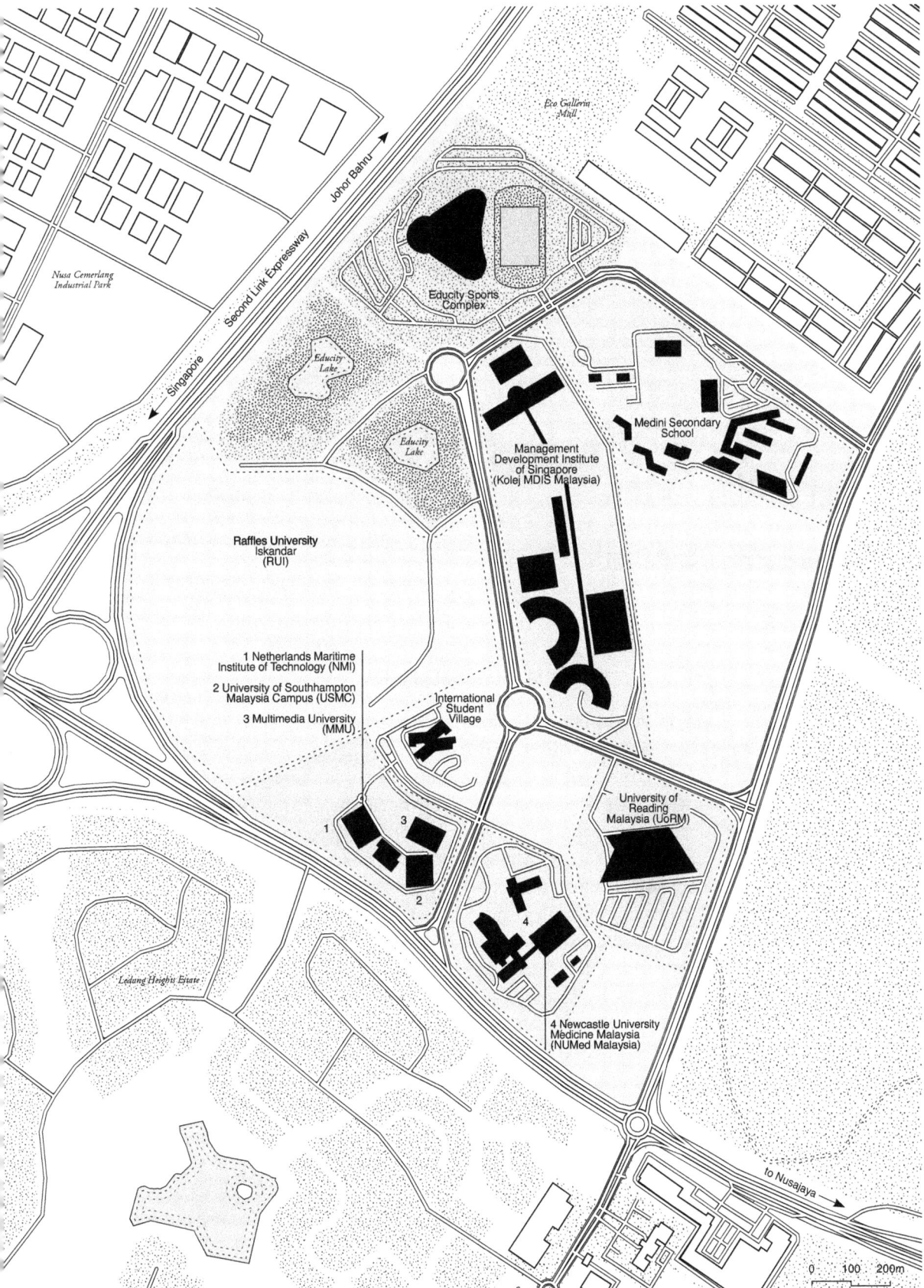

MAP 2.9
EDUCITY@ISKANDAR MALAYSIA
EDUCATION HUB

Eco Galleria Mall

Johor Bahru →

Second Link Expressway

Nusa Cemerlang Industrial Park

← Singapore

Educity Lake

Educity Lake

Educity Sports Complex

Medini Secondary School

Management Development Institute of Singapore (Kolej MDIS Malaysia)

Raffles University Iskandar (RUI)

1 Netherlands Maritime Institute of Technology (NMI)

2 University of Southhampton Malaysia Campus (USMC)

3 Multimedia University (MMU)

International Student Village

University of Reading Malaysia (UoRM)

1

3

2

4

Ledang Heights Estate

4 Newcastle University Medicine Malaysia (NUMed Malaysia)

to Nusajaya →

0   100   200m

2

AGRICULTURE IN JOHOR
What's Left?

Geoffrey K. Pakiam[1]

INTRODUCTION

For those living in Singapore or Peninsular Malaysia, accustomed to having fresh chicken eggs every other morning, chances are that your breakfast comes from one of 17 million broody hens raised in the Malaysian state of Johor (DVS 2017; AVA 2017).

If this comes as a surprise, you are probably not alone. Most recent commentaries concerning Johor's economic growth give the impression that agriculture is now a historical relic. The Iskandar Malaysia development project—accompanied by glittery real estate, oil and gas refining, complex manufacturing, mass tourism, and sophisticated healthcare offerings—now hogs the limelight.

Indeed, even for field-leading scholarship on greater Malaysia's economic development, agriculture has been conspicuous by its relative absence, sidelined by an overwhelming focus on manufacturing and services.[2]

This chapter represents an initial attempt to redress this imbalance. I ask two basic questions: what is left of agriculture in Johor? And why? My argument is similarly direct: although agriculture's share of Malaysian gross domestic product (GDP) and employment has fallen significantly, much remains, particularly in Johor. Amidst rapid urbanization and industrialization, agriculture's economic contribution in Johor has actually held steady and witnessed resurgence over the past decade. Johor's present-day agricultural strengths lie in oil palms, livestock farming, and certain forms of ornamental products. These agricultural activities are underlined both by high output and productivity relative to the rest of Malaysia. The clusters of trade networks and expertise underpinning these developments were already being developed in Johor prior to independence, and were given additional support from the 1960s onwards through policies linking industry with agriculture.

Johor's unusual situation can be best understood by comparing its present-day context with its past. The following section briefly outlines Southeast Asia's and Malaysia's agricultural transformations since the 1960s. A subsequent section places Johor squarely under the lens, comparing the size and productivity of its farm sector with the rest of Malaysia's. A third section examines the key historical drivers behind Johor's long-standing agricultural prominence. A fourth segment reviews the overarching roles that Malaysia's federal and state governments have played in shaping Johor's resource-heavy economy. I then offer some concluding remarks about Johor's past, present and future agricultural developments, pointing to a number of major uncertainties hanging over Johor's farmscape.

THE MALAYSIAN CONTEXT

In order to understand Johor's peculiar position, we first need to review developments across Malaysia and the surrounding region briefly. Compared with previous decades, agriculture now contributes a miniscule share of Malaysia's gross domestic product. This is largely thanks to the rapid expansion of local manufacturing and service activities. Indeed, the most recent publicly-available data show that similar trends have been occurring in neighbouring countries such as Indonesia, the Philippines, Thailand, and Vietnam (Table 2.1).

Malaysia, however, stands apart from these other economies due to the much lower proportion of workers currently involved in agricultural pursuits. Moreover, Malaysia's population is already much less rural. Johor, as will be discussed later, has been at the forefront these developments since at least the 1980s.

What kinds of activities underscore Malaysia's agricultural earnings? In 2016, just over half of Malaysia's agricultural production by value was derived from oil palm farming and, to a much lesser extent, rubber cultivation. Another fifth came from all other forms of cash cropping, including padi, vegetable, fruit, and food crop farming. Livestock husbandry and fishing together added another fifth to overall agricultural GDP, with forestry and logging activities accounting for the remainder (Figure 2.1).

Official international trade figures suggest a more sobering story. By one estimate, Malaysia registered an agricultural trade surplus of RM26 billion in 2015. But this gain was largely thanks to the oil palm sector (MAAI 2016, pp. 125–26). Palm oil and palm kernel oil net exports reached almost RM40 billion in 2015 (Figure 2.2). To be sure, the trade surplus was boosted by exports of wood-based manufactures, processed food, and agricultural chemical inputs. It would be even higher if manufactured goods made from natural rubber, such as footwear and tyres, were included in the official agricultural figures. But even with all these other products taken into consideration, Malaysia's agricultural trade balance would

TABLE 2.1

Value-Added in Agriculture, Employment Levels, and Rural Population, Selected Southeast Asian States, 1960–2015

Country	1960	1970	1980	1990	2000	2010	2015
Malaysia							
Agriculture, value added (% of GDP)	44	33	23	15	9	10	8
Employment in agriculture (% of total employment)	–	–	37	26	18	14	12
Rural population (% of total population)	73	67	58	50	38	29	25
Indonesia							
Agriculture, value added (% of GDP)	–	–	–	22	16	14	13
Employment in agriculture (% of total employment)	–	–	56	56	45	39	33
Rural population (% of total population)	85	83	78	69	58	50	46
Philippines							
Agriculture, value added (% of GDP)	27	30	25	22	14	12	10
Employment in agriculture (% of total employment)	–	–	52	45	37	33	29
Rural population (% of total population)	70	67	63	51	52	55	56
Thailand							
Agriculture, value added (% of GDP)	36	26	23	12	9	11	9
Employment in agriculture (% of total employment)	–	–	71	64	49	38	32
Rural population (% of total population)	80	79	73	71	69	56	50
Vietnam							
Agriculture, value added (% of GDP)	–	–	–	–	–	21	19
Employment in agriculture (% of total employment)	–	–	–	–	65	48	44
Rural population (% of total population)	85	82	81	80	76	70	66

Source: World Bank (n.d.).

FIGURE 2.1
Share of Agricultural Sector GDP, Malaysia, 2016 (%)

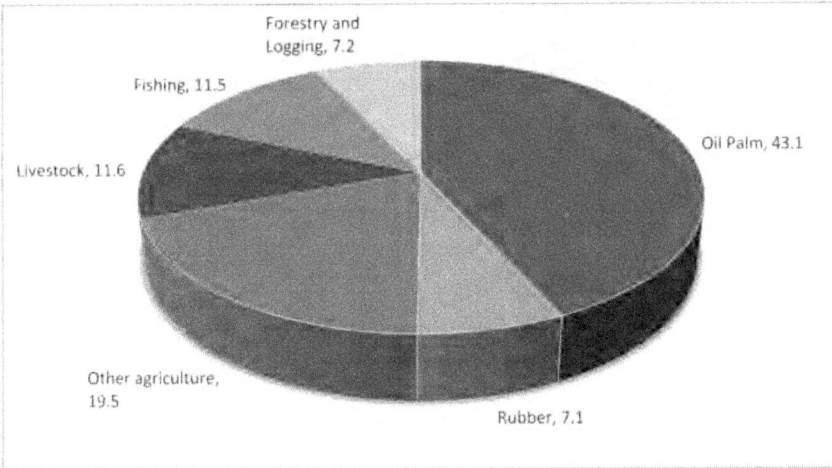

Source: DOSM (n.d.-b).

FIGURE 2.2
Malaysia's Agricultural Trade, Top 10 Exports and Top 10 Imports, 2015

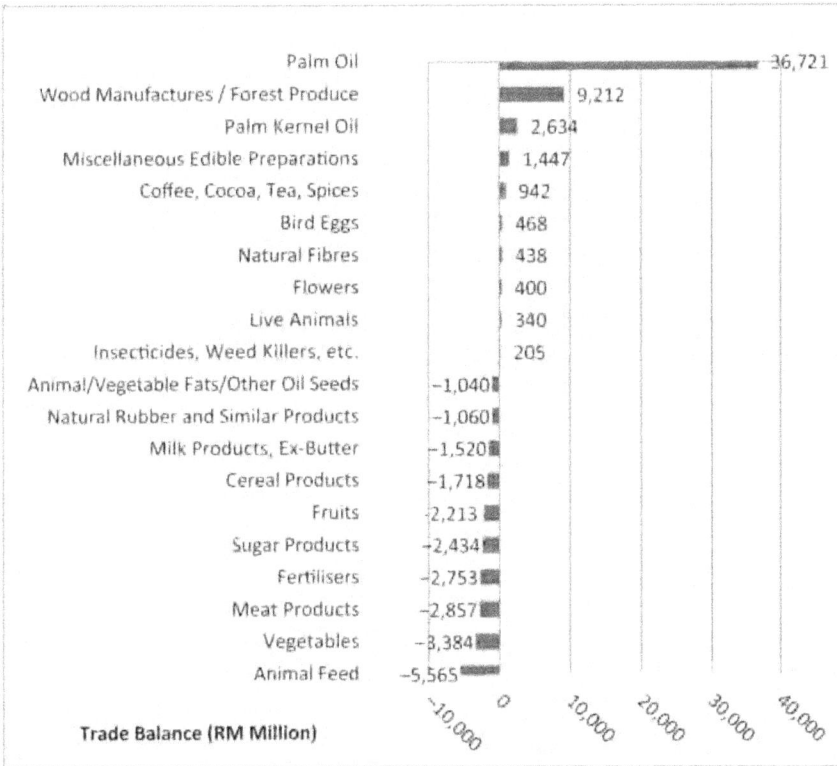

Sources: MAAI (2016), pp. 125–26.

still face dramatic shortfalls without the oil palm sector's support. Stripping out the palm oil/palm kernel oil trade surplus would leave the Malaysia agricultural trade balance in deficit, to the tune of roughly RM13.3 billion in 2015 (MAAI 2016). Moreover, these trade figures do not cover palm oil and palm kernels that were being retained within Malaysia to produce higher end exports, such as processed food, cosmetics, and lubricants.

One long-standing issue lies with Malaysia's general trade in foodstuffs. In 2015, the country's food trade registered a net loss of over RM18 billion, thanks to costly imports of meat, vegetables, fruits, cereals, dairy produce, as well as concentrated animal feed needed to keep large parts of Malaysia's domestic livestock industry commercially viable (MAAI 2016).

The stark contrast between Malaysia's heavy reliance on fresh food imports and the economy's overwhelming surplus from a single tree crop—in this case, oil palms—is not new. Since the rubber boom of the colonial period, policymakers and the general public have worried frequently about local food shortages. Staples like rice had to be imported in large quantities to meet the appetites of growing numbers of townsfolk, migrant labourers and rubber cultivators. Recent concerns, however, stem from a different dynamic: rising incomes from new manufacturing and service jobs have made agricultural work as a whole less attractive to locals, while at the same time encouraging greater household expenditure on larger quantities and varieties of food.

These shifting patterns of food consumption are especially pronounced when we look at the average Malaysian's food intake, coupled with the country's official food self-sufficiency levels (Table 2.2). The numbers do need to be viewed with some caution: not only are publicly available figures incomplete, but the complete range of food items selected to represent vegetables, fruits, and fish are not stated officially, and may have changed over time.

The figures nevertheless tell a forceful story. Malaysian rice intake per person has fallen since the 1970s, presumably due to greater access to alternative starchy staples, such as wheat- and potato-based fare. Meanwhile, Malaysian vegetable and meat consumption has risen with each successive decade. For chicken alone, the average Malaysian resident now eats the equivalent of an entire chicken every six days. Put another way, Malaysians today eat twice as much pork, 2.5 times as many eggs, 3.5 times as much beef, and 6.5 times as much chicken meat per person compared to forty years earlier. To their credit, Malaysian farms have generally managed to keep up with the public's growing appetite for eggs, poultry meat, pork, and to a lesser extent, certain types of fish, fruits and vegetables. But beef, mutton, and dairy production have continued to fall far short of local requirements.

Does Malaysia's current agricultural profile reinforce beliefs, held by many development economists, that countries generally follow an evolutionary pathway out of agriculture? In some ways, yes. According to these assumptions, as gross domestic product increases, agriculture in each country ceases to be a leading engine of economic growth. As farms shed labour, manpower is freed up to participate in the growing non-farm sector. With time, each country becomes highly urbanized, and

TABLE 2.2

Per Capita Food Consumption (kg/year) and Self-sufficiency Level (SSL) (%) in Main Food Types, 1975–2015

	1975		1985		1995		2005		2015	
	Per capita	SSL	Per capita	SSL	Per capita	SSL	Per capita	SSL	Per capita	SSL
Rice	117.8	89.8	102.3	73.3	86.9	76.3	80.5	72	93.2	72.3
Vegetables	18.1	56.6	40.8	36.1	48.5	71.6	45.9	74	N.A.	N.A.
Fruits	N.A.	N.A.	47.9	101.8	49.9	99.8	39.2	117	N.A.	N.A.
Eggs[a]	191.3	99.3	227.2	100	372.7	110.3	N.A.	113	465.9	112.3
Fish	47.6	84.5	45.7	71.1	N.A.	92	N.A.	91	N.A.	N.A.
Poultry	7.8	99.5	14.1	99.9	30	110.7	35.2	121	50.1	98.5
Beef	1.8	71.5	2.5	36.4	4.3	19.2	N.A.	23	6.4	24
Mutton	0.3	26.3	0.5	9	0.6	6	0.6	8	1.2	11.4
Pork	9.8	99.9	11.4	99.9	13.2	104	N.A.	107	18.2	93.7
Milk	N.A.	8	47.6	3	51.5	3.5	44.53	5	N.A.	N.A.

Note: a. Individual eggs as unit of measurement. Figures for 1995 and 2015 originally provided by weight, assumed to be medium- sized chicken eggs, and converted to individual egg units using Convert To website: http://convert-to.com/720/chicken-eggs-5-sizes-conversion-plus-nutrients-values.html (accessed 11 December 2017).

Sources: For years 1975 and 1985, see Arshad and Shamsuddin (2000), p. 110; for year 1995, see Ministry of Agriculture, Malaysia (1999), pp. 31, 33, and Arshad, Radam and Mohamed (2005), p. 3; for year 2005, FAOSTAT (n.d.); Mohamed Salleh, and Rokiah Yusof (2006), pp. 1–2, and Government of Malaysia (2006), p. 93; for year 2015, DOSM (2016), pp. 29, 67–71.

raw agricultural produce sales end up being dwarfed by the value contributed by local food manufacturing and associated services, which are in turn outweighed by the non-farm sector's overall growing heft (World Bank 2007, pp. 4–5; Vandergeest and Rigg 2012, p. 5). As we have already seen for Malaysia, agriculture has been steadily marginalized relative to manufacturing and services. What remains of Malaysia's agricultural trade now relies heavily on exports of processed (and semi-processed) agricultural goods, in turn made possible by massive imports of food and agricultural inputs for domestic use. The low proportion of Malaysia's workforce participating in agriculture, relative to other Southeast Asian economies, is also very striking. And as we shall now see, these tendencies are particularly acute in the case of Johor.

JOHOR'S PECULIAR POSITION

Why look at Johor? To begin with, it remains one of Malaysia's most substantial states, whether in terms of land area (third largest in the peninsula), population size (currently third highest in Malaysia), or the size of its economy (at present, third biggest in Malaysia, excluding Kuala Lumpur).[3] Johor's urbanization has also kept pace with general developments across Malaysia: in 2010, when the most recent population census was conducted, just under 72 per cent of Johor's population was classified as living in urban areas, compared to the national average of 71 per cent (DOSM 2013b, p. 11).

Indeed, if we think of urbanization not just as a measure of population density and built-up area (as the official estimates tend to do), and more as of a way of life, Johor's urban reach is probably far larger. Sociologists and anthropologists have long contended that Peninsular Malaysian villagers are already heavily integrated into "urban, industrial, national, and even international circuits" of living, by virtue of their heavy usage of modern communications, extensive commuting, as well as the socioeconomic sensibilities they share with city-dwellers (Thompson 2007; Preston and Ngah 2012). Rural households in Johor—including lower-income groups—now own a wide array of modern conveniences, ranging from cars, air conditioners, washing machines and refrigerators, to laptops, mobile phones, and Internet subscriptions, all at levels considerably higher than the national rural average, if not the highest in Malaysia (DOSM 2017f, Tables 4.10, 5.2a). These ownership patterns contrast sharply with those of 1980, when Johor's rural households tended to own major purchases at below-average national levels (DOSM 2013a, pp. 150–51).

Urbanization was driven in large part by the expansion of non-farm activities in Johor. While in 1980, three-fifths of Johor's GDP came from manufacturing and service activities, the proportion had increased to 85 per cent by 2016 (RMA Perunding Bersatu 1996, Table 3.1). The numbers employed in these pursuits also grew accordingly, from just over half of Johor's resident citizen population in 1980, to 93 per cent of all those working in 2016 (DOSM 1984; DOSM 2017g). Much of the workforce fuelling these non-farm activities was drawn from village households and Federal Land Development Authority (FELDA) settlements across Johor, ultimately enhancing material standards of living in home communities (Rogers 1992, pp. 96–99; Lie and Lund 1994, pp. 70–93). Unsurprisingly, able-bodied residents continued to spend less time farming in Johor: where in 1980, just under 235,000 people listed agriculture as their primary occupation, such individuals only numbered 101,000 by 2016, despite Johor's total workforce tripling during the same interval (DOSM 1984; DOSM 2017g). To be sure, such transformations were hardly unique to Johor, and have been witnessed in other states, not least Selangor.[4] But compared to the rest of Malaysia, Johor's development has been peculiar in several ways.

The first of these concerns a principal gauge of economic transformation: the productivity of those who remain farmers. If agriculture is to contribute, rather than detract from overall economic output, the value of agricultural produce churned out by each employee needs to rise and keep pace with the rest of the growing, diversifying economy. The official figures show that, in 2016, Johor's value-added per agricultural worker was two-and-a-half times higher than the Malaysian average, twice that of Pahang's, and nearly six times that of Sabah's (Table 2.3). Only Melaka's figures were significantly higher than Johor's. But Johor's agricultural sector is far larger than either Melaka or Penang's.

This brings us to the second unusual feature of Johor's agricultural economy: its sheer size. Between 2005 and 2016, Johor's share of Malaysian agricultural gross domestic product rose the most amongst all states, barring Melaka, from 13.8 to 15.7 per cent (Table 2.4). This expansion allowed Johor to draw level with Sabah (the largest agricultural economy in Malaysia in 2010), and close the gap with Sarawak (the largest state agricultural economy in 2016) to less than a percentage point; all this despite East Malaysia's much larger land area.

TABLE 2.3
Value-Added per Month, per Worker in Agriculture by State,
2010 Prices (RM)

	2010	2016
Melaka	14,142	16,158
Pulau Pinang	11,402	11,960
Johor	9,818	11,518
Perlis	7,668	7,466
Negeri Sembilan	5,624	7,342
Perak	6,055	7,287
Selangor	7,314	7,030
Pahang	6,732	6,017
Kelantan	3,910	5,330
Terengganu	4,722	4,750
Sarawak	3,631	4,076
Kedah	3,670	3,637
Sabah	3,048	2,020
National Average	4,823	4,631

Sources: DOSM (2017e), Tables 3, 26; DOSM (2013a), Tables 4.2–4.14; DOSM (2017g), Table B4.8.

TABLE 2.4
Share of Malaysia's Agricultural Gross Domestic Product,
by State, 2005–16

	2005	2010	2016
Johor	13.8	15.1	15.7
Kedah	4.9	5.3	5.6
Kelantan	5.2	5.4	5.7
Melaka	1.8	3.1	3.9
Negeri Sembilan	3.6	4.1	4.2
Pahang	12.0	12.1	12.2
Pulau Pinang	1.4	1.5	1.7
Perak	10.4	10.4	10.9
Perlis	1.6	1.4	1.2
Selangor	3.8	4.7	3.9
Terengganu	3.5	3.2	2.7
Sabah	21.5	19.2	15.8
Sarawak	16.2	14.3	16.5

Sources: DOSM (2017e), Tables 4, 28; DOSM (n.d.-a).

These shifts were both relative and absolute. In Johor's case, agriculture's share of state gross domestic product actually rose from 12.3 per cent in 2005 to 13.5 per cent in 2016, eating into the space occupied by non-agricultural activities (DOSM 2017e, Table 32; DOSM n.d.-a). Incredibly, this swing occurred despite the steady expansion of local manufacturing and service activities, including long-term investments in southern Johor's Iskandar Malaysia project (IRDA 2016, p. 66).

In sum, agriculture remains a major part of Johor's physical and economic landscape. For now, Johor's agriculturalists are outperforming the rest of Malaysia's growers in productivity *and* output. They are even increasing their lead over time, despite hard evidence of extensive urbanization and industrialization.

PRODUCT SPECIALIZATION

What secrets lie behind Johor's currently elevated agricultural profile? We can start by asking if Johor's labour demographics are atypical compared to other Malaysian states. On the whole, Johor's labour force composition is actually not that unusual, if the most recent official statistics are to be believed. Between 2000 and 2010, the age of those involved in Johor agriculture tended to be slightly elevated compared to the national average, but not glaringly so (DOSM 2003, Tables 4.1–4.14; DOSM 2013a, Tables 3, 4.1–4.14). Comparing agricultural employment between states by gender yields little of interest: the most productive agricultural states—Penang, Melaka and Johor—vary widely in their use of female labour (DOSM 2017g, Table B4.9).

By the same token, factors such as ethnicity and the proportion of agricultural employment in urban areas reveal little about Johor's dynamism, at least on their own. Like Penang and Melaka, Johor has had consistently elevated levels of Chinese involved in farming since the 1980s, as well as rising levels of agricultural work in urban areas. But states with far lower farm productivity levels, including Perak, Selangor and Pahang, have also had high levels of Chinese involvement, and plenty of agriculture in areas pigeonholed as urban (DOSM 1984, Tables 18–32.1; DOSM 1995, Tables 1.2–14.2; DOSM 2003, Tables 4.1–5.1; DOSM 2013a, Tables 3, 4.1–4.14; DOSM 2017g, Tables B4.8, B4.10). Even where foreign labour use is concerned, Johor's situation is not especially atypical, with official state figures running at slightly below the national average in 2010 (the most recent population census) (DOSM 2013a, Tables 3, 4.1–4.14). That being said, the situation regarding undocumented labour is trickier; we will return to this issue in the essay's penultimate section.

Instead of focusing broadly on *who* is producing Johor's crops, more rewarding answers can be found in *what* is currently being produced. In 2015, over half of Johor's entire land surface was being utilized for cultivating crops (DOSM 2013b, p. 11; JPBDNJ 2017, p. 2.32). Nearly three quarters of this landscape was devoted to oil palms, another sixth to rubber (mostly in northwest Johor), with the remainder dedicated mostly to fruit and vegetable cropping, including old-time cultivars like pineapples and coconuts (Table 2.5) (JPBDNJ 2017, p. 232).

Every district in Johor devotes significant amounts of land to crop farming, including the relatively built-up districts of Kulai and Johor Bahru. But Kluang, Segamat, Batu Pahat and Kota Tinggi currently lead the way (JPBDNJ 2017, p. 2.35). In other words, the western, central and eastern portions of the state tended to harbour the most expansive farmlands (Figure 2.3).

Focusing on land-hungry farming activities, however, only reveals part of the picture. In 2015, over 66 million chickens were housed in compact dwellings peppering the Johor landscape. This vast army of poultry, bred for their meat and eggs, constituted the bulk of Johor's livestock farming (Figure 2.4) (JPBDNJ 2017, p. 2.35; AVA 2016). There was also considerable pig-farming, duck-rearing, and cattle-raising activity occurring across the entire Johor state, as well as a significant number

TABLE 2.5
Crop Area and Output, Johor, 2015

Crop Type	Area Covered		Output	
	Hectares	%	Mt	%
Oil Palm	729,387	73.5	3,117,619	62.6
Rubber	172,831	17.7	562,492	11.3
Fruits	44,090	4.4	530,543	10.7
Vegetables	14,921	1.5	252,264	5.1
Pineapples	11,181	1.1	329,954	6.6
Coconuts	11,550	1.2	98,869	1.9
Other crops	8,902	0.9	91,331	1.7
Total	992,862	100	4,983,072	100

Source: JPBDNJ Johor (2017), p. 2.32.

FIGURE 2.3
Crop Land Use by District, Johor, 2015

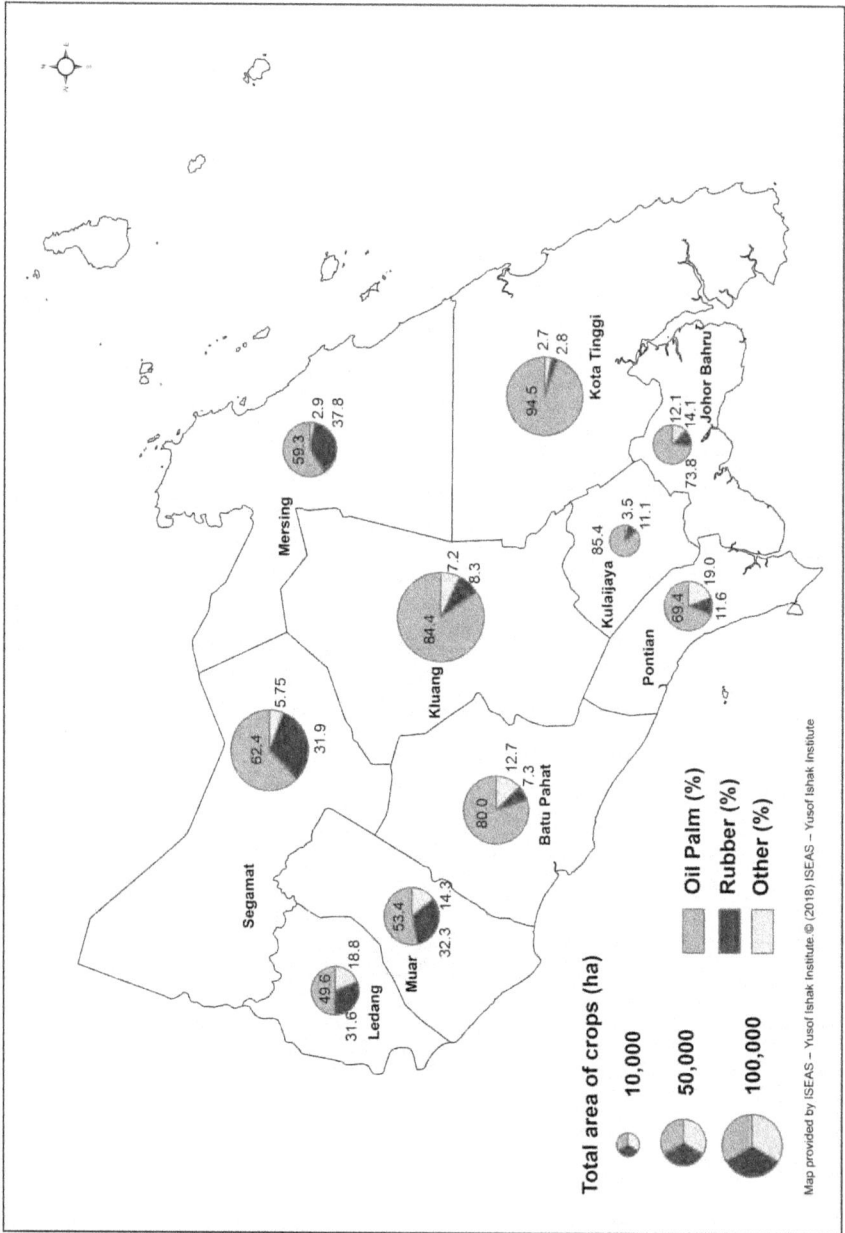

Kota Tinggi
94.5 / 2.7 / 2.8

Johor Bahru
73.8 / 12.1 / 14.1

Mersing
59.3 / 2.9 / 37.8

Kulaijaya
85.4 / 3.5 / 11.1

Kluang
84.4 / 7.2 / 8.3

Pontian
69.4 / 11.6 / 19.0

Segamat
62.4 / 5.75 / 31.9

Batu Pahat
80.0 / 12.7 / 7.3

Muar
53.4 / 32.3 / 14.3

Ledang
49.6 / 31.6 / 18.8

Oil Palm (%)
Rubber (%)
Other (%)

Total area of crops (ha)
10,000
50,000
100,000

Map provided by ISEAS – Yusof Ishak Institute. © (2018) ISEAS – Yusof Ishak Institute

Source: JPBDNJ (2017), p. 2.35.

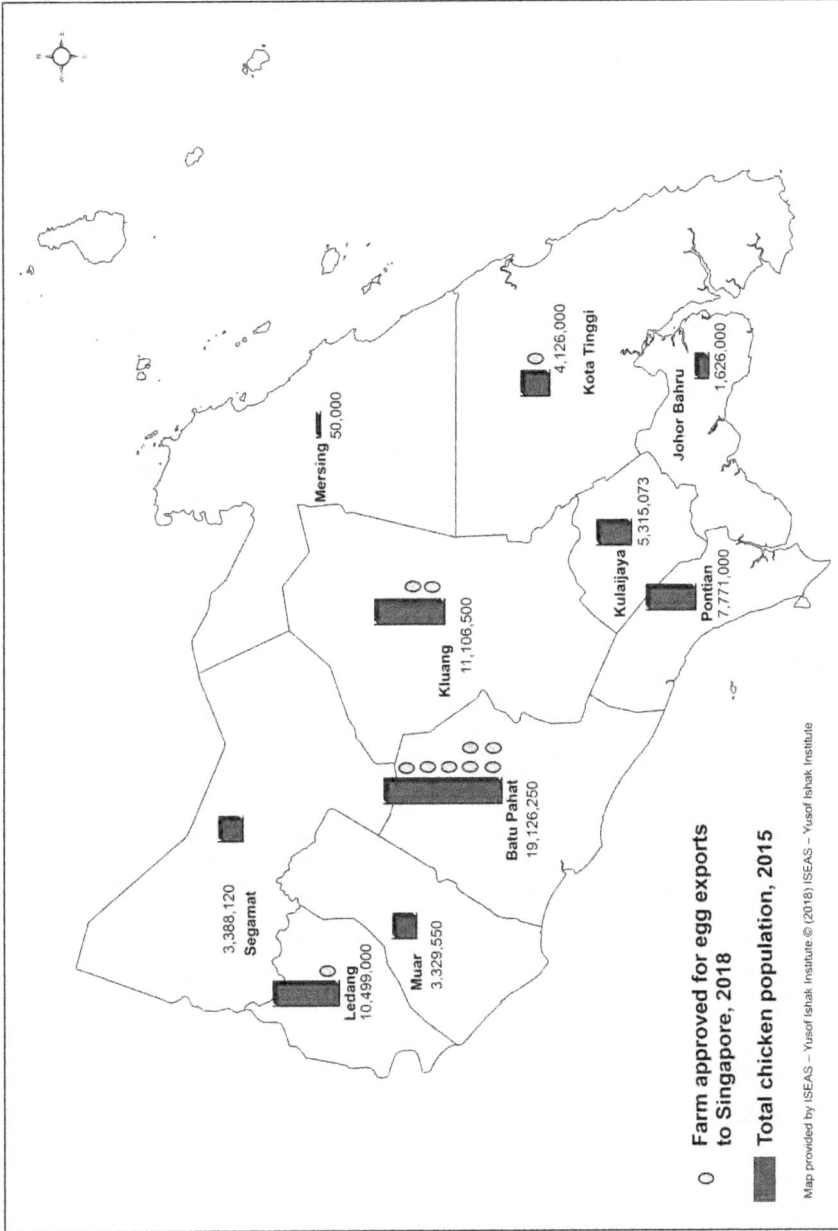

FIGURE 2.4
Chicken Population and Egg Farms by District, Johor

Kota Tinggi
4,126,000

Johor Bahru
1,626,000

Mersing
50,000

Kulaijaya
5,315,073

Pontian
7,771,000

Kluang
11,106,500

Batu Pahat
19,126,250

Segamat
3,388,120

Muar
3,329,550

Ledang
10,499,000

○ Farm approved for egg exports
    to Singapore, 2018

■ Total chicken population, 2015

Map provided by ISEAS – Yusof Ishak Institute © (2018) ISEAS – Yusof Ishak Institute

Sources: JPBDNJ (2017), p. 2.35; AVA (2016).

of fishery enterprises, including freshwater aquaculture, marine-based aquaculture and open-water fishing (JPBDNJ 2017, p. 2.36).

Things become even clearer when we compare Johor's agricultural profile with the rest of Malaysia's. The National Agrostatistics Compendium tells us that in 2015, Johor ranked among the leading Malaysian states in a wide variety of crops and livestock, including oil palm products, coconuts, various fruits, leafy and root vegetables, tubers, legumes, spices, flowers, pork, chicken meat and eggs, and ornamental fish. This dominance becomes especially apparent when we compare Johor's share of agricultural output with that of other states leading in agricultural productivity, such as Penang and Melaka (Figure 2.5).

As indicated in Malaysia's most recent national census of economic activity, the *Economic Census 2016*, considerable numbers of these above-mentioned agricultural products rank highly by value-added per worker. Table 2.6 shows that in 2015, the most productive forms of Malaysian agriculture included poultry farming (both eggs and meat), oil palm cultivation, pig and cattle farming, and freshwater aquarium fish rearing. These were all activities weighing heavily on Johor's agricultural profile. Oil palm produce accounted for the majority of Johor's earnings from arable activities (RM5.71 billion in 2015) (DOSM 2017a, p. 107). Thanks largely to this tree crop, Johor's cash crop sector remains one of Malaysia's greatest by output and employment (DOSM 2017a, p. 107).

FIGURE 2.5
Proportion of Malaysian Agricultural Production by State, Selected Commodities, 2015

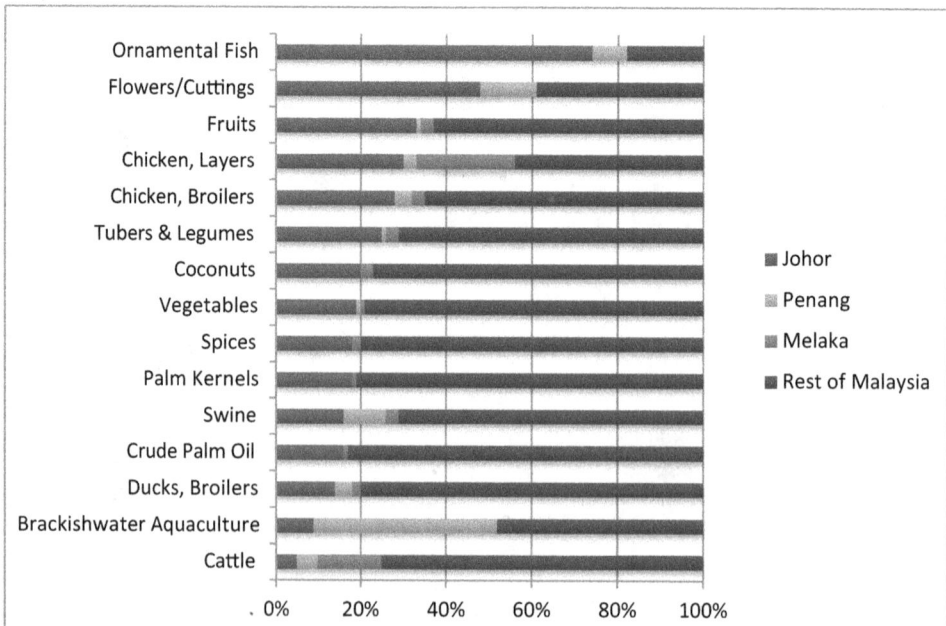

Sources: MAAI (2016); DVS (2017).

TABLE 2.6
Value-Added per Worker per Month, and Fixed Asset Values per Establishment, Selected Agricultural Products, Malaysia, 2015

Type of Agricultural Commodity	Value-Added per Worker per Month		Fixed Asset Value per Establishment	
	Average (RM)	Highest Rank (out of 82)	Average (RM '000)	Highest Rank (out of 82)
Chicken, eggs	10,025	5	7,346	6
Chicken, broilers	9,045	6	3,501	14
Oil palms (estates)	8,426	7	15,449	3
Ducks, broilers	6,685	10	3,000	17
Swine	5,612	13	1,468	37
Oil palms (smallholdings)	5,587	14	1,454	38
Coconuts (estates and smallholdings)	5,547	15	4,220	11
Cattle	4,908	19	322	69
Ornamental fish	3,665	32	459	65

Sources: DOSM (2017a), pp. 101–6; DOSM (2017b), pp. 101–3; DOSM (2017c), pp. 99–101.

Not to be overshadowed, Johor's livestock sector, led by chicken and pig husbandry, also made significant contributions to overall agricultural gains (RM0.89 billion in 2015). Indeed, because of these pastoral activities, Johor's livestock business has become Malaysia's largest, whether in terms of output value, or people employed (DOSM 2017b, p. 104).

It is probably no coincidence that many of Johor's leading agricultural activities also tend to be fairly capital-intensive, as indicated by the relatively high values of land, buildings, and equipment used to generate output (fixed asset values). We can thus safely infer that the more muscular features of Johor's agricultural sector are underpinned by selective specialization in high-earning, capital-intensive activities.

Focusing on present-day product specialization, however, does not tell us *why* such clustering has occurred in Johor. Answering this puzzle means turning to history, both of the more distant and recent varieties. Much of Johor's agricultural past still lies buried and unappreciated; that which is being progressively unearthed is fascinatingly complex, and only a brief outline can be provided here.

PRE-INDEPENDENCE ACTIVITIES

Most narratives of Johor's oil palm landscape usually emphasize how quickly oil palm cultivation expanded from the 1960s onwards. Much of this explosion was triggered by oil palm's increasing profitability relative to Malaysia's then-agricultural export mainstay, *Hevea* rubber. Large-scale land development initiatives pioneered by FELDA, Johor's own state schemes, as well as the replanting efforts of private estates and independent smallholders collectively fuelled a surge of oil palm planting (Rasiah 2006, pp. 164–65). These transformations, by and large, ensured that nearly three out of every ten acres of oil palms in Malaysia would be found in Johor by the mid-1980s (Malek bin Mansoor and Barlow 1988, p. 15). Until today, Johor's oil palm acreage remains Peninsular Malaysia's highest (MPOB n.d.).

While Johor's rapid ascendance certainly owes much to these recent developments, the speed, scope, and character of this expansion would have been impossible without two "gifts" from the more distant past. First, at independence, the territory inherited vast areas of suitable agricultural land for replanting—crucial to a land-hungry crop like the oil palm—as well as wide-ranging transport networks needed to convey heaps of bulky goods to the marketplace. As far back as the early nineteenth century, Johor's rulers demonstrated a predilection for encouraging wealth accumulation through extensive forest clearance for cash cropping. This began with awarding riverine concessions for Chinese-controlled pepper and gambier farming, followed by financial support to encourage Dutch East Indies immigrants to farm areca nuts and coconuts along Johor's lengthy coastlines. From the 1910s onwards, cheap land concessions for rubber and pineapple cultivation could be added to this list. Thus, over the course of one-and-a-half centuries, successive agricultural enterprises bequeathed independence-era Johor with over a million acres of already-cleared agricultural land suitable for oil palm cultivation (Pakiam 2017, pp. 54–71, 334).

Johor's denizens can also lay claim to a second legacy: privileged access to unrivalled flows of trade, investment, manpower, and commercial expertise, all tailored towards export-oriented agriculture. By the 1820s, two groups of merchant communities—one predominantly Western in origin, the other Asian—had begun converging on Singapore, after the island's re-emergence as a major entrepôt under British colonial rule. The Western segment specialized in supplying both capital inputs and skilled human resources to local planters and smaller merchants, while operating as gatekeepers to European markets. The Asian, Chinese-dominated segment used their intimate familiarity with regional trade networks to act as intermediaries for remote communities. In exchange for raw produce, they carved out niches supplying credit, consumer goods, and unskilled labour to smaller enterprises, especially those operating within Singapore's geographic vicinity, such as Johor and Sumatra. Both Asian and Western mercantile groups quickly developed complementary relations, in turn encouraging local cash croppers to quickly scale up production in tandem with rising global demand for agricultural commodities (Giacomin 2017, pp. 282–86). The aristocrats who oversaw Johor's agricultural development—and indeed, its transition from a maritime-based polity to a territorial state during the nineteenth century—did so leaning on the economic advantages of being physically proximate to Singapore (Trocki 2007, pp. 86–91, 98–123).

Western capital, Asian merchants, mobile labour, and local rule thus propelled rubber cultivation across Johor, Singapore and neighbouring areas during the early 1900s. When rubber markets slumped after the First World War, oil palms beckoned to estate planters and their mercantile backers, not least in Johor (Giacomin 2017, pp. 286–98). By 1940, Johor was already hosting nearly half of Malaya's oil palm lands, not to mention some of the most advanced (and costly) palm fruit processing technologies seen to date in Southeast Asia (Pakiam 2017, pp. 160, 334).

As local populations grew, so did their need for fresh food. By the 1930s, vast patchworks of Chinese market gardens were surrounding Johor's railway stations, enabling the swift despatch of leafy vegetables, tubers, beans, and other legumes (Grist 1936, pp. 242–48). These products catered directly to the appetites of Singapore and Johor's growing resident populations. Vegetables like *kangkong* were also nurtured to feed an expanding Johorean pig industry; pork had become one of the main sources of fresh protein for burgeoning Chinese communities in both Johor and Singapore during the 1930s. Pig farming also became more economically viable during this interval because of lower production costs. Protein-rich copra cake, a pulverized by-product of Singapore's rapidly expanding coconut kernel crushing industry, helped cheapen pig feed outlays, while simultaneously shortening the time needed to raise slaughter-ready hogs to just eight months (Pakiam 2017, pp. 209–10).

War and social upheaval brought Johor and Singapore even closer together. During the 1940s and 1950s, market gardens proliferated in response to local food shortages since the outbreak of the Second World War. Despite the illegal status of many such "squatter" farms, Johor's administrators condoned their expansion within southern Johor because of widespread hunger, as well as the need to provide livelihoods for otherwise unemployed Chinese labourers (Local Produce Working Committee 1951, pp. 7–11, 18, 23). Other Johor-based vegetable and pig farms were catalysed by federal efforts to relocate Chinese communities to new village sites, as part of a strategy to counter Malayan Communist Party guerrilla tactics (Pakiam 2017, pp. 283–84).

By the same token, Johor's ornamental fish farm industry appears to have been kick-started during the 1950s. Local entrepreneurs spied a market opportunity and started collecting fish from Johor's wetlands and peat swamps for breeding purposes and sale to nearby Singapore, long before such practices spread to other parts of Malaysia (Ng 2016, p. 9).

MORE RECENT TRENDS

Other prominent forms of Johor-based produce are more readily traced to recent times. Take the example of the poultry industry, now Malaysia's largest livestock offering: until the 1960s, local chicken meat and egg production was relatively insignificant. Malayan village holdings had played host to complementary flocks of fowls since antiquity, but there were apparently few specialist producers around using capital-intensive farming methods. Most poultry supplies before the Second World War apparently had to be sought from mainland Southeast Asia and China (Grist 1936, pp. 338–39). This all seems to have changed markedly by the 1980s, if not earlier (Figure 2.6).

Malaysian chicken meat saw production surge from the mid-1980s to the mid-1990s, before regaining momentum after the 1997–98 Asian Financial Crisis. Poultry egg output (of which chicken eggs constitute the vast majority) mirrored these gains. In fact, by the mid-1990s, local poultry farmers had turned Malaysia's long-standing national poultry product trade deficit into a surplus (see Table 2.2 earlier).

FIGURE 2.6
Production of Chicken Meat and Eggs, Malaysia, 1961–2015

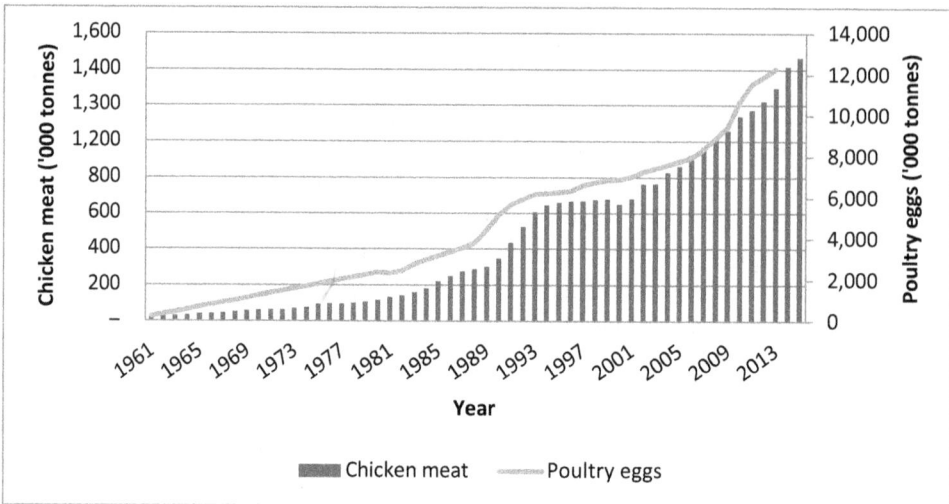

Source: FAOSTAT (n.d.).

Remarkably little seems to have been written on the recent histories of these Malaysian-based agribusinesses, let alone Johor's. In many ways the rise of Malaysia's poultry sector is encapsulated by the rise of Leong Hup (Malaysia) Berhad, today one of the country's largest home-grown poultry operations. Leong Hup apparently began operations in the early 1960s as a small Chinese family-run "backyard farm" in northwest Johor, eventually mutating into an incorporated business by 1979 (Munira binti Halili 2011, p. 10). By the early 1990s, the Lau family had successfully breached the other end of the poultry value chain, acquiring some 30 per cent of KFC (Malaysia) Holdings Berhad. They were eventually pressured into selling their stake to Datuk Ishak Ismail, a businessman linked with Malaysia's largest political party—United Malays National Organization—in 1996. The Laus reportedly used their sales proceeds to expand their chicken farm holdings (which, if true, may partly help explain the surge in poultry production after the Asian Financial Crisis) (Gomez 2001, p. 88; Jayaseelan and Ng 2015).

Today, Leong Hup Holdings is a leading Malaysian poultry industry integrator, breeding and rearing parent stocks, raising broiler day-old chicks, contracting farming out to smaller producers, slaughtering and processing broiler chickens, retailing produce, as well as farming eggs and supplying poultry inputs (Munira binti Halili 2011, p. 10). The firm currently controls a quarter of Malaysia's poultry market share, and continues to operate Johor-based facilities, including a large chicken farm in Desaru (Ho 2017). Its current executive chairman, Tan Sri Francis Lau Tuan Nguang, reportedly engages in occasional discussions with Malaysian government officials to ensure that Malaysian consumers are supplied with sufficient chicken meat during major local festivals (Ho 2017).

While Chinese-owned poultry farming enterprises such as Leong Hup's continue to dominate Johor's poultry sector, the state-linked Johor Corporation also commands a significant share of the domestic Malaysian sector. Through a controlling stake in QSR Brands (Malaysia) Holdings Sendirian Berhad—which in turn oversees the Ayamas group of companies—the Corporation manages a dense chain of large-scale poultry-based activities (Hutchinson 2012). To begin with, Ayamas Integrated Poultry Industry Sendirian Berhad operates Malaysia's largest single feedmill. Feed products are channelled towards the Group's own chicken farms, as well as contract broiler farms throughout Malaysia. Ayamas Integrated's breeder unit supplies chicks to some forty contract farms, and currently has its own farm units in Sedenak, Johor, and Mantin, Negri Sembilan. Taken together, Ayamas' farm network has the capacity to supply up to 36 million broilers per year to three processing plants owned by Ayamas Food Corporation Sendirian Berhad. Ayamas' plants are deliberately located close to densely populated areas, with facilities at Port Klang, Penang and Johor's Bandar Tenggara. Processed meat is then retailed through the open market under the Ayamas brand, or else channelled into QSR Brands' fast-food restaurant chains, especially KFC Malaysia (Johor Corporation 2016, pp. 16, 50–52, 249–53).

The domestic market for chicken is already fairly saturated. With each Malaysian consuming around 42 to 50 kilograms of chicken meat per year, per capita rates are among the world's highest, falling only slightly behind the United States, Saudi Arabia, and Israel (OECD 2018). Perhaps recognizing this limitation from early on, Malaysian poultry integrators have already gone regional in various ways. The Lau family has expanded Leong Hup's meat and egg supply chains to Indonesia, the Philippines and Vietnam (Wong 2011, p. 143). In Indonesia, for example, Leong Hup International has a controlling stake in twenty-year-old PT Malindo. A publicly listed firm that engages not just in chicken husbandry, but food processing and large-scale animal feed manufacture, PT Malindo had an estimated market capitalization of RM1 billion in 2015 (Jayaseelan and Ng 2015; PT Malindo Feedmill Tbk 2017, pp. 15–41).

Meanwhile, through QSR Trading, Johor Corporation has overseen the geographic expansion of its fast-food retail segment, notably through KFC Singapore, KFC Brunei and KFC Cambodia. Such transnational linkages do not show up easily via conventional statistical measurements of Malaysian agricultural trade. While considerable research has already been conducted on transnational business networks in Malaysia's oil palm sector (Pye and Bhattacharya 2012; Cramb and McCarthy 2016; Varkkey 2016), there is still nothing comparable for the Malaysia's poultry enterprises, which is surprising given their size, reach, and complexity.

Amidst these expansions, Singapore's market presence continues to weigh considerably on Johor's agricultural landscape. A contemporary account of Johor's economic development, written in 1995, noted that Johor's poultry sector output had been mounting, largely in response to recent demands from Singapore-based restaurants and households (Anon. 1995, pp. 83–84). These expansions were partly driven by Singapore-based entrepreneurs' overseas investments in livestock production, following Goh Keng Swee's decision (in his capacity as Singapore's Director of the Primary Production Department) to phase out Singapore's family-run farms from 1984 onwards (Chou 2014, pp. 234–36). As late as 2013, observers were still considering Singapore a "captive market" for Malaysian chicken eggs, with over 94 per cent of fresh eggs found in Singapore's wet markets, supermarkets and restaurants coming mostly from Johor (the proportion has since come down, mostly due to a resurgence of local production in Singapore, but still remained above 75 per cent in 2016) (Anon. 2013, p. 16; Mokhtar 2017).

Singapore's strong connections to markets beyond Southeast Asia also continue to shape Johor's farming options. In present-day Johor, proximity to Singapore's Changi Airport (one of the world's busiest and most efficient cargo airports) has been a boon to Johor's production of cut flowers and ornamental fish, destined for lucrative markets in Europe and the Pacific region. Changi Airport's unmatched reputation for cost-effective cargo-handling—crucial for sustaining production clusters of high-value perishable goods—has allowed Singapore-based entrepreneurs to retain footholds in the ornamental product business, even as local farm production declined. Singapore businesses have taken up the mantle of becoming middlemen to smaller Johor-based farm operators. Moreover, for the past three decades, a supportive Malaysian licensing regime has encouraged Singaporean entrepreneurs to relocate their farms, or establish subsidiaries within Johor (Gasco 2016, pp. 348–55). These trends all dovetail with the manner in which Johor's previous agricultural mainstays were sired, from pepper and gambier, to rubber and pineapples.

AGRICULTURE'S GOVERNMENT

Seen from history's vantage point, the various official strategies and initiatives undertaken by Malaysian authorities to support Johor's agricultural development fall into several interrelated channels. First, Johor's state government—throughout history—has sought to harness opportunities for "economic twinning" with Singapore. Through the provisioning of cheap land, liberal investment policies, and efficient transport networks, Malaysia's southernmost territory has consistently sought to capture gains from international trade in primary products, relying to a large extent on networks of capital, labour and marketing expertise via Singapore (Khazanah Nasional 2006, p. 4.15).

This internationalist orientation has not diminished significantly, despite Singapore's political independence since 1965. Malaysia's federal authorities have, in fact, helped prolong this economic interdependence through massive public infrastructural upgrades, not least through initiatives to widen the Singapore–Johor Causeway in 1976, as well as the early 1990s (UPENJ 1989, p. 145). At the same time, federal allocations directed towards Johor's internal transport networks and general development plans have been fairly generous. Those for Johor were amongst the highest of all states during the 1980s and 1990s (Anon. 1995, pp. 36–37). Such allocations suggest close political ties between Barisan Nasional-dominated Johor and federal political elites. All in all, this balance between internal and externally-oriented infrastructure has helped bolster agricultural expansion and intensification within Johor's countryside (UPENJ 1989, p. 145).

Second, federal and state authorities have gotten directly involved in Johor-based agricultural initiatives, whether in terms of research and development (R&D), producer cooperative formation, or through government-linked enterprises, such as FELDA, and the Johor Corporation (and its earlier incarnation, the Johor State Economic Development Corporation). These endeavours, especially those of government-linked enterprises, have tended to be coloured by ethno-nationalist considerations supporting greater bumiputra capital ownership, and attempts to wrest lucrative trade flows away from Singapore. Adding further to these tensions—as well as indirect pressures to speed up structural change within agriculture—have been efforts to accelerate industrialization in Johor since the 1970s, if not earlier.

These dynamics are encapsulated in the Johor government's past struggles to enlarge its economy by fostering a new industrial cluster at Pasir Gudang, operating in the shadows cast by Johor Bahru and Singapore. In 1966, the year following Singapore's separation from the Malaysian mainland (and even before the onset of the bumiputera-friendly New Economic Policy in 1970), Johor's government began planning for a new port near Johor Bahru, both in the interests of resource-based industrialization, as well as ensuring that Johor's rising flows of agricultural exports were not beholden to Singapore's own port facilities (Guinness 1992, p. 33). Backed by massive financial, technical, and regulatory support from Malaysia's federal government, the Johor authorities eventually established a modern harbour, Johor Port, and an accompanying industrial estate at Pasir Gudang in the late 1970s (Guinness 1992, p. 33–35). Cognizant of Singapore's incumbent advantages as a global trading centre, the Johor authorities had expended a total of $165 million on Pasir Gudang's industrial estate by 1987, developing local housing, a town centre, as well as ancillary railways and highways, all in order to attract manufacturing investment (Guinness 1992, p. 35). Chaired by the state's Chief Minister, the Johor State Economic Development Corporation became the de facto manager of Pasir Gudang Industrial Estate (Guinness 1992, pp. 34, 45). In addition, both the Johor Corporation and FELDA bought their way into a large number of resource-based manufacturing activities housed at Pasir Gudang, including food processing and palm oil refining (Guinness 1992, pp. 34–39).

Notwithstanding these combined efforts, Johor Port struggled to displace its Singapore counterpart during its opening decades. The exceptions to this trend lay in the trade of palm oil, fertilizers and rubber products. Between 1971 and 1985, Johor's overall share of primary exports dropped from 69.4 per cent to 6.5 per cent, displaced mostly by resource-based manufactures (UPENJ 1989, pp. 55–56). This outcome reflected Johor's agricultural strengths; not just a major site for tree crop cultivation and livestock husbandry, but as a rapidly ascending centre for the processing of bulky, perishable commodities. Johor's industrial development thus relied to a significant degree on the handling of live animals, meat, meat preparations, palm oil, palm kernels, rubber, as well as their derivatives and by-products, such as fertilizers and animal feed (Guinness 1992, pp. 39, 47; UPENJ 1989, p. 130).

By helping to propel Johor's industrialization, however, federal and state authorities indirectly contributed to a third major factor transforming Johor's agricultural scene: increasingly scarce labour. Thus, at Pasir Gudang Industrial Estate, roughly three-fifths of all workers by the mid-1980s were sourced from other parts of Johor. Nearby villages also saw labourers exit rubber tapping and weeding, seeking out better paying work in factories, construction and port-side activities. Large numbers of youth from FELDA settlements sought out job opportunities at Johor Port and Pasir Gudang, owing partly to underemployment on settler smallholdings (Guinness 1992, pp. 59, 126–27, 149–52, 156–57).

By the early 1990s, Johor's farmers were thus under heavy pressure to move into new crops and implement labour-saving technologies where possible (Anon. 1995, p. 79). "Fruits, vegetables, horticulture, aquaculture, and tropical fish are among sectors that are increasing in popularity," noted a major internal review of Johor's long-term development plans. "These sub-sector[s] are able to offer more value-added production with less labour requirement." (Anon. 1995, p. 80). With the international market for cut flowers booming, Johor's flower exports consequently quadrupled in value in just four years, reaching RM20 million in 1994. Similar booms occurred in poultry meat and egg production during the same interval (Anon. 1995, pp. 83–84, 91). To be sure, the Johor authorities also dedicated large sums of money to agricultural restructuring. Under the Fifth Malaysia Plan, the state government put aside RM10.4 million for "agricultural development" (UPENJ 1989, p. 125).

There were nevertheless distinct limits to how much labour could be displaced by new technologies and agricultural activities. The oil palm industry, for instance, remains heavily dependent until today on manual labour for fieldwork. Federal efforts to advance fruit harvesting technology beyond the predominant pole-mounted sickle/chisel combination have not been popular. The latest attempt to do so, the Malaysian Palm Oil Board's *CANTAS*—a petrol-powered, motorized version of the extended sickle—can potentially triple labour productivity. But the limited reach of current versions restricts their use to shorter (and hence less productive) palms, while vibrations from prolonged wielding can cause serious nerve tissue damage to a worker's upper limbs (Salleh et al. 2013; Guturu and Singh 2015).

Notwithstanding these genuine technological constraints, local firms have also had little incentive to improve labour productivity, thanks to the federal government's liberal foreign labour policies (Zunaira Saieed 2016). Lax migrant labour regulations have effectively repressed Malaysian agricultural wages, and enabled rapid agricultural labour shedding (mostly of the Indonesian variety) during commodity downcycles (Saravanamuttu 2013). Moreover, undocumented migrant workers have become a long-term social and economic concern in Malaysia; as many as 50,000 undocumented immigrants were thought to be employed in Johor plantations alone by the late 1980s (UPENJ 1989, p. 126).

To be fair, this situation is hardly unique to Johor's agricultural sector. Low-wage activities within construction, manufacturing and services are also affected. Pasir Gudang, a now long-time hive of industrial activity, is still heavily peppered by undocumented Indonesian migrants, some of whom have already been residing for over fifteen years in southern Johor (Ngah 2010, p. 4). But state and federal authorities—unable to provide credible estimates of migrant workers for decades—have turned a blind eye to the phenomenon (Lee and Khor 2018). Malaysia's publicly-available agricultural productivity figures are thus almost certainly overestimates. In other words, we do not know how many people actually work in Johor's agricultural sector each year, except to say that the numbers are probably underestimates. Until more accurate estimates (including previously undocumented workers) can be tabulated and publicly disseminated, Johor's agricultural productivity figures remain somewhat provisional in nature.

FINAL REMARKS

Many development economists, including those from the World Bank, have suggested that state-level economic growth usually follows an evolutionary path from agricultural-based production, to that of densely populated urban societies anchored in high-tech manufacturing and services, where agriculture contributes only around 5 per cent of gross domestic product (World Bank 2007, p. 4). At the sub-national level, however, Johor's present status complicates this assumption somewhat: despite being an already highly urbanized economy, agriculture still contributed almost 14 per cent of state gross domestic product in 2016. This paper has argued that such an aberration may not be a temporary phenomenon, but rather something structurally embedded within Johor's historical geography.

From early on, urban growth appears to have offered complex challenges and opportunities for Johor's agricultural sector. Since the nineteenth century, Johor's wealth creation through agriculture was based on deep engagement with international markets, not least through what the town of Singapore could offer through ancillary trade, labour, and services. Singapore's continued growth in population and prosperity has also created new agri-business opportunities for Johor, not least in food production. However, Singapore's economic growth has also seen various manufacturing and service activities relocate to cheaper locales in Johor since at least the 1980s. In turn, Johoreans have spent progressively less time in agriculture, in favour of higher earning non-farm occupations.

Nonetheless, as incomes within Johor and the rest of Malaysia have increased, so too has the domestic market for agricultural produce, especially food items, presenting new opportunities for growers to satisfy local appetites. But this dynamic lies in tension with accompanying pressures to convert increasingly expensive local farmland to higher value uses, often of non-farm varieties. This seems especially pertinent to Johor's Iskandar Malaysia region, whose regional development authority is only prepared to safeguard about three-fifths of all existing farmland within the Iskandar Malaysia development corridor by 2030, leaving the remainder to be converted to more lucrative urban purposes (Khazanah Nasional 2006, p. 11.2; IRDA 2015, pp. 6.6, 8.10, 8.56; JPBDNJ 2017, p. 2.97).

What might the future portend for agriculture in Johor? State planners, reflecting on recent growth trends since 2000, project that agriculture's footprint in Johor is likely to expand up to 2030. Most new cultivation will occur in districts that planners believe will be least affected by urban sprawl, namely Kota Tinggi, Batu Pahat, Kluang and Tangkak (JPBDNJ 2018, pp. 2.27–2.28). Oil palms are likely to increase their foothold in Johor by an additional 100,000 hectares in 2030 (13 per cent more than 2015 figures). Chillies, pineapples, vegetables and other food crops may see further additional planting in the next decade. Similar increases are projected for aquaculture (JPBDNJ 2018, pp. 2.27–2.28). There are also publicly and privately-funded moves afoot to expand Johor's already-considerable livestock sector—especially in the areas of chicken-rearing, beef cattle-ranching, and dairy-farming—and integrate it further into the oil palm industry's value chain (Ariff, Sharifah, and Hafidz 2015; Aruna 2017; *The Malaysian Insight*, 2 December 2017; *The Star*, 28 May 2018). In short, oil palm's continued expansion in Johor may actually benefit a number of other closely related high-earning agrofood activities, rather than crowd them out.

These synergies are also reinforced by the fact that Johor's still-expanding agrofood and oleo-chemical processing industries are likely to draw upon Johor-sourced agricultural offerings. This is especially pertinent where goods are either highly perishable (like poultry) or are bulky to transport, with a relatively low value-to-weight ratio (like crude palm oil) (Khazanah Nasional 2006, p. 4.11; IRDA 2015, pp. 4.3, 4.20–4.24). As Khaled Nordin, Johor's then Chief Minister and Chairman of the Iskandar Regional Development Authority declared in November 2016, "We are … banking on our position as one of the top three states in the country in [agricultural production] to develop the [industrial] bioeconomy sector." (Zazali Musa 2016). Iskandar Malaysia's ambition to supply the global halal consumer market (estimated to be worth over US$6 trillion a year by 2020) with processed foods is also likely to catalyse local agricultural expansion (IRDA 2015, pp. 4.17–4.20; IM BizWatch 2014). There is nothing quaint about such ambitions: in many urbanized economies today, agribusiness, food industry and services still account for much as a third of national-level gross domestic product (World Bank 2007, p. 4).

That being said, local complications abound. Coconuts, coffee, and rubber farming, having been either commercially stagnant or in retreat for decades, are likely to see croplands in Johor continue to shrink, or at least cease expansion (JPBDNJ 2018, pp. 2.27–2.28). Johor's cocoa growers are unlikely to revive production significantly, despite the fact that the state's cocoa grinders and chocolate-making industries are geared to expand production further, as part of government plans to make Malaysia Asia's next "King of Chocolate" (*Straits Times*, 8 October 2016; *The Iskandarian*, 8 May 2017). Pest and disease problems stemming from forest rent exhaustion, state neglect, competition from Indonesia's cocoa producers, and higher returns from oil palm cultivation have all discouraged local growers from remaining invested in cocoa (Arshad and Ibragimov 2015, pp. 1–14).

Water management issues also pose further conundrums. Although Johor's inhabitants receive far more rainfall that they will ever probably ever draw on for the conceivable future, their access to potable supplies continues to be problematic. As recently as April 2016, 85,000 Johorean residents and industrial users had water rationing imposed on them, triggered by a conjunction of drought, pollution, and saltwater infiltration of freshwater bodies (Ewing and Domondon 2016, p. 2). Worse still, Johor's near-term population growth and projected future water usage is set to smash earlier estimates by concerned observers. Iskandar Malaysia's gathering momentum is responsible for these revisions. The most recent figures from 2018, drawn from the state government's draft planning review for the period up until 2030, posit 6.2 million Johorean residents by 2030, a quarter higher than projections made in 2011. By the same token, projected state-level potable water demand for domestic, industrial and commercial purposes by 2030 (some 2,761 million litres/day) is set to surpass earlier projections that forecasted such levels being attained only after 2050 (JPBDNJ 2018, p. 2.35; Ewing and Hangzo 2016, p. 396).

Although most of this burgeoning water demand will come from urban activities, agriculture will also draw upon larger volumes of water as it expands. Future demand is less likely to come from Johor's cash crops (which require little irrigation, being predominantly rain-fed), and more likely to stem from Johor's rising livestock population. Most of the water used by poultry, cattle, pig and ruminant-keepers goes to keeping animals well-hydrated, with smaller amounts dedicated to livestock washing and abattoir cleansing. Should livestock population growth follow recent historical trends, Johor's water usage by livestock could almost treble from 2010 figures to constitute 6 per cent of Johor's total water demand by 2030 (Department of Irrigation and Drainage Malaysia 2011, pp. 1.4, 9.8). Moreover, unless additional measures are taken to stem water pollution from livestock farming and agro-processing in Johor, incidents such as 2017's multiple shutdowns of water treatment facilities at Semanggar and Sungai Johor are likely to happen again, if not on an even larger scale (Bernama 2018).

These uncertainties provoke further questions. To what extent does Johor's high agricultural productivity—far higher than oil palm-heavy states like Sabah and Sarawak—lie in specific synergies between agriculture, manufacturing and services that help agriculture to "stick around", as opposed to dependence on low-wage labour? And what more might studying the transnational linkages within Johor's other current agricultural mainstay—poultry farming—tell us about the persistence of agriculture within Johor, if not Malaysia itself? Further research should provide more refined answers to these puzzles.

Notes

1. An earlier version of this chapter was first published as *Agriculture in Johor: What's Left?*, Trends in Southeast Asia, no. 19/2018 (Singapore: ISEAS – Yusof Ishak Institute, 2018). I would like to thank Francis E. Hutchinson and an anonymous reviewer for their comments on an earlier draft, and Pearlyn Y. Pang for the maps accompanying this paper. The usual caveats apply.
2. Exceptions include Arshad (2007); Wong (2011).
3. For current land size, see DOSM (2013b), p. 11; for current population size, see DOSM (2017d); for current state-level GDP estimates, see DOSM (2017e).

4. For example, see Ariffin (1994); Ong (2010).
5. For instance, see Wong (2011), p. 131.

References

Agri-Food and Veterinary Authority of Singapore (AVA). 2016. "Country: Malaysia. Chicken Layer Farms Approved to Export Table Eggs to Singapore, MY180516". AVA website. https://www.ava.gov.sg/docs/default-source/tools-and-resources/resources-for-businesses/my_layerfarm.pdf (accessed 19 June 2018).

————. 2017. "Annual Report 2016/17". AVA website. https://www.ava.gov.sg/docs/default-source/publication/annual-report/ava-ar-2016-17>(accessed 20 November 2017).

Anon. 1995. "Review of Johor Long-Term Economic Development Plan 1995–2010". Mimeographed. Johor Bahru, December.

————. 2013. "Malaysian Poultry Industry: Past, Present & Future". 30 November 2013. http://www.vet.upm.edu.my/dokumen/90301_malaysian_poultry_industry.pdf (accessed 13 December 2017).

Ariff O.M., N.Y. Sharifah and A.W. Hafidz. 2015. "Status of Beef Industry of Malaysia". *Malaysian Journal of Animal Science* 18, no. 2: 1–21.

Ariffin, Jamilah, ed. 1994. *From Kampung to Urban Factories: Findings from the HAWA Study*. Kuala Lumpur: University of Malaya Press.

Arshad, Fatimah Mohamed, ed. 2007. *50 Years of Malaysian Agriculture: Transformational Issues, Challenges and Direction*. Serdang: University Putra Malaysia.

————, and Mad Nasir Shamsuddin. 2000. "Food Security and the Issue of Agricultural Land". In *Tanah Air Ku: Land Issues in Malaysia*, edited by Consumers' Association of Penang. Penang: Consumers' Association of Penang.

————, Alias Radam and Zainalabidin Mohamed. 2005. *The Fruits Industry in Malaysia: Issues and Challenges*. Serdang: Universiti Putra Malaysia Press.

———— and Abdulla Ibragimov. 2015. "Malaysia's Cocoa Beans Decline: A Prognosis". *International Journal of Agriculture, Forestry and Plantation* 1: 1–14.

Aruna, P. 2017. "Potential Game Changer: Palm Kernel Made into Chicken Feed". *The Star*, 11 May 2017.

Bernama. 2018. "Poultry Farm Linked to Ammonia Pollution Given 6 Months To Buck Up". 6 February 2018.

Chou, Cynthia. 2014. "Agriculture and the End of Farming in Singapore". In *Nature Contained: Environmental Histories of Singapore*, edited by Timothy Barnard. Singapore: NUS Press.

Convert To (website). n.d. http://convert-to.com/720/chicken-eggs-5-sizes-conversion-plus-nutrients-values.html (accessed 11 December 2017).

Cramb, Rob and John F. McCarthy, eds. 2016. *The Oil Palm Complex: Smallholders, Agribusiness and the State in Indonesia and Malaysia*. Singapore: NUS Press.

Department of Irrigation and Drainage Malaysia. 2011. *Review of the National Water Resources Study (2000–2050) and Formulation of National Water Resources Policy. Final Report. Vol. 17 — Johor*. Kuala Lumpur: Ministry of Natural Resources and Environment of Malaysia.

Department of Statistics, Malaysia (DOSM). 1984. *Population and Housing Census of Malaysia 1980: Population Report for Administrative Districts, Occupation, Industry*. Kuala Lumpur: Department of Statistics, Malaysia.

———. 1995. *Population and Housing Census of Malaysia 1991: Population Report for Administrative Districts: Occupation and Industry*. Kuala Lumpur: Department of Statistics, Malaysia.

———. 2003. *Population and Housing Census of Malaysia 2000: Economic Characteristics of the Population*. Putrajaya: Department of Statistics, Malaysia.

———. 2013a. *Population and Housing Census of Malaysia 2010: Economic Characteristics of the Population*. Putrajaya: Department of Statistics, Malaysia.

———. 2013b. *Population Distribution and Basic Demographic Characteristics, 2010*. Putrajaya: Department of Statistics, Malaysia.

———. 2016. *Supply and Utilization Accounts, Selected Agricultural Commodities, 2011–2015*. Putrajaya: Department of Statistics, Malaysia.

———. 2017a. *Economic Census 2016: Crops*. Putrajaya: Department of Statistics, Malaysia.

———. 2017b. *Economic Census 2016: Livestock*. Putrajaya: Department of Statistics, Malaysia.

———. 2017c. *Economic Census 2016: Fisheries*. Putrajaya: Department of Statistics, Malaysia.

———. 2017d. *Current Population Estimates, 2017*. Putrajaya: Department of Statistics, Malaysia.

———. 2017e. *GDP by State, National Accounts, 2010–2016*. Putrajaya: Department of Statistics, Malaysia.

———. 2017f. *Household Income and Basic Amenities Survey Report 2016*. Putrajaya: Department of Statistics, Malaysia.

———. 2017g. *Labour Force Survey Report, 2016*. Putrajaya: Department of Statistics, Malaysia.

———. n.d.-a. "Gross Domestic Product by Kind of Economic Activity at Constant Prices (2005=100), 2005–2013, Malaysia". DOSM website. http://www.epu.gov.my/sites/default/files/2.7.1.pdf (accessed 10 December 2017).

———. n.d.-b. "Selected Agricultural Indicators, Malaysia, 2017". DOSM website. https://www.dosm.gov.my/v1/index.php?r=column/pdfPrev&id=MDN YUitINm RKcENRY2FvMmR5TWdGdz09 (accessed 4 January 2018).

Department of Veterinary Services (DVS). 2017. "Livestock Statistics 2015/2016. P. Malaysia: Poultry Population". February. http://www.dvs.gov.my/index.php/pages/view/1743 (accessed 20 November 2017).

Ewing, Jackson J. and Pau Khan Khup Hangzo. 2016. "Development in Johor and Singapore's Water Access: Challenges and Opportunities". In *The SIJORI Cross-Border Region: Transnational Politics, Economics, and Culture*, edited by Francis E. Hutchinson and Terence Chong. Singapore: ISEAS – Yusof Ishak Institute.

Ewing, Jackson J. and Karissa Domondon. 2016. "Drought, Pollution and Johor's Growing Water Needs", *ISEAS Perspective* 47/2016, 26 August 2016.

FAOSTAT. n.d. "Food Supply: Crops, Livestock and Fish Primary Equivalent". FAOSTAT website. www.fao.org/faostat/en/#data (accessed 11 December 2017).

Gasco, Anna. 2016. "The Airport and the Territory: Transnational Flows in the Singapore-Johor-Riau Cross-Border Region". In *The SIJORI Cross-Border Region: Transnational Politics, Economics, and Culture*, edited by Francis E. Hutchinson and Terence Chong. Singapore: ISEAS – Yusof Ishak Institute.

Giacomin, Valeria. 2017. "The Emergence of an Export Cluster: Traders and Palm Oil in Early Twentieth-Century Southeast Asia". *Enterprise & Society* 19, no. 2: 272–308.

Gomez, Edmund Terence. 2002. "Political Business in Malaysia: Party Factionalism, Corporate Developmentalism, and Economic Crisis". In *Political Business in East Asia*, edited by Edmund Terence Gomez. London: Routledge.

Government of Malaysia. 2006. *Ninth Malaysia Plan, 2006–2010*. Putrajaya: Economic Planning Unit, Prime Minister's Department.

Grist, D.H. 1936. *An Outline of Malayan Agriculture*. Kuala Lumpur: Department of Agriculture, Straits Settlements and Federated Malay States.

Guinness, Patrick. 1992. *On the Margin of Capitalism: People and Development in Mukim Plentong, Johor, Malaysia*. Singapore: Oxford University Press.

Guturu, Kusuma and Vidhan Singh. 2015. "Harvesting of Oil Palm: An Ambitious Task Behind Ag. Engineers". *International Journal for Research in Emerging Science and Technology* 2, no. 7: 23–27.

Ho, Wah Foon. 2017. "Soaring High on Roosters". *The Star*, 12 February 2017.

Hutchinson, Francis E. 2012. "Johor and Its Electronics Sector: One Priority among Many?". ISEAS Working Paper no. 1. Singapore: Institute of Southeast Asian Studies.

IM Bizwatch. 2014. "Iskandar Malaysia Halal Technology Hub". 31 January 2014.

Ibrahim Ngah. 2010. "Pembangunan Komuniti di Pinggir Kawasan Metropolitan Kajian Kes di Kawasan Parlimen Pasir Gudang (Community Development on the Fringe of a Metropolitan Area: The Case of Pasir Gudang Parliamentary Constituency)". Unpublished research report. Iskandar Malaysia UTM Research Centre, Johor Bahru.

Iskandar Malaysia Regional Development Authority (IRDA). 2015. *Comprehensive Development Plan II 2014–2025: Iskandar Malaysia*. Johor Bahru: Iskandar Regional Development Authority.

———. 2016. *10 Year Progress Report*. Malaysia: Iskandar Regional Development Authority.

The Iskandarian. 2017. "Time to Celebrate with Hershey's Johor". 8 May 2017.

Jabatan Perancangan Bandar dan Desa Negeri Johor (JPBDNJ). 2017. *Johor 2030: Rancangan Struktur Negeri Johor 2030 (Kajian Semula)*. Kota Iskandar: Jabatan Perancangan Bandar dan Desa Negeri Johor.

———. 2018. *Draf Rancangan Struktur Negeri Johor 2030*. Kota Iskandar: Jabatan Perancangan Bandar dan Desa Negeri Johor.

Jayaseelan, Risen, and Ng Bei Shan. 2015. "Francis Lau on Chicken and Eggs". *The Star*, 7 March 2015.

Johor Corporation. 2016. *Annual Report 2016*. Johor Bahru: Johor Corporation.

Khazanah Nasional. 2006. *Comprehensive Development Plan for South Johor Economic Region 2006–2025*. Kuala Lumpur: Khazanah Nasional.

Lee Hwok-Aun and Khor Yu Leng. 2018. "Counting Migrant Workers in Malaysia: A Needlessly Persisting Conundrum". *ISEAS Perspective*, no. 2018/25, 25 April 2018.

Lie, Merete, and Ragnhild Lund. 1994. *Renegotiating Local Values: Working Women and Foreign Industry in Malaysia*. Richmond: Curzon Press.

Local Produce Working Committee. 1951. *Food Supplies for Singapore*. Singapore: Government Printing Office.

The Malaysian Insight. 2017. "Johor Agriculture Hub Gets RM500 million in New Investments". 2 December 2017. https://www.themalaysianinsight.com/s/25625.

Malaysian Palm Oil Board (MPOB). n.d. "Oil Palm Planted Area by State as at December 2016 (Hectares)". MPOB website. http://bepi.mpob.gov.my/images/area/2016/ Area_summary.pdf (accessed 24 January 2018).

Malek bin Mansoor, and Colin Barlow. 1988. "The Production Structure of the Malaysian Oil Palm Industry with Special Reference to the Smallholder Subsector". *PORIM Occasional Paper No. 24*. Kuala Lumpur: PORIM.

Ministry of Agriculture. 1999. *Third National Agricultural Policy (1998–2010)*. Kuala Lumpur: Ministry of Agriculture.

Ministry of Agriculture and Agro-based Industry (MAAI). 2016. *Agrofood Statistics 2015.* Putrajaya: Ministry of Agriculture and Agro-based Industry, Malaysia.

Mohamed Mohd Salleh, and Rokiah Mohd Yusof. 2006. "Tropical Fruits and Vegetables in Malaysia: Production and Impact on Health". Presented at "Fruits and Vegetables for Health" Workshop, 15–16 August 2006, Seoul, Korea.

Mokhtar, Faris. 2017. "Singapore Does Not Import Chicken and Eggs from Kelantan: AVA". *Today*, 9 March 2017.

Munira binti Halili. 2011. "The Factors Influencing Chicken Lovers in Malaysia, Race as the Moderating Variable". Master's Thesis, Universiti Sains Malaysia.

Ng, Casey. 2016. "The Ornamental Freshwater Fish Trade in Malaysia". *Agriculture Science Journal* 2: 7–18.

Ong, Aihwa. 2010. *Spirits of Resistance and Capitalist Discipline, Second Edition: Factory Women in Malaysia.* Albany: State of University of New York Press.

Organization for Economic Co-operation and Development (OECD). 2018. "Meat Consumption (Indicator)". https://doi.org/10.1787/fa290fd0-en> (accessed 25 January 2018).

Pakiam, Geoffrey Kevin. 2017. "Smallholder Involvement in Tree Crops in Malaya, with Special Reference to Oil and Coconut Palms in Johor, 1862–1963". PhD thesis, SOAS, University of London.

Preston, David and Ibrahim Ngah. 2012. "Interpreting Rural Change in Malaysia". *Singapore Journal of Tropical Geography* 33, no. 3: 351–64.

PT Malindo Feedmill Tbk. 2017. *Annual Report 2016: Stepping into a New Milestone.* Jakarta: PT Malindo.

Pye, Oliver, and Jayati Bhattacharya. 2012. *The Palm Oil Controversy in Southeast Asia.* Singapore: Institute of Southeast Asian Studies.

Rasiah, Rajah. 2006. "Explaining Malaysia's Export Expansion in Palm Oil and Related Products". In *Technology, Adaptation and Exports*, edited by Vandana Chandra. Washington, DC: World Bank.

RMA Perunding Bersatu. 1996. *Johor Operational Master Plan Study.* Johor Bahru: State Economic Planning Unit.

Rogers, Marvin L. 1992. *Local Politics in Rural Malaysia: Patterns of Change in Sungai Raya.* Boulder: Westview Press.

Salleh, S. MD, Erween Abd Rahim, Imran Hj Ghazali, Khairull Azmi, Abdul Razak Jelani, Mohd Fauzi Ismail and Mohd Rizal Ahmad. 2013. "Hand-Arm Vibration Analysis of Palm Oil Harvester Machine". *Applied Mechanics and Materials* 315: 615–25.

Saravanamuttu, Johan. 2013. "Migration and Flexible Labour in Malaysia". In *The Palm Oil Controversy in Southeast Asia: A Transnational Perspective*, edited by Oliver Pye and Jayati Bhattacharya. Singapore: Institute of Southeast Asian Studies.

Straits Times. 2016. "Malaysia Aims to Be Chocolate King of Asia". 8 October 2016.

Thompson, Eric C. 2007. *Unsettling Absences: Urbanism in Rural Malaysia.* Singapore: NUS Press.

Trocki, Carl A. 2007. *Prince of Pirates: The Temenggongs and the Development of Johore and Singapore, 1784–1885.* Singapore: NUS Press.

Unit Perancang Ekonomi Negeri Johor (UPENJ). 1989. *Pelan Ekonomi Negeri Johor, 1990–2005.* Johor Bahru: Government of Johor.

Vandergeest, Peter, and Jonathan Rigg. 2012. "The Restudy 'Problem' and Agrarian Change: Revisiting Rural Places in Southeast Asia". In *Revisiting Rural Places: Pathways to Poverty and Prosperity in Southeast Asia*, edited by Jonathan Rigg and Peter Vandergeest. Singapore: NUS Press.

Varkkey, Helen. 2016. *The Haze Problem in Southeast Asia: Palm Oil and Patronage*. London: Routledge.

Wong, Larry C.Y. 2011. "Agriculture". In *Malaysia: Policies and Issues in Economic Development*, edited by Khoo Siew Mun, Susan P.S. Teoh and Haji Ibrahim Ismail. Kuala Lumpur: Institute of Strategic and International Studies.

World Bank. 2007. *World Development Report 2008: Agriculture for Development*. Washington, DC: World Bank.

———. n.d. "World Development Indicators". World Bank website. http://databank. worldbank.org/data/views/variableSelection/selectvariables.aspx?source=World-development-indicators# (accessed 21 November 2017).

Zazali Musa. 2016. "3 Core Sectors to Spearhead Johor's Regional Economic Plan". *The Star*, 18 November 2016.

Zunaira Saieed. 2016. "Reducing Reliance on Foreign Workers". *The Star*, 2 May 2016.

3

JOHOR'S OIL PALM ECONOMY
Past, Present, and Future

Geoffrey K. Pakiam, Khor Yu Leng and Jeamme Chia[1]

INTRODUCTION

Introduced over a century ago, oil palms are currently Johor's most significant agricultural offering. Over one-third of Johor's entire landmass is planted with oil palms. Thirty per cent of these lands are farmed by independent smallholders, nearly twice the national average (MPOB n.d.-a; MAMPU n.d.). Further downstream, Johor's millers produced one-sixth of Malaysia's crude palm oil in 2018, worth nearly RM7 billion in revenue (MPOB n.d.-b). The territory hosts numerous downstream players pumping out refined palm oil, margarine, specialty fats, oleochemicals, and biodiesel. Johor's two major ports—Pasir Gudang and Tanjung Pelepas—anchor these production clusters, while also exporting RM15.5 billion of vegetable (mostly palm) oil products in 2017—an impressive 28 per cent of Malaysia's world-leading output (DOSM n.d.). Much of this global prominence stems from Johor's long history as an agricultural powerhouse, its forays into resource-based industrialization, and its relative success in becoming a trade hub for edible oils and chemical derivatives.

This essay will survey the oil palm's increasingly heavy presence within Johor's landscape, commerce, and political economy, grounding discussions in broader global and historical contexts where necessary. The paper's next section outlines the oil palm's importance to world trade, the crop's social and environmental complications in Southeast Asia, and the significance of independent smallholder farming arrangements. We then present a brief history of Johor's multilayered oil palm farm sector since its inception. A third section tracks the oil palm's journey through the value chain, mapping out the millers, crushers, refiners, merchants and equipment manufacturers that have consolidated Johor's status as an attractive locale for commodity processing. Having outlined the main commercial players involved, we then turn towards the more political dimensions of Johor's oil palm sector: the electoral significance of Johor's Federal Land Development Authority (FELDA) settler communities, other government-linked entities involved in oil palms, and land control issues, the latter especially dependent on close ties with Johor's state government. Land use concerns also connect with our final section, which looks at how urbanization, landowners and sustainability requirements are influencing the oil palm's future in Johor.

OIL PALM CONTROVERSIES AND THE SMALLHOLDER ALTERNATIVE

The oil palm has been subjected to some of the world's fiercest debates concerning social justice and environmental sustainability within agriculture, an age-old activity that has produced the mountains of food and many of the raw materials that have made modern civilizations possible. Approximately half of all packaged foods consumed globally today contain palm oil (Roundtable on Sustainable Palm Oil Secretariat n.d.). Oil palm products (including palm kernel oil, derived from the fruit's kernel) are used in a vast range of consumer goods now taken for granted, such as cleaning agents, cosmetics, plastics, herbicides, drugs, textiles and biofuels.

The environmental and social consequences of farming the palm fruits used to make these consumables are considerable. Recent large-scale conversions of tropical rainforests and coastal peatlands in both East Malaysia and parts of Indonesia to oil palm monocultures have led to substantial biodiversity loss, as well as significant chemical run-off from some mills and estates (Cramb and McCarthy 2016, pp. 7–8). These transformations are underpinned by extensive transfers of property rights into the hands of politically connected business elites, disadvantaging small landowners and local communities. Estate-centric oil palm farming in Malaysia and Indonesia typically relies on cheap migrant labour, often sowing tensions between locals and migrant workers (Cramb and McCarthy 2016, p. 5).

Some researchers have contended that it is the manner in which the oil palm is commodified, rather than the tree itself, which is the real problem. The key challenge, according to them, is to work out how the oil palm can "provide the greatest contribution to sustainable rural livelihoods", instead of undermining them (Cramb and McCarthy 2016, p. 2). In West and Central Africa, where the oil palm has been cultivated for millennia, small-scale growers still dominate the farming and processing of palm fruit for local diets and regional trade. In Thailand, Ecuador, and Costa Rica, independent smallholder participation in oil palm farming has been vigorous, due to strong competition between mills for growers' crops, competent support from grower cooperatives, secure land titles, or state-subsidized long-term credit (Potter 2016, pp. 177–78; Byerlee 2014, p. 584).

In response, non-government organizations, policymakers, and scholars have begun investigating ways to encourage more independent smallholder involvement in oil palms in Southeast Asia. Besides the incomes earned directly from cash cropping, independent smallholders usually retain control over their own labour power and its deployment, unlike estate labourers or scheme farmers. Some researchers contend that this arrangement leads to more skilled and cost-effective farming practices, since households retain intimate local knowledge of farm conditions, and do not need costly management structures to supervise (or motivate) them when working in the field (Ellis 1988, Ch. 10; Hayami 1996, p. 1158; Byerlee 2014, pp. 576–77). Many households address the labour question through sharecropping or by contracting labour from palm fruit dealers and other providers. Independent smallholders also adopt mixed farming practices geared towards crop diversification, building resilience to individual crop failures and price fluctuations, instead of trying to maximize farm yields via a single monoculture (Potter 2016, p. 166). Viewed from above, independent oil palm smallholdings appear markedly different from the profiles of government-managed schemes and corporate estates.[2] Even where oil palms are the dominant crop, independent holdings are often more irregularly planted, with large areas of mixed farming at the landscape level. Oil palm groves may be mixed with paddy (in Kedah and elsewhere), or fruit or rubber trees (Johor's western coastal region).

Like their independent counterparts, organized smallholders under Malaysian government managed schemes are officially classified as farming areas under 100 acres (roughly 40 hectares). The similarities tend to end there. Organized smallholders are mostly sheltered under federal agencies, notably FELDA, the Federal Land Consolidation and Rehabilitation Agency (FELCRA), and the Rubber Industry Smallholder Development Authority (RISDA). In today's context, government-organized smallholders' lands are frequently developed and managed by corporate entities, which in turn now employ migrant labour for work in the field. With their monocrop approach and disciplined symmetrical layout, the spatial profiles of government-managed schemes are difficult to distinguish from those of corporate plantations.

The muted presence of independent smallholders is accentuated by the fact that the oil palm is the only major tree crop in tropical Asia whose cultivation was still dominated by large-scale agribusinesses at the end of the twentieth century. Other prominent crops, notably *Hevea* rubber, coffee, coconuts, and cocoa, are now mostly grown by small-scale farmers (Barlow and Jayasuriya 1986, pp. 635–37; Clarence-Smith and Topik 2003; Dand 2010; Corley and Tinker 2016, pp. 19–20). In other words, there has been a historical tendency for most tree crops in the region to end up in the hands of independent smallholders, even where corporate estates led the initial charge decades (or centuries) earlier. The critical question is whether this disparity between the oil palm and other cultivars is a permanent feature of Southeast Asia, or whether it is only a matter of time before the oil palm follows the prevailing trend for other tree crops. While it is too early to offer any conclusive answers, the history of Johor—where oil palms have had an unusually long commercial run relative to the rest of Southeast Asia—suggests that small-scale oil palm farming is likely to expand further.

A BRIEF HISTORY OF OIL PALM AGRICULTURE IN JOHOR

A great deal of oil palm farming in Johor has taken place on soil that has already been subjected to other forms of agriculture. Rubber trees, coconut palms, areca nut palms and other fruit trees were all being farmed before the oil palm arrived, and they continue to be part of the landscape today, albeit as more minor crops. Geospatial analysis indicates that 55–60 per cent of Johor's current area under tree crops was already in use by 1970 (Khor 2018a). In all likelihood, over half of contemporary Johor's oil palm lands are on soil previously home to rubber, coconut and areca palms between the late nineteenth century and the 1970s, particularly the territory's western half (Figure 3.1).

Johor's earliest-known oil palm plantations date from the colonial period. Contrary to popular belief, Malaysia's first commercial oil palm estate was established in 1910 at Kluang, central Johor, roughly a year before Frenchman Henri Fauconnier planted his seedlings at Rantau Panjang Estate in Selangor. Little else is currently known about the provenance of the Kluang venture, save that the Guthrie Group found the property sufficiently "flourishing" by 1920, eventually purchasing and assimilating the venture into the core of a larger Elaeis Estate. Elaeis, in turn, became part of Guthrie's better-known Oil Palms of Malaya estate grouping by 1930 (Burkill 1966, p. 912; Cunyngham-Brown 1971, pp. 252, 320; Tate 1996, p. 464). Other prominent oil palm plantations established in Johor before the Second World War included Johore Labis Estate (which took over lands already partially degraded by nineteenth-century pepper and gambier farming), Oil Palm Plantations Ltd (also at Kluang), and a number of smaller Asian-owned concerns, all deep within Johor's interior, taking advantage of proximity to its main railway network (Pakiam 2017, pp. 152, 324). These early initiatives, aided by extremely generous concessionary terms for estates wishing to cultivate non-rubber crops in Johor during the 1920s and 1930s, set the scene for Johor's countrywide dominance as an oil palm-growing territory up until the late 1970s. Although growers in Sarawak and Sabah have since committed astounding amounts of land to oil palm cultivation, Johor continues to contribute a respectable 13 per cent of all oil palm lands found in Malaysia (Figure 3.2).

Prior to the 1960s, Johor's colonial authorities typically suppressed attempts made by independent smallholders to cultivate oil palms. Small-scale initiatives are known to have taken place near estate mills or through informal co-operatives owning their own mills. District officials would penalize growers who were discovered to be already farming oil palms, or otherwise refuse to grant smallholders land to do so in the first place. Official hostility stemmed from fears that "uncontrolled" cultivation by "backward" growers would drag down the overall quality and cost-effectiveness of Malaya's crude palm oil exports to North America and Western Europe (Pakiam

FIGURE 3.1
Areas Brought Under Tree Crop Farming, Johor, 1970 vs. 2013/4

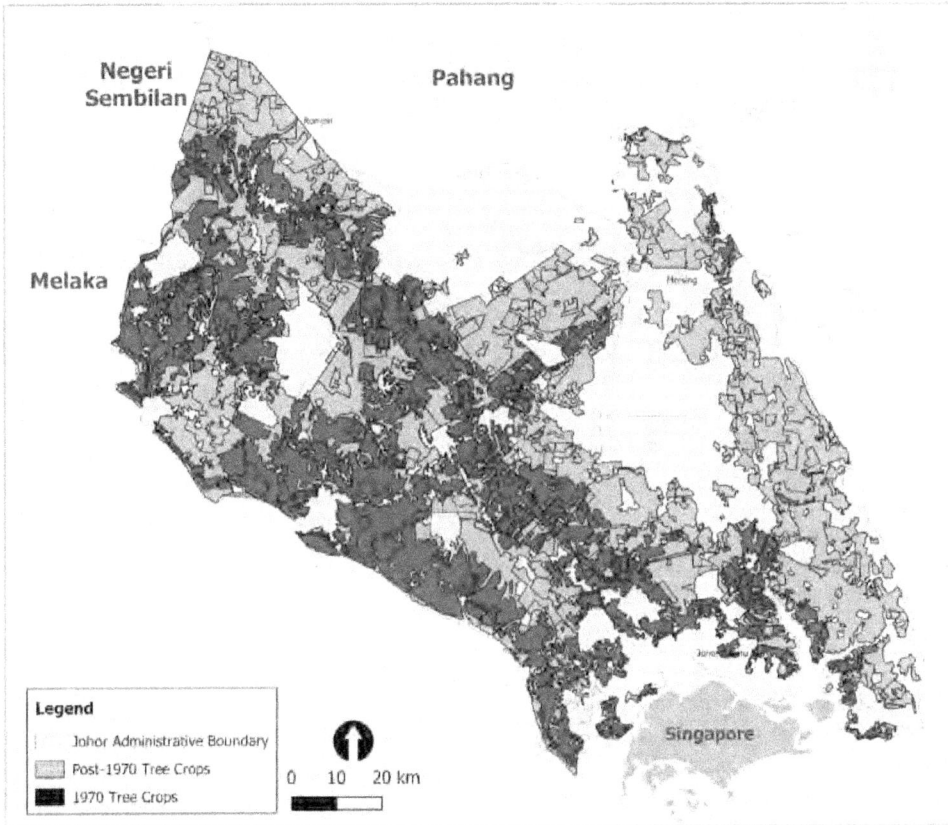

Sources: Analysis of data from Ministry of Agriculture and Lands Malaysia (1970); Petersen et al. (2016).

2017, Chs. 3–5). These same anxieties also pervaded the halls of federal government: amongst other things, they helped delay the inclusion of oil palms as crops eligible for government-sponsored rubber smallholder replanting grants until 1963, whereas rubber estates benefited from federal oil palm planting subsidies as early as 1954 (Pakiam 2017, p. 277).

In any case, the cultivation of rubber, coconuts, areca nuts and other cash crops usually offered Johor smallholders better incomes, more attractive marketing opportunities, and physically safer environments to work in during this period (Pakiam 2017, Ch. 2). In 1951, for instance, more than half of all Johor's rubber lands were worked by smallholders. Johor's coconut and areca nut farmlands were completely dominated by coastal smallholders, who in turn accounted for a quarter and a half of all of the Malay Peninsula's coconut and areca nut farmlands respectively (Pakiam 2017, p. 335).

The period following the Second World War saw another wave of oil palm expansion led by European- and Asian-owned rubber estates, with government-

FIGURE 3.2
Johor's Contribution to the Malay Peninsula's Oil Palm Hectarage, 1925–2018

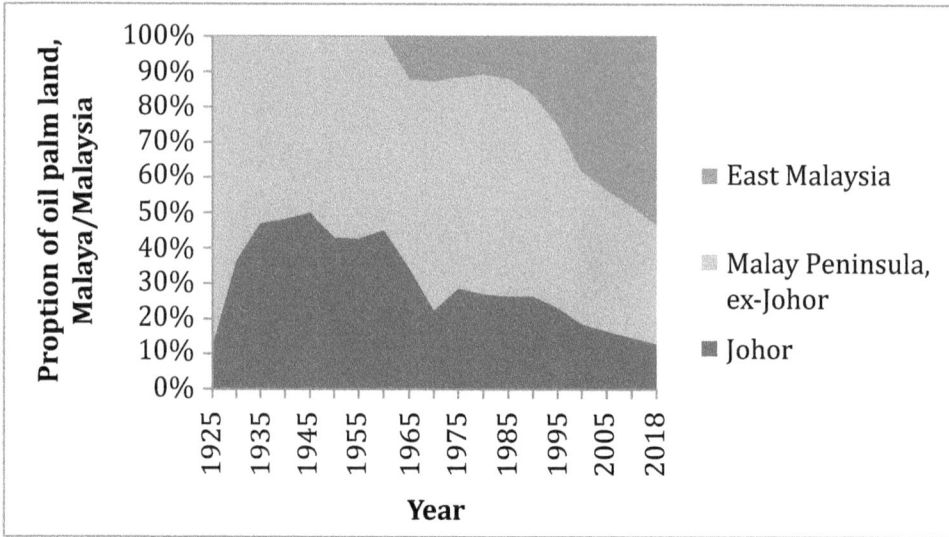

Sources: Pakiam (2017), p. 335; MPOB (n.d.-f); Department of Agriculture Johor, 1965–1980; Mansoor and Barlow (1986), p. 15; Khera (1976), p. 305; Teoh (2000), p. 35.

organized schemes gradually following suit. From the 1960s to the 1980s, Malaysia's federal authorities embraced large-scale oil palm-based group schemes as a way to diversify exports beyond tin and rubber, while reducing poverty and inequality at the same time (Rasiah 2006, pp. 183–87). As land development costs increased and popular interest in rural sector livelihoods waned during the 1980s, rural policy in Malaysia shifted from government-centric land development projects to increasing emphasis on private sector growth (Khor 2015). Johor's shifting oil palm farm structure exemplifies these trends: FELDA and FELCRA's oil palm expansion slowed down after the 1980s, local state schemes have shrunk, while private estates and independent smallholders have surged ahead (Table 3.1).

Today, independent smallholders occupy a central position in Johor's oil palm landscape, but their moves into oil palms faced considerable delays in the past. Besides encountering discrimination from federal and state governments, smallholders were spatially disadvantaged. In pre-1960s Johor, most oil palm estates (and their accompanying mills) parked themselves next to railway freight facilities in central Johor, where they could reap the benefits of modern bulk transport infrastructure for palm oil and heavy machinery. The majority of smallholder communities resided elsewhere, many strung out along Johor's western coastline, where they relied on time-honoured habits of maritime access for fishing, transport and water-based trade that pre-dated the railway's inception in the 1910s (Pakiam 2019a, p. 16). This geographic mismatch between littoral communities and inland mills helped retard independent involvement in oil palms until millers and dealers began extending

TABLE 3.1

Breakdown of Johor's Land Area Cultivated with Oil Palms, 1965–2017 (hectares)

	1965	1970	1975	1980	1984	1990	2000	2005	2010	2017
Private Estates	28,500	54,064	111,083	124,455	175,891	—	—	319,366	325,399	330,394
FELDA-FELDA Global Ventures (FGV)	4,201	12,747	50,886	92,712	98,035	—	—	118,658	126,399	131,812
State schemes	—	327	3,875	24,556	51,156	—	—	47,833	40,042	37,511
FELCRA	—	—	—	8,174	9,162	—	—	23,613	22,721	22,508
RISDA	—	—	1,894	2,833	2,482	—	—	5,213	4,774	3,211
Independent smallholders (licensed)	73	3,386	15,019	18,825	56,810	—	125,460	153,189	198,063	223,424
Total, Johor	32,773	70,525	182,758	271,556	393,536	455,672	671,046	667,872	717,398	748,860
Total, Malaysia	95,575	314,686	641,791	1,023,306	1,330,266	1,674,347	3,313,393	4,051,374	4,853,766	5,811,145

Sources: Department of Agriculture Johor, 1966–1984; Khera (1976), p. 305; Azman Ismail et al. (2003); MPOB (n.d.-f).

their reach to Johor's coastal districts (see Table 3.2) (Department of Agriculture Johor 1967, p. 9). An additional deterrent against crop-switching came from statutory boards such as RISDA, whose original mission to help smallholders replant old rubber trees saw the agency give out more generous smallholder replanting grants for rubber than oil palms during the 1980s, partly in order to safeguard RISDA's survival as Malaysia's main rubber-promoting agency.[3]

Even as relative earnings from rubber and other crops fell in the 1960s and 1970s, independents were discouraged by a lack of marketing opportunities for oil palm fruit. Palm oil's current exploitation as an "invisible ingredient" in processed food and chemical products places independent smallholders at a distinct disadvantage: the low-acid palm oil prized for such uses necessitates rapid delivery of palm fruit bunches to a large-scale processing facility within forty-eight hours. For estates with their own costly mills, these coordination issues are reduced significantly. Independent growers, however, may find it difficult to connect existing farmlands to a mill if there are no trader intermediaries willing to buy fruit and consolidate purchases from scattered smallholdings for sale to a nearby mill before the fruits rot. Smallholders and dealers have generally preferred to trade in crops that are more durable, stored with relatively less difficulty, and easily transported, such as rubber and coconuts (Pakiam 2017, pp. 85–88). Such crops are more compatible with smallholder livelihood strategies, as they are much less exacting in time requirements, and physically easier to harvest.

The steady rise of an oil palm-centric processing sector within Johor has changed the rules of the game for independent smallholders to some extent. By 2007, Johor had 584 licensed palm fruit dealers connecting growers with local factories, 31 per cent of the total number of dealers in Malaysia. A typical dealership might comprise of eleven lorry and trailer drivers, three clerks, and one manager (Ayat K. Ab Rahman et al. 2009, pp. 21, 24). Our own estimates and discussions with experts suggest competition between dealers in Johor has been fairly vigorous, with each mill being served by about twenty crop dealerships.[4] Smallholders in the first instance were

TABLE 3.2
Palm Fruit Mills in Johor, 1966–2017

Region	District	1966	1970	1975	1980	1984	2010	2017
West Johor	Muar	1	1	1	1	3	5	5
	Batu Pahat	0	0	1	0	2	6	5
	Pontian	0	0	0	0	0	1	1
Central Johor	Segamat	1	0	2	3	6	9	8
	Kluang	4	5	5	13	19	17	17
	Johor Bahru	2	4	7	7	8	5	5
East Johor	Mersing	0	0	0	0	2	5	5
	Kota Tinggi	0	1	4	8	10	15	15
Total		8	11	20	32	50	63	61

Source: Department of Agriculture Johor, 1966–1984; MPOB (n.d.-c).

thus probably incentivized to move into oil palm cash cropping by dealers competing to offer them more attractive returns for their produce. That being said, the 2013 Directory of Malaysian Oil Palm Fresh Fruit Dealers listed only 444 participants in Johor (still 31 per cent of Malaysia's total). This decline suggests that considerable consolidation had occurred within the dealer sector, and that better-resourced smallholders were making their own direct crop transport arrangements with mills during the post-2000 commodity boom.

Nevertheless, while growers are in theory free to sell their crops to either dealers or directly to mills, marketing opportunities are kept in check somewhat by the Malaysian Palm Oil Board's current policy to avoid excessive competition among millers (Ayat K. Ab Rahman et al. 2009, p. 20; MPOB n.d.-d). The policy prevents mills from being established too close to each other and competing directly for harvested fruit. Competition thus appears to be more vigorous at the dealer level. Independent smallholders managed to add over 72,000 hectares of oil palm to Johor's total in the past decade (equivalent to 93 per cent of all Johor-based additions), while areas managed by state schemes and government agencies shrank (MAMPU n.d.). All in all, we estimate that estates currently produce about 46 per cent of Johor's palm fruit, group schemes 22 per cent, and independent smallholders about 31 per cent, with the last figure likely to rise in future.[5]

MILLERS, CRUSHERS, REFINERS, MERCHANTS ... AND MACHINISTS

Johor's downstream oil palm sector appears to have been a prime beneficiary of federal efforts to shift Malaysia's focus from crude palm oil to processed palm oil exports. These included federal export taxes on crude palm oil from 1976 onwards, tax incentives on capital investment into refineries, financial incentives during the 1980s and 1990s to promote oleochemical industry growth, as well as R&D activities into new products and processing technology improvements (Rasiah 2006, pp. 183–87). The Johor government also helped facilitate resource-based industrialization locally, not least by seeding a processing and export industry cluster at Pasir Gudang in the 1970s and directly investing in food processing and palm oil refining activities there afterwards (Pakiam 2018a, pp. 29–31).

To map out contemporary downstream developments and key players in Johor, we have analysed business directories and interviewed some industry insiders. Recent information on mills (often paired with estates) can be derived from Malaysia Agribusiness Directories (2013 and 2017 editions). Johor's milling sector is Malaysia's largest, both in terms of mills (62 out of 454 nationwide) and processing capacity. The millers include owners of combined mill-estates (32 mills, drawing heavily on internal-owned crop supplies), milling owner-specialists (14 mills, with limited estate involvement) and stand-alone mill operators (16, with no estates owned). Mills do not undertake palm kernel processing, instead selling the kernels to Johor's nine palm kernel crushers who specialize in making palm kernel oil and palm kernel meal/expeller/cake.

The Johor milling scene is remarkably vibrant, with 99 per cent of existing mill capacity being utilized in 2017, compared to the national average of 90 per cent. The state hosted sixty-two palm fruit mills in 2017, a large number of whom were reliant on external, non-estate sources of palm fruit to survive and prosper. The major operators of estate-mill combos can theoretically process over 8 million tonnes of palm fruit per year, but only produce about 5 million tonnes of palm fruit themselves. This shortfall renders them reliant on external sources of palm fruit for 40 per cent of their total milling capacity (Table 3.3). Even more dependent are major millers with limited estate ownership: they process 4 million tonnes of palm fruit a year, but their fifty-one estates can only potentially supply about 1.3 million tonnes of fruit bunches. Meanwhile, independent millers process about 5.5 million

TABLE 3.3
Key Players in the Palm Fruit Milling and Kernel Crushing Segments, Johor, 2017

			Palm Fruit Harvested (tonnes/year)	Milling Capacity (tonnes/year)
Palm oil mill owners (62 mills)	Combined estate-mill owners (32 mills)	FELDA-FGV: 13 mills, 18 estates Sime Darby Plantations: 6 mills, 27 estates Kulim-Johor Corp: 5 mills, 30 estates IOI Corporation: 2 mills 15 estates Tradewinds: 2 mills, 14 estates KL Kepong (2 mills, 11 estates), Boustead: 1 mill, 6 estates Genting Plantations: 1 mill, 5 estates	About 5 million	Over 8 million
	Major millers with limited estate ownership (14 mills)	Chin Teck, FELCRA, Keck Seng, Kian Hoe, Kim Loong, RISDA/Espek, Southern/Bell Group, TH Plantations, YPJ Plantations.	1.3 million	4 million
	Standalone mill operators (16 mills)	Anglo Eastern, Kuantan Trading, Kumpulan Melayu, Lian Hup, Nam Heng, Negeri Johor, Rajendran, Soon Lee Huat. Those named for locations include Bukit Pasir, Kluang, Lenga, Malim, Muar, Padang, Selumpur, Sungei Kahang.	NIL	5.5 million

Source: Appendix 3.1.

tonnes of palm fruit annually, all from external sources. Part of overall crop shortfall is assuaged by owners of estates with no mills (about seventy entities in 2017), but they only produce around 1 million tonnes of palm fruit a year at best.[6] With Johor's total milling capacity hovering around 16.6 million tonnes of palm fruit per annum, and palm fruit production from Johor's private estates and group schemes only around 9.1 million tonnes, the balance is thus being addressed by independent smallholders (4.4 million tonnes) and fruit supplies from out of state (2–3 million tonnes).[7] A similar story arises with Johor's palm kernel crushers, who produced an even higher proportion of palm products than the national average in 2017.[8] In short, Johor's millers and crushers are head-and-shoulders above the national scene, pulling in regional fruit supplies to supplement an already-considerable stateside harvest.

Johor's oil palm industry is consolidated through links with local refineries (14 out of 54 in Malaysia, representing over a quarter of total national capacity), as well as commodity and financial traders. Pasir Gudang currently has the largest concentration of palm oil refining industries and downstream activities in the world. Crude palm oil and crude palm kernel oil are degummed, bleached and deodorized in refineries before being transformed into mass market food ingredients (cooking oil, fried and baked processed foods, dairy substitutes), energy (biodiesel, power generation), and oleochemicals (soap, detergents, toothpastes, cosmetics). Johor's processing infrastructure thus gives the state a regional edge in the production of value-added goods for export along the key trading route of the Straits of Melaka.

Moreover, much of Malaysia's palm processing equipment is actually manufactured within Johor. Three major palm oil equipment makers have origins in Muar: Muar Buan Lee, YKL Group, and Mvance Engineering. All are focused on equipment for the palm oil sector's midstream segment (palm fruit milling, kernel crushing and waste material processing), whereas downstream processing equipment manufacturing for refineries continues to be dominated by foreign engineering specialists such as Desmet Ballestra (Belgium), Alfa Laval (Sweden), Lurgi (Germany), and Southeast Asian entities like Lipco, Oiltek, Lipochem and Intersonikon.[9]

The Johor processor-trader segment can be divided in a similar manner between businesses with origins mostly outside Malaysia, as opposed to those with beginnings in Malaysia. Non-domiciled processor-traders with a significant presence in Johor include Wilmar (publicly listed in Singapore), Cargill (USA), Musim Mas (Indonesia), Archer Daniel Midlands (USA), Bunge (USA) and Golden-Agri Resources (Indonesia). Wilmar is by far the largest of these groups, and is said to control half of the global trade in palm products, as well as a quarter of the world's vegetable oil refining capacity. Wilmar and other transnational groups with trading backgrounds have tended to limit their involvement in estates and milling, with a stronger emphasis on processing and trading activity. Processor-traders of Malaysian origin have tended to come from the other direction. Although many are now regional players with interests in Indonesia and beyond, their attempts to vertically integrate have been shaped by their origins in primary production and milling. Domiciled processors in fact often sell their refined products to global giants like Wilmar and Cargill.

Johor's refining industry, housed mostly at Pasir Gudang, consists of both groups of processer-traders. The biggest refiners are two Singapore-listed groups, PGEO (Wilmar) and Mewah Oleo (Mewah Group), following IOI Pan Century (a subsidiary of IOI Corporation, listed in Malaysia). Other significant players include Sime Darby Kempas, a subsidiary of Malaysian government-linked company Sime Darby Plantations (Palm Oil Refiners Association of Malaysia, 2017). Taken together, Johor's refiners processed 4 million tonnes of crude palm oil and 0.3 million tonnes of crude palm kernel oil, about a fifth of national output in 2017. The refining segment is complemented by considerable storage infrastructure, with eight companies currently operating bulking installations in Johor. At Pasir Gudang alone seven bulk storage facilities received over 5.67 million tonnes of palm oil products in 2017, destined for both local upgrading and re-export.[10] The processing, storage and trading segment is marked by an oligopolistic market structure, which is unsurprising given the considerable cost economies involved in large-scale refining, bulk storage, and transport.

Anchored by the state's processing-storage clusters, Johor has successfully secured net gains both in terms of oil palm-based product volumes and value-added goods. In 2017, Johor exported RM15.5 billion worth of vegetable oil products (some 28 per cent of the national share). Pasir Gudang alone exported 2.8 million tonnes of crude and processed palm oil (17 per cent of the national share). Johor also receives and imports considerable amounts of palm products for further processing: crude palm oil, palm kernel oil, palm oil-based oleochemicals, palm kernel cake worth RM4.2 billion was imported in 2017. Even larger volumes were imported before Sarawak and Sabah established more local refineries, but in all likelihood Pasir Gudang continues to receive palm products from Indonesia as well. Although no precise breakdown of Johor palm exports by product is available, the territory's disproportionate share of Malaysian export values implies that Johor exports are skewed towards higher value-added produce (MPOB n.d.-e).

JOHOR'S OIL PALM GROWERS AS POLITICAL BENEFICIARIES

The lucrative, resource-intensive nature of Johor's oil palm sector has given it an unavoidably political edge. There are three prime channels through which oil palms in Johor have benefited politically. First, within Malaysia's federal system, state-level politicians control access to land and its development, making it imperative for corporate actors to foster close ties with political elites. Second, Johor is home to several major government-linked companies involved in oil palm enterprises. Third, group scheme oil palm settlers have become a significant voting base in some Malaysian rural areas, particularly those of Johor. Oil palms are thus intertwined with the interests of state capital as well as wider patron-client relations.

Politically Linked Private Sector Groups

Generally speaking, corporate plantation interests with close ties to Malaysian state elites have in the past successfully acquired forest-clearing licences and agricultural land (Nesadurai 2018, p. 209). In Johor, though, this dynamic has been somewhat diluted for oil palms because considerable swathes of current planted area were converted from older rubber farmland (see Figure 3.1). Even so, continued private long-term access to local farmland remains the prerogative of state-level land authorities, as well as federal politicians (who in the past have held significant stakes in private firms through government investment agencies).

Two examples may suffice for now. The first is Tradewinds Plantation Berhad, one of Malaysia's largest oil palm and rubber companies, as well as a significant player in Johor's oil palm sector. Tradewinds is part of the commercial empire of Syed Mokhtar Albukhary, a well-known bumiputra tycoon who gained favour in the mid-1970s by befriending Muhyiddin Yassin, then managing director of a government supply company that was a subsidiary of the Johor State Economic Development Corporation. The following decade saw Albukhary expand his business interests in shipping, construction, palm oil, sugar and property development, particularly in Johor, where Muhyiddin had become chief minister by 1986. Albukhary's clout continued to grow once he entered the good books of Mahathir Mohamad in the late 1990s, during the latter's first prime ministerial stint. Albukhary is widely believed to have been a major donor to the United Malays National Organization (UMNO) political party (Davidson 2018, pp. 108, 120–22). Bloomberg records state that Tradewinds currently maintains a landbank of 53,033 hectares in Peninsular Malaysia, with seventeen estates in Johor alone.

Another plantation company with a sizeable Johor landbank is Genting Plantations Berhad. The company is part of a group founded in 1965 by the late Lim Goh Tong, who was famous for establishing casino and gaming activities in Pahang's highlands. The Chinese-led group drew on support from key UMNO politicians to safeguard its continued growth and profits, particularly after the advent of the pro-bumiputra New Economic Policy in the early 1970s. The group co-opted former senior Malay public servants into company directorships, meanwhile enjoying government rents in the form of selectively awarded licences, contracts and projects (Gomez and Jomo 1999, p. 47; Gomez 2018, pp. 38–45). As of 2017, Genting owned a total planted area of 247,600 hectares across Malaysia and Indonesia, including 10,434 hectares in Johor, and one mill at Genting Sing Mah estate in Air Hitam (Genting Plantations n.d.-a). Genting also undertakes property development on three of its plantation concessions in Johor, while the Genting Kulai Besar Estate in Simpang Renggam hosts Genting Indahpura Car City and Genting Indahpura Sports City (Genting Plantations n.d.-b).

Government-Linked Corporations

One of the most outstanding features of Malaysia's national-era political economy is the extent to which government-linked investment companies own and control the corporate sector. Sime Darby, a Malaysian trading conglomerate whose largest stakeholders are government-linked investment holding companies Amanah Saham, Employees Provident Fund Board and Permodalan Nasional Berhad, in turn owns Malaysia's largest plantation group, Sime Darby Plantation Berhad. Through its subsidiaries, Sime Darby Plantation Berhad owns roughly 344,000 hectares of oil palms across Malaysia, divided among 124 oil palm estates, and also possesses numerous rubber estates. In Johor the group runs twenty-seven oil palm estates, six mills and a refinery, as well as three rubber estates and two rubber factories.

Sime Darby's presence in Johor has been boosted through its merger with the Guthrie Group in 2007. As seen earlier, Guthrie & Co. Ltd was one of Johor's earliest oil palm investors (and benefited from cheap land tenure courtesy of the colonial-era Johor authorities). In the decades following independence, government-owned holding companies stepped up their takeovers of Malaysia's most prominent European-owned rubber and oil palm plantation firms, including Sime Darby, Guthrie Corporation Ltd, and Harrison's & Crosfield. These manoeuvres during the 1970s and 1980s were spearheaded by several prominent Malay elites. The most outstanding include the late Tun Ismail Mohamed Ali, Permodalan Nasional Berhad's inaugural chairman from 1978 to 1996 (and Prime Minister Mahathir Mohamad's brother-in-law), as well as Tan Sri Hj. Basir Ismail, a Johor native who was eventually appointed by Mahathir as Food Industries of Malaysia Berhad's executive director in the early 1980s (Martin 2003, Ch. 9; Yacob and White 2010). The Permodalan link is especially significant, as the investment holding entity was established in 1978 as part of the federal government's pro-bumiputra New Economic Policy to address interethnic economic disparities. Oil palm investments via Sime Darby and other firms were thus seen by federal political elites as a crucial enabler in the creation of a Bumiputera Commercial and Industrial Community.

Johor's state authorities have pursued similar strategies through state-linked enterprises. The Johor Corporation, formerly known as the Johor State Economic Development Corporation, is the most prominent of these entities, not least thanks to its oil palm-related investments. The corporation was founded in 1968 to raise bumiputra earnings in Johor, embarking on a general asset accumulation strategy based on an initial state loan of RM10 million. Between the late 1960s and mid-1990s, the corporation expanded swiftly, acquiring profitable oil palm estates and land concessions. Plantations were purchased to generate operational revenues as well as for diversification into industrial parks (Hutchinson 2012).

Johor Corporation's ownership of Kulim (Malaysia) Berhad is a case in point. Kulim, one of Malaysia's largest palm oil interests, was progressively bought into by the Corporation until the latter acquired a majority share in the former. Under Johor Corporation, Kulim's primary business remains in plantations, but it also engages in intrapreneur ventures such as biofertilizers, agriculture machinery, and oil palm nurseries. As of 2017, Kulim held 47,098 hectares of oil palms (over 14 per cent of Johor's oil palm area held by estates) with a fruit yield per hectare of nearly 24 tonnes, far superior to Johor's and Malaysia's averages (20.66 and 18.70 tonnes respectively) (Kulim n.d.; Johor Corporation n.d.). The group's plantation interests extend to Indonesia, Solomon Islands and Papua New Guinea (*The Star,* 6 August 2014). Making use of the Corporation's ownership of Tanjung Langsat Port in Johor, Kulim also invested in palm product refining and storage facilities, becoming Malaysia's second largest oleo-chemical manufacturer until Kulim sold NatOleo to Wilmar in 2010. Although the Johor Corporation previously diversified into heavy industry, process manufacturing and services by the 1990s, it has since focused on core competencies in oil palm cultivation, palm processing and land development, having suffered severe losses during the 1997/98 Asian Financial Crisis (Hutchinson 2012, pp. 20, 28).

Oil Palm-Linked Rural Voters

Not all state capitalist forays into oil palms have proven successful, either in terms of commercial profits or electoral outcomes. The intricate nexus between political elites, business cronies and state-held funds has become particularly dysfunctional where FELDA settlers and the recently privatized FELDA Global Ventures (now FGV Holdings Berhad) are concerned.

The fact that FELDA's recorded history has been largely a success story makes recent developments more poignant. From the late 1950s to 1990, over 110,000 low-income land-starved households were recruited by FELDA into over 300 land development schemes scattered across the Peninsula. By 1990, when new settler schemes were terminated and FELDA's remaining land banks were converted into agency-run plantations, Johor had the one of the highest numbers of FELDA schemes and settler households in Malaysia, second only to Pahang. There were already 120,716 hectares of FELDA-owned oil palms in Johor by 1990, with smaller holdings of rubber (24,692 hectares). Much of FELDA's present-day agricultural imprint comes from the massive Johor Tenggara project in central and southeast Johor, with smaller settlements elsewhere in Segamat and Muar (Khor 2015).

Beyond resettlement and farming, FELDA has been an important vote bank for UMNO, and thus the Barisan Nasional coalition, particularly in Johor. Approximately 6 to 9 per cent of Malaysia's current eligible voter base consists of FELDA voters (including dependents, adult children and associated workers) (Khor 2014, p. 90; Pakiam 2018b, p. 2). FELDA schemes were politically motivated creations from the outset, spearheaded for the most part by senior UMNO politicians, and vested with the tasks of catalysing rural capital accumulation, modernizing peasant agriculture, and reducing Malay poverty (Hutchinson 2018, p. 20). The increasingly centrist bureaucratic structures used to perpetuate rural development from the 1950s onwards were themselves inspired by British Malaya's anti-Communist military campaigns during the late 1940s and 1950s (Harper 1999, pp. 366–67). Political geography also influenced the pacing and location of resettlement. For instance, the Kulai Oil Palm Scheme in Johor—FELDA's very first oil palm project in Malaysia—was launched partly to encourage Malay settlement in an area then dominated by Chinese pig farmers (Pakiam 2017, p. 286). In Johor and elsewhere, UMNO's presence coloured vital dimensions of settler life, including approving new scheme entrants, processing land claims, as well as structuring local governance and spreading party propaganda. UMNO's entrenched presence was backed by efficient administration at both the federal and state levels, especially in Johor, which was one of only two states in Malaysia to succeed in emplacing all selected settlers on time (Hutchinson 2018, p. 21). Settler electoral support for UMNO has consequently been astoundingly high in Johor (Table 3.4).

The results of Malaysia's 13th General Elections (GE-13) in 2013 showed that UMNO-BN's support had generally dwindled in urban areas, but the coalition retained parliamentary control due to support from rural seats. The FELDA "vote bank effect" in Johor was especially prominent. Not only did Johor's FELDA settlers poll the highest majorities favouring Barisan amongst all FELDA voting areas, but differences in voting preferences between FELDA and non-FELDA areas in Johor were the widest among Malaysia's states.

Even at this point, however, FELDA was becoming a victim of its hard-earned commercial success. The initial public listing of FELDA's former plantation subsidiary FGV on the Kuala Lumpur Stock Exchange in 2012 was dogged by controversies that deepened in the lead-up to GE-14. These included the fact that settlers were relinquishing direct ownership of some 356,000 hectares of mostly oil palm-based plantation lands run on their behalf by FELDA (thus losing a major revenue stream), FELDA and FGV's squandering of billions of ringgit raised from the latter's initial public listing on commercially dubious asset purchases, and FGV's plummeting share price shortly after the listing. All of these developments were presided over by former Negeri Sembilan Chief Minister Isa Samad, whose UMNO membership had been previously suspended for six years on corruption charges (Pakiam 2018b, pp. 10, 14n13; Pakiam 2019b, pp. 6–7; Rosli Yaakop 2018).

FELDA settlers were not necessarily distressed by these high-level corporate scandals, but they were certainly troubled by slack household income growth and

TABLE 3.4
Comparison of Support for Barisan Nasional Parliamentary Candidates, GE-13

Support for Barisan by Polling Centre	% votes for Barisan, GE13	vs. FELDA Areas in Same State
Johor, FELDA areas	90	N/A
Negeri Sembilan, FELDA areas	78	N/A
Pahang, FELDA areas	66	N/A
Other states, FELDA areas	64	N/A
Johor, near FELDA areas	76	–14
Negeri Sembilan, near FELDA areas	63	–16
Pahang, near FELDA areas	57	–9
Other states, near FELDA areas	62	–2
Johor, other areas	51	–39
Negeri Sembilan, other areas	49	–29
Pahang, other areas	48	–18
Other states, other areas	45	–19

Source: Khor and Chia (2018).

growing debts amidst tepid international palm oil prices since 2011. The impact of the global price slump on settler incomes was also worsened by the erosion of institutional safeguards set up to cushion the effects of these cyclical downturns. Corporate mismanagement within FELDA and FGV lay at the roots of these problems (Pakiam 2019b, pp. 4–6). Growing settler discontent prompted former Prime Minister Najib Razak—who had overseen Isa Samad's appointments to key FELDA leadership positions—to direct a barrage of financial incentives towards settlers in 2017. Proposals included a RM5,000 handout for each settler household, disposal of RM5,000 in replanting debt; disposal of FGV share loans for 77,000 settlers; interest-free home renovation loans of up to RM40,000 per settler; a replanting grant worth RM7,500 per hectare per household; and a special fund to help dispose of settler replanting debts exceeding RM40,000 (*New Straits Times*, 23 July 2017).

Despite these attempts to shore up rural support, settler discontent continued to grow in the lead-up to the 14th General Elections (GE-14). Highly-publicized management disputes at FGV in mid-2017 and further drops in FGV's share prices aggravated settler anxieties (Khor 2017; Khor 2018b). GE-14 in May 2019 thus saw an overall decline in support for Barisan candidates within FELDA settlements across Malaysia, compared with GE-13's results. The decline was steepest in Johor, but that was partly because support had been so high to begin with. All things considered, historical legacies remained intact, and Johor's FELDA settlers continued being one of Barisan's staunchest allies in GE-14 (Table 3.5). Indeed, GE-14's results suggest that FELDA voters remain critical vote banks for Barisan across much of the Peninsula, as differences in voting behaviour between FELDA and non-FELDA areas have grown even more stark.

Looking ahead, these growing political tensions surrounding oil palm enterprise are mirrored by commercial strains within Malaysia's oil palm sector. The future

TABLE 3.5
Change in FELDA Settler Support for Barisan Nasional Parliamentary
Candidates, GE-14 vs. GE-13

Support for Barisan in FELDA Areas	% votes for Barisan, GE-14	% votes for Barisan, GE-13	Change since GE-13
Johor	72	90	–18
Negeri Sembilan	63	78	–16
Pahang	53	66	–13
Other states with FELDA areas	52	64	–11
All states	59	74	–15
The "FELDA factor" (difference between FELDA and non-FELDA areas in same state)			
Johor	25	14	+11
Negeri Sembilan	15	16	–1
Pahang	3	9	–6
Other states with FELDA areas	8	8	+6
All states	12	12	0

Source: Khor and Chia (2020).

of agriculture and agribusiness within the country's increasingly urbanized and industrialized economy appears uncertain. Again, Johor's evolving landscape offers a fascinating window into these concerns.

LOOKING AHEAD: URBANIZATION, LABOUR, AND ENVIRONMENTAL SUSTAINABILITY

Just as oil palms were once a marginal crop in Johor, it is only a matter of time before commercial calculations and ageing trees prompt more estates and smallholders to sideline oil palm cultivation. This may be hard to imagine when one-third of present-day Johor is carpeted with these spiky trees. But it is worth remembering that as recently as the mid-1980s, Johor growers still devoted more soil to *Hevea* rubber than they did to oil palms (Department of Agriculture Johor 1984, p. 10). Low profitability, marketing difficulties, and the physical dangers associated with crop handling and harvesting held many farmers back from working with the latter cultivar. These barriers lessened as rubber and coconut trees aged and yields dropped, access to palm fruit milling facilities increased, relative prices for oil palm fruits improved, and cheap foreign labour took on increasing amounts of manual farm chores. But periodic commodity price slumps, persistent field labour shortages, and a widening range of urban activities have typically prompted growers to ask if they should switch from oil palms to a different crop—rubber, coconuts, other fruit trees, or vegetables—or exit agriculture completely.

On the surface, urbanization seems to pose a serious threat to Johor's oil palm economy. Johor's resident urban population has grown considerably: 72 per cent in 2010, compared with 64 per cent in 2000. Rural areas lost over 25,000 residents during the same interval, while urban areas gained nearly 671,000 denizens (DOSM 2000; DOSM 2013, p. 11). Considerable agricultural land has been converted to non-farm uses, including residential housing, integrated townships, and office/retail space; about 25,000 hectares between 1990 and 2014, to be precise.[11] Furthermore, oil palm enterprises themselves are often behind these manoeuvres, with the backing of federal and state governments keen on catalysing lucrative infrastructural and property development projects in Johor. With land and its development under the control of state-level politicians, the same cosy patron-client relationships that have helped corporate actors expand their landed oil palm interests under the watch of Johor's politicians have also been highly conducive to furthering real estate deals, as mentioned in the earlier cases of Genting and Johor Corporation.

Some oil palm growers have been unwilling parties to these land conversions. The most infamous case in recent memory, the Renong-United Engineers Malaysia "land grab", saw government-linked property developer United Engineers profit from a 1991 amendment to Malaysia's Land Acquisition Act allowing the Johor government to assume control over 13,350 hectares of land in Gelang Patah. The early 1990s acquisition facilitated the construction of the Second Link between Singapore and Malaysia and a nearby township by United Engineers, but affected landowners received only a quarter of the market price for their land (Fann 2012).

The de facto seizure affected nineteen villages, displaced some 10,000 residents, and saw several palm oil estates lose their concessions. A similar episode during the same decade saw Stamford Holdings, an oil palm-centric plantation firm co-owned by one Singaporean and two Malaysian families, sue the Johor government for allegedly abusing the Land Acquisition Act to acquire 6,500 acres of the firm's land for light industrial use. News reports alleged that Syed Mokhtar Albukhary had initially approached Stamford's directors with a private offer to buy the lands at less than half the going market rate for development. When the directors refused, Syed Mokhtar's close associate in Johor government, then Menteri Besar Muhyiddin Yassin, allegedly personally pressured Stamford to accept the offer in 1992. A year and a half later, the land was acquired by the state on behalf of the Johor Islamic Economic Development Corporation. An out-of-court settlement five years later saw RM405 million being paid to Stamford by both the Johor government and Syed Mokhtar's Kelana Ventures Sdn Bhd (*Kinibiz Online,* 18 September 2013*).*

On the whole, though, it appears that most large-scale oil palm enterprises in Johor have embraced property development themselves, focusing on southern Johor and opportunities within the Iskandar Malaysia investment corridor. The Sime Darby Group has been busy consolidating its status as a major property developer in Johor. Current projects include Bandar University Pagoh (an education hub with residential, retail and business properties 150 kilometres north of Johor Bahru) and Taman Pasir Putih (a residential development located 30 kilometres east of Johor Bahru, just beyond Pasir Gudang) (Sime Darby Properties Berhad n.d.). Smaller groups, such as Keck Seng (Malaysia) Berhad and the holdings of the Gooi family (Kim Loong Resources Berhad and Crescendo Corporation), are also running oil palm plantations and property development businesses concurrently, using their land banks to establish and run various townships, tourist resorts, hotels, commercial office space, and industrial properties in Johor Bahru (Keck Seng Berhad n.d.-a; Keck Seng Berhad n.d.-b; Crescendo Corporation Berhad n.d.).

Despite the recent real estate boom, Johor's sheer size suggests that urbanization per se is unlikely to endanger Johor's overall oil palm interests in the short- to medium-term, whether in terms of farm cultivation, or downstream processing activities. We estimate that less than 3 per cent of Johor's land area is currently built-up, leaving a vast amount under soil and water cover (Figure 3.3).

Most farmlands recently converted to non-farm uses run close to built-up clusters. 47 per cent of all conversions took place in the Johor Bahru and Kulai Jaya districts: the former currently hosts Johor's main urban conurbation, as well as the state administrative capital at Iskandar Puteri. Both districts accommodate a large number of Malaysians commuting to Singapore for work on a daily basis, as well as a range of businesses targeting Singaporeans looking for cheap weekend retail and tourism opportunities. Thus far, other parts of Johor have been largely left out of this commuter-centric dynamic between Johor and Singapore, and thus sheltered from pressures to urbanize.

Labour shortages might constitute a more serious long-term threat to Johor's oil palm economy. The farm segment of the oil palm value chain remains the largest

FIGURE 3.3
The Growth and Distribution of Built-up Areas in Johor, 1990–2014

Source: Appendix 3.3.

TABLE 3.6
Estimated Labour in Johor's Oil Palm Economy, 2010s

Oil Palm Value Chain Segment	Estimated Workers Employed
Farms	85,000
Crop dealers	At least 6,660 (15 per dealership)*
Mills	5,000 (60–100 per mill)**
Refineries	1,700 (Pasir Gudang only)***

Notes:
* 444 Johor dealers were listed in the 2013 Directory of Malaysian Oil Palm Fresh Fruit Dealers.
** Khor Yu Leng's interview with palm oil mill specialist, Johor, 24 February 2019.
*** Company reports suggest each factory in Pasir Gudang employs roughly 100 workers. There are currently 17 factories in Pasir Gudang involved in palm oil processing. See TPM Technopark Sdn Bhd (n.d.).

employer of manpower (Table 3.6). With a production area of almost 750,000 hectares and a labour-to-land ratio of about one worker for every 8 to 10 hectares, there may be as many as 85,000 oil palm labourers working in Johor.[12] Dealerships, mills and refineries require significantly less manpower.

The expansion of manufacturing and services in Malaysia, together with a growing local middle class, has sown conditions for heavy dependence on migrant labour, particularly in vocations considered dirty, dangerous or demeaning, such as agriculture (Saravanamuttu 2013, pp. 132–34). Official figures for non-citizens suggest that around 44,000 migrant workers are being employed to weed, fertilize, prune and harvest oil palms in the districts of Batu Pahat, Kluang, Kota Tinggi, Mersing, and Segamat, where three-quarters (561,465 hectares) of Johor's oil palms are cultivated. This implausibly low labour-to-land ratio of one worker per 12.7 hectares suggests that far higher numbers of workers are actually tending the fields. Given that local industry estimates of oil palm plantation industry's general reliance on foreign workers range from 70 to 90 per cent, the bulk of field labour in Johor estates clearly consists of both documented and undocumented migrants from Indonesia and Bangladesh, rather than Malaysian citizens doing low-paid work (Khor 2018c).

Complaints about labour shortages in oil palm plantations have been rife since the 1980s. What is often less appreciated by outsiders is how much of a difference skilled labour makes to field productivity, and how the techniques needed to prune palms cleanly, harvest fruit bunches efficiently, and avoid serious injuries along the way require months of practice and tutelage (Pakiam 2017, pp. 78–85; Adam Aziz 2018). Ongoing research into labour-saving devices such as retractable harvesting poles, improved motorized cutters and pulsed lasers will only intensify the need for skilled field workers in future (Mohd Ikmal Hafizi Azaman and Abdul Razak Jelani 2017). Failure to employ sufficient numbers of skilled field workers leads not only to permanent disfigurement and immobility for employees when accidents occur, but also significant crop losses and productivity for farm enterprises (Balasubramaniam and Prathap 1977; Wolf 1983; Sanderson 2016). The fact that Johor's farm sector has withstood labour shortages for decades by hiring undocumented workers does not detract from the fact that Johor's farmers have been keen to take up new livelihood opportunities if more attractive options are available. For example, oil palm group scheme participants in FELDA, FELCRA and RISDA projects have expressed interest in diversifying into more remunerative, less labour-intensive cash crops. However, they remain somewhat constrained by regulations imposed by their parent institutions, echoing RISDA's attempts to discourage rubber smallholders from switching to oil palms three decades earlier (Zunaira Saieed 2018).

Finally, environmental concerns have become a primary challenge to the Southeast Asian oil palm industry's continued prosperity. Both Malaysian and Indonesian businesses have come under sustained attack for violations relating to environmental damage (especially contributions to deforestation and climate change), as well as labour exploitation (child labour, indecent working conditions). The emerging regimes governing these issues are complex, involving a bewildering variety of industry players, non-government organizations and state authorities (Nesadurai 2018; Koay 2018). The most important development by far has been the European Union Parliament's preparations since January 2018 to limit palm oil's use within the European Union-based biofuels, with plans to begin enforcement from 2021. More recently, the European Union's push towards using "indirect land use" metrics to estimate emissions from crop-based biofuel production is likely to stymie palm oil's economic future further. Restricting energy-based uses for palm oil could initially reduce palm oil demand by 3 million tonnes, with possible further restrictions down the road within Asia itself as major buyers in Japan, China and Thailand sign up to the Roundtable for Sustainable Palm Oil (Hilton and Sugiura 2019).

While palm oil exporters and large refiners have been the main focus of media attention, forgotten in the push for more sustainable forms of palm oil are smallholders working in localities with longer farming histories. Here is where the independent smallholder story in Johor begins to take flight. Preliminary geospatial research and analysis indicates that 99 per cent of West Johor's dense belt of independent oil palm smallholdings was already put under agriculture by 1985 (Khor 2018a). With an estimated 1 million hectares of oil palm under cultivation, Malaysia's independent smallholders are theoretically able to produce 3 to 4 million metric tonnes of "no deforestation" crude palm oil. Once contributions from FELDA oil palm settlements are included, smallholder production would be equivalent to the European Union's annual demand. With the implementation of mandatory Malaysian Sustainable Palm Oil certification for smallholders by end-2019, there are significant opportunities for Johor and other Malaysian smallholders to deliver low-risk sustainable palm oil to the European Union and other discerning markets in the long term.

CLOSING REMARKS

Johor's oil palm industry has benefited immensely from the legacies left by other forms of agricultural production, especially rubber. Blessed with ample land, capital, know-how, migrant labour, processing technologies, trading clusters, and governments generally committed to upholding high-value export agriculture, Johor's moves up the oil palm-based value chain have occurred relatively smoothly.

The harder question to answer remains identifying specific synergies between different segments of the oil palm production chain in Johor. Physical proximity to palm processing facilities matters most at the farm stage when fruits need to be sent quickly to factories. Once milled, crude palm oil and kernel oil have longer shelf lives, making it less important for refiners to be close to millers. Yet vegetable oil refiners and speciality manufacturers choose to remain in Johor for many reasons beyond just closeness to Johor's growers and millers. These include the state's strategic location along major shipping routes, as well as the economies of scope gained by setting up dense production clusters at Johor's major industrial parks. The calculus behind these advantages will continue to shift as governments in East Malaysia and Indonesia seek to move up the oil palm value chain. But even if some of these higher-end processing facilities were to relocate out of Johor in future, many local farms and farmers supplying their raw materials would probably continue operations for years if not decades, thanks to their tree crops' long lives. Independent smallholders may yet prove integral to the persistence of oil palm farming in Johor and the rest of Malaysia, on both economic and environmental grounds. Such a shift might even prove politically beneficial for the governments of Johor and other Malaysian states.

APPENDIX 3.1

Summary Indicators for Oil Palm Subsectors in Johor, 2017

Subsectors	Key Statistics, 2017 (a)	Key Players and Locations, 2017 (b)	Notes and Sources
Estates (i)	330,394 hectares, with an estimated fresh fruit bunch (FFB) output of 6.5 million tonnes	By potential annual FFB output, Sime Darby and Kulim-Johor Corp have over 1 million tonnes, followed by IOI, Tradewinds, KL Kepong, Genting Plantations and Boustead.	Estimated FFB output is calculated using Johor's stated average FFB yield of 20.66 tonnes per hectare for 2017.
Government-managed group schemes (FELDA-FGV, FELDA, RISDA, state schemes) (ii)	195,042 hectares, FFB output estimated at 3.1 million tonnes	FELDA settlers are mostly in north, central, and southeastern Johor.	Johor's land area is about 1.91 million hectares. Over one-third of Johor is planted with oil palm.
Independent Smallholders (iii)	223,424 hectares, FFB output estimated at 4.4 million tonnes	A large zone of smallholders in western Johor, where oil palm is mixed with other tree crops such as rubber, coconuts, and other fruits	Estimated FFB sources from estates:scheme smallholders:independent smallholders are 46:22:31.
Total for Johor estates and smallholders (i to iii)	0.75 million hectares (9 per cent immature), FFB output estimated at 14 million tonnes		Johor hosts 13 per cent of Malaysia's total planted area of 5.8 million hectares for 2017; of which 2.7 million hectares is in Peninsular Malaysia (45 per cent), and 1.5 and 1.6 million hectares in Sabah and Sarawak respectively (about 27 per cent each).
Mills (often own significant private estate areas)	62 mills, 16.6 million tonnes' capacity and 16.3 FFB million tonnes of FFB actually processed	FGV (13 mills), Sime Darby (6); 2 mills each for IOI Corporation, Keck Seng, Taiko Plantations (KL-Kepong), EPA/Mahamurni Plantation, RISDA/ESPEK and Tradewinds.	Johor has 62 of the 454 mills of Malaysia (15 per cent of 112.2 million tonnes capacity). They processed 15.8 million tonnes of FFB (16 per cent of the national total's 97.8 million tonnes in 2017).
			Johor's milling capacity utilization rate was 99 per cent, considerably higher than the 90 per cent national average for 2017.
	Output of 3.1 million tonnes CPO, 0.9 million tonnes of palm kernels		Malaysia CPO production was 20.0 million tonnes, so Johor's output was almost 16 per cent of the total.

Palm kernel crushers	9 crushers with 1.3 million tonnes handling capacity. 0.4 million tonnes of CPKO output	The biggest crushers are Jin Lee, PGEO (Wilmar) and FELDA-FGV. Other key players include PYO, Sehcom, and Hok Kuat.	9 of the 45 Malaysian-based crushers (representing 18 per cent of 7.3 million tonnes national capacity) are located in Johor. Malaysia's CPKO production was 2.3 million tonnes, so Johor's output was 17 per cent of the total. (Khor Yu Leng's interview with palm oil mill specialist, Johor, 9 February 2019)
Refineries	14 refineries with 7.2 million tonnes handling capacity. 4 million tonnes of crude palm oil and 0.3 million tonnes of crude palm kernel oil processed.	The biggest refiners are PGEO (Wilmar), Mewah Oleo, and IOI Pan Century.	Johor hosts 14 out of 54 refineries in Malaysia (representing 26 per cent of 27.3 million tonnes national capacity). Johor's refiners' output represented about 25 per cent of the national total (16.2 million tonnes of crude palm oil and 1.5 million tonnes of crude palm kernel oil) in 2017. Johor evidently receives and/or imports palm oil and palm kernel oil for processing. It is the currently largest state for refining, just ahead of Sabah, Sarawak, and Selangor. (Khor Yu Leng's interview with downstream specialist, Kuala Lumpur, 9 February 2019)
Oleochemicals	6 oleochemical plants with 0.7 million tonnes capacity.	The largest are Evyap Sabun, IOI Pan-Century Oleo and Nat Oleo.	Johor hosts 6 out of 19 of Malaysia's oleochemical plants, representing 26 per cent of 2.7 million tonnes national capacity. Points to Johor receiving and/or importing products for processing. Selangor, however, still hosts a bigger plant capacity than Johor. (Khor Yu Leng's interview with downstream specialist, Kuala Lumpur, 9 February 2019)

continued on next page

APPENDIX 3.1 – cont'd

Subsectors	Key Statistics, 2017 (a)	Key Players and Locations, 2017 (b)	Notes and Sources
Biodiesel	5 biodiesel plants with 0.9 million tonnes capacity.	The top producers are Vance, Carotino, PGEO (Wilmar), and Supervitamins (Keck Seng).	Johor hosts five of Malaysia's 16 plants, representing 43 per cent of Malaysia's overall production capacity of 2.1 million tonnes. It leads in biodiesel capacity, ahead of Selangor with. Production data are not available, but capacity figures suggest that Johor receives and imports by-products for processing. Nevertheless, several larger biodiesel producers are no longer active, including AJ Oleo and YPJ. (Khor Yu Leng's interview with downstream specialist, Kuala Lumpur, 9 February 2019)
Palm kernel meal (animal feed for dairy cattle)	0.5 million tonnes were produced by Johor palm kernel crushers in 2017. 7 at Pasir Gudang alone.	New Zealand is the major global buyer and Wilmar is the dominant supplier.	Johor's share is 20 per cent of 2.5 million tonnes produced nationally. Again this points to Johor receiving and importing palm kernels.
Bulking installations		Key players are Pasir Gudang, Pelabuhan Tanjung Pelepas (both owned by MMC Group), and Tanjung Langsat Terminal (owned by Johor Corporation); Langsat Bulkers Sdn Bhd, Langsat Terminal (One) Sdn. Bhd, FELDA-Johor Bulkers (FJB)	Pasir Gudang: 460,000 MT capacity Tanjung Pelepas: containerized cargo only Tanjung Langsat: 31,200 MT (FJB).
Exports and imports	Exports of RM15.5 billion and imports RM4.2 billions' worth of vegetable (palm) oil products.		Johor's palm product exports constituted 28 per cent of the Malaysian total by value. Johor is receiving and importing palm products and also focusing on higher-value exports.

Notes:
At the time of writing, state-level information for Johor was only available for 2017.
Malaysia's national mill utilization rate was 90 per cent, palm kernel crushers 65 per cent, palm kernel crushers 65 per cent, refineries 65 per cent and oleochemicals 95 per cent in 2017 (utilization for biodiesel was not reported). State-level utilization rates were only available for mills.
There is variance in the two Malaysian Palm Oil Board (MPOB) sources. The MPOB directory (b) typically indicates a larger number of companies than the number of facilities counted in MPOB statistics (a). There is perhaps more than one company operating in "one facility" (per MPOB statistics count). Some non-operational companies are still listed in the MPOB directory, and miscategorization may also exist.
Sources: Summary, estimates and analysis based on various data: MPOB (n.d.-f); MPOB (2017); Rosnani Hashim and Mina Hattori (2016); Palm Oil Refiners Association of Malaysia (2017); SEDA (n.d.).

APPENDIX 3.2
Johor's Palm Oil Processing Equipment Makers

Muar Ban Lee group is a public-listed company founded and based in Muar, with seven subsidiaries related to oil palm industry equipment manufacturing. As of 2017, founder Dato Chua Ah Ba @ Chua Eng Ka was Executive Chairman (Muar Ban Lee Group Berhad 2018). The group's main activities involve manufacturing oilseed expellers and ancillary machinery for oilseed crushing plants (mainly palm kernels). The entity boasts over twenty years of experience in palm kernel expeller machines, with sales in over twenty-five countries. The group's expertise extends to designing and building palm oil mills and palm oil waste treatment plants. Muar Ban Lee describes itself as a "One Stop Service" for oilseed extraction, but is focused almost entirely on palm products. In 2017, it reported a total of RM183.61 million in revenue (Muar Ban Lee Group Berhad n.d.).

Also from Muar is the YKL Group, a third-generation family-owned business currently led by Yeo Koon Lian and his three sons. YKL had its origins in Koon Heng Engineering Works, a sole proprietorship established in 1973 to repair palm oil processing machinery, as well as supply and manufacture of palm kernel expeller machinery and equipment. Koon Heng expanded its operations to Indonesia in 1980, before breaking into Nigeria and other African states in 1985. Renamed Khun Heng Engineering Works in 1988, the firm diversified into other types of palm oil processing machine manufacturing. Fourteen years later, one of Koon Heng brothers set up a separate crushing equipment manufacturing business in Melaka named Mvance Engineering (Mvance Engineering Sdn Bhd n.d.). Meanwhile, in 2002, YKL Engineering was established by another brother with intentions of focusing on a new market segment: the design and manufacture of empty fruit bunch processing machinery and fresh fruit bunch splitting equipment. Finally, in 2009, the YKL Group set up a subsidiary named YTH Agri-Technology in order to develop and manufacture automated seed pressing machines. The Group is currently reaping a higher revenue stream than Muar Ban Lee, thanks to its expanding presence in Indonesia.[13]

Other major engineering outfits include Awan Timur Group, Johor's third major engineering outfit is based in Kluang. Founded in 1992, the group currently offers a patented ProAuto™ Vertical Sterilization System that claims to improve palm product recovery rates compared to conventional horizontal sterilization systems.

APPENDIX 3.3
Built-up Areas in Johor, 1990–2014

District	Total Area, square km	Built-up %, 1990	Built-up %, 2014	Built-up Change, times (x)	Built-up Change, hectares
Batu Pahat	1,873	1.8%	3.3%	1.8	2,829
Johor Bahru	1,064	13.3%	22.4%	1.7	9,687
Kota Tinggi	3,482	0.3%	0.6%	2.3	1,264
Kluang	2,865	1.1%	1.5%	1.4	1,308
Kulai Jaya	754	2.7%	5.5%	2.0	2,091
Mersing	2,838	0.2%	0.4%	2.0	562
Muar	1,376	1.5%	3.7%	2.5	3,008
Pontian	933	1.3%	2.5%	2.0	1,197
Segamat	2,807	0.7%	1.2%	1.9	1,645
Tangkak	970	1.3%	2.8%	2.2	1,493
TOTAL	19,102	1.6%	2.9%	1.8	25,084

Source: Summary and analysis of geospatial data from Pesaresi et al. (2015).

Notes

1. Assisted by Deborah Augustin and Jason Jon Benedict.
2. This tripartite production structure can also be found in other states in Malaysia, and also applies to other locally grown cash crops.
3. Geoffrey K. Pakiam's interview with smallholder representative, Kuala Lumpur, 21 April 2015.
4. Khor Yu Leng's interview with two mill specialists based in Johor (10 April 2019). While larger mills own palm fruit bunch ramps as collection points, most palm fruit dealers utilize a concrete flat surface for unloading, storage and loading of fruit bunches onto lorries. They are an important part of the supply chain as they serve the small holders. Some dealers provide harvesting and manuring services, on top of transport of fruit bunches to the mill. A mill may have 10–30 dealer accounts. Each dealer will have accounts with many mills.
5. See Appendix 3.1.
6. These estates include Lee Rubber (likely the largest), Dafa Estate, KUB Malaysia Berhad, Lum Trading, Perbadanan Islam Negeri Johor, Sayong Plantation, Steven Development, United Malacca, United Malaysia Pineapple, and three cooperatives (*Koperasis*).
7. See Appendix 3.1 for calculations.
8. Khor Yu Leng's interview with palm oil mill specialist, Johor, 9 February 2019.
9. Khor Yu Leng's interview with refinery processing specialist, Kuala Lumpur, 29 January 2019. See Appendix 3.2 for further details.
10. See Appendix 3.1.
11. See Appendix 3.3.
12. Khor Yu Leng's interview with plantation specialist, Kuala Lumpur, 24 February 2019.
13. Khor Yu Leng's interview with equipment manufacturing specialist, Kuala Lumpur, 21 August 2018.

References

Adam Aziz. 2018. "IOI Seeks More Flexibility in Hiring Foreign Plantation Workers". *The Edge Markets*, 9 October 2018. https://www.theedgemarkets.com/article/ioi-seeks-more-flexibility-hiring-foreign-plantation-workers (accessed 5 April 2019).

Ayat K. Ab Rahman, Ramli Abdullah, Mohd Arif Simeh, and Faizah Mohd Shariff. 2009. "Management of the Malaysian Oil Palm Supply Chain: The Role of FFB Dealers". *Oil Palm Industry Economic Journal* 9, no. 1: 20–28.

Azman Ismail, Mohd Arif Simeh, and M. Mohd Noor. 2003. "The Production Cost of Oil Palm Fresh Fruit Bunches: The Case of Independent Smallholders in Johor". *Oil Palm Industry Economic Journal* 3, no. 1: 1–7.

Balasubramaniam, P., and K. Prathap. 1977. "Pseudotumours Due to Oil Palm Thorn Injury". *Australian and New Zealand Journal of Surgery* 47, no. 2: 223–25.

Barlow, Colin, and S.K. Jayasuriya. 1986. "Stages of Development in Smallholder Tree Crop Agriculture". *Development and Change* 17, no. 4: 635–58.

Burkill, Isaac Henry. 1966. *A Dictionary of the Economic Products of the Malay Peninsula*. 2nd ed. Kuala Lumpur: Ministry of Agriculture and Cooperatives.

Byerlee, Derek. 2014. "The Fall and Rise Again of Plantations in Tropical Asia: History Repeated?". *Land Development Digest* 3, no. 3: 574–97.

Clarence-Smith, William Gervase, and Steven Topik, eds. 2003. *The Global Coffee Economy in Africa, Asia and Latin America, 1500–1989*. Cambridge: Cambridge University Press.

Corley, R.H.V., and P.B.H. Tinker. 2016. *The Oil Palm*. 5th ed. Hoboken, NJ: Wiley.

Cramb, Rob A., and John F. McCarthy. 2016. "Introduction". In *The Oil Palm Complex: Smallholders, Agribusiness and the State in Indonesia and Malaysia*, edited by Rob A. Cramb and John F. McCarthy. Singapore: NUS Press.

Crescendo Corporation Berhad. n.d. "Annual Report 2018". Crescendo Corporation Berhad website. <https://crescendo.com.my/core-files/uploads/2018/08/CCB_AR2018.pdf> (accessed 2 April 2019).

Cunyngham-Brown, Sjovald. 1971. *The Traders: A Story of Britain's South-East Asian Commercial Adventure*. London: Newman Neave.

Dand, Robin. 2010. *The International Cocoa Trade*. 3rd ed. Cambridge: Woodhead.

Davidson, Jamie S. 2018. "Stagnating Yields, Unyielding Profits: The Political Economy of Malaysia's Rice Sector". *Journal of Southeast Asian Studies* 49, no. 1: 105–28.

Department of Agriculture Johor. *Annual Reports*, various years.

Department of Statistics Malaysia (DOSM). "Selected Imports and Exports from 5 Major Ports, 2014–2017". Customised data request.

———. 2000. *Population and Housing Census of Malaysia 2000: Preliminary Count Report for Urban and Rural Areas*. Putrajaya: Department of Statistics, Malaysia.

———. 2013. *Population Distribution and Basic Demographic Characteristics, 2010*. Putrajaya: Department of Statistics, Malaysia,

Ellis, Frank. 1988. *Peasant Economics: Farm Households and Agrarian Development*. Cambridge: Cambridge University Press.

Fann, Thomas. 2012. "Land Grab Malaysian-Style". *Malaysiakini*, 14 October 2012. https://www.malaysiakini.com/letters/211658 (accessed 23 March 2019).

Genting Plantations. n.d.-a. "Plantation". http://www.gentingplantations.com/business-divisions/plantation/ (accessed 4 April 2019).

———. n.d.-b. "Annual Report 2017". http://www.gentingplantations.com/wp-content/uploads/2018/04/GENP_AR17.pdf (accessed 4 April 2019).

Gomez, Edmund Terence. 2018. *Minister of Finance Incorporated: Ownership and Control of Corporate Malaysia*. Singapore: Strategic Information and Research Development Centre.

———, and Kwame Sundaram Jomo. 1999. *Malaysia's Political Economy: Politics, Patronage and Profits*. Cambridge: Cambridge University Press.

Harper, Tim. 1999. *The End of Empire and the Making of Malaya*. Cambridge: Cambridge University Press.

Hayami, Yujiro. 1996. "The Peasant in Economic Modernization". *American Journal of Agricultural Economics* 78, no. 5: 1157–67.

Hilton, Sarah, and Eri Sugiura. 2019. "Asia's Palm Oil Industry Braces for Backlash at Home". *Nikkei Asian Review*, 9 February 2019. https://asia.nikkei.com/Business/Business-Trends/Asia-s-palm-oil-industry-braces-for-backlash-at-home (accessed 5 April 2019).

Hutchinson, Francis E. 2012. "Johor and Its Electronics Sector: One Priority among Many?". ISEAS Working Paper no. 1. Singapore: Institute of Southeast Asian Studies.

———. 2018. *GE-14 in Johor: The Fall of the Fortress?* Trends in Southeast Asia, no. 3/2018. Singapore: ISEAS – Yusof Ishak Institute.

Johor Corporation. n.d. "Kulim Businesses". Johor Corporation website. http://www.jcorp.com.my/introduction-47.aspx (accessed 1 April 2019).

Keck Seng (Malaysia) Berhad. n.d.-a. "2017 Annual Report". Keck Seng Berhad website. http://my.keckseng.com/annualreport/AnnualReport2017.pdf (accessed 4 April 2018).

———. n.d.-b. "The Keck Seng Collection". Keck Seng Berhad website. http://td.keckseng.com/ (accessed 2 April 2019).

Khera, Harcharan Singh. 1976. *The Oil Palm Industry of Malaysia: An Economic Study*. Kuala Lumpur: Penerbit Universiti Malaya.

Khor, Yu Leng. 2014. "The Political Tussle over FELDA Land Schemes: UMNO Strengthens Its Malay Rural Fortress in 13th General Election". *Kajian Malaysia* 32, no. Supp. 2: 89–121.

———. 2015. *High Carbon Stock Consulting Study 12: The FELDA Case Study*. Oxford: LMC International. http://www.simedarbyplantation.com/sites/default/files/sustainability/high-carbon-stock/consulting-reports/socio-economic/hcs-consulting-report-12-the-felda-case-study.pdf (accessed 26 March 2019).

———. 2017. "The FELDA Quarrel and Its National Ramifications". *ISEAS Perspective*, no. 51/2017, 12 July 2017.

———. 2018a. "My Say: The EU, Malaysian Smallholders and Big Data-Informed Sustainability". *The Edge Malaysia Weekly*, 23 January 2018. https://www.theedgemarkets.com/article/mysay-eu-malaysian-smallholders-and-big-datainformed-sustainability (accessed 27 March 2019).

———. 2018b. "Playing Palm Oil Politics Ahead of Malaysia's Elections". *East Asia Forum*. 26 April 2018. http://www.eastasiaforum.org/2018/04/26/playing-palm-oil-politics-ahead-of-malaysias-elections/ (accessed 2 April 2019).

———. 2018c. "Foreign Workers in Malaysia: Case Study of Oil Palm in Johor and Sabah". *Khor Reports Data & Maps*, 29 March 2018. https://www.khor-reports.com/data-analysis/2018/3/29/foreignlabour-johor-sabah (accessed 29 March 2019).

———, and Jeamme Chia. 2018. "FELDA in GE14: Access to the BN Fortress and a Takeover Rumour". *The Edge Markets*, 8 May 2018. https://www.theedgemarkets.com/article/felda-ge14-%E2%80%94-access-bn-fortress-and-takeover-rumour (accessed 2 April 2019).

——— and Jeamme Chia. 2020. "FELDA and Rural Voting Patterns in GE14: A Wake-up Call". *The Round Table* 109, no. 2: 126-154. https://doi.org/10.1080/00358533.2020.1741882 (accessed 4 May 2020).

Kinibiz Online. 2013. "EcoWorld's New Name with Baggage from the Past". 18 September 2013. http://www.kinibiz.com/story/issues/50225/ecoworld-%E2%80%94-new-name-with-baggage-from-the-past.html (accessed 4 April 2019).

Koay, Juliana. 2018. *Keep Palm ... Edible-Oil Sustainability in Asia*. New York: CLSA.

Kulim (Malaysia) Berhad. n.d. "Integrated Annual Report". http://integrated-report.kulim.com.my/files/document/1058/KULIM%202017%20AR%20-%20Copy.pdf (accessed 1 April 2019).

MAMPU. n.d. "Malaysia: Distribution of Oil Palm Planted Area". Public Sector Open Data Portal. http://www.data.gov.my/data/en_US/dataset/malaysia-distribution-of-oil-palm-planted-area-by-state-and-sector-in-2017-v2/resource/144039ff-dea6-466b-8c87-ef66e4a67dc8 (accessed 2 February 2019)

Malaysian Palm Oil Board (MPOB). n.d.-a. "Oil Palm Planted Area 2018". MPOB website. http://bepi.mpob.gov.my/images/area/2018/Area_summary.pdf (accessed 22 March 2019).

———. n.d.-b. "Production of Crude Palm Oil for the Month of December 2018". MPOB website. http://bepi.mpob.gov.my/index.php/en/statistics/production/186-production-2018/850-production-of-crude-oil-palm-2018.html (accessed 21 March 2019).

———. n.d.-c. "Palm Oil Industry Performance Status". MPOB website. http://econ.mpob.gov.my/economy/industry2/profile_menu.htm (accessed 4 April 2019).

———. n.d.-d. "Guidebook on the Licensing of the Oil Palm Industry". MPOB website. https://e-lesen.mpob.gov.my/document/CRITERIA%20AND%20GUIDELINES%20ON%20MPOB%20LICENSE%20APPLICATION%20cetakan%202018%20ENGLISH.pdf (accessed 11 April 2019).

———. n.d.-e. "Export Statistics 2017". MPOB website. http://bepi.mpob.gov.my/index.php/en/statistics/export/180-export-2017.html (accessed 28 March 2019).

———. n.d.-f. *Malaysia Oil Palm Statistics*. Bangi: MPOB, various years.

———. 2017. *Directory of Malaysian Palm Oil Processing Sectors*. 6th ed. Bangi: MPOB.

Ministry of Agriculture and Lands Malaysia. 1970. *Present Land Use. West Malaysia. Sheet 2.* Kuala Lumpur, Ministry of Agriculture and Lands.

Mohd Ikmal Hafizi Azaman and Abdul Razak Jelani. 2017. "Fundamental Study on the Development of Pulsed Laser System for Oil Palm Harvesting". ResearchGate website. https://www.researchgate.net/project/Fundamental-study-on-the-Development-of-Pulsed-Laser-System-for-Oil-Palm-Harvesting (accessed 11 April 2019).

Malek bin Mansoor and Colin Barlow. 1988. *The Production Structure of the Malaysian Oil Palm Industry with Special Reference to the Smallholder Subsector*. PORIM Occasional Paper No. 24. Kuala Lumpur: PORIM.

Martin, Susan M. 2003. *The UP Saga*. Copenhagen: NIAS Press.

Muar Ban Lee Group Berhad. 2018. "Annual Report 2017". 27 April 2018. https://www.mbl.com/pdf/27042018%20-%20Annual%20report%202017.pdf (accessed 28 March 2019).

———. n.d. "Muar Ban Lee Group Berhad". Muar Ban Lee Group website. https://www.mbl.com/ (accessed 28 March 2019).

Mvance Engineering Sdn Bhd. n.d. "Mvance". Mvance Engineering website. http://www.m-vance.com/ (accessed 28 March 2019).

New Straits Times. 2017 "Najib Unveils Six New Incentives for Felda Settlers". 23 July 2017. https://www.nst.com.my/news/nation/2017/07/260025/najib-unveils-six-new-incentives-felda-settlers (accessed 2 April 2019).

Nesadurai, Helen E.S. 2018. "New Constellations of Social Power: States and Transnational Private Governance of Palm Oil Sustainability in Southeast Asia". *Journal of Contemporary Asia* 48, no. 2: 204–29.

Pakiam, Geoffrey K. 2017. "Smallholder Involvement in Tree Crops in Malaya, with Special Reference to Oil and Coconut Palms in Johor, 1862–1962". PhD thesis, SOAS, University of London.

———. 2018a. *Agriculture in Johor: What's Left?* Trends in Southeast Asia, no. 19/2018. Singapore: ISEAS – Yusof Ishak Institute.

———. 2018b. "Voting Behaviour in FELDA Parliamentary Constituencies Since 2004". *ISEAS Perspective*, no. 26/2018, 26 April 2018.

———. 2019a. "Waterlands: Coconut Smallholders, Commodity Frontiers and Environmental Transformation on the Malay Peninsula, c.1862–1972". Commodities of Empire Working Paper No. 30. Milton Keynes: The Open University, https://commoditiesofempire.org.uk/publications/working-papers/working-paper-30/ (accessed 26 March 2019).

————. 2019b. "Addressing the FELDA Conundrum in Pakatan Harapan's First White Paper". *ISEAS Perspective*, no. 17/2019, 25 March 2019.

Palm Oil Refiners Association of Malaysia. 2017. *PORAM Directory 2.0*. Kelana Jaya: PORAM.

Pesaresi, Martino, Daniele Ehrlich, Aneta Florczyk, Sergio Freire, Andreea Julea, Thomas Kemper, Pierre Soille, and Vasileios Syrris. 2015. "GHS Built-up Grid, Derived from Landsat, Multitemporal (1975, 1990, 2000, 2014)". European Commission, Joint Research Centre (JRC), 2015. [Dataset] PID. http://data.europa.eu/89h/jrc-ghsl-ghs_built_ldsmt_globe_r2015b (accessed 2 April 2019).

Petersen, Rachael, Dmitry Aksenov, Elena Esipova, Elizabeth Goldman, Nancy Harris, Natalia Kuksina, Irina Kurakina, Tatiana Loboda, Alexander Manisha, Sarah Sargent, and Varada Shevade. 2016. "Mapping Tree Plantations with Multispectral Imagery: Preliminary Results for Seven Tropical Countries". Technical Note. Washington, DC: World Resources Institute. https://www.wri.org/publication/mapping-tree-plantations (accessed 29 April 2019).

Potter, Lesley M. 2016. "Alternative Pathways for Smallholder Oil Palm in Indonesia: International Comparisons". In *The Oil Palm Complex: Smallholders, Agribusiness and the State in Indonesia and Malaysia*, edited by Rob A. Cramb and John McCarthy. Singapore: NUS Press.

Rasiah, Rajah. 2006. "Explaining Malaysia's Export Expansion in Palm Oil and Related Products". In *Technology, Adaptation and Exports*, edited by Vandana Chandra. Washington, DC: World Bank.

Rosli Yaakop. 2018. "Should FELDA Be Turned into a Social Enterprise?". Paper presented at seminar at ISEAS – Yusof Ishak Institute, Singapore, 16 November 2018.

Rosnani Hashim and Mina Hattori. 2016. *Malaysia Agribusiness Directory 2016–2017*. Malaysia: Agribusiness Publishing.

Roundtable on Sustainable Palm Oil Secretariat. n.d. "Why Palm Oil Matters in Your Everyday Life: Consumer Fact Sheet". Roundtable on Sustainable Palm Oil website. http://bit.ly/2oWx4OP (accessed 3 May 2017).

Sanderson, Sunny. 2016. "Malaysian Oil Palm and Indonesian Labour Migration: A Perspective from Sarawak". In *The Oil Palm Complex: Smallholders, Agribusiness and the State in Indonesia and Malaysia*, edited by Rob A. Cramb and John McCarthy. Singapore: NUS Press.

Saravanamuttu, Johan. 2013. "Migration and Flexible Labour in Malaysia". In *The Palm Oil Controversy in Southeast Asia: A Transnational Perspective*, edited by Oliver Pye and Jayati Bhattacharya. Singapore: Institute of Southeast Asian Studies.

Sime Darby Properties Berhad. n.d. "What We Do". Sime Darby Properties website. https://www.simedarbyproperty.com/what-we-do (accessed 4 April 2019).

Star, The. 2014. "S&P Puts Sime Darby on CreditWatch Negative on Proposed Acquisition". 6 August 2014.

Sustainable Energy Development Authority Malaysia (SEDA). n.d. "Sustainable Energy development Authority Malaysia". SEDA website. http://www.seda.gov.my/ (accessed 3 April 2019).

Tate, Muzaffar. 1996. *The RGA History of the Plantation Industry in the Malay Peninsula*. New York: Oxford University Press.

Teoh Cheng Hai. 2000. *Land Use and the Oil Palm Industry in Malaysia: Abridged Report Produced for the WWF Forest Information System Database*. Kuala Lumpur: World Wildlife Fund.

TPM Technopark Sdn Bhd. "Biofuel". n.d. TPM Technopark Sdn. Bhd. website. http://www.tpmtechnopark.com.my/?page_id=1515 (accessed 5 April 2019).

Wolf, Joseph. 1983. *Injuries and Health Hazards Associated with Malaysia's Oil Palm Industry*. Kuala Lumpur: The Incorporated Society of Planters.

Yacob, Shakila, and Nicholas J. White. 2010. "The 'Unfinished Business' of Malaysia's Decolonisation: The Origins of the Guthrie 'Dawn Raid'". *Modern Asian Studies* 44: 919–60.

Zunaira Saieed. 2018. "CEO: Smallholders Should Be Allowed to Pull Out of Government-Controlled Schemes". *The Star*, 10 October 2018. https://www.thestar.com.my/business/business-news/2018/10/10/ceo-smallholders-should-be-allowed-to-pull-out-of-governmentcontrolled-schemes/ (accessed 2 March 2019).

4

JOHOR'S OIL AND GAS SECTOR
The Pengerang Integrated Petroleum Complex and Its Implications

Javier Revilla Diez and Serina Rahman[1]

INTRODUCTION

Malaysia`s Economic Transformation Program aims to propel the country to high-income status by 2020. Behind Indonesia, the country is the second largest oil and gas producer in Asia and aspires to become a regional hub in oil and gas (PWC 2017; MIDA 2017). Johor stands at the forefront of this endeavour, as the state aims to become a regional oil and gas storage and trading hub. This will be done by attracting major international investments and increasing petrochemical output.

These goals are also integrated into Iskandar Malaysia's development plan. The Iskandar Malaysia (IM) region was launched in 2006 and is one of five economic corridors promoted by the federal government. The Comprehensive Development Plan II (2014–25) for the region plans "to develop an environmentally friendly petrochemical and oil and gas cluster" and stresses the importance of its proximity to Singapore's petrochemical complex on Jurong Island.

The flagship project that will turn this vision into reality is the Pengerang Integrated Petroleum Complex (PIPC), a Petronas-led project with envisaged investments of US$27 billion. The PIPC was inspired by the Amsterdam-Rotterdam-Antwerp (ARA) model of maritime activity, port network and oil supply chain connectivity. The ARA is vital to Northern European oil and gas bunkering and transport. Partners of the PIPC such as the Dialog Group projected that "in 20 years Pengerang could surpass Rotterdam" (Huong 2012).

Against this background, the aims of this chapter are to explore the evolution of Johor's petrochemical industry vis-à-vis Singapore and to examine the developmental impacts of the PIPC. This chapter intends to answer the following research questions:

1. What are the functional and sectoral specializations of Johor's oil and gas industry?
2. What is the rationale behind the PIPC?
3. How does Johor compete or complement Singapore in attracting foreign direct investment?
4. What are the developmental impacts of the PIPC?
5. Can the PIPC succeed?

Methodologically, we applied a mixed methods approach. The FDI Markets database is used to illustrate investment flows to Johor on a quantitative basis. Qualitative insights have been gathered through literature and newspaper reviews. In addition, we conducted nineteen expert interviews with managers of multinational enterprises, consultants and development agencies between autumn 2016 and spring 2018 to gain a better understanding of the rationale behind the foreign investment. The interviewed enterprises cover all segments of the oil and gas production network, including upstream, midstream and downstream activities. The interview guidelines focus on the spatial organization of companies, location (dis)advantages, and the role of the state. In the following sections, we use codes to refer to the particular interviews. The first letter refers to the location where the interview took place (S = Singapore; J = Johor). The second letter provides information on the role of the interviewed organization (U = upstream; M = midstream; D = downstream; C = consultant).

PLACING JOHOR AT THE CENTRE OF THE REGIONAL OIL & GAS TRADE

The oil and gas sector is one of the core economic drivers of Johor, generating RM19 billion (US$4.57 billion) and RM2.8 billion (US$670 million) value-added, employing 35,446 workers (18 per cent of reported employment in manufacturing) in 2011 (Iskandar Regional Development Authority, 2014). Part of the strength of Johor's pitch for the new Pengerang development is its position at the centre of the region's oil and gas tradelines.

In addition to Johor's own geographical assets and abundance of land for development, Pengerang has easy access to major shipping lanes between the Middle East, Singapore and China. Given its proximity to Singapore's deepwater terminals, there is a good pool of Very Large Crude Carrier (VLCC) and Ultra Large Cruise Carrier (ULCC) traffic to tap on. Not only do 15.2 million barrels of oil pass through the Melaka Straits every day, the Malaysian government also offers myriad tax incentives for oil and gas companies that choose to use Malaysian ports of call and invest in the country's oil and gas industry. Figure 4.1 illustrates PIPC's fortunate position on regional maritime routes, as well as its proximity to various sites for oil and gas activity.

FIGURE 4.1
Pengerang as a Petrochemical Hub

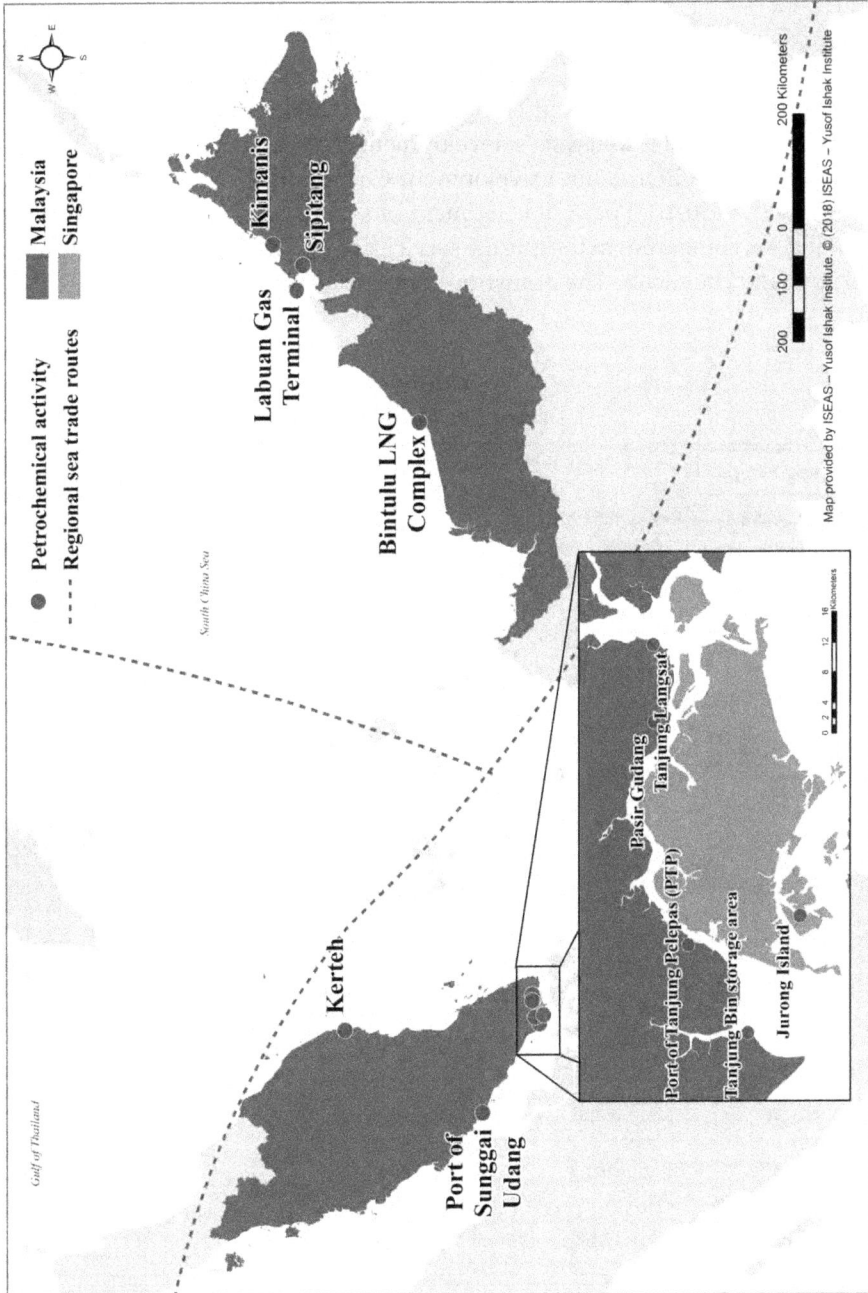

Map provided by ISEAS – Yusof Ishak Institute. © (2018) ISEAS – Yusof Ishak Institute

Malaysian oil and gas activities are located in Tanjung Bin, Pasir Gudang, Tanjung Langsat and Pengerang (see also Revilla Diez, Breul and Moneke 2019). Each of these locations fulfil different functions as explained below and are illustrated in Figure 4.2.

Tanjung Bin in the southwest of Johor, with a size of 913 hectares, was established as a free trade zone in 2012 and concentrates on storage. Vitol is a major player in the provision of the current storage capacity of 1.2 million cubic metres (cbm). According to Iskandar Malaysia's development goals, a final capacity of 3 million cbm is targeted (Johor Petroleum Development Corporation 2016).

Langsat's industrial park development of approximately 2,000 hectares began in 1993. It hosts companies in the marine services, steel, oil field services and equipment, and specialty chemicals. The industrial complex is supported by a port which has oil

FIGURE 4.2
Oil and Gas Activities in Johor

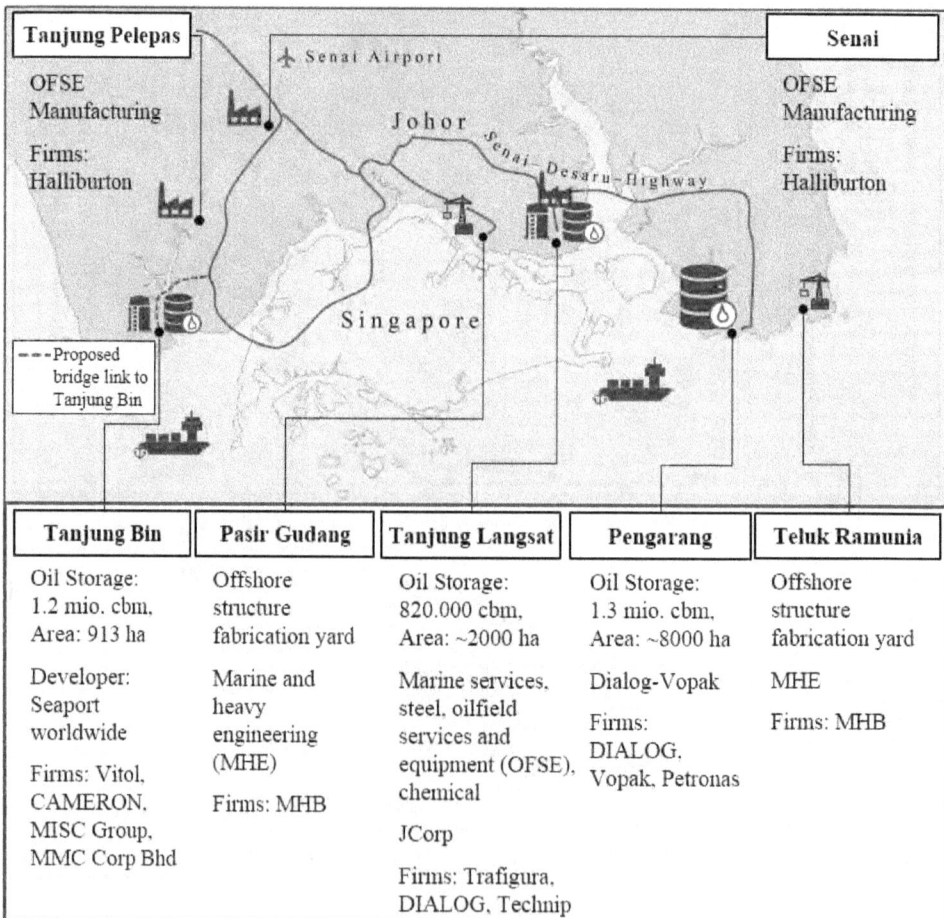

Tanjung Bin	Pasir Gudang	Tanjung Langsat	Pengarang	Teluk Ramunia
Oil Storage: 1.2 mio. cbm. Area: 913 ha	Offshore structure fabrication yard	Oil Storage: 820.000 cbm. Area: ~2000 ha	Oil Storage: 1.3 mio. cbm. Area: ~8000 ha	Offshore structure fabrication yard
Developer: Seaport worldwide	Marine and heavy engineering (MHE)	Marine services. steel, oilfield services and equipment (OFSE). chemical	Dialog-Vopak Firms: DIALOG. Vopak, Petronas	MHE Firms: MHB
Firms: Vitol, CAMERON. MISC Group. MMC Corp Bhd	Firms: MHB	JCorp Firms: Trafigura, DIALOG, Technip		

Source: Own illustration, based on JPDC (2016).

storage facilities, as well as liquid and dry jetties. Together with Tanjung Bin, these facilities aim to complement Singapore in adding independent storage and terminal capacity. To date, storage capacity lies at 820,000 cbm and should be expanded to 2 million cbm.

Pasir Gudang, a traditional industrial town, is the location for firms providing offshore structures like Malaysia Marine and Heavy Engineering (MMHE) and KTL Offshore and chemical firms like AMTech.

The Pengerang Integrated Petroleum Complex (PIPC) began in 2011 as the Refinery and Petrochemical Integrated Development (RAPID) project in response to the realization that gas resources in Peninsular Malaysia were finite, limiting the growth of the gas-based petrochemical industry.[2] It was thus decided that it would be more sustainable to enhance Petronas' petrochemical portfolio through an integrated refinery and petrochemical complex enabling Malaysia to move into downstream production of premium differentiated petrochemicals.

All in all, there are very high expectations of the PIPC. It is argued that: the complex will benefit from Malaysian oil and gas producing states such as Kelantan, Terengganu, Sabah and Sarawak; ongoing reviews of oil royalties are expected to further encourage greater participation in the oil sector. New developments in East Malaysia including an integrated liquefied natural gas (LNG) hub in Bintulu targeting underserved markets such as Brunei will also benefit the PIPC.

Petronas, the national oil company, plays a dual role in the Malaysian oil and gas industry. On the one hand, the company is Malaysia's host authority and resource owner. On the other hand, Petronas is active along the whole oil and gas value chain including upstream exploration and production of oil and gas to downstream activities like trading, oil refining, petrochemical manufacturing, and distribution of petroleum products. Table 4.1 provides details of other oil, gas and petrochemical facilities in other parts of Malaysia.

THE PENGERANG INTEGRATED PETROLEUM COMPLEX (PIPC)

According to the plans developed by the Johor Petroleum Development Corporation (JPDC) the US$27 billion mega project will house oil refineries, naphtha crackers, chemical plants and oil storage, as well as additional facilities like LNG import terminals, a regasification plant, a 1,220 MW power plant, air separation unit, and raw water supply unit. The RAPID project was launched in 2011, after which the project was expanded into the PIPC.

In 2012, then-Prime Minister Najib Abdul Razak declared that the Pengerang Integrated Complex, comprising RAPID and its associated facilities a "National Project of Strategic Importance".[3] The JPDC was thereafter formed in April 2012—a federal agency under the Malaysia Petroleum Resources Corporation, in collaboration with the Johor state government. As an indication of the importance of JPDC and this new petrochemical endeavour, the Board of Directors for JPDC is co-chaired by a Federal Minister and the Chief Minister of Johor.

TABLE 4.1
Existing Oil, Gas and Petrochemical (or Related) Activity in Malaysia

Location	OFSE manufacturing	Container port	Offshore struct fabrication & supply	Offshore services base	MHE	Oil storage	Marine services	Chemical	Oil Refinery	Petrochemical facility	LNG RGT
Senai, Johor	▓										
Port of Tanjung Pelepas, Johor		▓									
Teluk Ramunia, Johor			▓		▓						
Tanjung Langsat, Johor							▓	▓	▓		
Pasir Gudang (Johor Port)		▓				▓				▓	
Tanjung Bin, Johor						▓					
Pengerang (before PIPC)			▓								
Kertih, Terengganu			▓	▓						▓	
Kemaman, Terengganu			▓	▓							
Sungai Udang, Melaka									▓		▓
Port Dickson, Negri Sembilan									▓		
Nilai, Negri Sembilan										▓	
Gurun, Kedah										▓	
Prai, Penang										▓	
Gebeng, Pahang										▓	
Tanjung Agas, Pahang						▓	▓				
Lumut, Perak			▓								
Labuan						▓					
Bintulu, Sarawak			▓							▓	
Sipitang, Sabah										▓	

Notes:
These facilities support either the petrochemical process or the transport of feedstock or finished products.
Abbreviations: OFSE = Offshore field service & equipment; MHE = Materials handling & equipment; LNG RGT = Liquid natural gas regasification terminal.
Sources: Johor Petroleum Development Corporation Berhad; Pengerang Maritime Industrial Park website: International Trade Administration, www.export.gov; Calabrese (2014); Presentation by Frost and Sullivan on Malaysia LNG Outlook, 25 October 2011; Hydrocarbons Technology; PEMANDU; MIDA.

JPDC's role is to implement the vision that began with the Petronas RAPID project and coordinate the development of the wider Pengerang region under the auspices of the PIPC, a state government initiative in support of the national Economic Transformation Programme where oil, gas and energy are listed as a

National Key Economic Area (Petronas 2014). This task includes managing finances and funding, marketing and information dissemination, post-development operations and overseeing infrastructure and utilities development in the wider region.[4] The overarching goal of the entire endeavour was to transform Johor into a sustainable world class downstream oil and gas hub so as to derive greater value and investment from the oil and gas industry (Petronas 2014). The PIPC began with an overall start-up target of 2019 and 10 million cubic metres of oil and gas storage facilities by 2020.[5]

In January 2017, the Pengerang Local Authority, administered by Johor Corporation (JCorp) was launched to oversee the PIPC industrial zone and its surrounding areas. Its jurisdiction covers 128,830 hectares that were previously under Lembaga Bandaran Johor Tenggara and Kota Tinggi District (*New Straits Times*, 16 January 2017). Pengerang lies within the Penawar and Tanjung Surat state constituencies (Benjamin 2013).

CROSS-BORDER COMPETITION OR COOPERATION— WHAT NEXT?

One of the most common questions asked with regards to the PIPC is whether it will complement or compete with Singapore (for an in-depth study on the cross-border competition of oil and gas activities between Johor, the Indonesian Riau Islands and Singapore, see Revilla Diez, Breul, and Moneke 2019). Historically used as an oil storage facility for the British, the island-state has been actively involved in the oil and gas industry since the 1960s. Today it is one of the largest petrochemical hubs in the world, one of Asia's leading oil trading hubs and one of the world's top three export refining centres as well as a world-class research hub for oil and gas. Singapore is recognized by multinational firms in the oil and gas industry for its product quality, efficiency and ease of business (Breul and Revilla Diez 2018), but it suffers from land scarcity and could reach maximum capacity with no space to expand its facilities. Some industry analysts feel that there is more than enough business for Singapore and Pengerang to share, although PIPC will probably pick up on spillover business or attract traders that need less expensive alternatives. Others feel that Malaysia lags too far behind Singapore for collaboration to be truly effective or successful.

Over the course of forty years, Singapore has transformed into a world leading hub of the oil and gas industry. While Johor has ambitious plans to fully enter the oil and gas value chain, the success in the region has been limited to offshore equipment and storage facilities as explained before. After decades of heavy investment by the Singaporean state into industry specific infrastructure in transport and logistics and by multinational enterprises (MNEs) and local champions, a very efficient and competitive environment has emerged (Breul and Revilla Diez, 2018; Breul, 2019, 2020). As a result, Johor is finding it difficult to catch up to (or outcompete) its neighbour. This is particularly challenging because Singapore is far ahead in terms of business climate and institutional backing of MNEs and offering business functions related to infrastructure, technology, finance and trade.

A comparison of facilities between Malaysia, Singapore and PIPC is shown in Table 4.2. While PIPC will greatly expand Malaysia's capacity, some aspects will continue to lag behind Singapore. With Singapore's long-standing reputation, its substantial long-term investment in the oil and gas industry and its complete and seasoned ecosystem for oil and gas, Johor may have a steep climb to overcome before it can be on par with its southerly neighbour.

In order to demonstrate the enormous gap between Johor and Singapore in attracting foreign direct investment (FDI), we use the FDI Markets database provided by the *Financial Times*, which contains information on cross-border greenfield investment projects worldwide for the period between January 2003 and July 2016 (as shown in Table 4.3). Overall, our database contains 554 investments that were made from 2003 until 2016 into SIJORI by 414 different oil and gas-related MNCs worth US$44.4 billion. Looking at the geographical composition of the investments, we found that the majority of investments were made in Singapore (90 per cent), while less than 10 per cent of the greenfield projects involve the Malaysian state of Johor (fifty investments) and the Riau Islands of Indonesia (six investments).

Compared to Singapore, Johor's functional profile is relatively specialized in production and manufacturing plants for petroleum refined products (e.g., Lion Eco Chemicals invested in a plant that produces surfactants and chemicals) and offshore equipment (e.g., Halliburton established a manufacturing centre for completion equipment and cementing tools). Investments in more knowledge-intensive or high-end functions such as business services, headquarters and research and development are heavily linked to Singapore. Moreover, Singapore also seems to attract relatively more investments in service functions such as sales and marketing, operations providing customer support and servicing as well as oil and gas electric power plants (see also Revilla Diez, Breul, and Moneke 2019).

However, given Singapore's physical limitations and Johor's improving economic policy environment, the latter has been able to attract investment from Singapore-

TABLE 4.2
Comparison of Existing Capacity in Singapore and Malaysia (as of 2016)
as well as PIPC's Potential Capacity

	Malaysia's Capacity (as of 2016)	Singapore's Capacity (as of 2016)	PIPC Potential Capacity (When Complete)
Oil storage capacity (for trading)	2.93 million m^3	10 million m^3	5 million m^3
Oil refinery capacity	0.58 million bbl/day	1.45 million bbl/day	1 million bbl/day
Petrochemical production capacity	3.85 MTA	9.8 MTA	11.8 MTA
RGT (LNG) capacity	3.8 MTA	6 MTA	3.5 MTA

Notes: bbl/day = blue barrel (42 gallons/159 litres); MTA = million tonnes per annum
Source: Johor Petroleum Development Corporation Berhad presentation on PIPC, 25 August 2016.

TABLE 4.3
Frequency and Spatial Distribution of Greenfield FDI in SIJORI by Oil and Gas Subsectors, Functions and World Region of Origin, 2003–16

	Singapore		Johor		Riau Islands		Total	
Subsectors								
OG Extraction	2	(0.4)	1	(2.0)	2	(33.3)	5	(0.9)
Support activities	58	(11.6)	1	(2.0)	0	(0.0)	59	(10.6)
LNG	11	(2.2)	0	(0.0)	0	(0.0)	11	(2.0)
Petroleum refining	43	(8.6)	5	(10.0)	0	(0.0)	48	(8.7)
Midstream	13	(2.6)	1	(2.4)	2	(33.3)	16	(2.9)
Electricity	4	(0.8)	0	(0.0)	0	(0.0)	4	(0.7)
Refined products	367	(73.7)	42	(84.0)	2	(33.3)	411	(74.2)
Total	498	(100.0)	50	(100.0)	6	(100.0)	554	(100.0)
Functions								
Construction	0	(0.0)	0	(0.0)	0	(0.0)	0	(0.0)
Extraction	1	(0.2)	1	(2.0)	2	(33.3)	4	(0.7)
Energy	2	(0.4)	0	(0.0)	0	(0.0)	2	(0.4)
Production	168	(33.7)	41	(82.0)	1	(16.7)	210	(37.9)
Logistics	35	(7.0)	4	(8.0)	2	(33.3)	41	(7.4)
Sales and marketing	109	(21.9)	1	(2.0)	1	(16.7)	111	(20.0)
Support and servicing	5	(1.0)	0	(0.0)	0	(0.0)	5	(0.9)
Business services	41	(8.2)	1	(2.0)	0	(0.0)	42	(7.6)
Headquarters	40	(8.0)	0	(0.0)	0	(0.0)	40	(7.2)
Research & development	97	(19.5)	2	(4.0)	0	(0.0)	99	(17.9)
Total	498	(100.0)	50	(100.0)	6	(100.0)	554	(100.0)
World region of origin								
North America	144	(28.9)	5	(10.0)	1	(16.6)	150	(27.1)
Latin America & the Caribbean	4	(0.8)	0	(0.0)	0	(0.0)	4	(0.7)
West Europe	183	(36.7)	25	(50.0)	2	(33.3)	210	(37.9)
Rest of Europe	11	(2.2)	2	(4.0)	0	(0.0)	13	(2.3)
East Asia	114	(22.9)	17	(34.0)	3	(50.0)	134	(24.2)
Asia Pacific	38	(7.6)	1	(2.0)	0	(0.0)	39	(7.0)
Africa	4	(0.8)	0	(0.0)	0	(0.0)	4	(0.7)
Total	498	(100.0)	50	(100.0)	6	(100.0)	554	(100.0)

Note: For sectors, functions and source world regions, the column percentages are in parentheses.
Source: Own calculations, based on FDI Markets, a service from the Financial Times Limited (2016).

based MNEs, especially for offshore equipment and storage. In order to better understand the complementarities between Johor and Singapore, nineteen expert interviews were conducted with managers of MNEs, consultants and development agencies between autumn 2016 and spring 2018. The interviewed enterprises cover all segments of the oil and gas production network, including upstream, midstream and downstream activities. The interviewees were identified via FDI Markets database,

LinkedIn and by snowball sampling. The interviews provide clear indications that firms are strategically using differing regional assets in close spatial proximity in the upstream sector, especially oil and gas equipment manufacturers, and in the very intertwined trading and storage business.

The expert interviews reveal that firms with high land demand are coming under pressure in Singapore,

> the space is going to be limited and Singapore has by itself as an island, no matter how they are going to reclaim, they are going to end up having only limited square metres. (SU1)

The Riau Islands and Johor are definitely offering space to expand, and they also have the necessary work force in terms of professionals. One major oil and gas equipment supplier confirms that they *do a lot of outsourcing* and later in the interview mentioned the following,

> Right next door to Singapore we have also quite a few machining suppliers in Malaysia too. We reach out to and they are very competitive with the local suppliers here. (SU1)

Johor and also Batam attract low value-added activities, but the lead firm uses the sophisticated supplier base in Singapore to develop high-end products and services. It also profits from the excellent human capital base and business climate as well as from proximity to customers. The cross-border division of labour enables MNEs to strategically balance their activities according to the required regional assets. This particular spatial organization provides development impulses to the neighbouring regions.

This is especially so since the low crude oil price environment in 2014; the complementarities across SIJORI's subregions have been increasingly used by oilfield service and equipment companies in order to face intense cost pressures. The Singapore-based equipment supplier KTL Global, for example, announced the relocation of their rigging and steel rope production to Johor while keeping the administrative headquarters as well as more sophisticated activities in Singapore. The company intends to increase internal efficiency through the splitting up of activities across SIJORI (*Straits Times*, 4 April 2015).

A second activity where cross-border strategic coupling within SIJORI can be observed is in the intensively intertwined trading and storage of oil and gas. In recent years the independent storage capacity in Johor and the Riau Islands has expanded considerably, now reaching 26 per cent of total independent storage capacity in SIJORI. The reason behind the expansion is the availability of land in close proximity to Singapore as this quote illustrates,

> Now Malaysia has lots of land, they are riding on what Singapore is not able to provide. (SM2)

The additional capacity consequently increases competition for storage companies in Singapore. From a cross-border perspective this has a positive impact on costs,

So instead of raising terminal costs here in Singapore, it sort of puts a cap, puts a pressure on terminal fees here in Singapore. So, it is a win-win situation, because it keeps Singapore as trading hub. (SC2)

But more importantly, the capacity increases in storage will "lead to more flows of oil and gas, helping to meet the growing demand from traders [located in Singapore] for more liquidity to feed increasing pricing activity" (*Indian Express*, 20 September 2011). Interview partners involved in trading and centred in Singapore are very optimistic and see the region becoming an oil trading hub similar to Amsterdam-Rotterdam-Antwerp in Europe. The increased capacity

will add to what will reach 40 million cubes in the next few years. So that is encouraging for the market, but does it threaten Singapore's position as a trading hub? I do not think so. I think it will encourage the development and only cement Singapore as a trading hub, with all these outlying terminals. (SC2).

The reinforcement of the cross-border nature of the trading hub is also reflected by Platts' response to the growth of storage capacity in Johor and Riau Islands in how the value of oil products is assessed. Under the newly introduced Platts FOB Straits all the terminals in SIJORI are included in the oil benchmarking in an integrated manner, replacing the formerly used Platts FOB Singapore as shown in Table 4.4.

This cross-border strategic coupling is not happening automatically. Strategic decisions made by firms are also influenced by institutional conditions. In Singapore, the state is pushing firms to increase their value-added activities in a very proactive way contributing to what Breul, Revilla Diez, and Sambodo (2019) identify as an institutionally induced filtering process where high value-added functions are grounded in Singapore, while low value-added functions are deliberately pushed to the surrounding countries;

So, they are always talking to us about bringing more research, bringing new product, bringing new investments to be built here in Singapore. (SU1)

This orientation on high value-added functions is supported by the Singaporean state through schemes such as the Productivity and Innovation Credit Scheme (PIC), which grants 400 per cent tax deductions/allowances for expenditures in upgrading-related investments (e.g., training of employees, research and development activities, acquisition and leasing of IT and automation equipment) (IRAS 2017) and thus indirectly forces the firms to relocate their low added value activities;

Singapore is all based on one concept. And that concept is outsource as much as possible to the outside with the low income, keep the technology, keep the brain, the research, the money, the banking, keep it all inside. But the cheap stuff get it outside, do it in Batam, do it in Indonesia, do it in Malaysia, do it wherever you can. (SU1)

While these developments sound positive for the SIJORI region as a whole, cross-border strategic coupling is so far limited to offshore equipment and trade related

TABLE 4.4
The Evolution of Independent Storage Capacity in SIJORI

Terminal Name	Terminal Port	Total Capacity (cbm)	Founding Year
Vopak Terminals Singapore Pte Ltd (Penjuru)	Singapore	283,850	1970s
Vopak Terminals Singapore Pte Ltd (Sebarok)	Singapore	1263,079	1983
Tankstore Pte Ltd	Singapore	2000,000	1990
Singapore Petroleum Co. Ltd (Sebarok)	Singapore	220,000	1992
Vopak Terminals Singapore Pte Ltd (Sakra)	Singapore	288,070	1994
Oiltanking Odfjell Terminal Singapore Pte Ltd	Singapore	402,331	1999
Oiltanking Singapore Ltd (OTS, Seraya Av.site)	Singapore	717,500	2005
Horizon Singapore Terminals Pvt Ltd	Singapore	1252,184	2005
Vopak Terminals Singapore Pte Ltd (Banyan)	Singapore	1449,763	2006
Oiltanking Singapore Ltd (OTS, Jl Hwy site)	Singapore	649,500	2006
Universal Terminal (S) Pte Ltd	Singapore	2360,000	2008
Oiltanking Helios Singapore Pte Ltd	Singapore	503,400	2008
Senoko Services Pte Ltd (SSPL)	Singapore	260,000	2009
Stolthaven Singapore Pte Ltd	Singapore	237,252	2011
Banyan Caverns Storage Services Pte Ltd	Singapore	480,000	2014
Far East Oil Terminal One (Malaysia) Sdn Bhd	Pasir Gudang, Johor	231,000	2003
KIC Oil & Gas Sdn Bhd (Kadriah I)	Tanjung Pelepas, Johor	326,000	2011
Langsat Terminal (One) Sdn Bhd	Tanjung Langsat, Johor	476,000	2011
Langsat Terminal (Two) Sdn Bhd	Tanjung Langsat, Johor	171,000	2011
ATT Tanjung Bin Sdn Bhd (ATB)	Tanjung Pelepas, Johor	1153,000	2012
Pengerang Independent Terminals Sdn Bhd	Pengerang, Johor	1312,768	2014
PT Oiltanking Karimun	Karimun, Riau Islands	758,765	2016

Source: Own compilation, based on Tank Storage Magazine (2017).

storages. Strategic coupling in other oil and gas activities were not mentioned in the expert interviews. One potential area for collaboration could be petrochemicals as Jurong Island's capacities are limited. The RAPID project in Johor is seen as a potential expansion area by industry players, but up to now little foreign direct investments have been made in the further processing of oil and gas. According to the experts in the field, the reasons are twofold.

First, the business cycle is still difficult. The low oil prize since 2012 hurts the industry and the insiders are clear that

> We know the market has enough refining capacity, it is question of where is the demand coming from. (SC2)

Second, several interview partners were stressing the importance of political stability for long-term investments. The time horizon in downstream activities is often thirty to forty years (JD1). According to a representative of a leading German chemical company the most important precondition for attracting investments in the downstream segment is trust in the institutions.

> Johor's success will depend on whether Malaysia will be able to provide stable political conditions, stable, fiscal and tax conditions. And if this is achieved, Johor Bahru and the whole region will become a gigantic industrial cluster, which will be very successful. (SD1)

VIEWS FROM THE MALAYSIAN GROUND

Malaysian media consistently lauds the PIPC and its potential. It is projected that the development could generate RM1.6 billion (about US$409 million) to Malaysia's GNP by 2020 (Barrock and Ng 2017). Recent announcements of Saudi Aramco's commitment of US$7 billion for a 50 per cent equity share of RAPID's cracker and refinery is said to be an early indication of its future success. The agreement ensures that Saudi Aramco meets 70 per cent of RAPID's refinery feedstock needs, while the refinery's output becomes feed for the polymer plant. Saudi Aramco has also taken a 50 per cent equity stake in PRPC Polymers Sdn Bhd, giving it exposure to the full cycle of PIPC's petrochemical activities, helping Saudi Arabia to diversify its dependence on oil for its government budget (*Star Online*, 2 September 2017).

However, as shown by the interviews discussed earlier, some analysts are more hesitant to predict success too soon. An informant from the Johor Petroleum Development Corporation (JPDC) conceded that the PIPC is at the "infancy stage", and that there is no prior expertise or human capital development in Johor for the skills that are needed.[6] In order to attract higher level talent, however, a more complete residential and leisure ecosystem needs to be in place so as to meet the lifestyle needs of the relevant specialists.[7] It remains to be seen whether this deficiency will inhibit the progress and success of PIPC.

Plans for the PIPC were made in 2010 when crude prices were on their way down and policymakers realized that there was a need to offset reduced incomes from falling crude prices with diversification into the downstream sector. While the prediction was for better economic returns from refined products (International Trade Administration), the approach seemed to be more of the old-school economic style of creating the infrastructure and product first, then the demand second. These plans did not foresee new global trends such as the move towards electric cars, increasing bans on plastic and disposable products and the move towards alternative energy sources. It is possible that by the time PIPC is fully online, the plans would have been a decade too late to tap onto these rising trends. The expectation that lower crude prices will lead to lower processing costs only lasts as long as prices remain low. As the price of crude oil increases, it is unclear how much of a negative impact this will have on refining costs.[8]

An understanding of investor tentativeness is clear at all levels of JPDC. Its chief operating officer Izhar Hifnei Ismail revealed that many investors were "still taking a wait-and-see approach" (Barrock and Ng 2017). Other staff commented that there were a number of reasons for the unfulfilled search for investors. One of the main reasons behind unwillingness to invest is the time needed to relocate existing residents. While the overall 20,000 acres has been allocated to the PIPC by the state, land ownership remains in the hands of the local community. Although JPDC takes care of the relocation procedure, compensation and the costs of relocation are paid for by the investor. Not only is upfront payment required for the process to begin, groundworks cannot take place until about two years later, when relocation is complete.

Staff also hint at difficulties in consolidating announcements made at the federal level and action taken on the ground. For example, while the Saudi Aramco deal is a boon for the PIPC, the substantial refinery output commitment tied into the contract hampers negotiations with other potential investors who might also expect a pledged feedstock supply.[9] The JPDC is currently engaging with parties from Korea, Taiwan, Japan and China as prospective investors in the remaining available areas (as shown in Figure 4.2). Industrial and maritime parks such as those developed by Benelac, JCorp and Serba Dinamik will accommodate smaller investors who need only ten to fifty acres of ready land.[10]

While there are many naysayers, there are also those who seem excited about the PIPC. Conversations with SME businessmen from Singapore revealed their surprise that analysts were doubtful about the PIPC. Their view was that Jurong Island was getting smaller and that there are no new investments. The PIPC will rejuvenate the market in the region and provide fresh opportunities; they are keen to get involved. These businessmen provide maintenance, manpower and support services to the oil and gas industry.[11]

Others see huge potential in the storage business; a sector that provides quick returns on investments. With Jurong Island limited in space, there will be a need for more storage facilities, especially with the United States coming into the LNG market and attempting to sell its products to China (Moeller 2018). The presence of the new RGT2 will greatly enhance PIPC's ability to tap into these opportunities.[12] With regional energy demand set to grow and LNG seen as a cleaner source of fuel, experts foresee that its demand will increase by 150 per cent in the Asia-Pacific region (Foo 2014). Malaysia's own LNG reserves may make it more competitive in the long run, even though Singapore has already established itself as an LNG hub. Malaysia has also taken other steps to expand its LNG business. New laws that allow third party access will open the market to foreign suppliers, making LNG prices more competitive (*New Straits Times*, 2 January 2018). Several collaborations by Petronas in LNG has created movement in the market. Its agreement with Pavilion Gas Singapore diversifies its LNG portfolio, integrates the LNG value chain and provides a link to Singapore's LNG market (Adilla 2017). The Secretary-General of the Malaysian Gas Association, Rosman Hamzah sees good growth prospects in expanding local use of LNG, as well as in the business of pipeline infrastructure to new areas such as Kelantan (*New Straits Times*, 2 January 2018).

Analysts from the carrier business also see growth potential. With increased shipments of LNG in the region, and Saudi Aramco's commitment of feedstock, there will be increased need for VLCCs and ULCCs, both of which will be able to dock at PIPC when construction is complete. Finished products will also have to be shipped to receiving parties.[13] As it is, Johor Port is reported to have increased traffic, partly due to increased activity related to the PIPC (*Star Online*, 2 January 2018).

Some JPDC insiders feel that even if wider plans are unfulfilled, the presence of RAPID and DIALOG alone will provide enough economic benefits and spillover for Malaysia. While Malaysia's sweet crude reaps better economic benefits by being exported, the import and processing of cheaper sour crude will also help to meet local demands for Euro 5 quality products. Support and maintenance services alone could take up another 2,000 acres of the PIPC land allocation. There is also a general optimism that once RAPID is fully online in 2019, investments will begin to come in.[14] As at August 2017, Petronas spending has mostly been on RAPID. With positive projections on its potential returns, RAPID is seen as a high source of growth and profit in the medium term (*Star Online*, 17 August 2017).

DECONSTRUCTING THE PIPC

The Pengerang Integrated Petroleum Complex covers about 20,000 acres in a single piece of land allocated by the Johor state government—about 80 km² and equivalent to about 10 per cent of Singapore's size.[15] The PIPC is made up of several parts; the Pengerang Integrated Complex (PIC) by Petronas which comprises RAPID and other ancillary facilities; the Pengerang Deepwater Terminal (PDT), a joint venture between Petroliam Nasional Bhd (Petronas), Dialog Group Bhd, the Johor state government and Royal Vopak; and the Pengerang Maritime Industrial Park (PMIP) by Benelac Holdings Bhd.

RAPID is a refinery and a petrochemical integrated complex on an area of 2,000 hectares worth US$16 billion. It includes a crude oil refinery with a capacity of 300,000 b/d, a naphtha cracker and a petrochemical complex that will begin operations in Q1 2019. The petrochemical complex will produce 3.4 Mtpa of differentiated and specialty chemicals such as synthetic rubbers and high-grade polymers. The refinery will produce gasoline and diesel and will supply feedstock for the petrochemical complex. In February 2017, Saudi Aramco signed a share purchase agreement (SPA) for US$7 billion. In addition, Saudi Aramco will assure 70 per cent of the crude oil supply for the refinery. In order to expand their downstream activities Petronas signed tentative partnership agreements to jointly develop, construct and operate production facilities in specialty chemical products such as ASITOCHU Cooperation of Japan, PTT Global Chemical from Thailand, Malay Dialog group, Italy-based Versalis SpA, Evonik Industries AG. After having signed an agreement, BASF terminated its interest in 2013 (Hydrocarbons Technology 2018).

Another catalytic project within the PIPC is the Pengerang Deepwater Terminal (PTDT). The PDT was completed in 2013 and has been in operation since 2014. A joint venture between Dialog, Royal Vopak and S.S.I., the PDT sits on approximately

60 hectares and has a storage capacity of 1.3 million cbm; six berths were built in its first development phase. The current storage capacity is undergoing an expansion of a further 430.000 cbm in order to add capacity for independent storage operators. In addition, storage capacity for the exclusive use of Petronas' RAPID project will be commissioned in 2019. The terminal also includes an LNG terminal and regasification facility which has already been in operation since 2017 (Johor Petroleum Development Corporation 2016).

Further investments into PIPC are through large integrated projects such as the Pengerang Integrated Development Project (PIDP) by Serba Dinamik Holdings Bhd, comprising the Pengerang Eco-Industrial Park (PEIP) and Pengerang International Commercial Centre (PICC). Flanking the development are numerous townships and other infrastructural developments that surround the area and extend towards Bandar Penawar, Kota Tinggi and Desaru. Sungai Rengit is the main town closest to the PIPC development and the main node for existing amenities and facilities. Residents of the original five villages within the PIPC boundaries were moved to Taman Bayu Damai (*Malaysian Insider*, 29 February 2016) and the wider Punggai area[16] about 20 km away. Total investment in the PIPC is said to be RM97 billion (~US$25 billion) (Hydrocarbons Technology). Figure 4.3 illustrates the overall make-up of the area.

The PIPC also has non-refinery sectors that support the main industrial areas. Details of these sectors and the acreage allocated to them are listed in Table 4.5 below.

FIGURE 4.3
Illustration of the Wider Pengerang Area and the Extent of
Associated Development Projects

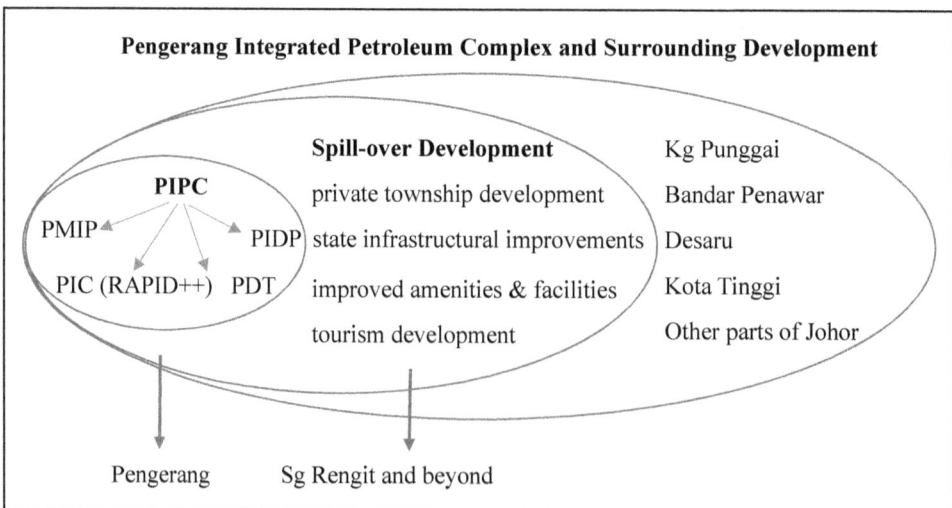

Pengerang Integrated Petroleum Complex and Surrounding Development

Spill-over Development   Kg Punggai

PIPC   private township development   Bandar Penawar

PMIP   PIDP   state infrastructural improvements   Desaru

PIC (RAPID++)   PDT   improved amenities & facilities   Kota Tinggi

tourism development   Other parts of Johor

Pengerang   Sg Rengit and beyond

TABLE 4.5
Non-Refinery Segments within the PIPC

Non-refinery Sector	Details	Acreage
Emergency Coordination Centre	Emergency coordination, hospital and clinic, PIPC security coordination	
Waste Management Centre	Waste water treatment, solid waste conversion	60 acres
Emergency Response Centre	Fire response team, ambulance base	10 acres
Centralised Tank Farm	Crude & product handling, sulphur and coke handling	1,400 acres
Commercial Services Hub	Professional services, banking and finance	180 acres
Downstream Finished Product Zone	Plastics and fine chemicals, SMEs	1,081 acres
Medium and Light Industry Hub	Support industries, testing and metering	700 acres
Solid Logistics Hub	Container facilities, sulphur and coke	125 acres

Source: Johor Petroleum Development Corporation Bhd.

WHY PENGERANG?

Before the advent of the PIPC, the wider Pengerang area comprised seven fishing villages and adjacent smallholdings in a relatively rural part of Johor with limited access and infrastructure. Its selection for the site of the PIPC is attributed to a number of natural and fortunate circumstances. The Pengerang coastline enjoys a safe and sheltered harbour where no breakwater is required for coastal development.[17] Coastal waters are deep (between 20 to 24 metres) resulting in cost savings from ample available anchorage area with minimal need for maintenance dredging and minimal capital outlay for shorter jetty trestles for VLCC berthing.[18]

Pengerang is accessible via a number of highways and airports (both in Johor and in Singapore)[19] and is in close proximity to other deepwater port facilities and regional demand centres, enabling easy transport of finished products to end markets (Hydrocarbons Technology). The 633 million strong ASEAN population and the overall Asian population of 3 billion people are highly accessible via international shipping lanes for which Pengerang is already en route.[20] Existing facilities in Malaysia are scattered, further away from international ports and non-integrated. Many do not have deepwater ports, are unable to produce according to Euro 4 and Euro 5 specifications, and have no space for expansion.[21]

PIPC AS A CATALYST FOR DEVELOPMENT

Even as the potential success of PIPC is being debated, domestic questions as to the development's impacts on the surrounding region, its residents and the natural environment have been raised. According to Khaled Nordin, Johor's then Chief Minister, the PIPC was cited as the starting point of development on Johor's east coast (Astro Awani 2017). Even as the technical aspects of the PIPC are still being finalized and built, steps have been taken to improve connectivity between Pengerang and the surroundings. Existing roads have been widened and new roads have been built to either improve access or to cater specifically to heavy vehicles (Ng 2017). Federal government investment in supporting infrastructure for the PIPC has amounted to RM2.49 billion (about US$640 million),[22] and included new roads, improved drainage, new fire and police stations, the Sungai Rengit clinic, a new secondary school, new public low-cost houses, and a new fishery complex.[23] The Rapid City Centre is a 196-acre development launched in 2015 in Sungai Rengit comprising shop houses and office lots.[24] Other new amenities are located around the relocation site of displaced villagers and are meant to specifically benefit the original local community of the area.

Given the scale of the PIPC, it is projected that by 2020, the population of the area will more than double from 30,008 people in 2010 to 70,043 people. Housing demand will thus increase from accommodation needed for 7,280 families in 2010 to about 14,000 families in 2020.[25] Petronas direct staff numbers alone are expected to increase from 59 in 2016 to 4,483 people in 2010.[26] Local rental opportunities are very scarce and rental costs are high given the scarcity;[27] there is a great need to develop housing and other associated facilities for this new migrant PIPC working population. In response, a number of new townships catering to various strata of society have sprung up. The locations of these townships are shown in Figure 4.2.

Also not too far from the PIPC, other recently announced residential developments include the Innocity Residence and Vivo Cove City. Bandar Penawar is now the nearest satellite town and is currently the main township beyond Sungai Rengit to support PIPC housing needs. In Kota Tinggi, Sungai Papan is a 3,160-hectare growth area slated to be yet another satellite town that will serve the needs of the PIPC. Johor Corporation will build 60,000 units of housing of various types as well as facilities for trade, marine industries, education and research and development (Othman 2016). In order to provide for second-generation families of those displaced from the original seven villages that existed in the area before the PIPC was built and to meet future relocation needs, a new settlement is being built in Kampung Punggai, not far from Taman Bayu Damai.

Before the arrival of the PIPC, Pengerang was designated an ecotourism destination anchored around its quiet seaside villages, popular lobster restaurants and the rare dugong sighting. However, tourism did not take off (Barrock and Ng 2017). With PIPC completely transforming the economic targets of this area, tourism in nearby Desaru and Pantai Timur are being reinvigorated. While existing resorts and attractions are being spruced up, Khazanah Nasional Bhd is focusing on Desaru as an integrated tourism hub. An area of about 4,114 acres along a 17-km coastline along the South China Sea (The Malaysia Project) is being transformed into 5-star resorts, golf courses and theme parks (*Sun Daily*, 31 October 2017. Marketed under the brand name Desaru Coast, golf courses headlined by Ernie Els and Vijay Singh are already open for business.

PIPC IMPACTS ON THE LOCAL COMMUNITY

When the RAPID project was first announced in 2011, there was substantial pushback from Pengerang local communities as there had been no earlier warning that their land would be taken for the project (*Free Malaysia Today*, 26 September 2012). As they were also unaware of the state plan to allocate 20,000 acres to the larger PIPC, they also questioned the need to take more than the 6,424 acres reported to make up just RAPID. More than 3,000 Malay and Chinese fishermen and smallholders were relocated to Taman Bayu Damai, a newly constructed settlement area built on land reclaimed from coastal mangroves between Teluk Ramunia and Punggai. A thousand Muslim graves and 1,500 Chinese graves had to be relocated as part of the process. According to a representative of JPDC,[28] the law actually states that relocated villagers are to be given only cash compensation but, in this case, they were also given subsidized housing and replacement agricultural lots for lost smallholdings.

At the time, however, the community was not appeased. Many claimed that the allocation of compensation was not transparent, and that promises were not guaranteed in writing (and therefore unfulfilled). Fishermen were given RM4,000 or less if they were unlicensed and smallholders of between 1–2 acres were paid between RM65,000 to RM105,000. While they were offered subsidized housing, many complained that the quality of the houses was poor (as the newly reclaimed land was still settling) and that the new houses were very small compared to the homes that they were used to, and never had to pay for. Some families who had lived in Pengerang for generations did not have land titles, while others shared land with many siblings. This meant that they were either not eligible for compensation or received very little, and few had money set aside to pay for the new homes, which cost between RM35,000 and RM105,000 (*Free Malaysia Today*, 26 September 2012). Taman Bayu Damai is also about 20 km away from where many parked their fishing boats, which can mean an hour's travel by motorbike and additional petrol costs; in the past it only took the fishermen five minutes to get to the sea (*Malaysian Insider*, 1 March 2016).

After the initial furore died down, however, there was little news of the plight of the local community in terms of displacement and livelihoods lost. Instead, efforts by Petronas and various state agencies to assist the community and provide amenities, infrastructure and job training dominated the public discourse.

Petronas' Sustainability Reports (2014, 2016) consistently list their contributions to the communities of Pengerang; job matching for main contractors, entrepreneurship training, school programmes and sponsorship for vocational training. Publicity material for PIPC from various agencies list its potential to create 4,000 high skilled jobs (Petronas 2014), and 8,600 other jobs (Petronas 2016). While at the time of writing 60,000 jobs had already been created in the development, many of these are construction related and thus taken up by foreign workers. The local community had already questioned the possibility of their residents getting jobs in the development as few had the required skill sets (*Free Malaysia Today*, 26 September 2012). By sheer numbers, the local population of about 10,000 people in the wider Pengerang area is insufficient to meet the needs of the PIPC.

JPDC has a unit specifically devoted to human capital development, but because plans for the PIPC took off so quickly, they currently focus on providing upgrading skills to available candidates to fill knowledge gaps. Petronas is moving qualified staff from other centres to PIPC to provide start-up guidance while newly hired staff are sent to long-running facilities for training.[29] JPDC runs several programmes with a variety of entities such as Yayasan Peneraju Pendidikan Bumiputera (Bumiputera Education Foundation), TERAJU, SME Bank, and the Bandar Penawar Community College, among others, to train and certify vocational and supervisory staff as well as provide entrepreneurial training, assistance and financing.[30] While nearby Universiti Teknologi Malaysia (UTM) has a petroleum engineering programme, there seems to be a gap between jobs available, skills required and the quality of graduates entering the market. New groups such as NrgEdge, a network of oil and gas professionals help to bridge the gap between study and work by providing internships, boot camps and networking opportunities for fresh graduates to the industry (Bahari 2017). Private initiatives such as this will help to meet the needs of the PIPC and provide job-matching facilities for the wider Malaysian population.

Beyond jobs and compensation, Petronas has also set up KOPEJA (Koperasi Pengarang Jaya Johor Berhad), a cooperative with membership comprising mostly displaced residents from Taman Bayu Damai. The cooperative operates a retail station within the PIC and members are also provided with entrepreneurship and job training. In response to grievances that came about because of the relocation exercise, a Social Impact Management Plan was devised and a Community Leadership Committee comprising village heads, women and youth groups' representatives are involved in project disclosure sessions and participate in arranged visits to Petronas' Kerteh Integrated Petroleum Complex. Petronas has also set up a grievance mechanism through which residents can channel complaints directly to an assigned Community Liaison Officer (Petronas 2015).

In spite of all these efforts, however, news broke in 2016 of continued dissatisfaction in Pengerang. With the influx of foreign workers, Sungai Rengit town is now derogatively referred to as "Pekan Bangla" (Bangladeshi Town); residents complain that local mosques are overrun with foreigners who have also set up shops and homes there (*Malaysian Insider*, 1 March 2016). This is in spite of Temporary Workers' Villages built and already being used within the PIC (Petronas 2015). A drive through the edges of Sungai Rengit town reveals a number of workers' quarters fashioned out of refurbished containers and other improvised facilities.[31]

Fishermen report that their earnings have plunged from RM200–RM1,000 per day to RM25 after three days of fishing and increased petrol costs of RM50 per day for motorbike travel to their boats and having to go further to put down their nets. Others say that their fishing nets, which cost them between RM1,500 to RM2,500 each, have not been used in years and supplementary incomes are no longer available with the loss of their home gardens and smallholdings (*Malaysian Insider*, 1 March 2016). There have also been reports of increased crime and fatal accidents as a result of speeding contractor vehicles and lorries (*New Straits Times Online*, 25 January 2017).

ENVIRONMENTAL IMPACTS OF THE PIPC

In marketing collateral for the PIPC, a brief reference to the surrounding natural environment is made in these terms: "limited environmentally sensitive areas that are easily protected".[32] No matter how it is positioned, the oil and gas industry is always perceived as an environmentally unfriendly endeavour. The sight of raw red earth from hills, forests and other natural habitats being cleared and piles of sand dumped at sea for coastal reclamation do not help to alleviate these negative perceptions. Yet, apart from the initial protests by Kekalkan Pengerang Lestari (Keeping Pengerang's Sustainability, a civil society group), rumours of a purported nuclear plant in the area and complaints about bias in the Detailed Environmental Impact Report (*Free Malaysia Today*, 26 September 2012), there has been very little in the news about the environmental impacts of the PIPC.

Environmentalists will be quick to point out that hill and forest clearing on land translates into major run-off and erosion into rivers and seas. An examination of Google satellite maps and drone photos of the area clearly indicate that the coasts around Pengerang suffer severe siltation. Coastal reclamation by nature results in sedimentation, damage and, sometimes, total loss of marine environments.

Local fishermen say they not only have to travel further to get to their boats, but they also have to risk choppier waters and pirate encounters when they head out to sea as inshore and coastal waters are now severely polluted and there is less fish to catch. On top of that, fishing areas have shrunk as previously popular fishing holes are now out of bounds for safety or blocked by new structures at sea (*Malaysian Insider*, 1 March 2016). While less fish catch translates into economic difficulties for the local community, increased boat traffic from sand barges and other vessels leads to increased dangers for fishermen in their small fishing boats. Increased vessel traffic can also result in oil dumping or oil spills in the event of accidents (*Straits Times Online*, 18 August 2017).[33]

On land, there are also environmental issues. Development-related flooding during heavy rains have been reported,[34] and dust from cleared land, lorries transporting earth and sand and general construction material have resulted in severe air pollution. Residents have complained that their shops and houses are constantly covered in red dust, stinging their eyes and causing many to have respiratory problems and asthma attacks (*New Straits Times Online*, 25 January 2017).

These sentiments were corroborated in a survey of Johoreans' opinions conducted in 2017;[35] of 300 residents in East Johor, comprising Johoreans living between Pengerang and Mersing, 76 per cent expressed concern about the environmental impacts of the PIPC (Rahman 2017). With construction in this area set to continue for at least the next ten years, these impacts will be prolonged, and will add to prevailing environmental issues that come with the sudden materialization of a petrochemical complex in an area that was once deemed an idyllic ecotourism destination.

CONCLUSION

Johor's economic development in oil and gas so far has relied on rather generic assets—cheap labour and land. Notwithstanding the impacts that the PIPC has had on the local environment and surrounding residents, the question now arises as to whether partnership between Singapore and Johor is also possible in higher value-added activities such as petrochemicals. Several interviewees have acknowledged Johor's potential to attract investments in the processing of oil and gas (downstream), especially in relation to the RAPID project. However, this strategic coupling will not happen automatically. This is because, first, long-term investment requires trust in the institutional conditions. In this respect, Malaysia is still not considered a very "safe" place to do business.

With the recent change of government in Malaysia, questions now emerge on the future of the PIPC (as with any other large infrastructure projects) given new revelations on the state of the country's finances. It was announced that Petronas would have new leadership, which usually implies new directions or a revision of past objectives. While PIPC does not face the same uncertainty as foreign-led projects, it remains to be seen how the new regime will affect the development of this new oil and gas hub even as it comes to close to its targeted commissioning date.

Second, in order to form a symbiotic relationship, Johor has to complement the strategic needs of Singapore-based MNEs through more than mere provision of low-cost land and labour. Commitment by national and regional authorities to support the strategic coupling through investment in education, training, and infrastructure will help to attract investment in higher value-added activities.

Third, external factors will also play a crucial role in the success of the Johor's ambitious PIPC project. Oil and gas experts warn that there is already an overcapacity in refining; so the central question is where the demand will come from. In addition, a lot depends on the decisions taken by MNEs that have already invested massively in Singapore. Only if these MNEs expand to Johor, provide capital, develop skills and share the market, can Johor successfully take-off.

Notes

1. Parts of this chapter were previously published in the following: Javier Revilla Diez, "Territorial Complementarities or Competition for FDI? Johor, Singapore and the Oil and

Gas Sector", *ISEAS Perspective*, no. 2018/23, 19 April 2018; Javier Revilla Diez, Moritz Breul, and Jana Moneke, "The SIJORI Growth Triangle: Territorial Complementarities or Competition for FDI in the Oil and Gas Industry?", *Journal of Southeast Asian Economies* 36, no. 1 (2019): 71–90; and Serina Rahman, *Developing Eastern Johor: The Pengerang Integrated Petroleum Complex*, Trends in Southeast Asia, no. 16/2018 (Singapore: ISEAS – Yusof Ishak Institute, 2018).

2. Juniwati Rahmat Hussin, Vice President and Venture Director of the Pengerang Integrated Complex (under Petronas), quoted from the Petronas Sustainability Report 2014, p. 70.

3. Johor Petroleum Development Corporation (JPDC) website, www.jpdc.gov.my (accessed 13 April 2018).

4. Ibid.

5. Ibid.

6. Personal communication, JPDC staff (name withheld by request , Pengerang, 12 September 2017.

7. Discussion during seminar on "Johor Economic Update", at ISEAS – Yusof Ishak Institute, 23 February 2018.

8. Personal communication, oil and gas industry player (name withheld by request).

9. Personal communication, JPDC staff (name withheld by request), Pengerang, 12 September 2017.

10. Personal communication, Abd Rahim Ahad, Manager, Investor Management, JPDC, Pengerang, 8 March 2018.

11. Personal communication, oil and gas SME representatives (names withheld by request), Pengerang, 8 March 2018.

12. Personal communication, oil and gas industry player (name withheld by request), Pengerang, 8 March 2018.

13. Personal communication, Sameer C. Mohindru, Senior Editor, S&P Global Platts, Singapore, 16 July 2018.

14. Personal communication, JPDC staff (name withheld by request), Pengerang, 12 September 2017.

15. Johor Petroleum Development Corporation (JPDC) website, www.jpdc.gov.my (accessed 13 April 2018).

16. Personal communication, Pengerang local informant (name withheld by request), Pengerang, 12 September 2017.

17. JPDC website, www.jpdc.gov.my (accessed 17 November 2017).

18. Personal communication with representative of Benalec Holdings Berhad who declined to be named, 3–4 October 2017, Iskandar Puteri, Johor.

19. PIPC is only 100 km away from Senai International Airport in Johor (by land) and 26 km away from Changi International Airport in Singapore.

20. Johor Petroleum Development Corporation Berhad presentation at the 30th Annual General Meeting of the Malaysian Gas Association, Kuala Lumpur, 12 May 2016.

21. Johor Petroleum Development Corporation Berhad presentation on PIPC, Kuala Lumpur, 25 August 2016.

22. Pengerang Maritime Industrial Park website, http://pengerangmaritime.com.my/johor-pipc/ (accessed 17 November 2017).

23. Johor Petroleum Development Corporation Berhad presentation on PIPC, Kuala Lumpur, 25 August 2016.

24. Malton Berhad Group, http://www.malton.com.my/portfolio-items/rapid-city-centre/ (accessed 17 November 2017).
25. Johor Petroleum Development Corporation Berhad presentation on PIPC, Kuala Lumpur, 25 August 2016.
26. Petronas presentation on "Accommodation and Amenities Readiness for Pengerang Integrated Complex", Pengerang, 24 March 2016.
27. Personal communication, Pengerang local informant (name withheld by request), Pengerang, 13 September 2017.
28. Personal communication, JPDC staff (name withheld by request), Pengerang, 12 September 2017.
29. Personal communication, Abd Rahim Ahad, Manager, Investor Management, JPDC, Pengerang, 8 March 2018.
30. Johor Petroleum Development Corporation Berhad presentation on PIPC, Kuala Lumpur, 25 August 2016.
31. Personal observation.
32. JPDC website, www.jpdc.gov.my , 11 November 2017.
33. Accidents already frequently take place around Pengerang due to heavy vessel traffic. One recent example can be found at this link: *Straits Times Online*, "Two Vessels Collide Near Johor, Causing Oil Spill", 18 August 2017, http://www.straitstimes.com/asia/se-asia/two-vessels-collide-near-johor-causing-oil-spill
34. Personal communication, local informant (name withheld by request), Pengerang, 13 September 2017.
35. Commissioned by ISEAS – Yusof Ishak Institute and implemented by the Merdeka Institute.

References

Adilla F. 2017. "Petronas LNG Inks MOU with Pavilion Gas". *New Straits Times*, 31 March 2017 https://www.nst.com.my/news/2017/03/225989/petronas-lng-inks-mou-pavilion-gas (accessed 10 June 2018)

Astro Awani. 2017. "Pengerang Poised to Be Catalyst for East Johor Corridor Development". Quote by Johor's Chief Minister, Mohamed Khaled Nordin, 16 January 2017. english. astroawani.com/business-news/pengerang-poised-be-catalyst-east-johor-corridor-development-129167

Bahari, F. 2017. "A Head Start in the Oil and Gas Industry". *New Straits Times Online*. 16 August 2017. https://www.nst.com.my/education/2017/08/268382/head-start-oil-and-gas-industry (accessed 17 June 2020).

Barrock, J., and J. Ng. 2017. "Petronas in the Spotlight". *The Edge Markets*, 10 August 2017 www.theedgemarkets.com/article/cover-story-petronas-spotlight (accessed 10 June 2018)

Benjamin, N. 2013. "Development in Pengerang Will Be Fed by Its Oil and Gas Industry Which Will Create Jobs and Opportunities". *Star Online*, 18 February 2013. www.thestar.com.my/news/community/2013/02/18/development-in-pengerang-will-be-fed-by-its-oil-and-gas-industry-which-will-create-jobs-and-opportun/ (accessed 14 June 2018).

Breul, M. 2019. "Cities in 'Multiple Globalizations': Insights from the Upstream Oil and Gas World City Network". *Regional Studies, Regional Science* 6: 25–31.

———. 2020. *Gateway Cities in Global Production Networks. Insights from the Oil and Gas Industry in Southeast Asia*. Cham, Switzerland: Springer.

———, and J. Revilla Diez. 2018. "An Intermediate Step to Resource Peripheries: The Strategic Coupling of Gateway Cities in the Upstream Oil and Gas GPN". *Geoforum* 92: 9–17.

———, J. Revilla Diez, and M.T. Sambodo. 2019. "Filtering Strategic Coupling: Territorial Intermediaries in Oil and Gas Global Production Networks in Southeast Asia". *Journal of Economic Geography* 19, no. 4: 829–51.

Calabrese, J. 2014. "Positioning Malaysia Within the Global Energy Landscape". Middle East Institute, 19 August 2014.

Foo, A. 2014. "Malaysia's Oil Hub: Will It Be a Threat to Singapore?". *Straits Times*, 17 July 2014. http://www.straitstimes.com/opinion/malaysias-oil-hub-will-it-be-a-threat-to-singapore (accessed 10 June 2018).

Free Malaysia Today. 2012. "10 Questions on the Pengerang Project". 26 September 2012. www.freemalaysiatoday.com/category/opinion/2012/09/26/10-questions-on-pengerang-project (accessed 1 November 2018).

Huong, T. 2012. "Malaysia Can Complement Singapore and Create Another Amsterdam-Rotterdam-Antwerp (ARA)". *Star Online*. 4 June 2012. https://www.thestar.com.my/business/business-news/2012/06/04/msia-can-complement-spore-and-create-another-amsterdamrotterdamantwerpara (accessed 17 June 2020).

Hydrocarbons Technology. 2018. "Petronas RAPID Project, Southern Johor". Kable Intelligence Limited. www.hydrocarbons-technology.com/projects/petronas-rapid-project-malaysia/ (accessed 17 November 2017).

Income Revenue Authority of Singapore (IRAS). 2017. "Productivity and Innovation Credit Scheme". https://www.iras.gov.sg/irashome/Schemes/Businesses/Productivity-and-Innovation-Credit-Scheme/ (accessed 21 February 2018).

Indian Express. 2011. "Malaysia Expansion Sets the Stage for 'Greater Singapore' Oil Hub". 20 September 2011. https://indianexpress.com/article/news-archive/web/malaysia-expansion-sets-the-stage-for-greater-singapore-oil-hub/ (accessed 6 August 2019).

International Trade Administration, USA. www.export.gov/article?id=Malaysia-Oil-and-Gas-Equipment (accessed 17 November 2017).

Iskandar Regional Development Authority (IRDA). 2014. *Iskandar Malaysia Comprehensive Development Plan II 2014–2025*. Johor Bahru: Iskandar Regional Development Authority.

Johor Petroleum Development Corporation (JPDC). 2016. "Oil and Gas in Johor". www.jpdc.gov.my/development/oil-and-gas-in-johor/ (accessed 17 November 2017).

Malaysia Project. "Pengerang's Property Play", 9 January 2013. http://malaysiaproject.blogspot.sg/search/label/sg%20rengit (accessed 20 November 2017).

Malaysian Insider, "Once Tranquil, Pengerang Now Dusty, Overrun with Migrants and Crime". 1 March 2016. https://sg.news.yahoo.com/once-tranquil-pengerang-now-dusty-230013347.html (accessed 11 November 2017).

Moeller, J.O. "Oil, LNG, and Fracking Defines a New Power Game: US Main Exporter, China and India Main Importers; New Alliances in the Middle East". Seminar by the Regional Strategic and Political Studies (RSPS) Programme at the ISEAS – Yusof Ishak Institute, Singapore, 6 February 2018.

MIDA. 2017. "Oil and Gas". www.mida.gov.my/home/oil-and-gas/posts/ (accessed 3 February 2018).

New Straits Times Online. 2017a. "A Head Start for Oil and Gas Industry". 16 August 2017.

https://www.nst.com.my/education/2017/08/268382/head-start-oil-and-gas-industry (accessed 5 June 2018).

———. 2017b. "It Causes Watery, Itching Eyes". 25 January 2017. https://www.nst.com.my/news/2017/03/207081/actionline-it-causes-watery-itchy-eyes (accessed 8 June 2018).

New Straits Times. 2018. "Local LNG Price Expected to Be More Competitive by 2019". 2 January 2018. https://www.nst.com.my/business/2018/01/320540/local-lng-price-expected-be-more-competitive-2019> (accessed 5 June 2018).

Ng, S. 2017. "The Elements Needed for Iskandar Malaysia's Success". *Edge Property*, 7 May 2017. https://www.edgeprop.my/content/1128646/elements-needed-iskandar-malaysia%E2%80%99s-success (accessed 8 June 2010).

Othman A.F. 2016. "JCorp Set to Roll Out 11 Major Development Projects in Johor". *New Straits Times Online*. 20 November 2016. https://www.nst.com.my/news/2016/11/190295/jcorp-set-roll-out-11-major-development-projects-johor (accessed 8 November 2018).

———. 2017. "New Local Authority Launched to Oversee Johor's PIPC". *New Straits Times*, 16 January 2017. www.nst.com.my/news/2017/01/204574/new-local-authority-launched-oversee-johors-pipc (accessed 1 June 2018).

Petroliam Nasional Berhad (Petronas). 2014. *Petronas Sustainability Report, 2014*. Kuala Lumpur, Malaysia. https://www.petronas.com/ws/sites/default/files/downloads/Sustainability%20Report%202014.pdf (accessed 12 November 2017).

———. 2015. *Petronas Sustainability Report, 2015*. Kuala Lumpur, Malaysia. https://www.petronas.com/ws/sites/default/files/downloads/SustainabilityReport2015.pdf (accessed 4 February 2018).

———. 2016. *Petronas Sustainability Report, 2016*. Kuala Lumpur, Malaysia. https://www.petronas.com/ws/sites/default/files/2018-07/sustainability-report-2016.pdf (accessed 3 February 2018).

PwC 2017. "Oil and Gas in Indonesia". Investments and Taxation Guide. https://www.pwc.com/id/en/pwc-publications/industries-publications/energy--utilities---mining-publications/oil-and-gas-in-indonesia-.html (accessed 3 February 2018).

Rahman, S. 2017. "Johor Survey 2017: Johorean views on Iskandar Malaysia and Investments in Johor". *ISEAS Perspective*, no. 2017/82, 8 November 2017.

Revilla Diez, J., M. Breul, and J. Moneke. 2019. "The SIJORI Growth Triangle: Territorial Complementarities or Competition for FDI in the Oil and Gas Industry?". *Journal of Southeast Asian Economies* 36, no. 1: 71–90.

Star Online. 2017. "Leaner, Meaner Petronas Targets Key Markets Growth". 17 August 2017. https://www.thestar.com.my/business/business-news/2017/08/17/leaner-meaner-petronas-targets-key-markets-for-growth/ (accessed 11 June 2018).

———. 2018. "Rakuten Calls a Buy on Straits Inter Logistics". 2 January 2018. https://www.thestar.com.my/business/business-news/2018/01/02/rakuten-calls-a-buy-on-straits-inter-logistics/ (accessed 9 June 2018).

Straits Times. 2015. "KTL Global Relocating Bulk of Singapore Operations to Johor". 4 April 2015. http://www.straitstimes.com/business/companies-markets/ktl-global-relocating-bulk-of-singapore-operations-to-johor (accessed 9 June 2018).

Straits Times Online. 2017. "Two Vessels Collide Near Johor, Causing Oil Spill". 18 August 2017. http://www.straitstimes.com/asia/se-asia/two-vessels-collide-near-johor-causing-oil-spill (accessed 9 June 2018).

Sun Daily. 2017. "Desaru Coast Unveiled: Malaysia's First Premium Integrated Destination". 31 October 2017. http://www.thesundaily.my/news/2017/10/31/desaru-coast-unveiled-malaysia%E2%80%99s-first-premium-integrated-destination-itb-asia-2017 (accessed 10 November 2018).

Zainul, I.F. 2017. "Dialog Propelled by Rapid Development". *Star Online*, 2 September 2017. https://www.thestar.com.my/business/business-news/2017/09/02/dialog-propelled-by-rapid-development/ (accessed 12 June 2018).

5

THE PRIVATE HEALTHCARE SECTOR IN JOHOR
Trends and Prospects

Meghann Ormond and Lim Chee Han[1]

INTRODUCTION

The Iskandar Malaysia (IM) special economic zone (SEZ) was established in Malaysia's southernmost state, Johor, in 2006 and is now beginning its third and final phase of development, with a targeted completion in 2025. IM is jointly operated and regulated by the Malaysian federal government and Johor state government under the statutory body called Iskandar Regional Development Authority (IRDA), which is charged with the development of IM as a "strong and sustainable metropolis of international standing" (IRDA 2016a).

To do this, IRDA focuses on economic sector and infrastructural planning, the promotion of IM to the general public and potential investors, and coordinating and facilitating investment in the SEZ. It promotes nine economic sectors within IM: healthcare, financial and business services, tourism, education, logistics and creative services make up the service sector; while electrical and electronics, petrochemical and oil and gas, as well as food and agro-processing comprise the manufacturing sector.

From IM's inception in 2006 to mid-2016, the manufacturing sector (27 per cent), retail/mixed-development (26 per cent) and residential property segments (20 per cent) comprised the bulk of investment in IM, with the services sector accounting for only 8 per cent during that period (IRDA 2016a, p. 64). Healthcare made up only 1 per cent of total investment, or RM3.16 billion, in the same period (IRDA 2016a, p. 65).

Despite its relative insignificance in the SEZ's broader investment portfolio, healthcare—a driver for other health-related industries (e.g., biotechnology, medical devices and equipment, pharmaceuticals and education)—has been thought to be a steadier source of growth over the last decade than others that IRDA initially saw as significant growth catalysts (Whang and Lim 2016). This is due in part to healthcare functioning, like schools and transport, as a key infrastructural anchor and "enabler" to render retail/mixed-development and residential property development more attractive to investors and consumers.

In the following pages, we provide a contemporary snapshot of the key policies and players shaping the development of private healthcare in Johor in order to inform policymakers, current commercial stakeholders and potential investors, and residents and civil society actors in the region about the latest trends, concerns and opportunities linked to the private healthcare sector in Johor. We also offer an overview of healthcare demand, facilities and human resources available in Johor that enables readers to compare the dimensions and competitiveness of Johor's private healthcare services sector with other leading states in Malaysia. This information draws on documentary sources, interviews with key private health and aged-care sector representatives, and participant observation. This chapter concludes with reflections on the future challenges and opportunities the private healthcare services sector faces in Johor.

POLICIES

The private healthcare services sector is a significant contributor to the Malaysian economy, equivalent to 1.4 per cent of the country's total GDP (2015).[2] The Economic Transformation Programme (ETP), launched in 2011 and focused on transforming Malaysia into a high-income country by 2020, recognizes this sector's significance and potential. Earmarked as one of the ETP's twelve National Key Economic Areas (NKEAs), the private healthcare sector is expected to create 26,966 jobs and generate RM6.59 billion by 2020 (Pemandu 2013b). The ETP's Healthcare NKEA focuses on medical devices and equipment, clinical and pharmaceutical research and product development, diagnostic services, health insurance for foreigners, medical tourism and senior living (Pemandu 2013a). Of these, most relevant to IM is medical tourism and senior living. The Wholesale and Retail NKEA should also not be ignored, as one of its foci—wellness—intersects with private healthcare services in developments throughout Malaysia. In this section, therefore, we outline the contours of the main national policies shaping the development of private medical care, ageing, and wellness and lifestyle services in Johor and, more specifically, in IM.

Private Medical Care

Malaysia's changing epidemiological and demographic profiles have been used in recent decades by the federal government to frame publicly financed healthcare as increasingly financially unsustainable. In the 1980s and 1990s, the Malaysian healthcare system began the process of privatization and corporatization. With the growth of Malaysia's middle class and neoliberal policy reform favouring privatization, private hospitals have since expanded in size and number throughout the country (Chee and Barraclough 2007). The introduction and enforcement of the Private Healthcare Facilities and Services Act (PHFSA) of 27 August 1998 (Commissioner of Law Revision Malaysia 1998) reflects the government's recognition of the private healthcare sector's growing significance in Malaysia from the late 1990s onwards. The PHFSA regulates private healthcare facilities and services by ensuring quality, setting fee ceilings and monitoring compliance.

The Malaysian private healthcare market is subject to national, regional and global economic volatility. The Asian financial crisis in the late 1990s, for example, left many private hospitals with fewer patients when many middle-class Malaysians again turned to the public sector to meet their healthcare needs. In 1998, therefore, the federal government also recognized the potential of the foreign patient market (so-called "medical tourism") to support private healthcare providers in Malaysia, especially during moments of economic crisis. From that point onwards, the federal government has fostered medical tourism via promotional campaigns, land grants and fiscal incentives (Ormond 2013). Since 2009, the corporatized national promotional body Malaysia Healthcare Travel Council (MHTC) has assumed responsibility for the coordination and promotion of Malaysian hospitals as medical tourism destinations.

The ETP's "Reinvigorating healthcare travel" Entry-Point Project has further enshrined medical tourism as a national economic driver. Under the Income Tax (Exemption) Order 2012 (renewed by Parliament in 2017), companies anywhere in Malaysia that establish new private healthcare facilities or existing private healthcare facilities undertaking expansion, modernization or refurbishment for purposes of promoting medical tourism are eligible to apply for an Income Tax Exemption equivalent to an Investment Tax Allowance (ITA) of 100 per cent on the qualifying capital expenditure incurred within a period of five years (MIDA 2011). The ITA has been extended until 31 December 2020, following the announcement of the 2018 Federal Budget of the Malaysian government (*New Straits Times*, 27 October 2017). The government also announced an increase in the medical tourism incentive from 50 per cent to 100 per cent of the incremental value of private healthcare services exports, from the year of assessment (2018) to 2020 in the Budget. We outline in detail how Johor and IM are specifically affected by the government's pro-healthcare privatization policies in later sections of this report.

Ageing

Some 15 per cent of the Malaysian population will be aged 60 and above by 2035, a figure which will grow to 23.6 per cent by 2050 (Alfian 2017). It is estimated that three-fourths of Malaysians are not saving enough for retirement and few have sufficient funds to cover the costs of long-term care needs (i.e., medical and non-medical needs associated with chronic illness, disability and dependency) (EPF Annual Report 2016).

Furthermore, while demographic changes have extended life expectancy among Malaysians, economic transformations within the country have led to the growth of nuclear families and dual-earner households and the decline of multi-generational households, leaving many older people without the intergenerational care upon which previous generations relied.

Yet, the Malaysian government has only recently started to prepare for population ageing, having few policies in place to address its specific medical and long-term care needs (e.g., the National Health Policy for Older Persons and Plan of Action for Older Persons and the National Plan of Action for Health Care of Older Persons (Ruhaini 2013)). Commentators in the national press argue for the need for greater public-private collaboration to reduce care costs associated with ageing, like institutional care services, retirement homes, products and services for senior living, and long-term care insurance coverage (see, for example, Yip, in Khairani 2017).

There is growing worldwide recognition that conventional institutional care homes pose challenges to supporting care-dependent seniors' quality of life (Gawande 2014), resulting in a push to enable seniors to live in their own homes for as long as possible. However, despite the continuing stigma in Southeast Asia associated with outsourcing elder care due to beliefs about filial piety (Ormond 2014), there appears to be a growing lobby to develop and transform private-sector aged-care facilities in Malaysia (see, for example, the Aged Care Group 2016). Indeed, in 2014, the Malaysian government identified a need for

> appropriate facilities, professional care and the availability of trained care givers to look after this increasing segment of population.... While still a new concept in Malaysia, the seniors living sector offers great potential growth and can help address the outpatient and community-based care needs of the elderly. It allows for seniors to live in a respectable and dignified facility allowing them to "age-in-place" in a secured environment where they can remain active and socially connected and be assured of care when the need arises. (Pemandu 2014).

Yet the government is not only interested in responding to Malaysian nationals' growing elder care needs. There is also clear interest in complementing Malaysia's growing medical hub status with senior living and aged-care facilities and in using public–private partnerships to do so, catering to both middle-class Malaysian nationals and international retirement migrants in the Malaysia My Second Home (MM2H) programme.

The ETP places specific emphasis on senior living and aged-care facility models imported from abroad (e.g., Singapore and Australia) "to answer this pressing need for quality and dependable senior active living and aged care which can be sustainable in the long term under a non-government funded or non-welfare regime" (Pemandu 2014). How this manifests in Johor and IM can be seen in later sections. Currently, most long-term care in Malaysia is offered by government welfare homes, private nursing homes, private care centres, voluntary aged-care organizations and charitable centres. However, most of these are thought to be unlicensed.

Recognizing a need for care standards to be streamlined and standardized, the ETP Healthcare NKEA's "Institutional aged care" Entry-Point Project led to the development of new specific legislation that builds on the Private Healthcare Facilities and Services Act (PHFSA) of 27 August 1998 and the Care Centre Act (CCA) of 7 July 1993 (Commissioner of Law Revision Malaysia 1993) to further regulate and monitor aged-care centres throughout the country and identify skills requirements for employed caregivers.[3]

The resulting Private Aged Healthcare Facilities and Services Bill (PAHFSB) of 29 November 2017 (previously the Aged Healthcare Act) requires private elderly care centres (i.e., private centres caring for four or more people aged 60 and above) to possess an operating licence issued by the Ministry of Health and renewed every three years. Private aged-care centre operators must ensure that caregivers working on their premises hold the Malaysian Skills Certificate (SKM) and are trained in basic life support. Premises must be built in accordance with standards set by the Ministry of Urban Wellbeing, Housing and Local Government. Operators are to be subject to inspection and, in cases of non-compliance, liable to fines. Unlike with the PHFSA, however, the government has not set a fee ceiling on private aged care, though this may be considered in the future (Carvalho et al. 2017).

Wellness and Healthy Lifestyles

Businesses around the world are increasingly seeking to tap into the rapidly growing "Lifestyles of Health and Sustainability" (LOHAS) market segment focused on the elusive concept of "wellness", which involves health and fitness, the environment, personal development, sustainable living and social justice (Emerich 2011). The industry offers goods and services linked to complementary and alternative medicine (CAM), preventive and personalized medicine, fitness and mindfulness, healthy eating and weight loss, beauty and anti-ageing, spa and thermal/mineral springs, and "wellness lifestyle" real estate and tourism.

The Malaysian government and diverse commercial actors aligned with the mission of developing Malaysia as a care hub have increasingly developed strategies to capture, expand and capitalize on the LOHAS market segment in the fields of healthcare; lifestyle, wellness and active ageing; and assisted living and institutionalized aged care. This is seen by the Wholesale and Retail NKEA "Setting up wellness resorts" Entry-Point Project, which "aims to establish wellness resorts at strategic locations … to tap into the booming medical tourism industry" (Pemandu 2013a). In Kuala Lumpur, for instance, the Country Heights Group is developing a 120-acre "integrated health and wellness resort" called Mines Wellness City (MWC), which will include hospitals, specialist clinics, aged-care facilities, a health-screening centre, residential units, office spaces and retail space. It was gazetted as a Special Wellness Zone by the federal government, entitling developers, operators, managers and promoters that provide healthcare- and wellness-related facilities or services to tax incentives.

In Johor, where it is expected that IM will be home to 3 million residents by 2025 (double its 2006 population), IRDA has identified a handful of programme areas to improve the SEZ's liveability, such as "integrated health facilities improvement" and "healthy lifestyles" (IRDA 2014, p. 6). This has led to the launch of IM's "Smart Healthy City and Communities" programme as well as a slew of developments in IM billing themselves as "health and wellness" destinations for well-heeled older people. Examples of these will be described in greater detail below.

CURRENT HEALTHCARE SERVICES IN JOHOR

According to the *Economic Census 2016*, the gross output value of health services in Johor in 2015 was RM1.55 billion, or 1.5 per cent of the state GDP (Table 5.1). Hospitals contributed about half (Table 5.2). While the contribution to state GDP is higher than the national average, it is lower than the most significant medical tourism destination states (e.g., Melaka, 2.1 per cent; Pulau Pinang, 2.4 per cent; Selangor, 1.7 per cent; and the Federal Territory of Kuala Lumpur, 2.1 per cent).

From 2010 to 2015, the size of the private health sector in Johor grew 60.7 per cent, compared to 44 per cent in GDP (Figure 5.1), indicating that the sector's growth is faster than general growth of the state economy. In 2015, 9,967 people were employed in health services in Johor across 1,254 establishments. Of these, 44.3 per cent were employed by 32 hospitals.[4]

From 2010 to 2015, 412 new health service establishments were set up in Johor and gross output increased by 60.7 per cent, faster than Melaka (49.8 per cent), Pulau Pinang (43.5 per cent) and the Federal Territory of Kuala Lumpur (57.3 per cent). Six hospitals opened in Johor during that time, while four closed in Pulau Pinang and one opened in Melaka. However, if we look at value added over value of gross output, an indicator of efficiency and profitability, we see that Johor only achieved 45.5 per cent (39.6 per cent for hospitals) in 2015, lower than the national average and other key states (Tables 5.1 and 5.2). This indicator could be a concern for potential healthcare investors coming to Johor. Yet it could also present an opportunity for investors to develop the sector from the lower baseline if operators are confident in their market efficiency and believe that they could outperform their competitors in Johor.

Healthcare Facilities and Capacity

While there has been steady growth in the numbers of public health clinics, private medical clinics and dental clinics in Johor over the years, the actual number of Johor private hospitals has been on the decline, dropping from thirty-eight hospitals in 2008 to twenty-one in 2014 (Table 5.3). Despite this, Johor experienced a general increase in total (public and private) hospital bed capacity from 2008 to 2016. Yet one interviewee representing a major private hospital group suggests that, given the forecasted population growth in IM, the number of public and private hospital beds in Johor is not yet sufficient. In 2016, while the number of hospitals per 100,000

TABLE 5.1
Principal Statistics of Health Services by Selected States, 2010 and 2015

	No. of Establishments			No. of Persons Engaged (During December of Last Pay Period)			Value of Gross Output, RM million			% Value Added/Value of Gross Output			% Value of Gross Output/State GDP		
	2010	2015	% Change	2010	2015	% Change	2010	2015	% Change	2010	2015	% Change	2010	2015	% Change
MALAYSIA	6,739	11,018	63.5%	77,742	101,056	30.0%	10,052	16,218	61.3%	45.8%	47.2%	1.4%	1.2%	1.4%	0.18%
Johor	842	1,254	48.9%	7,729	9,967	29.0%	963	1,548	60.7%	41.8%	45.5%	3.7%	1.3%	1.5%	0.15%
Melaka	275	418	52.0%	3,936	4,558	15.8%	508	761	49.8%	41.5%	51.0%	9.5%	2.1%	2.1%	0.05%
Pulau Pinang	517	909	75.8%	9,219	11,143	20.9%	1,299	1,864	43.5%	47.8%	45.6%	-2.2%	2.5%	2.4%	-0.01%
Selangor	1,617	2,779	71.9%	20,630	25,912	25.6%	2,555	4,428	73.3%	44.9%	48.5%	3.6%	1.4%	1.7%	0.24%
F. T. Kuala Lumpur	937	2,022	115.8%	13,318	20,169	51.4%	2,378	3,740	57.3%	48.6%	47.7%	-0.9%	2.1%	2.1%	0.01%

Source: Economic Census 2016 (Department of Statistics Malaysia 2017b) and authors' calculations.

TABLE 5.2
Principal Statistics of Hospital Services by Selected States, 2010 and 2015

	No. of Establishments			No. of Persons Engaged (During December of Last Pay Period)			Value of Gross Output, RM million			% Value Added/ Value of Gross Output			% Value of Gross Output (Hospital Services/Total Health Services)		
	2010	2015	% Change	2010	2015	% Change	2010	2015	% Change	2010	2015	% Change	2010	2015	% Change
MALAYSIA	198	232	17.2%	37,273	46,362	24.4%	5,995	9,007	50.2%	41.0%	42.4%	1.5%	59.6%	55.5%	−4.10%
Johor	26	32	23.1%	2,704	3,901	44.3%	514	749	45.8%	34.0%	39.6%	5.6%	53.4%	48.4%	−4.95%
Melaka	4	5	25.0%	2,378	2,426	2.0%	329	428	30.0%	31.3%	43.6%	12.3%	64.8%	56.2%	−8.57%
Pulau Pinang	25	21	−16.0%	6,539	7,316	11.9%	1,046	1,290	23.3%	45.5%	40.3%	−5.2%	80.5%	69.2%	−11.31%
Selangor	48	60	25.0%	10,477	11,338	8.2%	1,547	2,438	57.6%	39.0%	44.9%	5.9%	60.5%	55.1%	−5.49%
F. T. Kuala Lumpur	41	46	12.2%	7,057	9,663	36.9%	1,461	2,231	52.7%	47.4%	44.9%	−2.5%	61.4%	59.7%	−1.80%

Source: *Economic Census 2016* (Department of Statistics Malaysia 2017b) and authors' calculations.

FIGURE 5.1
Johor's GDP and Size of Private Health Sector, 2010–15

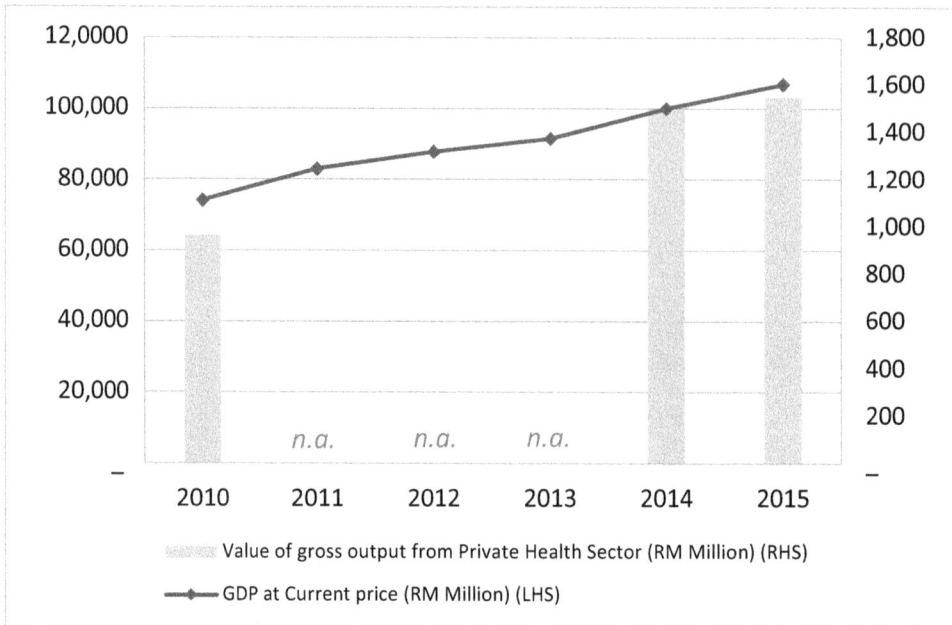

Value of gross output from Private Health Sector (RM Million) (RHS)
GDP at Current price (RM Million) (LHS)

Source: Economic Census 2016 (Department of Statistics Malaysia 2017b).

TABLE 5.3
Number of Health Facilities in Johor, 2008–16

Type of Facilities	2008	2009	2010	2011	2012	2013	2014	2015	2016
Public Hospitals	12	13	13	13	12	12	12	12	12
Private Hospitals	38	37	37	30	27	27	21	25	26
Total Hospitals	50	50	50	43	39	39	33	37	38
Public Beds	4,917	4,953	4,941	5,046	4,766	4,968	4,968	4,968	5,185
Private Beds	1,059	1,070	1,110	1,006	1,025	1,153	831	1,146	1,202
Total Beds	5,976	6,023	6,051	6,052	5,791	6,121	5,799	6,114	6,387
Health Clinics (Public)	87	90	88	94	94	94	94	94	95
Community Clinics (Public)	265	265	267	262	262	262	261	261	261
Maternal & Child Health Clinics (Public)	4	4	3	3	3	3	3	3	3
Medical Clinics (Private)				786	803	821	842	868	894
Dental Clinics (Private)				162	169	173	184	202	211

Source: Health Indicators 2008–2017, Ministry of Health Malaysia (Ministry of Health Malaysia, 2017).

population in Johor was comparable with that of Melaka and Selangor (Figure 5.2) its bed-to-population ratio (174.9 per 100,000 people), though higher than Selangor (145.2), was lower than the national average (188.5) and significantly lagged behind the already well-established medical tourism destinations of Pulau Pinang (250.7), Melaka (251.2) and Kuala Lumpur (439.3) (Figure 5.3).

With the predicted population growth in IM, it will be necessary to open more hospitals. Public hospitals will be necessary in Nusajaya and expansion of the existing hospital in Kulai should be considered along with the construction already slated for a new public hospital in Pasir Gudang (Musa 2014b). With 83.8 per cent of all private beds in Johor currently concentrated in private hospitals and specialist clinics in IM (Table 5.4) and six of Johor's eight MHTC member institutions promoting medical tourism being located in IM,[5] the clustering of private healthcare resources in the SEZ attests to IM's status as the state's foremost healthcare hub (see Map 2.3). This percentage will grow, as more private hospitals are slated for construction, with two new KPJ hospitals and TMC Life Sciences Bhd's Thompson Medical Centre to be built in the coming years.

Healthcare Demand

From 2010 to 2017, Johor's state population steadily rose from 3,362,900 in 2010 to 3,700,500 in 2017 (Department of Statistics Malaysia 2017a). Home to approximately 11.5 per cent of the national population, Johor's demographic profile by age closely resembles that at the national level (Department of Statistics Malaysia

FIGURE 5.2
Number of Hospitals per 100,000 Population, 2010 and 2016

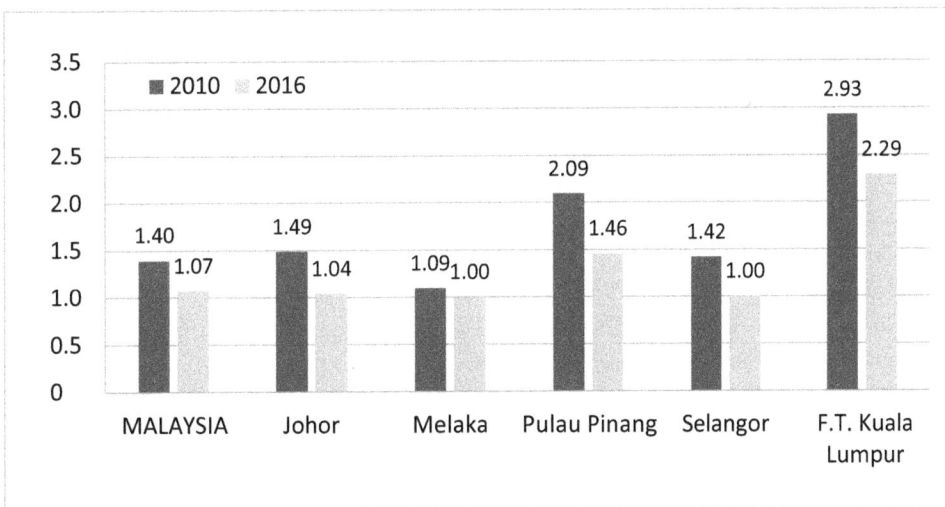

Source: Health Indicators, Ministry of Health Malaysia, Department of Statistics Malaysia and authors' calculations (Ministry of Health Malaysia 2017; Department of Statistics Malaysia 2017a).

FIGURE 5.3
Number of Beds per 100,000 Population, 2010 and 2016

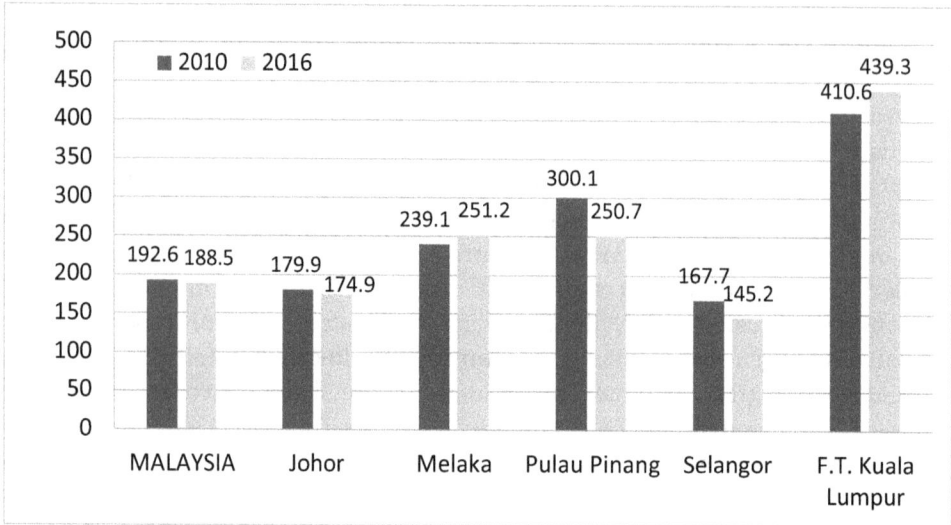

Source: Health Indicators, Ministry of Health Malaysia, Department of Statistics Malaysia and authors' calculations (Ministry of Health Malaysia 2017; Department of Statistics Malaysia 2017a).

2018) (Figure 5.4). However, IM's population is expected to grow significantly over the coming decades. When IM was first established, it was home to 1.5 million residents; by 2025, some 3 million people—coming from other parts of Malaysia and abroad—are expected to be living in the region alone (Othman 2017). Also, by 2025, some 799,000 people aged 55 and over will be residing in Johor, accounting for 19.1 per cent of the total state population. Being highly urbanized and complemented with many advanced healthcare and long-term care facilities, it is expected that IM will host the highest concentration of seniors in Johor. This demographic would be expected to place significant demands on local healthcare and long-term care services in Johor.

Hospital admissions require the most intensive use of healthcare resources. In both the public and private sectors, hospital admissions (per 1,000 population) across Malaysia are slowly increasing (Figure 5.5). However, in terms of utilization of private inpatient healthcare resources, Johor has the lowest private inpatient hospital admission-to-population ratio when compared with Selangor, the Federal Territory of Kuala Lumpur, Melaka and Pulau Pinang (Figure 5.5). In 2016, Johor residents were three times more likely to be admitted to public hospitals than private ones for inpatient care. The number of inpatients per 1,000 people in Johor (27) was approximately one-third of that in Pulau Pinang (92) and Kuala Lumpur (92). This trend suggests that the private hospital sector has ample room for improvement not only as regards the development of medical tourism but also when it comes to attracting and persuading local patients to cross over from public hospitals to make use of private ones.

TABLE 5.4

List of Hospitals and Specialist Clinics in Johor According to MHTC and APHM Membership and Location

Name of Institution	Located in Iskandar Malaysia?	Membership		No. of Beds*	Notable Ownership
		MHTC (Sept 2017)	APHM (June 2016)		
1. Gleneagles Medini	Yes	Ordinary		300	IHH
2. KPJ Bandar Maharani Specialist Hospital	No	Ordinary	Yes	63#	KPJ
3. KPJ Johor Specialist Hospital	Yes	Ordinary	Yes	252	KPJ
4. KPJ Pasir Gudang Specialist Hospital	Yes	Ordinary	Yes	136	KPJ
5. Pantai Hospital Batu Pahat	No	Ordinary	Yes	106	IHH
6. KPJ Puteri Specialist Hospital	Yes	Ordinary	Yes	158	KPJ
7. Regency Specialist Hospital	Yes	Ordinary	Yes	218	HMI
8. TMC Fertility & Women's Specialist Centre (Johor)	Yes	Ordinary			TMC Life Sciences
9. Columbia Asia Hospital Iskandar Puteri	Yes		Yes	80	Columbia Asia
10. KPJ Kluang Utama Specialist Hospital	No		Yes	30	KPJ
11. Medical Specialist Centre (JB) Sdn Bhd	Yes		Yes	45	
12. Pelangi Medical Centre Sdn Bhd	Yes			12	
13. Pusat Pakar Perbidanan & Sakitpuan Raja	No			11	
14. T.K. Tan O&G Specialist Clinic	Yes			10	
15. Tey Maternity Specialist & Gynae Centre	No			19	
16. Kempas Medical Centre	Yes			130	
17. Putra Specialist Batu Pahat	No			84	
18. Penawar Hospital Pasir Gudang	Yes			80	
19. Penawar Hospital Pandan City	Yes			200	
20. ECON Medicare Centre (Nursing Home)	Yes			200	ECON Healthcare Group
21. Jeta Care Centre (Nursing Home)	Yes			80	

Notes: MHTC – Malaysia Healthcare Travel Council; APHM – Association of Private Hospitals of Malaysia.

Source: Malaysia Healthcare Travel Council, 2018; The Association of Private Hospitals of Malaysia, 2018 and authors' findings;

* IM BizWatch, Healthcare @ Iskandar Malaysia: Opportunities in Private Healthcare in Iskandar Malaysia", April 2016 (IRDA 2016d) and APHM website; # Number is taken from the hospital website.

FIGURE 5.4
Demographic Profile by Age in Johor and Malaysia

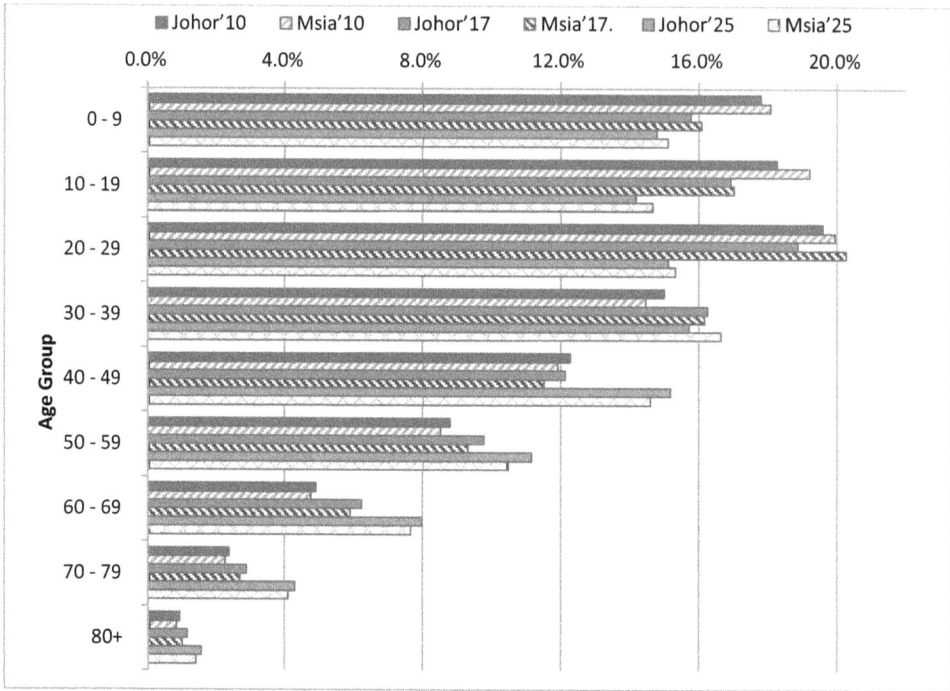

Source: Department of Statistics Malaysia and authors' calculations.

FIGURE 5.5
Number of Admissions per 1,000 Population by Selected State, 2011–16

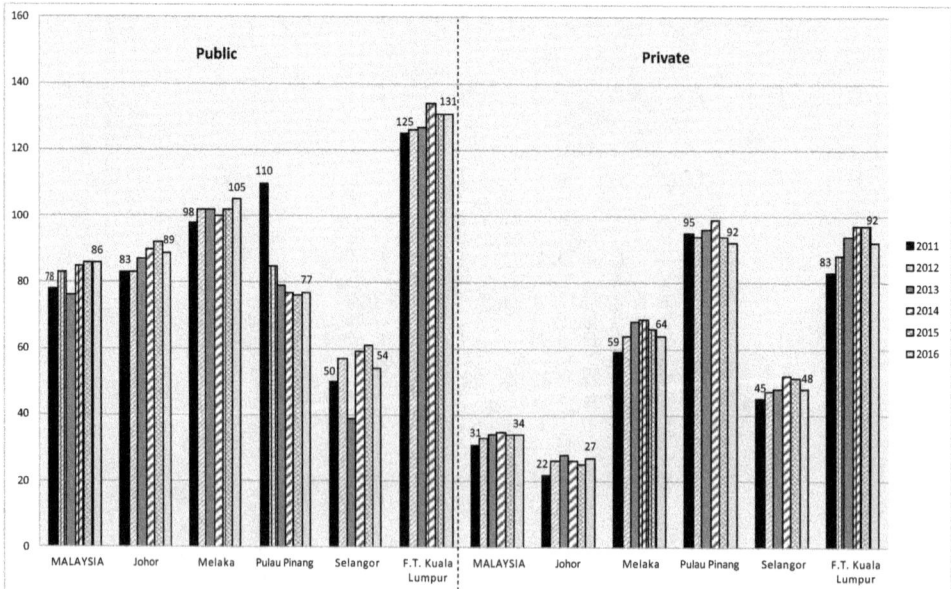

Source: Health Indicators, Ministry of Health Malaysia, Department of Statistics Malaysia and authors' calculations (Ministry of Health Malaysia 2017; Department of Statistics Malaysia 2017a).

Healthcare Workforce

Doctors, nurses and pharmacists are the core pillars of the healthcare workforce. Any increase in healthcare capacity would normally require the recruitment of a larger workforce. From 2008 to 2016, the number of doctors in Johor rose across the board, though more substantially in the public sector (from 1,067 to 2,887) than in the private sector (1,085 to 1,496). The state's doctor-to-population ratio has improved tremendously, dropping from 1:1,571 in 2008 to 1:834 in 2016 (Figure 5.6) and narrowed Johor's gap with other states. However, Johor's doctor-to-population ratio remains higher than Selangor, the Federal Territory of Kuala Lumpur, Melaka and Pulau Pinang (Figure 5.6). In light of current and future developments in Johor, however, the ratio may drop below the national average. From 2011 to 2016, more nurses began to work in public and private hospitals, leading to a marked improvement in the nurse-to-population ratio from 1:536 in 2011 to 1:368 in 2016 (Figure 5.7). However, as with the pharmacist-to-population ratio, Johor's ratio remains higher than the national average (Figure 5.8). In conclusion, the state's healthcare workforce must keep up with the projected rising patient demand by both local residents and medical tourists.

Doctors—especially specialists—are typically private hospitals' most valuable assets for attracting patients. Hospitals' physical size, facilities and finances are the main limiting factors affecting their ability to house a larger number and more diverse range of specialists. Figure 5.9 compares fifteen Johor private hospitals with four private hospitals in the much smaller, neighbouring state of Melaka, which is a well-established, thriving medical tourism destination and Johor's main private healthcare competitor in southern Peninsular Malaysia. Johor private hospitals

FIGURE 5.6
Ratio of Doctors to Population by Selected States, 2008–16

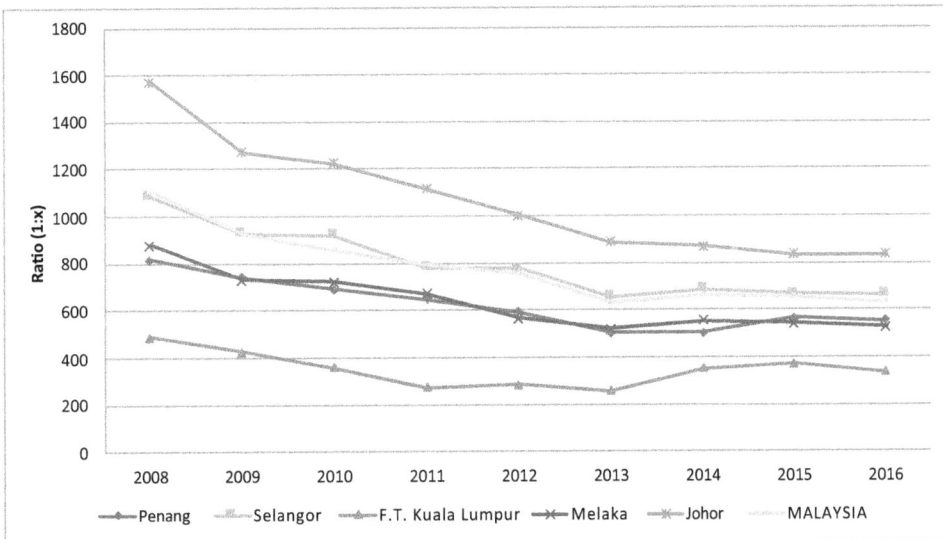

Source: Health Indicators, Ministry of Health Malaysia (Ministry of Health Malaysia 2017).

FIGURE 5.7
Ratio of Nurses to Population by Selected States, 2011–16

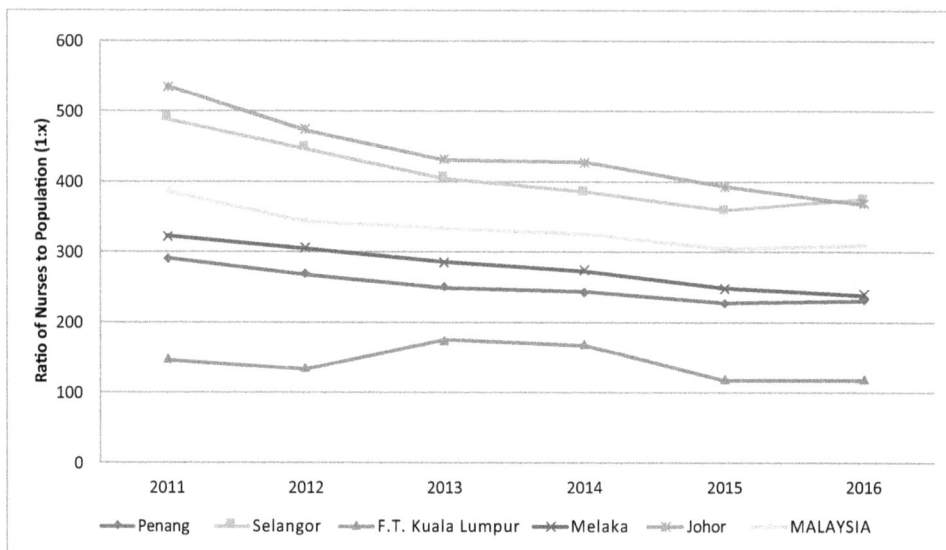

Source: Health Indicators, Ministry of Health Malaysia (Ministry of Health Malaysia 2017).

FIGURE 5.8
Ratio of Pharmacists to Population by Selected States, 2008–16

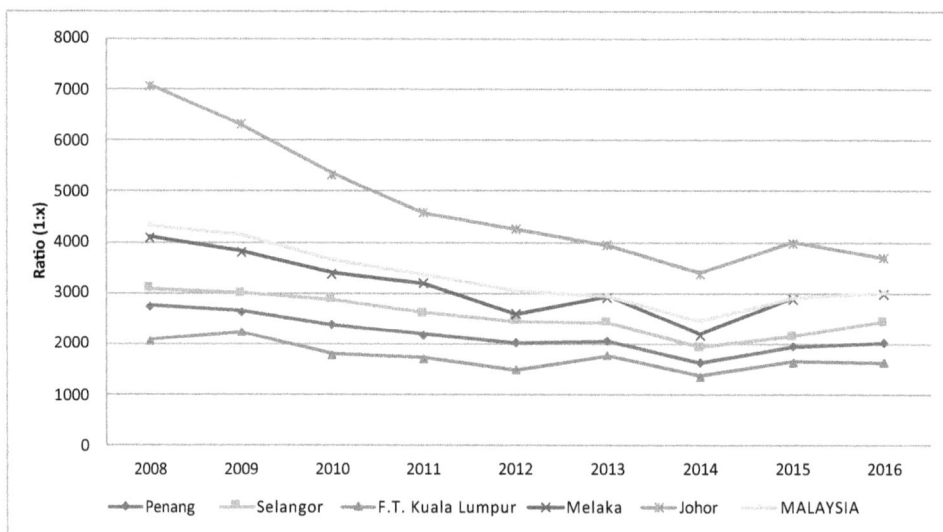

Source: Health Indicators, Ministry of Health Malaysia (Ministry of Health Malaysia 2017).

FIGURE 5.9
Demographics of Doctors and Specialists in Johor and
Melaka Private Hospitals, January 2018

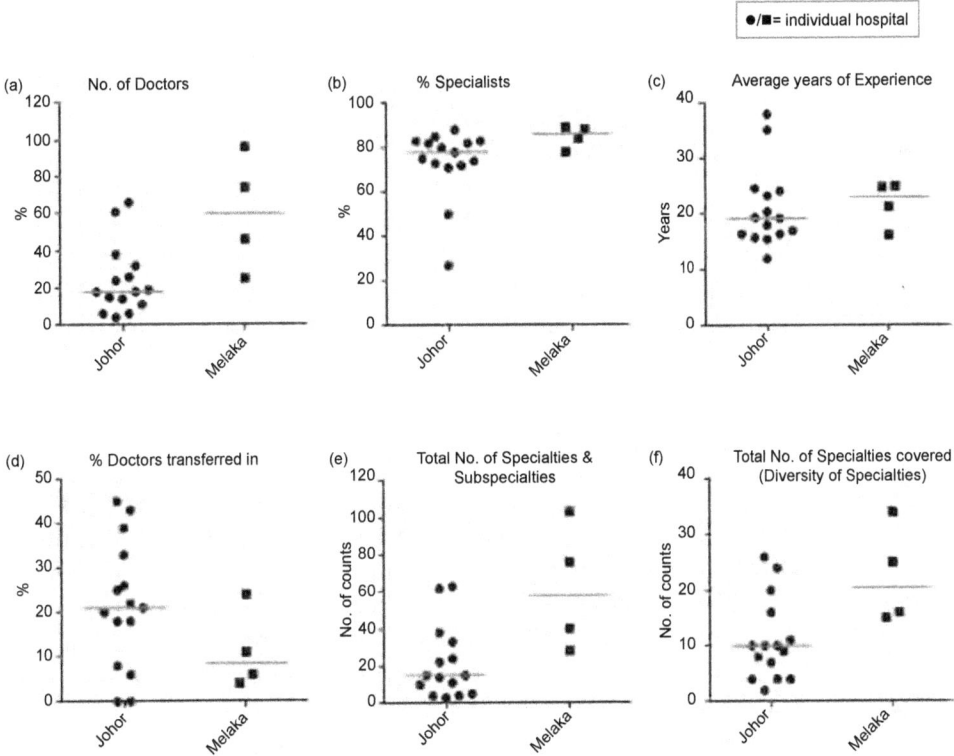

Source: Medical Register, National Specialist Register and authors' calculations (Malaysian Medical Council 2018a; Malaysian Medical Council 2018b).

generally have fewer doctors per hospital than those in Melaka (Figure 5.9a). Only two Johor private hospitals have 40 or more doctors (i.e., KPJ Johor Specialist Hospital (66) and Regency Specialist Hospital (61)), though Gleneagles Medini (38) is not too far behind. By contrast, Melaka's Mahkota Medical Centre (96) and Pantai Ayer Keroh Hospital's (74) physician workforce is comparable to hospitals in Malaysia's capital.

Most doctors in Johor and Melaka private hospitals are specialists (70–90 per cent) (Figure 5.9b). However, Johor still has a lot of catching up to do in order to provide a comprehensive range of specialist care to residents and medical tourists. While KPJ Johor Specialist Hospital (63) and Regency Specialist Hospital (62) lead the pack in Johor for hosting the largest number of specialties, more than half of all Johor hospitals have less than 20 (Figure 5.9e). Of the 88 specialties and subspecialties areas listed in the National Specialist Register, half of all Johor hospitals have covered less than ten specialty areas and only four of all Johor private hospitals have more than fifteen specialties (Figure 5.9f). Statistics may skew more towards specialized private medical institutions in the near future in light of a trend towards institutions focused on providing specialty treatment in IM (e.g., the National Heart Institute (IJN) and TLICC which will be discussed in the next section).

Due to the length of specialist training, specialists usually already have several years of experience when recruited by hospitals: a median of nineteen years of experience for doctors in Johor and twenty-three for those in Melaka (Figure 5.9c).[6] Melaka's lower recruitment rate indicates that most specialists have chosen to stay where they are, signalling a stabilized workforce. By contrast, in the last three years, over 20 per cent of all doctors were absorbed by more than half of Johor's private hospitals were responsible for recruiting, due in part to the opening of new hospitals in IM (Figure 5.9d). Johor hospitals' current recruitment strategies clearly indicate private healthcare expansion in the state, and interviews with major hospital groups suggest that there is growing competition for recruiting and retaining talented specialists.

HEALTHCARE PLAYERS AND HORIZONS

The Malaysian private healthcare economy is currently believed to be negatively affected by inflation and currency volatility and competition for health human resources (MIDF 2016). However, while cost-sensitive patients may seek out cheaper or public-sector healthcare alternatives, the private healthcare market is held to remain relatively stable because it targets middle- to upper-class populations with higher disposable incomes and are covered by private health insurance (MIDF 2016, p. 4).

This belief that private healthcare is and will remain a profitable, relatively stable growth sector has brought about an array of players in private healthcare in Johor, including well-established large healthcare groups, established and increasingly prominent smaller- and medium-sized healthcare providers, and a crop of major investors seeking to expand and diversify their portfolios that increasingly see hospitals as key assets for real estate development (e.g., Malaysian real estate development companies like Tropicana Corp). In this section, we offer an overview of the key players and developments shaping the landscape of medical and long-term care services in Johor and IM now and in the future.

Medical Care

IM is today home to several major hospitals and numerous small and medium-sized specialist clinics and diagnostic centres (Figure 5.10 and Table 5.4). As noted in an earlier section, it is estimated that there are 1,500 private hospital beds in IM currently and that this number will grow to 2,500 in the coming years. Of IM's five flagship development zones, Johor Bahru City Centre and Iskandar Puteri are those within which the majority of private healthcare services are most heavily concentrated (see Figure 5.10) and will continue to grow. Most of the hospitals and clinics in Johor Bahru City Centre were established prior to IM (e.g., KPJ Johor Specialist Hospital (1981), KPJ Puteri Specialist Hospital (1986 [1993]) and TMC Fertility and

FIGURE 5.10
Map Location of Private Healthcare Institutions in Iskandar Malaysia, Johor

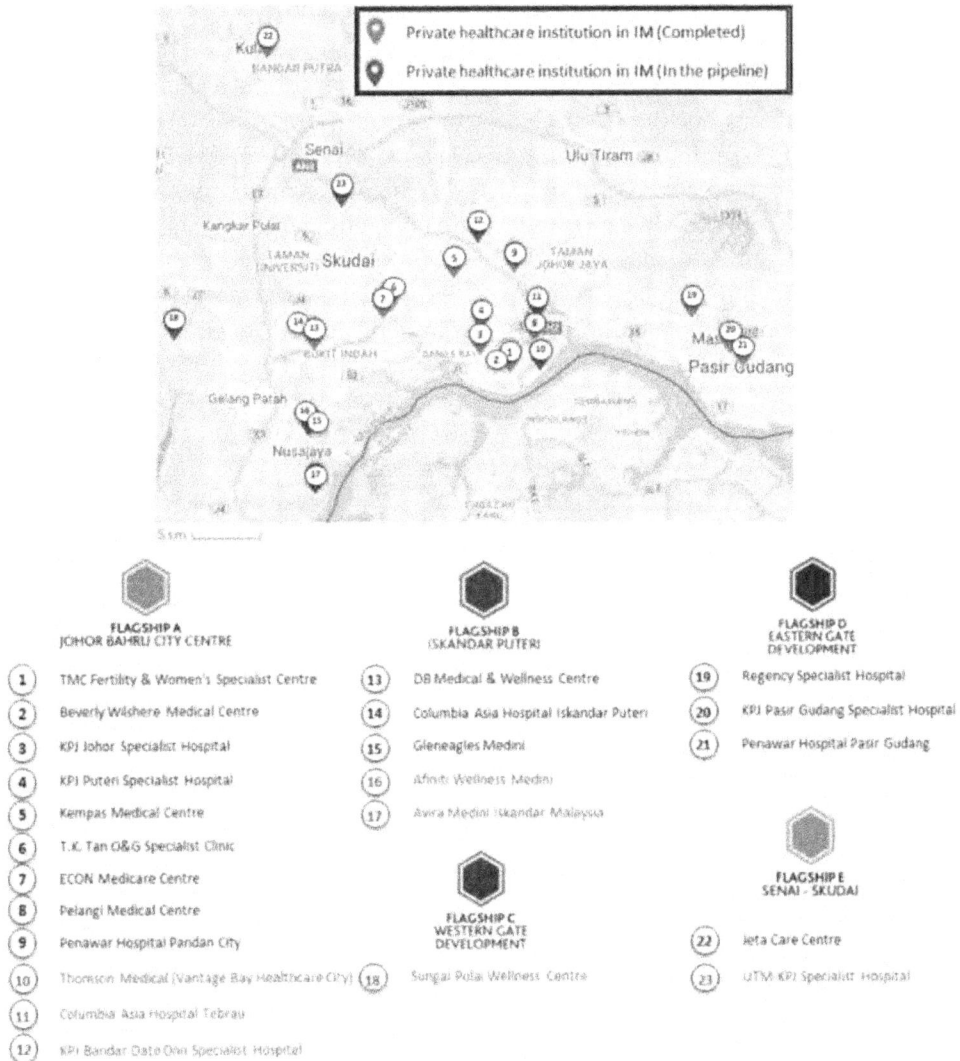

FLAGSHIP A
JOHOR BAHRU CITY CENTRE

(1) TMC Fertility & Women's Specialist Centre
(2) Beverly Wilshere Medical Centre
(3) KPJ Johor Specialist Hospital
(4) KPJ Puteri Specialist Hospital
(5) Kempas Medical Centre
(6) T.K. Tan O&G Specialist Clinic
(7) ECON Medicare Centre
(8) Pelangi Medical Centre
(9) Penawar Hospital Pandan City
(10) Thomson Medical (Vantage Bay Healthcare City)
(11) Columbia Asia Hospital Tebrau
(12) KPJ Bandar Dato Onn Specialist Hospital

FLAGSHIP B
ISKANDAR PUTERI

(13) DB Medical & Wellness Centre
(14) Columbia Asia Hospital Iskandar Puteri
(15) Gleneagles Medini
(16) Afiniti Wellness Medini
(17) Avira Medini Iskandar Malaysia

FLAGSHIP C
WESTERN GATE
DEVELOPMENT

(18) Sungai Pulai Wellness Centre

FLAGSHIP D
EASTERN GATE
DEVELOPMENT

(19) Regency Specialist Hospital
(20) KPJ Pasir Gudang Specialist Hospital
(21) Penawar Hospital Pasir Gudang

FLAGSHIP E
SENAI - SKUDAI

(22) Jeta Care Centre
(23) UTM-KPJ Specialist Hospital

Women's Specialist Centre (2004)). A more recent wave of hospital construction took place after IM was set up, largely clustered in Iskandar Puteri (e.g., Columbia Asia Hospital (2010) and Gleneagles Medini Hospital (2010)). However, KPJ Pasir Gudang Specialist Hospital (2013) and Regency Specialist Hospital (2009) are both located in IM's Eastern Gate Development Zone.

Several major well-established private-sector healthcare players currently involved in Johor and IM and a number of new players with projects in the pipeline are set to have significant impact on the region. In this subsection, we present this wide array of players, the nature of their current holdings and their plans for development in the region. Across the board, we see optimism and robust growth. All the major well-established players are vigorously working to expand their existing operations in Johor and, more specifically, in IM. New players, mostly foreign investors, are seeking to establish a foothold in Johor's rapidly developing private healthcare services sector, catering to the expected needs of IM's future residents. Even the federal government decided in mid-2017 to set up a branch of the corporatized National Heart Institute (Institut Jantung Negara, IJN) in Iskandar Puteri in order to reach a larger customer base from Malaysia, Singapore and Indonesia (Rao 2017).

Part of the Malaysian state economic development corporation Johor Corporation (JCorp), Kumpulan Perubatan (Johor) Sdn Bhd (KPJ) is the largest healthcare group in Malaysia and the fifth largest in the Asia-Pacific region, managing twenty-six hospitals in Malaysia, two in Indonesia, one in Bangladesh, one in Thailand. It also holds a 57 per cent 2015 to 2,929 in 2016, amounting to one-fourth of all private hospital beds in the country. Its average bed occupancy rate (BOR) went from 68 per cent in 2015 to 66.2 per cent in 2016 due in part to "economic uncertainty" (KPJ 2017, p. 34), though this is roughly still on par with the national public hospital average BOR of 68.2 per cent (MIDF 2016). In Johor, five KPJ hospitals currently provide 531 beds, and there are plans to open two more (e.g., the sixty-bed Bandar Dato Onn Specialist Hospital and the UTM KPJ Specialist Hospital) in IM.

IHH Healthcare Bhd (IHH) is the world's second largest listed hospital group, with fifty hospitals as well as medical centres, clinics and ancillary healthcare businesses across ten countries (Brunei, Bulgaria, China, India, Iraq, Macedonia, Malaysia, Singapore, Turkey and the United Arab Emirates). Its brands include Mount Elizabeth, Pantai, Parkway, Gleneagles, Acibadem and ParkwayHealth. Malaysia is home to fourteen IHH hospitals. IHH was established in 2010 as a result of a merger between Singapore's Parkway Group and Malaysia's Pantai Group; numerous global acquisitions followed. Today, Malaysia's sovereign wealth fund, Khazanah, holds the majority stake (41.17 per cent) (Khoo 2016). In Johor, it owns and operates Gleneagles Medini Hospital and Pantai Hospital Batu Pahat. Seeing Malaysia as a high-growth market, IHH has plans to add 160 medical clinic suites in the next phase of the Johor hospital's development (IHH 2017, p. 35).

Singapore-based Health Management International (HMI) owns Regency Specialist Hospital (RSH) in Johor and Mahkota Medical Centre in Melaka. While RSH currently has 166 beds, this will grow to 200 beds in 2018, and HMI plans to expand RSH to a 500-bed hospital, given strong patient demand (HMI 2017). Mahkota will also grow from 266 beds to 340 beds in the coming years. Across their hospitals, they note that inpatient growth is higher than outpatient growth due to the weak economic situation, and that foreign patient load growth is more than double (6.7 per cent) that of the local patient load (2.8 per cent) (HMI 2017, p. 6). They wish to continue attracting medical tourists from the neighbouring countries of Indonesia and Singapore in order to maximize their BOR and to offset dips in local patient volumes (HMI 2017, p. 10). Columbia Asia Hospitals are jointly owned by the U.S.-based International Columbia USA LLC (70 per cent) and the Malaysia-based Employees Provident Fund (EPF) (30 per cent). EPF also holds an 8.55 per cent stake in IHH and a 20 per cent stake in Iskandar Investment Berhad. With more than thirty hospitals across Asia (India, Indonesia, Malaysia and Vietnam), there are fourteen Columbia Asia hospitals in Malaysia, one of which is in Johor (2010) (Columbia Asia 2018). These are mainly mid-sized hospitals (100–200 beds). Patient demand was especially high at Columbia Asia Hospital-Iskandar Puteri (an estimated 80–90 per cent BOR in 2015), leading the hospital to develop a new wing with an additional eighty-five beds and to build Johor's second Columbia Asia Hospital in Tebrau (*The Edge Property*, 11 May 2015; *The Iskandarian*, 16 March 2017). With the new expansion and construction projects, Columbia Asia seeks to become a more prominent healthcare player in IM, serving a different value-segment of the population.

While KPH, IHH, HMI and Columbia Asia are the most significant major private healthcare providers in the region today, we cannot ignore the significance of small- and medium-sized private healthcare providers in the IM and Johor private healthcare landscape. Daiman Development Bhd, a company majority-owned by the Singaporean Tay family, for example, has launched an integrated medical hub at Menara Landmark Medical Suites, positioned as a "one-stop centre for medical services without a single operator" (Loh 2014), that brings together an ambulatory care centre, general clinic and medical services with medical tourism-friendly services (e.g., a DoubleTree Hotel, shopping, and food and beverage outlets) only 2 km from the Johor Causeway. Aesthetics and plastic surgery (Beverly Wilshire Medical Centre), fertility and gynaecology (TMC Fertility Centre), cancer treatment centre, physiotherapy and pain management, MRI and medical imaging, pathology, and dental services are all located at the Medical Suites (Daiman 2015, 2016). Likewise, the Tunku Laksamana Johor Cancer Centre (TLICC) to be built near Horizon Hills in Iskandar Puteri and operational by the end of 2020. The Cancer Centre, led by Singapore-headquartered healthcare specialist Asian American Medical Group (AAMG), will include a thirty-bed ambulatory cancer facility targeting 7,000 patients annually. Phase Two of its development is pegged to include inpatient services, including a *shariah*-compliant women's wing, a laboratory for medicine and advanced molecular diagnostics, and a medical mall with specialist retail outlets (*Bernama*, 1 April 2018). These two developments—Menara Landmark Medical Suites and TLICC—demonstrate how specialty treatment healthcare providers can compete with major conventional private hospitals. They offer an innovative model that may enable small- and medium-sized providers to band together in order to better compete with the bigger hospitals not only for local patients but also for Singaporean and Indonesian medical tourists, most of whom travel to Malaysia for diagnostic and specialist outpatient care needs.

A number of significant developers are also seeking to establish medical facilities in IM. Among the most anticipated is the 11-ha Vantage Bay Healthcare City, jointly developed by Singapore's Rowsley Ltd and Singapore-based Thomson Medical's Malaysian subsidiary, TMC Life Sciences Bhd.[7] It is billed as a "cradle-to-grave healthcare hub" or precinct comprising healthcare, education and research arms (e.g., a 500-bed specialist hospital (Thomson Medical Centre) set to open in 2020, a community hospital, health sciences education and training facilities for nurses and allied health professionals, wellness retail services and a hotel catering to medical tourists) as well as lifestyle and wellness arms (e.g., long-term care facilities, a purpose-built urban wellness resort and wellness retail services) (Rowsley Ltd 2017, p. 11; see also Lai 2016). Reflecting the volatile nature of property development in IM, in 2015, Vantage Bay Healthcare City was—like other developments in the region, as we shall see below—repositioned from an integrated residential, office and retail project to a healthcare hub.

Mainland Chinese investors also have stakes in IM's private healthcare services sector. Forest City, a 1,400-ha Chinese-backed mixed-development township built on reclaimed land with an estimated gross development value of RM450 billion, for example, is being developed by Country Garden Pacific View Sdn Bhd (CGPV), a joint venture between Guangdong-based, Hong Kong-listed Country Garden Group and local Malaysian partner Esplanade Danga 88 Sdn Bhd, a company actually owned by Johor's Sultan Ibrahim Ismail. Developers aspire for it to ultimately accommodate 700,000 residents by 2035, many of whom are expected to be mainland Chinese. CGPV's promotional materials cite Gleneagles Medini, KPJ Specialist and Regency Specialist Hospital (RSH) as anchors relevant to prospective buyers. CGPV and the Chinese state-owned Greenland Group are also planning to attract renowned Traditional Chinese Medicine (TCM) facilities to IM (Jaipragas 2017). Forest City will be home to the first international branch of the Foshan Hospital of Traditional Chinese Medicine (Lee 2017). Typical of IM's eclectic mix of entertainment and healthcare infrastructure, the Tebrau Bay Waterfront City project in IM's Eastern Corridor, a joint venture between Greenland Group and the Johor state government-linked company Iskandar Waterfront City Berhad (IWCB), over the next fifteen years will come to include a "snow world" theme park, an opera house and a TCM hospital (Whang 2015b).

Medical Tourism

Private Malaysian hospitals received some 921,500 foreign patients in 2016. Half of these were already residing in Malaysia (i.e., expatriate workers, retirement migrants and international students), while the other half (what the Ministry of Health Malaysia calls "health tourists") travelled expressly to Malaysia for treatment (*New Straits Times*, 27 October 2017). The medical tourism destination heavyweights in Malaysia are Pulau Pinang (with 40 per cent of all foreign patients and 60 per cent of "health tourists"), the Klang Valley (comprising Selangor and the Federal Territory of Kuala Lumpur, and accounting for 34 per cent of all foreign patients but only 12 per cent of all "health tourists") and Melaka (11 per cent of all foreign patients and 19 per cent of all "health tourists").

The state of Johor is a minor player by comparison, accounting for only 4 per cent of all foreign patients and 4 per cent of all "health tourists" treated in Malaysia in 2016 (Marini 2017). Focusing on three popular disease treatment categories for medical tourism, Johor only recorded a 2.7–6.7 per cent foreign patient volume in

2015 (Figure 5.11), which is minor when compared with Pulau Pinang (15.2–35.8 per cent) and Melaka (8.8–21.6 per cent). Compared with other key states in Malaysia, foreign patients to Johor contributed approximately 5.7 per cent (RM43 million) of Johor's total private hospital revenue in 2015, this was only half the national average (10.2 per cent) and a mere one-sixth of Pulau Pinang's (31.6 per cent). While foreign patient numbers in Johor private hospitals are increasing on the whole, the rate of increase does not outpace the national average.

For more than a decade, Johor has been pegged as the country's up-and-coming medical tourism destination in light of its proximity to Indonesia and Singapore. This is evidenced by IRDA identifying healthcare as an important driver and component for the IM region's growth, seeking to position IM as "the next medical destination for patients who are seeking quality and cost-effective healthcare across the region" (IRDA 2016b). Yet Johor's role in medical tourism has been relatively minor to date. Not yet in competition with other better-established Malaysian medical tourism destinations like Pulau Pinang and Melaka for foreign patients from further afield, Johor private hospitals currently largely cater to the healthcare needs of those who already have or are developing ties to Johor (e.g., Indonesians from nearby islands, patients or patients' family members already living in Johor, Singaporean seniors and international expatriates planning to settle in Johor, patients of Malaysian origin who live in Singapore, etc.). Roughly half of all medical tourism in Johor comprises foreigners residing in Malaysia, while the other half comprises "health tourists". Indonesians made up 90.5 per cent of all "health tourists" in Johor in 2015, while Singaporeans, the second largest group of "health tourists" in Johor, comprised only

FIGURE 5.11
Percentage Share of Malaysian and Foreign Inpatients by
Selected Disease Treatment Categories in Johor, 2015

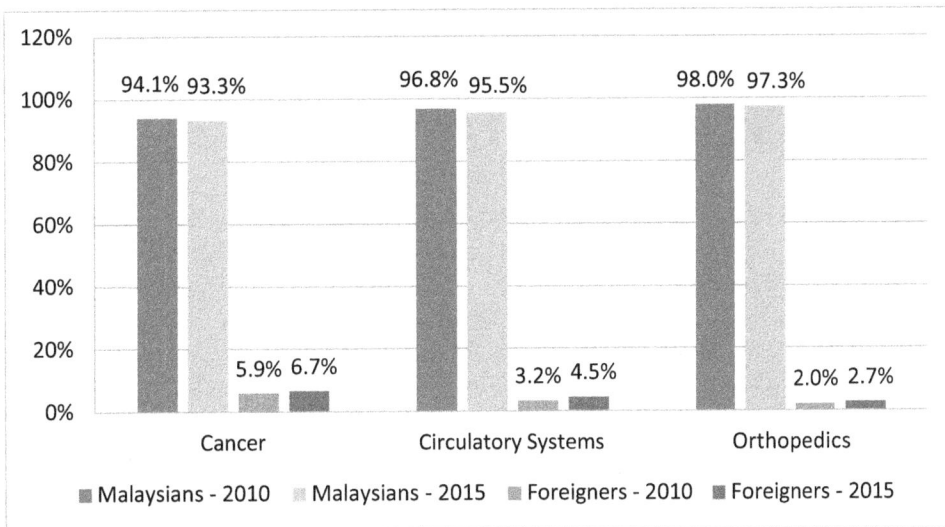

Source: Ministry of Health Malaysia (Ministry of Health Malaysia 2018) and authors' calculations.

4.3 per cent. These figures suggest that poor access to reliable, high-quality medical care in nearby Indonesia remains the most crucial push factor for Indonesians to pursue healthcare in nearby Johor, a trend that will likely persist long into the foreseeable future and on which many private hospitals promoting medical tourism in the region continue to strongly rely.

The persistently small number of Singaporean "health tourists" has troubled the region. There were initially hopes that this number would grow in the wake of Singaporean legislation that, starting on 1 March 2010, enabled Singapore residents to use their Medisave funds[8] on hospitalization and day surgeries in selected Malaysian hospitals with an approved working arrangement with a Medisave-accredited institution or referral centre in Singapore (Ministry of Health Singapore 2010).

To date, this cross-border care scheme has relied solely on two Singapore-linked hospital groups—Health Management International (HMI) and Parkway Holdings Pte Ltd—that have facilities in both Singapore and Malaysia. HMI hospitals in Malaysia include Mahkota Medical Centre (Melaka) and Regency Specialist Hospital (IM). Parkway Holdings (later IHH) hospitals are spread around Malaysia and include those under the Pantai and Gleneagles brands, and Johor is home to Gleneagles Medini Hospital.

As of 2018, only three hospitals in Johor have qualified for Singaporean Medisave use: Pantai Hospital Batu Pahat, Regency Specialist Hospital (IM) and Gleneagles Medini Hospital (IM). These hospitals promote themselves as offering strong value for money for Singaporeans and other international patients, given that procedures cost 30–50 per cent less in Malaysia than in Singapore and that they are geographically, linguistically and culturally close to Singapore (Whang 2015a). In the six months following the policy implementation, newspapers reported that a significant proportion of Singapore residents pursuing care in Malaysia were doing so for obstetrics and giving birth. Others sought coronary angiograms, cataract surgery, total knee replacement and total hip replacement (Lim 2010). However, the proportion of Singaporean "health tourists" in Johor appears to have remained relatively small since 2010. Further research is necessary to identify the potential effects of the Medisave cross-border care scheme on both care providers and patients in Singapore and Malaysia, especially in the states most likely to be most heavily affected: Johor and Melaka.

Despite Johor's comparatively minor role on the national stage in medical tourism, a number of hospitals located in the state—especially those in the IM zones of Johor Bahru City Centre and Iskandar Puteri—actively promote themselves as medical tourism destinations. This enables them to benefit from government policies supporting medical tourism which qualify them for a range of fiscal incentives mentioned earlier in this report. However, Johor does not have a state-based association equivalent to Pulau Pinang's Penang Centre of Medical Tourism (PMED), which coordinates hospital marketing efforts and promotes Penang as a unified medical tourism destination. While many of IM's major hospitals promoting medical tourism are MHTC members, it may be a wise move to emulate the PMED model in order to promote IM as Malaysia's southern medical tourism hub.

Wellness, Lifestyle and Ageing

Numerous players in Johor are deploying "health", "wellness" and "lifestyle" narratives to pitch their services and property developments. IRDA, for instance, frames IM as a global "smart city" that avails residents and visitors of state-of-the-art medical and health facilities and services as well as "healthy" housing and a "health-supportive" physical (i.e., "green" and "clean") and social environment (e.g., via public-private nutrition and exercise initiatives to encourage healthy lifestyles and workplaces) (IRDA 2016c). In the realm of private healthcare, we also see preventive health services and screenings being packaged as "wellness" offerings (e.g., KPJ Johor Specialist Hospital's Wellness Clinic).

This trend is most prominent among Khazanah-owned healthcare and property developers, who have deployed a "wellness" theme to make a number of major mixed-use developments in Iskandar Puteri more attractive. These developments are generally anchored by major hospitals. The Afiniti Medini Wellness Project, anchored by Gleneagles Medini Hospital and developed by Pulau Indah Ventures (PIV), a 50:50 joint venture between Khazanah and Temasek, is expected to include residential units, serviced apartments, a corporate training centre, a wellness centre and wellness-themed retail.

During our October 2017 visit, we found that the Afiniti Medini Wellness project was most likely in its final phase, with at least four companies having set up shop there. In a similar vein, Khazanah-subsidiary UEM Sunrise's 67-acre Afiat Healthpark, anchored by Columbia Asia Hospital, is framed as a future "integrated medical hub", offering traditional Chinese medicine (TCM) and modern medicine as well as wellness opportunities, set within "lush manicured environs" with golf courses, a hotel and a care centre. When UEM put the empty DB Wellness & Medical Suites "care centre" property on the market, it was promoted as ideal for diverse specialist medical services, diagnostic medical services, psychotherapy, ozone therapy (banned in 2017), physiotherapy, traditional and complementary medicine, beauty and wellness services, and pharmacy. A number of smaller developers are building near it. However, during our October 2017 visit, we noted that, despite the DB Kompleks having been long completed, there appeared to be limited interest in occupying the medical and commercial units.

Intriguingly, "wellness" and "lifestyle" are also strategically deployed to make retirement village-style developments more appealing in IM (see, e.g., Lee, in *The Edge Property*, 8 April 2015). Take, for instance, Avira Medini Iskandar (previously called the "Urban Wellness Project" and "Medini Integrated Wellness Capital" (Medini IWC, 2013)). It is a 207-acre mixed-development resort-like "wellness township" developed by Nuri Merdu Sdn Bhd, a joint venture between Galaxy Prestige Sdn Bhd (a subsidiary of E&O Bhd) and Pulau Indah Ventures Sdn Bhd (a joint venture between wholly owned subsidiaries of Khazanah and Temasek). This gated community with different residential offerings, a retail "village" and a 12.5-acre "Wellness Sanctuary" is, according to the *2016 E&O Annual Report*, focused on "prolonging active years by promoting physical vitality and mental clarity through holistic, non-invasive programmes backed by scientifically-proven methods, technologies and diagnostics" (E&O Bhd 2017, p. 38).

The number of facilities for more frail dependent seniors is also growing in Johor. One of the "model" aged-care projects identified by the ETP (Pemandu 2013a) is led by Singapore-based Econ Healthcare Group, which has facilities in Singapore, Kuala Lumpur and a 199-bed facility in the Taman Perling area of IM's Iskandar Puteri zone. Another is JetaCare, a 66-bed purpose-renovated "mid-range" care facility in Kulai that brings together elements of an Australian aged-care home model with the Confucian value of filial piety (*xiào dào*). JetaCare has one facility in Australia (a joint venture with KPJ), two in China and four in Malaysia.[9]

Facilities like these in Johor, which seek to attract not only locals from Johor but also Singaporeans, struggle to combat societal taboos surrounding the outsourcing of elder care in both countries (Ormond 2014). Notes one anonymous sector representative interviewed, "if one wants to be successful in [this sector in] Asia, one has to adapt [an aged-care facility] and integrate it with the local culture demanding the services". This means detaching deeply seated notions of what it means to be a "good" son or daughter from beliefs that children themselves must physically care for their ageing parents as well as being affordable for seniors' families.

There are concerns in the sector about what the 2017 Private Aged Healthcare Facilities and Services Bill (PAHFSB) will require of existing and forthcoming aged-care facilities, especially since compliance with building and care-giving standards may require many facilities to raise residents' costs. Local facilities currently cost between RM1,000–3,000 per month. Differences in price are linked to the quality of residential conditions and the quantity and quality of care labour (i.e., staff-to-resident ratios are lower in more expensive facilities). Profit margins for such facilities are minimal. Another anonymous sector representative interviewed notes, "Senior care is not like general medical care. [With m]edical care, for example one operation can cost a lot of money. But, with senior care, we don't do operations."

However, if paired with other kinds of services and retail in a retirement village model, developers believe that such facilities could function as anchors and yield greater profitability. It is reportedly difficult to attract well-trained care-givers due to societal beliefs that aged-care facilities are equated with low-wage, depressing work. However, there are initiatives to train local people in order to acquire the required level of care-giving skill and the sector is pushing for greater governmental support in the form of fiscal incentives for training and retaining care-givers.

Aged-care facilities in Johor mainly attract Malaysians, although they also are home to some Singaporeans and Westerners. As with medical care, IM is seen as an especially strategic location for attracting older Singaporeans because of its geographical proximity (Ormond 2014). In one facility we studied, 20 per cent of the residents were Singaporean.

Medical Education

Iskandar Puteri's EduCity was developed as an education hub and is an ETP Entry Point Project (EPP). It comprises universities, research and development (R&D) centres and student accommodation. It is meant to feed talent into IM's industries. Invited by the Malaysian Federal Government to set up in IM, Newcastle University Medicine Malaysia (NUMed Malaysia) was an early anchor tenant for this development (2011). It, like other universities in the area, benefits from a favourable land price, leasing the land for thirty years from Iskandar Investment Bhd before receiving rights to purchase the land for £1. NUMed Malaysia offers an MBBS programme (Bachelor of Medicine, Bachelor of Surgery), and a biomedical sciences degree. It is not currently operating at its full capacity of 1,000 students, and only 7–10 per cent of its current 600 students are international students. The limited number of foreign students has been attributed in an interview with us by NUMed's Provost and CEO Prof Roger Barton to these students not being permitted to work in Malaysia after 2011 upon graduating and students' home countries (e.g., Singapore) not always recognizing degrees earned on the NUMed Malaysia campus.

NUMed intends to build more labs to develop its research potential and a primary care centre to expand its campus and provide staff the chance to continue clinical practice to ensure high-quality, up-to-date education. As at August 2017, NUMed Malaysia had four to five ongoing research collaborations with partners like the Institute of Medical Research (IMR), Universiti Teknologi Malaysia (UTM), National University of Singapore (NUS) and University of Malaysia (UM). Barton expects more research grants to come in for international collaborative work. In the near future, NUMed Malaysia expects to enrol more students for the biomedical science degree programme, contributing to medical research work. NUMed already works together with public hospitals in the area for compulsory clinical attachments, but it would like to partner up with private healthcare providers. Private hospitals are, however, thought to be reluctant because they believe that patients do not want to be treated by students.

FUTURE PROSPECTS AND CHALLENGES

In seeking to capitalize on global and national private healthcare growth trends, the Federal and Johor State Governments and the private sector have jointly collaborated in a number of ways to enhance the development of Iskandar Malaysia's (IM) private healthcare services sector so that it may become a dynamic, integrated and world-class healthcare destination for local residents and foreign visitors alike. To reach these objectives, as we have seen throughout this chapter, IM's development intersects and frequently aligns with national strategies and policies in the medical care, aged care, and lifestyle and well-being sectors. It becomes clear, however, that a number of issues must be addressed by policymakers and commercial and civic actors in order to ensure continued positive development in this sector.

First, IM's economic volatility and the eclectic idealism of its developments must be reduced. With the planned construction and expansion of many new hospitals and developments targeting a growing, more diverse and rapidly ageing population, stakeholders in the private healthcare industry are showing very strong signs of optimism. However, IM's troubling economic volatility, brought on by political scandals (e.g., 1MDB) and fears about real estate investment stoked by limited corporate settlement, Singapore's unwillingness to relax border control to facilitate easier cross-border movement, and China's 2016–17 capital outflow controls have led to a glut of property development and a massive drop in sales (Tan and Yong 2017; Vasagar 2017).

The future of private healthcare in Johor and in IM in particular is intimately tied to these much larger property developments and trends, both because private healthcare developers are increasingly the same as property developers (e.g., Khazanah, Thomson Medical, etc.) and because IM's future population growth relies heavily on corporate settlement in IM and the jobs that such settlement generates.

Second, because Johor and IM are not (yet) significant medical tourism destinations, private healthcare providers in the region depend by and large on local residents as their consumer base. Economic forecasts suggest that private providers are at least somewhat buffered from temporary economic downturns in the sense that they do not easily lose their target middle- and upper-class customer bases. Hence, and given the current rate of expansion of existing hospitals and construction of new ones in Johor and specifically in IM, it will be essential to secure local demand.

To do this, the government will need to develop measures that increase the Johor household income base and bring more families into the middle-income bracket as well as to foster interstate migration from within Malaysia that will attract higher-income talent in larger numbers to work, live and play in IM. Improving the liveability of Johor and IM (e.g., reduction of crime rates, transportation infrastructure, etc.) is paramount to the region's success. Safe access to high-quality healthcare and active lifestyle amenities is one step towards making the region more attractive to new residents. While housing is cheap and plentiful, poor transport infrastructure makes the region undesirable, hindering specialist workforce recruitment. Developers need to work more with existing government bodies to create better plans and infrastructure. Public amenities such as schools, green spaces and parks, public activity/assembly halls, market places, local bus and rail services linking different areas of IM and high-speed Internet connection cables would be the cornerstone for creating a feasible and liveable environment for more residents and health workers to stay in IM. Such infrastructure would sustain private healthcare sector growth in the region.

Third, significant deviation from current private healthcare policy, development and promotional practices is unlikely in the foreseeable future and medical tourism is expected to remain a key government interest. To strengthen medical tourism, which could play a major strategic role in filling up Johor private providers' unutilized capacity, private players—both large and small—require greater coordination and cooperation at the state level and perhaps specifically at the SEZ level in promoting medical tourism and in setting up centres of excellence and medical tourist-friendly services that cater to the actual needs of international patients, most of whom are middle-class Indonesians. Relaxing regulations in IM on hiring foreign medical professionals would be useful to draw greater medical expertise to the region and, while it is widely believed in the industry that national and international accreditation (e.g., Malaysia Society for Quality in Healthcare (MSQH) and U.S.-based Joint Commission International (JCI)) are useful tools for attracting foreign patients to hospitals and clinics, the actual significance of such schemes in international patient decision-making remains largely unknown.[10]

Further study is necessary to identify the specific draws of Johor as a medical tourism destination relative to other better established destinations within Malaysia (e.g., Melaka, Klang Valley and Pulau Pinang) and Southeast Asia (e.g., Singapore and Thailand) and the extent to which accreditation schemes are useful in increasing destination prestige and use among specific international patient markets.

Fourth, despite the IM's SEZ status relaxing restrictions on foreign equity (e.g., foreigners can own 100 per cent of equity in private hospitals, specialist medical clinics and specialist dental clinics), the majority of private hospitals in Malaysia and IM are locally owned and/or a result of joint ventures with foreign investors. This suggests there may be barriers to full foreign investment in IM's private healthcare services sector. Since the healthcare industry is highly regulated, there remain challenges for new investors to understand and navigate the approval processes to set up new private healthcare facilities as well as to bring in foreign doctors and practitioners.

In light of these challenges, IRDA has developed a one-stop centre to fast-track the process of obtaining approval and licences for catalytic healthcare-related projects in IM. However, while the privileges and tax exemptions granted to foreign investors have been extended (Musa 2014a), it appears that these continue to be mostly made use of within the scope of foreign-local partnerships. Tracking the impact of these federal fiscal incentives and monitoring actual demand for private-sector capacity are essential to assess the value and utility of such incentives (e.g., return on investment (ROI) for the government), especially given the potential for such incentives policies to promote the generation of excessive private-sector hospital and clinical capacity if left unchecked.

Finally, greater attention should be paid to opportunities to forge greater linkages between IM's healthcare services sector and other health sectors like medical education and biosciences training, medical devices and pharmaceutical product manufacturing as well as other non-health sectors like logistics and information technology in order to create multiplier effects. Given IM's proximity to Singapore and potential for functioning as a strategic overflow site for Singaporean research and development, connections with Singapore's Biopolis should not be overlooked.

Because it is sandwiched between Singapore and Melaka, simply being home to a handful of excellent hospitals cannot propel Johor towards becoming a renowned regional medical care hub. We argue that the confidence of investors, employers, patients and residents in Johor's private healthcare services sector must be boosted by a comprehensive, integrated and well-structured development plan that considers subnational, national and regional demographic, social, economic and political factors.

Notes

1. This chapter was first published as *The Private Healthcare Sector in Johor: Trends and Prospects*, Trends in Southeast Asia, no. 17/2018 (Singapore: ISEAS – Yusof Ishak Institute, 2018).
2. Authors' calculation is based on the data obtained from the Economic Census 2016 (Department of Statistics Malaysia 2017b) and Department of Statistics Malaysia.
3. The PHFSA only covers healthcare services provided in hospitals, clinics and diagnostic centres and, while the CCA covers childcare, rehabilitation centres and elderly care homes, limited enforcement has meant that care quality is highly variable.
4. The difference in the number of hospital institutions is due to different definitions used by the Department of Statistics and Ministry of Health Malaysia.
5. MHTC and the Association of Private Hospitals of Malaysia (APHM) membership affiliation with the Johor hospitals (see Table 5.4) is often seen as an indicator for any private hospital to be considered serious in promoting medical tourism and enhancing the hospital network, respectively. There are currently eight MHTC-affiliated and thirteen APHM-affiliated hospital members in Johor, among them six are affiliated to both. Nevertheless, a few prominent local independent hospitals such as Kempas Medical Centre, Penawar Hospital Pasir Gudang and Putra Specialist Centre Batu Pahat do not hold affiliations to either, suggesting that they have different value proposition, marketing and operational strategies.
6. Two notable exceptions in Johor where doctors have a median of over thirty-five years of experience are Pelangi Medical Centre (38) and Medical Specialist Johor Bahru (35), both being institutions that have long provided niche treatment.
7. Thomson Medical owns hospitals in Indonesia, Malaysia and Singapore.
8. Compulsory personal health savings scheme derived from 8 per cent of an employee's monthly income and that can only be drawn on for health-related payments.
9. In addition to the one in Johor, there is an eighty-eight-bed facility in the Klang Valley and two more are in the pipeline in Johor.
10. Seven Johor private hospitals in Johor were MSQH-accredited as at 3 January 2018 and, while Malaysia has twelve JCI-accredited facilities, only one Johor hospital—KPJ Johor Specialist Hospital—holds JCI accreditation.

References

Aged Care Group. 2016. "About Us". http://agedcare.com.my/about/ (accessed 13 February 2018).

Alfian, H. 2017. "9.6 million Senior Citizens Expected in M'sia by 2050, Why This Is Worrying". *Malaysian Digest*, 31 October 2017. http://malaysiandigest.com/frontpage/282-maintile/705341-malaysia-s-population-is-aging-at-a-rapid-rate-are-we-prepared.html (accessed 13 February 2018).

Association of Private Hospitals of Malaysia. 2018. "APHM Member Hospitals". http://www.hospitals-malaysia.org/portal/eventsasp?menuid=3 (accessed 13 February 2018).

Bernama. 2018. "Tunku Laksamana Johor Cancer Centre operational by end 2020". 1 April 2018. http://bernama.com/en/general/news.php?id=1450029 (accessed 13 April 2018).

Carvalho, M., H. Sivanandam, L. Shagar, and R. Ghazali. 2017. "Bill on Aged Healthcare Services Tabled". *The Star Online*, 24 October 2017. https://www.thestar.com.my/news/nation/2017/10/24/bill-on-aged-healthcare-services-tabled/ (accessed 13 February 2018).

Chee, H.L., and S. Barraclough, eds. 2007. *Health Care in Malaysia: The Dynamics of Provision, Financing and Access*. London: Routledge.

Columbia Asia. 2018. "About Us". https://www.columbiaasia.com/about-us (accessed 13 February 2018).

Commissioner of Law Revision Malaysia. 1993. "Care Centres Act 1993". http://www. commonlii.org/my/legis/consol_act/cca1993121/ (accessed 13 February 2018).

———. 1998. "Private Healthcare Facilities and Services Act 1998". http://www.commonlii. org/my/legis/consol_act/phfasa1998367/ (accessed 13 February 2018).

Daiman. 2015. "Healthcare Beyond Hospitality". 12 June 2015. https://menaralandmark. wordpress.com/2015/06/12/healthcare-beyond-hospitality/ (accessed 13 February 2018).

———. 2016. "Menara Landmark Johor Bahru". 3 October 2016. https://menaralandmark. wordpress.com/2016/10/03/menara-landmark-medical-suites-the-new-specialist-hub-in-johor-bahru/ (accessed 13 February 2018).

Department of Statistics Malaysia. 2017a. "Time Series Table of Mid-Year Population Estimate by State and Sex, Malaysia, 1970–2017". Release date 14 July 2017.

———. 2017b. "Economic Census: Table 2.1 Principal Statistics in Services Sector by Sub-sectors and State of Johor, 2015". Release date 22 December 2017.

E&O Bhd. 2016. "Annual Report". https://www.easternandoriental.com/uploads/annual-reports/EO_AR_2016.pdf (accessed 13 February 2018).

The Edge Property. 2015a. "From Industrial to Wellness Concept Projects". 8 April 2015. https:// www.edgeprop.my/content/industrial-wellness-concept-projects (accessed 13 February 2018).

———. 2015b. "Iskandar Malaysia Making Progress". 11 May 2015. https:// www.edgeprop. my/content/iskandar-malaysia-making-progress (accessed 13 February 2018).

Emerich, M.M. 2011. *The Gospel of Sustainability: Media, Market and LOHAS*. Urbana-Champaign: University of Illinois Press,

Gawande, A. 2014. *Being Mortal: Illness, Medicine and What Matters in the End*. New York: Picador.

HMI. 2017. "4Q17 Results Presentation". 24 August 2017. http://hmi.com. sg/index.php/ highlights/4q2017-results-presentation/ (accessed 13 February 2018).

Ibrahim, P. and M. Ali. 2013. "Foreign Direct Investment Affluences in Iskandar Malaysia".

IHH. 2017. "Expanding Opportunities, Consolidating Strengths: Annual Report 2016". http://www.insage.com.my/ir/cmn/downloading.aspx?sFileName=17118000023463&s ReportType=AR&sCompanyC ode=IHH (accessed 13 February 2018).

Iskandar Regional Development Authority (IRDA). 2014. "Smart City Iskandar Malaysia". http://www.iskandarmalaysia.com.my/SCIM/ (accessed 13 February 2018).

———. 2016a. "Iskandar Malaysia 10-year Progress Report". http://iskandarmalaysia.com. my/downloads/IM10%20Progress%20Report_V5.pdf (accessed 13 February 2018).

———. 2016b. "Healthcare". http://iskandarmalaysia.com.my/healthcare/ (accessed 13 February 2018).

———. 2016c. "Our Development Plan". http://iskandarmalaysia.com.my/our-development-plan/ (accessed 13 February 2018).

———. 2016d. "Healthcare @ Iskandar Malaysia: Opportunities in Private Healthcare in Iskandar Malaysia". *IM BizWatch*, April 2016. http://iskandarmalaysia.com.my/ wp-content/uploads/2016/06/IM_BizWatch_April_2016_Special_Edition_Healthcare.01. pdf

Iskandarian, The. 2017. "March Drill: Rahani Yaacob – General Manager". 16 March 2017. http://www.theiskandarian.com/web/march-drill-rahani-yaacob-general-manager-columbia-asia-hospital-iskandar-puteri/ (accessed 13 February 2018).

Jaipragas, B. 2017. "Malaysia's Forest City Adds Traditional Chinese Medicine to Its Grant Plan". *South China Morning Post*, 4 August 2017. http://www.scmp.com/week-asia/article/2105507/malaysias-forest-city-adds-traditional-chinese-medicine-its-grand-plan (accessed 13 February 2018).

Khairani, A.N. 2017. "Retirement Planning: 'Malaysians Need a Wake-up Call'". *The Edge Markets*, 22 November 2017. http://www.theedgemarkets.com/article/retirement-planning-malaysians-need-wakeup-call (accessed 13 February 2018).

Khoo, D. 2016. "Khazanah Realises Value in IHH". *The Star Online*, 2 June 2016. https://www.thestar.com.my/business/business-news/2016/06/02/khazanah-realises-value-in-ihh/ (accessed 13 February 2018).

KPJ. 2017. "2016 Annual Report". http://kpj.listedcompany.com/misc/ar2016.pdf (accessed 13 February 2018).

Lai, L. 2016. "Thomson Medical to Build Hospital in JB". *Straits Times*, 27 December 2016. http://www.straitstimes.com/singapore/health/thomson-medical-to-build-hospital-in-jb (accessed 13 February 2018).

Lee, X.E. 2017. "TCM Hospital, Co-working Spaces and Data Centre For Forest City as It Struggles to Keep up Home Sales". *Straits Times*, 4 August 2017. http://www.straitstimes.com/business/traditional-chinese-medicine-hospital-co-working-spaces-and-a-data-centre-for-johors-forest (accessed 13 February 2018).

Lim, Meng Kin. 2010. "Extension of Medisave for Overseas Hospitalisation". *Health Policy Monitor*, October 2010. http://www.hpm.org/survey/sg/a16/1 (accessed 13 February 2018).

Loh, J. 2014. "Daiman, Former Sunrise Owners Plan RM1.4bil Publika-style project in Johor". *The Star Online*, 10 May 2014. https://www.thestar.com.my/business/business-news/2014/05/10/daiman-plans-rm14b-johor-project-former-sunrise-owners-eye-publikastyle-development/#QALQSHdZECpHaUSI.99 (accessed 13 February 2018).

Malaysia Healthcare Travel Council (MHTC). 2018. "Elite Partner Membership and MHTC Ordinary Members". https://www.mhtc.org.my/services/mhtc-partners/ (accessed 13 February 2018).

Malaysian Medical Council. 2018a. "Medical Register". http://www.mmc.gov.my/index.php/medical-register (accessed 13 February 2018).

———. 2018B. "National Specialist Register". https://www.nsr.org.my/list1.html (accessed 13 February 2018).

Malaysian Industrial Development Finance (MIDF). 2016. "Healthcare: Resilient Amidst Cost Pressures". MIDF Research, 30 September 2016. http://www.midf.com.my/images/Downloads/Research/Sector/Healthcare/Healthcare-Resilient-amidst-cost-pressure-MIDF-300916.pdf (accessed 13 February 2018).

Malaysian Investment Development Authority (MIDA). 2011. "Incentives for Service Sectors". http://www.mida.gov.my/env3/uploads/Services/IncentivesSept2011.pdf (accessed 13 February 2018).

Malaysian Parliament. 2017. "Private Aged Healthcare Facilities and Services Bill 2017". http://www.cljlaw.com/files/bills/pdf/2017/MY_FS_BIL_2017_35.pdf (accessed 13 February 2018).

Marini M.S. 2017. "Medical Travel Statistics". Malaysia Healthcare Travel Council (MHTC),

Insight 2017: "Malaysia Healthcare: Going Beyond", Kuala Lumpur, 27 September 2017. https://www.mhtc.org.my/insigHT2017/ (accessed 13 February 2018).

Ministry of Health, Malaysia. 2017. "Health Indicators 2009–2017". http://www.moh.gov.my/english.php/pages/view/56 (accessed 13 February 2018).

———. 2018. "Malaysian Health Data Warehouse (MyHDW)". https://myhdw.moh.gov.my/public/home (accessed 13 February 2018).

Ministry of Health, Singapore. 2010. "Medisave for Approved Overseas Hospitalisation". 10 February 2010. https://www.moh.gov.sg/ content/moh_web/home/pressRoom/pressRoomItemRelease/2010/Medisave_for_Approved_Overseas_Hospitalisation.html (accessed 13 February 2018).

Musa, Z. 2014a. "Medini Gets 10-year Extension on Special Tax Holidays and More". *The Star Online*, 31 March 2014. https://www.thestar.com.my/business/business-news/2014/03/31/incentives-for-medini-to-continue-10year-extension-for-special-tax-holidays-and-other-packages-for-i/#8dJPpMp6Y4sH47Ew.99 (accessed 13 February 2018).

———. 2014b. "New Hospital in Pasir Gudang". *Star Online*, 23 October 2014. https://www.thestar.com.my/news/community/2014/10/23/new-hospital-in-pasir-gudang/ (accessed 13 February 2018).

New Straits Times. 2017. "2018 Budget: Medical Tourism Set to Grow". 27 October 2017. https://www.nst.com.my/news/nation/2017/10/296023/2018-budget-medical-tourism-set-grow (accessed 13 February 2018).

Ormond, M. 2013. *Neoliberal Governance and International Medical Travel in Malaysia*. Abingdon: Routledge.

———. 2014. "Resorting to Plan J: Popular Perceptions of Singaporean Retirement Migration to Johor, Malaysia". *Asian and Pacific Migration Journal* 23, no. 1: 1–26.

Othman, A.F. 2017. "Growing Population Spurs Demand in Iskandar Malaysia". *New Straits Times*, 20 April 2017. https://www.nst.com.my/property/2017/04/232342/growing-population-spurs-demand-iskandar-malaysia (accessed 13 February 2018).

Pemandu (Performance Management Delivery Unit). 2013a. "EPP 10: Setting up Wellness Resorts". http://etp.pemandu.gov.my/Wholesales_-%E2%97%98-_Retail-@-Wholesale_and_Retail_-_EPP_10-;_Setting_Up_Wellness_Resorts.aspx (accessed 13 February 2018).

———. 2013b. "Healthcare". http://etp.pemandu.gov.my/Healthcare-@-Healthcare.aspx (accessed 13 February 2018).

———. 2014. "Eden-on-the-Park Integrated Senior Active Lifestyle and Care Residence Resort". http://etp.pemandu.gov.my/26_June_2014-@-Eden-on-the-Park_Integrated_Senior_Active_Lifestyle_and_Care_Residence_Resort.aspx (accessed 13 February 2018).

Rao, M. 2017. "IJN, PNB to Open JB Heart Centre". *The Malaysian Reserve*, 16 August 2017. https://themalaysianreserve.com/2017/08/16/ijn-pnb-open-jb-heart-centre/ (accessed 13 February 2018).

Rowsley Ltd. 2017. "Annual Report 2016". http://infopub.sgx.com/FileOpen/Rowsley%20Annual%20Report%202016_20170411.ashx?App=Prospectus&FileID=31479 (accessed 13 February 2018).

Ruhaini binti Haji Zawawi. 2013. "Active Ageing in Malaysia". The 2nd Meeting of the Committee on International Cooperation on Active Ageing, 19 July 2013. http://www.mhlw.go.jp/stf/shingi/2r98520000036yla-att/2r98520000036yqa_1.pdf (accessed 13 February 2018).

Tan, S.M., and Y. Yong. 2017. "Cover Story: China's Liquidity Squeeze Casts Shadow over Iskandar Malaysia". *The Edge Malaysia*, 25 May 2017 http://www.theedgemarkets. com/article/cover-story-chinas-liquidity-squeeze-casts-shadow-over-iskandar-malaysia (accessed 13 February 2018).

Vasagar, J. 2017. "Iskandar: 'Malaysia's Shenzhen' Takes Shape". *Financial Times*, 2 July 2017. https://www.ft.com/content/5b57aa20-40fe-11e7-9d56-25f963e998b2 (accessed 18 June 2018).

Whang, R. 2015a. "Patients Can Use Medisave at Gleneagles Medini". *Straits Times*, 11 December 2015. http://www.straitstimes.com/business/companies-markets/patients-can-use-medisave-at-gleneagles-medini (accessed 13 February 2018).

———. 2015b. "Up Next at Iskandar Malaysia: A Snow World Theme Park and an Opera House". *Straits Times*, 21 January 2015. http://www. straitstimes.com/business/up-next-at-iskandar-malaysia-a-snow-world-theme-park-and-an-opera-house (accessed 13 February 2018).

———, and J. Lim. 2016. "Iskandar's Challenges, 10 Years On". *Straits Times*, 10 February 2016. http://www.straitstimes.com/business/iskandars-challenges-10-years-on (accessed 13 February 2018).

6

EDUCITY, JOHOR
Its Promise and Challenges

Chang-Da Wan and Benedict Weerasena[1]

INTRODUCTION

Private higher education in Malaysia has seen robust growth since the introduction of the Private Higher Education Institutions Act (1996) (Act 555), which legalized these institutions. To transform Malaysia into a global higher education hub, as first outlined by the National Higher Education Strategic Plan (2007–20), the government has sought to offer a wide range of courses and programmes through private universities and colleges as well as international branch campuses with competitive tuition fees.

This chapter examines the development of EduCity, an integrated learning hub situated in Iskandar Malaysia in the state of Johor. The idea for an integrated learning hub built around multiple universities was first hatched in 2007, and in 2011 the first institution moved in. In exploring the challenges and underlying issues involved, this chapter aims to shed light on the private higher education sector in the country in general.

Several site visits were made to the EduCity campus and to the temporary city campus. On 17–23 August 2017, we conducted interviews with academics and administrators in the various universities and with policymakers. In addition, policy documents from the Malaysian government, Johor State government, Iskandar Regional Development Authority, and the respective universities were consulted.

The chapter first outlines how EduCity was conceptualized and discusses the role of EduCity Iskandar Sdn Bhd (EISB) as the "driver" and "owner" of EduCity.

It then studies the huge challenges that the creation of an integrated learning hub involves.

JOHOR AND ISKANDAR MALAYSIA

Over the past five decades, the economic structure of Johor has evolved substantially. The state started off as an agriculture-based economy, as its flat and fertile land was well suited for the production of primary products for export such as palm oil, rubber, pineapple and coffee. But faced with volatile commodity prices in the 1980s, Johor sought to develop its manufacturing sector (Hutchinson 2012).

The Economic Plan for Johor (1990–2005) advocated greater commercialization of agriculture and encouraged more knowledge- and capital-intensive industries (UPEN Johor 1989). In the subsequent Johor Operational Master Plan (1996–2010), the service sector was added as a target growth area. This highlighted strategic investment in infrastructure and skill provision to foster high-value services (RMA Perunding Bersatu 1996).

The Iskandar Malaysia Comprehensive Development Plan (CDP) was launched in 2006, with the aim of creating "A Strong and Sustainable Metropolis of International Standing". The CDP covers the southern region of Johor, and it sought to advance the economy from being manufacturing-based to being services-based (Hutchinson 2012). Electrical and electronics, petrochemical, oil and gas, food and agro-processing, logistics and tourism were selected as core sectors. Finance, insurance, real estate and business services (FIREBS), the creative industry, health services and education services were identified as major emerging sectors. The horizontal and vertical linkages across these industries were to constitute a complete economic ecosystem for Johor.

To correspond with the federal administration's Government Transformation Programme and Economic Transformation Programme and to factor in the challenges raised by the Global Financial Crisis, the CDP was reviewed; and the CDPii 2014–2025 was subsequently launched. According to a review of performance indicators within this framework, education services contributed 2 per cent to gross output, 5 per cent to value-added services and 5 per cent to employment by 2011 (Iskandar Regional Development Authority 2014). Iskandar Malaysia is being marketed as a regional education hub with twenty colleges and institutions of higher learning within EduCity, Bandar Seri Alam and Bandar Dato' Onn. The latter two hubs are predominantly made up of local colleges and institutions of higher education, while EduCity is an integrated learning hub with branch campuses of international colleges and universities.

IMAGINING EDUCITY

EduCity, developed by EISB, also promotes Malaysia as a centre of educational excellence in line with the main objectives of the Ninth Malaysia Plan. In addition, it is considered an Entry Point Project (EPP) under the Economic Transformation

Programme. As the 11th EPP for the education sector, EduCity is expected to contribute RM1 billion to the Gross National Income, and is projected to create 1,100 jobs by the year 2020 (*The Edge*, 31 January 2011).

This 305-acre fully integrated education hub is located within Nusajaya (Flagship Zone B of Iskandar Malaysia), adjacent to Medini Iskandar which is the central business district of Iskandar Puteri. EduCity is accessible via the Coastal Highway that links Medini to Johor Bahru city centre and to the Tuas Customs, Immigration and Quarantine Complex (CIQ) in Singapore. Iskandar Malaysia as a whole seeks to become a "Strong and Sustainable Metropolis of International Standing" by leveraging on its close proximity to Singapore, and EduCity tries to make the most of its strategic location. In fact, EduCity is situated less than 30 minutes away from Singapore via the Tuas Second Link, and is also within a six-hour flight radius of major Asian cities.

EduCity aims to become a best-in-class higher education destination, providing an avenue for local Malaysian students to pursue tertiary education and obtain foreign qualifications at an affordable price without leaving their home soil. Indirectly, EduCity can potentially slow the flow of Malaysians going overseas for their tertiary education and subsequently remaining abroad.

EduCity is also meant to become a feeder system for the economic pillars of Iskandar Malaysia, and contribute to Malaysia's aspiration of becoming a regional hub for education by providing relevant talent for economic activities in Iskandar Malaysia. High-tech companies based in Johor, such as Dyson, Lloyd's Register and BAE Systems, are being encouraged to employ students from EduCity institutions. Furthermore, EduCity is also intended to be a catalyst for the development of Iskandar Malaysia, once its economic and demographic impact spills over to surrounding areas.

Currently, EduCity comprises the following higher education institutions (see Map 2.9):

- Kolej MDIS Malaysia (MDIS)
- Multimedia University (MMU)
- Netherlands Maritime Institute of Technology (NMIT)
- Newcastle University Medicine Malaysia (NUMed)
- Raffles University Iskandar (RUI)
- University of Reading Malaysia (UoRM)
- University of Southampton Malaysia Campus (USMC)

When the idea of EduCity was first suggested, different institutions were to offer programmes in an area of specialist expertise, with a pre-agreed exclusivity clause. In other words, certain institutions were to enjoy a monopoly on delivering EduCity-based programmes in a particular subject area for a number of years. For instance, only NUMed was permitted to offer programmes in medicine, and only the USMC may offer courses in the engineering sciences.

THE ROLE OF EDUCITY ISKANDAR SDN BHD

EISB was incorporated in 2007 and is solely owned by Iskandar Investment Berhad (IIB), while IIB is co-owned by Khazanah Nasional Berhad, Employees' Provident Fund and Kumpulan Prasarana Rakyat Johor. Khazanah Nasional Berhad is the biggest shareholder. IIB was established in 2006 as a catalytic developer for Iskandar Malaysia, while EISB functions as the catalytic driver for education.

EISB seeks to create a superior urban environment to attract local and international students and visitors (Iskandar Investment n.d.; Zazali 2009). As such, they see themselves as a facility provider first and foremost. In 2008 when the project first took off, EISB was predominantly development-driven. They built and completed the roads, street lighting, turfing and landscape, and constructed some of the buildings. Kolej MDIS Malaysia and Raffles University Iskandar (RUI) bought land from EISB to construct their own buildings and facilities, but the buildings used by other institutions are leased. EISB constructed buildings according to specifications provided by each institution, and leases them out over a period of twelve, fifteen or thirty years. The management and operation of each building is left to the institution concerned.

EISB is also responsible for the outer structures and shared facilities between institutions, and hence EISB sees itself as a facility driver, providing the necessary real estate and amenities for the smooth running of EduCity. Among the shared facilities under the management of EISB are an international student village, student accommodation, a sports complex featuring a 6,000-seat stadium with a Grade 2 International Association of Athletics Federations (IAAF) track and football pitch, a 1,500-seat indoor arena, a 500-seat aquatic centre with an Olympic-sized swimming pool, and several outdoor courts.

However, as the infrastructure development of EduCity reached a relatively mature phase, EISB began to see itself as a partner to the institutions in bringing in students, and to ensuring that students receive a good learning experience. In this respect, EISB is focusing on promoting a livelier social environment and on creating spaces for students from the different institutions in EduCity. Among the key initiatives undertaken by EISB are being the liaison for the EduCity Student Council, which has representatives from all the student councils on the campus, as well as creating a common student area or complex within EduCity.

The role of EISB, ideally, is also to act as a base to unite all the institutions in the campus. In addition, EISB coordinates the marketing and promotion for EduCity where EISB strives to advertise EduCity as a whole without focusing on individual programmes offered or institutions present. To achieve this, EISB invites all partners to participate in its promotional activities and ensures information on each institution is available for the international marketing fairs in which they participate, such as the ones conducted in China, South Korea and Kazakhstan. The belief is that when one institution prospers, the whole of EduCity will attain a greater level of success. As part of its Corporate Social Responsibility (CSR) initiatives, EISB provides monetary incentives amounting to RM1,000 to the best student in each programme across EduCity.

After almost a decade, EISB has seen its role evolve from a mere facility and infrastructure developer into an entity that both shapes the learning experience and environment for students in EduCity and manages a multi-institution organization of higher education. Hence, the current roles of EISB are somewhat blurred, overlapping and difficult to define, and in a state of flux. Nevertheless, the ways in which the roles of EISB evolve will have an important bearing on the future direction of EduCity in moving forward.

THE CURRENT STATUS OF EDUCITY AND THE INSTITUTIONS

EduCity targets having 16,000 students by 2025; and as of January 2017, it has more than 3,500 students enrolled.[2] For comparison, only 530 students were enrolled in 2012. Of those enrolled in January 2017, about 2 per cent are international students, mainly from the ASEAN region, South Asia and selected countries in Africa. Most of the Malaysians who make up 98 per cent of the student population are from Johor.

Newcastle University Medicine Malaysia (NUMed) is the branch campus of Newcastle University in Malaysia, specializing in medicine and biomedical sciences. NUMed was the first institution to move into its own campus in EduCity, which it did in 2011 on a lease agreement from IIB. It is wholly owned by Newcastle University. Currently 670 students are enrolled in the institution, 550 of whom are in the medicine programme. To date, NUMed has had four cohorts of medical students and two cohorts of students in the biomedical sciences. Of the students enrolled in NUMed, 10 per cent are international students. NUMed has about eighty academic staff members, almost a quarter of whom are from the United Kingdom while 15 per cent are from Malaysia. The rest of the academic staff are most notably from the Philippines, Myanmar and India.

Netherlands Maritime Institute of Technology (NMIT) is a joint venture between a local entrepreneur and the Dutch government, and specializes in the "dry side" of the maritime industry, such as port management, logistical support and law. It welcomed its first intake of 240 students in 2011 at its temporary city campus located in Johor Bahru. By 2012, the institution had moved to its permanent campus in EduCity's Multi-Varsity Complex. This complex houses several institutions, each with its own building with joint facilities. In other words, it is an integrated mini-campus within EduCity. As of 2017, NMIT has supported nearly 2,000 students in their pursuit of maritime education.

Multimedia University (MMU) Faculty of Cinematic Arts is another institution located in the Multi-Varsity Complex. This MMU branch campus houses a single faculty, unlike its two other campuses in Cyberjaya and Melaka. Due to the fact that it is only a single faculty with two programmes and that the faculty specializes in a highly niche area, the student population has been growing at a much slower pace. However, the relocation of this faculty from its Cyberjaya campus to EduCity has been driven by a strategic consideration: that of being located nearer to the creative industry in Iskandar Malaysia which comprises leading players like the Pinewood

Iskandar Studios. Currently, MMU in EduCity has 170 students, of whom twelve are international students. There are eight academic staff members, of whom four are Malaysian.

University of Southampton Malaysia Campus (USMC) is also housed in the Multi-Varsity Complex. It is wholly owned by University of Southampton in the United Kingdom and offers only programmes in engineering. This institution has 250 students with an estimated twelve to fifteen international students. The relatively smaller number of students is due to the fact that USMC only has students pursuing the foundation programme and the first two years of the undergraduate programmes. For the remaining two years, students of USMC move to University of Southampton in the United Kingdom. It has twenty-five academics with six international lecturers, of whom three are seconded from the United Kingdom.

University of Reading Malaysia (UoRM), like NUMed, has its own campus within EduCity through a lease agreement with IIB. Like the other two UK universities, UoRM is wholly owned by its mother university, in this case the University of Reading. This institution started out in the temporary city campus and only moved to EduCity recently. At the moment, UoRM is the most comprehensive institution in EduCity offering programmes in sciences, applied sciences and social sciences. It also has a branch of its business school on site. In addition, it is the only institution in EduCity to offer doctoral programmes in four areas of study. Currently it has about 550 students and this number is expected to increase to 900 by 2018. Out of the 550 students, 95 per cent are Malaysian, two-thirds of whom are from Johor. Of the sixty academic staff, 40 per cent are from a range of countries including Iran, Italy, France, the Philippines, Bangladesh, and the United Kingdom (specifically Reading).

Kolej MDIS Malaysia (MDIS) and Raffles University Iskandar (RUI) are the two institutions which have purchased part of EduCity to construct their own full-fledged campus. The construction of the MDIS campus in EduCity is almost complete and the institution is expecting 2,000 students when it moves into the new campus with its own accommodation and sports facilities. In the meantime, it operates in the temporary city campus. MDIS is owned by a Singapore corporation and the campus in EduCity is its second international branch campus outside Singapore. MDIS's niche is in providing professional and lifelong education in applied areas of management at the diploma level. It offers a franchised Bachelor's programme of the University of Wolverhampton in EduCity.

RUI is a joint venture between Raffles Education Corporation Limited from Singapore and EISB (Raffles University Iskandar 2017). It is one of the two institutions operating in the temporary city campus and has purchased a piece of land in EduCity on which to build its own campus. Construction of the RUI campus in EduCity has not started and the institution seems likely to continue its operation from the temporary city campus, with recent initiatives to upgrade existing facilities such as studios and laboratories. Currently, RUI has an enrolment of 400 students. Most of them are from Johor. Only 10 of the 400 students are foreign. RUI has twenty-two academic full time academic staff members and thirty part-timers.

Tables 6.1 and 6.2 list the programmes offered by institutions in EduCity as well as their fee structure.

EDUCITY@ISKANDAR MALAYSIA—A STRATEGIC LOCATION?

One major benefit of the close proximity to Singapore is the possibility of tapping into the Singaporean student market. At EduCity, it is possible for students to obtain a British qualification with lower tuition and living costs due to the favourable exchange rate of the Malaysian ringgit in relation to major foreign currencies. In addition, institutions in EduCity can also leverage on Singaporean companies and industries to offer training, consultancy and short courses at a more reasonable cost and with the benefit of geographical proximity.

However, for some of these institutions the close proximity poses a challenge, since they have to compete for students and academic staff with the two top universities in Asia, namely the National University of Singapore (NUS) and Nanyang Technological University (NTU). This makes it particularly difficult to attract students into programmes with high academic entry requirements.

Apart from Singapore, EduCity also has to contend with competition from private higher education institutions in Kuala Lumpur. Given the concentration of private institutions in the capital of Malaysia, which offers students a better social environment outside the classroom, the less vibrant social environment in EduCity has, to some extent, been an obstacle to student recruitment. There remains a lack of food and beverage options and entertainment outlets in EduCity and in Nusajaya in general. Limited connectivity, due to the absence of public transportation, has also been a challenge for EduCity in its bid to live up to its selling point of providing a holistic educational experience for students.

Attracting academic staff to work in EduCity has also been a challenge for some institutions. Like the challenge of attracting students, EduCity's close proximity to Singapore can be a disadvantage in terms of the more favourable Singapore dollar as compared to the Malaysian ringgit. Furthermore, some academic staff also have difficulties adjusting to life in Nusajaya, an area still undergoing major development. Particularly for foreign academic staff, the lack of expatriate clubs and associations has further added to the difficulties in making these academic staff feel at home.

Thus, like a double-edged sword, the location of EduCity poses some strategic advantages to institutions in terms of recruiting students and academic staff, but there is also the challenge of providing an urban environment.

EDUCITY AND LOCAL DEVELOPMENT

EduCity has been relatively successful in providing opportunities for Johoreans to access not only higher education but, more specifically, foreign higher education without leaving the state. This has been reflected in the fact that across all the institutions, Johoreans make up the bulk of the students.

TABLE 6.1
Programme by Level across Institutions in EduCity

Institution	Foundation	Certificate	Diploma	Bachelor	Postgraduate Certificate	Master	Doctorate
Kolej MDIS Malaysia	Business & Technology, Science	English	Business Management, International Business Accounting, Marketing, Mass Communication, Information Technology, Tourism Management	Event Management,[a] Business Management,[a] International Business[a]	Nil	Nil	Nil
Multimedia University	Cinematic Arts	Nil	Nil	Cinematic Arts	Nil	Nil	Nil
Netherlands Maritime Institute of Technology	Nil	Nil	Maritime Transportation Management, Shipping Management, Port Management, Maritime Law, Maritime Occupational Safety & Health	Nil	Nil	Nil	Nil
Newcastle University Medicine Malaysia	Biological & Biomedical Sciences	Nil	Nil	Medicine & Surgery, Biomedical Sciences	Cancer Studies, Medical Education	Clinical Research, Oncology, Palliative Care, Oncology for Pharmaceutical Industry	Nil

Raffles University Iskandar	Business, Liberal Arts	Nil	Business, Interior Design, Visual Communication	Nil	Multimedia Design, Graphic Design, Interior Design, Fashion Design, Business Administration, Accountancy, Supply Chain Management, Psychology	Nil	Business Administration	Nil
University of Reading Malaysia	Business, Science	English	Nil	Nil	Finance & Business, Management & Business, Accounting & Finance, Real Estate, Quantity Surveying, Construction Management, Psychology, Pharmacy[b]	Nil	Investment Banking & Islamic Finance, Business Administration	Built Environment, Pharmacy, Psychology, Business & Management
University of Southampton Malaysia Campus	Engineering	Nil	Nil	Nil	Aeronautics & Astronautics Engineering,[b] Mechanical Engineering,[b] Electrical & Electronic Engineering[b]	Nil	Nil	Nil

Notes: Nil = No programme offered.
a. Offers by University of Wolverhampton, UK.
b. This programme is a four-year (2+2) twinning Bachelor's degree.
Source: Websites of all institutions.

TABLE 6.2
Fee Structure of Programmes per annum across Institutions in EduCity (2017/18)

Institution	Foundation	Certificate	Diploma	Bachelor	Postgraduate Certificate	Master	Doctorate
Kolej MDIS Malaysia Multimedia University	NA RM13,200 (RM16,500)	NA Nil	NA Nil	NA RM20,000 (RM25,000) Additional RM2,700 (RM14,925) as admission fees	NA Nil	NA Nil	NA Nil
Netherlands Maritime Institute of Technology	Nil	Nil	RM21,200– RM35,200	Nil	Nil	Nil	Nil
Newcastle University Medicine Malaysia	RM26,000 (RM29,380)	Nil	Nil	RM40,240–RM95,000 (RM44,100–RM105,000)	GBP2,700	GBP4,980– GBP5,400	Nil
Raffles University Iskandar	NA	NA	NA	NA	NA	NA	NA
University of Reading Malaysia	RM19,000– RM21,650 (RM22,000– RM24,875)	NA	Nil	RM36,750–RM37,900 (RM43,500–RM54,000) RM46,250 (RM52,500)[a]	Nil	RM44,750– RM77,250 (RM51,500– RM77,250)	RM48,000 (RM52,250) 45% discount if students pursue the course on part-time basis
University of Southampton Malaysia Campus	RM27,200 (RM32,100)	Nil	Nil	RM48,700 (RM55,400)	Nil	Nil	Nil

Notes: Figure in parentheses for international students; Nil = No programme offered; NA = Not available.
a. Fees for twinning programme in Malaysia. For the second part of the programme, students will pay international fees in GBP.
All fees have been converted to "per annum", and if there is more than one fee-structure for multiple programmes at the same level, a range will be reported.
Source: UoRM website, NUMed website, MMU website, USMC booklet, Edverty.my website for NMIT.

In this regard, it is important to highlight the efforts that have been made by NMIT. This institution mainly focuses on diploma-level programmes in the maritime field, specifically the dry side of the industry. Therefore, it has invested in recruiting students from rural Johor, particularly targeting the ethnic Malay community. With financial support from Majlis Amanah Rakyat (MARA) and the National Higher Education Fund Corporation (PTPTN), these students obtain the necessary qualifications for them to work in the two international seaports of Johor, namely Johor Port and the Port of Tanjung Pelepas, and in other parts of Malaysia and in Singapore.

The development of Iskandar Malaysia comprises nine pillars—agro-processing, oil and gas, electrical and electronics, education, finance, healthcare, creative, logistics and tourism. The most direct contribution that EduCity can make may be in education but the individual institutions can also leverage on these sectors to play a bigger role beyond just talent development. For instance, NMIT can leverage on its Dutch connection to develop the logistics sector, given that the Netherlands is a world leader in logistics. Through its niche in engineering and British connection, USMC is well positioned to develop closer collaboration with leading British businesses like Dyson and Lloyds' Registrar. As illustrated earlier, MMU Faculty of Cinematic Arts is also poised to work more closely with Pinewood Iskandar Studios as the leading industry player for the creative sector in Iskandar Malaysia. While NUMed currently has clinical arrangements for its students with public hospitals in Johor Bahru and neighbouring districts, there is potential for it to extend beyond teaching and clinical training into research and development with hospitals and healthcare providers in strengthening the healthcare sector underlined by Iskandar Malaysia.

Although there is vast potential for institutions in EduCity to play their part beyond education and talent development, it is important to point out that many of these institutions are still young and in the midst of developing their academic programmes. For instance, USMC has just graduated their first cohort of students, and some programmes in UoRM are just about to begin recruiting the first cohort of students. Thus, the research and service component across these institutions are understandably underdeveloped, and research and development as well as industrial collaboration and community engagement remain secondary priorities.

MARKET FORCES AT PLAY

While EduCity is intended to be a catalytic driver for the economic development of Iskandar Malaysia, through talent development as well as benefits accruing from the spillover effect of an education hub, it is in turn also susceptible to market forces. The development of EduCity, especially with regard to its facilities and infrastructure, has to be sensitive to both demand and supply. EISB and the institutions can project certain levels of demand and supply, but utilization and sustainability undoubtedly will depend on actual demand.

The development of facilities in EduCity, such as accommodation, is also highly sensitive to demand. At the moment, the occupancy rate for the 800-bed accommodation has been approximately 75 per cent. And even while there are plans in the pipeline to construct another accommodation block to house the projected increase of students enrolling in EduCity, many of the current students are already opting to stay in the surrounding areas, including the neighbouring zone of Gelang Patah, due to lower prices and fewer residential requirements.

Thus, as a whole, the provision of facilities and support services faces a Catch-22 situation. Should these provisions be supplied to anticipate the projected demand, or should supply only be provided when the demand is present? At the moment, the situation seems to be the latter, and as a result there have been some complaints from students and staff concerning facilities and support services, such as the lack of variety in food and beverage outlets, accommodation, space for social activities and so on. Even with a well-equipped sports complex that opens once a week for free to the students, the relatively high costs for utilizing the facilities have been a barrier to some students and staff. For EduCity to become a complete integrated learning hub, the provision of facilities and support services is as crucial as the quality of academic programmes provided. There is tremendous room for improvement in the former.

ACADEMIC COORDINATION

Ideally, EduCity should be seen as a comprehensive university and the various institutions as faculties or schools. In this "university", the Faculty of Medicine and Biomedical Sciences is operated by NUMed, the Faculty of Engineering by USMC, the Faculty of Business and Social Sciences by UoRM, the Faculty of Design by RUI, the Faculty of Maritime by NMIT, the Faculty of Arts and Cinematic by MMU, and the Faculty of Foundational Studies by MDIS. Importantly, for this ideal concept to become a reality, some form of coordination is needed, especially across the institutions.

However, such coordination is missing. EduCity may not be a higher education institution with award-granting authority as each of the institutions based there award their own respective diplomas and degrees. All that is needed then, is a common academic direction and coordination if EduCity is to develop as a whole.

Currently, whatever academic coordination there is in EduCity is rather ad hoc. The relationship between EISB and the individual institutions is similar to a partner relationship—or, more specifically, a landlord and tenant in terms of the academic facilities. All academic matters are left purely to the institutions. Furthermore, the inter-institution relationship is also conducted on a piecemeal basis, and almost every representative of the institutions has highlighted some degree of difficulty in terms of academic coordination.

One of the main issues concerns the exclusivity clause. While every institution in EduCity has been invited to become part of this project in a particular niche area, there remain a number of niches and specializations that are undefined. For instance, UoRM, RUI and MDIS offer programmes in business (see Table 6.1). Both UoRM and RUI offer Foundation in Business, while MDIS also offers Foundation in Business and Technology. At the degree and postgraduate levels, these three universities also compete with one another for prospective students in the field of business. UoRM offers BA Management and Business, RUI offers Bachelor of Business Administration (Hons.), while MDIS offers BA (Hons.) Business Management through twinning arrangements with the University of Wolverhampton. This overlap in programmes also happens at the postgraduate level between RUI and UoRM's Henley Business School, where both offer a Master's degree in Business Administration.

It is unclear if the exclusivity clause has been breached, because although each institution signed individual agreements with EISB in an agreed area of expertise, the details of the arrangements are not made known to the other institutions. If they were, then it may have been an easy matter for the institutions to agree on an initial course offering, with leeway given to the offering of other programmes further down the road. Furthermore, it is unclear to what extent EISB has legal authority and right to act when there is a breach of the exclusivity clause, due to the fact that programme registration is agreed to between the institution and the Ministry of Higher Education and Malaysian Qualifications Agency, and not with EISB.

At present, there is a sense of competition between the institutions, making academic coordination almost impossible on many different levels. Institutions have become divided into cliques, to the point that some have chosen to stay away from collaborative marketing fairs and ad hoc partners' meetings because they have begun to see other institutions in EduCity as competitors.

As a result, several institutions are now embarking on their own promotional activities, holding open days and participating in educational fairs as individual universities and not as part of EduCity. This is problematic. EduCity is supposed to be a destination, and all marketing and promotional efforts should be anchored under the EduCity brand, and not occur in a piecemeal fashion. Intensified individual promotional efforts will only reinforce stronger competition between the institutions, making the learning experience a far cry from the initial ideals of EduCity. The lack of coordination has also pushed institutions to focus on their own academic direction. Students as well as academics are unable to cross their disciplinary boundaries to learn and conduct research. For instance, an engineering student at USMC will not be able to attend any courses in cinematic arts at MMU or maritime-related courses at NMIT. No doubt, there have been some positive changes in this respect ever since the three British institutions began to explore some forms of collaboration such as allowing students to do language courses at UoRM, with NUMed and USMC not needing to duplicate these courses.

Having initially secured the commitment and participation of world-renowned universities, EISB seems at this moment to be taking a hands-off approach towards coordinating these institutions. But as noted by an institutional leader, the absence of an active umbrella body to coordinate the direction of the institutions towards a common goal will remain the biggest obstacle to EduCity becoming the "best-in-class" higher education destination it set out to be.

A DIVIDED AND REGIMENTED ENVIRONMENT

Another issue to consider is the fact that the environment and landscape on the campus is also fairly divided. Institutions that have their own compounds have fenced them off. One must first pass through a security barrier when entering the EduCity campus, and then through another layer of security as one enters the compound of each institution. Vehicles have to be registered at each point. At some institutions, security guards will escort the visitors' vehicles to designated parking spaces. In other institutions visitors are either escorted by a security guard to the specific meeting venue, or they have to wait for their host to meet them. The general feeling is similar to that of a military camp or high-security prison.

While the institutions may exercise tight security, the common area within the EduCity campus provides a contrasting experience. As parts of the campus are still under construction, there are many areas which are not fenced off, which are dusty and seem abandoned, and which do not promise safety or comfort, especially for students who have to walk around the campus. There is also a lack of connecting walkways between buildings to shield pedestrians from the rain or sun. Connectivity within the campus is also a problem. There is no public/common transport or facilities and support for those with limited mobility.

FINAL THOUGHTS

While EduCity has been successful in providing educational opportunities, especially for Johoreans, its future development cannot be taken for granted. As highlighted, the need for coordination between the institutions is crucial. The branding and solidarity of all institutions under the umbrella of EduCity need to be strengthened, and importantly the sense of competition among institutions needs to be transformed into a spirit of collaboration. More specifically, the role of EISB must also evolve, from constructing and setting up EduCity to managing and governing EduCity like a university (although without the authority to award qualifications).

Looking into the future, the concept of EduCity may be further enhanced through the provision of an even more diversified and holistic learning experience for students. Situated as it is in the heart of Southeast Asia, EduCity should consider expanding beyond Western higher education institutions. As pointed out in the Johor Development Report 2015, Asian and Islamic higher education institutions are needed to complement the existing Western institutions (Wan et al. 2016). Major universities in China, Japan, Korea, India, Turkey and Iran can be brought in to work alongside the existing Western-based institutions from the United Kingdom, the Netherlands and Singapore.

Not only should different types of institutions be considered, EduCity should also put in place structures and mechanisms to allow and encourage students, who may be enrolled in one particular institution, to expand their learning across EduCity. Only when this happens will EduCity live up to its claim to be the "best-in-class" integrated higher education hub.

Having articulated the challenges and issues underlying the development of EduCity, we would like to point out some limitations of our study. Due to constraints on time and access to participants, we are not in a position to shed light on the learning experience of students, specifically the quality of education in lecture halls, classrooms and laboratories as such a focus would require an ethnographic study. Our limited insights on the learning experience have mainly been confined to the views of academics and administrators. We are also unable to devote more attention to specific areas such as research and development activities, industry collaboration, community service, or governance, management and funding of these institutions. These specific areas about the institutions within EduCity are, nonetheless, interesting and important and should be taken up by future research.

Notes

1. This chapter was first published as *EduCity, Johor: A Promising Project with Multiple Challenges to Overcome*, Trends in Southeast Asia, no. 4/2018 (Singapore: ISEAS – Yusof Ishak Institute, 2018). This research is supported by the ISEAS – Yusof Ishak Institute. The authors would also like to thank Bait al-Amanah for its support. The usual disclaimer applies.
2. This figure does not include primary and secondary school students from Raffles American School and Marlborough College Malaysia.

References

Edge, The. 2011. "The Roadmap for Malaysia: A Special Report". 31 January 2011. http://etp. pemandu.gov.my/upload/ETP_TheEdge_Pull_out.pdf (accessed 14 November 2017).

Hutchinson, F.E. 2012. "Johor and Its Electronics Sector: One Priority Among Many?". ISEAS Working Paper Series no. 1. Singapore: Institute of Southeast Asian Studies.

Iskandar Investment. N.d. "Iskandar Puteri". https://www.iskandarinvestment.com/master-planned-development-projects/ surrounding-developments/ (accessed 14 November 2017).

Iskandar Malaysia Investment. N.d. "Iskandar Malaysia—Development Overview". http:// www.iminvestors.com/iskandar-malaysia.html (accessed 14 November 2017).

Iskandar Regional Development Authority. 2014. *Comprehensive Development Plan ii 2014–2025*.

Khor, Y.L. 2011. *Iskandar Malaysia: Policy, Progress and Bottlenecks*. Singapore: S. Rajaratnam School of International Studies.

Kolej MDIS Malaysia. 2017. "About Us". http://www.mdis.edu.my/ about-us.php (accessed 7 September 2017).

Multimedia University. 2017. "About Us". https://www.mmu.edu.my/ faculty/faculty-of-cinematic-arts/ (accessed 7 September 2017).

Netherlands Maritime Institute of Technology. 2017. "Overview". http:// nmit.edu.my/ about-nmit/overview/ (accessed 7 September 2017).

Newcastle University. 2017. "About Us". http://nmit.edu.my/about-nmit/overview/ (accessed 7 September 2017).

Raffles University Iskandar. 2017. "About Us". http://www.raffles-university.edu.my/about-us/about-rui (accessed 7 September 2017).

RMA Perunding Bersatu. 1996. *Johor Operational Master Plan Study*. Johor Bahru: State Economic Planning Unit.

UPEN Johor. 1989. *Pelan Ekonomi Negeri Johor 1990–2005* [The Economic Plan for Johor 1990–2005]. Johor Bahru: Kerajaan Negeri Johor Darul Ta'zim.

University of Reading Malaysia. 2014. "About Us". https://www. reading.edu.my/about-us (accessed 7 September 2017).

University of Southampton. 2017. "Our Malaysia Campus". https://www.southampton. ac.uk/my (accessed 7 September 2017).

Wan, C.D., N. Abdillah, A. Abdul Razak, and M.D. Mohd Daud. 2016. *Johor Development Report 2015*. Kuala Lumpur: Bait Al-Amanah.

Zazali, M. 2009. "EduCity to Be Top of the Class". *The Star*, 14 September 2009. http://www. thestar.com.my/business/business-news/2009/09/14/educity-to-be-top-of-the-class/ (accessed 8 September 2017).

7

TOURISM IN JOHOR AND ITS POTENTIAL

Serina Rahman and Goh Hong Ching

INTRODUCTION

As the southernmost state in Peninsular Malaysia, bordering on Singapore, Johor serves as an entry point for a substantial number of tourists. In 2016, the state ranked third of those that contribute to tourism industry incomes, generating RM11,406 million in 2016. This figure represents an annual average growth rate (or added value) of 6.9 per cent (Department of Statistics 2018a). Johor's ranking in terms of tourism income banks heavily on Singaporean visitors. Malaysia's overall inbound tourism receipts contributed to 6.7 per cent of the national GDP in 2016 (*Nikkei Asian Review*, 31 October 2017), with 26.8 million tourists arriving in the country in that same year. Of these arrivals, Singaporeans made up the bulk of the visitors (13.3 million or 49.6 per cent), with Indonesians in a distant second place with 3.1 million (11.5 per cent) visitors. Many of these Singaporeans enter Malaysia through Johor.

Domestic tourism also generates economic revenue for Malaysia, with 189.3 million local arrivals registered in 2016 with a total expenditure of RM74.8 billion. It was reported that Tourism Malaysia listed Johor as the most popular destination for domestic tourists with 7.4 million recorded local visitors in 2016 compared to the next favourite local destination (Perak) at 7.2 million in the same year (Mohd Farhaan Shah 2018). However, a domestic tourism survey conducted in 2017 (Department of Statistics Malaysia 2018) did not place Johor in the top five states preferred by domestic visitors. Instead, Selangor ranked the highest at 25.5 million domestic visitors with Perak coming in second with 20.1 million voters. The remaining favoured domestic destinations in the top five according to this survey were Kuala Lumpur, Sabah and Sarawak.

Johor enjoys one of the fastest economic growth rates in Malaysia, often attributed to the establishment of the southern economic corridor, Iskandar Malaysia, in 2006. However, while Johor enjoys high international tourist arrivals through its land bridges to Singapore, it does not seem to retain these tourists within the state. In order to examine tourism in Johor, this chapter will first set out the relevant context regarding the structure of tourism management and policy-making in Malaysia. From there, it will provide an overview of the industry within the state, and then look at its approaches to both domestic and international tourism, as well as the policies that support or prohibit tourism development across Johor. Future developments, opportunities and challenges will also be discussed.

OVERALL TOURISM STRUCTURE, STATISTICS AND POLICY HIGHLIGHTS

The organization and management of tourism in Malaysia is a multifaceted one, confined within a federal, state and local government hierarchy. Overall tourism planning is a federal prerogative undertaken by the Ministry of Tourism and Culture (MOTAC). MOTAC's mission is to develop Malaysia into a world-class tourism and cultural destination by 2020, as well as to build a national identity based on arts, culture and heritage. Tourism and culture are seen as catalysts for sustainable socio-economic growth, which in turn will strengthen and preserve the national cultural heritage and arts. Tourism Malaysia is a federal agency under MOTAC that focuses on promoting tourism both domestically and internationally. Other federal agencies also contribute to tourism planning and development depending upon the respective areas of expertise as shown in Table 7.1.

There are several policy documents at the national level that influence tourism planning and which, at the state level, are transformed into action plans for implementation on the ground.

Five-Year Economic Plan

These national plans are formulated by the incumbent government to set the economic direction of the country. The Eleventh Malaysia Plan 2016–20 highlighted ecotourism as one of the main tools to enhance national economic growth (Iskandar Regional Development Authority 2015, p. 5). At the national level, the goal is to leverage on Malaysia's position as a biodiversity hotspot, supported by action taken for conservation and protection, coupled with targeted branding and marketing for high-yield tourism investments for premier ecotourism destinations.

National Tourism Policy

First published in 1992, this document recommends broad policies for the planning,

TABLE 7.1
Tourism-Related Agencies in Malaysia and Johor

Federal Level			
Ministry of Tourism and Culture (MOTAC) Overall policy and direction Licencing, regulations and ticketing Hotel ratings and standards		(with other relevant authorities) Ministry of Rural Development Department of Agriculture Department of Forestry Department of Fisheries	
Tourism Malaysia (federal agency under MOTAC) Marketing and promotion Domestic tourism		Department of Marine Parks Department of Wildlife and National Parks Department of Orang Asli (Indigenous People) Development Department of Museums Department of Natural Heritage	

Johor State			
MOTAC Branch	*State Economic Planning Unit*	*Johor Tourism*	*Johor Land Office and Other Relevant State Departments*
Overall tourism direction and regulation	State tourism policy and budget allocation	State action plan, implementation and specific promotion	All related land matters and infrastructural support

in collaboration with:	
Local Authorities Facility maintenance, waste management, landscaping. Etc. (e.g., MBJB, MBIB) *Associations* Tour agencies, guides and other service providers (e.g., MATA, MITA, JTGA, MANAGA, etc.) *Businesses and Developers* Private tourism investments and tourism components of catalytic developments (e.g., Johor Corporation, Sunway Iskandar and Iskandar Investment Berhad)	*Iskandar Regional Development Authority (IRDA)* (for Iskandar Malaysia: federal entity that also reports to the Johor Chief Minister) Economics and Investment Department Subject Matter Expert (Tourism) bridging, brainstorming and facilitation catalytic tourism ideas Social Development Department Kawan Iskandar Malaysia (KIM) cooperatives: small-scale community tourism *Southeast Johor Development Authority (KEJORA)* (by the Ministry of Rural Development)

development and marketing of tourism. While the second edition of this original policy is in use today, a revised third edition is currently being drafted and is due for release in early 2019.

Economic Transformation Programme (ETP)

Launched in 2010, the ETP identifies National Key Economic Areas (NKEAs) as areas for focused development, and to reduce the country's reliance on oil and gas revenues. Tourism has been identified as a key sector for economic diversification.

The Economic Transformation handbook indicates that Malaysia's growth in tourism relies on an increase in visitor arrivals rather than yield (PEMANDU 2014, p. 35).

Based on the above documents and several planning workshops by MOTAC, Figure 7.1 illustrates the areas identified as key entry point projects for tourism to boost yield and revenues.

Extracting from Figure 7.1, Malaysia tourism focused on the following niche areas in 2016:

1. shopping tourism;
2. ecotourism (especially birding);
3. lifestyle (especially cruises);
4. sports tourism (especially golf); and
5. marine tourism

(*source*: Tourism Malaysia 2016).

Given these focuses, several other documents are relevant to tourism planning.

National Ecotourism Plan (NEP)

First prepared in 1996, the NEP does not address national level strategies but details comprehensive guidelines for ecotourism site development. More of a blueprint than a strategic policy document, there was a lack of a buy-in from industry players on this document and little integration between federal and state entities on its implementation (World Wildlife Fund for Nature (WWF) Malaysia 2016). The second

FIGURE 7.1
Key Entry Points for Tourism According to the Malaysian Ministry of Tourism and Culture

Source: Adapted from Tourism Malaysia *Annual Report 2016*.

edition of the NEP (2016–25) comprises a review of the implementation of the original NEP, formulates new strategic directions and focuses on the implementation of best practices of key stakeholders (Ministry of Tourism and Culture 2016, p. 22).

Rural Tourism Master Plan

Often geographically overlapping with ecotourism destinations, this plan serves to remove existing barriers to tourism in rural areas. It focuses on preventing poor product quality, proliferation of litter, low service quality and emphasizing the concept of "beautiful countryside and friendly people" (Ministry of Rural and Regional Development 2001, p. 1). The plan aims to create long-staying, high-spending visitors. While the document is tourism-centred, the rural transformation statement released by the ministry emphasized "urbanization of rural areas", generation of higher incomes through private involvement and partnership, entrepreneurship and employment opportunities. It also aims to reduce out-migration of youths from rural areas in search of jobs and better prospects.

Table 7.2 provides a summary of some available tourism statistics for Malaysia. Malaysia's tourism revenue is significantly lower than Thailand and Singapore (for the latter, this comparison is made given that Singapore is a far smaller city-state). Although there are high tourist arrival numbers, because of shorter average lengths of stay, lower spending per day and a high dependence on short-haul markets, Malaysia's tourism revenue lags behind in comparison to its neighbours. The focus now is thus on growing yields per tourist.

JOHOR TOURISM STATISTICS

As the southern gateway of Peninsular Malaysia, Johor receives substantial numbers of visitors from Singapore. In 2016, a total of 15,868,064 international tourist arrivals were recorded entering Johor, of which 12,075,881 (76.1 per cent) were Singaporean tourists. Tables 7.3 and 7.4 illustrate the source markets for Johor and the number of overnight tourists in the state. Most visitors were from Asian countries, followed by the United Kingdom and Australia.

These figures indicate a decrease in total arrivals by 2.9 per cent. Of the international tourist arrivals (total 15,868,064 people: Table 7.3), 16.3 per cent were overnight tourists (2,581,983 people: Table 7.4). Of the total 7,013,784 overnight tourists in 2016 (Table 7.4), 4,431,801 or 63.2 per cent were domestic tourists. This indicates that few international tourist arrivals (mostly Singaporeans) stay in Johor, but instead drive or fly through to other states. A larger percentage of domestic tourists, on the other hand, come to Johor with the intention of staying there for its tourism attractions.

A HVS Global Hospitality Services (Chee, Bernhard and Teo 2017, p. 8) report indicates that hotel guest numbers in Johor have been increasing every year, with 2017 registering a 6.5 per cent increase from the previous year comprising an increase of 5.3 million guests, of which 60 per cent are domestic tourists.

TABLE 7.2
Summary of Available Tourism Statistics for Malaysia

Indicator	Year	Value	Note	Source
Inbound tourism receipts	2016	6.7% of GDP	Thailand: 11.4% of GDP	Nikkei Asian Review (2017)
Inbound visitors	2016	26.8 million	Singapore: 16.4 million visitors[a]	Nikkei Asian Review (2017)
International tourist expenditure	2016	RM82.1 billion	Singapore: S$24.8 billion (RM77.376 billion)[a]	Tourism Malaysia (2016)
International per capita expenditure	2016	RM3,068	14.2% increase from 2015	Tourism Malaysia (2016)
Top international per capita expenditure: Saudi Arabia	2016	RM10,185.7		Tourism Malaysia (2016)
Top tourist generating market: Singapore	2016	13.3 million visitors	49.6% of total visitors	Tourism Malaysia (2016)
Top market for tourist expenditure: Singapore	2016	RM38,069.2 million	29% increase from 2015	Tourism Malaysia (2016)
ASEAN market overall	2016	20.3 million visitors	75.8% of total visitors	Tourism Malaysia (2016)
Average international visitor length of stay	2016	5.9 nights		Tourism Malaysia (2016)
Domestic tourism expenditure	2016	RM74.8 billion	10.2% increase from 2015	Tourism Malaysia 2016
Domestic tourism arrivals	2016	RM189.3 million	7% increase from 2015	Tourism Malaysia, 2016
Average domestic visitor length of stay	2016	2.31 nights		Tourism Malaysia (2016)
Tourism contribution to national economy	2016	RM182.4 billion	14.8% of total national economy / 13.7% of total GDP	Tourism Malaysia (2016)
Travel and tourism contribution to GDP	2016	RM40 billion	Thailand: 2,906.8 billion baht (RM363.35 billion) or 20.6% of total GDP[b]	World Travel and Tourism Council (2017)

Sources for Singapore and Thailand statistics:
a. Singapore Tourism Board, Year-in-Review 2016, published 14 February 2017, https://www.stb.gov.sg/news-and-publications/Documents/Year-in-review%202016%20presentation%20slides_14Feb2017.pdf (accessed 31 December 2018).
b. World Travel and Tourism Council, "Travel and Tourism Economic Impact 2017 Thailand", March 2017, https://www.wttc.org/-/media/files/reports/economic-impact-research/countries-2017/thailand2017.pdf (accessed 31 December 2018).

TABLE 7.3
International Visitor Arrivals to Johor, 2014–16

Nationality	Year		
	2014	2015	2016
Singapore	16,922,023	12,096,066	12,075,881
Indonesia	1,260,174	1,339,065	1,173,690
China	628,087	797,862	888,714
Philippines	422,201	458,468	317,541
India	299,446	221,037	311,454
Japan	218,343	192,787	138,730
Thailand	161,385	154,977	79,881
South Korea	108,739	149,202	116,444
United Kingdom	114,696	91,427	52,855
Australia	100,634	84,836	74,176
Brunei	11,444	8,980	6,659
Other countries	731,576	745,268	632,039
Total	20,978,748	16,339,975	15,868,064

Source: Tourism Johor (2017).

TABLE 7.4
Overnight Tourists in Johor

Year	Overnight Tourists		Total
	Domestic	International	
2010	2,051,955	1,566,977	3,618,932
2011	2,003,611	1,781,765	3,785,376
2012	2,162,130	1,794,729	3,956,859
2013	3,138,895	2,631,675	5,770,570
2014	4,023,691	2,402,884	6,426,575
2015	4,388,235	2,565,092	6,953,327
2016	4,431,801	2,581,983	7,013,784

Source: Tourism Johor (2017).

Iskandar Malaysia (IM) covers 12 per cent of Johor's southernmost land area, stretching between the western bank of the Johor River in Pasir Gudang and Pontian on the western coast, and reaching as far north as Kulai. The Iskandar Malaysia ten-year Progress Report indicates that IM's GDP grew at a rate of 6.9 per cent between 2006 and 2014, higher than Johor's GDP growth of 6.5 per cent and Malaysia's overall GDP growth of 6 per cent. This higher growth rate was attributed mainly to new tourism destinations such as the Johor Premier Outlet (JPO), Legoland, and the Puteri Harbour Family Theme Park (Hello Kitty Land), as well as EduCity. There were RM1.083 billion worth of tourism investments in this region (3.4 per cent of total investments) within this same time period (IRDA 2015, p. 3).

According to the Iskandar Malaysia Comprehensive Development Plan II (2014–25), most visitors to Iskandar Malaysia in 2014 were business excursionists or day visitors (25.1 per cent). The average length of stay in IM in 2015 was 2.3 days. Of these visitors, the highest source country was Singapore, comprising 82 per cent of all visitors (IRDA 2014, p. 4.30). This large percentage of Singaporean visitors is clearly due to the country's proximity and ease of access to these IM destinations; most within half an hour's drive from the border (not including the time taken to get through both countries' immigration and customs procedures).

JOHOR TOURISM POLICIES AND MANAGEMENT

The overarching driving force behind tourism planning and subsequent tourism arrivals in Johor comes from the National Tourism Policy. This has been transformed into the Tourism Johor Master Plan 2014–23. The state government's goal for tourism is to position Johor as a high-value destination. The following targets have been set for 2021:

1. increased tourist arrivals (30.3 million);
2. increased tourist receipts (RM7.14 billion); and
3. increased tourist expenditure per capita (RM1,030 per person).
(*source:* Johor Economic Planning Unit 2013, p. 4.)

According to the Master Plan, the state aims to achieve these goals through product development, infrastructure and supporting facilities, destination management and human resource development. It was also explicitly stated that tourism development should be balanced out between IM, the East Coast Economic Region and other districts in Johor. Increased tourism revenue will be raised by increasing length of stay and increased tourist spending on iconic and international tourism products that enhance the depth of tourist experiences.

While Singaporeans are the largest market of international visitors to Johor, the state recognizes that it must position its tourism efforts in parallel and in competition with Singapore. It also intends to attract new markets from China, India and the Middle East. Internally, reorganization of tourism destinations into Tourism Development Clusters is intended to enable the state to prioritize and enhance existing flagship offerings, with renewed focus on specific market segments such as families, students, groups and special interests. Tourism standards will be set and maintained through the creation of the Johor Tourism Flagship Standard and sustainability certification to encourage mindset change and service quality as well as human capital development and management. Appendix 7.1 provides a summary of the designated Tourism Development Clusters.

There are also a number of other documents that contribute to tourism development and management. Given the state's sole control over land matters, the Johor State Structure Plan 2030 (PLAN Malaysia 2018, pp. 6–82) is the key document that outlines policies and proposals for land use within the state. The plan emphasizes balanced development throughout the state with some areas highlighted for specific tourism niches as shown in Table 7.5.

TABLE 7.5
Areas Identified for Tourism by the Johor State Structure Plan, 2030

Within IM	Area	Tourism Niche	Status
	Mersing	Ecotourism	Key economic driver
	Batu Pahat	Cuisine tourism	Supporting economic driver
	Tangkak	Lifestyle and adventure tourism	Key economic driver
	Tangkak	Ecotourism in the legendary Gunung Ledang forest	High impact project
	Kluang	Agro- and ecotourism	Supporting economic driver
	Segamat	Ecotourism	Supporting economic driver
✓	Pontian	Ecotourism	Supporting economic driver
✓	Kota Tinggi	Beach/eco-heritage/health/ education tourism	Supporting economic driver
✓	Kota Tinggi	Historical tourism	High impact project
✓	Pulai River	Ecotourism[a]	High impact project
	Segamat	Eco-adventure park	High impact project
✓	Kukup Island and Tanjung Piai	Gazettement as permanent forest reserve[a]	Sustainability value
	Kota Tinggi to Mersing	Wildlife corridor along the central forest spine	Sustainability value
	Mersing	Sultan Iskandar Marine Park	Sustainability value

Note: a. Kukup Island's status as a national park was revoked in September 2018 and the island has been redesignated as Sultanate Land. Kukup Island, the Pulai River and Tanjung Piai are gazetted as Ramsar sites (wetlands of international importance), however parts of the Pulai River mangrove forest have recently been degazetted for golf course and resort development.
Source: Draf Rancangan Struktur Negeri Johor 2030 (PLAN Malaysia 2008).

Most of the plans for the listed areas are relatively in line with the Tourism Development Clusters allocated to existing tourism attractions across Johor. Both documents indicate an intention to expand tourism beyond the Iskandar Malaysia boundaries. Added to that is the allocation of budgets to the following areas at the district level (three out of five districts listed are outside IM borders):

1. Kluang: to develop integrated agro- and ecotourism packages.
2. Kota Tinggi: to establish a specialized portal for existing tourism attractions and initiatives for local community empowerment and involvement in tourism.
3. Mersing: to develop new ecotourism products focussed on traditional villages.
4. Pontian: to increase and strengthen tourism activities and fisheries.
5. Tangkak: to develop facilities in support of the tourism sector.

Aside from the relevance of the National Ecotourism Plan and the Rural Tourism Master Plan discussed earlier, the Johor Sustainability Policy 2016–20 also has a direct effect on tourism development in Johor. This policy spells out the need for economic development to be balanced with social well-being and environmental sustainability. The conservation of natural heritage, responsible lifestyles, a green economy, improvements to governance and local community empowerment are emphasized (UPEN Johor 2016, p. vi). This policy is in line with IRDA's Circles of Sustainability, a strategic framework that outlines the need for a balance between wealth generation, wealth sharing and inclusiveness, resource optimization and use, environmental conservation and community well-being and equitability (IRDA 2014, p. 5.1).

PROSPECTS AND PROJECTIONS FOR TOURISM IN JOHOR

There are many indications that the future of tourism in Johor is positive. Prior to 2006, before the launch of the Iskandar Malaysia economic corridor, Johor was a sleepy border town that many Singaporeans and other arrivals through its land bridges simply passed through on their way to other states or Kuala Lumpur. The launch of IM, combined with Sultan Ibrahim Iskandar's goal to make Johor Bahru the next Shenzhen (Ellis 2017), and the arrival of major attractions such as Hello Kitty Land, the Johor Premium Outlets and Legoland were a big boost to tourism in the state.

The development of more well-known hotels such as Double Tree by Hilton, the Somerset Serviced Apartments and Jen Hotel (formerly Traders Hotel) were also an endorsement of the city and its business and tourism potential. Prior to these changes, maximum room rates per night could only reach RM450; this has since changed. Average length of stay has also increased to 3 nights from 1.8 nights.[1] More hotels are planned for Johor with a focus on midscale and upscale offerings such as Melia, Holiday Inn, Novotel and Ibis Styles. These developments in the works are also an indication of the industry's confidence in future demand growth in Johor (Chee and Teo 2018, p. 9).

Current public transportation options between Singapore and Malaysia include a KTM train service between Johor Bahru Railway Station and Woodlands, Singapore and several public bus options, managed by both Singapore and Malaysia. More bus routes have been added in recent years, serving many who live in Malaysia and work in Singapore, as well as day-trippers and other tourists who travel from Singapore to Senai Airport. Plans to develop the Malaysia-Singapore Rapid Transit System (an additional train service that is planned to connect to Singapore's Mass Rapid Transit (MRT) system) will further enhance connectivity across the Johor Straits. Planned improvements to transportation within Johor Bahru through the Iskandar Malaysia Bus Rapid Transit system will also provide positive infrastructural support to tourism in Johor (Chee and Teo 2018, p. 9).

Senai Airport's international connectivity is an asset for tourism in Johor. In 2017, 3 million passengers travelled through Senai by air to eleven domestic cities and eight international cities (Mohd Farhaan 2018). These include stops in Indonesia (Jakarta and Surabaya), which is the second largest market for Malaysia, as well as Guangzhou and Macao. The Chinese market is one that Tourism Malaysia is targeting to increase to 8 million visitors by 2020, a goal deemed achievable given the number of large Chinese mixed developments, especially in Johor, such as Forest City, Princess Cove and Country Garden at Danga Bay. The highest year-on-year increase in visitor arrivals are tourists from Thailand, with figures rising by 26.4 per cent in 2016 (Chee, Bernhard, and Teo 2017, p. 6). The direct connectivity between Senai and Bangkok will support further increases in Thai visitor numbers to the state.

IRDA has clearly had a positive impact on tourism development and support in Johor. The agency does not focus on domestic tourism, but its objective is to drive tourism investments in IM, with a goal of RM10.87 billion investments by 2020. As a catalyst for tourism development, IRDA helps to bridge gaps between various entities that might otherwise work in silos, such as between various government agencies, between the private and public entities, as well as between federal and state authorities. While IRDA does not necessarily have the authority to dictate tourism development, management or policy in Johor, its role of bringing in and brainstorming new ideas for the state through its subject matter expertise and providing facilitation and support for both the state government and investors has shown significant results.

IRDA also creates platforms for tourism collaborations between Malaysia and Singapore, such as one that was recently established between Tourism Johor and the Singapore Tourism Board. Study tours have been facilitated by IRDA for Johor tourism officials to learn from Singapore, and a new "passport programme" that encourages twinning visits between venues in both Singapore (Sungai Buloh Nature Reserve) and Johor (Kukup Island) has been launched. This is the first collaboration of its kind in Malaysia.

According to Wan Suziana Wan Othman, Vice-President of Economics and Investment at IRDA, the future of tourism in Johor lies in the Ibrahim International Business District (IIBD), and its potential contribution to business and MICE (meetings, incentives, conferences and events) tourism. Other areas of potential growth include halal tourism and the global halal travel market; Malaysia has yet to fully exploit this niche even though it is a Muslim country, while countries like Japan and Korea are steps ahead in drawing Muslim tourists. Another potential tourism revenue source is in medical tourism. A number of reputable international hospital brands have recently opened in Johor, but for now there are still insufficient hospital beds to meet expansive tourism needs.

Wan Suziana also noted that Johor could, in future, improve Singaporean overnight visitors by focusing on offerings that may be of specific interest to the market. These include offerings that focus on unique traditional village experiences, ecotourism (such as those offered by Johor Corporation in the Johor River area) and food tourism. IRDA is currently working with the Johor Heritage Foundation (Yayasan Warisan Johor) and Think City to enhance cultural and heritage tourism, with a focus on Johor Bahru City. Johor Bahru is already known to have a thriving arts scene, with a number of arts and cultural festivals throughout the year. Most importantly, Wan Suziana feels that Johor needs to enhance its branding as a safe family destination, especially with new theme parks opening in Medini City and Sunway Iskandar.

Beyond large-scale attractions and in line with its principles of inclusivity and community well-being, IRDA has also focused on developing small-scale community tourism efforts through its Kawan Iskandar Malaysia (KIM) community cooperative network. Run by IRDA's Social Development unit, these initiatives train, support and sometimes fund villages to develop, nurture and maintain small tourism efforts throughout IM. These programmes enable tourism benefits to reach beyond the usual big business players and at the same time meets Tourism Johor's goals of identifying small service providers scattered throughout the state to support them with access, marketing and other expertise.[2] As part of these efforts, IRDA, Johor Tourism and MOTAC have worked to train and license community guides as well as promote these more experiential tourism offerings to international markets. The growth of grassroots tourism associations and entities such as the Pontian Tourism Association and Kelab Alami have not only contributed to local tourism efforts and revenue, but also meet the community empowerment and inclusivity goals of both IRDA's Circles of Sustainability and the Johor Sustainability Policy.

On paper, Johor's plans for tourism development indicate a clear move beyond the IM boundaries to ensure balance with the rest of the state. With a new government in power, there have been definite indications of action to fulfil these plans. Almost immediately after the 14th General Elections, announcements were made with regards to the cancellation of two big ticket tourism developments in the Kota Tinggi area (Daniel 2018) and a move to focus on existing natural attractions, as well as to spread tourism focus to areas such as Batu Pahat, Muar and Kluang.

Private developers also have a large role to play in future tourism development in Johor. Desaru Coast on the eastern shore of Johor, funded by Khazanah Nasional Berhad, recently launched its integrated tourism development comprising golf courses and water parks. This injects renewed interest in a part of Johor that was once a favourite cycling and dining destination, but fell to neglect with the rise of the Pengerang Integrated Petroleum Complex (PIPC) in the vicinity. Forest City in the west of Johor has also recently launched its new golf course along the Pulai River.

Some developers are focusing on preserving and promoting Johor's natural assets. The Iskandar Puteri area is host to forty-five parks, gardens and lakes. Within it, Medini City has developed the Edible Park and the Heritage Forest, which host regular events and festivals throughout the year. Iskandar Investment Berhad (IIB), the catalytic developer for the Iskandar Puteri area, is also planning to preserve some of its mangrove forest areas, with a view to developing low-impact nature-based tourism attractions. Frequent organic food festivals and other similar health and lifestyle events in Iskandar Puteri also generate both local and Singaporean tourism interest.

Private developers' efforts at increasing traffic and building communities in their respective developments will also drive tourism in Johor. Puteri Harbour has regular festivals, events and countdowns, often featuring international attractions such as the Moscow Circus. Sports tourism is also growing in Johor, with a number of international events such as marathons and triathlons, as well as kayaking and fishing competitions. These events have shown to be popular with regional visitors (from Singapore and Indonesia) as well as foreigners living in Malaysia, adding to domestic tourism numbers.

OVERCOMING CHALLENGES TO SUCCESS IN JOHOR

While the future of tourism in Johor is undeniably bright, there are a number of issues that will need to be resolved to ensure that ambitious goals can be achieved, and Johor's huge potential fulfilled.

With the arrival of international hotel chains and standards of service, local manpower may not be deemed qualified for hire. In the east coast Mersing and Sibu-Tinggi archipelagos, there has been some out-migration of local youths from the islands in search of jobs. With the arrival of large hotels or resorts on these islands, the youth that remain or those who return, have often found that they do not have the required skills to participate in new tourism opportunities. More qualified, often foreign, and cheaper labour, is then hired to fill the gap. The same situation arose in Forest City where its Phoenix Hotel personnel were initially all brought in from China. The reason given for the lack of local hires was their lack of relevant qualifications or experience, and the need to quickly get the hotel up and running. Forest City has since begun hiring locals for its new Golf Resort which had more lead time to provide the necessary training.

Training, capacity-building and certification for tourism, leisure and hospitality needs to be improved and enhanced in Johor. While there are a number of private polytechnics offering courses in hospitality, this field is not yet seen as an attractive or lucrative one for many locals. At times, culture and tradition deem it morally inappropriate for women to work in the industry, and many families would rather their daughters work in a factory than in a hotel or leisure attraction. Capacity-building also needs to be conducted for government agencies that manage or administer tourism matters, as not all civil servants have the relevant qualifications or understanding of the industry. Local council staff also need to be provided training so that they are able to grasp how to better manage their districts to attract tourism revenue. IRDA, Universiti Teknologi Malaysia (UTM) and Tourism Johor have run workshops and conferences to this effect, but the effective application of the information disseminated has not yet been studied.

Even as training is provided for local council or district officers, work culture and attitudes can stand in the way of more cohesive approaches to tourism administration and implementation on the ground. Department heads and the state executive committee are either frequently rotated or are political appointments, meaning that short-term easy-to-achieve goals are often favoured over harder long-term adaptations to improve tourism services or product development. With IRDA and Tourism Johor's recent efforts to license community guides, older "professional" guides have baulked at the potential entrance of competitors to their field, and have at times been less than cooperative in the endeavour.

Misunderstandings between federal and state entities, as well as between state departments have also arisen in the efforts to create platforms for sharing and collaboration. Some state agency staff (who do not wish to be identified) have questioned IRDA's right to advise them on their work, a misunderstanding of the agency's efforts to suggest new ideas and provide access to broader opportunities. IRDA staff have also commented on the reluctance of some agency or local council personnel to do more than what they are used to, although they too understand how overwhelming it can be to be suddenly introduced to new initiatives that may lead to additional work and overtime hours.

Mohd Shukri bin Misbah, the former Director of Johor Tourism opined that the department cannot do everything alone. In order for Johor to fulfil its tourism potential, all parties must work together, especially at the local level. Since retiring from office, he has set up the Pontian Tourism Association as a model of how local service providers can take the initiative to mobilize themselves and benefit from opportunities provided by the state and IRDA. However, this association is in the unique position of having at its helm a person well-versed in the mechanics of the state and what it offers. Other grassroots organizations in Johor may not have such access, connections or knowledge.

Mohd Shukri himself is fully aware of this, but he pointed out that one of the biggest obstacles to the success of tourism in Johor is the lack of ideas. Tourism operators and service providers need to learn how to understand foreign needs, interests and tastes. This can boil down to the simplest of factors such as souvenir sizes and how simple village products can be packaged to attract foreign tourists' interest. While marketing and branding are the key weaknesses of the state and its people, digital marketing is an even bigger challenge.

HVS Global Hospitality Services recommends that Johor adapt its offerings to meet the interests of the millennial traveller (Chee, Bernhard, and Teo 2017, p. 9). However, they note that these travellers will frequent destinations that provide easy-to-access online information and booking services. Johor's tourism operators and service providers would have to quickly improve their digital marketing abilities in order to benefit from this market. While the millennial traveller is known to have limited spending power, they look for more meaningful experiences that allow them to spend a longer time getting to know communities and local heritage; a potential source of longer-staying tourism revenue.

A lack of tourism data is also a challenge for Johor and tourism-related decision-making. Both Mohd Shukri and Wan Suziana pointed out this problem; there are no structured means of retrieving information from homestay providers, for example, or even general feedback from the average tourist. Accurate raw data on accommodation, destination and activity choices is lacking and this affects the efficient and effective provision of tourism services and attractions, and could lead to the misdirection of effort and funding to areas of little actual interest to tourists.

Sustainability is a term frequently used in tourism material and policy publications. According to the Malaysian constitution, land is a state prerogative, and in Johor it is also a lucrative source of income. Lofty federal goals of sustainability in tourism views land and other natural resources as a shared commodity that needs to be conserved, but at the state level, land is often seen as a resource that is to be effectively maximized for economic benefit. As a result, wealth generation will always take precedence over environmental protection. In Johor, the practice has been to use tourism in natural areas as a tool to encourage habitat protection, by demonstrating its importance to local livelihoods and economies in contrast to incomes lost should the areas be destroyed for physical development.

This then leads to the question of inclusivity. While IRDA's efforts under its KIM network and Johor Tourism's efforts at supporting small players have enabled small-scale operators to participate in tourism, there can be a conflict when land is arbitrarily bought over or redesignated for private or large-scale business use. This issue has arisen in the recent past with the approval for some parts of the Pulai River Ramsar area to be turned into a golf course and the redesignation of Kukup Island, also a Ramsar site and formerly designated as a national park, to Sultanate Land.

The setting up of the Sultan Iskandar Marine Park in the Sibu-Tinggi archipelago has also raised questions as to how the local fishing community benefits from the endeavour, as opposed to the resort owners (who are not originally from the island), whose tourism earnings stand to improve from better habitat management. Top-down dictation of policy and regulation by hired consultants who have not effectively engaged with the community can lead to conflict in tourism areas and could jeopardize the multiple benefits of such initiatives.

Inclusivity also pertains to the tourists who are able to benefit from new tourism development. Domestic tourism makes up a large percentage of Johor's tourism revenue. If new attractions such as the Johor Premium Outlet and Legoland are priced beyond local consumers' budgets, it may affect domestic tourist interests in the state. Thus, while tourism in Johor needs to draw big-ticket investment and international clientele, strategies need to also accommodate the local traveller who will also need attractions and initiatives that they can afford.

While Johor's prime asset is its location as the southern gateway of Peninsular Malaysia, the time taken to cross the border at its land bridges have recently outweighed the benefit of being in such close proximity. Over the last festive season, some travellers took eight hours to get to and through both immigration and customs complexes for a journey that could take a mere half hour without traffic (Choo 2018). Average weekend traffic across the border is also known to stretch to three or four hours. In 2017, analysts noted that the imposition of a foreign vehicle fee could dissuade Singaporeans from travelling north (*Nikkei ASEAN Review*, 31 October 2017), but this fee has less of an impact than the time taken to cross the border. Potential visitors could eventually decide to avoid Johor altogether and instead opt to fly to Melaka, Kuala Lumpur or other parts of Malaysia.

While HVS Global Hospitality Services recommends an improvement of flight connectivity in order to further enhance tourism in Johor (Chee and Teo 2018, p. 9), the issues related to the land-border crossing need to be resolved before visitors from the south can benefit from Senai's connectivity. The High-Speed Rail (HSR) was another infrastructural development linking Singapore and Malaysia that was slated to improve tourism and other opportunities in other parts of Johor beyond Iskandar Malaysia. With plans for the HSR temporarily shelved under the new government, this source of potential tourism revenue will also be put on hold for now.

CONCLUSION

The prospects for tourism in Johor are bright. In spite of complications in the overall tourism hierarchy in Malaysia, MOTAC, Johor Tourism and IRDA are able to come together to find the best way forward for tourism in the state. Statistics have shown that tourism in Johor has increased since 2006, with a bulk of visitors coming from the domestic market. Although Singaporeans make up a large percentage of the international visitor arrivals through Johor's land bridges with the island-state, most travel through Johor to other destinations. More work needs to be done to tweak Johor's tourism offerings to cater to the specific interests of this market, emphasizing more experiential packages around traditional village culture, heritage and food tourism. Other areas of tourism growth will come from the Ibrahim International Business District, halal tourism and the global halal travel market, as well as medical tourism. Tourism in Johor is a multipronged effort, with grassroots entities, tourism associations and private developers and businesses working with state and federal government agencies to promote the state and attract more visitors. More involvement and initiatives by local councils and district officers can enhance this effort to make all areas of the state, especially those beyond Iskandar Malaysia, attractive to both domestic and international visitors.

APPENDIX 7.1
Johor Tourism Development Clusters

No.	Tourism Development Cluster (TDC)	Areas	Tourism Driver	Market Segments	Focus
1.	Family Fun	Nusajaya, Gelang Patah and Pendas	*Flagship product:* LEGOLAND Family Entertainment Centre	High income; Middle income; Children (2–12 yrs); Youths	Entertainment-based; Boat cruise; Orang Asli village visit; Seafood
2.	Urban Heritage and Lifestyle	JB City Centre, Tampoi and Kempas	*Flagship product:* Danga Bay Johor Bahru City Centre	Family; Businessmen; Specific interest; Tour groups	Heritage tourism; City entertainment; One Stop Centre; Hop On-Off bus; Tanjung Puteri Heritage Trail
3.	Leisure Shopping	Kulaijaya, Senai and Skudai	*Flagship product:* Johor Premium Outlets	High and middle income; Sophisticated office ladies; Brand-conscious	Shopping; Golf; Fashion
4.	Mangrove and Rural Getaway	Pekan Nenas, Bandar Pontian, Kukup, Tanjung Piai and Sungai Pulai	*Major product:* Ramsar Triangle (Taman Negara Tanjung Piai – Pulau Kukup – Sungai Pulai)	Family; Students; Nature enthusiasts; Researchers; Tour groups	Nature and rural-based Agrotourism; Seafood
5.	Coastal Retreat	Desaru, Sedili, Pengerang and Johor Lama	*Flagship product:* New Desaru	Family; Package loyalty card members; High-end MICE; Businessmen; Specific interest: golfers, water sports lovers, surfers, cyclers	Family recreation; Cultural heritage; Ecotourism; Agritourism; Agro and ecotourism trail
6.	Marine and Island Escapade	Mersing, Tanjung Leman and Mersing Islands	*Major product:* Mersing Laguna *Support products:* Mersing Islands	Businessmen; Golfers; Yachting; Family; Organizations; Scuba diving; Leisure fishers	Island tourism; Golf; Community-based tourism (Pulau Sibu Besar); Educational tourism (Pulau Tinggi); Family picnic (Pulau Besar); Deep sea fishing (Pulau Pemanggil); Scuba diving (Pulau Aur)

continued on next page

APPENDIX 7.1 – cont'd

No.	Tourism Development Cluster (TDC)	Areas	Tourism Driver	Market Segments	Focus
7.	Eco Adventure Challenge	Endau-Rompin National Park	*Major product:* Endau-Rompin National Park	Students; Extreme sports enthusiasts; Exploration groups; Bird watchers; Researchers	Nature-based tourism; Ecotourism; Educational and research-based tourism
8.	Cradle of Johor Heritage	Parit Raja – Batu Pahat – Yong Peng – Pagoh – Sungai Mati – Muar	*Major product:* Royal Town Muar and Batu Pahat	Family; Students; Tour groups; Researchers; Culture and heritage enthusiasts	Culture heritage; Birding activity; Royal Town of Muar Heritage and History Trail; Trail Park and Garden Bakri Food trail
9.	Mystical Nature	Tangkak, Grisek, Kundang Hulu and Durian Chondong	*Major product:* Gunung Ledang National Park	Family; Youths; Extreme sports enthusiasts; Religious organizations	Adventure tourism; Spiritual tourism; Cultural heritage
10.	Agri Delights	Ayer Hitam – Bandar Kluang – Kahang	*Major product:* Zenxin Organic Farm UK Farm KOREF	Family; Students; Researchers; Specific interest; Tour groups	Agrotourism
11.	Orchard Route	Bandar Segamat, Labis and Bekok	*Major product:* Kg Sermin Kg Gelang Chin-Chin Kg Pauh	Family; Students; Fruit entrepreneurs	Agrotourism (fruits)

Source: Johor Tourism (2017).

Notes

1. Personal communication, Wan Suziana Wan Othman, Vice-President, Economics and Investment at the Iskandar Regional Development Authority, 14 November 2018.
2. Personal communication, Mohd Shukri bin Misbah, former Director of Tourism Johor, 12 November 2018.

References

Chee Hok Yean, and Jeremy Teo. 2018. "In Focus Malaysia—Reinvigorated Opportunities". HVS Global Hospitality Services, 3 July 2018. https://www.hvs.com/article/8311-in-focus-malaysia-reinvigorated-opportunities (accessed 16 November 2018).

———, Stephanie Bernhard, and Hatta Teo. 2017. "In Focus: Malaysia—A Rising Opportunity". HVS Global Hospitality Services, 15 May 2017. https://www.hvs.com/article/8008-in-focus-malaysia-a-rising-opportunity (accessed 16 November 2018).

Choo Yun Ting. 2018. "Long Waits at Tuas and Woodlands Checkpoints, with Some Delays Hitting 8 Hours". *Straits Times*, 16 December 2018. https://www.straitstimes.com/singapore/travellers-endure-long-waits-at-tuas-and-woodlands-checkpoints-over-the-weekend (accessed 12 December 2018).

Department of Statistics, Federal Government of Malaysia. 2018a. "Economic Census 2016: Tourism Statistics". 29 January 2018. https://www.dosm.gov.my/v1/index.php?r=column/pdfPrev&id=WEVEUi8zaytMbFpncC9vTDN4TmZQQT09 (accessed 16 November 2018).

———. 2018b. "Domestic Tourism Survey 2017". 29 June 2018. https://www.dosm.gov.my/v1/index.php?r=column/pdfPrev&id=dU9zUGtzRG15dXUrODRUNFQ2cENRQT09 (accessed 16 November 2018).

Economic Planning Unit, Federal Government of Malaysia. 2015. *Eleventh Malaysia Plan 2016–2020*. Putrajaya: Prime Minister's Office.

Ellis, Eric. 2017. "Malaysia's Sultan Seeks to Create a New Shenzhen". *Asiamoney*, 4 October 2017. https://www.euromoney.com/article/b150kykbcvdlv4/malaysia39s-sultan-seeks-to-create-a-new-shenzhen (accessed 16 November 2018).

Iskandar Regional Development Authority (IRDA), Federal Government of Malaysia. 2014. *Iskandar Malaysia Comprehensive Development Plan II 2014–2025*. Johor Bahru: Iskandar Regional Development Authority.

———. 2015. "Eleventh Malaysia Plan". *IM Biz Watch* 5, 31 May 2015.

Johor Economic Planning Unit, State Government of Johor, Malaysia. 2013. *Johor Tourism Master Plan 2014–2023*. Iskandar Puteri: Johor.

———. 2016. *Johor Sustainability Policy*. Iskandar Puteri: Johor.

Ministry of Rural and Regional Development, Federal Government of Malaysia. 2001. *Rural Transformation Master Plan*. Putrajaya: Ministry of Rural and Regional Development.

Ministry of Tourism and Culture, Federal Government of Malaysia. 2004. *Review of the National Tourism Policy*. Putrajaya: Ministry of Tourism and Culture Malaysia.

———. 2016. "Executive Summary". *National Ecotourism Plan 2016–2025*. Putrajaya: Ministry of Tourism and Culture Malaysia. 2016.

Mohd Farhaan Shah. 2018. "Johor Now a Top Tourism Destination". *The Star Online*, 13 January 2018. www.thestar.com.my/news/nation/2018/01/13/johor-now-a-top-tourism-destination/ (accessed 16 November 2018).

Nikkei Asian Review. 2017. "Malaysia Struggles to Attract More Tourists". 31 October 2017. https://asia.nikkei.com/Economy/Malaysia-struggles-to-attract-more-tourists' (accessed 16 November 2018).

PEMANDU, Federal Government of Malaysia. 2014. *Economic Transformation Programme Handbook.* Putrajaya: Performance Management and Delivery Unit, Prime Minister's Office.

———. 2016. *National Transformation Programme Annual Report 2016.* Putrajaya: Performance Management and Delivery Unit, Prime Minister's Office.

PLAN Malaysia. 2018. *Draf Rancangan Struktur Negeri Johor 2030.* Johor Bahru: PLAN Malaysia.

Daniel, Steven. 2018. "Johor May Axe Two Big Tourism Plans". *The Star Online,* 29 May 2018. https://www.thestar.com.my/news/nation/2018/05/29/johor-may-axe-two-big-tourism-plans-exclusive-unsure-future-for-projects-worth-over-rm3bil/ (accessed 16 November 2018).

Tourism Johor, State Government of Johor, Malaysia, 2017. *Annual Report.* Johor Bahru: Tourism Johor.

Tourism Malaysia, Federal Government of Malaysia. 2016. *Annual Report.* Putrajaya: Tourism Malaysia.

World Tourism Council. 2017. *Benchmarking Report 2017—Malaysia.* June 2017, London. https://www.wttc.org/-/media/files/reports/benchmark-reports/country-reports-2017/malaysia.pdf (accessed 31 December 2018).

World Tourism Organization. 2017. *Yearbook of Tourism Statistics.* Madrid: World Tourism Organization.

World Travel and Tourism Council. 2018. *Travel and Tourism Economic Impact 2018.* London: World Travel and Tourism Council.

World Wildlife Fund for Nature (WWF), Malaysia. 2016. *Malaysian National Ecotourism Plan.* Petaling Jaya: World Wildlife Fund for Nature, Malaysia.

II

Politics

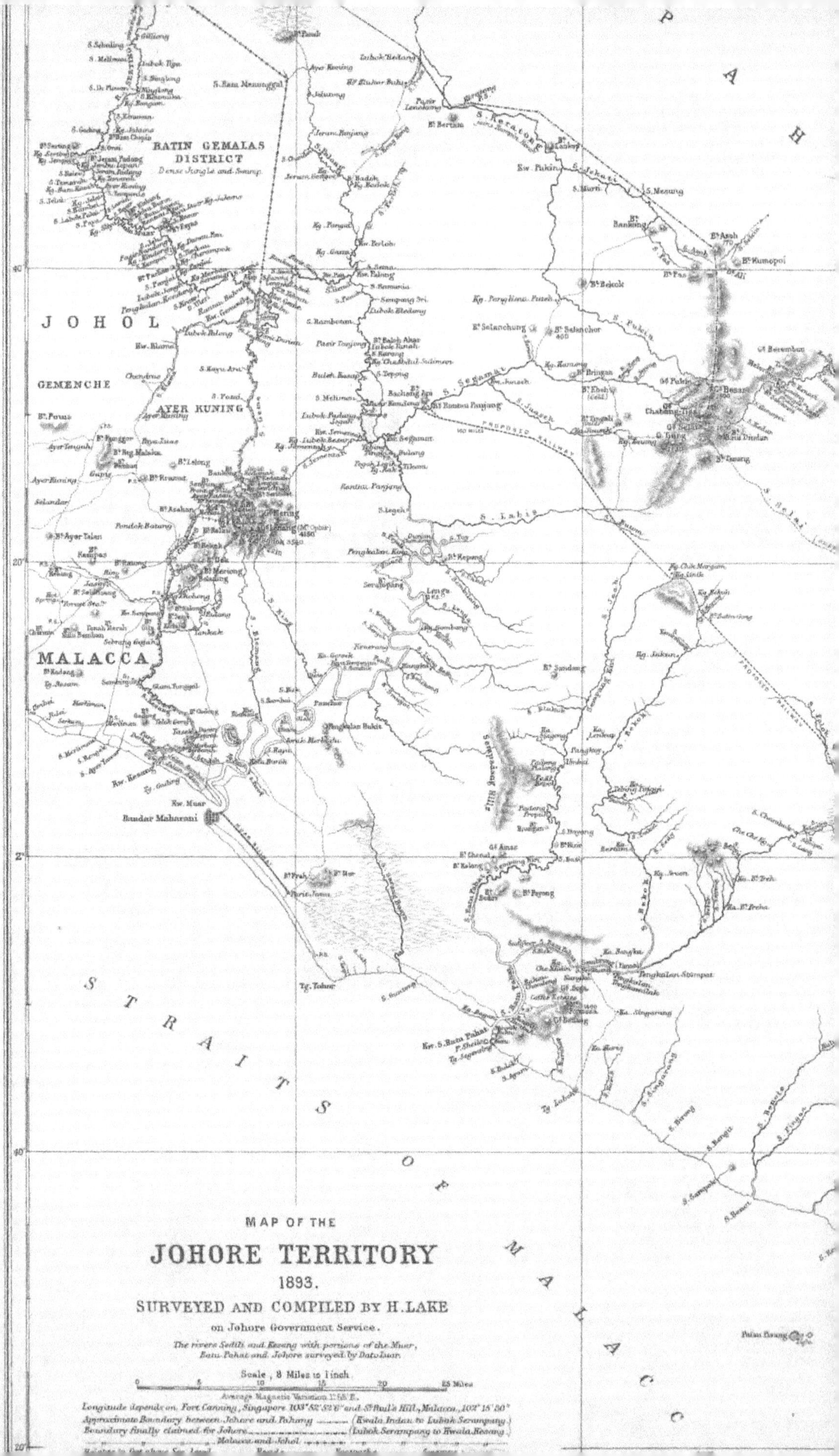

MAP OF THE

JOHORE TERRITORY

1893.

SURVEYED AND COMPILED BY H. LAKE

on Johore Government Service.

The rivers Sedili and Kesang with portions of the Muar,
Batu-Pahat and Johore surveyed by Dato Luar.

Scale, 8 Miles to 1 inch.

Average Magnetic Variation 1°55′E.

Longitude depends on, Fort Canning, Singapore, 103°52′52″E and St Paul's Hill, Malacca, 102°15′30″

Approximate Boundary between Johore and Pahang (Kuala Indau to Lubok Serampang)

Boundary finally claimed for Johore (Lubok Serampang to Kwala Kesang)

Malacca and Johol

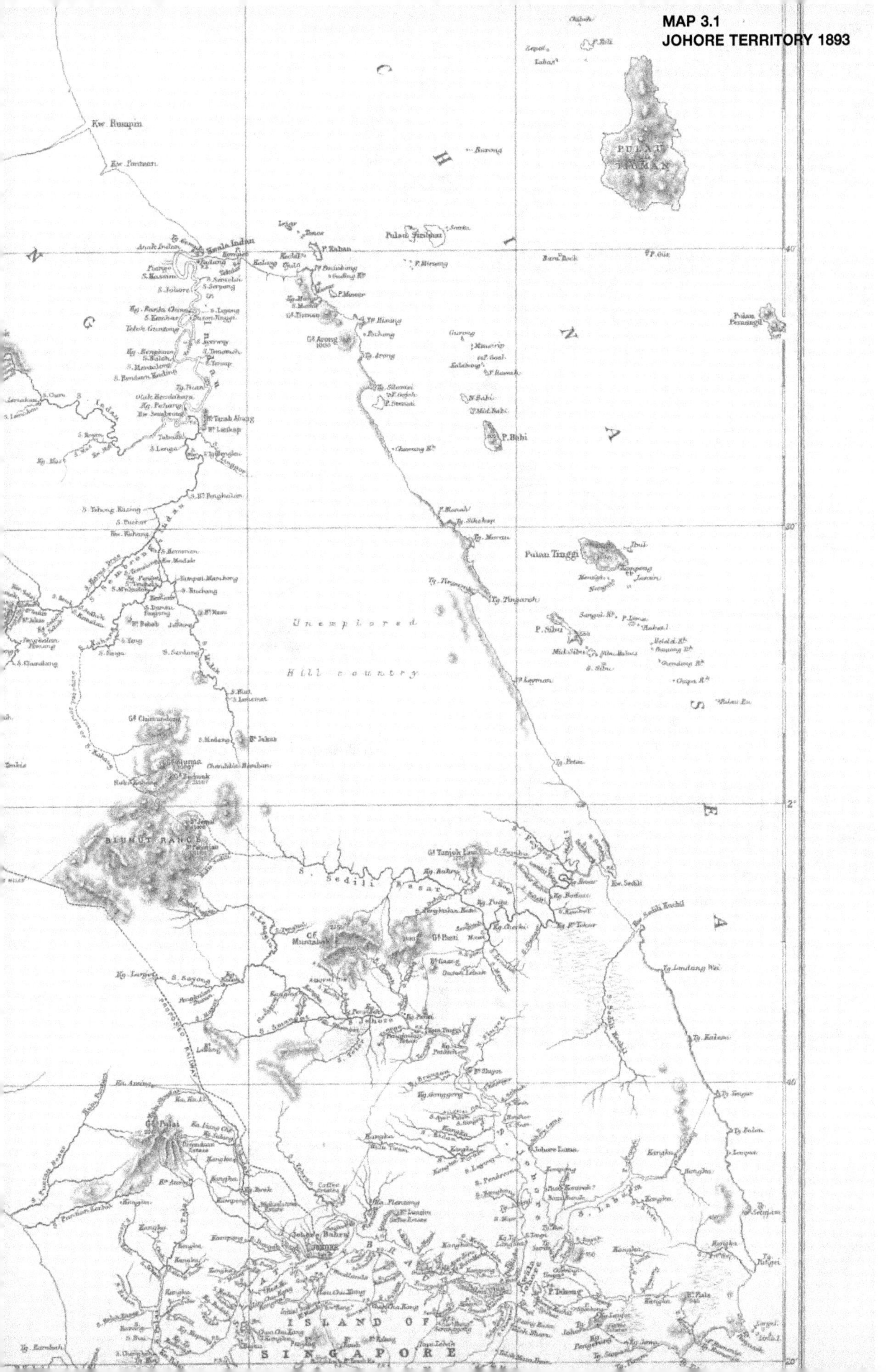

MAP 3.1
JOHORE TERRITORY 1893

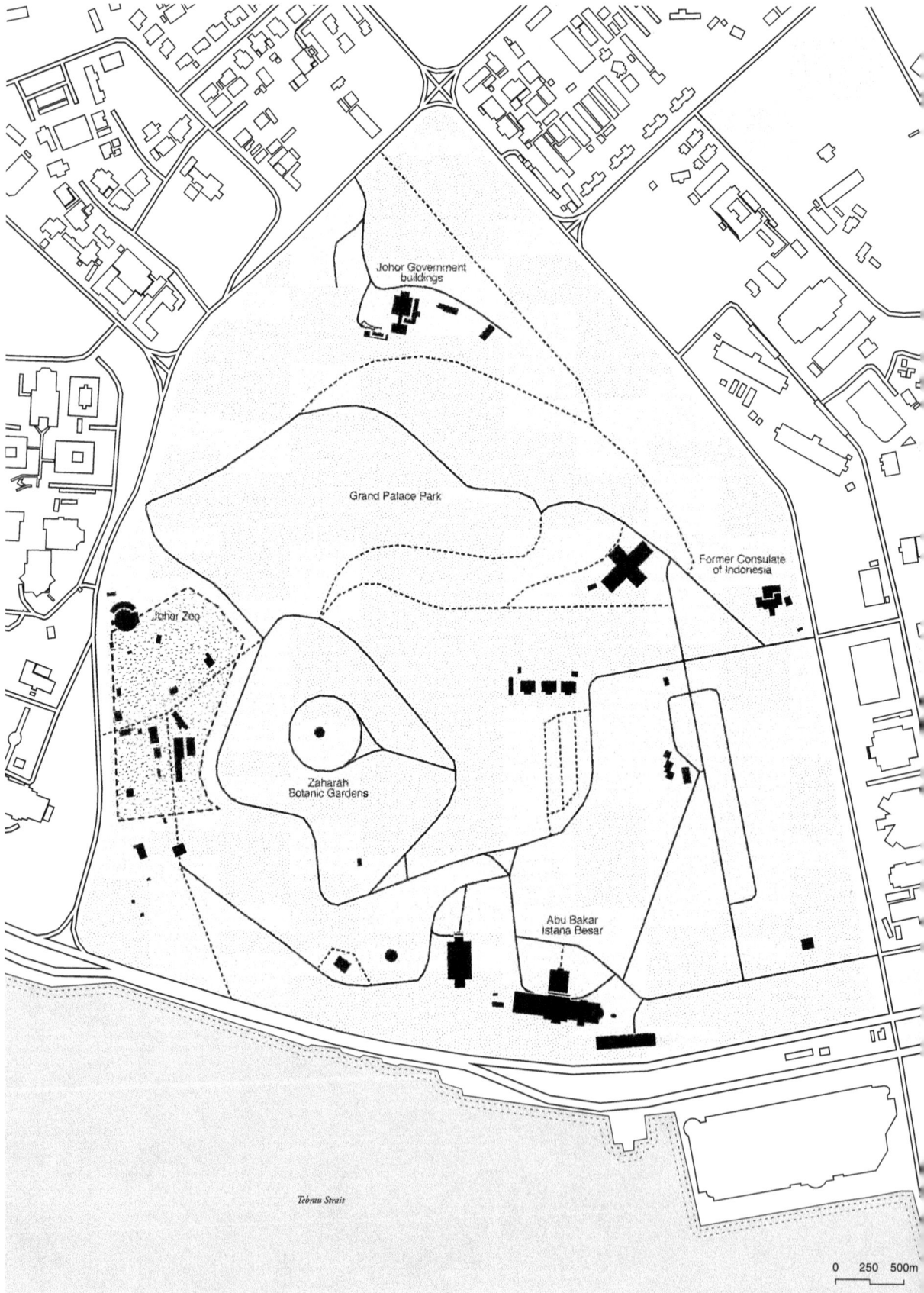

MAP 3.2
ISTANA BESAR AND
THE GRAND PALACE PARK

Johor Government
buildings

Grand Palace Park

Former Consulate
of Indonesia

Johor Zoo

Zaharah
Botanic Gardens

Abu Bakar
Istana Besar

Tebrau Strait

0   250   500m

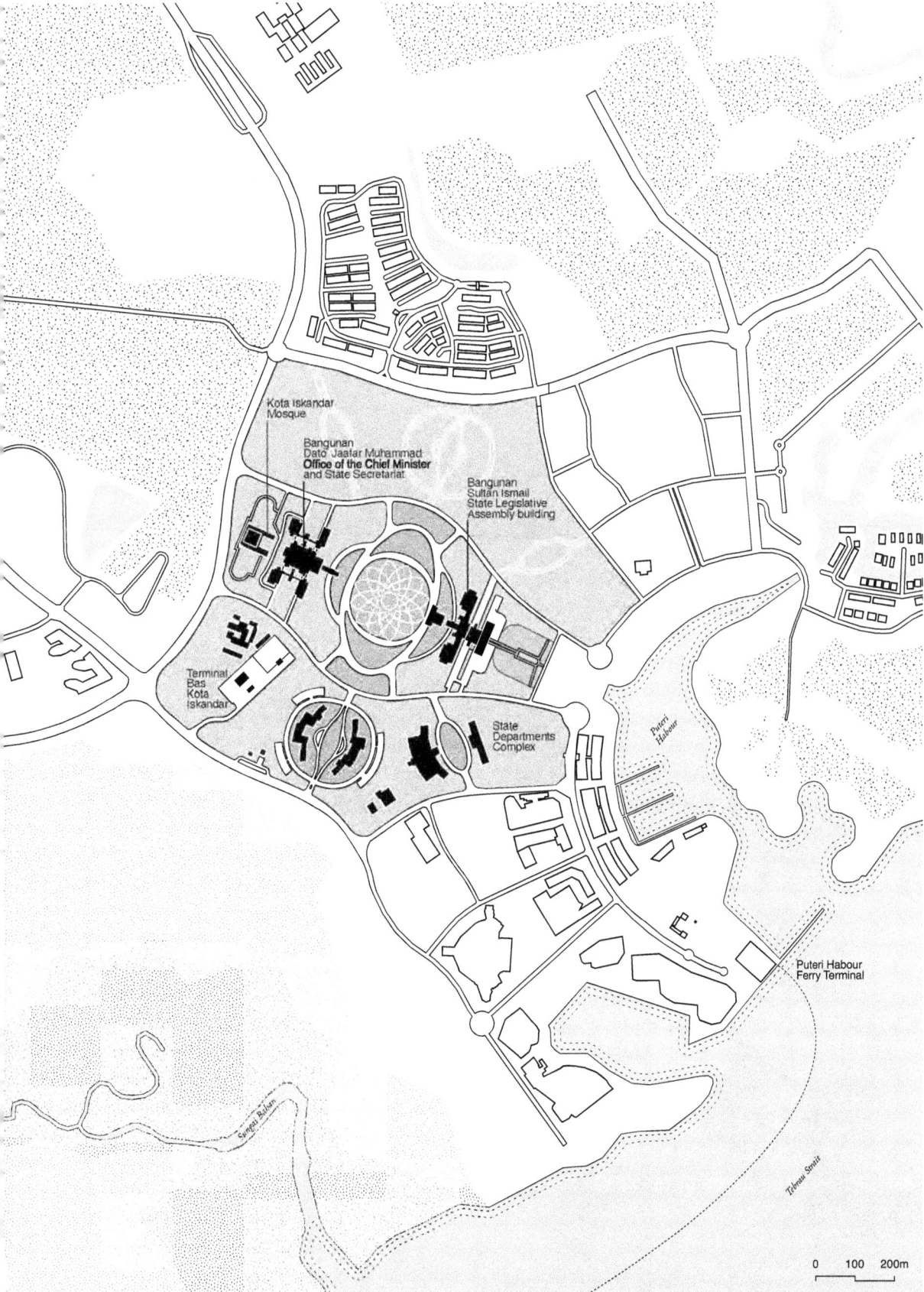

MAP 3.3
KOTA ISKANDAR, NUSAJAYA CITY
JOHOR'S NEW GOVERNMENTAL SEAT

Kota Iskandar
Mosque

Bangunan
Dato Jaafar Muhammad
Office of the Chief Minister
and State Secretariat

Bangunan
Sultan Ismail
State Legislative
Assembly building

Terminal
Bas
Kota
Iskandar

State
Departments
Complex

Puteri
Habour

Puteri Habour
Ferry Terminal

Sungei Bahan

Tebrau Strait

0   100   200m

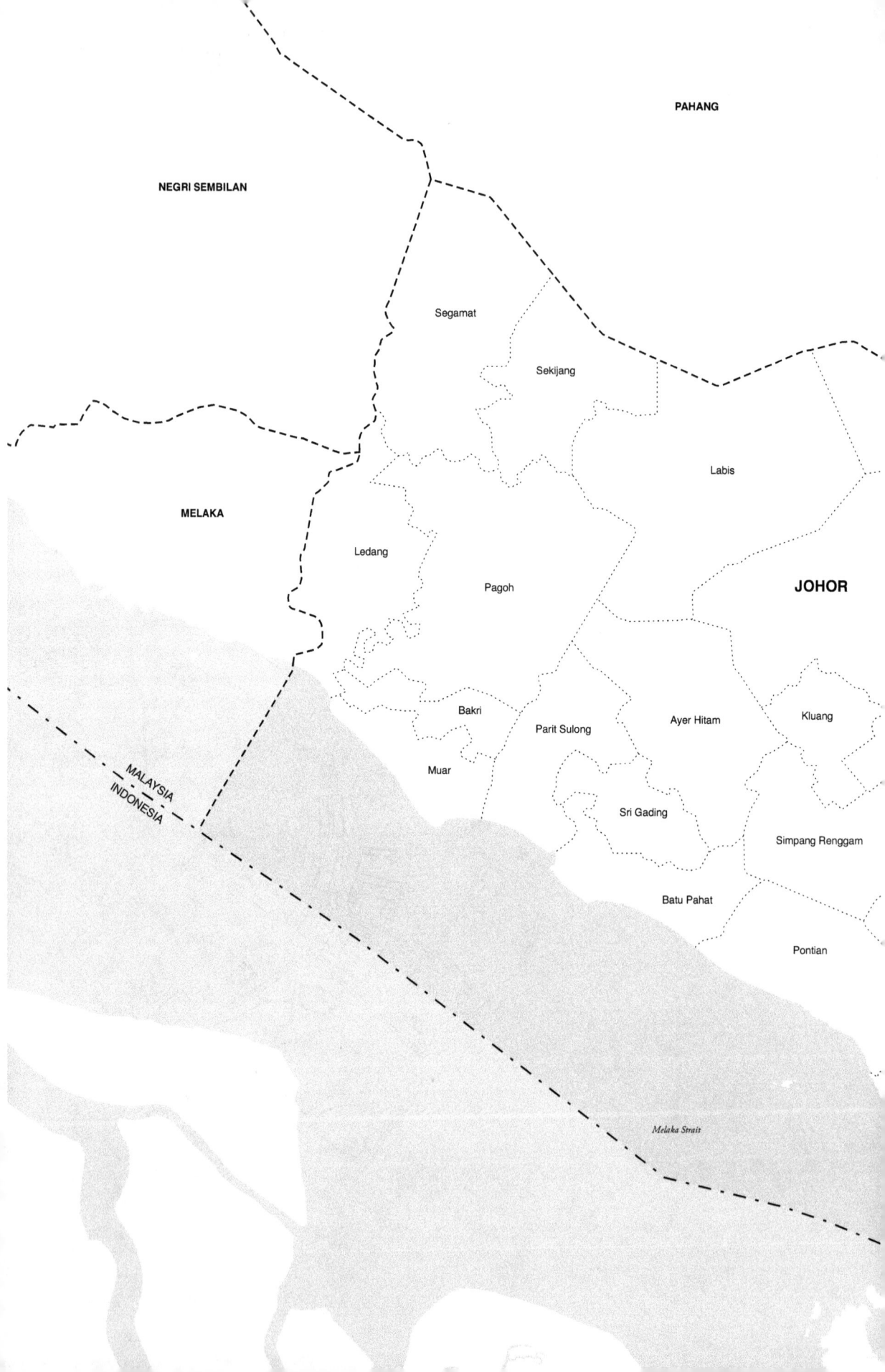

PAHANG

NEGRI SEMBILAN

Segamat

Sekijang

Labis

MELAKA

Ledang

Pagoh

JOHOR

Bakri

Ayer Hitam

Kluang

Parit Sulong

Muar

Sri Gading

Simpang Renggam

MALAYSIA
INDONESIA

Batu Pahat

Pontian

Melaka Strait

MAP 3.4
**PARLIAMENTARY CONSTITUENCY
BOUNDARIES IN JOHOR**

Mersing

Sembrong

*South China
Sea*

Kota Tinggi

Tenggara

Kulai

Tebrau

Pasir Gudang

anjong Piai

Pulai

Johor
Bahru

Iskandar Puteri

Pengerang

*Singapore
Strait*

SINGAPORE

0   10   20km

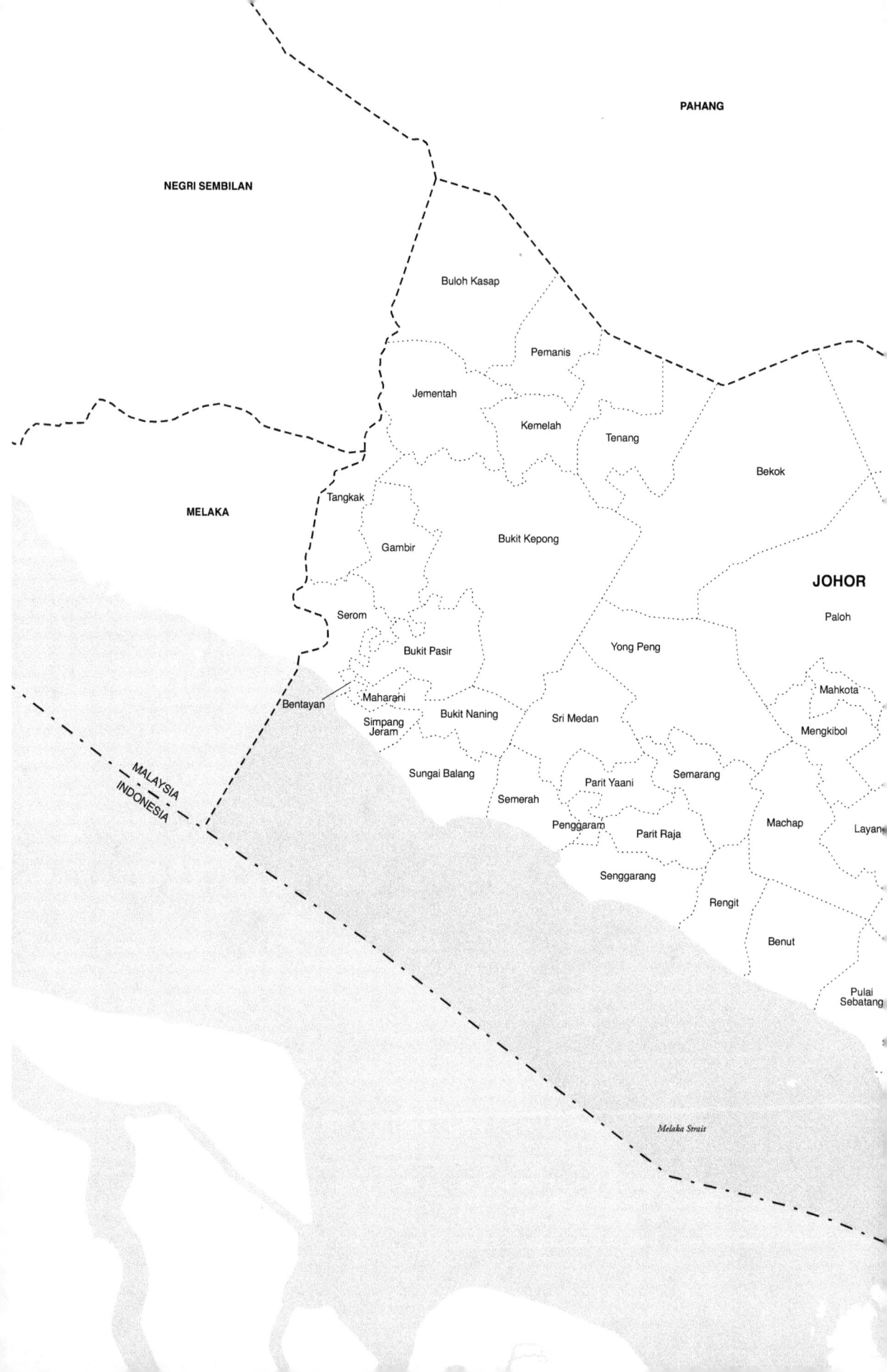

PAHANG

NEGRI SEMBILAN

Buloh Kasap

Pemanis

Jementah

Kemelah

Tenang

Bekok

MELAKA

Tangkak

Gambir

Bukit Kepong

JOHOR

Paloh

Serom

Bukit Pasir

Yong Peng

Mahkota

Bentayan

Maharani

Bukit Naning

Sri Medan

Mengkibol

Simpang
Jeram

Sungai Balang

Parit Yaani

Semarang

Semerah

Machap

Layan

Penggaram

Parit Raja

Senggarang

Rengit

Benut

Pulai
Sebatang

MALAYSIA
INDONESIA

Melaka Strait

MAP 3.5
STATE LEGISLATIVE
CONSTITUENCIES IN JOHOR

Endau

Kahang

Tenggaroh

*South China
Sea*

Panti

Sedili

Layang

Bukit Permai

Johor Lama

Pasir Raja

Bukit Batu

Senai

Penawar

Puteri Wangsa

Tiram

Skudai

Johor Jaya

Pekan Nanas

Perling

Permas

Kota Iskandar

Stulang

Tanjung Surat

Larkin

Kempas

Kukup

*Singapore
Strait*

SINGAPORE

0   10   20km

MAP 3.6

- Urban
- Semi-urban
- Rural

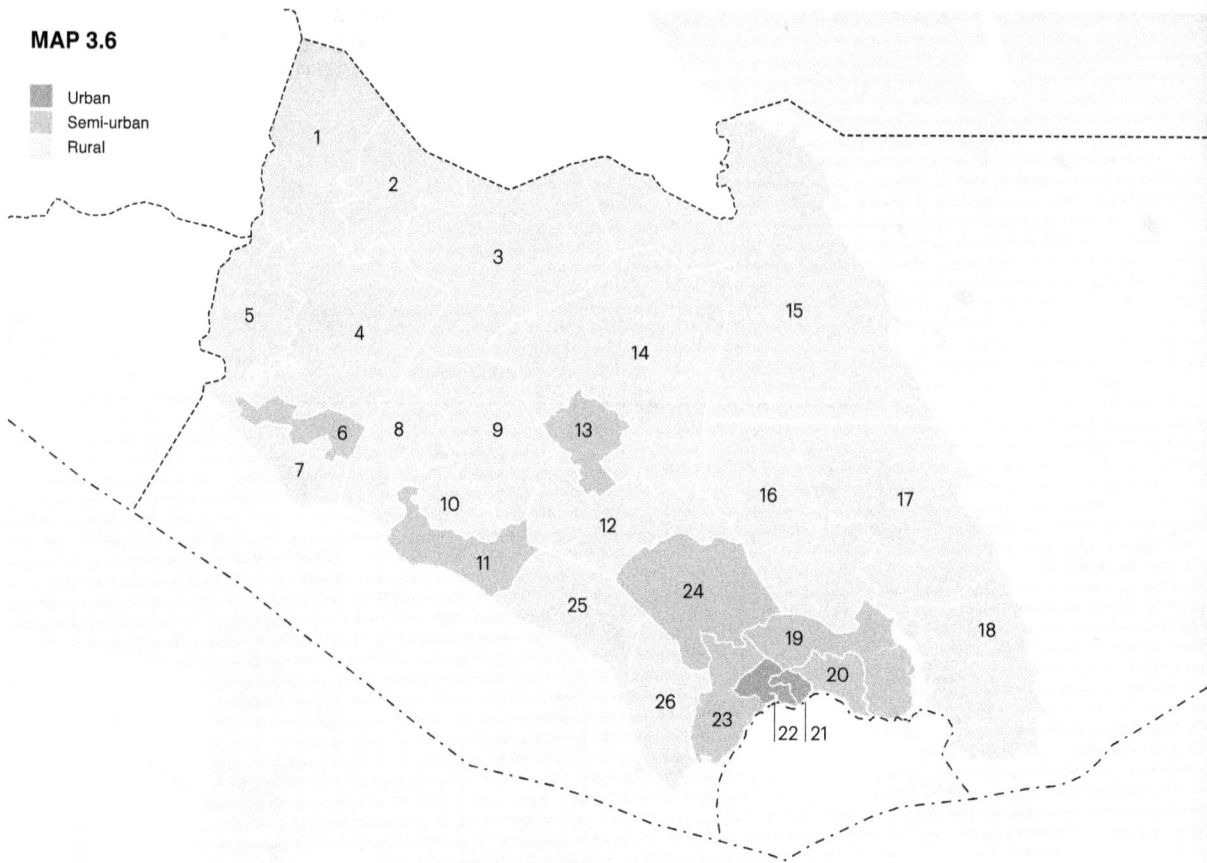

MAP 3.7

- Malay >60%
- Malay 55-60%
- Malay 50-55%
- Malay <50%

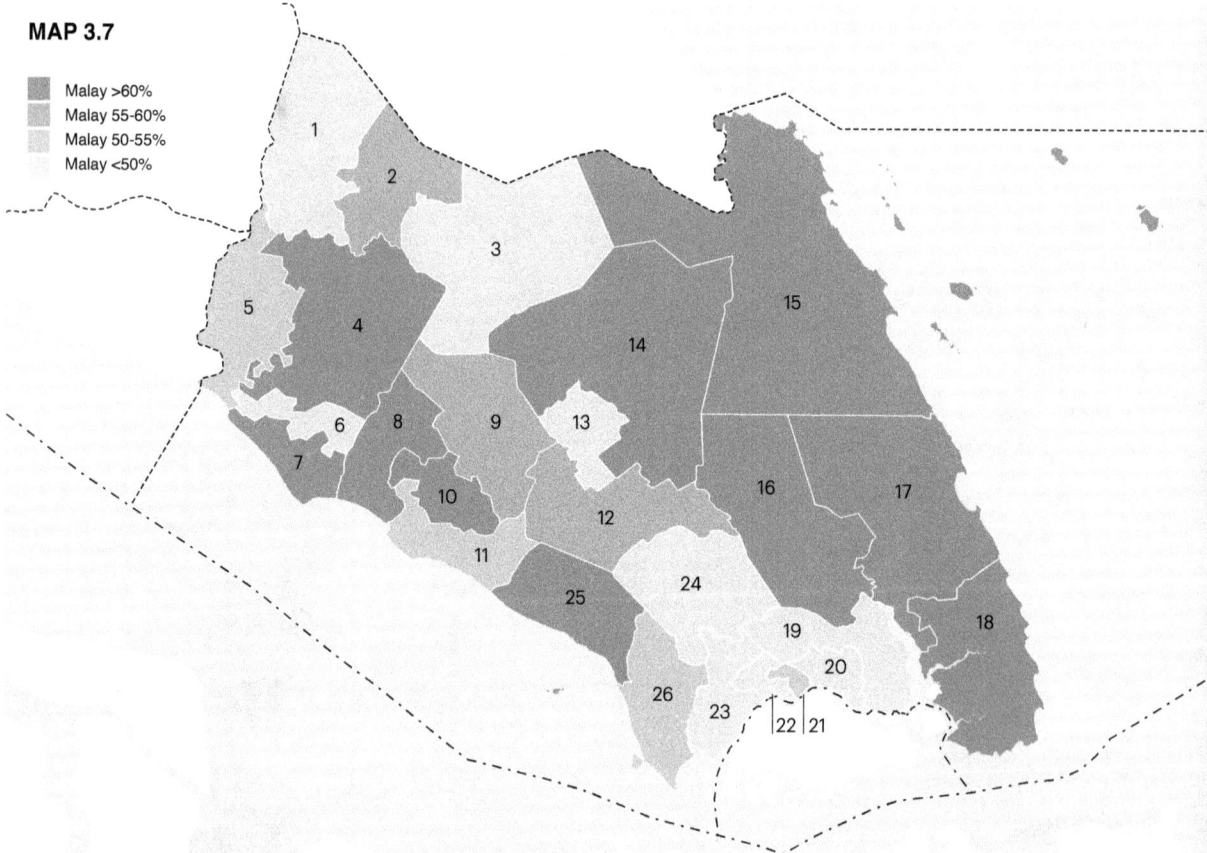

1	Segamat	14	Sembrong
2	Sekijang	15	Mersing
3	Labis	16	Tenggara
4	Pagoh	17	Kota Tinggi
5	Ledang	18	Pengerang
6	Bakri	19	Tebrau
7	Muar	20	Pasir Gudang
8	Parit Sulong	21	Johor Bahru
9	Ayer Hitam	22	Pulai
10	Sri Gading	23	Iskandar Puteri
11	Batu Pahat	24	Kulai
12	Simpang Renggam	25	Pontian
13	Kluang	26	Tanjong Piai

MAP 3.8

- Won by Barisan Nasional
- Won by Pakatan Harapan

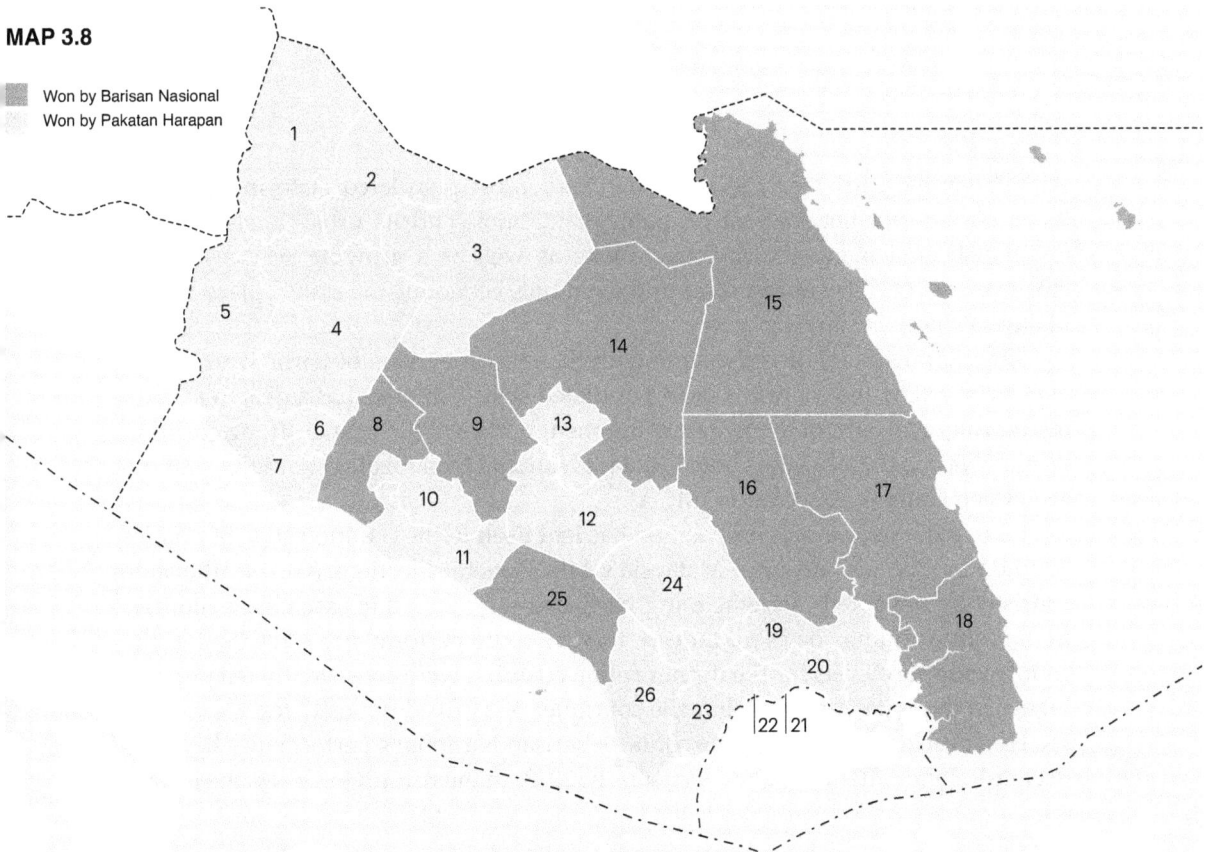

8

UMNO AND BARISAN NASIONAL IN JOHOR
A Time-Bound Fixed Deposit?[1]

Francis E. Hutchinson

INTRODUCTION

With 3.7 million residents, Johor is the third most populated state in Malaysia. Its ample interior houses vast oil palm plantations, and its urban areas are host to sophisticated manufacturing operations as well as a growing services sector. However, beyond its contribution to the nation's economy, the state's place within Malaysia's political context is key.

After Sarawak, Johor is the state with the most members of parliament, ahead of even Selangor, the country's most populated state. The state has a deep historical relationship with two of the largest component parties of the former ruling coalition Barisan Nasional (BN)—the United Malays National Organization (UMNO) and the Malaysian Chinese Association (MCA).

Johor's diverse ethnic composition has lent itself to the coalition style of politics adopted by BN and, up until Malaysia's 14th General Elections (GE-14), the state consistently delivered overwhelming parliamentary and state assembly majorities to the former ruling coalition. Indeed, relative to its performance elsewhere in the country, support levels for the former ruling coalition were consistently ten per cent higher in the state, earning Johor the sobriquet of a "fixed deposit" for BN.

However, as in the rest of the country, Barisan Nasional's performance began to decline in Johor after 2008 and, particularly, 2013. In the run-up to GE-14, the former ruling coalition was looking weak in the state, particularly in urban, semi-urban, and mixed rural seats.

The state's size, prestige, and ethnic heterogeneity made it of interest to other parties. The DAP had been active in urban and Chinese-majority areas in the state since the 1960s. Following schisms in the Islamic party PAS and UMNO in 2015, Johor's sizeable Malay population was important for fledgling parties such as Parti Pribumi Bersatu Malaysia (PPBM) and Parti Amanah Negara (Amanah).

Consequently, the opposition coalition, Pakatan Harapan (PH) declared the state a key battleground for the 2018 elections and made sure to deploy a number of heavy hitters to contest in key constituencies. Nonetheless, the conventional wisdom going into GE-14 was that although BN was looking vulnerable, the long track record and advantages of incumbency meant that they would still retain the state.

Yet, in May 2018, the seemingly invincible BN suffered a stinging defeat in Johor, including in many of its heartland constituencies. In order to shed light on this unexpected turn of events, this chapter asks two questions. First, why was BN so successful for so long in the state? Second, which of the structural factors that favoured the former ruling coalition in Johor came undone in GE-14?

In order to shed light on these questions, this chapter is comprised of five sections. Following this introduction, the second section will look at BN's track record in Johor from 1959 to 2013, compare it with national trends, and establish reasons underpinning this exceptional performance. The subsequent section will ask if there were any state-level factors that contributed to BN's exceptional performance in Johor. The fourth section will analyse the outcomes of GE-14 in the state. The fifth and final section will analyse which mechanisms underpinning Johor's exceptionalism were undone and which, if any, still remain relevant today.

BARISAN NASIONAL'S TRACK RECORD IN JOHOR (1959–2013)

While BN has performed very well in electoral terms across Malaysia, its track record in Johor has been outstanding. Figures 8.1 and 8.2 set out BN's share of parliamentary and state assembly seats in Johor from 1959 to 2013. With regard to parliamentary seats, the ruling coalition secured a clean sweep in ten out of the thirteen elections during this period. In two elections, it lost one seat, Kluang, to the Democratic Action Party (DAP) in 1978 and another, Bakri, to the same party in 2008. This performance is unmatched in other large peninsular states such as Selangor and Perak, which witnessed significant Opposition inroads as early as 1969. Other elections which saw large national reversals for BN such as 1990, 1999, and 2008 also had a muted effect in Johor. It was only in 2013 that the opposition garnered a significant number of seats—five—for the first time.

This performance is mirrored—albeit to a lesser degree—at the state level. In nine elections, BN secured more than 90 per cent of state seats in Johor. In three more, namely those of 1959, 1990, and 2008, the ruling coalition secured no less than 85 per cent of the total, conceding only four to six seats to the Opposition. In

FIGURE 8.1
Parliamentary Seats in Johor, 1959–2013

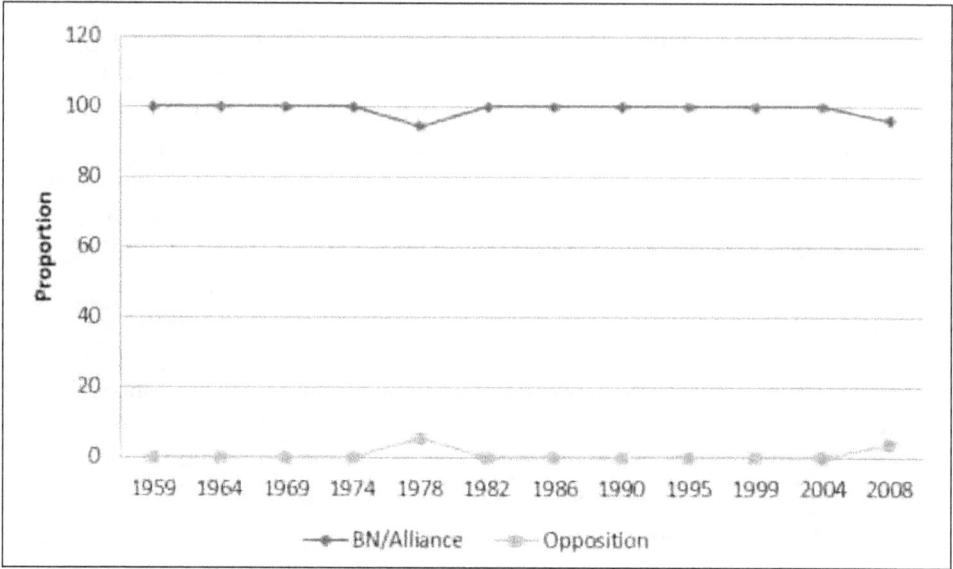

Source: NSTP (1990); Election Commission Malaysia, various years.

FIGURE 8.2
SLA Seats in Johor, 1959–2013

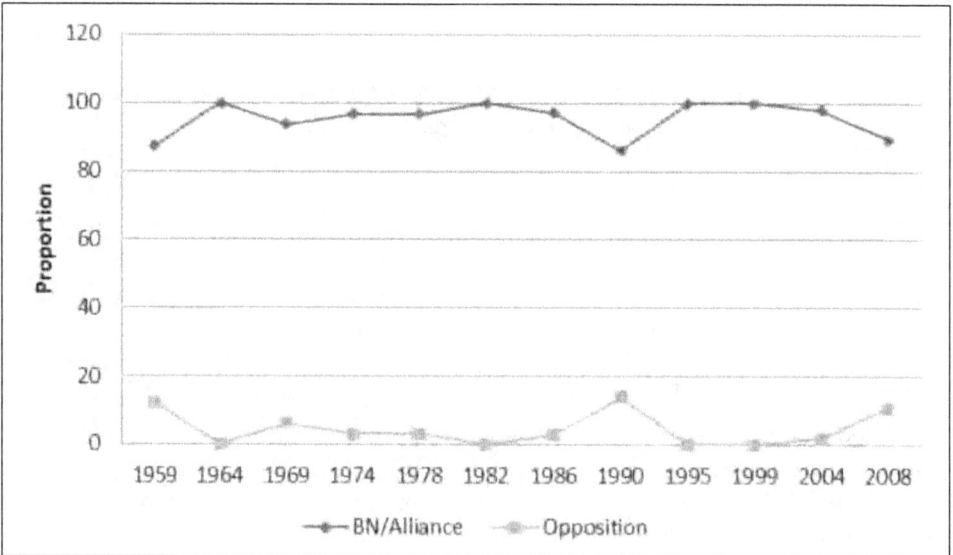

Source: NSTP (1990); Election Commission Malaysia, various years.

1969, Johor was a rare exception to the large swing against the ruling coalition, as it yielded a mere two seats to the Opposition that year. In contrast, the coalition lost fourteen state seats in Selangor, twenty in Penang, and twenty-one in Perak. In 2008, another bad year for BN nationally, the Opposition gained state-level majorities in Kelantan, Kedah, Penang, Perak, and Selangor. In contrast, in Johor, this downturn constituted an increase from one to six state seats—out of a total of fifty-six seats in the legislative assembly. Only in 2013, when BN lost a total of eighteen seats did it begin to look vulnerable.

At one level, BN has performed so well in Johor because of its effective embodiment of the "consociational model" of politics. This term, according to Lijphart (1977), refers to a framework for governing plural societies—those characterized by cleavages due to language, religion, or ethnicity. Under this mechanism, societies with substantial internal divisions are able to avoid conflict and maintain stability through the representation of the main interest groups in government as well as effective negotiation between their leaders. Thus, even though the various communities remain divided, peace and stability are maintained.

This "grand coalition", comprising the elite of each of the communities, can effectively mediate if three additional requirements are met. First, there is a mutual veto in decision-making—meaning that the majority is unable to unilaterally impose its will on all groups. Second, important positions such as public office or the civil service are allocated proportionally. Third, the various groups possess a significant degree of autonomy to manage their own affairs (1977, p. 25).

A number of academics have argued that Malaysia largely, if not completely, meets these conditions (Milne and Mauzy 1999, pp. 17–18; Crouch 1996, pp. 152–53). The grand coalition can be seen in the Alliance, founded in 1954 and comprising UMNO, Malaysian Chinese Association (MCA), and the Malaysian Indian Congress (MIC)—each representing a numerically significant community. This coalition was motivated by electoral incentives, as it allowed the three parties to pool and then field candidates in all seats. The component parties and candidates usually—but not always—matched the largest community in each constituency. Negotiations between the parties were held at the elite level prior to elections, with agreements on the sharing out of candidatures for parliamentary and state seats, ministerial positions, and quotas in the civil service. This same dynamic also privileged moderate and consensual policies, which then enabled voters from different communities to vote across ethnic lines for the local representative of the Alliance, as they knew that their interests were represented within the grouping (Horowitz 1993, p. 33).

This logic has been retained in the post-1969 period, albeit in a more limited sense. Following the ethnic unrest in 1969 and ensuing declaration of emergency, the compact between the component parties was reformulated. On one hand, the Alliance was expanded to incorporate a larger number of parties and renamed Barisan Nasional. On the other, within the coalition, UMNO's share of power and cabinet positions increased significantly. Thus, while the other component parties lost relative power, UMNO's unfettered access to resources constituted the main incentive for other coalition members to cooperate (Mauzy 1993, p. 110). In addition, the coalition mechanism continued to act as a "guarantee" against total exclusion (Horowitz 1993, p. 33).

In Johor, the "grand coalition" model was put in place in the run-up to the 1959 general elections. UMNO, MCA, and MIC leaders agreed on the allocation of seats between the parties, and this formula has been used—with very minor variations—in every election since then. Under this formula, UMNO candidates contest in roughly two-thirds of parliamentary and 60–65 per cent of state seats. The other BN component parties compete in the remainder.

With the exception of minor modifications made following the four electoral redelineation exercises, these seat allocations have remained unchanged (Figure 8.3). In particular, the proportion of candidatures for UMNO and non-UMNO component parties has rarely been altered, although changes have occurred between non-UMNO BN component parties more frequently. And, relative to parliamentary seats, modifications in the allocation of state seats also occur more often. For example, the 2004 and 2008 allocation of parliamentary seats between the coalition members was identical, but at the state level, one constituency—Bukit Batu—was contested by Gerakan in 2004 but passed to an MCA candidate in 2008.

In Johor, under the grand coalition model, UMNO contested in two types of parliamentary seats. Following the 2002–3 re-delineation exercise (which increased the number of parliamentary seats from 20 to 26), UMNO fielded 16 candidates in the 2004 and 2008 elections and 17 in 2013. The first and numerically most important type of constituency consisted of 13 Malay-majority and predominantly rural seats along the eastern coast such as Pengerang, Kota Tinggi, and Mersing, and in the

FIGURE 8.3
UMNO Share of BN Candidatures, 1959–2013

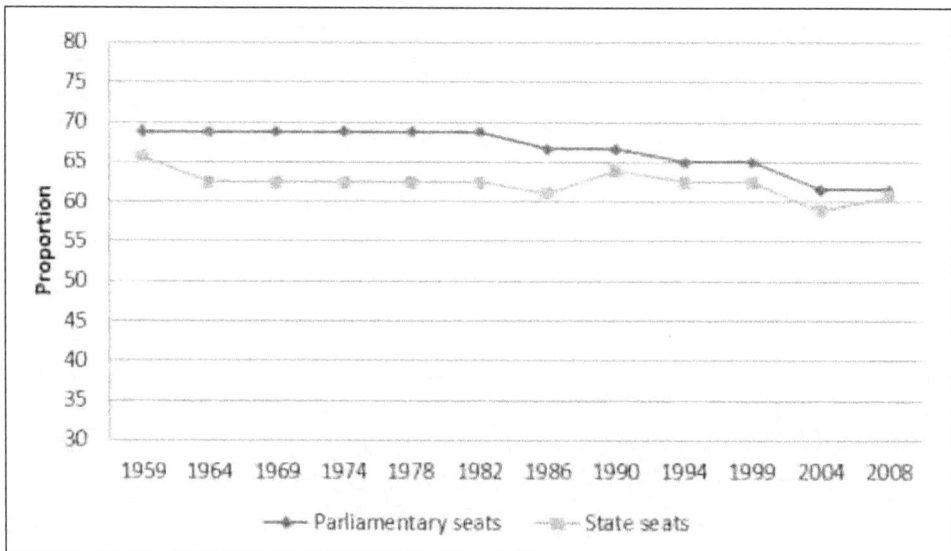

Source: NSTP (1990); Election Commission Malaysia, various years.

FIGURE 8.4
UMNO Seats in Johor

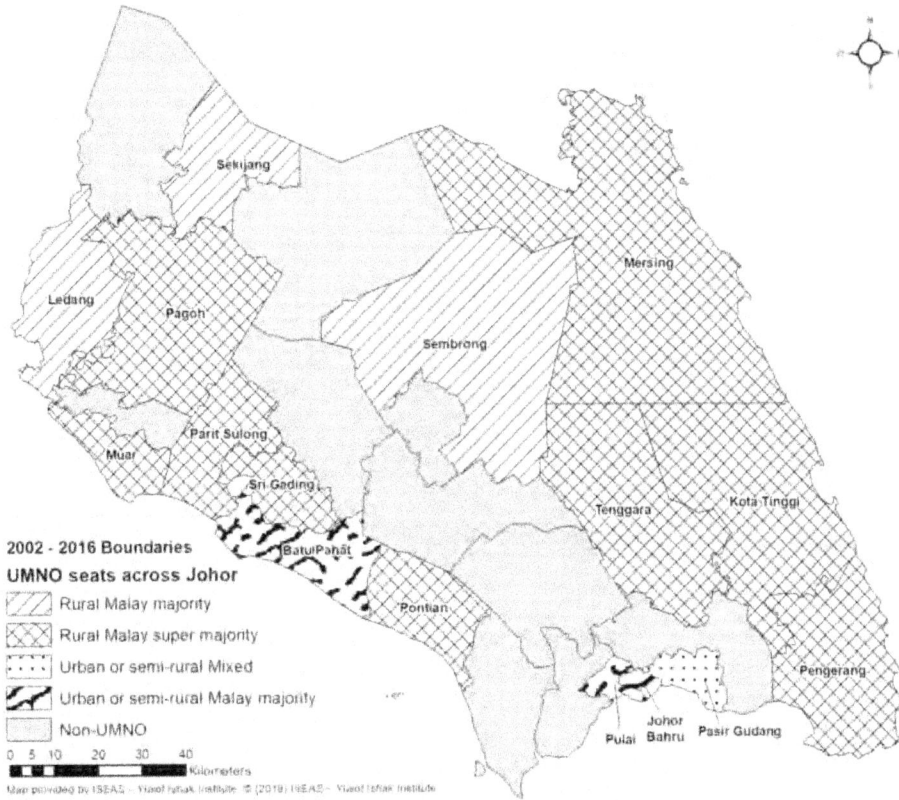

state's interior such as Sembrong, Pagoh, and Sri Gading. The second group consisted of three mixed seats in urban and semi-urban areas near the state capital, such as Johor Bahru, Pulai, and Pasir Gudang.

In turn, the non-UMNO component parties active in Johor—MCA, MIC, and Gerakan—shared the remaining ten seats. These parties contested in mixed seats in semi-urban areas such as Kluang, Batu Pahat, Gelang Patah and Segamat. There were two notable exceptions to this pattern. Gerakan fielded candidates in Simpang Renggam and MCA did the same in Ayer Hitam. Unlike the other seats, which were mixed, these were Malay-majority constituencies.

It is by focusing on these seats that the workings of the "grand coalition" are made manifest. The number of candidates from the different component parties enabled BN to field Malay candidates in Malay-majority seats and non-Malay candidates in mixed seats. However, because of its unified front, the coalition was also able to attract votes across communal lines. Thus, the candidates from non-UMNO BN parties were able to win solid majorities in Malay-majority areas. For example, despite

FIGURE 8.5
Non-UMNO Seats in Johor

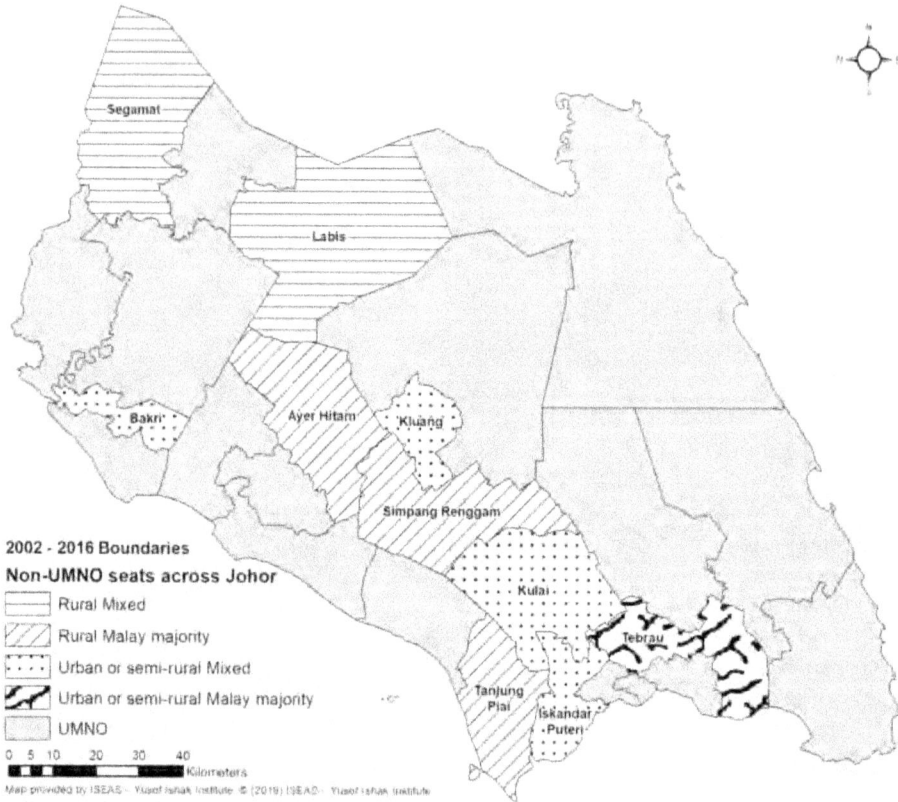

ethnic Indians only comprising 13 per cent of voters in Segamat, BN traditionally fielded candidates from MIC in the constituency and won every time. Conversely, this mechanism allowed UMNO candidates to carry the day in mixed seats such as Johor Bahru, Pulai, and Pasir Gudang.

This mechanism was replicated at the state level, with UMNO contesting 60–65 per cent of seats and the other coalition partners the remainder. As with the parliamentary model, the candidates usually—but not always—matched the dominant ethnic community in each constituency. And, in constituencies where this was not the case, BN was still able to garner sufficient votes across the various communities to form a majority.

The effect of BN's majorities was then magnified by Malaysia's first-past-the-post parliamentary system. Thus, in 2004, the coalition's 79.6 per cent of the popular vote in Johor translated into 100 per cent of parliamentary seats. And, its significantly lower share of 65.3 per cent in the 2008 elections still resulted in it getting 96 per cent of parliamentary seats. Likewise, its 54.9 vote share in 2013 was converted into 81 per cent of parliamentary constituencies in Johor.

This electoral performance has been further supported by significant mal-apportionment across the various parliamentary and state constituencies. The Reid Commission, which designed Malaysia's parliamentary system and drafted the Constitution, sought to ensure a degree of proportionality across seats, arguing that there should be no more than a 15 per cent discrepancy in size. However, these strictures were bypassed through a series of measures that reduced the power and independence of the Electoral Commission and transferred decisions regarding electoral delimitation issues to Parliament. Furthermore, the Electoral Commission has had a very flexible and liberal definition of what constitutes undue weightage (Saravanamuttu 2016, pp. 36–41).

Looking at the voting population across the various constituencies in Johor in 2004, it can be seen that there was indeed a significant variation in their size. The smallest constituency, Tenggara, had 29,800 voters and the largest, Johor Bahru, 91,100—yielding a factor of three. Allowing for a difference of 15 per cent from the average number of voters (48,000), there were actually only six seats out of twenty-six that were not over- or under-represented. In contrast, eleven were over- and nine under-represented. The over-represented constituencies were all rural. Conversely, of the state's nine urban or semi-urban constituencies, only one was of average size, and eight was under-represented.

Looking at the split between UMNO and non-UMNO component parties, the former had the bulk of the under-size and over-represented constituencies—eight out of the total. UMNO and the other component parties split the average-size seats. Regarding the over-size seats, UMNO had five and the other parties four. Thus, while UMNO clearly benefitted from having a substantial number of over-represented seats, it also fielded candidates in the two largest and, consequently, under-represented parliamentary constituencies of Pulai and Johor Bahru.

Prior to the 2018 redelineation exercise, previous adjustments took place in 1974, 1984, 1994, and 2002–3 (Saravanamuttu 2016, p. 41). These exercises did not directly tackle the most glaring cases of malapportionment, and often exacerbated them—in many cases creating new constituencies that cut across natural barriers or ignore natural conglomerations of voters (Ostwald 2017, p. 9).

Consequently, from 1959 to 2018, BN was able to dominate in Johor at the parliamentary and state legislative assembly levels due to: its effective use of the

TABLE 8.1
Parliamentary Constituencies in Johor, 2004

Constituencies	Number	UMNO	Non-UMNO	Rural	Urban, Semi-Urban
Over-represented	11	8	3	11	0
Average size	6	3	3	5	1
Under-represented	9	5	4	1	8

Source: Election Commission Malaysia (2004); categorization of rural and urban parliamentary constituencies follows Politweet, https://docs.google.com/spreadsheets/d/1avEv-WaeZwcYsq48GtieTrlh5fdsIVUliBeFGRI8-C0/edit#gid=0 (accessed 24 November 2017).

consociational "grand coalition" model; Malaysia's first-past-the-post electoral system; and significant malapportionment that favoured a disproportionate number of Malay-majority and smaller, rural seats.

In essence, these structural advantages were replicated across the country and underpinned BN's dominance at the national level. Nevertheless, even by these standards, BN's dominance of the Johorean political scene was exceptional. Figure 8.6 sets out the level of popular support for UMNO at the national level as well as for Johor from 1959 to 2013. While broadly following the national trend, with significant dips in 1969, 1999, 2008, and 2013 popular support for BN in Johor is consistently some 10 per cent higher than it is at the national level—at an average 70 per cent as opposed to the national level of 60 per cent.

Consequently, this indicates that, even taking into account the structural factors outlined above, Johor is unique within the national context. The next section will analyse reasons for BN's exceptional performance in Malaysia's southernmost state.

JOHOR'S EXCEPTIONALISM

This section will advance three reasons for the exceptionally high level of support that BN has enjoyed in the state. The first two are directly linked to the state's pattern of development during the pre-independence period, and the third is the localized outcome of a national policy implemented following independence.

FIGURE 8.6
BN Vote Share Nationally and in Johor, 1959–2013

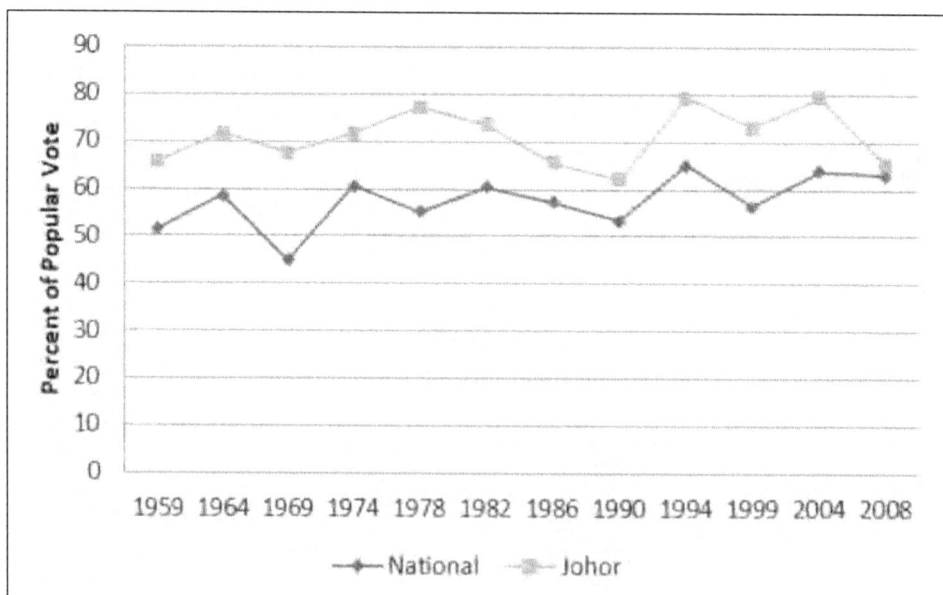

Source: NSTP (1990); Election Commission Malaysia, various years.

UMNO's Legacy

More than any other state in Malaysia, Johor has a deep relationship with UMNO. The party was founded in Johor Bahru by a Johorean, and the state has produced a disproportionate number of the organization's leaders. The positive association of UMNO with nation-building at the local level has enabled the party to build up an uncommonly large membership base and extensive grassroots network in the state. The resulting higher level of competition for elected posts, coupled with an effective mechanism for grooming and deploying leaders at both state and federal levels, has enabled Johor to produce both effective local-level leaders as well as national-level party cadres and politicians.

The roots of this relationship lie in Malaysia's pre-independence period and Johor's unique model of development under its traditional rulers. In order to maximize their autonomy and pre-empt British intervention, Johor's sultans were committed to state-building, good governance and providing high levels of public services. Of key importance was the Johor government's Malay Officers' Scheme, an initiative which sought to train local cadres for top-level civil service positions. Consequently, prior to the Second World War, a full 90 per cent of administrative positions in the sultanate were occupied by local Malays—a much higher figure than elsewhere in Malaya, where the process of grooming locals for leadership positions was only in its infancy. Much of this cohort of senior civil servants remained in the Johor government during the Japanese occupation (Hutchinson 2015).

When the British returned to Malaya, the relaxation of controls on political activity and subsequent ill-fated attempt to establish the Malayan Union led to the profusion of local political organizations. The declaration of the Malayan Union led to the first visible manifestation of Malay ethno-nationalism. Fearing the loss of their status as the indigenous inhabitants of the country, the Union was stridently opposed by the Malays. During the first period of opposition to the Malayan Union, a large number of Malay political organizations were established or revived. Beyond their opposition to the Malayan Union, these groups had very diverse political aims, ranging from state-based associations led by the Malay elite to pan-Malayan movements that were more anti-colonial and ethno-nationalist (Amoroso 2014).

Johor's well-developed education system and high level of literacy, central position between Singapore and the Federated Malay States, and sheer mass of civil servants with senior-level experience made it fertile ground for grassroots organizations. For example, Onn Jaafar, a District Officer in the Johor Government, founded the Peninsular Malay Movement of Johor. Abdul Rahman Yassin, the State Commissioner, established the Johor Malay Union, and Sardon Jubir, who worked in the Public Prosecutor's Bureau, set up the Singapore Malay Union. All of these became feeder parties for UMNO upon its founding.

Due to these factors, members of the Johor government dominated UMNO's national leadership and membership base in its formative period. During the party's first ten years, Johor contributed fifteen out of sixty-one Supreme Council members—one quarter of the total and more than any other state. Other first-generation leaders from Johor include: Hussein Onn, third Prime Minister; Abdul Rahman Yassin, first President of the Senate; Mohamad Noah Bin Omar, first Speaker of the Lower House; Suleiman Abdul Rahman, first Local Government, Housing, and Town Planning Minister; Awang Hassan, Deputy Speaker of the House; and Sardon Jubir, first Public Works Minister. All of these leaders had their professional debut in the Johor government in the pre-war period or during the Japanese occupation (Hutchinson 2015, p. 127).

Beyond UMNO's central leadership, people from Johor dominated the Youth and Women's sections of the party. The first and third Presidents of the Youth Wing as well as the second, third, and fourth Presidents of the Women's section were from the state (Funston 1980, pp. 298–303; Arifful 2000). Despite leadership of UMNO passing to Tunku Abdul Rahman in 1951, the party headquarters remained in Johor Bahru until 1955. In addition, Johoreans remained at the head of the Youth and Women's wings until the mid-1960s and early 1970s, respectively (Hutchinson 2015, p. 128).

Consequently, Johor's connection with UMNO is deep, and the party is associated with the protection of Malay rights, the royalty, nation-building, and a tradition of public service.[2] The state's estimated party membership of 400,000 is the largest in the country and UMNO-Johor has an extensive grassroots network—particularly among the Women's wing.[3] Furthermore, in Johor, there are a considerable number of ulama who are UMNO members, which is unusual in Malaysia and further attests to the party's ability to attract community leaders.[4] This positive association and large membership base, in turn, result in high levels of competition for leadership positions.[5]

This leadership base has been effectively deployed at both the state and national levels. During the 1970s, under the second Mentri Besar, Othman Saat, the state-level party machinery established a dual track for promising leaders. Those with more grassroots and community liaison ability were encouraged to run in state seats, develop community outreach activities, and build social capital with voters. In contrast, those that had more developed strategic skills were fielded for parliamentary seats, and even placed in safe constituencies to allow full concentration on national matters. This ensured that UMNO had good representation at the national level, so that the state could push for federal investment.[6]

Consequently, throughout the years, Johor was able to maintain its high membership numbers in the state as well as producing an important number of senior UMNO figures. Beyond the independence leaders mentioned above, this includes the following senior-level politicians and cabinet members with their current or former positions: Musa Hitam, Deputy Prime Minister; Mohamed Rahmat, Information Minister; Shahrir Samad, Domestic Trade and Consumer Affairs Minister; Muhyiddin Yassin, Deputy Prime Minister; Syed Hamid, Minister of Foreign Affairs; Abdul Ghani Othman, Minister of Sports, Youth, and Culture; Hishamuddin Hussein, Minister of Defence; Azalina Othman, Minister in the Prime Minister's Department; and Nur Jazlan, Deputy Home Minister.

Control of Islam

The second reason that BN, and more particularly UMNO, have done well in Johor is that the party's main rival for Malay voters, the Pan-Malaysian Islamic Party (PAS), has had relatively little traction. This was due to the tight control over religious issues exercised by the Sultan of Johor, which then entailed a less hospitable environment for the religious outlook favoured by PAS.

As with UMNO's local-level legacy, the reasons for this lie in Johor's development during the colonial period. Prior to independence, Malaysia's traditional rulers, or sultans, were the unquestioned authorities on religious matters. Despite pervasive British involvement in many areas of governance, Malaya's colonizers were reluctant to interfere in matters pertaining to religion. This sphere of influence was clearly established in treaties signed between the British and the sultans, where the latter had authority over this matter as well as Malay custom (Winstedt 1931, p. 9).

In the case of Johor, this prerogative was zealously guarded. Prior to British control being established, Abu Bakar, the traditional ruler who laid the foundations for Johor's development, had a Constitution drafted in 1895. While never explicitly recognized by the British, this document established the institutional foundations of the Johor government and specified the role and prerogatives of the Sultan, including over religious matters. Besides stating that Islam was the religion of the sultanate, the Constitution also stipulated that the Sultan was the head of religion and had the authority to appoint the Mufti and members of the Johor Islamic Council (Milner 1995, pp. 220–21).

This authority over religious affairs allowed Johor's sultans to promote their variant of Islam, which is traditionalist in orientation, more suffused with local customs and traditions as well as more amenable to a prominent role for the royalty (Norshahril 2017, p. 3). Johor's rulers hand-picked promising local scholars and sent them overseas to specific institutions possessing a compatible religious outlook. Upon their return, they were then charged with setting up Islamic schools in the state (Milner 1995, p. 198).

Following the establishment of British control in Johor in 1914, the Sultan and the British Advisers based in Johor engaged in a protracted battle over control of key government departments. While the British were able to secure control over finance, lands and mines, and public works, this did not extend to religion, which remained a royal prerogative throughout the colonial period (Gray 1978, pp. 142–43).

In the early twentieth century, the rubber industry was established in Johor with great success. Through taxing exports of the commodity, the Johor government was able to expand the education system considerably—including religious instruction. By the end of the 1930s, Johor's government-funded religious education system was the largest among the Unfederated Malaysian States, comprising a network of 88 schools and almost 10,000 students. In comparison, Kelantan's religious school system comprised 13 schools and 910 students, and Terengganu's 9 schools and 815 students (Malayan Yearbook 1939, pp. 143–44).

The legacy of royal control over religion continues today, as does Johor's emphasis on traditionalist Islam. Under the Federal Constitution, sultans are the heads of religion and Malay custom in their respective states. This entails the prerogative to: appoint key positions in the Islamic bureaucracy, notably the Islamic Religious Council, as well as the mufti—the prime religious authority; and oversee the religious police. These authorities also issue fatwas, or religious rulings, that influence the everyday conduct of Islam in the state (Norshahril 2017, p. 5).

As in the pre-independence period, Johor's sultans continue to promote a traditionalist Islamic outlook through: the religious bureaucracy; the rulings of the Mufti and other notables; and the licensing of preachers active in the state. The state has a network of boarding schools (*pondoks*) that provide traditionalist religious education and, as in the past, aspiring religious scholars are sent to centres of higher learning which are amenable to traditionalist Islam such as Al-Azhar University. Furthermore, visiting religious scholars that want to preach in the state need to obtain permission from the state Islamic authority (Norshahril 2017, pp. 5 and 10).

Conversely, although there are some boarding schools run by PAS in Johor, the party has been unable to establish an extensive network of boarding schools in the state.[7] Consequently, the traditionalist variant of Islam practised in Johor and its close identification with local level identity, as well as the limited network of religious schools compatible with PAS' outlook, have been directly linked to the party's limited inroads in the state.

Figure 8.7 sets out the electoral fortunes of PAS in Johor since the 1959 elections. Indeed, the party has a long history in opposition campaigning in the state, running two candidates for state seats in the first election. Despite fielding candidates in every election—1974 excepted—PAS only won its first state seat, Senggarang, in 2004—on a technicality. Indeed, in that year, PAS fielded a total of thirty-six candidates. Only in 2008 did the party win two contested seats—out of a total of thirty-three candidatures. And, only in 2013 as part of a wider coalition did PAS win an unprecedented four seats.

While PAS has traditionally targeted UMNO-held seats, on the rare occasions it has chosen to contest against non-UMNO component parties in Malay-majority seats, it has also fared badly. For example, in 2004, the Malay-majority state seats of Gambir, Kahang, and Tenggaroh were won with large majorities by MIC candidates. Pemanis and Pulai Sebatang, also with substantial Malay majorities, were won by Gerakan and MCA, respectively. This, again, attests to the strength of Barisan Nasional's grand coalition model.

FELDA Seats

The third reason that UMNO and, by extension, BN have done so well in Johor is the phenomenal scale and success of the Federal Land Development Agency (FELDA) programme in the state. Established in 1956, FELDA was established to deal with high levels of poverty and pent-up demand for land in rural areas in Malaysia.

FIGURE 8.7
PAS Candidates Contesting in Johor, 1959–2013

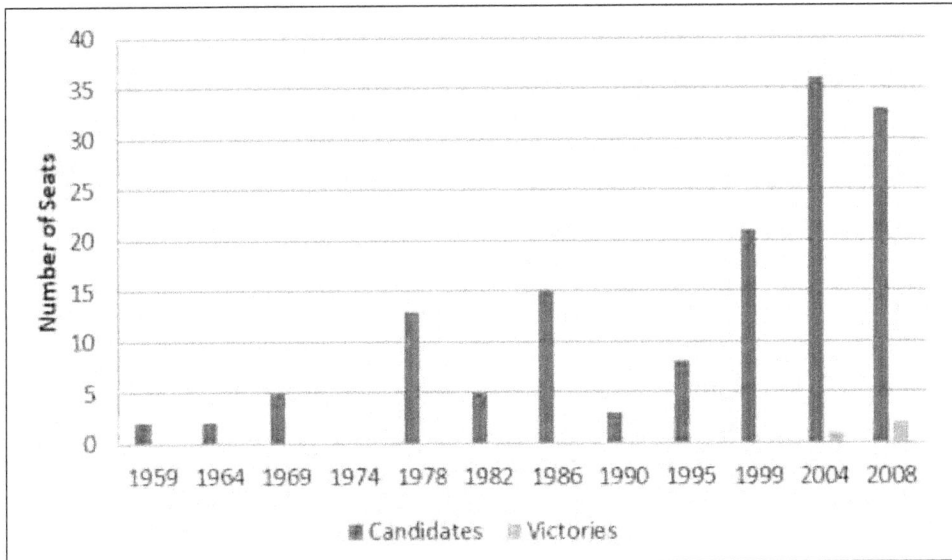

Source: NSTP (1990); Election Commission Malaysia, various years.

Through populating largely uninhabited frontier areas, the initiative sought to create livelihoods for settler families with few or no assets from agricultural areas. The selected participants, the vast majority of whom were Malay, were allocated plots of cleared land, a house, technical training to produce oil palm and rubber, as well as credit to begin planting. The settlers also were paid an allowance until harvesting could begin, after which they were charged with repaying their loans (McAndrews 1977, p. 2; Henley 2015, pp. 131–32).

Eager to spearhead development, foster social change, and reduce poverty, the newly independent Malaysian state invested high levels of economic and political capital in the initiative, creating a new ministry of Rural Development, helmed by the Deputy Prime Minister (Henley 2015, pp. 131–34). Due to its efficient administration and consistent follow-through, FELDA has been labelled as "the most successful resettlement programme of its kind in the world" (Sutton 1989 in Henley 2015, p. 118).

Over the 1959–1990 period, the initiative settled 120,000 families, largely from peninsular Malaysia, on some 471,000 hectares of smallholding land. This population has grown, with estimates that there are now some 1.2 million voters who live in FELDA settlements or work for the agency (Khor 2015, pp. 91–92).

Beside the fact that the programme was launched by a senior UMNO leader and geared towards the Malay population, the party and FELDA have become intertwined at an operational level. During the selection process, successful candidates needed to be recommended by local UMNO officials (Khor 2015, p. 96). In addition, the party has a branch within every plantation, enabling it to maintain a high-profile presence and monitor local-level developments. And, UMNO is also interwoven into the governing structures of the plantations. For many FELDA settlers, the party has become "interchangeably recognized as the government". Furthermore, due to high levels of indebtedness, settlers are vulnerable to changes in government policy—making them a captive vote bank. Consequently, FELDA members have voted overwhelmingly for BN over the years. In 2013, this translated into secure majorities in 85 per cent of the fifty-four parliamentary seats that have settler populations (Maznah 2015, pp. 135, 148–50).

Due to the extent of available frontier land, as well as the willingness and technical capacity of state governments to work with the federal government, FELDA was implemented to differing degrees in different parts of the country. Due to its large size, tracts of unoccupied land, and substantial numbers of rural poor, Johor was, bar Pahang, the state that implemented the programme on the largest scale.

Thus, over the 1960–74 period, some 38,000 people moved onto FELDA plantations in Johor. This was second only to Pahang and constituted one-quarter of the total population of FELDA settlers. However, unlike Pahang, which sought to increase its population by inviting settlers from other states, in Johor a full 96 per cent of settlers were local (McAndrews 1977, p. 71). The programme continued to expand in the state and, by 1987, Johor had about one-quarter of the national settler population (Bahrin and Lee 1988, p. 83).

An additional element of the initiative's success at the local level was the Johor state government. The local administration's processing of land claims were done more quickly than elsewhere, with Johor one of only two states to completely allocate all targeted settlers on schedule (Guyot 1974, p. 385; Bahrin and Lee 1988, p. 83). This efficiency was further enabled by good access between the state government and FELDA, due to the agency's second and third Chairmen—Taib Andak and Musa Hitam—Johoreans who collectively ran the agency from 1958 to 1972 (Bahrin and Lee 1988, App IV).

As elsewhere, FELDA came to be closely intertwined with UMNO in Johor. State legislative assemblymen and UMNO officials approved settler applications and land claims, with specific cases even being referred directly to the Mentri Besar. In turn, these position-holders let their choices be "strongly guided by political considerations" (Guyot 1974, p. 385).

The success of the programme and its association with BN has translated into exceptionally high levels of support among FELDA areas in Johor. In 2013, 86 per cent of voters in FELDA districts in the state voted for BN, versus 73–78 per cent in Selangor, Kedah, Melaka, Perak and Negri Sembilan; and 61–67 per cent in Kelantan, Pahang, and Terengganu (Figure 8.8).

Given its expansive FELDA programme, there are a recorded seventy-two settlements in thirteen of the state's parliamentary constituencies. Of these, four seats (Tebrau, Simpang Renggam, Labis and Segamat) have three or fewer settlements and a modest number of settlers (Pakiam 2019). The other nine constituencies have a much higher number of settlements and more sizeable settler populations

FIGURE 8.8
Support for BN in FELDA Districts, 2013

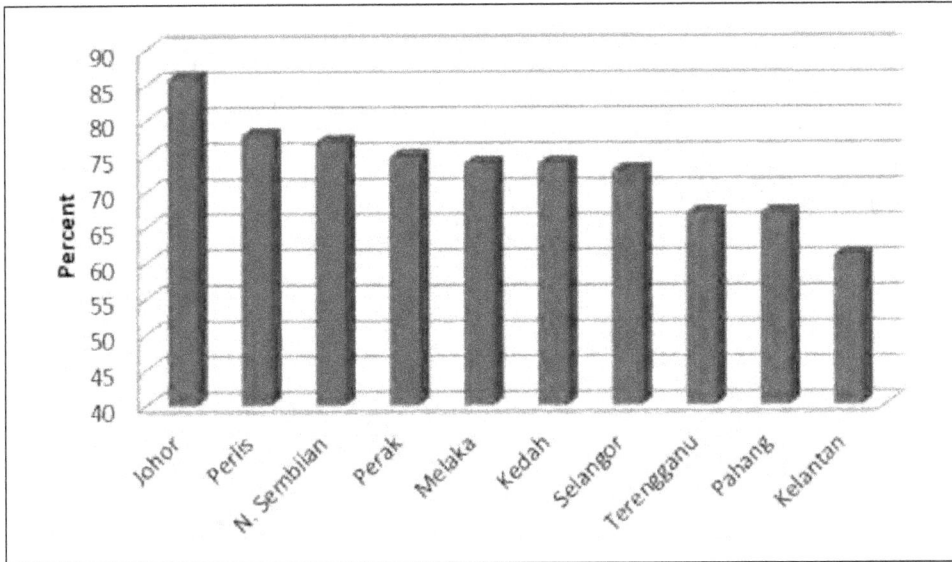

Source: Merdeka Center in Khor (2015), p. 106.

(Figure 8.9). Unlike the first group of seats, which is more mixed, the demographic of this second group of super-FELDA seats is rural and heavily Malay-majority. In the cases of seats such as Tenggara, Kota Tinggi, Mersing, and Pengerang, Malays made up 75 per cent of more of voters. Prior to 2018, most of these seats were held by UMNO, and in some cases not even contested by opposition candidates, as in the cases of Pengerang and Kota Tinggi in 2004 and Pengerang again in 2008.

Thus, this section has argued that the exceptionally high levels of support that BN enjoyed in Johor were due to: the local-level legacy of UMNO; the state's strong traditionalist Islamic orientation; and the large-scale success of FELDA. The next section will look at the results of GE-14.

THE DEFEAT IN GE-14

Despite BN retaining Johor in 2013 with a popular majority and a solid, if not overwhelming majority in the state legislature, the ruling coalition was looking weak in the run-up to GE-14.[8] Pakatan Harapan's (PH) five parliamentary seats were joined by a sixth, Pagoh, after Muhyiddin Yassin, the former Deputy Prime Minister co-founded the Parti Pribumi Bersatu Malaysia (PPBM) party with Mahathir Mohamad. At the state level, PH's fifteen state seats were bolstered by another PPBM member leaving UMNO. And, coupled with PAS' three more state representatives, this meant that BN no longer had a two-thirds majority in the state legislature for the first time ever.

FIGURE 8.9
FELDA Status of Parliamentary Seats in Johor

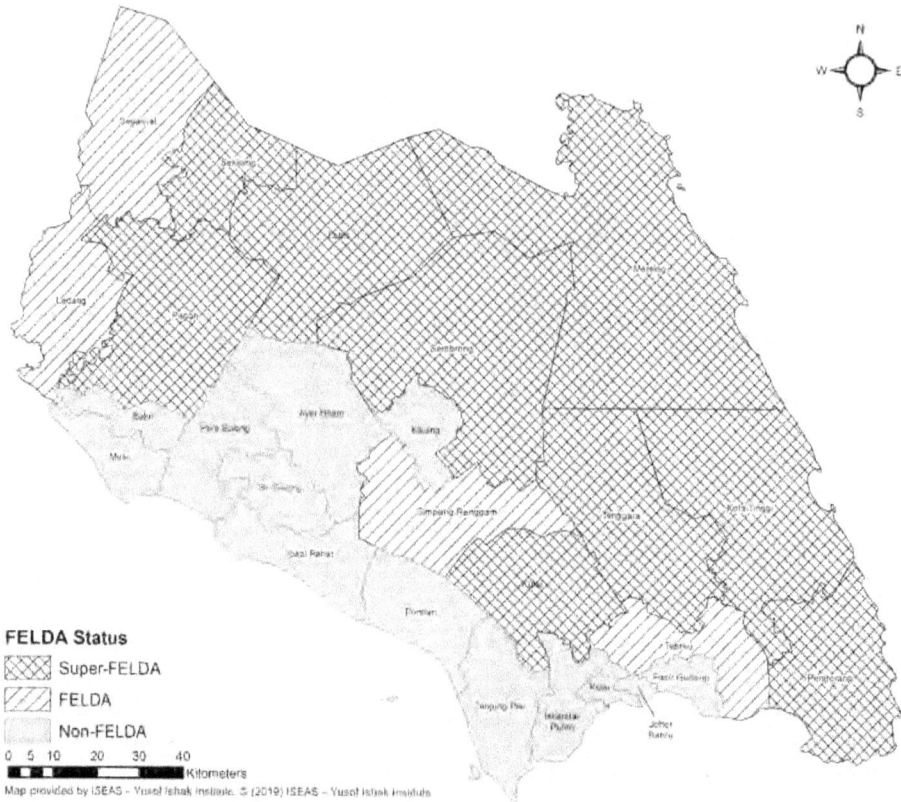

FELDA Status
- Super-FELDA
- FELDA
- Non-FELDA

0 5 10 20 30 40 Kilometers

Map provided by ISEAS – Yusof Ishak Institute. © (2019) ISEAS – Yusof Ishak Institute

In electoral terms, BN looked weak in urban and semi-urban areas, as well as mixed rural areas in the north of the state. However, despite the former ruling coalition also looking vulnerable in some rural western Malay-majority seats, it was largely held that, due to the substantial structural advantages favouring the ruling coalition, BN would retain Johor. Furthermore, opinion surveys released in the run-up to the elections consistently reported that a substantial number of voters had not made up their mind (Merdeka Center 2018).

Yet, in the end, the defeat was decisive for BN. BN garnered only 38.6 per cent of the popular vote, versus PH's 54.4 per cent and PAS' 7 per cent (Figure 8.10). Compared to national trends, PH and BN both did better in Johor than they did elsewhere, and PAS' performance was considerably below its national-level average.

Barisan Nasional only secured eight parliamentary seats, of these seven were won by UMNO and one by MCA. In the process, the former ruling coalition yielded an unprecedented eighteen constituencies to PH. Beyond the expected nine urban and semi-urban seats, this also included more than half of Johor's rural seats (Table 8.2).

FIGURE 8.10
Popular Support in Johor and Nationally (GE-14)

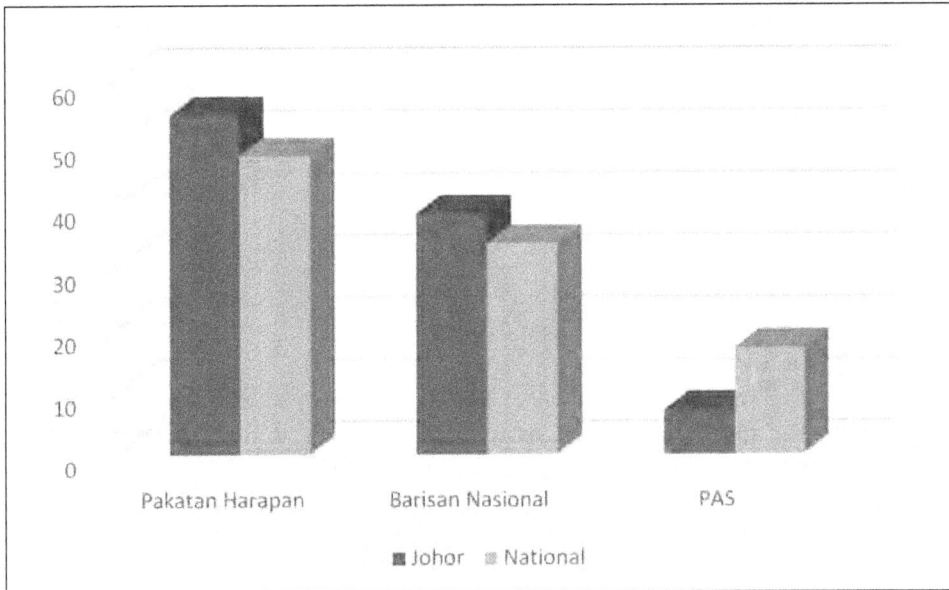

Source: https://graphics.straitstimes.com/STI/STIMEDIA/Interactives/2018/05/malaysia-general-elections-live-results/
index.html (accessed 26 December 2018).

TABLE 8.2
2018 Parliamentary Results (Urban/Rural)

Coalition	Urban/Semi-Urban	Rural
Pakatan Harapan	9	9
Barisan Nasional	0	8

Source: Results from http://www.undi.info/ (accessed 26 December 2018);
classification of urbanization from https://docs.google.com/spreadsheets/
d/1avEv-WaeZwcYsq48GtieTrlh5fdslVUliBeFGRl8-C0/edit#gid=0
(accessed 26 December 2018).

This latter category marked a clear departure from tradition, as rural seats used to be the heartland of UMNO support.

In terms of the ethnic composition of the seats, PH won in all mixed constituencies, all Malay-majority seats, and five out of the thirteen Malay super-majority seats. This latter result meant that a significant proportion of Malay votes swung to PH and, more worryingly for BN, that their hegemony in Malay-majority constituencies is no longer guaranteed (Table 8.3).

In geographic terms, PH took the centre and western parts of the state, with three exceptions, Pontian, Parit Sulong, and Ayer Hitam. These seats were retained

TABLE 8.3
Parliamentary Results by Type of Seat, 2018

Coalition	Mixed	Malay Majority (51–55)	Malay Majority (56–60)	Malay Majority (61+)
Pakatan Harapan	9	4	2	3
Barisan Nasional	0	0	2	6

Source: Results from http://www.undi.info/ (accessed 26 December 2018).

by BN, but Pontian and Ayer Hitam were held with razor-thin majorities. In contrast, BN retained its heartland in the eastern part of the state, particularly the Malay-majority and rural areas.

At the state level, BN did similarly poorly, losing an additional eighteen seats and retaining a rump of nineteen constituencies. Pakatan Harapan, in contrast, did very well, more than doubling its holdings from sixteen to thirty-six seats. These results broadly map on to the parliamentary seats that each coalition won, with PH doing well in the more mixed and urbanized state seats, and BN doing well in the more rural and Malay majority state constituencies within the various parliamentary districts. The only discrepancy between the different types of seats is the sole state seat won in 2018 by PAS. The seat, Bukit Pasir, was within an opposition stronghold, but the PH candidate for the seat was disqualified based on a technicality. Consequently, the constituency's protest vote went to PAS.

Looking at the results in aggregate, there were a number of messages from the electorate in GE-14.

First, urban and semi-urban areas are no longer hospitable constituencies for UMNO, which lost overwhelmingly in its traditional urban strongholds of Pulai, Pasir Gudang, and Johor Bahru. Indeed, the overall swing against the UMNO candidates occurred despite their reputation and substantial popularity. The candidate for Pasir Gudang and incumbent state Chief Minister, Khaled Nordin, enjoyed positive ratings in surveys carried out before the elections. Shahrir Samad, the UMNO MP for Johor Bahru had been based in that constituency since 1978. Yet, their prestige did not deter a massive swing against them, obliterating previously attained majorities. Indeed, the victors of both Pasir Gudang and Johor Bahru were relatively unknown political figures.

Second, non-UMNO BN parties are no longer electorally viable in Johor. The Malaysian Indian Congress (MIC) lost its parliamentary contests and only retained two state seats, and Gerakan was wiped from the map. However, MCA suffered the most dramatic reversal in fortunes. Relative to its heyday in 2004, when MCA contested in eight parliamentary constituencies and won all, in 2018, the party lost all of its contests bar one. Its sole victory was Ayer Hitam, which it retained by a mere 303 votes.

Third, UMNO is now only viable in rural, Malay-majority areas largely on the eastern part of the state. The six constituencies that the party won with sizeable

FIGURE 8.11
Parliamentary Results in Johor in GE-13 and GE-14

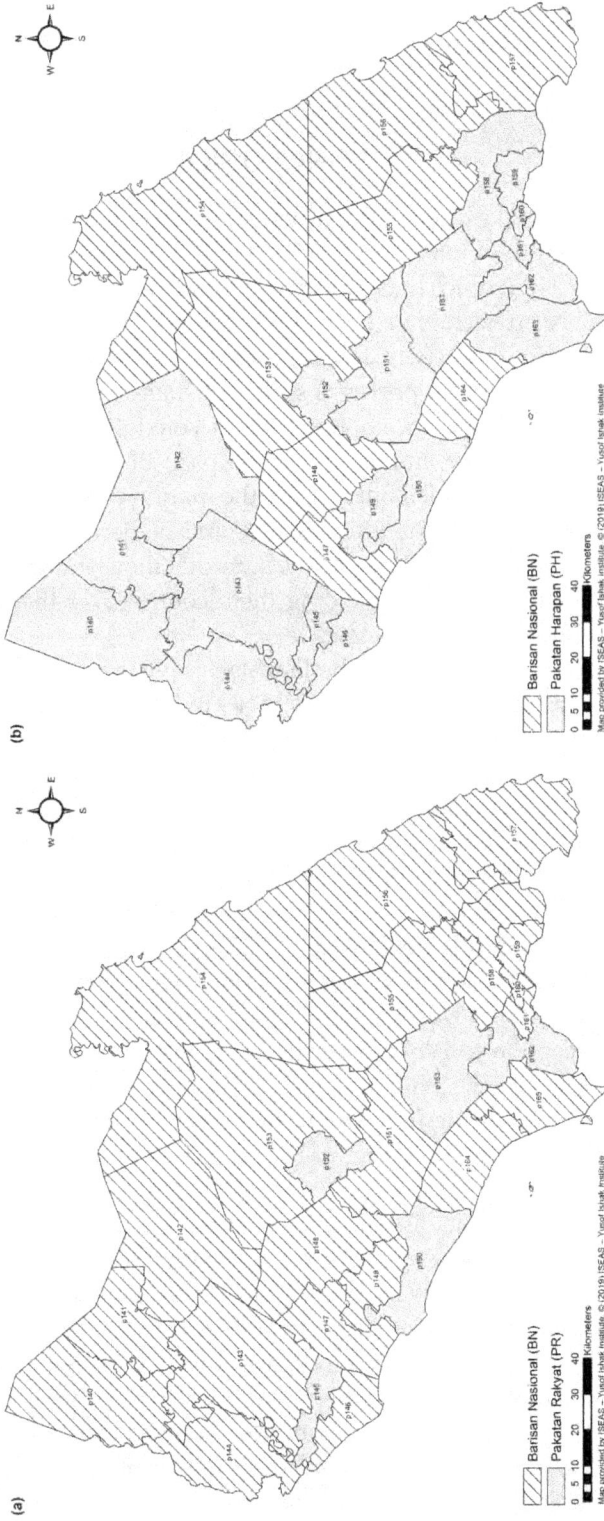

majorities are all rural, and had at least 55 per cent Malay voters. Yet, despite these victories, in all cases, these parliamentary majorities were only half as large as they were in 2013.

CONCLUSION

What then does GE-14 say about the structural underpinnings of BN and particularly UMNO's dominance in Johor?

As was the case in much of the rest of Malaysia, the overall structural advantages underpinning BN's trajectory in Johor came undone. The grand consociational model no longer worked for the erstwhile ruling coalition, as the quasi-totality of non-Malays deserted BN and Malay support was split. Thus, all mixed seats went to PH and, in many Malay-majority seats, enough Malays voted against BN to tip the balance towards PH. Furthermore, in contrast to the past, BN's meagre performance was not magnified by FPTP, which only boosts the margin of victory for the winner, but does not change or reverse the ultimate outcome. Nevertheless, malapportionment did still help BN and UMNO, because the seats that they won were over-represented and geographically very large, yielding them control over the scarcely populated eastern and central parts of the state.

What then, can be said about the local-level dynamics that used to boost BN's performance? The state-level legacy of UMNO in Johor, which was important in the past, is no longer determinant. In part, the deterioration of the "brand" effect was due to the governance issues associated with the apex of UMNO, embodied by party president Najib Razak, rather than local-level leaders. The decline of the UMNO brand was further accelerated by the departure of senior leaders such as Mahathir Mohamed as well as Muhyiddin Yassin, the former Deputy Prime Minister and Johor Chief Minister, to the newly formed Parti Pribumi Bersatu Malaysia.

In contrast, the local control of Islam is still an important factor in Johor's political context. In 2018 as in every other election in the state, PAS did not do well. Indeed, in GE-14, the party fared worse in Johor than elsewhere in the country. However, the rather chilly reception to PAS did not translate into support for BN. In contrast to the past, where the choice in many seats, particularly at the state level, was between BN and PAS, in GE-14 the fights were three-way. In this context, lower levels of support for BN and scarce backing for PAS allowed PH to secure an unprecedented number of seats.

Last, the FELDA legacy is still an important factor in Johor's political context, as it further shored up BN and UMNO's performance in the eastern and central constituencies in the state. Work by Pakiam (2019) illustrates that, in GE-14, there was considerable diversity in voting outcomes across seats with FELDA settlements within them. However, much of this diversity was due—not to uncertain levels of support for BN among FELDA settlers—but rather the proportion of voters within each constituency that they comprised. Of the eight constituencies in Johor that UMNO retained in GE-14, five were super-FELDA seats that between them housed almost two-thirds of all FELDA settlements in the state.

Consequently, while BN benefited from both national and local structural dynamics for much of Malaysia's recent history, a substantial number came undone in GE-14. The coalition's "fixed deposit" has now lapsed, and UMNO as well as any of its partners will need to rethink of a model to remain viable in Malaysia's and Johor's changed political landscape.

Notes

1. This chapter draws on *GE-14 in Johor: The Fall of the Fortress?*, Trends in Southeast Asia, no. 3/2018 (Singapore: ISEAS – Yusof Ishak Institute, 2018).
2. Interview with UMNO party member from Kelantan working in Johor, Johor Bahru, 21 April, 2010. For an interesting account of the contribution of one prominent family of Johorean civil servants to nation-building, consult *Legacy of Honour* by Zainah Anwar (2011).
3. Interview with Nur Jazlan, UMNO party member and member of parliament for Pulai, Johor Bahru, 18 May 2010; Wan Saiful (2018).
4. Interview with an UMNO party member from Kelantan resident in Johor, Singapore, 3 March 2010.
5. Interview with an UMNO party member from Kelantan resident in Johor, Johor Bahru, 21 April, 2010; Guyot also found high levels of internal competition within UMNO Johor in the 1960s (1974, p. 381).
6. Interviews with: Shahrir Samad, UMNO party member and former member of parliament for Johor Bahru, 18 June 2010; and Tawfik Ismail, former UMNO member of parliament for Sungai Benut, Kuala Lumpur, 8 September 2011.
7. Interviews with: Johor PAS member, Johor Bahru, 29 April 2010; and Shahrir Samad, Johor Bahru, 18 June 2010.
8. For a more extensive analysis of the GE-14 campaign and election results, consult F.E. Hutchinson, "GE-14 in Johor: Shock or Just Awe?", in *The Defeat of Barisan Nasional: Missed Signs or Late Surge?* edited by F.E. Hutchinson and Lee H.-A. Singapore: ISEAS Yusof Ishak Institute, 2019.

References

Amoroso, Donna. 2014. *Traditionalism and the Ascendancy of the Malay Ruling Class in Malaya.* Singapore: NUS Press.

Arriful Ahmadi. 2000. *Wira Bangsa Dalam Kenangan: Sejarah Perjuangan UMNO dan Profil Ahli Majlis Kerja Tertinggi 1946–2000.* Kuala Lumpur: Duracase Products.

Crouch, Harold. 1996. *Government and Society in Malaysia.* Ithaca: Cornell University Press.

Department of Statistics (DOS), Malaysia. 2013. *Population Distribution and Basic Demographic Characteristics, 2010.* Putrajaya: Department of Statistics.

———. 2017. *Current Population Estimates 2017.* Putrajaya: Department of Statistics.

Election Commission Malaysia. 2013. *Report of the 13th General Election.* Putrajaya: Election Commission.

Funston, John. 1980. *Malay Politics in Malaysia: A Study of UMNO and PAS.* Kuala Lumpur: Heinemann.

Gray, Christopher. 1978. "Johore, 1910–1941, Studies in the Colonial Process". PhD dissertation, Yale University, Newhaven.

Guyot, Dorothy. 1974. "The Politics of Land: Comparative Development in Two States of Malaysia". *Pacific Affairs* 44, no. 3: 366–89.

Henley, David. 2015. *Asia-Africa Development Divergence: A Question of Intent*. London: Zed Books.

Horowitz, Donald L. 1993. "Democracy in Divided Societies". *Journal of Democracy*, 4, no. 4: 18–38.

Hutchinson, Francis E. 2015. "Malaysia's Independence Leaders and the Legacies of State Formation under British Rule". *Journal of the Royal Asiatic Society* 25 no. 1: 123–51.

———. 2018a. *GE-14 in Johor: The Fall of the Fortress?*. Trends in Southeast Asia, no. 3/2018. Singapore: ISEAS – Yusof Ishak Institute.

———. 2018b. "Malaysia's 14th General Elections: Drivers and Agents of Change". *Asian Affairs*, 49, no. 4: 582–605.

Khor Yu Leng. 2015. "The Political Economy of FELDA Seats: UMNO's Rural Fortress in GE-13". In *Coalitions in Collision: Malaysia's 13th General Elections*, edited by Johan Saravanamuttu, Lee Hock Guan, and Mohamed Nawab Mohamed Osman. Singapore: ISEAS – Yusof Ishak Institute.

Lijphart, Arend. 1977. *Democracy in Plural Societies: A Comparative Exploration*. New Haven, Yale University Press.

MacAndrews, Colin. 1977. *Mobility and Modernisation: The Federal Land Development Authority and Its Role in Modernising the Rural Malay*. Yogyakarta: Gadjah Mada University Press.

Mauzy, Diane K. 1993. "Malaysia: Malaysia Political Hegemony and 'Coercive Consociationalism'". In *The Politics of Ethnic Conflict Regulation*, edited by J. McGarry and B. O'Leary. London: Routledge,

Maznah Mohamad. 2015. "Fragmented but Captured: Malay Voters and the FELDA Factor in GE13". In *Coalitions in Collision: Malaysia's 13th General Elections*, edited by Johan Saravanamuttu, Lee Hock Guan, and Mohamed Nawab Mohamed Osman. Singapore: ISEAS – Yusof Ishak Institute.

Merdeka Center. *Johore Opinion Survey*. Singapore: ISEAS – Yusof Ishak Institute, 2017.

———. 2018. "Malaysia General Elections XIV Outlook: Prospects and Outcome". Merdeka Center, Kuala Lumpur, 26 April 2018.

Milne, R.S., and Diane K. Mauzy. 1999. *Malaysian Politics under Mahathir*. London: Routledge.

Milner, Antony. 1995. *The Invention of Politics in Colonial Malaya: Contesting Nationalism and the Expansion of the Public Sphere*. Cambridge: Cambridge University Press.

Norshahril Saat. 2017. *Johor Remains the Bastion of Kaum Tua*. Trends in Southeast Asia, no. 1/2017. Singapore: ISEAS – Yusof Ishak Institute.

NSTP Research and Information Services. 1990. *Elections in Malaysia: Facts and Figures*. Kuala Lumpur: Balai Berita.

Ostwald, K. 2017. *Malaysia's Electoral Process: The Methods and Costs of Perpetuating UMNO Rule*. Trends in Southeast Asia, no. 19/2017. Singapore: ISEAS – Yusof Ishak Institute.

Pakiam, G. 2019. "The Making and Breaking of Malaysia's FELDA Vote Bank" . In *The Defeat of Barisan Nasional: Missed Signs or Late Surge?* edited by F.E. Hutchinson and Lee H.-A. Singapore: ISEAS – Yusof Ishak Institute.

Saravanamuttu, Johan. *Power Sharing in a Divided Nation: Mediated Communalism and New Politics in Six Decades of Malaysia's Elections*. Singapore: ISEAS – Yusof Ishak Institute and SIRD, 2016.

Statistics Department, Straits Settlements and Federated Malay States. 1939. *Malayan Yearbook 1939*. Singapore: Government Printing Office.

Sutton, Keith 1989. "Malaysia's FELDA Land Settlement Model in Time and Space". *Geoforum* 20, no. 3: 339–54.

Tunku Shamsul Bahrin, and Lee Boon Thong. 1988. *FELDA: 3 Decades of Evolution*. Kuala Lumpur: FELDA.

Wan Saiful Wan Jan. 2017. *Parti Amanah Negara in Johor: Birth, Challenges, and Prospects*. Trends in Southeast Asia, no. 9/2017. Singapore: ISEAS – Yusof Ishak Institute.

———. 2018. *Party Pribumi Bersatu Malaysia in Johor: New Party, Big Responsibility*. Trends in Southeast Asia, no. 2/2018. Singapore: ISEAS – Yusof Ishak Institute.

Winstedt, R.O. 1931. *The Constitution of the Colony of the Straits Settlements and of the Federated and Unfederated Malay States*. London: Royal Institute of International Affairs.

Zainah Anwar. 2011. *Legacy of Honour*. Kuala Lumpur: Yayasan Mohamed Noah.

9

ELECTORAL POLITICS AND THE MALAYSIAN CHINESE ASSOCIATION IN JOHOR

Lee Hock Guan and Nicholas Chan[1]

INTRODUCTION

Until the shocking results in the 14th General Elections (GE-14) that saw the long-ruling Barisan Nasional (BN) being defeated in parliament and most states by the opposition coalition, Pakatan Harapan (PH) Johor was always regarded as BN's electoral bastion. Historically, Johor has the highest number of parliamentary seats contested and won by the two largest BN parties, namely the ethnic Malay-Muslim-based United Malays National Organization (UMNO) and its Chinese partner, the Malaysian Chinese Association (MCA). With a mixed racial make-up (60 per cent bumiputra, 33 per cent Chinese, and 7 per cent Indian), clear urban-rural divides, an influential royal house, and a growing and relatively industrialized economy (Hutchinson 2018, p. 2; van Grunsven and Hutchinson 2016), Johor is often deemed to be the bell-wether of BN's support, or rather, its "jewel in the political crown" (Reme Ahmad and Cheong 2017).

UMNO's strength in and dependence on Johor as its point of origin, a forging ground for leaders, and base of support has been convincingly documented (Hutchinson 2015b, 2018; Funston 1980). Yet, the same cannot be said for the MCA. The party's relative resilience in Johor, despite its notable decline from 2008 to 2018, remains unexplored. Its resilience can be seen from the fact that Johor MCA managed to hold onto most of its seats in the 2008 elections despite BN as a whole suffered massive losses nationwide. The importance of Johor can also be intimated from the fact that most MCA presidents are in some way connected to Johor—some for the fact that they are Johor-born (Neo Yee Pan, Chua Soi Lek); some for standing for office in the state (Lee San Choon, Ling Liong Sik); and almost all—with the exception of Tan Siew Sin, Tan Koon Swan, and Liow Tiong Lai, for having at some point of time been appointed chairman of the MCA Johor State Liaison Committee.

This chapter examines the MCA's electoral performance in Johor in relation to its history, Malaysia's national politics in general, the state's changing socio-economic landscape, and most importantly, the unique ethnic-pooling formula that worked in the MCA's favour. It argues that the MCA's fate in Johor, while at first secured by its local Chinese networks and affiliations, was soon undermined by the party's changing membership structure and the party's progressive loss of influence within BN, especially vis-à-vis UMNO. Thus, as the party faced an across-the-board drop in popularity nationwide, its constituencies in Johor were retained only through the pooling of support across multiple ethnic groups and not through reliance on its traditional "Chinese" base. This signifies that the MCA's performance was contingent on UMNO's strength within the state, and as UMNO lost the state in the 2018 elections, the MCA's fate in Johor was also sealed.

This chapter is organized as follows. The first and second sections provide an outline of the history of the MCA in national politics and in Johor state. The third section discusses the institutionalized ties the MCA once enjoyed with rural Chinese in Johor through its control of local councils and overlapping membership with local commercial and educational associations. The fourth section reviews the MCA's electoral performance in Johor and analyses its relative resilience. The final section concludes the chapter with the fall of Johor to PH and offers some reflections on the MCA's future prospects.

THE MCA AND NATIONAL POLITICS

The MCA was established in February 1949 to provide Malayan Chinese with institutional means to articulate their grievances as well as to protect and defend their interests.[2] The party's founding "bridged the divide between modern and traditional modes of community organization in both ideological and structural terms ... and the gap between the Laukeh and Peranakan political cultures to produce a synthesized Malaya-centred Chinese world-view" (Heng 1988, p. 54). English-educated Peranakan and English-Chinese bilingual-educated Chinese representing the professional and business elites of the community dominated the party's national leadership. But it was only with the inclusion and participation of the multitude of local Chinese guilds and associations (CGAs)[3] that the party was truly transformed into a credible political force with a mass base and support (Hara 1997, p. 71).

With the participation of local and national CGAs in the party, the MCA managed quickly to expand its membership base. When the MCA was established in 1949 it had 103,000 members, but by the time of independence in 1957, its membership exceeded

300,000 (Heng 1988, p. 78). In 2006, the party claimed to have about 1.08 million members, making it the second largest party in the country after UMNO, with its 3.65 million members. But, this 1 million figure is deceptive as it was revealed that "70 per cent of its 4,900 branches were in a state of hibernation" and that there were all sorts of problems with the membership list, such as the presence of phantom members, illegal members such as those who were registered without their knowledge, and so on (*Nanyang Siang Pau*, 28 September 2016).

While the MCA founding leaders shared the common stance of collaborating with the Malays, one group was willing to do so in a non-ethnic/multiethnic party and another group insisted on doing so only as an ethnic Chinese party. This difference in approach came to a head in the Kuala Lumpur municipal election in 1952. Several leaders, led by Tan Cheng Lock, allied with the multiethnic Independent Malayan Party (IMP) to contest in the Kuala Lumpur election,[4] while some leaders of the Kuala Lumpur MCA branch, led by H.S. Lee, formed an alliance with the KL UMNO branch to contest in the same election.[5] The UMNO-MCA alliance, with each component party adopting a communal, or ethnic, approach successfully defeated the IMP and thus "found a winning formula that was to be applied throughout the country" (Khong 1984, p. 173). That winning formula came in the form of pooling votes across ethnicities, thus enabling the UMNO-MCA alliance to overcome the ethnic bloc voting behaviour for racially mixed constituencies. As opposed to the Indian National Congress that functioned as a catch-all party in multiethnic India, the winning formula of the alliance of ethnic parties became the defining feature of the ruling coalition in the Malaysian electoral system.

In the pre-independence constitutional negotiations, the MCA successfully obtained "more liberal requirements in acquiring citizenship eligibility and rights for Chinese immigrants" and safeguards for Chinese business, but triggered vigorous disagreements about and objections to the compromises the party made regarding Chinese language, education and culture.[6] Popular Chinese opinion was clamouring for cultural pluralism, especially the elevation of Chinese to official language status and the equal treatment of Chinese education. The MCA leadership's failure to fight for these issues led to the departure of many Chinese-educated leaders and their supporters, and many CGAs either withdrew their support or severed their ties with the party.[7]

Throughout the 1960s, the MCA's increasing ineffectiveness in influencing the Alliance Government's decision-making and policies gradually eroded the support it had garnered from the Chinese.[8] An increasing portion of middle- and working-class Chinese also became dissatisfied with the business class–dominated MCA leadership's failure to address their socio-economic welfare. Unsurprisingly, the MCA's popularity suffered a precipitous decline throughout the 1960s, culminating in the disastrous 1969 elections when the party failed to win a majority of the Chinese votes. The MCA hence lost its claim as the legitimate representative of the Chinese community (Vasil 1972).

As a result of its poor performance in the 1969 elections, the MCA's role and influence in the ruling coalition and government greatly diminished. It could no longer negotiate with UMNO as the legitimate representative of the Chinese community, since it had lost most of its support. The party also lost its most important cabinet portfolios, namely Finance as well as Commerce and Industry. Its diminished role in the coalition was further eroded by the inclusion of the Chinese-dominated Malaysian People's Movement Party (Gerakan) and the People's Progressive Party (PPP) in the new coalition Barisan Nasional (BN).[9]

From 1971 to 1990, the vital issues faced by the party were the New Economic Policy (NEP), Chinese education including the Merdeka University controversy, and Chinese culture. Chinese educational opportunities were greatly curtailed by the introduction of Malay preferential policies especially in relation to admission to tertiary education and the allocation of scholarships.[10] In 1978, the CGAs, led by Chinese educationists, applied to establish the Chinese-medium Merdeka University, but this was rejected and their court case in 1982 also ended in failure.[11] With the implementation of the NEP, Chinese business groups also started to turn away from the MCA and instead forged ties with UMNO and new business groups to advance their interests (Lee Kam Hing 2008).

From 1969 onwards, the MCA essentially lost its previously close connection with the Chinese traditional clan, guild and business associations, including the powerful Chinese educationist lobby. In 1982, the MCA and Gerakan performed better because of a significant Chinese swing towards the party. This was due partly to the new dynamic Mahathir-Musa leadership and partly due to the decision of a large number of Chinese associations—particularly the educationists—to work within the BN coalition in order to achieve their objectives. The CGAs' collaboration with the BN was demonstrated by the fact that several key CGA leaders such as Koh Tsu Khoon, Kerk Choo Ting and others left civil society and joined the MCA/Gerakan to contest in the 1982 elections.

However, after the elections, the CGAs very quickly became disappointed with the failures of MCA and Gerakan in making significant changes in the BN government's discriminatory policies against the Chinese community. In 1985, more than 5,000 CGAs representing all classes and backgrounds endorsed the Malaysian Chinese Union Declaration, a document that opposed a whole range of BN policies. To counter declining support from the CGAs, the MCA marshalled its allies and supporters to gradually take over the leadership of several major CGAs and registered new pro-MCA CGAs such as the Federation of Chinese Assembly Halls in Malaysia (Thock 2008).

From 1990 to 2004, Chinese support for the MCA/BN experienced an upward trend due to a number of positive developments, key of which was the country's high economic growth. The liberalization of education policies enhanced Chinese educational opportunities especially at the tertiary level, and Chinese schools were given more recognition and better treatment by the BN government. In addition, the privatization of the mass media enabled and empowered Chinese culture and language in society. Above all, Chinese employment opportunities and businesses benefited from the expanding economy and the relaxation of the implementation of Malay preferential policies. Growing Chinese support for the MCA peaked in the 2004 elections when the party achieved its best-ever results—winning thirty-one parliament seats and fifty-six state seats. The high hopes of a transition from Mahathir's strong-armed rule to Abdullah Badawi's perceivably less corrupt and more open government, bolstered by a timely, if not temporary, détente of the party's conflicting factions, gave the MCA its biggest electoral victory post-1969 (Chin 2006, p. 75).

Since the 2004 elections, however, worsening political and socio-economic conditions coupled with internal tensions within BN and UMNO resulted once more in a sense of alienation amongst the Chinese community (Moten 2009). Badawi's perceived softer rule, had, ironically, resulted in UMNO veering towards a more ethno-supremacist position that placed Malaysian Chinese at the centre of its *pendatang* (outsiders) rhetoric and sabre-rattling threats (Chin and Wong 2009, p. 78). The MCA's (as well as Gerakan's) inability and failure to fight for Chinese rights and interests very rapidly led to the party losing the majority of the Chinese vote in the elections in 2008 and 2013. Consequently, the number of seats held by the MCA dwindled to fifteen parliamentary and thirty-two state seats and only seven parliamentary seats and eleven state seats respectively after these two elections. Trapped in a mutually reinforcing cycle of seat and influence loss, the MCA became irrelevant in the eyes of both its coalition partner, UMNO, and the Malaysian Chinese voters.

THE MCA IN JOHOR

While the community's Malayan-born, English-educated professional and business elites dominated national leadership, in Johor it was mostly the Chinese-educated and non-educated businessmen[12] who mobilized and led the Chinese in the state to form Johor MCA. The Chinese business leaders' dominance of Johor MCA resulted in the party taking on a more traditional function and outlook, somewhat similar to the CGAs, at the state level. Unsurprisingly, Chinese business leaders were also leaders of a large number of the CGAs in the state. For the first thirty years after independence, the majority of Johorean Chinese resided in the semi-urban and rural areas, in the New Villages in particular. The crucial role played by the MCA Johor in providing relief and welfare to Chinese villagers in the state brought party loyalty and support from the rural Chinese community.

MCA's establishment in Johor can largely be attributed to Wong Shee Fun (Table 9.1), a banker, businessman, and philanthropist who served as chairman of the MCA Johor State Liaison Committee from 1949 to 1961. Wong was widely regarded as the leader of the Chinese community, evidenced from the fact that he was the president of the highly influential Chinese Association of Johor Bahru (*gonghui*) and a number of prominent CGAs in Johor.[13] As a member of the Council of the State in Johor, he also represented the Chinese community in various state committees and had worked closely with Malay officials and the palace. By virtue of Wong's many "hats" and stature, Johor MCA enjoyed a synergistic relationship with the local CGAs, which saw MCA politics and community development being

TABLE 9.1
Chairmen of the MCA Johor State Liaison Committee, 1949–present

	Johor MCA	National MCA	Background
Wong Shee Fun	1949–61	CWC 1949–57	businessman
Chua Song Lim	1961–73	Vice-President	businessman
Lee San Choon	1973–77	President, 1975–83	school teacher; civil servant
Teo Ah Kiang	1977–83	–	businessman
Neo Yee Pan	1983–84	Acting President, 1983–85	academic
Tan Peng Khoon	1984–87	Vice-President	
Ling Liong Sik	1987–2002	President, 1986–2003	medical doctor
Chua Soi Lek	2002 – Jan 2008; Nov 2009 – Jan 2014	President, 2010–13	medical doctor
Ong Ka Ting	Mar 2008 – Nov 2008	President, May 2003 – Oct 2008	school teacher
Ong Tee Keat	Nov 2008 – Nov 2009	President, Nov 2008 – Nov 2009	engineer
Wee Ka Siong	Jan 2014 – present	Deputy President, 2013–18 President, 2018–	urban planner

Note: Names in italics indicate that the individual was born in Johor.

intimately linked. This relationship was gradually lost after Wong's demise in 1979, as we shall see below (Lim 2006, p. 36).

Wong Shee Fun's successor Chua Song Lim (chairman, 1961–73) was a prosperous rubber baron and leader of various CGAs, and the state assemblyman for Bandar Maharani (1959–64, 1964–69, 1969–74, and 1974–78). As the majority of the prominent early Johor MCA leaders were not English-educated or proficient in English, they did not play important roles at the national level. One exception was the bilingual Lee San Choon (MCA 2011). A former teacher and civil servant, he was the first Johor MCA parliamentarian appointed as a minister. This was in 1971. Lee went on to succeed Chua Song Lim as MCA state leader (1973–77) and Tan Siew Sin as president of MCA (1975–83).

With business leaders bringing in the CGAs, Johor MCA grew its membership rapidly and helped the party in its efforts to secure broad support from the state's largely rural-based Chinese. The CGAs cooperated with the MCA to help disseminate its message and programmes, as well as to mobilize Chinese support for the party.[14] Nevertheless, Johor MCA initially capitalized on, but eventually supplanted, the central role the CGAs played in representing and conveying Chinese interests to the Johor state government and the federal government.

Since the 1970s, however, Johor MCA saw the proliferation and growing dominance of professional politicians in, first, the party ranks, and gradually in its leadership. Since 1973, professional politicians had occupied and dominated the Johor MCA leadership. In fact, Teo Ah Kiang was the last businessman to hold the state party's chairmanship, from 1977 to 1983. Unlike the Chinese businessmen with their extensive network and support in the Chinese CGAs and the community at large, the professional politicians usually did not enjoy such linkages and networks. Thus, the dominance of the professional group can be said to have come at the cost of the party's social capital vested within the Johor CGAs, business and the larger Chinese community.

Nevertheless, Johor remained pivotal to the MCA, as a significant number of national leaders of the party were either Johorean, contested a Johor parliamentary seat, the chairman of Johor MCA, or a combination of all three, as in the case of Lee San Choon, Neo Yee Pan, and Chua Soi Lek (see Table 9.1). For example, Johor became the base for Ling Liong Sik, the longest-serving president of the MCA (September 1986 – May 2003). Originally a Penang parliamentarian, he was the chairman of Johor MCA for more than a decade (1987–2002). Ling contested in one of the safest parliament seats in Johor, namely Labis, where he won easily and was its parliamentarian for four terms (1986, 1990, 1995, 1999). Ling's long tenure may have weakened the party in Johor, as being non-Johorean and English-educated, Ling had few connections to the local Chinese communities. Being a federal minister, he had to spend much time and energy on national issues.

Johor's proximity to the MCA's national leadership also meant that it was particularly vulnerable to factional politics. One notable episode involved the Muar-born Bakri parliamentarian (1986–2008) and former Health Minister Chua Jui Meng contesting for the party presidency unsuccessfully in 2005 and 2008.[15] The split caused Chua to be dropped from his seat in Bakri, which was the only parliamentary seat the MCA lost in Johor in 2008—a seat that Chua had won with 70 per cent of the total votes in 2004. Chua Soi Lek, another Johorean MCA politician was later involved in a leadership struggle with Ong Tee Keat, which led to him winning the presidency in 2010 but he then had to withdraw from contesting the position in 2013, following another disastrous showing by the MCA in the 13th General Elections.

In any case, the factions congregated around personalities rather than state boundaries. For example, Chua Soi Lek, a supporter of Ling Liong Sik, helped deliver the Johor vote to his protégé, Perak-born Ong Ka Ting, in the 2005 party elections (Chin 2006, p. 77). Nevertheless, the two soon fell out when Ong's associates were rumoured to have engineered Soi Lek's sex scandal–led downfall (Chin 2010, p. 154). As the chairman of the MCA state liaison committees is an appointed position, Soi Lek's clashes with Ong Tee Keat during the latter's short-lived MCA presidency (2008–9) also saw him being denied the position of Johor chairman despite being a popular figure in the state (Chin 2010, p. 156). He soon recaptured the position following his ascendency to the presidency, but relinquished it again following his decision not to contest the position in late 2013.

THE MCA AND RURAL CHINESE IN JOHOR

The resilience of the MCA in Johor cannot be addressed without reference to the party's institutional linkages to the rural Chinese. Historically, and well after Malaysia gained political independence in 1957, the legacy of the Kangchu system meant that the majority of the Chinese population in Johor resided in rural villages and was engaged in agricultural activities (Trocki 1976). The advent of the Emergency in 1948 led the British to establish many New Villages as a counter-insurgency tactic. As a result of the suppression of opposition Chinese political groups, such as the Malay(si)an Communist Party (banned in 1948), and the Labour Party (officially dissolved in 1972 but inactive after 1965), the MCA was the most active and, for a while, the sole political party in the New Villages.

Through its network and linkages with CGAs, the MCA actively assisted in the resettlement of squatters in the New Villages in the state. With British support, the MCA played important roles in helping to maintain peace and security, and to alleviate the hardships of and provide various amenities and facilities for the villagers. Over time, the MCA built up a strong political base among the Chinese in the New Villages.[16] Recognizing the importance of the New Villages to the MCA, the New Villages were placed under the care of the Ministry of Housing and Local Government with the Minister traditionally appointed from the MCA after independence.

Initially, the CGAs played crucial roles in liaising and serving Chinese New Villagers, which helped to secure broad support for the MCA. The MCA would also have direct links to the New Villages where they invariably maintained a branch office. Gradually, however, the CGAs' roles and functions were undermined and replaced by the appointment of MCA members or operatives to liaise with and serve the local Chinese communities. MCA members were appointed to, and dominated, the New Village committees, in particular, the village security and development committees (JKKK). While the party itself raised and provided considerable funds to develop the New Villages, the government also contributed funding to the New Villages through the Ministry of Housing and Local Government.

After independence in 1957, 70 per cent of the local committees in the rural areas were converted to MCA-controlled Local Councils.[17] Through its control of the Local Councils, the MCA could confer patronage through the allocation of licences, the provision of jobs, and the commissioning of public works not just in the New Villages but also generally in the Chinese-dominated small towns. In the mainly agricultural New Village communities, the pressing issues had to do with land and agriculture such as land tenure and acquisition of new land. For instance, since the 1990s, the growing scarcity of land in the state due to the shrinking availability of uncultivated land and growing competition for land from both Federal Land Authority schemes and commercial players meant that it was unlikely that there would be new lands for the Chinese. The MCA played a key role in liaising between New Villagers and the state government over the extension of land tenure and the acquisition of new land.[18]

Such developments are important because, after Perak, Johor has the second largest number of New Villages in the country, 94 in 1954 but declining to 92 in 1970 and 84 in 2002 (Lim and Fong 2005, p. 53). In Johor, the Chinese residing in the New Villages totalled 130,613 in 1954 and increased to 216,441 in 1970 and 435,557 in 1995 but decreased to 322,141 in 2002. In 2002, Chinese residing in the New Villages still comprised about a third of the total Chinese population in the state.

Since the 1990s several factors and developments have led to a growing scarcity of economic and employment opportunities for the Chinese in the New Villages and the small towns in the state. The agriculture-based occupations in the New Villages no longer appeal to young Chinese, and there is also an infusion of cheaper foreign labour displacing the more expensive local labour force. Increased urbanization and the outmigration of rural Chinese led to a dramatic decline in the rural Chinese population of Johor from 305,861 (51.5 per cent of the total Chinese population in the state) in 1980 to 240,793 (34.2 per cent) in 1991 and to 154,963 (15 per cent) in 2010.[19] Correspondingly, the percentage of Chinese aged fifteen to sixty years working in the agricultural sector shrank from 73,292 (34.8 per cent) to 42,907 (16.4 per cent) in 1991 and 22,227 (6.7 per cent) in 2010.

The marginalization of the agricultural sector became more acute as alternative economic activities failed to develop in the New Villages and small towns (Pang and Tan 2012). Voon (2009) argues that the outflow of the younger Chinese population gradually undermined the economic and social viability of the New Villages. Due to Johor's proximity to Singapore, local Chinese (and increasingly other ethnic groups) also experienced tremendous outmigration pressures, with a reported 150,000 out of the 350,000 Malaysians working in Singapore as daily commuters from Johor Bahru (Koh 2010, p. 48). Relocating and working outstation meant that the younger Chinese New Villages would no longer be dependent on the MCA to serve their interests. Without the institutional linkages that integrated the MCA with the economic opportunities and welfare of the local Chinese, the erosion of support of the MCA among the Chinese, including those from the New Villages and small towns, was inevitable. Yet, Johor remained a stronghold for the MCA until 2013, at least electorally that is, for reasons we will see below.

MCA ELECTORAL PERFORMANCE IN JOHOR

Until 2008, Johor was UMNO's unassailable fortress, illustrated by the fact that the party has won every state and parliament seat it had contested in every election except for the Parit Bakar state seat that it lost to Semangat 46's Abdul Kahar Ahmad in 1990 and the Johor Bahru parliament seat it lost to the then ex-UMNO parliamentarian Shahrir Samad in a by-election in 1988 (Shahrir Samad contested as an independent candidate).[20] In 1999, when UMNO suffered a major erosion in Malay support down to around 75 per cent, the party still won all the seats it contested in Johor.

The MCA also won nearly all the parliament and state seats it contested in every election from 1974 until 2008. It only lost the Kluang parliament seat in 1978 and the Bandar Kluang state seat in 1974 and 1978 to Lee Kaw of the Democratic Action Party (DAP). Other losses to the DAP include the Maharani state seat in 1986 and 1990, and the Bekok and Jementah state seats in 1990. While all those seats that MCA lost to the DAP were Chinese-majority seats, the party, nevertheless, managed to win the majority of the Chinese parliamentary and state seats in every election until 2013. Indeed, in the 11th General Elections (GE-11) in 2004, echoing the nationwide strong support for BN across all ethnicities during Abdullah Badawi's first electoral outing as prime minister, the MCA won all of the eight parliament seats and the fifteen state seats it contested in Johor.

Cracks in BN's Johor fortress emerged in the 2008 elections (GE-12) when an anti-incumbent sentiment, especially among Chinese voters, swept across Peninsular Malaysia. The BN lost one parliament seat (Bakri) and six state seats (Bentayan, Mengkibol, Senai, Skudai, Sungai Abong, Maharani) to the opposition Pakatan Rakyat (PR) in Johor. While the BN garnered more than 80 per cent of the Malay vote, the state also experienced a sizeable Chinese vote swing towards the PR; it was estimated that the BN won only 35 per cent of the Chinese vote in Johor in 2008. A contributing factor to the BN retaining most of its seats was the voter turnout of about 75 per cent, with a significant percentage of outstation Chinese voters not returning to cast their vote.

Nevertheless, the MCA won seven of the eight parliament seats and twelve out of the fifteen state seats the party contested in Johor in 2008. It lost the Chinese-majority Bakri parliament seat and the Chinese-majority state seats Bentayan, Mengkibol and Senai to the DAP. Although the MCA won the other Chinese-majority seats of Gelang Patah and Kulai, the winning margins were reduced by 19 and 6 per cent respectively. Even the Malay-majority parliament seats Ayer Hitam and Tanjung Piai and the mixed parliament seats Labis, Kluang and Tebrau were all won by the MCA by reduced margins; Labis—4,094 majority in 2008 from 10,729 in 2004; Ayer Hitam—13,909 majority in 2008 from 15,763 in 2004; Kluang—3,781 majority in 2008 from 18,698 in 2004; Tebrau—14,658 majority in 2008 from 26,011 in 2004; and Tanjung Piai—12,371 majority in 2008 from 23,615 in 2004. Similarly, the MCA won the state seats Jementah, Bekok, Tangkak, Yong Peng, Parit Yaani, Penggaram, Paloh, Johor Jaya, Stulang, Pengkalan Rinting, Pulai Sebatang and Pekan Nanas by reduced margins. Thus, while the MCA lost the support of the majority of the Chinese, it managed to win most of the Chinese-majority parliament and state seats in Johor on the back of strong Malay bloc voting, a point we will return to later.

In the 2013 General Elections (GE-13), however, Johor BN retained control of the state government but by only narrowly retaining a two-thirds majority when it lost eighteen state seats to PR. With respect to parliamentary seats, the coalition performed much better, winning twenty-one out of the twenty-six constituencies contested. Merdeka Center (2013) estimated that the BN garnered about 81.8 per cent of the Malay vote in Johor in GE-13 (*The Edge Markets*, 26 April 2018). However, because Chinese support for the BN/MCA remained at a low (20.1 per cent) in GE-13, the MCA was almost decimated in Johor in the 2013 elections. The MCA lost the Chinese-majority parliament seats Bakri, Gelang Patah and Kulai and even the mixed seat (with a Chinese plurality) Kluang to the DAP. It won the mixed seat Labis by a mere 303 votes and the Malay-majority seats Ayer Hitam and Tanjung Piai albeit with even a smaller margin than in GE-12; for Ayer Hitam from 7,853 votes in 2008 to 5,706 votes in 2013 and Tanjung Piai from 12,371 votes in 2008 to 5,457 votes in 2013.

At the state level, the MCA suffered shocking losses, managing to win only two of the fifteen state seats allocated to the party to contest. The MCA was only successful in winning the Malay-majority seat Pulai Sebatang by a margin of 3,412 votes, down from 5,765 votes in 2008 and the mixed seat Paloh by a mere 103 votes. The party was also defeated by the Islamist Malaysian Pan-Islamic Party (PAS) in the Malay-majority state seat of Parit Yaani by 1,188 votes. A significant contributing factor was the high turnout among outstation voters returning to cast their votes in the 2013 elections and the fact that a huge majority of outstation Chinese most likely voted for the opposition.[21] The voter turnout for GE-13 was a high 86.7 per cent.[22]

EXPLAINING MCA'S RELATIVE RESILIENCE IN JOHOR

In terms of BN (and by extension, MCA) support, Johor may be considered an anomaly. The consistently strong electoral performance of BN in Johor until 2018 happened against the backdrop of Johor being an ethnically heterogeneous state, which tended to be a liability for the BN during periods of electoral upheaval, as exemplified by what happened in Perak, Selangor, and Penang in 1969 and in 2008 onwards (Ratnam and Milne 1970 p. 206). According to the 2010 census, Johor has the third highest proportion of Chinese inhabitants in Malaysia (33 per cent), after Penang (45 per cent) and Kuala Lumpur (43 per cent) (*Oriental Daily*, 30 April 2017). Johor also stood out for letting the MCA hold onto its four parliamentary seats during the widely named "Chinese tsunami'" of 2013, which constituted little more than half its total parliamentary yield nationally.

Understanding this trend requires an overview of the seats that the MCA contested in Johor. One feature that stands out for the MCA Johor is that, when compared to other states with substantial Chinese populations, the seats it contested in the state are on the lower spectrum in terms of Chinese voter concentration (see Table 9.2). The most obvious point is that the MCA was only contesting one seat that has a Chinese supermajority in Johor—the Bentayan state seat. This is in marked difference to Selangor, Penang, and Perak, which had Chinese supermajority seats forming a substantial if not majority portion of the seats contested by the MCA, as seen in the case of Penang and Perak (Table 9.2). Of all four states, MCA Johor also contested in the highest number of Malay-majority seats, two at the parliamentary level and one at the state level. One such seat is Ayer Hitam (58 per cent Malay voters), the only MCA-controlled seat that remains in parliament today.

Therefore, it is not wrong to say that the logic behind the MCA's resilience in Johor lies in Johor BN's traditionally huge Malay voting bloc. This meant that the racially mixed parliament and state seats invariably benefited the BN parties including the MCA, Gerakan and the Malaysian Indian Congress (MIC).[23] In particular, since Malay bloc voting for the BN had consistently exceeded 70 per cent, it meant that the MCA would not need to garner a majority of the Chinese votes in order to win the Chinese-majority parliamentary seats of Bakri, Gelang Patah and Kulai. The MCA needed to garner only 26, 32 and 33 per cent of the Chinese votes to win Bakri, Gelang Patah and Kulai, respectively (see Figures 9.1 and 9.2). For the Chinese-majority state seats of Jementah, Bekok, Tangkak, Bentayan, Yong Peng, Penggaram, Mengkibol, Stulang, Skudai, Bukit Batu, Senai and Pekan Nanas, the BN parties would have had

TABLE 9.2
Seats Contested by the MCA Delineated by the
Concentration of Ethnic Chinese Voters, 2013

	Johor	Selangor	Penang	Perak
Parliament				
Chinese supermajority (>70% Chinese)	0	1 (14%)	3 (75%)	2 (28.5%)
Chinese majority (>50% Chinese)	4 (50%)	0	0	2 (28.5%)
Mixed (no single majority)	2 (25%)	5 (72%)	1 (25%)	3 (43%)
Malay majority (>50% Malay)	2 (25%)	1 (14%)	0	0
State Assembly				
Chinese supermajority (>70% Chinese)	1 (7%)	2 (14%)	7 (70%)	8 (53%)
Chinese majority (>50% Chinese)	10 (66%)	8 (57%)	3 (30%)	6 (40%)
Mixed (no single majority)	3 (20%)	4 (29%)	0	1 (7%)
Malay majority (>50% Malay)	1 (7%)	0	0	0

Notes: Figures from undi.info. The 2013 figures are used to demonstrate the longer term trends in terms of seat-type allocation as the redelineation passed in 2018 has significant impact on voter composition in many seats following the BN government's acknowledgement that it has lost the Chinese vote. While Selangor is arguably the most affected by the redelineation, one of the state seats contested by the MCA in Johor, Pekan Nanas, was changed from a Chinese-majority seat to a Malay-majority seat. On the redelineation before GE-14, see Ooi (2018).

to garner only 28 to 41 per cent of the Chinese votes to win. Also, as the logic goes, because of vote pooling, the MCA would have received a higher percentage of the Malay votes than UMNO as their candidates would contest against those from the perceived Chinese party, the DAP.[24]

Not having to defend a high proportion of Chinese-supermajority seats meant that the kind of electoral gains the DAP made at the expense of the MCA in Penang and Perak, which occurred even during the height of the BN's popularity in 2004,[25] was never a problem for the MCA in Johor. It is worth noting that in 2008 when the MCA managed to retain most of its seats in Johor in the face of massive losses in other states, all the seats it lost, with the exception of Bakri (53 per cent Chinese),[26] were on the upper end of the Chinese-majority category—Bentayan (74 per cent), Mengkibol (62 per cent), and Senai (68 per cent). The higher proportion of Chinese-majority seats at the state level (80 per cent of total state seats) as compared to the parliamentary level (50 per cent) also saw the MCA losing ten out of the twelve state seats it held in 2013, as compared to losing three out of seven in parliament.

To be sure, it is the combination of having both a strongly BN-leaning Malay (and somewhat less DAP-leaning Chinese) electorate and more ethnically mixed seat that explained the MCA's relative resilience in Johor, at least until 2013, that is. Such strategic dependence on the Malay BN-voting bloc could not be replicated in Selangor, where the MCA had a slightly higher combined proportion of mixed and Malay-majority seats—86 per cent of the total number of seats contested at parliament, and 29 per cent for state seats (although the MCA did not contest in any Malay-majority state seats). This is because, according to one estimation, BN

FIGURE 9.1

Parliamentary Seats in Johor and the Percentage of Chinese Votes Needed for MCA to Win if Malay Support is (A) >70% and (B) >80%

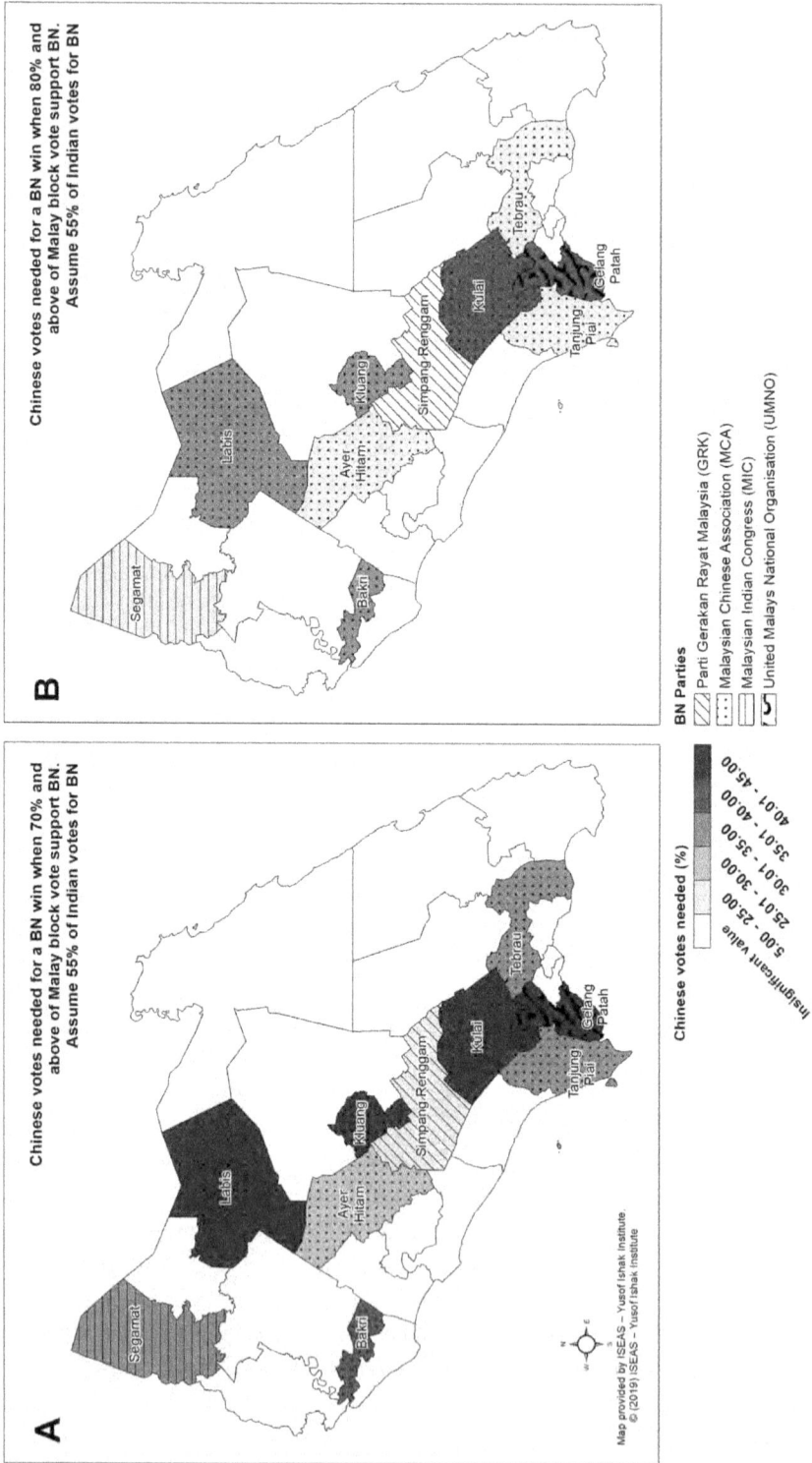

Note: Calculations can be found in Appendix 9.1.

FIGURE 9.2
State Assembly Seats in Johor and the Percentage of Chinese Votes Needed for MCA to Win if Malay Support is (A) >70% and (B) >80%

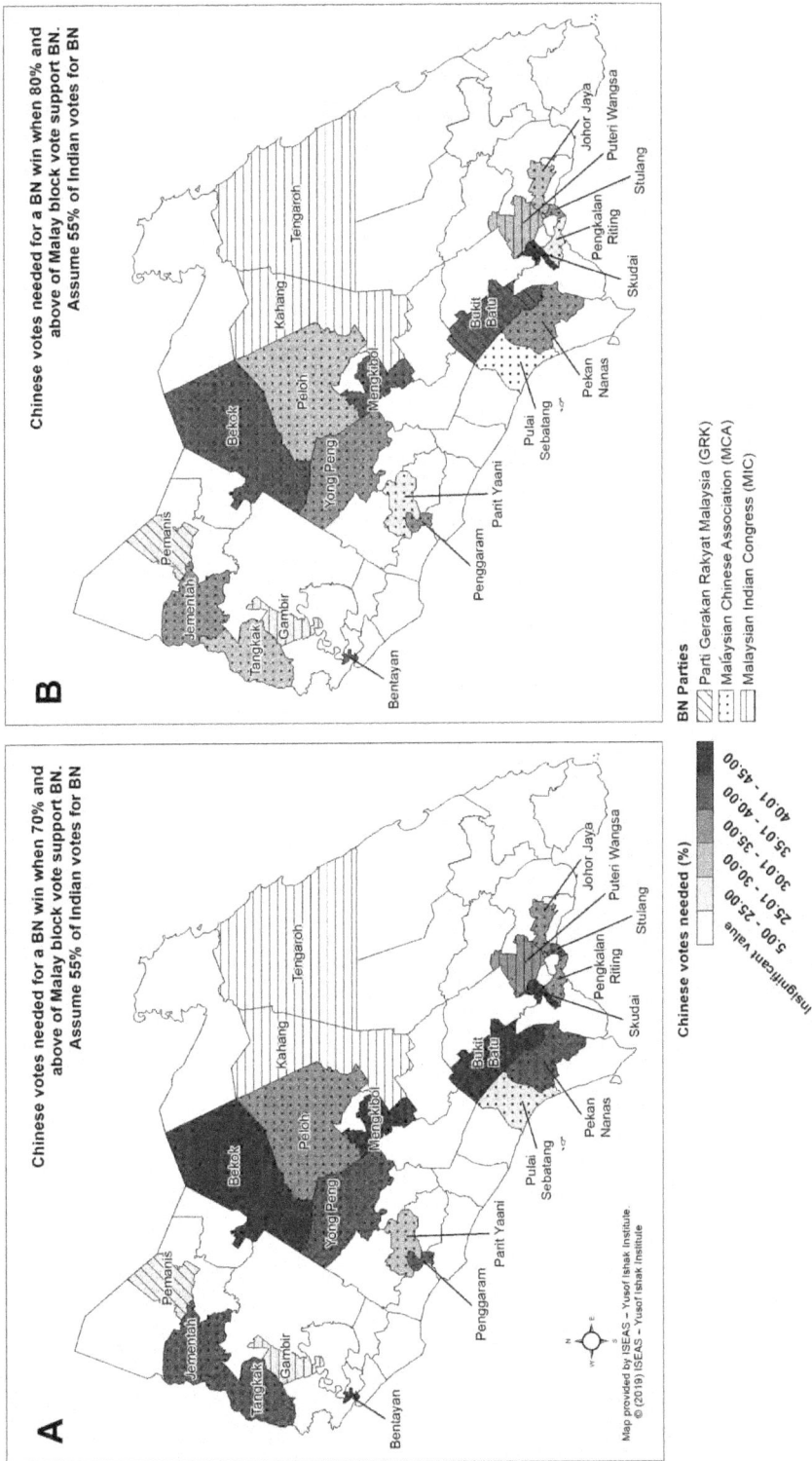

Chinese votes needed for a BN win when 80% and above of Malay block vote support BN. Assume 55% of Indian votes for BN

Chinese votes needed for a BN win when 70% and above of Malay block vote support BN. Assume 55% of Indian votes for BN

BN Parties

Parti Gerakan Rakyat Malaysia (GRK)
Malaysian Chinese Association (MCA)
Malaysian Indian Congress (MIC)

Chinese votes needed (%)

Insignificant value
5.00 - 25.00
25.01 - 30.00
30.01 - 35.00
35.01 - 40.00
40.01 - 45.00

Map provided by ISEAS – Yusof Ishak Institute
© (2019) ISEAS – Yusof Ishak Institute

Note: Calculations can be found in Appendix 9.2.

support in Selangor was only a paltry 44 per cent in 2008 as compared to Johor's 65 per cent, thereby diluting the Malay support that could be "borrowed" by the MCA (Ong 2013). The fact that the BN could not even win all of the Malay-majority seats in Selangor points to the futility of replicating the strategy in Johor.[27]

THE JOHOR MCA DEMOLISHED IN THE 2018 ELECTIONS

In the 2018 elections (GE-14), the opposition Pakatan Harapan (PH) surprisingly breached the BN Johor fortress to gain control of the state assembly, winning thirty-six out of the fifty-six seats—nearly a two-thirds majority. In terms of the popular vote, the BN vote share dropped to its lowest at 36 per cent, an 11 per cent reduction from its performance in 2013 (*Malay Mail Online*, 11 May 2018). Days before the elections, Merdeka Center estimated that Johor would experience the biggest drop in Malay support "falling 20.9 percentage points to 60.9 per cent of Malay votes in GE14, compared with 81.8 per cent in GE13" (*The Edge Market*, 26 April 2018). After the elections, Ong Kian Ming (2018), a DAP leader, estimated that for the first time in history, BN support in Johor at the parliamentary level dropped below the 50 per cent threshold, landing at 38 per cent.

The significant reduction in Malay bloc voting and the persistent small Chinese vote support for the BN dramatically affected the MCA's electoral performance in GE-14, furthering its trend of declining returns in Johor (see Figure 9.3). While UMNO remains formidable in the state by winning seven of the sixteen parliament seats contested, its fellow BN coalition parties only won one of the ten parliament seats allocated to them; the MCA won the Malay-majority parliament seat Ayer Hitam with a meagre 303 votes. PAS, while never having a formidable presence in Johor, managed to play its role as a potential spoiler. It obtained a total of 4,975 votes in Ayer Hitam and 2,962 votes in Tanjung Piai. These are votes that could have altered the winner of the aforementioned seats although it is difficult to say at this point if those votes were solidly for PAS and would have gone to PH if it had stayed in the coalition, or if they were non-PH protest votes that would have stayed with BN had PAS not contested.

For the state assembly, the MCA failed to win a single seat out of the fifteen seats allocated to the party. With its failure to win any significant Chinese votes,[28] the slight Malay vote swing to the PH ensured that the MCA would have almost no chance of winning any of the Chinese-majority and mixed parliamentary and state constituencies. It was even defeated in the Malay-majority state seat, Pulai Sebatang, by Amanah and the Malay-majority parliament seat, Tanjung Piai, by PPBM. Indeed, the MCA was decimated despite the possibility that fewer outstation Chinese voters returned to cast their vote in this election; the Election Commission estimated a voter turnout of 74 per cent, much lower than the 86.7 per cent in GE-13 (*New Straits Times*, 9 May 2018).

In the aftermath of the devastating GE-14 results, MCA leaders from Johor were reportedly vying to take over the MCA leadership from the incumbents, namely party president Liow Tiong Lai (who is also the chairman of the MCA Melaka State

FIGURE 9.3
The Parliamentary and State Seat Count of the MCA in Johor, 2004–18

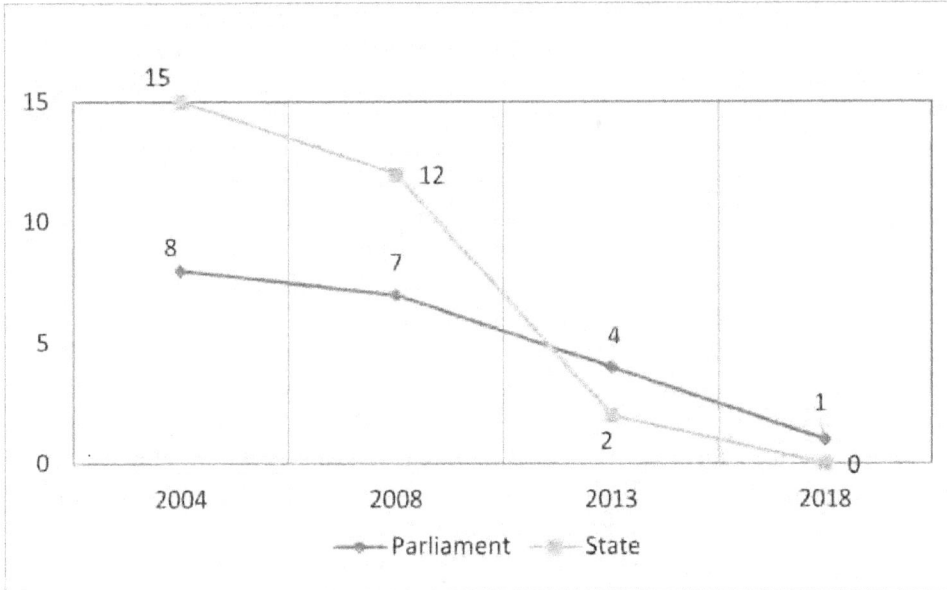

Source: undi.info.

Liaison Committee) and his deputy, Melaka-born Wee Ka Siong (chairman of the MCA Johor State Liaison Committee), who was eyeing for the party's presidency. Many of the interested parties were supporters of Chua Soi Lek's faction,[29] including Tee Siew Kiong (deputy to Wee in the MCA Johor), who eventually contested for the post of deputy president but lost to Wee's running mate Mah Hang Soon (*Sin Chew Daily*, 28 April 2018). Wee similarly prevailed over MCA Kluang division chief Gan Ping Sieu, who received an endorsement from Soi Lek, ultimately cementing his position over the southern challengers through a landslide victory of his team (*The Star*, 28 September 2018; *The Malaysian Insider*, 6 November 2018).

CONCLUSION

In the past decade, the MCA became very dependent on its historically strong support from the Malay voting bloc, therefore subjecting its fate to UMNO's performance within Johor. In fact, there are very few seats contested by the MCA in Johor during GE-14 that can be considered competitive (in which a 10 per cent vote change could alter the winner), and those that were, such as Tanjung Piai, Paloh and Pekan Nanas, were mixed if not Malay-majority seats. As the UMNO parliamentary and state assembly seat count dropped close to half—seven and seventeen (from fifteen and thirty-two) respectively in 2018—the near-elimination of the MCA in Johor was inevitable, considering it lost both the ethnic Chinese and Malay votes.

At the time of writing, any conjecture of MCA's fate can only be premature. However, two factors will be pivotal to the MCA's prospects. Internally, the party will have to undergo reorganization and rejuvenation. While the party has expanded its party election system from one that is dependent on over 2,000 delegates to one dependent on over 40,000 delegates, the system of having the party leader appoint state-level leaders remains unchanged (*Sin Chew Daily*, 29 May 2018). This hampered the dynamism of the party as its internal politics continued to revolve around high-stakes contests at the centre, as seen in the Team A–Team B split that began in Ling Liong Sik's time, and the later struggles between Chua Soi Lek and Ong Ka Ting, and subsequently Ong Tee Keat which almost paralysed the party (Chin 2010, pp. 155–59). Without elections that foster the rise of young capable leaders at the local level, such as that of the DAP's Liew Chin Tong who managed to take over the DAP Johor leadership at the relatively young age of thirty-seven, the local party machinery will continue to depend on patronage and winner-picking from the national level (*The Star*, 12 January 2014).

Moreover, it is uncertain how in the foreseeable future, young ethnic Chinese leaders will be attracted to join a party with an ossified leadership and tarnished reputation after a "near total failure" in three consecutive elections (Weiss 2013, p. 26). Since the 2008 political tsunami, both the PKR and the DAP have emerged as the more enticing avenues for young ethnic Chinese political aspirants. The MCA's key challenger, the DAP, had reportedly fielded the highest number of young candidates in GE-14, with many under the age of thirty elected into office (*Malaysian Insight*, 12 January 2018; *Star2.com*, 7 May 2018).

Externally, the party will have to reconsider its position within the BN and its cooperation with the coalition's hegemon, UMNO. The latter is observed to be moving towards forming a Malay-Muslim exclusivist alliance with PAS—a party the MCA is uneasy with due to its call for conservative Islamist policies, including the implementation of *hudud* punishments. Hints of a break were suggested when Wee Ka Siong, then deputy president, declared that the BN "ceased to exist except in name" (*Malay Mail Online*, 2 June 2018). Yet soon enough, in a by-election that was the MCA's to run, the party continued to receive endorsement and support from the BN, and even from PAS (*New Straits Times*, 24 August 2018; *Malay Mail Online*, 5 September 2018). If the MCA breaks off from the BN, it will have to wean off its dependence on the coalition's consociational model that delivered the compensating Malay votes it needed so badly. In addition, a stand-alone Chinese party in Malay-majority Malaysia would compel the party to adopt a more hardline position in championing perceived "Chinese" rights, as seen in PAS's drift towards Malay and Muslim issues when it decided not to join the PH. Yet, there are multiple reasons that may prevent the success of such a rebranding for the MCA.

First, there are no signs that as a minority that is often reminded of the spectre of the May 13 racial riots,[30] the Malaysian Chinese electorate is in demand of a more chauvinistically "Chinese" party, even if reactionary voices are sometimes appreciated for the purpose of pushing back against the Malay supremacy discourse.[31] Also, there is significant diversity within the Chinese population, with many, most prominently the English-speaking intelligentsia and the many Mandarin-speaking civil society activists, unlikely to be attracted to a more communal approach to politics.[32] Second, even if someone were to step up to lead such an insurgency, there are no credible figures in the MCA with a strong following among the Malaysian Chinese.[33] Third, in Malay-Muslim majority Malaysia such a strategy will almost definitely backfire—as has been the case historically[34]—possibly leading to the party's dissolution.

Ultimately, MCA is not (or at least is no longer) a party with strong local roots, such as PAS in the northern states of east coast West Malaysia, or Parti Pesaka Bumiputera Bersatu (PBB) in Sarawak, or even Sabah's recent wunderkind, Parti Warisan Sabah. MCA support in Johor appears to have no association whatsoever with locally rooted sentiments. As we have demonstrated, its Johor base is tied to the BN's overall strength in the state, and by extension, West Malaysia. The strong identification with *Bangsa Johor* ("Johor national"; or someone of Johor origins) and the Johor royal family shown in survey results of the Chinese Johoreans did not translate into votes for the BN (Lee 2017), despite the tacit support given by the royal family (*Channel News Asia*, 8 April 2018). Alas, unable to break free from Malaysia's centralized federalism and pervasive ethnic politics,[35] the MCA's survival in Johor will inevitably be linked to its survival in Malaysian politics in general.

APPENDIX 9.1
Parliamentary Seats Contested by MCA, MIC and Gerakan, 2013

	Constituency	Votes	Malay Votes (%)	Chinese Votes (%)	Indian Votes (%)	A (%)	B (%)
P140	Segamat	MIC	44	46	10	30.00	19.35
P142	Labis	MCA	36	47	15	35.43	29.36
P145	Bakri	MCA	44	53	2	34.34	26.23
P148	Ayer Hitam	MCA	56	38	4	22.89	8.68
P151	Simpang Renggam	GRK	57	33	9	15.91	—
P152	Kluang	MCA	39	49	10	35.31	28.37
P158	Tebrau	MCA	47	38	13	26.45	15.79
P162	Gelang Patah*	UMNO	34	52	12	37.88	32.50
P163	Kulai	MCA	33	56	10	38.39	33.39
P165	Tanjung Piai	MCA	51	47	2	28.30	17.66

Notes: A refers to the Chinese votes needed for a BN win when 70 per cent and above of the Malay bloc vote supports the BN.

B refers to Chinese votes needed for a BN win when 80 per cent and above Malay bloc vote supports the BN. Assume 55 per cent of Indian votes for the BN.

* Gelang Patah was traditionally an MCA seat, but in 2013 the outgoing Mentri Besar of the state, Abdul Ghani Othman, took on DAP's Lim Kit Siang in this seat.

APPENDIX 9.2
State Constituencies Contested by MCA, MIC and Gerakan, 2013

	Constituency	Party	Malay votes (%)	Chinese votes (%)	Indian votes (%)	A (%)	B (%)
N2	Jementah	MCA	36	55	9	36.27	30.55
N3	Pemanis	GRK	56	39	3	23.72	9.74
N6	Bekok	MCA	26	54	18	40.74	37.59
N9	Gambir	MIC	55	40	4	23.50	10.25
N10	Tangkak	MCA	38	51	10	35.29	28.82
N12	Bentayan	MCA	25	73	2	43.15	39.86
N19	Yong Peng	MCA	32	60	7	39.75	35.00
N21	Parit Yaani	MCA	54	43	2	26.05	13.72
N23	Penggaram	MCA	35	62	2	39.52	34.03
N28	Mengkibol	MCA	27	58	14	40.52	37.07
N30	Paloh	MCA	37	44	17	33.75	27.27
N31	Kahang	MIC	74	21	3	0.00	—
N33	Tengaroh	MIC	80	13	5	0.00	—
N41	Puteri Wangsa	MIC	40	47	12	32.98	25.74
N42	Johor Jaya	MCA	43	47	7	34.36	25.96
N45	Stulang	MCA	39	55	4	37.45	30.73
N46	Pengkalan Riting	MCA	43	45	11	31.00	22.67
N48	Skudai	MCA	22	65	12	43.23	40.77
N51	Bukit Batu	GRK	30	62	7	40.73	36.45
N52	Senai	MCA	23	65	11	43.00	40.31
N54	Pulai Sebatang	MCA	62	35	2	16.00	—
N55	Pekan Nanas	MCA	39	58	2	37.41	30.86

Notes: A refers to the Chinese votes needed for a BN win when 70 per cent and above of the Malay bloc vote supports the BN; and B refers to Chinese votes needed for a BN win when 80 per cent and above Malay bloc vote supports the BN. Assume 55 per cent of Indian votes for the BN.

Notes

1. This chapter was first published as *Electoral Politics and the Malaysian Chinese Association in Johor*, Trends in Southeast Asia, no. 20/2018 (Singapore: ISEAS – Yusof Ishak Institute, 2018).
2. See Roff (1965), Heng (1988) and Tan (2015) for more in-depth analyses of the MCA.
3. Chinese communal organizations include traditional guilds, clan and regional dialect groups, trade/business associations, and religious and cultural societies. See Ho (1992) and Thock (2008).
4. Onn Jaafar, the founding president of UMNO, also wanted to convert the party into a multiethnic one. His proposal to open up the party to non-Malays who qualified as citizens was rejected by an overwhelming majority. Subsequently, Onn Jaafar resigned from UMNO in mid-1951 and, in September of the same year, established the first intercommunal party in Malaya, the Independence Malayan Party (IMP). Partly because of its intercommunal politics, the IMP did not attract much support from the Malay and Chinese communities. Indeed, its intercommunal ideas were too radical as they were anathema to the predominantly conservative and communal-minded ethnic communities. Hence, before its demise in 1954, the IMP failed to defeat the communal approach adopted by UMNO and MCA in successive elections.
5. The beginning of the UMNO-MCA coalition has been shown to have come about more by accident than by design, especially given that at the national leadership level there existed no signs of the two parties coming to work together (Heng 1988, p. 159). Specifically, it had its origins in the Kuala Lumpur municipal elections in February 1952 when the local MCA decided to form an informal front with KL-UMNO to challenge the IMP. Working together, the informal alliance divided the constituencies among themselves based on the ethnic composition of the constituency; the MCA contested in the Chinese-dominated seats while the UMNO candidates contested in the Malay-dominated ones. Appealing to and manipulating communal fears and anxieties, the MCA and UMNO successfully defeated the IMP in ten of the twelve seats.
6. As both came from the business-class group, the English- and Chinese-educated leaders could not afford to remain disunited as it would irreparably weaken their class bargaining position vis-à-vis UMNO. Consequently, the two groups reconciled their differences immediately after independence; this was publicly formalized by the Conference of Chinese Associations on 10 November 1957.
7. Many leaders of the powerful Perak Chinese Associations and Guilds became disenchanted with, and felt betrayed by the MCA which supported the Razak Report and subsequently the Talib Report. A failed attempt to raise Chinese as an official language by the Laukeh group led by Lim Chong Eu resulted in the first major split in MCA with Lim resigning from the MCA and establishing a new political party, the United Democratic Party (UDP). A number of MCA leaders also left the party and contested as independent candidates in the 1964 elections. The Lim-led group also wanted the power to decide on the selection and the transfer of MCA federal and state candidates from the Alliance National Council to the MCA Executive Council. If the MCA retained the autonomy to pick its candidates, it would make the process more "democratic", and allow Lim and his supporters to pick their own people. Lastly, pressured by the Chinese middle-class, the group proposed that the government increase the intake of qualified Chinese into the Malayanized civil service; the existing recruiting quota was four to one in favour of the Malays. Obviously,

if the above demands had been accepted, it would have greatly strengthened MCA participation in the Alliance's decision-making process. Nevertheless, before Tan Siew Sin, the new MCA president, and the other English-educated leaders could reorganize the party and remobilize their mass support, they were dealt another severe blow by the Alliance Government's new education policy, the Talib Report (1960), named after Abdul Rahman Talib, then Minister of Education. For the reactions of Chinese educationists, see Ang (2014).

8. When the 1967 National Language Bill was passed by parliament, it led to many more Chinese becoming disenchanted with the MCA. It reinforced their view that the party was politically impotent, and incapable of protecting and looking after the Chinese community's rights and interests. For example, when the Chinese Associations and educationists proposed the establishment of a Chinese-medium tertiary institution, the Merdeka University in 1968, the MCA opposed the idea. Consequently, Chinese support for the party fell dramatically towards the late 1960s, and ultimately led to the disastrous MCA showing in the 1969 general elections, except in Johor.

9. After losing substantial Chinese support in the 1969 elections, the MCA tried to revive its link to the Chinese associations which had abandoned the party. Post-1969 saw many young English-educated Chinese joining the party. These young MCA leaders actively sought to revive support for the party among the Chinese grassroots, especially in the new villagers in Perak. In 1971, an emerging group of young leaders, such as Lim Keng Yaik and Alex Lee, helped to organize a meeting among the leaders of Chinese associations, with more than 1,000 delegates in attendance, and thus was born the Chinese Unity Movement. The MCA-backed Chinese Unity Movement tried to revive active support for the party as well as provide active leadership in the aftermath of the 1969 debacle. However, this unity movement was short-lived when internal MCA party rivalry led Tan Siew Sin, president of MCA, to expel several of the young leaders. A majority of the Young Turks eventually joined Gerakan, as they wished to continue working with the BN coalition formula.

10. The MCA launched a scholarship fund called Kojadi and applied for the expansion of Tunku Abdul Rahman (TAR) College. However, the two moves could only assist a small number of Chinese students with a majority denied the opportunity to further their studies. TAR was set up on 4 February 1969 in Kuala Lumpur to cater mainly for Chinese students who did not have the opportunity to pursue tertiary education locally or overseas. In 1991, the Government allocated RM20 million under the Sixth Malaysia Plan for the college. Under Ling's leadership, a total of RM30 million was raised by MCA in a series of fund-raising campaigns. This was matched by the Government on a ringgit-to-ringgit basis, bringing the total to RM60 million. Under a massive development plan, TAR spread its campuses to Johor, Penang, Perak and Pahang. In 1997, the government issued the MCA the licence to establish the bilingual-medium University Tunku Abdul Rahman.

11. It was estimated that it received supporting signatures of some 4,238 Chinese guilds and associations throughout the country, and copies were sent to the Prime Minister, the Minister of Education and all members of parliament.

12. For example, twenty-seven of the twenty-nine members of the Johor Working Committee for the years 1953–55 were either Chinese-educated or non-educated businessmen with the remaining two being doctors. Due to the small number of top English-educated members in the party, Johor MCA politicians did not play prominent roles at the national level until

the 1970s. By the 1970s, Johor MCA had a more balanced membership of Chinese- and English-educated individuals (MCA 1974, p. 8).

13. Wong Shee Fun served as the President of the Johor Chinese Chamber of Commerce, 1949–66, chairman of the Boards of both Foon Yew Primary and High Schools, 1951–53, chairman of the board of Guangzhao Huiguan, 1946–78, as well as the chairman of the Singapore Chinese newspaper, *Chung Shing Jit Pau* (Lim 2006, p. 49).

14. The CGAs had long played the role as guardian and intermediator for Chinese welfare in Johor, predating even the founding of the MCA. One such organization as singled out by Lim (2000) was the Ngee Heng Kongsi, and its successor after it was banned, the Chinese Association of Johor Bahru. The association was credited with connecting the Chinese community with Malay officials especially, above all, the Sultan.

15. To read about Chua Jui Meng's challenge in the context of the MCA's internal party politics and the infamous Team A–Team B split between Ling Liong Sik and his deputy, Lim Ah Lek, see Chin (2006, 2010).

16. The relationship between the MCA and the New Villages was once described as, in the words of Wee Ka Siong, a "nail and finger" interdependency for mutual interests.

17. Johor was the first state to introduce Chinese citizens' committees with proportional representation for different dialect groups, which through co-operation with *penghulu* (headmen) were absorbed into local administration in 1951.

18. Lee Kaw, a veteran opposition politician, referred to the link between land acquisitions and support for MCA/BN in explaining why the rural Chinese continued to support the MCA. See *The Edge Markets*, 3 May 2013.

19. These figures are calculated from the National Population and Housing Censuses of 1980, 1991, and 2010.

20. UMNO also lost the Senggarang state seat to the Islamic party PAS on a technicality in 1990.

21. Liew Chin Tong, the DAP candidate for Kluang in GE-13, mentioned that he knew he could win when his informants told him of massive traffic jams in and around Kluang. The traffic jams indicated huge numbers of outstation Chinese returning to cast their vote (private conversation).

22. In Johor, the percentage of ethnic Chinese electorate on the electoral roll was 38 per cent in late 2017, about 5 per cent higher than the population as reported by the census, see *China Press Johor*, 5 April 2018.

23. Maznah (2003) shows that UMNO consistently received strong support from Malay voters in the Malay-majority parliamentary constituencies in Johor. UMNO garnered 79, 86 and 79 per cent of the Malay votes in the 1990, 1995 and 1999 elections respectively. The Merdeka Center estimated that Malay voter support for the BN in the 2008 and 2013 elections were 81.1 and 81.9 per cent respectively.

24. It was revealed in a survey that 85 per cent of Malays in Johor were "not in favour" of the DAP (Wan Saiful 2018, p. 28).

25. Split voting between the BN at the state level and the opposition at the federal level had been a key feature of Chinese voting patterns in a state like Penang until 2008. This explained the DAP's relatively high parliamentary seat count in Penang, even in 2004 (when it won four, which is more than what the MCA and Gerakan had won separately), while only winning one seat at the state assembly.

26. As alluded to above, the MCA loss of Bakri may be postulated as the consequence of dropping Chua Jui Meng, former Minister of Health and five-term Bakri parliamentarian, as the seat's candidate.

27. This is due no less to the sizeable influence of the PKR, the PAS, and Amanah amongst the Malay-Muslim electorate in Selangor. The same cannot be said for these parties in Johor. PKR and Amanah only made substantial gains in the state by GE-14 through their partnership with the DAP and more importantly, the Mahathir-led Parti Pribumi Bersatu Malaysia (PPBM) that had a strong presence in Johor due to party president Muhyiddin Yassin's influence.

28. It was reported that the PH won a total of 95 per cent of the Chinese vote, see *Straits Times*, 14 June 2018.

29. Soi Lek himself was rumoured to be plotting a comeback, but he denied such news. See *Nanyang Siang Pau*, 26 June 2018.

30. The resounding failure of the *Suqiu* movement of the late 1990s that saw many Chinese CGA leaders coming together to demand for "Chinese" and wider Malaysian rights is a good indication of how far "Chinese" communitarian politics can advance in Malaysia. The movement had to drop its appeal after being told "if racial riots broke out they would be held responsible" (Collins 2006, p. 311).

31. The same can be said about UMNO too, as seen in its massive losses in GE-14 despite the increased tenor in UMNO's ethnoreligious exclusivism, the essence of which can be seen in the *"apa lagi Cina mahu"* [what else do the Chinese want?] lament by former Prime Minister Najib after the 2013 General Elections. See Norshahril (2016) for a discussion of UMNO's role in promoting exclusivist readings of Islam in Malaysia.

32. The lack of traction by the Chinese education group, the *dongjiaozong*, in opposing the now-defunct government programme to use English at the medium of instruction in science and mathematics in all primary schools also points to the lack of consensus among the Malaysian Chinese about what constitutes "Chinese" rights (Collins 2006, pp. 311–17).

33. MCA's President, Wee Ka Siong, has only about 9,000 likes in his Facebook account. On the contrary, Khairy Jamaluddin, who is playing is the role of a potential reformer for UMNO, has 1.2 million likes on his Facebook page. Lim Guan Eng, the secretary-general of DAP and current Finance Minister, has 650,000 likes. Figures are taken in September 2018.

34. The rising ethnic tensions after Chinese education interest groups, as well as the MCA and DAP, protested what was perceived to be government infringements into Chinese primary schools—which was followed by an UMNO counter-protest—became the pretext to *Operasi Lalang* in 1987. The massive clampdown was said to have included the arrest of MCA leaders. See Julian Lee (2008); *New Straits Times*, 30 October 2017.

35. For a discussion of how Malaysia's centralized federalism affected intraparty politics of another BN party, UMNO, see Hutchinson (2015a).

References

Ang Ming Chee. 2014. *Institutions and Social Mobilization: The Chinese Education Movements in Malaysia, 1951–2011*. Singapore: Institute of Southeast Asian Studies.

Chin, James. 2006. "New Chinese Leadership in Malaysia: The Contest for the MCA and Gerakan Presidency". *Contemporary Southeast Asia* 28, no. 1: 70–87.

———. 2010. "Malaysian Chinese Association Politics a Year Later: Crisis of Political Legitimacy". *The Round Table* 99, no. 407: 153–62.

———, and Wong Chin Huat. 2009. "Malaysia's Electoral Upheaval". *Journal of Democracy* 20, no. 3: 71–85.

Collins, A. 2006. "Chinese Educationalists in Malaysia: Defenders of Chinese Identity". *Asian Survey* 46, no. 2: 298–318.

Funston, John. 1980. *Malay Politics in Malaysia: A Study of UMNO and PAS*. Kuala Lumpur: Heinemann Educational Books.

Hara, Fujio. 1997. *Malayan Chinese and China: Conversion in Identity Consciousness, 1945–1957*. Tokyo: Institute of Developing Societies.

Heng Pek Koon. 1988. *Politics in Malaysia: A History of the Malaysian Chinese Association*. Oxford University Press.

Ho Khai Leong. 1992. *The Malaysian Chinese Guilds and Associations as Organized Interests in Malaysian Politics*. Working Paper No. 4, Department of Political Science, National University of Singapore.

Hutchinson, Francis E. 2015a. "Centre-State Relations and Intra-Party Dynamics in Malaysia: UMNO and the Case of Johor". *Asian Journal of Political Science* 23, no. 2: 111–33.

———. 2015b. "Malaysia's Independence Leaders and the Legacies of State Formation under British Rule". *Journal of the Royal Asiatic Society* 25, no. 1: 123–51.

———. 2018. *GE-14 In Johor: The Fall of the Fortress?* Trends in Southeast Asia, no. 3/2018. Singapore: ISEAS – Yusof Ishak Institute.

Khong Kim Hoong. 1984. *Merdeka! British Rule and the Struggle for Independence in Malaya, 1945–1957*. Petaling Jaya: Institute for Social Analysis.

Koh Sin Yee. 2010. *Towards a Theory of "Skilled Diasporic Citizenship": Tertiary-Educated Chinese-Malaysians in Singapore as Citizens, Diasporas, and Transnational Migrants Negotiating Citizenship and Migration Decisions*. LSE Migration Studies Unit Working Papers. London: Migration Studies Unit, LSE.

Lee Hock Guan. 2017. "Johor Survey 2017: Views on Identity, Education and the Johor Royal Family". *ISEAS Perspective*, no. 84/2017, 13 November 2017.

Lee, Julian C.H. 2008. "The Fruits of Weeds: Taking Justice at the Commemoration of the Twentieth Anniversary of Operasi Lalang in Malaysia". *Round Table* 97, no. 397: 605–15.

Lee Kam Hing. 2008. "Politics of the Chinese in Malaysia: Fifty Years On". In *Malaysian Chinese and Nation-Building: Before Merdeka and Fifty Years After*, vol. 2, edited by Voon Phin Keong. Kuala Lumpur: Centre for Malaysian Chinese Studies.

Lim Hin Fui, and Fong Tian Yong. 2005. *The New Villages in Malaysia: The Journey Ahead*. Kuala Lumpur: Institute of Strategic Analysis & Policy Research.

Lim Hong Hai. 2003. "The Delineation of Peninsular Electoral Constituencies: Amplifying Malay and UMNO Power". In *New Politics in Malaysia*, edited by Francis Loh Kok Wah and Johan Saravanamuttu. Singapore: Institute of Southeast Asian Studies.

Lim, Patricia Pui Huen. 2000. "Continuity and Connectedness: The Ngee Heng Kongsi of Johor, 1844–1916". ISEAS Working Paper: Visiting Researchers Series, no. 2. Singapore: Institute of Southeast Asian Studies,

———. 2006. "Between Tradition and Modernity: The Chinese Association of Johor Bahru, Malaysia". In *Voluntary Organizations in the Chinese Diaspora*, edited by Kuah Khun Eng and Evelyn Hu-debart. Hong Kong: Hong Kong University Press.

Malaysian Chinese Association. 1974. *MCA 25th Anniversary Souvenir Publication*. Kuala Lumpur: MCA.

———. 2011. "Tan Sri Lee San Choon", 20 April 2011. https://web.archive.org/web/20110420234247/http://www.mca.org.my/en/about-us/about-mca/history-zone/former-presidents/tan-sri-lee-san-choon/

Maznah Mohamad. 2003. "The Contest for Malay Votes in 1999: UMNO's Most Historic

Challenge". In *New Politics in Malaysia*, edited by Francis Loh Kok Wah and Johan Saravanamuttu. Singapore: Institute of Southeast Asian Studies.

Moten, Abdul Rashid. 2009. "2004 and 2008 General Elections in Malaysia: Towards a Multicultural, Bi-party Political System?". *Asian Journal of Political Science* 17, no. 2: 173–94.

Norshahril Saat. 2016. "Exclusivist Attitudes in Malaysian Islam Have Multifarious Roots". *ISEAS Perspective*, no. 39/2016, 5 July 2016.

Ong Kian Ming. 2013. "GE2013 Results Shows That it Was a Malaysian Tsunami and Not a Chinese Tsunami That Increased Pakatan's Popular Vote and Number of Parliament and State Seats", 10 May 2013. https://ongkianming.com/2013/05/10/media-statement-ge2013-results-shows-that-it-was-a-malaysian-tsunami-and-not-a-chinese-tsunami-that-increased-pakatans-popular-vote-and-number-of-parliament-and-state-seats/

———. 2018. "GE14: A Truly Malaysian Tsunami", 17 May 2018. https://ongkianming.com/2018/05/17/media-statement-ge14-a-truly-malaysian-tsunami

Ooi Kok Hin. 2018. "How Malaysia's Election Is Being Rigged". *New Naratif*, 19 May 2018. https://newnaratif.com/research/malaysias-election-rigged/

Pang Siew Nooi, and Tan Teck Hong. 2012. "New Villages in Malaysia: A Boon or Bane?". Conference Proceeding for the Conference on Malaysian Chinese in Historical Context: Interpretation and Assessment, Kajang, Malaysia.

Ratnam, K.J., and R.S. Milne. 1971. "The 1969 Parliamentary Election in West Malaysia". *Pacific Affairs* 43, no. 2: 203–26.

Roff, Margaret. 1965. "The Malayan Chinese Association, 1948–1965". *Journal of Southeast Asian History* 6, no. 2: 40–53.

Tan Miau Ing. 2015. "The Formation of the Malayan Chinese Association (MCA) Revisited". *Journal of the Malaysian Branch of the Royal Asiatic Society* 88 pt. 2, no. 309: 105–24.

Thock Ker Pong. 2008. "Discoursing Nation-Building and Civil Society Formation: The Role of Malaysian Chinese Guilds and Associations". In *Malaysian Chinese and Nation-Building: Before Merdeka and Fifty Years After*, vol. 2, edited by Voon Phin Kheong. Kuala Lumpur: Centre for Malaysian Chinese Studies.

Trocki, Carl A. 1976. "The Origins of the Kangchu System 1740–1860". *Journal of the Malaysian Branch of the Royal Asiatic Society* 49, no. 2: 132–55.

van Grunsven, L. and Francis E. Hutchinson. 2016. "Revisiting Industrial Dynamics in the SIJORI Cross-Border Region: The Electronics Industry Twenty Years On". In *The SIJORI Cross-Border Region: Transnational Politics, Economics, and Culture*, edited by Francis E. Hutchinson and Terence Chong. Singapore: ISEAS – Yusof Ishak Institute.

Vasil, R.K. 1972. *The Malaysian General Election of 1969*. Singapore and Kuala Lumpur: Oxford University Press.

Voon Phin Keong. 2009. "The Chinese New Villages in Malaysia: Impact of Demographic Changes and Response Strategies". In *Study on Regional and Ethnic Diversities of Poverty Problems in Malaysia*, edited by M. Fujimaki. Kyoto: College of Letters, Ritsumeikan University.

Wan Saiful Wan Jan. 2018. *Parti Pribumi Bersatu Malaysia in Johor: New Party, Big Responsibility*. Trends in Southeast Asia, no. 2/2018. Singapore: ISEAS – Yusof Ishak Institute.

Weiss, Meredith. 2013. "Coalitions and Competition in Malaysia: Incremental Transformation of a Strong-party System". *Journal of Current Southeast Asian Affairs* 32, no. 2: 19–37.

Newspapers

Channel News Asia. 2018. "Don't 'Bring Down' Government, Trust The Royal Family: Johor Crown Prince". 8 April 2018.

China Press Johor. 2018. "柔總選民182萬617人 僅華裔比例下滑" [Johor's Electorate at 1.8 Million People, with Only the Chinese Ratio Dropping]. 5 April 2018.

Edge Markets, The. 2013. "#GE13* DAP Veteran Says Chinese in Johor 'No Longer Indebted' ", 3 May 2013.

———. 2018. "GE14 to see 8% Malay vote swing to Pakatan in peninsula, but BN will prevail, says Merdeka Center", 26 April 2018.

Malay Mail Online, The. 2018a. "At 36.42pc, BN Records Lowest Popular Vote i1n History". 11 May 2018.

———. 2018b. "Ka Siong: MCA Won't Carry Water for UMNO Anymore, BN Only Alive in Name". 2 June 2018.

———. 2018c. "PAS Sec-Gen Stumps for MCA Candidate in Balakong". 5 September 2018.

Malaysian Insight, The. 2018a. "Will Younger Candidates Pull in the Youth Vote?". 12 January 2018.

———. 2018b. "Wee Ka Siong, MCA Leader in Troubled Times". 6 November 2018.

Nanyang Siang Pau. 2016. "MCA Members That Existed in Name Only". 28 September 2016. http://www.malaysianchinesenews.com/2016/09/mca-members-that-existed-in-name-only/

———. 2018. "吃饱没那么空闲，蔡细历不攻马华会长" [I Am Not So Free: Chua Soi Lek Not Vying for MCA Presidency]. 26 June 2018.

New Straits Times. 2017. "Ops Lalang Allegedly Carried out Under Dr M's Orders, Says MCA Man". 30 October 2017.

———. 2018a. "74 percent Cast Their Votes In Johor". 9 May 2018.

———. 2018b. "Balakong By-election Candidate Says BN, NGOs Giving Full Support". 24 August 2018.

Oriental Daily. 2017. "大马华人的人口变化" [The Changes in Chinese Demographics in Malaysia]. 30 April 2017.

Reme Ahmad and Danson Cheong. 2017. "Johor: The Jewel in the Political Crown". *Straits Times*, 23 October 2017.

Sin Chew Daily. 2018a. "首次采扩大代表制，马华各级党选七月掀幕" [First Time Using an Expanded Delegate System, MCA's Party Elections at the Multiple Level to Begin in July]. 29 May 2018.

———. 2018b. "证实将竞选马华高职，郑修强攻老大或老二" [Teh Kiong Confirming His Interest in the Party's Top or Second Top Posts]. 28 August 2018.

Star, The. 2014. "Liew Is New Johor DAP Chief, Dr Boo Ousted". 12 January 2014.

———. 2018. "Chua: Gan Has My Backing For President". 28 September 2018.

Star2.com. 2018. "10 Young New Politicos in GE14 Looking to Serve Their Communities". 7 May 2018. https://www.star2.com/people/2018/05/07/looking-to-serve-their-communities-better/

Straits Times, The. 2018. "Most Malaysian Chinese Voted PH in Polls, but Malays in 3-Way Split". 14 June 2018.

10

PARTI PRIBUMI BERSATU MALAYSIA IN JOHOR
New Party, Big Responsibility

Wan Saiful Wan Jan[1]

INTRODUCTION

On 9 September 2016 the Malaysian Registrar of Societies (RoS) gave approval for the establishment of Parti Pribumi Bersatu Malaysia (PPBM), following the splintering of the main party in the country's ruling coalition, the United Malays National Organization (UMNO). PPBM was then officially launched on 14 January 2017, boasting some of the most famous names in Malaysian politics today as its top leaders. Malaysia's longest-serving Prime Minister Mahathir Mohamad was named as Chairman, and former Deputy Prime Minister Muhyiddin Yassin as President. Former Chief Minister of the northern Malaysian state of Kedah, Mukhriz Mahathir, who is Mahathir's son, was named Deputy President.

Right from the start, PPBM projected itself as a party that champions the Malay agenda. This is a position traditionally dominated by UMNO, who has always been able to fend off other contenders.[2] PPBM's Malay agenda also bucks the trend among Malaysian opposition parties who usually prefer to take a more multiracial and multicultural approach. This is a bold strategy, and makes clear that PPBM aims to replace UMNO as the political party for ethnic Malays in Malaysia. Bearing in mind that UMNO today is led by Prime Minister Najib Razak, who is suffering from various allegations of corruption and whose popularity rating has been very low for many months (*Time*, 23 May 2017), the establishment of PPBM is a development that cannot be ignored.

Soon after the party obtained the RoS approval, Muhyiddin declared that it would work towards wresting the southern state of Johor from the ruling coalition, Barisan Nasional (BN) (*Bernama*, 9 October 2016). This announcement was not surprising. Johor is after all Muhyiddin's home ground. Not only is he member of parliament for the Johor constituency of Pagoh, he was Chief Minister of the state from 1986 to 1995. Johor is also the birthplace of UMNO and has remained the party's bastion since 1946, which makes the proclamation by Muhyiddin worth scrutinizing further. Is this a realistic target for the fledgling party? This chapter seeks to answer that question.

It presents the author's analysis of media coverage and academic literature on the topic, together with findings from extensive fieldwork conducted between April and August 2017. During the fieldwork, interviews were conducted with national, state and divisional leaders and activists of PPBM, other parties in the opposition coalition, and UMNO. More time was spent in rural areas with a high proportion of Malay voters because these are the areas where PPBM is expected to focus. The author also travelled to various parts of rural Johor to interview community leaders and villagers, including eight FELDA[3] settlements, to gauge grassroots reactions to PPBM.

Following this introduction, the chapter is divided into five sections. Section 2 provides a brief description of Johor's demography, economy, and political history. Subsequently, it looks into the formation and the organization of PPBM, and the external and internal dynamics shaping the party. The next two sections examine the likelihood of PPBM achieving its ambition of capturing Johor in the next elections and how UMNO reacts to PPBM's presence. The chapter ends with a summary.

JOHOR: A BRIEF OVERVIEW

Demography and Economy

Johor is the third largest Malaysian state in terms of population size, after Selangor and Sabah (Department of Statistics Malaysia, July 2016). Of its 3.6 million inhabitants, 54 per cent is ethnic Malay, 33 per cent is Chinese, and 6 per cent is Indian. It has a rather substantial number of non-Malaysians. The 2010 Census recorded a total of 271,899 foreigners, or 8 per cent of the population at that time. But that was before the influx of more foreign workers involved in the various mega construction projects launched in the state.[4] Malaysia as a whole is facing a serious problem in handling illegal migrant workers, and it is estimated that for every one legal foreign worker, there are two illegals (*Straits Times*, 17 September 2016). By that measure, Johor today may have more than 800,000 illegal foreign workers, equivalent to a staggering 22 per cent of its total population.

Johor is also a relatively urbanized state with a young population. More than 70 per cent of Johoreans live in urban areas and the number is increasing. Fifty per cent of the population is aged between fifteen to forty-four years old (Department of Statistics Malaysia; Johor State Investment Centre), creating a significant demand for jobs. The state's consistent economic growth has helped meet that demand thus far, especially as it evolves from one that is mainly based on agriculture into one based on industry and services. GDP per capita increased from RM21,116 in 2010 to RM26,399 in 2014, recording a healthy growth rate of between 4 to 6 per cent annually for the past several years (Oxford Business Group 2016). In March 2016, the state government published a four-year Johor Strategic Growth Plan with the ambitious target of growing per capita income by 8.7 per cent per annum to enable it to become a "high-income state" by 2020.

Four ongoing mega projects make Johor a state that is being closely watched not just by Malaysians but also by the wider world. Two of them are part of China's Belt and Road Initiative: The RM60 billion high-speed rail linking Singapore and Kuala Lumpur, which will have stops in several Johor towns and cities, and which is pivotal to the relationship between the two countries; and the RM9 billion electrified double-tracking of the train line connecting Gemas in Negeri Sembilan and Johor Bahru, due to be constructed and then operated by state-owned enterprises from China. Then there is the RM430 billion Forest City, a mixed-use development being built on four reclaimed islands in the Johor Strait, also run by a company from China. In addition, Malaysia's national oil company Petronas is investing RM90 billion into a major oil and gas refinery in Johor's eastern district of Pengerang.

Politics

Although Johor is governed by Barisan Nasional (BN), which is a national coalition of thirteen political parties led by UMNO, only four BN parties have seats in the state. In the last general election (GE-13) at the state legislative assembly level, UMNO led the BN bloc by winning thirty-two seats, the Malaysian Chinese Association (MCA) gained two seats, the Malaysian Indian Congress (MIC) three seats, and the People's Movement Party (Gerakan) one seat. On the opposition side, the Democratic Action Party (DAP) won thirteen seats, the National Justice Party (PKR) one seat, and the Islamic Party of Malaysia (PAS) four seats.[5] At the federal parliamentary level, BN won twenty-one seats, with UMNO having the lion share of fifteen seats, followed by MCA with four seats, and one each for the MIC and Gerakan. The DAP, in turn, won four parliamentary seats, and PKR one.

Figures 10.1 and 10.2 show that there is a relationship between ethnic distribution—more specifically the percentage of Malay voters in a constituency—and election results. Non-Malay areas are more likely to vote for non-UMNO parties and vice versa. In Figure 10.1, it can be seen that of the fifty-six seats in the state legislative assembly, sixteen have less than 45 per cent Malay voters, twenty-six have between 45 to 70 per cent Malay voters, and fourteen have more than 70 per cent Malay voters. In GE-13, the mainly Chinese DAP dominated constituencies with high numbers of non-Malay voters, while UMNO dominated those with a larger Malay population.

The same is reflected in federal parliamentary constituencies. Figure 10.2 shows that of the twenty-six parliamentary seats in the state, six have less than 45 per cent

FIGURE 10.1
Distribution of Johor State Legislative Assembly Seats Following GE-13

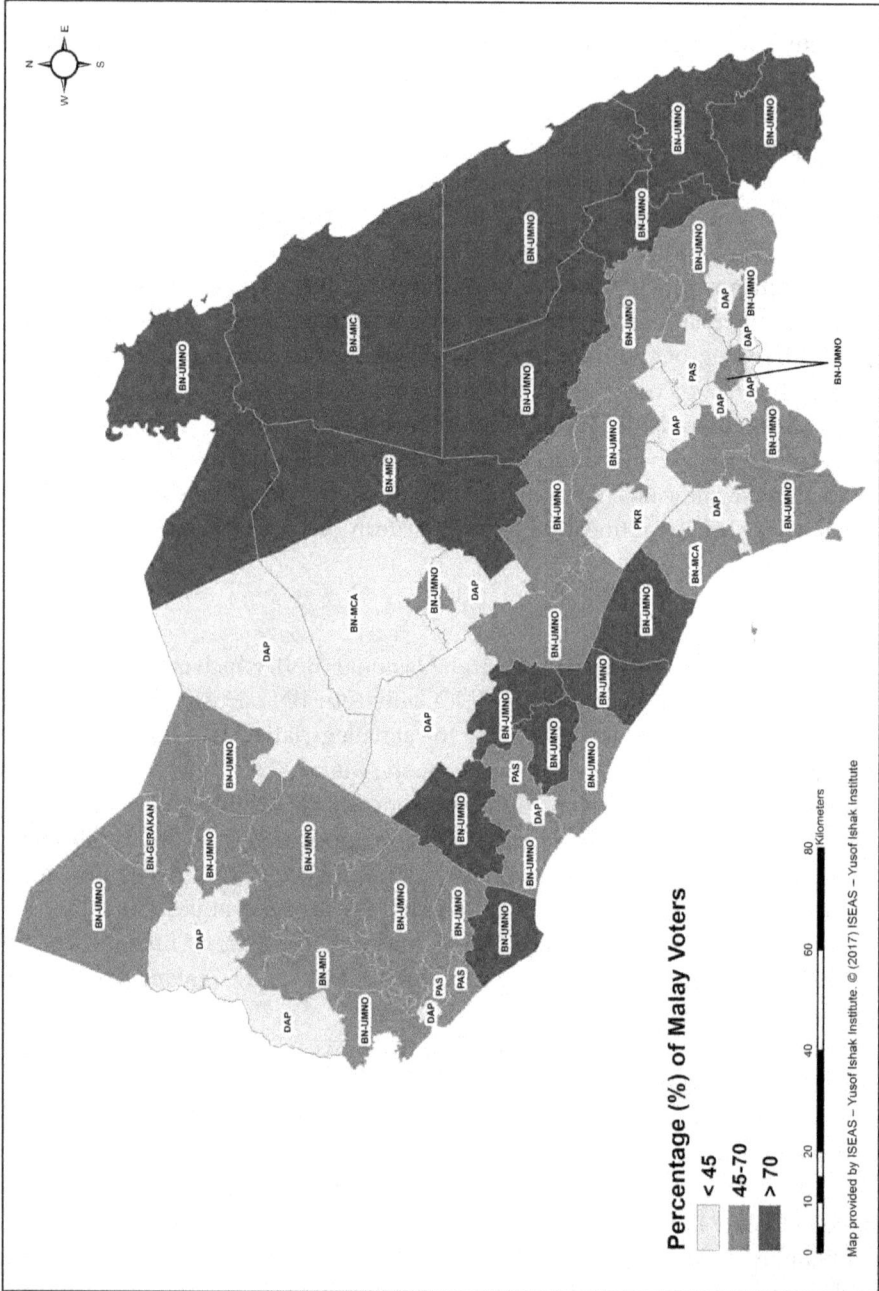

Percentage (%) of Malay Voters

< 45
45–70
> 70

0   10   20   40   60   80
                                    Kilometers

Map provided by ISEAS – Yusof Ishak Institute. © (2017) ISEAS – Yusof Ishak Institute

FIGURE 10.2
Distribution of Parliamentary Seats in Johor Following GE-13

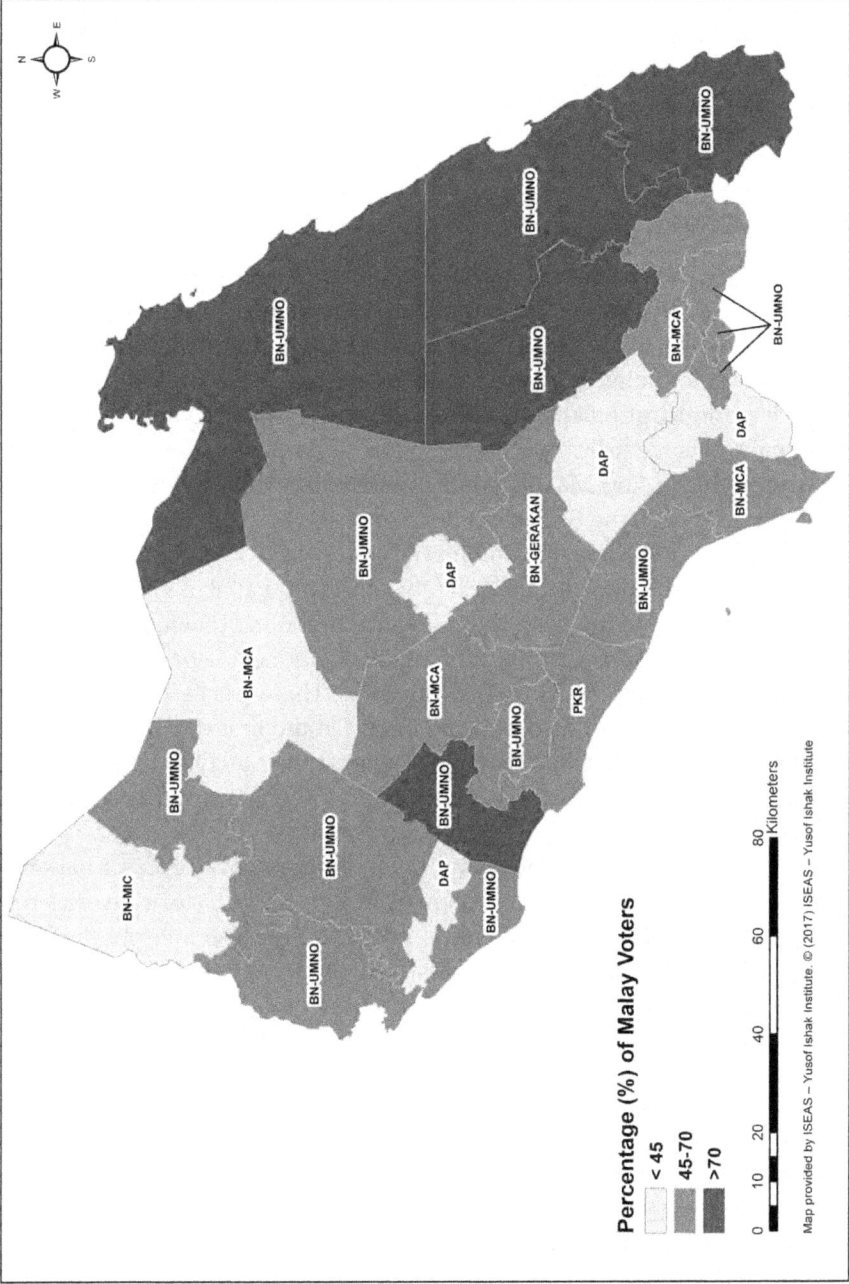

Percentage (%) of Malay Voters

< 45
45-70
>70

Map provided by ISEAS – Yusof Ishak Institute. © (2017) ISEAS – Yusof Ishak Institute

Malay voters, fifteen seats have between 45 to 70 per cent Malay voters, and five seats have more than 70 per cent Malay voters. DAP and PKR won four and one seats respectively, all in constituencies with high percentage of non-Malay voters. Non-Malay BN parties, namely the MCA, MIC and Gerakan, won in six constituencies, but UMNO once again dominates with fifteen seats, especially in areas with a higher Malay population. In fact, data from the Malaysian Election Commission show that in nine of the fifteen seats won by UMNO, their margin of victory was sizeable, at more than 10,000 votes in each.

UMNO in Johor

UMNO has been the dominant party in Johor since the party was first launched in 1946. It traces its history to the anti-colonial movement in the early 1900s, which peaked in the 1940s when the British proposed to set up the Malayan Union. Under this proposal, the Malay monarchs were to surrender the bulk of their powers to the British administration and everyone who wished to apply for citizenship would enjoy equal rights regardless of their ethnicity and religion. Refusing to allow equal citizenship rights to non-Malays, Malay nationalists nationwide quickly organized themselves to oppose the British proposition.

In Johor,[6] the anti-Malayan Union campaign was led by Onn Jaafar, a respected Malay aristocrat who was also District Officer in Batu Pahat, a town in northwestern Johor. But Onn did not just lead the resistance in Johor. He widened his leadership to the whole of Malaya by calling for a Malay Congress[7] to be held on the grounds of the Johor Royal Palace on 11 and 12 May 1946. This attracted representatives from Malay organizations from across the country. On the first day of the Congress, the delegates agreed to strengthen their fight against the Malayan Union by creating a political platform. That was the beginning of UMNO, and Onn was elected as its first President.

Onn's rise as a national leader and his founding of UMNO as a national party reflect how the socio-political environment in Johor was historically different from that in other states. From the late 1800s until the Japanese invasion in 1942, Johor under British rule was largely administered by a civil service staffed by locals, especially from the aristocratic class. This created a group of experienced and capable Malay administrators (Hutchinson 2015). It was within this environment of relative administrative freedom that Onn grew into a "national leader" who transcended "state boundaries, constructed political opinion and connected with Malays throughout the peninsula" (Amoroso 2014). Many other Johor Malay administrators soon followed Onn into UMNO and they too quickly rose to become national leaders through the party.[8] The environment in the state at that time allowed local Malays not just to grow into charismatic leaders, but, at variance with Malay leaders in other states, the Johor Malay leadership went on to contribute to the growth of political consciousness and political activism nationwide, beyond Johor's borders.

UMNO and the Malay nationalists continued to mobilize opposition to the Malayan Union, and the British were eventually forced to reconsider. Following negotiations with UMNO and the Malay Rulers, they agreed that the Malayan Union would be replaced with the Federation of Malaya, starting from 1 February 1948 (Stockwell 1979). Onn thus scored a major political victory, and this encouraged him to think about what UMNO should do next. He started exploring two areas: navigating Malaya towards independence from Britain and getting Malaya's various ethnic groups to work together. The independence agenda was adopted by UMNO without much hesitation, although the speed at which independence should be gained and the actual form of independence continued to be debated. Onn, however, faced a tremendous backlash from UMNO when he pushed for non-Malays to be accepted as equal members of the party. His failure to persuade UMNO to become a multiracial party led to his resignation from the presidency as well as from the party in August 1951 (Funston 1980). Soon after that, on 16 September 1951, he launched the ambitiously non-communal Independence of Malaya Party (IMP). The first splinter party from UMNO was thus born, led by none less than UMNO's founding president himself.[9]

Despite being founded and led by a towering Johorean, the IMP failed to make any mark in the state, or, for that matter, anywhere else in the country. Various authors have offered reasons to explain IMP's failure (Shaharom 1985; Ramlah 1992). One was that UMNO, contrary to Onn's expectations, regrouped rather than disintegrated following his departure (Puthucheary 1992, p. 298). Additionally, during his tenure as president of UMNO, Onn had several confrontations with the Malay Rulers. He was scathing in some of his attacks, and he was once even quoted as saying "We must find ways and means to end feudal rule" in an obvious reference to the Malay Rulers (Puthucheary 1992, p. 148). These created the impression that his IMP was also an anti-Royal party, which was anathema to the Malay psyche at that time (Puthucheary 1992, p. 300).

Onn dissolved the IMP in 1953, and formed another party—Parti Negara (National Party). This also suffered a similar fate, however. The fate of both IMP and Parti Negara showed that even a highly respected Johorean, and the founding President of UMNO to boot, could not muster enough support to shake the party's influence in Johor. This historical background, combined with the fact that UMNO is still strong in the state today, raises the question if it is realistic for a fledgling party like PPBM to capture Johor so quickly. But before we attempt to tackle that question, we need to consider PPBM's history and the internal and external dynamics affecting it in Johor today.

THE STORY OF PPBM

The story of PPBM started with discontent within UMNO towards the way its President and Malaysia's current Prime Minister Najib Razak handled the various allegations of mismanagement and corruption surrounding the state-owned enterprise 1Malaysia Development Berhad (1MDB). Some party members and leaders were upset when it was disclosed that a political donation of US$700 million had been deposited into Najib's personal bank account rather than the party's account

(*The Guardian*, 4 August 2015). Much to Najib's chagrin, several UMNO national leaders went public to voice their concerns on these issues. Najib reacted decisively by removing them from their government posts through a cabinet reshuffle on 28 July 2015 (*Utusan*, 28 July 2015). Unhappy with Najib's actions, Malaysia's longest-serving Prime Minister Mahathir Mohamad declared on 29 February 2016 that he was resigning from the party (*Astroawani*, 29 February 2016). Najib eventually sacked two other critics, Muhyiddin Yassin[10] and Mahathir's son Mukhriz, from UMNO, and suspended the membership of Shafie Apdal,[11] on 24 June 2016 (*Utusan*, 25 June 2016).

Throughout that tumultuous period, and especially after the July 2015 cabinet reshuffle, the affected UMNO leaders started talking to leaders of Malaysia's opposition parties and to civil society groups. The conversations morphed into an agreement to organize a rally called the People's Congress (Kongres Rakyat) on 27 March 2016 at the Shah Alam Convention Centre in Shah Alam, Selangor. As an invited guest to the Congress, this author witnessed how more than 2,000 people thronged the grand hall to listen to Malaysia's top opposition and civil society leaders welcoming Muhyiddin and Mahathir into their fold. Following this Congress, various closed-door discussions were hosted by the duo, during which inputs were invited from stakeholders on what their next steps should be. It was during this stage that the idea that a new political party needed to be formed started to gain strength. The seeds for the founding of PPBM were thus planted.[12]

Since the main movers for this new party were almost all from UMNO, one big issue that cropped up was whether it should be ethnocentric. A significant portion of opposition politicians and civil society activists feel that Malaysia needs to move away from ethnic-based politics and therefore the new party must be non-communal. However, an equally large number of stakeholders believed that Mahathir's and Muhyiddin's main advantage is their ability to capture the Malay votes because of their credentials as Malay nationalists. If the new party were non-communal, that advantage would be lost because they would become just like the existing non-communal opposition parties. An alternative Malay party would be more apt to complement the existing set of opposition parties. Ultimately, and upon advice from various civil society leaders, this argument won the day, resulting in the PPBM having the form it has today.[13]

But not everyone agreed with that position. Many among the younger generation who sympathized with the anti-Najib agenda insisted on maintaining their non-communal idealism despite appreciating the political realities. Even though they understood that in the immediate term they must become a Malay party to capture the Malay votes, they asserted their desire to see the party eventually becoming a party for all Malaysians.[14] As a compromise, two categories of membership were created: Normal and Associate. Normal membership gives the person full rights as a member and is only for "Pribumi", while Associate Membership is for non-"Pribumi", who are not given the right to vote or contest for party positions. This was put into the new party's constitution, in which they defined "Pribumi" as "a Malaysian citizen who is a Malay and Bumiputera, including the Orang Asli and those from Sabah and Sarawak as stated in the Federal Constitution, the respective State constitutions, and the laws of Malaysia."[15]

The party's registration was eventually approved by the RoS on 9 September 2016, with seven founding members, as listed in Table 10.1. The official launch of the party took place on 14 January 2017 at Stadium Malawati, Shah Alam, Selangor. The objectives of the party, as per its constitution, clearly make it a party that targets the Malay Muslim voters. The first four of its thirteen objectives talk about upholding Islam as the religion of the Federation, upholding the sanctity of the Malay Rulers, defending the special position of the Malays, and strengthening the Malay language (see Appendix 10.1). The importance of this position will become apparent later in this chapter, when the politics of Malay identity is discussed.

Party Organization and Financing

PPBM's constitution describes the party's structure as outlined in Table 10.2. In addition to the main body of membership, PPBM also has two wings, the women's wing, Srikandi, for their female members of all ages and the youth wing, Angkatan Bersatu Anak Muda (Armada), for male youths under thirty-five years of age.

In Johor, the current Head of the State Leadership Council is Shahruddin Salleh, state assemblymen for Jorak who simultaneously is also the party's national Secretary General. Shahruddin is known as a trusted associate of Muhyiddin. His political career started to rise when Muhyiddin appointed him Political Secretary from 1998 to 2009. Muhyiddin also helped secure Shahruddin's nomination as candidate for Jorak, a state seat under the former's parliamentary constituency of Pagoh. It is therefore not a surprise when, on 4 July 2016, Shahruddin resigned from his post as the Vice-Head of UMNO Pagoh Division in protest against Muhyiddin's

TABLE 10.1
Founding Members of PPBM

Name	Background
Mahathir Mohamad	Former President of UMNO and former Prime Minister
Muhyiddin Yassin	Former Deputy President of UMNO and former Deputy Prime Minister
Mukhriz Mahathir	Former Chairman of Kedah UMNO Liaison Committee and former Chief Minister of Kedah
Kamarul Azman Habibur Rahman	Spokesperson for Coalition of UMNO Branch Leaders
Akhramsyah Muammar Ubaidah Sanusi	Candidate for national UMNO Youth Leader in 2013 but lost
Anina Saadudin	UMNO member from Kedah who, claiming to act on behalf of UMNO, sued Najib in 2015 to recover the political donation that was banked into the latter's personal account
Syed Saddiq Syed Abdul Rahman	Former student leader, not from UMNO

TABLE 10.2
PPBM's Organizational Structure

Level	Name	Composition and Criteria
National	Supreme Leadership Council	• Chairman (elected by the general assembly) • President (elected by the general assembly) • Deputy President (elected by the general assembly) • Five Vice-Presidents including the heads of the Srikandi Women's Wing and the Armada Youth Wing (elected by the general assembly) • Secretary General (appointed by the President following consultation with the Chairman) • Treasurer (appointed by the President following consultation with the Chairman) • Information Chief (appointed by the President following consultation with the Chairman) • Maximum of 15 members elected by the general assembly • Maximum of 7 more members appointed by the President after consultation with the Chairman, • 3 representatives each from Srikandi and the Armada, appointed by their respective wings.
	Presidential Council	• President • Deputy President • Five Vice-Presidents including the heads of Srikandi and Armada • Secretary General • Treasurer • Information Chief
State	State Leadership Council	• Head (appointed by the President following consultation with the Chairman, but must be from among the Divisional Heads) • Deputy Head (appointed by the President following consultation with the Chairman, but must be from among the Divisional Heads) • Head of State Srikandi (appointed by national Srikandi Head) • Head of State Armada (appointed by national Armada Head) • Secretary (appointed by the State Head) • Treasurer (appointed by the State Head) • Information Chief (appointed by the State Head) • All other Divisional Heads in the state as members
Division (one per parliamentary constituency)	Divisional Leadership Committee	• Head (elected by the Division general assembly) • Deputy Head (elected by the Division general assembly) • Vice Head (elected by the Division general assembly) • Head of Division Srikandi (elected by the wing's general assembly) • Head of Division Armada (elected by the wing's general assembly) • Secretary (appointed by the Division Head) • Treasurer (appointed by the Division Head) • Information Chief (appointed by the Division Head) • Maximum of 10 members elected by Division general assembly • Maximum of 4 members appointed by the Division Head

Branch	Branch	• Head (elected at the Branch general assembly)
(sub-units	Committee	• Deputy Head (elected at Branch general assembly)
under the		• Vice Head (mechanism for appointment not stated)
Division)		• Head of Branch Srikandi (elected by the wing's general assembly)
		• Head of Branch Armada (elected by the wing's general assembly)
		• Secretary (appointed by Branch Head)
		• Treasurer (appointed by Branch Head)
		• Information Chief (appointed by Branch Head)
		• Maximum of 8 members elected by the Branch general assembly
		• Maximum of 3 members appointed by the Branch Head

Source: PPBM Constitution (2017).

sacking from the party. When interviewed for this study, Shahruddin admitted that he left UMNO with a heavy heart, but he felt compelled to do so after seeing how Muhyiddin was treated and especially when he discovered further details of Najib Razak's alleged corruption.[16]

With Shahruddin spending most of his time in Kuala Lumpur fulfilling his duties as national Secretary General, the day-to-day operations of PPBM in Johor is left to two former veteran UMNO politicians. The first is Deputy Head Nasir Hashim, a businessman who was formerly Deputy Head of Johor's Gelang Patah UMNO Division. The second is Osman Sapian, Secretary of Johor PPBM. Osman was a three-term UMNO state legislative assembly member for Kempas, before retiring from public life in GE-13 to focus on his business. The two are tasked with building PPBM's state machinery and ensuring it is well-lubricated, and supported by other State Leadership Council members.[17] Thus far, PPBM has Divisions in all twenty-six parliamentary constituencies across Johor, and all are holding regular activities.

In Johor, the party is mainly funded by contributions from members. The party's membership fee is low, at just RM2.00 per annum or RM100.00 for life membership. This forces the party to depend on additional contributions from its members and leaders to pay for their activities and the day-to-day operations of the party. When the party wanted to open its state headquarters in early 2017, its state leaders had to pay for the rental and renovation of the premise themselves. Daily operating costs for the state headquarters is the responsibility of Osman Sapian, the Secretary of Johor PPBM, and he relies on his own money as well as money that he raises from his network for the purpose.[18] At divisions and branches, the leaders and activists in the respective levels too must make regular contributions in order to cover the costs of their activities, complemented by public donation drives.

Key Dynamics Experienced by Johor PPBM

Winning the Hearts of Johor's Younger Voters

PPBM has been successful in attracting younger members, so much so that the majority of the party members are under thirty-five years of age. This is true both at the national level and in Johor. The current estimate is that nationally, PPBM has almost 200,000 members, and 55 per cent of these are under thirty-five years old.[19] In Johor, PPBM has around 7,000 approved members while approximately 8,000 more are still being processed. More than 50 per cent of that number are under thirty-five years old. In fact, quite a few of the party's state and divisional leading activists are from the under-35 age group, with many still in tertiary education.[20]

Youth activism in PPBM started even before the party was officially launched. Its origin can be traced back to March 2016, when a group of twenty-five student and youth leaders signed a statement calling for Prime Minister Najib to resign. The group called themselves "Challenger" and their spokesperson was twenty-three-year old Johorean Syed Saddiq Syed Abdul Rahman. This group came out of the blue and many of the names were not known in the national arena prior to the statement. But Challenger successfully organized themselves into a cohesive group and travelled the country to meet other students and youth leaders, recruiting many more into their cause. Syed Saddiq then became one of the seven founding members of PPBM. Twelve more members of Challenger, from the original twenty-five, soon followed him into the party, and they continue to play important roles to bring more of their peer group into PPBM. One of them, Mohamad Fahim Mohamad Farid, was appointed Head of Armada PPBM in Gelang Patah Division, and is considered one of the more active leaders of the party in Johor and nationally.

To understand why PPBM has been attractive to the young in the state, this author interviewed several leaders and members of Armada PPBM.[21] Three themes emerged as the most cited reasons. Top of the list is their admiration of Mahathir. The maximum age to be a member of Armada is thirty-five. Thus, the oldest of them were born in 1982, a year after Mahathir became Prime Minister. For the next twenty-two years, they lived under Mahathir's administration and they grew up seeing and enjoying the high level of physical and economic development that Mahathir brought to the country. But they were also too young to understand the criticisms that were levelled at Mahathir throughout this time in office. Hence for many of them, Mahathir is a hero.

Second is their anger against the current administration, related to the rising cost of living. They experience difficulties in finding well-paying employment, let alone buying a house, or even a car which they feel is necessary in a state like Johor where the coverage and frequency of public transportation is unsatisfactory. Those in higher education as well as fresh graduates have to deal with relatively high student debts. But while they face these challenges, they regularly read from online platforms about the extravagant lifestyle of Najib's family and the many corruption allegations surrounding other UMNO leaders. This leads them to search for a platform through which they feel they can stop the problems. Being a new party, PPBM enables them to champion this cause through a platform that has minimal red tape since the party does not yet have an extensive bureaucracy. In PPBM, the youngsters quickly found a political party that is open to their ideas and participation.

The third factor is the role played by the current head of Armada PPBM, Syed Saddiq. This law graduate from the International Islamic University Malaysia built a name as a champion debater both in Malaysia and internationally while still at university. He became well known when he became the spokesperson for Challenger and when he acted as the emcee for the People's Congress in March 2016. While building up support for Challenger, he travelled from one university campus to another, garnering support for the cause, and today he continues to do the same for PPBM's Armada in Johor as well as nationally. In October 2017, he even announced that he had turned down a full scholarship offer from the University of Oxford, United Kingdom, in order to continue PPBM's political struggle (*Malaysiakini*, 2 October 2017). This endeared him to many youths and young professionals, and attracted even more young people into the party.

Female Voters a Major Hurdle

In GE-13, half of the voters in Johor were female (*Malaysiakini*, 27 April 2013), making them an important component of the electorate. In her commentary on female voting patterns in Malaysia, political scientist Bridget Welsh (*Malaysiakini*, 27 April 2013) argued that female voters are more likely to vote for BN for four reasons. First, UMNO's women wing, the Wanita UMNO, has been a formidable force in campaigning for the party for decades and they are rooted in the social structures of many local communities. Second, women have less access to alternative sources of information, relying mainly on mainstream media that is usually pro-BN. Third, women, especially those from the lower classes, are more responsive to monetary incentives and they feel more obliged to repay the assistance given by the BN government. And fourth, women are more responsive to the fear tactics adopted by the BN, as they usually worry about how political change may impact their families. Another analyst, Maszlee Malik,[22] added that winning over female votes is crucial for PPBM if they want to become a credible threat to UMNO in Johor. If PPBM can swing women voters their way, especially in seats where BN won only marginally, Maszlee believes that the party will certainly have a good chance of winning the state.[23]

But although PPBM has been relatively successful in attracting the young, this experience is not replicated when it comes to female voters. PPBM leaders interviewed in this study openly acknowledge this shortcoming. They are well aware of the effectiveness of Wanita UMNO, especially in rural areas of the state. Hence, PPBM Srikandi is working hard to penetrate Johor villages. Its members also organize ad hoc membership registration and information booths in strategic locations across the state, to enable them to engage with female members of the public directly. The main issue they raise with female voters is the increasing cost of living in the state. The assumption is that women are more sensitive to the rising cost of living, especially when it affects the price of household goods because they are the ones who make the daily purchases for their families.[24]

Yet the response to Srikandi's campaign has been relatively slow and they are not yet a real challenger to Wanita UMNO. The biggest hurdle is in rural areas and villages, especially the FELDA areas, where the Wanita UMNO infrastructure is deeply entrenched and they have regular, almost weekly activities. One example are the Quran recitation meetings organized in small groups by Wanita UMNO activists in villages across the state, rotating from house to house, usually once a week. The same group also plays active roles whenever there are deaths in the village, or at wedding receptions and other community functions. Such small group activities have been going on for decades under Wanita UMNO, creating a sense of belonging and loyalty among the members. They are also a visible although indirect way to campaign for UMNO to other women in the village. More importantly, if a member were to jump to PPBM, they might be ostracized from the group and this is a big deterrent for many.[25] Johor's Srikandi has not been able to penetrate this network of informal women groupings.

In the more urban areas of the state, there are some signs that Srikandi's efforts are paying off, albeit only very slowly, especially among those who are more educated. For example, in the Tebrau parliamentary constituency, which is an urban area just next to the capital city of Johor Bahru, the majority of Srikandi members are new to party politics, with PPBM being the first party that they have joined. They are relatively young, many below forty years old, and are still building their careers. For many of them, while the cost of living remains the top complaint that drives them to join PPBM, they are also unhappy with the state of governance and corruption in the country. They have better access to non-mainstream media and they are better informed about the various allegations of misconduct especially those surrounding 1MDB and FELDA. While they do keep an eye on issues directly affecting them in their local environment, they are also influenced by national issues. In the Tebrau Division alone, out of the 1,500 or so members and activists that they have today, around 400 are in Srikandi, and many of them fit this description.[26]

In fact, if one were to use attendance at opposition events in Johor as a yardstick, it is quite visible that Srikandi still has a long way to go. This author observed several public events[27] across the state between April and August 2017, and it was rather obvious that most attendees, by far, were male. Female attendees were small in number, and even when they were seen in the audience, the vast majority were non-Malays, implying that they are not from PPBM. Given the limited time before GE-14, this situation does raise the question if PPBM will be able to make sufficiently large gains among Malay female voters. Nevertheless, it should be noted that Malay women generally do not attend political talks, or *ceramah*, anyway. These events tend to take place in the evenings and they often go on well after midnight. This is a deterrent especially if their husbands are attending the event. This is also why the Wanita UMNO approach as described above, where they run daytime small group activities in the neighbourhood itself, have been more effective.

The ISEAS – Yusof Ishak Institute commissioned the 2017 Johor Opinion Survey,[28] and its findings confirms that PPBM is still quite far behind in terms of winning female voters (Figure 10.3). Only 17 per cent said that they are in favour of the party, while 44 per cent rejected them outright. The offside, however, is that 39 per cent of female voters could potentially still be persuaded, since they refused to answer the question, or they stated that they are neutral or unsure.

FIGURE 10.3
Favourability towards PPBM among Female Voters

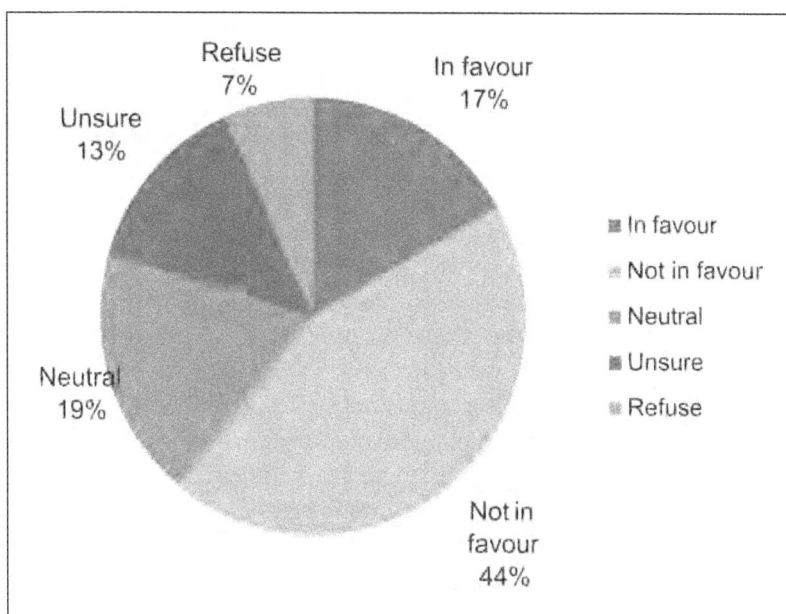

Source: Johor Opinion Survey commissioned by ISEAS – Yusof Ishak Institute, 2017.

The Politics of Malay Identity[29]

Race and religion are two issues that are pervasive in Malaysian politics. Among the ethnic Malays, the perceived threat of losing their political influence is often posed by those with vested interests as a threat to the survival of the entire ethnic group. UMNO[30] has always played up this issue, maintaining and exploiting ethno-religious fear while presenting themselves as the only party that can guarantee Malay survival. For example, in the 2016 UMNO General Assembly, Prime Minister Najib Razak in his Presidential Address claimed that Malaysians are presented with only two options, a government that is led by Malays through UMNO on the one hand, or non-Malays through DAP on the other. He also said that if the country were to fall into DAP's hands in GE-14,

> surely the rights and special position (of the Malays) championed by UMNO … will become extinct and will disappear … This is why if the Malays … can understand the implicit meaning of my speech, especially with regards to the horrific fate that will fall onto them, I am confident the Malays … will be fearful and concerned, and they will hold on as strongly as they can to UMNO as the only party that can defend their children and grandchildren … (*Najibrazak.com*, 1 December 2016)

This fear, and fear-mongering, are well recognized by PPBM founders. Hence, nationally, PPBM is firmly positioning themselves as a Malay party and this is formalized in their party constitution. This strategy is embraced by its Johor state leaders as they too recognize the importance of winning the hearts of Malay voters. Especially in rural Johor, the fear of losing Malay political power is a strong influence on voting intentions. Almost always, the fear directly contributes to voting intentions in favour of BN and UMNO, as reflected in the maps shown in Figures 10.1 and 10.2, where the more rural and largely Malay constituencies are dominated by the BN coalition.

The analogy most often cited by the villagers interviewed is that the Malays in Johor may become like the Malays in Singapore if the DAP wins more seats because the party is a remnant of Singapore's People's Action Party (PAP). They perceive the Malays in Singapore as being discriminated against by the Chinese-led PAP government. No evidence was supplied to back up this claim, and when pressed for specifics, many simply stated that they heard this from political leaders, or this was their understanding from media coverage and media commentaries. When pressed further, none of them could cite which media report they were referring to or which politician made those claims. However, there are three media platforms mentioned by everyone met by this author, the most common being the UMNO-linked television channel TV3, followed by two Malay newspapers *Utusan Malaysia* and *Berita Harian*. At the same time, all the politicians they quoted are either from UMNO, or are from UMNO but now have left for PPBM. Interestingly, even though many of them cited the example of Singapore Malays, none of the villagers interviewed have visited the country or know any Malays from Singapore.

All the interviewees associate the Chinese-majority DAP with the risk of further erosion of Malay special privileges, and they insist that they, as Malays, will only vote for a political party that will guarantee these privileges. Interestingly, in all the interviews, the name DAP and the phrase *"orang Cina"* (ethnic Chinese) were used interchangeably by the villagers. It was as if for them, the rise of the DAP is equated to rising ethnic Chinese political power, and by extension the erosion of Malay political power. When these villagers read media coverage or hear speeches from politicians about the DAP, they almost instinctively treat it as a code word for ethnic Chinese. Johor being a state that borders Singapore serves to heighten that fear because the danger feels more immediate to them. Thus, voting for any party that helps DAP get into government is the equivalent of jeopardizing Malay special position. The truthfulness of this assumption will be surely challenged by many. But, when it comes to political sentiment, at least among the interviewed villagers, their fear of the DAP and the ethnic Chinese is palpable, and they do not hide the fact that this fear influences how they vote.

The fear plays directly into the way PPBM is perceived by Malay voters in Johor because of DAP's membership in the Pakatan Harapan (Harapan) opposition coalition, which includes PPBM, Parti Amanah Negara (Amanah) and Parti Keadilan Rakyat (PKR). DAP holds thirteen state seats in Johor, making them the biggest party in the coalition. While this may be a strength to the DAP, it is ironically a risk to the Harapan coalition, especially in the eyes of rural Malay voters. The problem is particularly acute for PPBM because rural Malay voters are their core target. This sentiment among the Malays is supported by findings from the Johor Opinion Survey commissioned by the ISEAS – Yusof Ishak Institute. As shown in Figure 10.4, 85 per cent of Johor Malays says that they are not in favour of the DAP. This contributes significantly to the low acceptance (14 per cent, see Figure 10.5) of Harapan among Johor Malays, indicating a huge challenge for PPBM.

DAP recognizes this challenge, and argues that, at most, they are likely to contest and win in only fourteen to fifteen seats in GE-14, making it impossible for them to become a dominant party if Harapan wins the state.[31] That notwithstanding, the current strength of DAP in the state still generates fear among rural Malay voters there. They see a vote for PPBM as a vote for DAP, since both are in the same coalition. UMNO too continues to exploit this fear by highlighting the PPBM-DAP relationship (*Astroawani*, 18 March 2017).

FIGURE 10.4
Favourability towards DAP among Malays

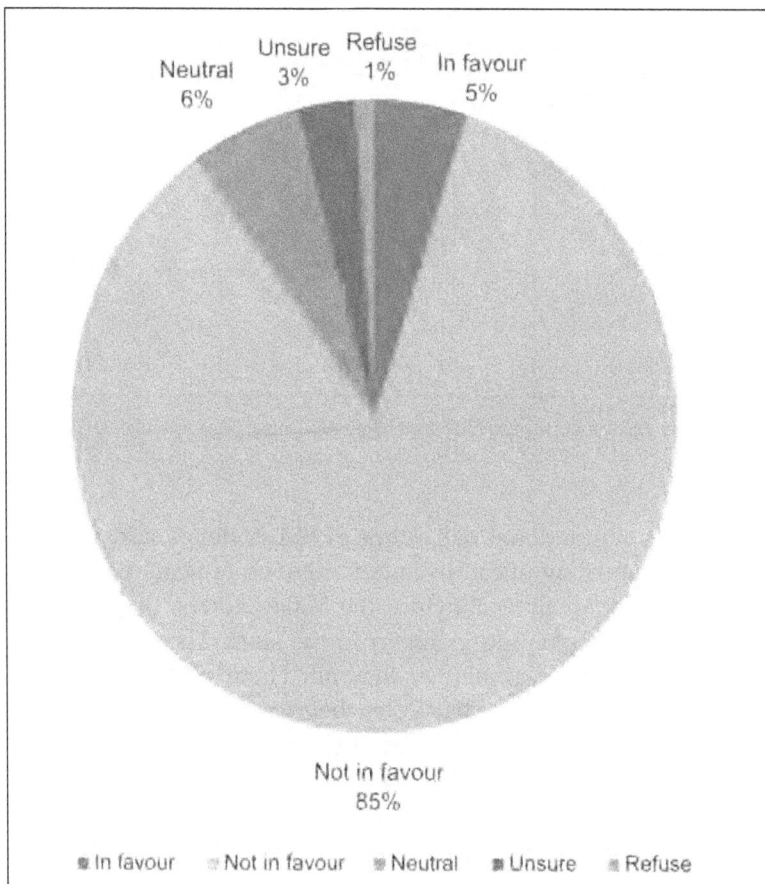

Source: Johor Opinion Survey commissioned by ISEAS – Yusof Ishak Institute, 2017.

FIGURE 10.5
Favourability towards Pakatan Harapan among Malays

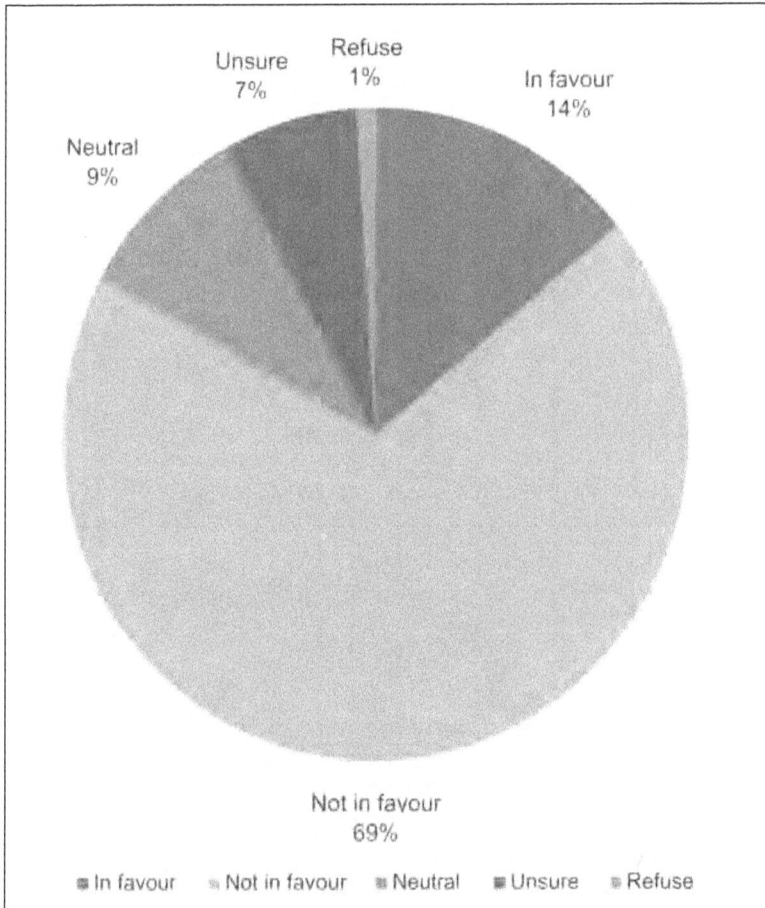

Source: Johor Opinion Survey commissioned by ISEAS – Yusof Ishak Institute, 2017.

To manage this reputational risk, Johor PPBM leaders are insisting that their party must be given a significantly larger number of seats in Johor by other Harapan partners. For them to convince the Malay voters, they must be visibly seen as leading and dominating Harapan in the state. They believe that if they are not put in the driving seat, neither they nor Harapan will be able to sway a sufficiently large proportion of Malay votes their way. Negotiations on this matter are still ongoing and signs indicate that DAP, PKR and Amanah are gradually accepting PPBM's point of view. The biggest indicator so far is that on 22 August 2017, Muhyiddin was named as Chairman of Johor Harapan, putting him as the leader of the state opposition coalition (*Sinar Harian*, 26 August 2019). But, as of the date of writing this chapter, PPBM's desire for a significantly larger number of seats remains unresolved.

The Dynamics between Mahathir and Muhyiddin

As shown in Table 10.2, PPBM's Supreme Leadership Council is the highest executive body, with Mahathir as Chairman. Next is the Presidential Council, chaired by Muhyiddin. When this structure was first announced, almost immediately tongues started to wag about how there was a tussle between "Mahathir's men" and "Muhyiddin's men". This provided early ammunition for critics eager to argue that a ship with two captains will never sail far. This structure, however, was designed to ensure proper checks and balances within the party, especially when the founding members knew that the presence of the two towering figures could become a challenge if not managed properly. To accommodate both leaders, the drafters of PPBM's constitution decided to adopt a structure similar to any well-governed organization, where the Chairman and the CEO are two different people, and the Board and the Management are two different teams as well.[32]

While those within the party feel that this structure exemplifies PPBM's commitment to good governance, observers continue to look into the politics behind such an arrangement. Some criticisms go deeper. Several commentators have said that the dynamics between the two figures have led to Muhyiddin having to stand behind Mahathir.[33] There is quiet rumbling in the background that Muhyiddin is not assertive or popular enough compared to Mahathir, even in Johor, where Mahathir is perceived as generating more excitement whenever he visits the state.[34] When asked about this situation,[35] Muhyiddin argues that critics either misunderstand the division of responsibilities in the party, or they are trying to score political points against him. To Muhyiddin, Mahathir has always been the more aggressive person, even from the time he first entered politics decades ago. Therefore, it is illogical for anyone to compare Mahathir to any other politician, himself included.

According to Muhyiddin, the correct way to assess his performance is by looking at how he fulfils the role of party President. In less than one year he has been able to create a fully staffed and well-equipped national head office for the party. He has also identified and appointed committed individuals into various posts at the national level. And more importantly, he has set up divisions in more than 145 parliamentary constituencies across the country, including the twenty-six in Johor. He has also successfully identified and appointed the right people into various party posts, both at national and state levels. He further argues that Mahathir's assault needs to be supported by a strong and credible infrastructure, which now exists as a result of the machinery that he has built. He refuses to be drawn into the discussion about who is more powerful, believing instead that both he and Mahathir have important roles to play. He argues that they are effective now as a team, complementing each other in turning the new party into a credible challenger to the ruling regime, including in Johor.

At this point it is useful to bring data from another set of survey conducted by independent research house EMIR Research and several local Malaysian academics.[36] Using random stratified sampling, 2,440 respondents were interviewed from across peninsular Malaysia, controlled by quota for ethnicity, age and gender. One of the questions was who would they favour to lead the country, implying the favourability or popularity of a particular leader in the eyes of the respondents. Nationally, Mahathir came top at 42.7 per cent, while Muhyiddin was second with 34.5 per cent. However, when the findings are analysed by state, as shown in Figure 10.6, the level of popularity is not uniform as it varies from one state to another, with Muhyiddin leading in Johor with 41.1 per cent against Mahathir's 29.5 per cent. This shows that while Mahathir might be more popular at the national level but in Johor itself, despite the criticisms thrown against him, Muhyiddin's popularity is higher.

FIGURE 10.6
Popularity Ranking by State in Peninsular Malaysia

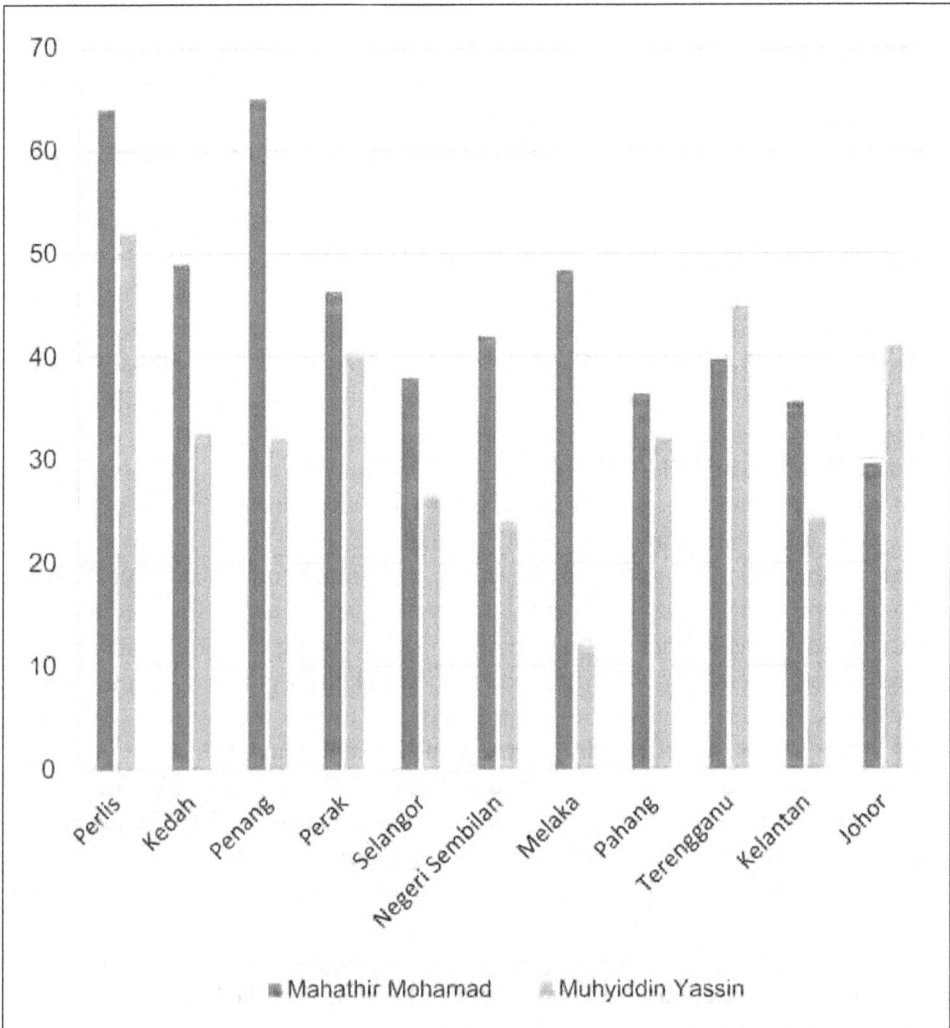

Source: Author's compilation of data from EMIR Research, Malaysia

Muhyiddin's popularity in the state may have contributed to him becoming Chairman of Johor Harapan. But despite that, it is intriguing that the question has been raised whether Muhyiddin should defend his Pagoh parliamentary seat or move to a safer one. All the leaders of other Harapan component parties interviewed for this study raise this issue because they believe UMNO will expend all necessary resources to unseat Muhyiddin from a constituency that is considered his personal base in order to make a statement to the country at large.[37] In fact, this is an issue that has been asked since even before PPBM was officially registered as a political party (*Malaysiakini*, 15 August 2016).

Looking at the electoral numbers, in GE-13, Muhyiddin won Pagoh with a handsome majority of 12,842. But Harapan leaders still consider this risky if assaulted by UMNO in the expected fashion. The seat considered safer for Muhyiddin is Muar, where the incumbent is UMNO's Razali Ibrahim, whose majority in GE-13 was slim at 1,646. The suggestion is that Muhyiddin will be able to win all the non-UMNO votes in Muar, while stealing sufficient votes from UMNO to help him win, albeit potentially with a smaller majority than what he obtained in Pagoh in GE-13. When interviewed for this study, Muhyiddin denied that he is considering moving to Muar[38] but in a later press interview (*Berita Harian*, 22 August 2017) his answer was less definitive, implying that his thinking may still be evolving.

HOW REALISTIC ARE PPBM'S AMBITIONS?

Scramble for Mixed Seats

UMNO won thirty-two Johor state seats[39] in GE-13. These seats are also the ones targeted by PPBM for GE-14 and PPBM claims to be ready to contest in all of them.[40] This situation may sound like a straightforward scenario because, after all, PPBM was created with the purpose of taking away the Malay votes from UMNO and hence, by simple logic, PPBM should be able to stake a claim on all the thirty-two UMNO seats. Unfortunately for PPBM, there are overlapping claims from their two coalition partners, PKR and Amanah. Both are eyeing mixed seats that have between roughly 30 to 45 per cent Chinese voters. There are twenty-four seats (Table 10.3) that fit into this category, and in GE-13, seventeen of these seats were contested by PAS, five by PKR and two by DAP. For GE-14, there are many overlapping claims. Amanah wants to take over all the PAS seats (Wan Saiful 2017) while DAP and PKR want to keep theirs. Additionally, PKR feels that they have a better chance to win more seats this time round, and they would like to put candidates in twenty seats in total, mostly in the mixed areas as well.[41]

The overlapping claims make seat negotiations complicated, and include disagreements between the other Harapan parties. Parallel to that, PKR and Amanah believe that PPBM should focus solely on the areas with larger Malay populations, and especially on the FELDA areas. PKR and Amanah want the mixed areas to be left to them, while DAP wants to focus on areas with a large Chinese population. PPBM, on the other hand, feels that they are being dealt a short hand that is not

TABLE 10.3

Mixed State Seats in Johor, Arranged by Percentage of Chinese Voters

State Code	State Name	Total Voters	Malay (%)	Chinese (%)	Indian (%)	Others (%)	BN Candidate	PR Candidate	Winner in GE-13	Victory Majority
N44	Tanjong Puteri	51,442	61.3	31.6	5.3	1.7	UMNO	PKR	UMNO	9,097
N26	Machap	22,221	62.4	31.7	5.0	0.9	UMNO	PAS	UMNO	3,902
N01	Buloh Kasap	18,779	55.0	32.2	11.6	1.2	UMNO	PAS	UMNO	3,370
N11	Serom	24,540	65.5	32.8	0.9	0.8	UMNO	PAS	UMNO	2,264
N17	Semerah	31,046	63.2	33.6	0.6	2.6	UMNO	PKR	UMNO	2,649
N50	Bukit Permai	21,619	52.4	33.9	11.9	1.7	UMNO	PAS	UMNO	3,369
N54	Pulai Sebatang	28,170	61.8	34.5	1.4	2.2	MCA	PAS	MCA	3,412
N08	Jorak	25,364	59.0	34.8	5.4	0.8	UMNO	PAS	UMNO	3,726
N27	Layang-Layang	17,922	49.0	34.9	14.7	1.5	UMNO	PKR	UMNO	2,518
N47	Kempas	39,273	54.2	35.2	8.9	1.7	UMNO	PAS	UMNO	3,947
N24	Senggarang	24,048	60.5	37.4	0.5	1.6	UMNO	PAS	UMNO	1,855
N05	Tenang	16,940	49.4	37.6	11.3	1.7	UMNO	PAS	UMNO	1,586
N49	Nusa Jaya	50,183	47.0	38.4	12.7	2.0	UMNO	PAS	UMNO	2,201
N14	Bukit Naning	15,502	58.7	38.4	1.0	1.8	UMNO	PKR	UMNO	1,455
N04	Kemelah	20,449	54.6	38.6	5.7	1.1	UMNO	PKR	UMNO	2,260
N03	Pemanis	22,617	56.2	39.3	3.4	1.0	GERAKAN	PAS	GERAKAN	1,329
N09	Gambir	21,382	54.6	39.7	3.8	1.8	MIC	PAS	MIC	310
N29	Mahkota	44,352	50.5	40.6	5.9	3.0	UMNO	PAS	UMNO	1,108
N15	Maharani	27,090	54.7	42.0	2.5	0.8	UMNO	PAS	PAS	3,136
N21	Parit Yaani	24,609	54.0	43.1	1.1	1.9	MCA	PAS	PAS	1,188
N30	Paloh	18,222	37.3	43.6	17.1	2.0	MCA	DAP	MCA	103
N46	Pengkalan Rinting	61,217	42.5	44.7	10.6	2.1	MCA	DAP	DAP	1,970
N13	Sungai Abong	28,262	51.0	45.2	3.0	0.8	UMNO	PAS	PAS	3,813
N41	Puteri Wangsa	43,824	39.6	47.2	11.7	1.4	MIC	PAS	PAS	3,469

Source: General elections data obtained from Dr Ong Kian Ming, member of parliament for Serdang.

commensurate with the expectation and responsibility placed on them to win Malay voters. They argue that the mixed seats can only be won by Harapan if Malay voters in those areas are persuaded to switch sides. This will only happen by virtue of PPBM presence and leadership, not through the strengths of the other three parties. They added that even to attract Malays to Harapan events, the presence of PPBM leaders like Mahathir, Muhyiddin or Mukhriz are needed because leaders from the other Harapan parties are not sufficiently attractive to the Malays yet. Thus, if PPBM is the reason for Harapan to win in mixed seats, their vital contribution must be reciprocated in the form of seats in mixed areas as well. At the same time, they also know that the high-Malay areas are not going to be an easy fight. They will be fighting against the resource-rich UMNO that has been dominant in those areas for sixty years. They are willing to take on the heavy responsibility of challenging UMNO in the most challenging areas, but in return they want to be rewarded with seats with higher probability of victory, namely, the mixed areas.[42]

PPBM's desire to contest at least in some of the mixed seats becomes more apparent when its chances for parliamentary seats are examined. Winning a large number of parliamentary seats in Johor is a crucial part of its plan to become the main party in office (i.e., the successor to UMNO's role in BN) if Harapan should form the next federal government. Hence their opening bid in the seat negotiations is twenty to twenty-two parliamentary seats out of the twenty-six in the state.[43] But this requires PPBM to contest in both high-Malay as well as mixed parliamentary areas. As shown in Figure 10.2, the bulk of Johor parliamentary areas are mixed. In GE-13, the majority that UMNO obtained in parliamentary areas with more than 70 per cent Malay voters was very large, upwards of 11,000 votes. UMNO also dominates the middle section where Malays form 45 to 70 per cent of the voters, holding ten out of the fifteen parliamentary seats in this category, albeit with a much smaller majority. In six of those seats, they only had a majority of less than 3,500 votes. If PPBM were to contest only in high-Malay areas while PKR and Amanah take the mixed areas, then its struggle to break UMNO's dominance would be a tough one compared to what its Harapan partners will face. This means that the other Harapan parties will benefit from the wave, or the Malay Tsunami, that may be generated by PPBM's involvement. But PPBM itself may end up with an unfairly low number of seats.

Therefore, PPBM wants the added value that they bring to be acknowledged and reciprocated with a commensurate number of seats with a high probability for victory. Apart from its opening bids for thirty-two state and twenty to twenty-two parliamentary seats, PPBM also wants its allies to accept its leadership in Johor Harapan. Judging from the interviews with the leaders with all Harapan parties in the state, it appears that they are open to these demands and are willing to negotiate, both on seat allocation and leadership position. On the former, even though all the parties have laid down their cards on the table, they are unanimous in asserting that the final decision must be made by their national leaders after taking into consideration the picture for Malaysia as a whole. Where the state leadership role is concerned, all the other Harapan partners have already agreed to Muhyiddin being

Chairman of Johor Harapan. This is a major shift from their previous convention of having all the respective state party leaders as joint chairmen of the coalition,[44] indicating that the other parties are indeed appreciative of PPBM's importance and the value of Muhyiddin's leadership.

Johor and PPBM's Long-Term Survival

PPBM is not the first splinter party from UMNO. Far from it. Earlier in this chapter, the experience of the IMP, the party founded and led by UMNO's founding President Onn Jaafar, has been discussed. UMNO experienced several more break-ups after the IMP, and essentially, there are two patterns to the splinter parties. First, just like the IMP, are the parties that were formed directly by UMNO leaders and their followers immediately after they had left the mother party. Examples include the National Convention Party[45] that was formed in 1963 and the Spirit of 46 Malay Party,[46] formed in 1989. Second are the parties formed as a result of the coming together of multiple additional forces in support of the departing UMNO leaders. This includes PAS[47] which was formed in 1951 by Islamists from inside and outside of UMNO, and PKR[48] in 1999 by Anwar Ibrahim following his sacking from the party, after he successfully mobilized various civil society groups as well as other opposition parties to support his agenda.

None of the splinter parties have ever had any real traction in Johor. Even when they were able to make a mark nationally or in other states, Johor remained an UMNO stronghold. Nevertheless, it is interesting to note that the splinter parties that followed the second model have proven more successful in building their own support base, albeit in states other than Johor.[49] On the other hand, none of the parties from the first model created any real impact or caused damage to UMNO. Just like the IMP, all of them suffered electoral failures and were eventually dissolved. This raises the question about the sustainability of PPBM—former UMNO leaders created it immediately after their exit from the mother party, and its current leadership is almost completely dominated by former UMNO members. Its genesis has thus much in common with the IMP-like model, and this has historically failed to survive.

Having said that, there is also the argument that PPBM was formed on the back of internal anger over alleged massive corrupt practices within UMNO. Thus, PPBM's establishment took place at a time when UMNO, so the suggestion goes, had lost its legitimacy as the champion of the Malay agenda because the leaders are now only pursuing their personal agenda. This arguably makes PPBM different from the IMP.[50] Regardless of that view, PPBM leaders still acknowledge the sustainability risk they face, and this is why they are determined to win at least one state, if not the federal government, with Johor being high on their target list. The intention is for Johor to become the base from which the party can survive and expand in the long run, just like PKR in Selangor, PAS in Kelantan and DAP in Penang.[51] Johor therefore is not just another state. It is the state that may decide if PPBM will exist in the long run, and that is the party is working so diligently there.

PPBM and the Malay Vote

The establishment of PPBM raised the hopes of Malaysian opposition supporters. Although some concerns have been expressed,[52] but overall the reaction has been positive. The expectations heightened when PPBM officially joined the Harapan coalition on 20 March 2017. The presence of PPBM in Johor as part of Harapan is particularly important for the opposition parties there because PPBM is expected to attract more Malay votes for the coalition as a block. In GE-13, the opposition coalition benefited tremendously from what was dubbed as the Chinese tsunami, wherein the majority of ethnic Chinese voted for them. But Malay votes did not swing in their favour and this contributed to UMNO staying in power. This time round, Harapan has high hopes that PPBM, being a Malay party, will bring the Malay votes, creating a Malay tsunami to complement the Chinese support that they already have.[53]

Of particular interest to Harapan is PPBM's potential influence in constituencies that have FELDA settlements. FELDA areas are seen as an UMNO bastion so much so that a Johor UMNO Member of Parliament, Ahmad Maslan, once estimated that as much as 90 per cent of FELDA settlers support his party (Zubaidah 2010). There are fifteen Johor state seats[54] that have at least one FELDA settlement, and in GE-13, UMNO won ten of them. For parliament, there are eleven FELDA seats[55] in the state and UMNO won ten of them. Keeping that in mind, it is obvious that only PPBM has a reasonable chance in FELDA areas since they are the only party in Harapan that can present themselves as a Malay substitute to UMNO.

In her study of the voting patterns of FELDA settlers, Maznah Mohamad posited that:

> the economic basis of Malay support for UMNO is patronage, while its socio-cultural corollary is usually attributed to Malay voters' fear of a decline in Malay political supremacy … The dependency–patronage relations between UMNO and FELDA voters played the biggest role in sustaining the Malay vote bank (Maznah Mohamad 2015).

Maznah's argument echoes the discussion earlier in this chapter on how identity politics shape the voting preferences of rural Malays, especially their attitude towards the DAP and the Harapan coalition. This also means the hurdle is even higher for PPBM in FELDA areas because the fear of losing Malay political power is more prevalent there. The problem for PPBM is that these are exactly the areas where their Harapan partners and their own members expect to deliver. In other words, they are to win where UMNO is strongest and where Harapan is weakest. This is a very big responsibility indeed for a fledgling party to shoulder.[56]

PPBM seems willing to take up the challenge though. They appreciate that for Harapan, winning the Malay and FELDA votes is crucial, and that in the immediate term, only they have the potential to do it. As can be seen in Figure 10.1 in the earlier part of this chapter, there are fourteen state constituencies that have more than 70 per cent Malay voters.[57] BN holds all the seats in this category, and UMNO has twelve of them. The other two seats are held by the Malaysian Indian Congress (MIC), but in both areas the percentage of Indian voters is tiny, at less than 3 per cent. Thus, it is safe to assume that the MIC won these areas not because of its own strength, but simply because UMNO supporters voted for it. These two are essentially still UMNO areas. All these are the seats that PPBM would like to claim as theirs to contest.

In order to win the heart of the Malay voters, PPBM is devising manifesto pledges that prioritize socio-economic well-being. They envision policy offers that will alleviate the economic hardships faced by the bottom 40 per cent, plus measures that can help enhance the livelihoods of the middle 40 per cent as well. The areas they are studying include enabling more home ownership, increasing the number of scholarships for education, and providing greater financial and institutional support for Islamic affairs.

As mentioned earlier, there are major projects being carried out involving investments from China. There are concerns over the impact of these on land ownership and displacement of people in traditional villages.[58] However, while this study is being done, the Johor PPBM leaders are still formulating their election promises and not many details on this front were available.

Identity Politics Makes It Challenging

So how well has PPBM fared in winning over its target group? Much depends on how Harapan is presented, and how the Malays respond to that presentation. The most pertinent issue is how Malay voters view the DAP, and much will therefore depend on PPBM's ability to convince Malay voters that the DAP is not a threat.

Telephone polling data show that the trend is not in PPBM's favour. In the Johor Opinion Survey 2017 commissioned by the ISEAS – Yusof Ishak Institute, when Malay voters were asked to state their level of favourability towards political parties, PPBM's rating was poor. As seen in Figure 10.7, 69 per cent said that they were outright not in favour of PPBM. This was second only to the DAP who saw 85 per cent of the Malay sample not favouring them. The numbers were worse when the sample was asked who they would vote for if elections were held today (Figure 10.8). Across all ethnic groups in the state, while only 34 per cent said that they would vote for BN, the number for PPBM was abysmal at just 2 per cent. Worse, among the Malays, only 2.2 per cent and 2.7 per cent said they would vote for Harapan and PPBM respectively, while BN enjoys support from 48.4 per cent of the Malays.

The Malays' distrust of the DAP, coupled with their insecurity when it comes to the future position of their ethnic group and their religion, plays a significant role in shaping Malay political attitude. Figure 10.9 shows that ethno-religious identity is a major influence among the Malays. They even think the DAP is controlling the Harapan coalition. Even though it is premature without a deeper study to say that the DAP is the Achilles Heel for PPBM and Harapan in the state, it can be argued that the Harapan coalition is not necessarily the most beneficial partnership for PPBM in terms of winning political mileage among their target Malay population.

FIGURE 10.7
Favourability of Johor Malay Voters towards Political Parties in the State

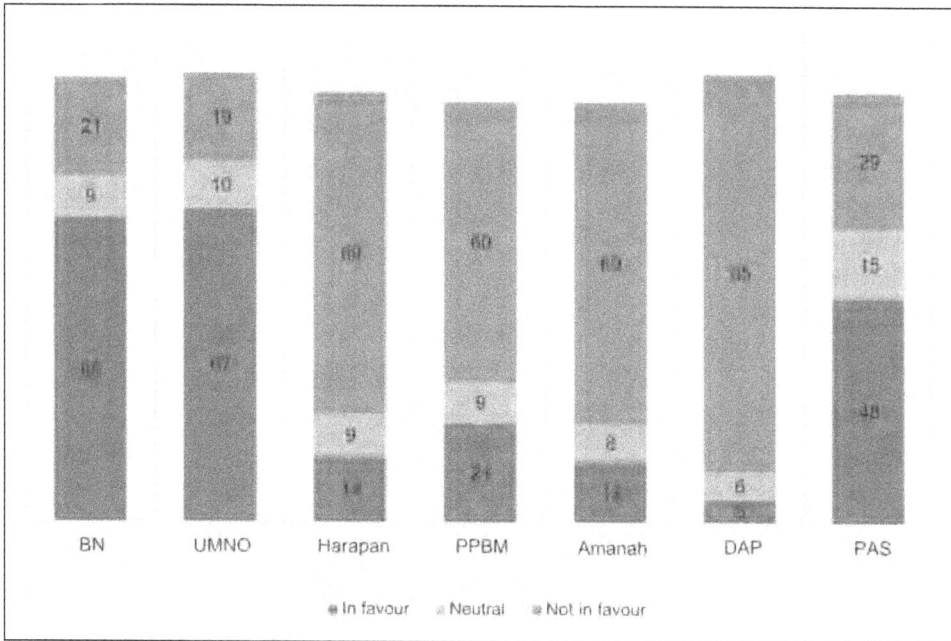

Source: Author's compilation of data from Johor Opinion Survey commissioned by ISEAS –Yusof Ishak Institute, 2017.

FIGURE 10.8
How Would People Vote if Elections Were Called Today?

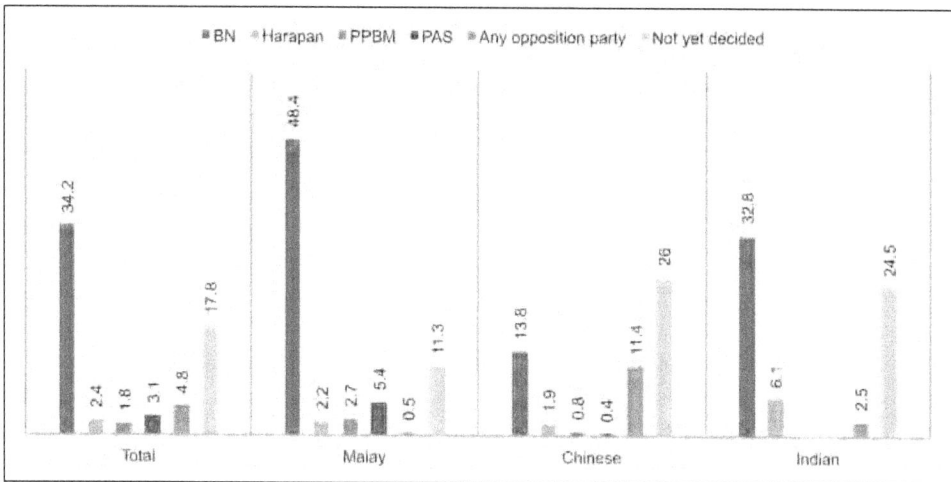

Source: Johor Opinion Survey commissioned by ISEAS – Yusof Ishak Institute, 2017.

FIGURE 10.9
Attitude towards Selected Issues among Johor Malays

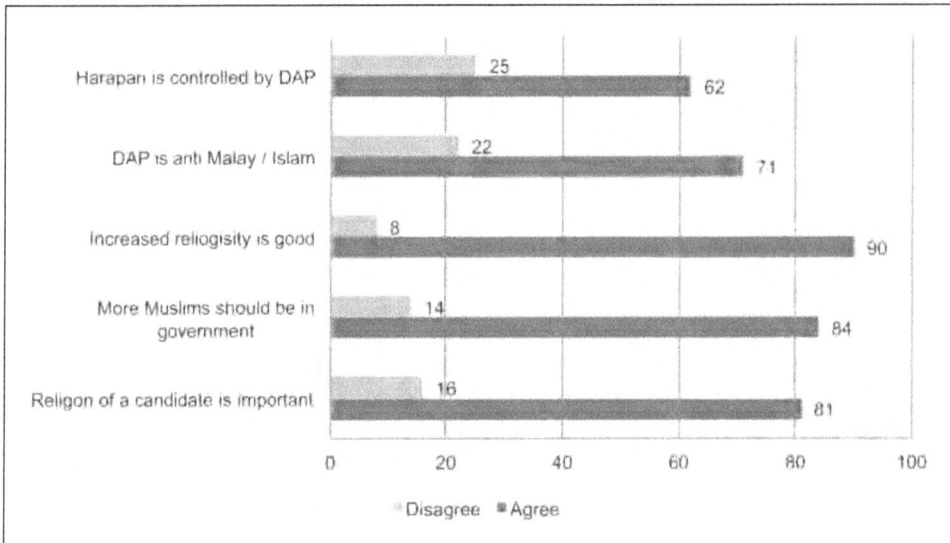

Source: Author's compilation of data from Johor Opinion Survey commissioned by ISEAS-Yusof Ishak Institute, 2017.

Having said that, caution must be exercised when reading the telephone poll data. It is the experience of this author, not just during the fieldwork for this study, that the Malays and Malaysians generally are cautious in expressing their political preferences. It takes time to get them to open up in conversations, especially if they had not known the interviewer before the meeting. This is particularly the case in rural areas where people frequently fear being victimized if they show a differing political attitude. To get beyond this restraint, it is usually necessary to spend time to "warm up" the conversation with informal chit-chats before delving into the more political questions. Therefore, even though the telephone poll data indicate that PPBM in Johor would likely be wiped out by UMNO in GE-14, the latter cannot yet rest on their laurels. During the face-to-face interviews in the fieldwork for this study, the general sentiment was much less certain than what the survey captured. Many of those who started off by expressing loyalty to UMNO gradually changed their tone as they become more comfortable in the conversation. They became more amenable to the possibility of voting for PPBM, with some even admitting that they were only retaining the public façade of being loyal to UMNO to avoid being victimized. These nuances may be missed in telephone polls, making it necessary to use information from both to inform judgement.

HOW UMNO RESPONDS TO PPBM

The difficulty in gauging the real sentiment among voters, especially Malay voters, is appreciated by UMNO leaders in the state. Although confident that UMNO will still win comfortably, they acknowledge that they can no longer ignore the potential threat posed by the opposition coalition, especially with Muhyiddin leading the charge. One of the concerns is the impossibility of measuring how many UMNO members remain in the party but intend to vote for PPBM. The silent protest can be a threat if Johor UMNO leaders fail to quell it properly, especially among rural voters who are traditionally staunch UMNO voters.[59] To counteract the threat, Johor UMNO seems to be deploying a three-pronged strategy.

The first is by answering the allegations thrown at them in a coherent and easy-to-digest fashion. Chief Minister Khaled Nordin has been actively touring the state to deliver speeches to defend UMNO's record, as well as his personal record as head of the state government. Members of his administration have been doing the same, supported by visits by national leaders as well. In fact, on 16 July 2017, a grand event attended by almost 30,000 people was held in the parliamentary constituency of Sembrong, featuring a host of top leaders including Prime Minister Najib Razak, Deputy Prime Minister Zahid Hamidi, UMNO Vice-President Hishammuddin Hussein, Minister for Tourism Nazri Aziz, and Chief Minister Khaled Nordin. Even the Chief Secretary to the Government Ali Hamsa was there. At all these events, UMNO leaders usually provide direct responses to the allegations made by the opposition, aimed at appeasing the crowd.

Second is by reminding voters of UMNO's successes in bringing physical and economic developments to the state, while at the same time providing a vision of how Johor can develop further under them. The main slogan used for this purpose is *"Muafakat Johor"* (Johor Consensus). Perhaps learning from the way Prime Minister Najib uses the 1Malaysia[60] brand to promote his political standing, Chief Minister Khaled also uses *Muafakat Johor* as a brand for his activities in the state. Various welfare programmes are branded as *Muafakat Johor*, such as the free *Muafakat Johor* Bus Services covering fifteen routes in the southern part of the state and various types of assistance under the *Muafakat Johor* Work Commitment Programme (Azam Kerja Muafakat Johor) covering those who are looking for employment, grants for micro-entrepreneurs, and the disabled who would like to work from home. There was even a *Muafakat Johor* Arts Festival held in November 2017. *Muafakat Johor* comes complete with its own logo and official song, which are used in almost all state government functions. Additionally, the state government through its various agencies, as well as the UMNO-linked think-tank Bait Al Amanah, are actively creating and circulating simple infographics, also under the *Muafakat Johor* brand, to highlight UMNO's previous successes and future plans. Arguably, the brand is being used to project Khaled's personal image as a successful and visionary leader for the state. The assumption is that by doing so, the fate of UMNO in Johor can be detached from that of UMNO in other states and nationally.[61]

Third is by highlighting the dominance of DAP in Harapan. UMNO leaders regularly claim that voting for any party that would strengthen DAP further is not in the interest of Malays in the state. The reason for this approach, and the possible implications, are already discussed at length in previous sections. This author observed several activities organized by UMNO in the state during this study, and more often than not the speeches delivered in those activities served to remind the audience of the potential rise of the DAP if support were given to PPBM.

CONCLUDING REMARKS

At the end of the day though, this author feels that it is still impossible to make a conclusive prediction about how PPBM will fare in GE-14. The ground is still, to put it simply, too confusing with some findings from the various surveys contradicting findings from face-to-face interviews. Most voters are reluctant to disclose their political leanings, and many may still be assessing the situation before making up their mind.

What is certain, however, is that PPBM leaders feel the long-term survival of their party hangs on their ability to win at least one state should they fail to take the federal government in GE-14. Johor is among their priority states. But their main target audience, the Johor Malays, are not yet jumping onto their bandwagon. The main concern among this group seems to be the DAP and the future of the Malay agenda if the DAP were to come into government with PPBM through Harapan. The fear is reflected in the relatively slow response to PPBM's membership drive. PPBM leaders are quick to point out though that all political parties in Malaysia receive a much higher number of votes than the size of their membership, and therefore membership is not an indicator of support.[62]

Between now and GE-14, the most crucial factor is the seat division between Harapan parties. If PPBM gets only the high-Malay seats and less of the mixed seats, then it will be highly unlikely they will achieve their ambition of capturing the state. UMNO's majority in these areas is large, and it is not easy to imagine a scenario where the Malay votes would swing to a significant enough extent. If PPBM wants a fighting chance, having a healthy share of the mixed seats is crucial. However, the high-Malay areas are the areas where PPBM is expected by their Harapan partners to focus on and to win. This creates a real dilemma for the party—the areas where they are expected to win are also the areas that are hardest to win. Thus, even though PPBM seems to be taking the challenge and the responsibility in their stride, this is clearly one heavy burden for a fledgling party to shoulder.

APPENDIX 10.1
Objectives of PPBM as Listed in Its Constitution

Malay Text	Translation in English
Menegakkan Islam sebagai agama bagi Persekutuan dan menghormati hak orang bukan Islam untuk menganut dan mengamalkan agama masing-masing secara aman dan harmoni.	To uphold Islam as the religion of the Federation and to respect the rights of non-Muslims to believe in and practise their religions peacefully and harmoniously.
Menjunjung kemuliaan dan kedaulatan institusi Raja-Raja Melayu.	To uphold the sanctity and sovereignty of the institution of the Malay Rulers.
Mempertahankan kedudukan istimewa orang Melayu dan anak negeri Sabah dan Sarawak dan hak-hak yang sah untuk semua kaum.	To defend the special position of the Malays and the natives of Sabah and Sarawak and the legitimate rights of all ethnic groups.
Memperkasa Bahasa Melayu sebagai bahasa kebangsaan dan memelihara hak semua kaum untuk mempelajari bahasa ibunda masing-masing.	To strengthen Malay Language as the national language and to defend the rights of all ethnic groups to learn their mother tongues.
Menegakkan sistem demokrasi berparlimen dan doktrin pemisahan kuasa dengan memperkukuhkan institusi demokrasi menerusi reformasi institusi yang menyeluruh.	To champion parliamentary democracy and the doctrine of the separation of powers by strengthening democratic institutions through holistic institutional reforms.
Memperkasa agenda memerangi rasuah dan salah guna kuasa untuk mewujudkan amalan tadbir urus yang baik dan pemerintahan yang bersih, beramanah dan berintegriti.	To galvanize the efforts to fight corruption and abuse of power so as to create good governance and an administration that is clean, honest, and with integrity.
Memelihara hak-hak asasi rakyat sepertimana yang termaktub di dalam Perlembagaan Persekutuan, menjunjung nilai-nilai keadilan sejagat yang selari dengan agama Islam,serta menjunjung keluhuran perlembagaan, kedaulatan udang-undang serta prinsip keadilan dan kesaksamaan.	To ensure the basic rights of the citizens as enshrined in the Federal Constitution are protected, to uphold universal values that are in line with Islam, and to defend the sovereignty of the constitution, the rule of law, and the principles of fairness and equality.
Membentuk masyarakat Malaysia yang inklusif, progresif, dinamik dan saintifik serta menghargai seni, budaya dan tradisi sebagai acuan membina sebuah negara maju yang sejahtera.	To create a Malaysian society that is inclusive, progressive, dynamic, and scientific, and appreciative of the arts, culture and traditions as moulds to shape a developed and prosperous country.
Memperjuangkan keadilan sosial,mengagih kekayaan negara secara adil dan saksama, membela kebajikan rakyat dan membasmi kemiskinan tanpa mengira kaum dan agama.	To champion social justice, ensuring the nation's wealth is shared fairly and equitably, looking after the welfare of the people and eradicating poverty among people of all races and religions.

continued on next page

APPENDIX 10.1 — *cont'd*

Malay Text	Translation in English
Mendokong prinsip bahawa setiap rakyat berhak untuk berjaya dengan memperolehi pendidikan yang berkualiti dan sempurna menerusi satu sistem pendidikan yang mementingkan pengembangan bakat, kreativiti, inovasi dan amalan nilai-nilai murni serta melaksanakan dasar dan inisiatif yang konsisten untuk merapatkan jurang pendidikan antara bandar dan luar bandar.	To uphold the principle that all citizens have the right to succeed through good quality and complete education, through an education system that prioritizes talent development, creativity, innovation, and good values, as well as to implement policies and initiatives that are consistent to reduce the educational rural-urban divide.
Memupuk perpaduan dan keharmonian antara masyarakat pelbagai kaum dan agama, memelihara kestabilan politik dan keselamatan negara, dan memacu pembangunan ekonomi yang mapan demi kepentingan rakyat dan negara.	To foster unity and harmony between people of different races and religions, securing political stability and national security, and to drive a sustainable economic growth for the benefit of the population and the country.
Mengamalkan prinsip-prinsip Rukunegara serta mendukung Perlembagaan Persekutuan dan Perlembagaan NegeriNegeri.	To practise the principles of Rukun Negara and uphold the Federal Constitution as well as the constitutions of the states.
Menyertai pilihanraya umum Persekutuan dan Negeri serta pilihanraya kecil dengan tujuan untuk menghantar wakil parti ke Dewan Undangan Negeri, Dewan Rakyat dan Dewan Negara.	To participate in federal and state elections as well as by-elections with the purpose of sending the party's representatives to the Dewan Undangan Negeri, Dewan Rakyat and Dewan Negara.

Notes

1. This chapter was previously published as *Parti Pribumi Bersatu Malaysia in Johor: New Party, Big Responsibility*, Trends in Southeast Asia, no. 2/2018 (Singapore: ISEAS – Yusof Ishak Institute, 2018).

2. A notable previous contender was the Parti Melayu Semangat 46 formed in 1988 by former Finance Minister and former vice-president of UMNO, Tengku Razaleigh Hamzah. But the party survived for just eight years. Razaleigh dissolved the party and rejoined UMNO in 1996.

3. Federal Land Development Authority (FELDA), a federal statutory body tasked with resettling poor Malays into new areas.

4. For example, construction work for Forest City, Danga Bay and Petronas RAPID Project were all ramped up after the 2010 Census. A large number of foreign workers work on these projects.

5. This composition changed slightly following the formation of two new Malay parties, Parti Amanah Negara (Amanah) and Parti Pribumi Bersatu Malaysia (PPBM). For the purpose of this chapter, data from GE-13 will be used, since the change does not significantly affect the composition.

6. For a more detailed history of UMNO in Johor, see Abu Bakar Hamid et al., *UMNO Johor 50 Tahun: Memartabatkan Bangsa Melayu* (Kuala Lumpur: Berita Publishing, 1996).

7. Within the national context, this was actually the third of a series of Malay Congresses held in Malaya.

8. For example, Hutchinson (2015) identifies seventeen Malay figures from Johor who became UMNO's early national leaders.

9. A more detailed account of Onn's departure from UMNO to form the IMP is provided in Puthucheary (1992).

10. At the time Deputy President of UMNO and Deputy Prime Minister of Malaysia.

11. At the time Vice-President of UMNO and Minister of Rural and Regional Development.

12. Interview with Sufi Yusof, Special Officer to PPBM Chairman Mahathir Mohamad, 2 August 2017.

13. Interview with Ambiga Sreenevasan, former leader of the Coalition for Clean and Fair Elections (Bersih) and current President of Malaysian National Human Rights Society (HAKAM), 8 August 2017. Ambiga attended several of these meetings.

14. Interview with Syed Saddiq Syed Abdul Rahman, current head of PPBM's Youth Wing (Armada), 11 July 2017.

15. Constitution of PPBM, clause 2.

16. Interview with Shahruddin Salleh, PPBM Secretary General and Head of Johor PPBM, 3 August 2017.

17. Interview with Osman Sapian, Secretary of Johor PPBM, 8 July 2017, and Nasir Hashim, Deputy Head of Johor PPBM, 16 July 2017.

18. Interview with Nasir Hashim, 16 July 2017.

19. Interview with Mukhriz Mahathir, PPBM Deputy President, 30 May 2017.

20. Interview with Osman Sapian, 8 July 2017.

21. Interviews with national Armada Head Syed Saddiq Syed Abdul Rahman on 11 July 2017; Head of Armada Gelang Patah Division in Johor, Mohamad Fahim Mohamad Farid on 8 July 2017; as well as five other Johor Armada activists in Kota Tinggi (16 July 2017), Tebrau (11 August 2017), and Pontian (11 August 2017).

22. Associate Professor at the International Islamic University Malaysia.

23. Interview with Maszlee Malik, 11 August 2017.
24. Interview with Shahruddin Salleh.
25. Interview with three Wanita UMNO activists at branch level, one each in Tanjung Piai (10 August 2017), Pontian (11 August 2017) and Gelang Patah (12 August 2017). All requested anonymity.
26. Interview with Noorlihan Arifin, Head of Recruitment, Srikandi PPBM Johor, 13 August 2017.
27. The events were in Pengerang on 13 May 2017, Kota Tinggi on 15 July 2017, Pontian on 12 August 2017, and Kulai on 13 August 2017.
28. The survey was conducted between May and June 2017. A sample size of 2,011 respondents was interviewed via fixed-line and mobile phones. Respondents consisted of Malaysian citizens aged eighteen and above who resided in Johor, selected on the basis of random stratified sampling across district of residence, controlled by quota for ethnicity, age and gender. A "Johor resident" is defined as one who is registered as a voter in the state. There were 1,104 (55 per cent) ethnic Malay respondents, 758 (38 per cent) ethnic Chinese respondents, and 149 (7 per cent) ethnic Indian respondents. 340 respondents were between the ages of 21 and 30 years old; 455 respondents were between the ages of 31 and 40 years old; 546 respondents were between the ages of 41 and 50 years old; 409 respondents were between the ages of 51 and 60 years old; and 261 respondents were 61 years old and above. The survey's estimated margin of error is +2.18.
29. The discussion in this subsection is primarily based on focus group discussions conducted with four to eight randomly selected villagers in each of the following villages across Johor: FELDA Ayer Tawar 1 (Panti constituency, 11 May 2017), Kampung Sungai Rengit (Pengerang constituency, 12 May 2017), Kampung Mohd Noor (Sri Gading constituency, 10 May 2017), Kampung Serkat Timur (Tanjung Piai constituency, 11 August 2017), FELDA Taib Andak (Kulai constituency, 12 August 2017).
30. To be fair, all ethnic- and religion-based political parties in Malaysia have always played up ethno-religious sentiments for their partisan benefit, not just UMNO. But since this chapter focuses more on PPBM, UMNO, and Malay politics, the discussion is intentionally restricted.
31. Interview with Liew Chin Tong, Chairman of Johor DAP, 13 July 2017.
32. Interview with Rais Hussin Mohamed Arif, Head of National PPBM Policy and Strategy Bureau, 3 June 2017.
33. See, for example, Azizul Osman, "Tun Mahathir Lebih Berkuasa Daripada Muhyiddin dalam PPBM" [Tun Mahathir Is More Powerful Than Muhyiddin], *AntaraPos*, 26 Januari 2017.
34. Multiple interviews with various Johor opposition leaders from PKR, Amanah and DAP, conducted in July and August 2017.
35. Interview with Muhyiddin Yassin, President of PPBM, 9 August 2017.
36. The survey is not released to the public but this author was granted a closed-door briefing on the findings. The data is used here with permission.
37. Multiple interviews with various Johor opposition leaders from PKR, Amanah and DAP, conducted in July and August 2017.
38. Interview with Muhyiddin Yassin.
39. The defection of Shahruddin Salleh from UMNO to become PPBM's Secretary General has reduced this number by one. However, for this chapter, the results from GE-13 are used as the benchmark.
40. Interview with Osman Sapian.

41. Interview with Hassan Abdul Karim, Chairman of Johor State PKR, 11 August 2017.
42. Interviews with PPBM President Muhyiddin Yassin; Head of Johor PPBM Shahruddin Salleh and Deputy Head of PPBM Johor Nasir Hashim.
43. Interview with Shahruddin Salleh and Osman Sapian.
44. Interview with Salahuddin Ayob, Deputy President of Amanah, 9 August 2017; Liew Chin Tong; and Hassan Abdul Karim.
45. Parti Perhimpunan Kebangsaan formed in 1963 by former UMNO Minister for Agriculture and Cooperatives. The party was dissolved in 1965.
46. Parti Melayu Semangat 46 was formed in 1989 by Tengku Razaleigh Hamzah, a senior UMNO leader who held various posts in the party as well as several ministerial posts including Minister of Finance. The party was dissolved in 1996 and Razaleigh rejoined UMNO together with his followers.
47. PAS was formed in 1951 with the Head of UMNO Religious Bureau Haji Ahmad Fuad Hassan as its first President, with other UMNO members who held dual membership in both parties for several years. The party today claims to have more than 750,000 members and it remains a challenger to UMNO, especially in rural Malay seats.
48. PKR was formed in 1999 with former UMNO Deputy President and former Deputy Prime Minister Anwar Ibrahim as its leader. The party today leads the coalition government in Selangor and is a leading member of the opposition coalition.
49. PAS and PKR have formed state governments in Kelantan and Selangor, respectively.
50. Interview with Marzuki Mohamad, Associate Professor at International Islamic University Malaysia, and former Special Officer to Muhyiddin Yassin when he was Deputy Prime Minister, 13 August 2017.
51. Interview with Shahruddin Salleh, PPBM Secretary General and Head of Johor State Leadership Council. 3 August 2017.
52. For example, a small loose grouping of pro-opposition activists who call themselves "Otai Reformis" issued a statement in July 2017 rejecting Mahathir's potential leadership of the opposition coalition. Additionally, on 28 October 2017, a group of activists detained without trial during Mahathir's premiership under the Internal Security Act (ISA) also issued a statement protesting his leadership of Harapan and demanded that he formally apologize for their detention.
53. Interview with Aminolhuda Hassan, Amanah Johor State Chairman, 29 May 2017; Liew Chin Tong; and Hassan Abdul Karim, Johor PKR State Chairman, 11 August 2017.
54. N03 Pemanis, N04 Kemelah, N05 Tenang, N07 Bukit Serampang, N26 Machap, N27 Layang-Layang, N31 Kahang, N32 Endau, N33 Tenggaroh, N34 Panti, N35 Pasir Raja, N37 Johor Lama, N41 Puteri Wangsa, N50 Bukit Permai, N51 Bukit Batu.
55. P141 Sekijang, P143 Pagoh, P144 Ledang, P147 Parit Sulong, P149 Sri Gading, P151 Simpang Renggam, P153 Sembrong, P155 Tenggara, P156 Kota Tinggi, P157 Pengerang, P163 Kulai.
56. Interview with Shahruddin Salleh.
57. The electoral data in this chapter is based on official figures from GE-13. It is expected that a redelineation will be introduced prior to GE-14. However, this chapter uses GE-13 data.
58. Interviews with Muhyiddin Yassin, and Shahruddin Salleh.
59. Interview with Associate Professor Dr Abdul Razak Ahmad, Founding Director of Bait Al Amanah, a think-tank of UMNO Johor that works closely with the state government, 13 July 2017.
60. The 1Malaysia concept was introduced by Prime Minister Najib Razak when he became

Prime Minister in 2009 as a slogan to promote national unity but it gradually evolved into a brand for various welfare programmes offered by the federal government. Examples include the cash handout Bantuan Rakyat 1Malaysia, the low-cost shops such as 1Malaysia Fishmongers, 1Malaysia Textile Shops, and 1Malaysia Grocery Shop, as well as the free tyres for taxi drivers under the Tyre Assistance 1Malaysia.

61. Interview with a prominent Johor Malay businessman who claims to be a regular donor to UMNO, 22 June 2017. The respondent requested anonymity.
62. Interviews with Shahruddin Salleh and Nasir Hasim.

References

Amoroso, Donna J. 2014. *Traditionalism and the Ascendancy of the Malay Ruling Class in Colonial Malaya*. Petaling Jaya: SIRD; Singapore: NUS Press.

Astroawani. 2016. "Tun Mahathir dan Isteri Umum Keluar UMNO". 29 February 2016. http://www.astroawani.com/berita-politik/tun-mahathir-dan-isteri-umum-keluar-umno-96732 (accessed 24 July 2017).

———. 2017. "PPBM Lahir Hasil Sokongan DAP—Annuar Musa". 18 March 2017. http://www.astroawani.com/berita-politik/ppbm-lahir-hasil-sokongan-dap-annuar-musa-135970 (accessed 15 August 2017).

Bait Al Amanah. http://baitalamanah.com/?page_id=171

Berita Harian. 2017. "Belum Pasti Muhyiddin di Pagoh". 22 August 2017. https://www.bharian.com.my/berita/politik/2017/08/315958/belum-pasti-muhyiddin-di-pagoh (accessed 20 September 2017).

Bernama. 2016. "Muhyiddin's Statement Is Like 'Counting Chicken Before They Hatch'—Salleh". 9 October 2016.

Guardian, The. 2015. "Malaysian Prime Minister Had $700m of 'Donations' in Bank Account —Watchdog". 4 August 2015. https://www.theguardian.com/world/2015/aug/04/malaysia-corruption-watchdog-najib-razak-donations-1mdb (accessed 24 July 2017).

Funston, John. 1980. *Malay Politics in Malaysia: A Study of UMNO and PAS*. Kuala Lumpur: Heinemann Educational Books.

Hutchinson, Francis E. 2015. "Malaysia's Independence Leaders and the Legacies of State Formation under British Rule". *Journal of the Royal Asiatic Society*, Series 3, No. 25, Vol. 1: 123–51.

Keputusan Pilihan Raya Umum. http://resultpru13.spr.gov.my/module/keputusan/paparan/paparan_Laporan.php

Malaysiakini. 2016. "Muhyiddin Losing Support in Pagoh, May Contest Muar in GE-14?". 15 August 2016. https://www.malaysiakini.com/news/352337 (accessed 20 September 2017).

———. 2017. "Syed Saddiq Turns Down Oxford to Remain in Politics". 2 October 2017. https://www.malaysiakini.com/news/396975 (accessed 5 October 2017).

Maznah Mohamad. 2015. "Fragmented but Captured: Malay Voters and the FELDA Factor in GE-13". In *Coalitions in Collision: Malaysia's 13th General Elections*, edited by Johan Saravanamuttu, Lee Hock Guan, and Mohamed Nawab Mohamed Osman. Petaling Jaya: Strategic Information and Research Development Centre; and Singapore: ISEAS – Yusof Ishak Institute.

Najib Razak. 2016. "Ucapan Dasar Presiden di Perhimpunan Agung UMNO 2016". *Najibrazak.com*, 1 December 2016. https://www.najibrazak.com/bm/blog/ucapan-dasar-presiden-di-perhimpunan-agung-umno-2016/> (accessed 2 August 2017).

Oxford Business Group. 2016. *The Report, Malaysia 2016*. https://www.oxfordbusinessgroup. com/overview/state-readiness-wide-range-investment-opportunities-await (accessed 25 July 2017).

Puthucheary, Juita. 1992. "Dato Onn, UMNO and the Independence of Malaya Party 1948–1952". Doctor of Philosophy thesis, School of Oriental and African Studies, London.

Ramlah Adam. 1992. *Dato' Onn Jaafar: Pengasas Kemerdekaan*. Kuala Lumpur: Dewan Bahasa dan Pustaka.

Shaharom Husain. 1985. *Biografi Perjuangan Politik Dato' Onn Jaafar*. Petaling Jaya: Fajar Bakti.

Sinar Harian. 2019. "Muhyiddin dilantik Pengerusi Pakatan Harapan Johor". 26 August 2019. http://www.sinarharian.com.my/politik/muhyiddin-dilantik-pengerusi-pakatan-harapan-johor-1.723005 (accessed 22 August 2017).

Straits Times. 2016. "The Dilemma of Having Foreign Workers in Malaysia". 17 September 2016. http://www.straitstimes.com/opinion/the-dilemma-of-having-foreign-workers-in-malaysia (accessed 29 July 2017).

Stockwell, A.J. 1979. *British Policy and Malay Politics During the Malayan Union Experiment, 1945–1948*. Kuala Lumpur: Malaysian Branch of the Royal Asiatic Society.

Time. 2017. "Najib as Among the Five World Leaders Whose Ratings Are Lower Than President Donald Trump". 20 May 2017. http://time.com/4785127/michael-temer-nicolas-maduro-donald-trump/

Utusan. 2015. "Rombakan Kabinet: Muhyiddin Gugur, Zahid Hamidi TPM Baharu". 28 July 2015. http://www.utusan.com.my/berita/nasional/rombakan-kabinet-muhyiddin-gugur-zahid-hamidi-tpm-baharu-1.117963 (accessed 24 July 2017).

———. 2016. "Muhyiddin, Mukhriz dipecat". 25 June 2016 http://www.utusan.com.my/berita/politik/muhyiddin-mukhriz-dipecat-1.346795 (accessed 24 July 2017).

Wan Saiful Wan Jan. 2017. *Parti Amanah Negara in Johor: Birth, Challenges, Prospects*. Trends in Southeast Asia, no. 9/2017. Singapore: ISEAS – Yusof Ishak Institute.

Welsh, Bridget. 2013. "BN's Femme Fatale: The Power of Women". *Malaysiakini*, 27 April 2013. https://www.malaysiakini.com/news/228256

Zubaidah Abu Bakar. 2010. "PAS, PKR out to win FELDA settlers' votes". *New Straits Times*, 23 July 2010.

11

PARTI AMANAH NEGARA IN JOHOR
Birth, Challenges and Prospects

Wan Saiful Wan Jan[1]

INTRODUCTION

Islam has always been an important factor in Malaysia's politics. Even political parties whose members are mainly non-Muslim cannot run away from debating the role of Islam in public policy. Since its establishment in 1951, the Islamic Party of Malaysia (PAS) has dominated the discourse on political Islam, and many others have had to respond and compete with it. It would not be wrong to say that the deepening Islamization in Malaysia over the years is the result of political competition between PAS and the ruling coalition. However, a new development took place in 2015 when a group of senior PAS leaders left the party to form Parti Amanah Negara (Amanah).[2] PAS suddenly found a competitor who is also staking a claim on the right to define and shape the discourse on political Islam in the country.

This chapter looks into the break-up and its implications on the politics in the southern state of Johor, since this was the state where much of the groundwork to form Amanah took place. Following this introduction, a brief history behind the break-up is provided. Attention is then given to Johor, with a discussion on the role of activists in the state that led to the formation of Amanah, the party's current organization, and their likely electoral potential. The chapter concludes with a discussion on how the emergence of Amanah may affect PAS in Johor.

FROM PAS TO AMANAH

To understand how Amanah came to be, a brief review of the evolution of Islamist thoughts in Malaysia is useful, as it has heavily influenced PAS' own evolution. The history behind PAS' establishment in 1951 is a contested one.[3] Arguably, it was closely tied to the strategy of the United Malays National Organization (UMNO) which was founded five years earlier, especially to the latter's desire to widen its support base. UMNO at that time was worried that it was losing support from conservative Malay Muslims and wanted therefore to reposition itself as a champion of Islam. Thus, UMNO sponsored two Ulama Congresses (Perjumpaan Alim Ulama Tanah Melayu), on 20–22 February 1950 and 23 August 1951. The purpose was to bring together conservative Muslim scholars to discuss, among others, steps that they could take to bring the country towards independence. When the Ulama Congress met for the third time on 24 November 1951, the delegates agreed to the formation of the Persatuan Islam Se-Malaya (Pan-Malayan Islamic Organization), which is widely regarded as the starting point for PAS.

The linkage between PAS and UMNO in the former's early years is clear, even though many PAS activists today tend to dislike this notion since they prefer to distinguish themselves from UMNO. In reality, in addition to being a gathering of Malay conservatives, the founding ideas of PAS revolved around Malay nationalism and Malay unity, echoing UMNO's founding principles. Members of PAS were allowed to hold dual membership in UMNO. And PAS' founding President, Haji Ahmad Fuad Hassan, simultaneously held the position of head of UMNO's Religious Affairs Bureau, thereby providing a direct linkage to UMNO head office.

Throughout its history, PAS has seen its members and leaders leave to form a new party on several occasions. Their founding president left in 1953 together with many top leaders to join the newly established but short-lived Independence of Malaya Party. Later, new political parties were formed as a direct result of the splintering of PAS' factions from the main party. Two significant ones were when their fourth president Mohamad Asri Muda left in 1983 to form Hizb al-Muslimin (HAMIM, or Party of Muslims), and prior to that when Barisan Jemaah Islamiah SeMalaysia (BERJASA) was formed in 1977 by Muhamed Nasir, a state leader from the northeastern state of Kelantan. Neither of these splinter parties survived for very long as their fate was tied to that of their respective founders. There were also smaller and less significant ones like Parti Islah Malaysia and Angkatan Keadilan Insan Malaysia (AKIM). As its history shows, PAS is not new to splintering and factionalism.[4]

Being the oldest and biggest political party that publicly champions the creation of an Islamic state in Malaysia, PAS is the natural home for activists and political actors interested in advocating political Islamism through a party platform. Consequently, PAS members consist of people from diverse backgrounds, worldviews and ideologies. These groups compete to bring their ideas to the fore in the party by forming factions internally. Most of the time, the internal rivalries occur silently and behind the scenes. Only sometimes do they surface publicly. In the latest crisis, PAS leaders failed to manage long-standing ideological differences, especially between the two main factions in the party—the conservatives and the progressives. This eventually led to the progressive faction leaving to form Amanah.[5]

The conservative faction in PAS has been commonly called the *ulama* camp. But it consists not just of *ulama*, or religious scholars. There are also those who are not religiously educated in the group. Regardless of their backgrounds, when it comes to political strategy, this faction generally adheres to a conservative interpretation of how Islam should be applied to public policy, and they more often than not focus on the legalistic aspects of Islam, especially on the need to immediately implement the Islamic shariah law or *hudud*. They also hold an exclusivist view when it comes to dealing with non-Muslims, believing that major policy decisions affecting Islam—be it at party or government levels—must be mainly, if not solely, in the hands of Muslims.[6] Since ethnicity and religion are frequently mixed in Malaysian public policy debates,[7] the conservatives are naturally more comfortable with a Malay-centric agenda as they see it as an extension of their Islamist campaign. Among the current thought leaders of the conservative group are the party's President Abdul Hadi Awang, Vice-President Nik Mohamad Ammar Abdullah, Information Chief Nasruddin Hassan and central committee member Mohamad Zuhdi Marzuki.

The progressive faction in PAS on the other hand are commonly called the "professional camp", implying that they come from professional backgrounds as opposed to the usually traditionally educated *ulamas*. All the leading figures from this group have left PAS and they now hold top posts in Amanah, including current Amanah President Mohamad Sabu, Deputy President Salahuddin Ayub, Director of Strategy Dr Dzulkefly Ahmad, and Information Chief Khalid Samad. When Turkish leader Recep Tayyip Erdogan was still seen in a positive light and still considered an influential political Islamist thought-leader by the global Islamist movement in the 1990s and 2000s, the PAS progressives were also labelled the "Erdogans", to distinguish them from the conservatives who were seen as more aligned with the views of Turkey's previous conservative president Necmettin Erbakan. The progressives, too, consist of individuals who have both secular and Islamic education backgrounds. They differ quite significantly from the conservatives in their political outlook, especially when it comes to their emphasis on good governance and human rights, or what they consider the higher purpose of the shariah law (*maqasid al-shariah*), instead of being narrowly focused on the immediate implementation of the shariah law itself.

The progressives are also more inclusive towards non-Muslims. They acknowledge that it is necessary to respect all views regardless of whether they come from Muslims or non-Muslims, and that all these ideas need to be negotiated within a liberal democratic framework.[8] The progressives still believe in the need to create an Islamic state that implements the shariah law, but they prioritize the creation of a supportive ecosystem first before introducing the law itself. In other words, there are still elements of conservatism in their agenda, but they use more gradual and inclusive strategies, and are willing to be flexible and accommodative where necessary. Hence some scholars use the term neoconservative to describe this group, arguing that progressivism is in fact a feature of neoconservatism.[9]

The *Reformasi* era[10] that started in 1998 saw PAS actively forging partnerships[11] with other political parties in its quest to take over power in Malaysia. This move helped PAS make significant gains among non-Muslims especially between 1998 and 2015, thanks to the softening of their attitude towards non-Muslims and non-Malays, as well as their partnership with the Chinese-dominated Democratic Action Party (DAP). The progressives within PAS quickly moved to institutionalize the relationship with non-Muslims as they wanted PAS to become a truly inclusive party. Among their first moves was to create the PAS Supporters Club, a platform for non-Muslims who are supportive of PAS' agenda. The club was upgraded to an official wing of the party called the Dewan Himpunan Penyokong PAS (DHPP, or PAS Supporters Wing) on 23 May 2010. However, although the progressives' original proposal was to give equal membership rights to non-Muslims, this idea was rejected by the dominant conservatives, resulting in non-Muslims being allowed to join the DHPP but without being accorded equal membership rights.[12]

The progressives then took another bold step to shape PAS in their mould. In 2010 they mooted the idea of reforming how the concept of *Kepimpinan Ulama* (Leadership by the Ulama) is to be practised. Believing that the model as it was then implemented provided no effective check-and-balance mechanism, they suggested that PAS needed to adopt a framework that was more democratic and more accountable.[13] This touched on the conservatives' raw nerve because it would affect their grip on power in the party. The *Kepimpinan Ulama* concept ensures the highest offices are firmly, albeit unofficially, reserved for individuals from the conservative group whereas the progressives' suggestion would open those positions to non-ulama, and hence the progressives, too. This proposal sparked a strong reaction from the conservatives, and they started to organize themselves and to mobilize their supporters.

The conservatives mounted repeated challenges against the progressives, including by contesting for more seats in the central committee. Their main battle cries were twofold: that the progressives were bowing too much to the demands of non-Muslims, and that the progressives wanted to change the very nature of the party when they proposed reforms to the *Kepimpinan Ulama* concept. Throughout this period the progressives benefited from the patronage of Nik Abdul Aziz Nik Mat, the revered chairman, or *Mursyidul Am*, of PAS' Syura Council. Many times, Nik Abdul Aziz publicly backed the progressives and chided the conservatives, especially when the latter attempted to bring PAS towards a more Malay-centric and exclusivist agenda. However, old age and health issues caught up with Nik Abdul Aziz from 2010 onwards, reducing his ability to intervene effectively in the ongoing debates, especially during the period leading to his demise on 12 February 2015.

This resulted in fierce internal battles for party positions taking place at all levels from 2010, and the contestation was visible especially at the 2011 and 2013 national annual conferences.[14] Finally, after taking over the majority of key positions in the state and divisional layers of the party, on 4–6 June 2015, in PAS' 61st annual conference, the conservatives completely wiped out all progressive leaders from the central national committee. Eighteen progressive figures lost their central committee seats, decisively ending any remaining influence they had in PAS. The all-out campaign against them, as well as the drastic "cleansing"[15] at the June 2015 party conference, forced the progressives to regroup and rethink their overall strategy, and this eventually led to the formation of Amanah, as will be described further below.

JOHOR: DEMOGRAPHY AND ELECTORAL DATA

Johor has a population of 3.6 million. The 2010 census shows that 71.9 per cent of the population is urbanized. Ethnic Malays make up 54 per cent of the population, followed by 33 per cent Chinese and 6 per cent Indians. The population is also relatively young, with 50 per cent aged between fifteen to forty-four years old (Department of Statistics Malaysia 2011). As can be seen from Table 11.1, the ethnic distribution of voters is also very mixed. Out of the fifty-six state seats, sixteen have less than 45 per cent Malay voters, twenty-six seats have between 45 to 70 per cent Malay voters, and only fourteen seats have more than 70 per cent Malay voters. Out of the twenty-six parliamentary seats, six have less than 45 per cent Malay voters, fifteen seats have between 45 to 70 per cent Malay voters, and only five seats have more than 70 per cent Malay voters.

TABLE 11.1
Ethnic Distribution of Voters in Johor (in percentages)

State Code	State Name	Malay	Chinese	Indian	Others	
N48	Skudai	21.8	64.9	12.2	1.1	
N52	Senai	22.9	65.0	11.0	1.1	
N12	Bentayan	24.7	72.6	2.2	0.4	
N06	Bekok	25.6	53.6	18.0	2.7	
N28	Mengkibol	27.3	58.3	13.8	0.6	
N51	Bukit Batu	30.4	61.6	7.2	0.8	
N19	Yong Peng	31.8	60.4	6.8	1.0	
N23	Penggaram	35.2	61.5	2.3	1.1	Below 45%
N02	Jementah	36.3	54.5	8.7	0.6	Malay
N30	Paloh	37.3	43.6	17.1	2.0	
N10	Tangkak	37.7	51.2	9.7	1.5	
N45	Stulang	38.7	55.1	4.5	1.7	
N55	Pekan Nanas	39.3	57.8	1.2	1.7	
N41	Puteri Wangsa	39.6	47.2	11.7	1.4	
N46	Pengkalan Rinting	42.5	44.7	10.6	2.1	
N42	Johor Jaya	42.8	47.1	7.5	2.7	
N49	Nusa Jaya	47.0	38.4	12.7	2.0	
N27	Layang-Layang	49.0	34.9	14.7	1.5	
N05	Tenang	49.4	37.6	11.3	1.7	
N29	Mahkota	50.5	40.6	5.9	3.0	
N13	Sungai Abong	51.0	45.2	3.0	0.8	
N43	Permas	51.6	29.4	14.7	4.2	
N50	Bukit Permai	52.4	33.9	11.9	1.7	
N40	Tiram	53.2	29.7	14.5	2.6	

N21	Parit Yaani	54.0	43.1	1.1	1.9	
N47	Kempas	54.2	35.2	8.9	1.7	
N04	Kemelah	54.6	38.6	5.7	1.1	
N09	Gambir	54.6	39.7	3.8	1.8	
N15	Maharani	54.7	42.0	2.5	0.8	
N01	Buloh Kasap	55.0	32.2	11.6	1.2	
N03	Pemanis	56.2	39.3	3.4	1.0	
N14	Bukit Naning	58.7	38.4	1.0	1.8	
N08	Jorak	59.0	34.8	5.4	0.8	45–70%
N24	Senggarang	60.5	37.4	0.5	1.6	Malay
N35	Pasir Raja	61.1	25.5	9.2	4.2	
N44	Tanjong Puteri	61.3	31.6	5.3	1.7	
N54	Pulai Sebatang	61.8	34.5	1.4	2.2	
N26	Machap	62.4	31.7	5.0	0.9	
N17	Semerah	63.2	33.6	0.6	2.6	
N11	Serom	65.5	32.8	0.9	0.8	
N56	Kukup	69.0	27.6	0.8	2.6	
N07	Bukit Serampang	69.9	26.1	2.1	1.9	
N16	Sungai Balang	71.6	26.9	0.2	1.3	
N37	Johor Lama	72.1	22.7	3.9	1.2	
N22	Parit Raja	73.1	22.2	1.8	3.0	
N31	Kahang	73.6	21.0	2.6	2.9	
N32	Endau	76.0	18.9	0.7	4.4	
N39	Tanjong Surat	76.7	20.7	0.9	1.6	
N53	Benut	77.7	18.3	0.2	3.9	More than
N25	Rengit	79.1	18.3	0.3	2.4	70%
N33	Tenggaroh	80.2	13.4	1.7	4.7	Malay
N20	Semarang	82.2	13.3	0.8	3.7	
N18	Sri Medan	83.0	9.1	0.3	7.6	
N34	Panti	85.9	7.2	4.0	2.9	
N36	Sedili	95.5	2.1	0.8	1.6	
N38	Penawar	97.0	0.3	0.8	1.9	

Note: Highlighted are seats won by PAS in GE-13.
Source: General elections data obtained from Dr Ong Kian Ming, Member of Parliament for Serdang.

Despite Malays making up only just over half of the population, Johor has always been a bastion of Barisan Nasional (BN), and UMNO is by far the dominant party. In the 13th General Elections (GE-13), out of the fifty-six state seats, BN won thirty-eight seats, with UMNO having a lion's share of thirty-two of those seats, or 58 per cent of the total. The opposition coalition Pakatan Rakyat[16] won eighteen state seats, with DAP holding thirteen, PAS four, and Parti Keadilan Rakyat (PKR) just one. This composition has changed slightly in recent times due to the splintering of Amanah from PAS and Parti Pribumi Bersatu Malaysia (PPBM) from UMNO, but for the purpose of this chapter we will use the results of GE-13 as a benchmark since the recent changes do not have a significant impact on the overall picture.

THE SIGNIFICANCE OF JOHOR TO AMANAH

Johor is a significant state for Amanah as it was in the state that the foundational steps towards forming the party were taken. Months before the June 2015 PAS party election, the progressives were already sensing that the internal tide was moving against them. At the same time, the conservatives were becoming more agitated with their partners in the Pakatan coalition, especially the Chinese-majority DAP. As stated above, the conservatives are more naturally inclined towards a Malay-centric agenda, making them uncomfortable whenever non-Muslims become assertive. Worried that the rising strength of the conservatives and their vocal public spat with the DAP may split Pakatan, a non-government organization (NGO) called Persatuan Ummah Sejahtera Malaysia (PasMa) was formed on 11 August 2014, led by a state-level PAS leader from Kedah, Phahrolrazi Mohd Zawawi. PasMa's stated purpose was to advocate from within the party for PAS to stay as a loyal partner in Pakatan (*Free Malaysia Today*, 9 September 2014). But the group was not able to establish itself as a sustainable organization and fizzled away soon after its establishment.

Parallel to that, starting from early 2015, a group of PAS leaders from the southern state of Johor was also becoming increasingly concerned about the rising conservatism in the party. To them, the development was neither healthy for the party, nor good for the propagation of Islam generally. The individuals voicing this concern were mainly from the progressive side who believe that Islam is an inclusive and moderate religion. To them political Islamism too should adhere to the same principles of inclusiveness and moderation. When the top leaders of PAS started expressing more conservative and exclusivist attitudes, it could only be expected that the progressives would feel uncomfortable. The direction of the party was fast diverging from their worldview.[17]

The PAS Johor progressives also believed that the nature of voters in the state made it a non-starter if a party did not want to compromise and partner with others. Johor has many seats that are mixed in terms of their ethnic composition. Any party that wants to succeed electorally must work with other parties representing other ethnic groups. Thus, for the Johor progressives, rhetoric and policies that alienate non-Muslim voters could only be detrimental to the growth of Islamist ideas in the state, as well as to the electoral prospects of PAS. As highlighted in Table 11.1, in GE-13, PAS won four seats in Johor, all in constituencies with a relatively large percentage of Chinese voters. But their margin of victory was not big. Even in the constituency of Sungai Abong where PAS gained the largest majority out of the four seats, the margin of victory was only by 3,813 votes or just 13.5 per cent. Chinese voters make up 45.2 per cent of the electorate there and even if just half were to swing away from the party, PAS would have a very slim chance of retaining the constituency. Chinese voters are not natural supporters of PAS. But since PAS was the sole representative of Pakatan Rakyat, they had no choice but to vote for the party even if they were actually PKR or DAP supporters. For the opposition pact, only by using this strategy could they present a credible challenge to the ruling coalition. PAS clearly benefited from this arrangement. It was only logical to think that any opposition party that wants to pose a real challenge again in GE-14 needs to adopt the same strategy, and the progressives were aware of this.

Fearful that the conservatives' attitude would scare away non-Muslims not just from PAS but also from Islam itself, the progressives in Johor began to moot the idea of creating a new Islamist yet inclusive political party. This proposition started to be discussed more openly among Johor progressives in the early half of 2015, before PAS' party conference in June. They took inspiration from the success of another Islamist party in Tunisia, the Ennahda led by Rachid Ghannouchi, who had embraced inclusivism as a defining aspect of their struggle.[18]

A prominent Johor activist for the rights of FELDA[19] settlers and then-PAS central committee member Mazlan Aliman took the initiative to speak to other progressives in the party, both nationally as well as in the state, on the need to set up a new platform that championed progressive and inclusive Islamism.[20] The operationalization of the idea was taken up by Aminolhuda Hassan, state legislative assembly member for Parit Yaani and Johor PAS State Commissioner (2013–15). Prior to the June 2015 party conference, while still holding the post of PAS State Commissioner, Aminolhuda was invited by the party's grassroots leaders from across Johor to discuss how to handle the growing conservatism in the party. It was at these meetings that the idea to form a new party began to take shape. Not all grassroots leaders agreed to the proposition, but a sizeable portion was supportive.[21] Many were open to leaving PAS for a new party if one were to be formed, and they also asked Aminolhuda to continue gauging support for this proposition from other PAS divisional leaders in the state.

Aminolhuda continued to tour the state, accepting invitations from many more PAS' division and branch heads. The fact that he was invited to the meetings, and seeing the frankness of the division and branch leaders that he met, Aminolhuda came to the conclusion that the PAS grassroots members and activists themselves were not comfortable with the rising conservatism and exclusivist attitude in the party. It was the grassroots members themselves were calling for a new party to be set up. Bolstered by these findings, immediately after the decisive June 2015 PAS party conference, Aminolhuda, Mazlan Aliman, and several others invited all the progressive leaders from across Malaysia who had lost their central committee seats to an event in Bakri, Johor, on 16 June 2015. The event was themed "Jasamu Dikenang" (Your Deeds are Remembered),[22] and it was scheduled to take place in the evening (see Figure 11.1).

Prior to the event, a meeting was held in the afternoon of the same day, at Muar Traders Hotel, attended by 118 invited delegates mainly from Johor, together with all the eighteen national PAS leaders who had just lost their central committee seats. Aminolhuda chaired the meeting, and he explained his belief that the progressives had two options: remain in PAS but work in a more strategic way within the party; or only some of them would remain in PAS with the rest leaving to form a new party. He also explained that the progressive leaders in Johor were ready to form their own party, and they already had candidates for the various posts in the new set up. He even listed the names of the proposed post holders for Johor in his presentation. The full set of slides used in that meeting is included in Appendix 11.1.

Following a heated discussion, the meeting concluded with a "Bakri Declaration" (see Table 11.2). This landmark declaration outlines the summary of their discussion, their agreement to form a new national party instead of one just for Johor, as well

FIGURE 11.1
Poster Advertising the "Jasamu Dikenang" Event in Bakri

TABLE 11.2
Full Text of the Bakri Declaration and Its Translation in English

Original text in Malay	Translation in English
Jawatan kuasa bertindak dibentuk di peringkat pusat hari ini dengan diketuai Yang Berbahagia Tuan Haji Mohamad bin Sabu sebagai Pengerusi dan Tuan Haji Salahuddin Ayub sebagai Timbalan.	A national action committee is formed today, with Mohamad Sabu as Chairman and Salahuddin Ayub as Deputy Chairman.
Wadah baru dibentuk melibatkan kebangkitan rakyat, NGO dan pertubuhan masyarakat dengan segera. Pembentukan jawatankuasa bagi wadah baru ini akan dibentuk hari ini juga di Bakri.	A new platform is formed to garner support from the public, civil society organizations, and community groups as soon as possible. The committee for this new platform will be formed today in Bakri.
Deklarasi ini disaksikan oleh 118 orang ahli yang hadir pada petang ini. Kepada Allah kita berserah, semoga semua kita dirahmati Allah.	This declaration is witnessed by the 118 delegates who attended the meeting this afternoon. To God we surrender, may we all receive blessings from Him.
Dibentang pada jam 6.45 petang di Dewan Seminar Muar Traders, Muar, Johor. InshaAllah wujud satu parti baru di Malaysia dalam masa terdekat. Amin.	This declaration is presented at 6.45 p.m. at the seminar room at Muar Traders, Muar, Johor. God willing, a new party will be formed in the nearest future. Amen.
Asas kepada pembentukan wadah baru ini adalah: • Memelihara dan menjaga nama baik Islam yang tercalar oleh fitnah kepartian dan politik terdahulu. • Mengambil alih peranan dakwah PAS dan mengembalikan kepercayaan rakyat terutama non-Muslim kepada keindahan Islam sebagai cara hidup seluruh Umat. Mengambil pendekatan Islam Rahmatan lil Alamin. • Menggunapakai kaedah demokrasi yang ada di Malaysia dengan memasuki pilihanraya untuk menang dan mendapat kuasa bagi melaksanakan pemerintahan yang paling hampir menurut Islam serta menghapuskan segala bentuk kezaliman kerajaan yang ada sekarang.	The bases for the formation of this new platform are: • To defend and retain the good name of Islam which has been damaged by prior partisanship and politicization. • To take over PAS' role in spreading Islam (dakwah) and to regain the trust of the people, especially non-Muslims, in the beauty of Islam as a way of life for all. To use the approach of Islam as a blessing to all. • To utilize democratic means in Malaysia by contesting in elections to win and obtain power, with a view to govern using methods that are the nearest to Islam and to abolish all oppression practised by the current regime.

Source: Original slides presented at the meeting in Bakri on 16 June 2015, obtained from Haji Aminolhuda Hassan.

as the key principles that this new party will subscribe to. It also specifically named former PAS Deputy President Mohamad Sabu and former PAS Vice-President Salahuddin Ayub, both of whom lost their party posts following the onslaught at the 2015 PAS party conference, respectively as chairman and deputy chairman of the committee tasked with laying the grounds for the new party.

The decision to form a new party was not immediately announced to the public as they wanted to build the foundations first. That same evening, on the grounds of PAS Bakri Division office, at the event that was supposedly to thank the defeated PAS leaders for their service to the party, it was announced that a new, progressive platform had been established, called Gerakan Harapan Baru (New Hope Movement). Three months later, on 16 September 2015, the group morphed into Amanah, which was officially launched at the Ideal Convention Centre (IDCC) Shah Alam, Selangor. The leadership line-up at the time of the new party's official launch reflected the significance of Johor in the formation of the party. Five of the twenty-seven national leaders were from Johor: Deputy President Salahuddin Ayub, Organizing Secretary Suhaizan Kaiat,[23] as well as central committee members Aminolhuda Hassan, Mazlan Aliman and Hu Pang Chow.[24] At that event, it was also announced that Johor was second only to Kelantan in terms of membership in the new party.

AMANAH'S ORGANIZATIONAL STRUCTURE

Clause 36(a) of Amanah's constitution (Constitution of Parti Amanah Negara, 15 August 2016) states that the party is governed according to the following structure, starting with the layer that has the highest authority:

(a) Annual National Convention or Special National Convention
(b) National Leadership Committee
(c) National Management Committee
(d) Annual State Convention or Special State Convention
(e) State Leadership Committee
(f) State Management Committee
(g) Annual Division Meeting or Special Division Meeting
(h) Division Leadership Committee
(i) Division Management Committee
(j) Annual Branch Meeting or Special Branch Meeting
(k) Branch Leadership Committee
(l) Branch Management Committee.

The party allows full and equal membership to all Malaysians above the age of seventeen, regardless of race or religion. Additionally, the constitution also states that there shall be an Expert Advisory Council at the national level whose role is to make recommendations to the National Leadership Committee. The Council can have up to fifteen members. At the state level, the operations are run by a State Leadership Committee led by a Chair, a Deputy Chair, up to three Vice-Chairs, up to twenty-two committee members, plus other appointees as necessary. All posts are open to Muslims and non-Muslims.

In Johor, the first and current Chair for Johor is Aminolhuda Hassan, who won the Parit Yaani state seat in 2013 when he contested as a PAS candidate. He chairs the Johor's State Leadership Committee. Below the state committee, Amanah follows a structure similar to almost all other Malaysian political parties, where they have divisions (covering a parliamentary constituency) and then branches (as subunits within a division).

AMANAH'S INFRASTRUCTURE IN JOHOR

Amanah now has twenty-six divisions in the state, one each for every parliamentary constituency, and twenty-five of them have regular active programmes run by their respective branches.[25] The only division that is not yet fully active at the time of writing this chapter was Sembrong. Many of the divisions that quickly established their activities were able to do so because the majority of their activists were previously active campaigners from PAS. As explained by the Amanah leaders interviewed for this study, when they crossed over to the party, they brought the infrastructure, manpower, as well as the resources with them, enabling relatively easy and quick mobilization.[26]

Realizing that Johor has a relatively young, urbanized, multiracial and multi-religious voter demographic, Amanah tries to accommodate the different demands from Malays and non-Malays, Muslims and non-Muslims alike. They also want to move beyond the rhetoric around the Islamic state, preferring to focus on real governance issues and solving the day-to-day problems faced by the population regardless of race and religion. To them, this is not merely a necessary political strategy if they want to see a repeat in GE-14 of the massive Chinese voters swing against the ruling BN that took place in GE-13, but it is also a religious obligation.[27] Salahuddin Ayub stated in a speech:[28]

> We are a party that carries the torch of political Islamism such that we want to prove that Islam can be trusted by non-Muslims, and that they can show us that trust by giving us their votes. We recognize all the roles played by the different groups in multiracial Malaysia that includes both Malays and non-Malays. But we are also progressive in that we learn from universal values from outside of Malaysia. For example, we know that the values of good governance, integrity, and accountability are imperative for the success of countries like Norway, Sweden, Denmark, New Zealand, Japan, Korea and Singapore. These countries show Islamic values too and we recognize their success in governance.

While the party is quite clear about the direction they want to take, building a new party proves to be an arduous task. In terms of membership, while Amanah leaders like to talk about their success in attracting key activists from PAS into their fold, the number of lay members is still not very high. The latest estimate puts Amanah membership in Johor at just under 10,000, with less than 200 being non-Muslims.[29]

But the relatively small membership seems not to deter Amanah Johor leaders. They argue that this is a norm for all political parties and what is more important is to have activists and campaigners working across the state. Not all of them need to formally become a member of the party as long as they assist in the campaign.

While they acknowledge that having a larger membership is desirable, they argue that in all previous elections membership numbers do not reflect the number of votes a party gets in elections. On top of votes from non-member supporters, they expect a lot more votes to come from supporters of other Pakatan member parties.[30] This is supported by experience from previous elections. For example, in GE-13, Salahuddin Ayub contested as a PAS candidate in the southern parliamentary constituency of Pulai, against Nur Jazlan Muhamed of UMNO. According to Salahuddin, the PAS division in Pulai at that time had less than 500 active members. Yet he received 40,525 votes, just 3,226 votes short of the 43,751 received by Nur Jazlan. Similarly, current Amanah Johor Information Chief Onn Jaafar contested in the parliamentary constituency of Kota Tinggi which has nine FELDA settlements, indicating that it is an UMNO stronghold. According to Onn, the Kota Tinggi PAS division at that time had less than 100 active members. He however managed to gather 5,799 votes. This is significantly behind the 30,373 votes received by the victorious UMNO candidate but it still proved the point that party membership is not necessarily indicative of votes that can be gained.

Financially Amanah is not well resourced, and it is unable to depend on membership fees because the rate is very low, at just RM5 per person per year. Nevertheless, the presence of former PAS leaders and activists is a boon. PAS grassroots activists are well known for their financial generosity and commitment to the party. When they crossed over to Amanah, they brought that culture with them. They are willing to work for free and to contribute towards paying for party activities as and when necessary.

Amanah benefits from the support of some PAS members and supporters too. For example, this author observed an Amanah public event at Kampung FELDA Air Tawar 1, in the parliamentary constituency of Pengerang, on the eastern coast of Johor. The event took place on the evening of 13 May 2017 on the front lawn of a first-generation FELDA settler who had been a PAS member since the 1970s. When queried why he agreed to host an event by Amanah despite being a member of PAS, he explained that he was not at all troubled by the fact that Amanah is a splinter party from PAS. To him the top priority was to defeat UMNO and he would support any party aiming to do so.[31] Several others who helped with logistical arrangements for the event, when asked, also stated that they were still PAS members. The same sentiment was expressed by PAS supporters interviewed at another PAS event on 10 May 2017, in Kampung Bindu, in the parliamentary constituency of Sri Gading, on the northwest side of Johor. Even though the speakers at that event were emphasizing the importance of staying loyal to PAS, some of the lay members[32] were open to the idea of helping Amanah in their quest to defeat UMNO, even saying that if Amanah were to ask for their help, they would be happy to assist. They expressed disappointment and anger for the defection of Amanah from PAS, but most of them stated that the priority was to defeat UMNO rather than fight Amanah.

Additionally, at the same event in FELDA Air Tawar 1, it was observed that the Pakatan coalition model was effective at the functional level. The organizer, who is also Head of Amanah Pengerang Division, explained[33] that he received generous non-financial support from activists from other Pakatan parties to organize the event. Activists from the UMNO splinter party Parti Pribumi Bersatu Malaysia (PPBM) helped in dealing with FELDA authorities and with logistics, while those from Parti Keadilan Rakyat (PKR) assisted with publicity. During that event, FELDA settlers themselves donated cash to pay for the rental of the audio system and chairs. The event attracted circa 250 people, which is not a bad achievement for an opposition event in a FELDA area in Pengerang where UMNO won more than 80 per cent of the votes in GE-13.

The limited resources means it is uncertain how strong a challenge Amanah can mount against the offers that UMNO and their BN partners will make to voters in the run-up to GE-14. A study on money politics in Malaysian elections has identified four main categories of gifts and patronage common to Malaysian campaigns: "sweets and treats" like T-shirts and other token gifts; cash and subsistence aid to the poor and needy; promises of infrastructure and other projects needed by the community; and financial assistance programmes usually dished out as government initiatives (Weiss 2014, pp. 10–13). At the time of this study, Amanah did not have sufficient resources even to offer the "sweets and treats", let alone the other types of gifts. As a new party working in a coalition that is not yet certain to win either the federal or the state government, Amanah leaders feel it is unlikely that they can match the costlier offers they expect BN to make.[34]

On top of that, PAS is still contesting some of the assets that Amanah claims belong to them. When they crossed over to Amanah, some of the activists took with them assets that were long assumed to belong to PAS. And PAS is now making legal claims on these. Publicly known disputes are ongoing in three parliamentary areas—Bakri, Tenggara and Pontian—revolving around the question of how to divide the assets when the owner of the land joined Amanah but the building on that land was built using PAS resources. When the landowner asked PAS to vacate the land, the ownership of building came into question. In addition, there are also education initiatives, such as the PAS-owned kindergarten PASTI that are operated by those who have now crossed over, that are being challenged by PAS too. The legal battles are ongoing and lawyers from both sides have yet to find a resolution.[35]

In terms of campaign issues, at the time of this study Amanah was still in the process of finalizing their main policy offerings. They have plans to hold state-wide consultations with stakeholders, and they are also holding closed-door discussions in which they invite respected figures to present their thoughts. This author was invited to observe the first of such meetings on 13 May 2017 at Kulai Jaya. The topics covered by the speakers[36] were cost of living and wages, housing, jobs and foreign workers, access to quality education, and environmental damage caused by Johor's many construction projects. Participants were selected representatives from across the state, most of whom were professionals and academics, and some party workers. The party expects to have a set of election promises ready before the general election, but the issues discussed in their first seminar are indicative of the topics they will use in the campaign.

THE ELECTORAL POTENTIAL OF AMANAH IN JOHOR

As can be deduced from Table 11.3, the ethnic composition of voters in the constituencies can have a significant impact on the electoral outcomes. Constituencies with a higher percentage of Malay voters tend to opt for UMNO, and this is generally true at both parliamentary and state levels, with only small exceptions (e.g., the state seats of Tenang, Layang-Layang, and Nusa Jaya, as well as parliamentary seats of Pasir Gudang and Pulai). DAP won thirteen state seats, all in areas where the majority voters are non-Malays. PAS on the other hand won four state seats, all in areas that are highly mixed where Malay voters are less than 55 per cent of the total electorates, and 40 to 50 per cent of the voters are Chinese. In other words, the results of GE-13 show that while seats with a substantial number of Malay voters are likely to be easier for UMNO and BN to win, Pakatan has better chances in mixed seats. The exception to this is PPBM, Pakatan's latest member, as they are targeting Malay-majority seats. However, PPBM is outside of the scope of this chapter and will not be discussed in much depth here.

With that background, it is only logical that Amanah aims for state seats that have a mixed ethnic composition, especially those with circa 30 to 45 per cent Chinese voters, plus all the four PAS seats.[37] If the 2013 electoral boundaries are followed, then there are twenty-four seats that fit these criteria, as listed in Table 11.4. In GE-13, within these twenty-four seats, seventeen were contested by PAS, five by PKR and two by DAP.[38] Based on the criteria stated earlier, it can be expected that Amanah is eyeing all the seventeen seats in this category that were previously contested by PAS.

At the parliamentary level (Table 11.5), out of the twenty-six parliamentary seats, UMNO holds fifteen of the twenty-one BN seats, while on the opposition side DAP holds four and PKR has one. PAS contested eight parliamentary seats in GE-13 but did not win any.[39] In seven of those seats, PAS suffered rather big losses, with a vote deficit ranging from just under 6,000 in Simpang Renggam to almost 25,000 in Kota Tinggi. The exception was Pulai, where the then-PAS candidate Salahuddin Ayub, who is now Deputy President of Amanah, gained 48 per cent of the votes, and was just 3,226 votes shy of winning. With the defeat suffered by PAS before, it is unsurprising that Amanah leaders interviewed in this study are not as excited about their parliamentary chances other than in Pulai. In the bigger scheme of things, much of Amanah's focus is on state seats, not the parliamentary ones.

By remaining strategically focused on state seats, Amanah is optimistic about their chances. They feel that if non-Malays retain their rejection of UMNO, then the overall trend is on their side. It is easier to understand this optimism by looking at the total number of votes collected by BN and non-BN parties in Johor state elections from 1978[40] as shown in Figure 11.2. The overall trend shows that, from 2004 the gap between the total votes obtained by the two sides is narrowing, and the opposition coalition in its various forms is catching up at a faster rate. Between 2004 and 2013, BN was not able to increase its total share of votes by much. If Pakatan can maintain the same momentum, and if the new electoral boundaries do not disrupt the ethnic

TABLE 11.3
Electoral Performance of the Main Political Parties in GE-13 in Johor

State Code	State Name	Total Voters	Malay (%)	Chinese (%)	Indian (%)	Others (%)	BN Candidate	PR Candidate	Winner	Winning Majority	BN or PR	FELDA Area?
N01	Buloh Kasap	18,779	55.0	32.2	11.6	1.2	UMNO	PAS	UMNO	3,370	BN	–
N02	Jementah	28,230	36.3	54.5	8.7	0.6	MCA	DAP	DAP	2,196	PR	–
N03	Pemanis	22,617	56.2	39.3	3.4	1.0	GERAKAN	PAS	GERAKAN	1,329	BN	YES
N04	Kemelah	20,449	54.6	38.6	5.7	1.1	UMNO	PKR	UMNO	2,260	BN	YES
N05	Tenang	16,940	49.4	37.6	11.3	1.7	UMNO	PAS	UMNO	1,586	BN	YES
N06	Bekok	20,774	25.6	53.6	18.0	2.7	MCA	DAP	DAP	1,401	PR	–
N07	Bukit Serampang	21,429	69.9	26.1	2.1	1.9	UMNO	PKR	UMNO	7,845	BN	YES
N08	Jorak	25,364	59.0	34.8	5.4	0.8	UMNO	PAS	UMNO	3,726	BN	–
N09	Gambir	21,382	54.6	39.7	3.8	1.8	MIC	PAS	MIC	310	BN	–
N10	Tangkak	23,394	37.7	51.2	9.7	1.5	MCA	DAP	DAP	1,537	PR	–
N11	Serom	24,540	65.5	32.8	0.9	0.8	UMNO	PAS	UMNO	2,264	BN	–
N12	Bentayan	23,438	24.7	72.6	2.2	0.4	MCA	DAP	DAP	6,847	PR	–
N13	Sungai Abong	28,262	51.0	45.2	3.0	0.8	UMNO	PAS	PAS	3,813	PR	–
N14	Bukit Naning	15,502	58.7	38.4	1.0	1.8	UMNO	PKR	UMNO	1,455	BN	–
N15	Maharani	27,090	54.7	42.0	2.5	0.8	UMNO	PAS	PAS	3,136	PR	–
N16	Sungai Balang	21,118	71.6	26.9	0.2	1.3	UMNO	PAS	UMNO	1,635	BN	–
N17	Semerah	31,046	63.2	33.6	0.6	2.6	UMNO	PKR	UMNO	2,649	BN	–
N18	Sri Medan	25,850	83.0	9.1	0.3	7.6	UMNO	PAS	UMNO	9,430	BN	–
N19	Yong Peng	22,484	31.8	60.4	6.8	1.0	MCA	DAP	DAP	2,475	PR	–
N20	Semarang	20,429	82.2	13.3	0.8	3.7	UMNO	PAS	UMNO	8,075	BN	–
N21	Parit Yaani	24,609	54.0	43.1	1.1	1.9	MCA	PAS	PAS	1,188	PR	–
N22	Parit Raja	20,207	73.1	22.2	1.8	3.0	UMNO	PAS	UMNO	3,956	BN	–
N23	Penggaram	45,157	35.2	61.5	2.3	1.1	MCA	DAP	DAP	10,051	PR	–
N24	Senggarang	24,048	60.5	37.4	0.5	1.6	UMNO	PAS	UMNO	1,855	BN	–
N25	Rengit	19,067	79.1	18.3	0.3	2.4	UMNO	PAS	UMNO	5,492	BN	–
N26	Machap	22,221	62.4	31.7	5.0	0.9	UMNO	PAS	UMNO	3,902	BN	YES
N27	Layang-Layang	17,922	49.0	34.9	14.7	1.5	UMNO	PKR	UMNO	2,518	BN	YES
N28	Mengkibol	42,380	27.3	58.3	13.8	0.6	MCA	DAP	DAP	10,001	PR	–
N29	Mahkota	44,352	50.5	40.6	5.9	3.0	UMNO	PAS	UMNO	1,108	BN	–

continued on next page

TABLE 11.3— cont'd

State Code	State Name	Total Voters	Malay (%)	Chinese (%)	Indian (%)	Others (%)	BN Candidate	PR Candidate	Winner	Winning Majority	BN or PR	FELDA Area?
N30	Paloh	18,222	37.3	43.6	17.1	2.0	MCA	DAP	MCA	103	BN	–
N31	Kahang	23,366	73.6	21.0	2.6	2.9	MIC	PKR	MIC	7,801	BN	YES
N32	Endau	19,040	76.0	18.9	0.7	4.4	UMNO	PAS	UMNO	3,110	BN	YES
N33	Tenggaroh	25,457	80.2	13.4	1.7	4.7	MIC	PKR	MIC	13,014	BN	YES
N34	Panti	17,358	85.9	7.2	4.0	2.9	UMNO	PAS	UMNO	10,270	BN	YES
N35	Pasir Raja	22,336	61.1	25.5	9.2	4.2	UMNO	PAS	UMNO	6,666	BN	YES
N36	Sedili	24,716	95.5	2.1	0.8	1.6	UMNO	PKR	UMNO	18,127	BN	–
N37	Johor Lama	17,178	72.1	22.7	3.9	1.2	UMNO	PAS	UMNO	7,022	BN	YES
N38	Penawar	19,881	97.0	0.3	0.8	1.9	UMNO	PAS	UMNO	12,818	BN	–
N39	Tanjong Surat	18,118	76.7	20.7	0.9	1.6	UMNO	PKR	UMNO	9,035	BN	–
N40	Tiram	46,658	53.2	29.7	14.5	2.6	UMNO	PAS	UMNO	7,443	BN	–
N41	Puteri Wangsa	43,824	39.6	47.2	11.7	1.4	MIC	PAS	PAS	3,469	PR	YES
N42	Johor Jaya	51,648	42.8	47.1	7.5	2.7	MCA	DAP	DAP	1,460	PR	–
N43	Permas	49,393	51.6	29.4	14.7	4.2	UMNO	PAS	UMNO	5,752	BN	–
N44	Tanjong Puteri	51,442	61.3	31.6	5.3	1.7	UMNO	PKR	UMNO	9,097	BN	–
N45	Stulang	44,879	38.7	55.1	4.5	1.7	MCA	DAP	DAP	3,296	PR	–
N46	Pengkalan Rinting	61,217	42.5	44.7	10.6	2.1	MCA	DAP	DAP	1,970	PR	–
N47	Kempas	39,273	54.2	35.2	8.9	1.7	UMNO	PAS	UMNO	3,947	BN	–
N48	Skudai	56,543	21.8	64.9	12.2	1.1	MCA	DAP	DAP	18,050	PR	–
N49	Nusa Jaya	50,183	47.0	38.4	12.7	2.0	UMNO	PAS	UMNO	2,201	BN	–
N50	Bukit Permai	21,619	52.4	33.9	11.9	1.7	UMNO	PAS	UMNO	3,369	BN	YES
N51	Bukit Batu	22,262	30.4	61.6	7.2	0.8	UMNO	PKR	PKR	4,015	PR	YES
N52	Senai	40,110	22.9	65.0	11.0	1.1	MCA	DAP	DAP	11,227	PR	–
N53	Benut	21,463	77.7	18.3	0.2	3.9	UMNO	PAS	UMNO	6,572	BN	–
N54	Pulai Sebatang	28,170	61.8	34.5	1.4	2.2	MCA	PAS	MCA	3,412	BN	–
N55	Pekan Nanas	32,486	39.3	57.8	1.2	1.7	MCA	DAP	DAP	2,669	PR	–
N56	Kukup	19,389	69.0	27.6	0.8	2.6	UMNO	PAS	UMNO	6,946	BN	–

Source: General elections data obtained from Dr Ong Kian Ming, Member of Parliament for Serdang.

TABLE 11.4

State Seats That Can Be Targeted by Amanah in GE-14, Arranged According to Percentage of Chinese Voters

State Code	State Name	Total Voters	Malay (%)	Chinese (%)	BN Candidate in GE-13	PR Candidate in GE-13	Winner in GE-13	Winning Majority
N44	Tanjong Puteri	51,442	61.3	31.6	UMNO	PKR	UMNO	9,097
N26	Machap	22,221	62.4	31.7	UMNO	PAS	UMNO	3,902
N01	Buloh Kasap	18,779	55.0	32.2	UMNO	PAS	UMNO	3,370
N11	Serom	24,540	65.5	32.8	UMNO	PAS	UMNO	2,264
N17	Semerah	31,046	63.2	33.6	UMNO	PKR	UMNO	2,649
N50	Bukit Permai	21,619	52.4	33.9	UMNO	PAS	UMNO	3,369
N54	Pulai Sebatang	28,170	61.8	34.5	MCA	PAS	MCA	3,412
N08	Jorak	25,364	59.0	34.8	UMNO	PAS	UMNO	3,726
N27	Layang-Layang	17,922	49.0	34.9	UMNO	PKR	UMNO	2,518
N47	Kempas	39,273	54.2	35.2	UMNO	PAS	UMNO	3,947
N24	Senggarang	24,048	60.5	37.4	UMNO	PAS	UMNO	1,855
N05	Tenang	16,940	49.4	37.6	UMNO	PAS	UMNO	1,586
N49	Nusa Jaya	50,183	47.0	38.4	UMNO	PAS	UMNO	2,201
N14	Bukit Naning	15,502	58.7	38.4	UMNO	PKR	UMNO	1,455
N04	Kemelah	20,449	54.6	38.6	UMNO	PKR	UMNO	2,260
N03	Pemanis	22,617	56.2	39.3	GERAKAN	PAS	GERAKAN	1,329
N09	Gambir	21,382	54.6	39.7	MIC	PAS	MIC	310
N29	Mahkota	44,352	50.5	40.6	UMNO	PAS	UMNO	1,108
N15	Maharani	27,090	54.7	42.0	UMNO	PAS	PAS	3,136
N21	Parit Yaani	24,609	54.0	43.1	MCA	PAS	PAS	1,188
N30	Paloh	18,222	37.3	43.6	MCA	DAP	MCA	103
N46	Pengkalan Rinting	61,217	42.5	44.7	MCA	DAP	DAP	1,970
N13	Sungai Abong	28,262	51.0	45.2	UMNO	PAS	PAS	3,813
N41	Puteri Wangsa	43,824	39.6	47.2	MIC	PAS	PAS	3,469

Note: Highlighted are seats won by PAS in 2013.
Source: General elections data obtained from Dr Ong Kian Ming, Member of Parliament for Serdang.

TABLE 11.5
Electoral Performance of the Main Political Parties in GE-13 at Parliamentary Level

Parliament Code	Parliament Name	Total Voters	Malay (%)	Chinese (%)	Indian (%)	Others (%)	BN Candidate	PR Candidate	Winner	Winning Majority	BN or PR
P140	Segamat	47,009	43.8	45.6	9.8	0.8	MIC	PKR	MIC	1,217	BN
P141	Sekijang	43,066	55.5	39.0	4.5	1.0	UMNO	PKR	UMNO	3,007	BN
P142	Labis	37,714	36.3	46.5	15.0	2.2	MCA	DAP	MCA	353	BN
P143	Pagoh	46,793	64.0	30.8	3.9	1.3	UMNO	PAS	UMNO	12,842	BN
P144	Ledang	69,316	52.8	41.1	4.8	1.4	UMNO	PKR	UMNO	1,967	BN
P145	Bakri	67,202	43.6	53.2	2.3	0.9	MCA	DAP	DAP	5,067	PR
P146	Muar	48,208	62.1	35.4	1.5	1.0	UMNO	PKR	UMNO	1,646	BN
P147	Parit Sulong	56,896	72.2	22.5	0.4	4.9	UMNO	PAS	UMNO	11,753	BN
P148	Ayer Hitam	42,913	55.8	38.0	3.9	2.3	UMNO	PAS	UMNO	7,310	BN
P149	Sri Gading	44,816	62.6	33.6	1.4	2.4	UMNO	PKR	UMNO	5,761	BN
P150	Batu Pahat	88,272	51.5	45.6	1.4	1.5	UMNO	PKR	PKR	1,524	PR
P151	Simpang Renggam	40,143	56.4	33.1	9.3	1.2	GER	PAS	GERAKAN	5,706	BN
P152	Kluang	86,732	39.1	49.3	9.7	1.8	MCA	DAP	DAP	7,359	PR
P153	Sembrong	41,588	57.7	30.9	8.9	2.5	UMNO	PKR	UMNO	10,631	BN
P154	Mersing	44,497	78.4	15.8	1.3	4.5	UMNO	PAS	UMNO	15,747	BN
P155	Tenggara	39,694	72.0	17.5	6.9	3.6	UMNO	PAS	UMNO	17,196	BN
P156	Kota Tinggi	41,894	85.9	10.5	2.1	1.5	UMNO	PAS	UMNO	24,574	BN
P157	Pengerang	37,999	87.4	10.1	0.9	1.7	UMNO	PKR	UMNO	22,508	BN
P158	Tebrau	90,482	46.6	38.2	13.2	2.0	MCA	PKR	MCA	1,767	BN
P159	Pasir Gudang	101,041	47.1	38.4	11.0	3.5	UMNO	PKR	UMNO	935	BN
P160	Johor Bahru	96,321	50.8	42.6	4.9	1.7	UMNO	PKR	UMNO	10,495	BN
P161	Pulai	100,490	47.1	41.0	9.9	2.0	UMNO	PAS	UMNO	3,226	BN
P162	Gelang Patah	106,726	33.7	52.4	12.4	1.5	UMNO	DAP	DAP	14,762	PR
P163	Kulai	83,991	32.5	56.1	10.2	1.2	MCA	DAP	DAP	13,450	PR
P164	Pontian	49,633	68.7	27.5	0.9	3.0	UMNO	PKR	UMNO	13,727	BN
P165	Tanjong Piai	51,875	50.4	46.5	1.1	2.0	MCA	DAP	MCA	5,457	BN

Source: General elections data obtained from Dr Ong Kian Ming, Member of Parliament for Serdang.

FIGURE 11.2
Total Share of Votes at State Level, 1978–2013

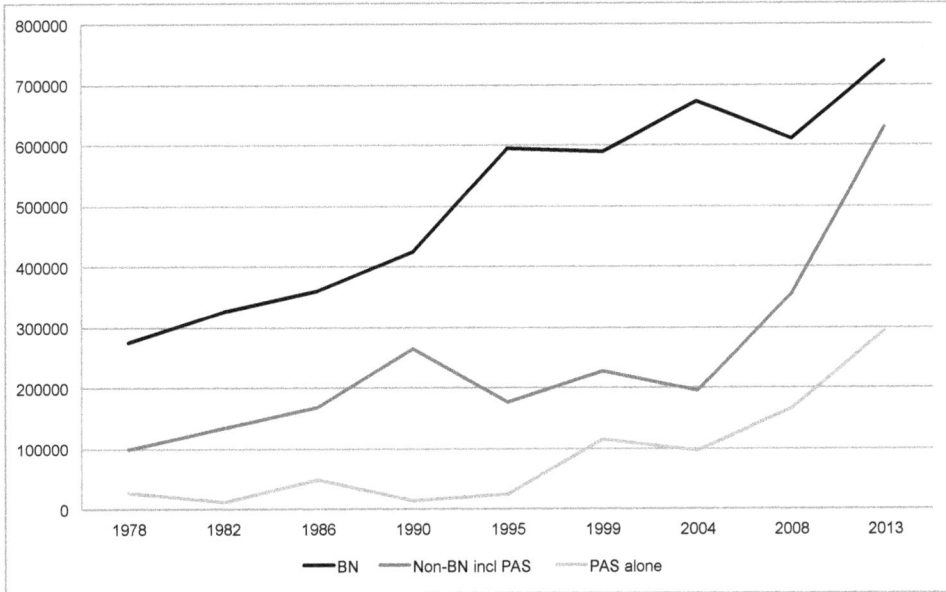

Source: General elections data obtained from Dr Ong Kian Ming, Member of Parliament for Serdang.

composition too significantly, the opposition parties are on a trajectory that will see it posing a real threat to UMNO in Johor.

No discussion about Johor is complete without touching on the issue of seats in FELDA settlements. As marked in Table 11.3, there are fifteen Johor state seats that have at least one FELDA settlement. Even though the voting patterns in FELDA areas have become less predictable due to improvements in the socioeconomic situation of the settlers, generally FELDA seats remain BN strongholds, especially for UMNO (Khor 2016; Saravanamuttu, Lee and Mohamed Nawab 2015). In GE-13, PAS won the seat of N41 Puteri Wangsa and PKR won N51 Bukit Batu. In Puteri Wangsa, 47 per cent of the voters are Chinese while 40 per cent are Malay. In Bukit Batu 62 per cent of the voters are Chinese and only 30 per cent are Malay. Thus, these two are anomalies because, despite the presence of FELDA settlements, Malay voters are still in the minority. The other thirteen FELDA seats have between 49 per cent to 86 per cent Malay voters and they were all won by BN, with UMNO winning ten of them. The trend confirms that in areas where Malay voters form the majority, BN and UMNO have the upper hand. Pakatan, on the other hand, has a better chance in mixed seats that have a high number of Chinese voters. Amanah's desire to contest in mixed seats with circa 30 to 45 per cent Chinese voters fits well into this pattern. The seats with a higher percentage of Malay voters seem more suitable for a Malay party like PPBM to contest in.

A major challenge for Amanah, and for Pakatan as a whole, is actually from PAS. Even if a large portion of non-Malay voters remains with Pakatan, the coalition will still need Malay votes to win. Even though some lay PAS members may assist Amanah in their quest to defeat UMNO, this attitude is not unanimous and many are still loyal to PAS regardless of the party's attitude to UMNO. If PAS goes ahead with its intention to field candidates in more than 40 state seats and eight parliamentary seats (*The Star*, 16 April 2017), Amanah and Pakatan as a whole will be affected because the Malay votes will be split. In the eighteen state seats won by DAP, PAS and PKR in GE-13 (see Table 11.4), five[41] were won with a majority of less than 2,000 votes, and another eight[42] with a majority of between 2,000 and about 4,000 votes. These thirteen are relatively high-risk seats. Three-cornered fights in these seats between BN, Pakatan and PAS will most likely result in a BN victory because PAS can pull away some of the Malay votes from Pakatan. Interestingly, the BN party that may benefit from PAS' presence in these seats is the Malaysian Chinese Association (MCA). Issues such as voter turnout and the willingness of Chinese voters to vote for the BN again will be important factors.[43] But within the thirteen seats, nine[44] are currently held by DAP and they could go to the MCA if PAS' presence reduces the level of Malay support to the DAP. Thus, PAS may inadvertently be giving a lifeline to the ailing Chinese party, at least in some of those seats.

Therefore, in the areas targeted by Amanah, the fate of both Amanah and Pakatan is quite dependent on whether an arrangement can be made with PAS. If PAS still refuses to enter into an agreement, and assuming that non-Malays continue to not vote for BN, the only option for Amanah is to work hard to capture Malay votes to such an extent that they can win even if there is a three-cornered fight. Looking at the way PAS and Amanah behave towards each other currently, reaching an arrangement before GE-14 is a very tall order. Amanah is therefore preparing for three-cornered fights against both BN and PAS, and their focus is two-pronged: to safeguard non-Malay support and to carve away a bigger share of Malay support from PAS and UMNO.[45]

One other factor raised by the Amanah leaders interviewed for this study is the role of PPBM. For Amanah, PPBM is a valuable partner that can reduce UMNO's grip on Malays in rural areas. Thus, Amanah feels that PPBM should be given a respectable number of seats in Malay majority areas, especially in FELDA seats, as they have a better chance of winning there. Amanah is also open to the possibility of PPBM being at the forefront of the campaign. The key consideration for Amanah is not whether they or PPBM gets more seats, but to ensure that both they and PPBM—i.e., the Malay parties—contest more seats than the DAP. This is to prevent UMNO claiming that the DAP would be the dominant party if Pakatan won the state. This concern comes at the back of UMNO's persistent allegation that the DAP has a hidden agenda to eradicate Malay political power. This propaganda seems to have worked among conservative Malay voters including in Johor. Amanah leaders are aware that this could be Pakatan's Achilles heel if not tackled strategically. Thus, even though seventeen seats or more would be ideal, they are willing to lower their demand to around fifteen seats, which is still more than DAP's allocation of fourteen seats, so as to accommodate PPBM's demands if necessary.[46]

IMPLICATIONS FOR PAS

Historically, PAS has always been small in Johor. When Malaya held its first general election in 1955, PAS did not have enough support or resources to field even one candidate in Johor. The party soldiered on to enlarge its support base and eventually fielded three parliamentary candidates and nine state legislative assembly candidates in the 1959 general elections. Every single one lost badly, and the cumulative number of votes they received was not even 3 per cent of the total votes cast.[47]

PAS Johor's electoral performance shows negligible improvements over the successive four decades of elections. Until 2004 none of their candidates won, and their share of votes showed no significant increase compared to previous years (Figure 11.2). The first ever victory was in 2004, when PAS' candidate Mohamad Ramli Mad Kari won unopposed after the nomination paper for his UMNO opponent was rejected due to technicalities. If not due to this technicality, arguably Mohamad Ramli would have almost no chance to win the contest because PAS' influence throughout the state was still very low, as shown by the fact they lost in all the other seats that they contested in. A breakthrough was achieved in 2008 when PAS managed to win two state seats in Sungai Abong and Maharani in a fiercely fought election. These two early victories inspired PAS activists, and they continued to campaign hard in Johor even when it was not election season. The hard work paid off when in GE-13, as stated earlier in this chapter, they won four state seats. And in twelve of the seats that they lost, the majority was less than 3,500 votes.

However, all the achievements between 2004 and GE-13 occurred when PAS worked within a wider coalition of opposition parties. Even the two seats that they won in 2008 were only possible because PAS was in a wider pact with other opposition parties at that time and they benefited from a surge in Chinese support. In 2013, again, increased support was seen in mainly mixed seats where ethnic Chinese form between 40 to 50 per cent of the electorate. The four seats PAS won that year all fall under this category, and Figure 11.2 shows there was a spike in the numbers of total votes received by the party in 2008 and 2013 in line with the rising popularity of Pakatan. However, in constituencies that have a large Malay population, PAS lost to UMNO with a relatively large majority (Table 11.3). These imply that the new votes came from non-Malays who were very likely to have voted for PAS because they were in a pact with others like DAP and PKR, and not from a real increase in PAS' own support base. PAS is weak in Johor and their actual strength, if they were to stand alone, is highly questionable.

One factor that limits PAS' growth in Johor is the fact that the state authorities hold a tight grip on all matters pertaining to Islamic administration. There are 578 Islamic schools in the state, and all of them are administered and funded directly by the state government (Azlina Othman 2017). There are no major independent *madrasah, tahfiz* or *pondok* schools in the state. These types of education institutions are important recruitment grounds for PAS in other states in Malaysia, but in Johor, they are controlled by the state government. The state religious authority also tightly regulates and controls the religious teachers who are allowed to speak at mosques in the state. Those who speak without an official permit issued by the state will face legal prosecution and even those who do have the permit may see it revoked if they give speeches that are perceived to be political in nature.[48] PAS does not have much room to manoeuvre, and this is likely to remain a major challenge. There are no signs that the authorities in Johor will be relaxing their grip on Islamic matters any time soon.

The departure of many of their most active members and leaders to Amanah since 2015 has hit PAS badly. Speaking at the party's 2016 annual conference in Kelantan, a delegate representing Johor declared that 80 per cent of the state's more active members have left, especially from among those who are better educated.[49] It is not possible to ascertain the accuracy of this claim but the speech does reflect how dejected the remaining PAS state leaders felt at that time.

Since PAS is no longer in the formal opposition pact, it is unlikely that they will continue to enjoy the same level of support from the non-Malays, especially the Chinese. Amanah has taken over PAS' position in the opposition coalition, inheriting that support. PAS is thus left in a quandary because their entry into the electoral contest would create a three-cornered fight between BN, Pakatan, and PAS, which will likely split the Malay non-BN votes to BN's advantage. As stated earlier, in Johor the BN party most likely to benefit from PAS' refusal to work with Pakatan is MCA.

PAS Johor is also adversely affected by the actions of their national leaders, especially their President Abdul Hadi Awang. All the lay members of PAS interviewed for this study mentioned[50] that Abdul Hadi's friendliness with UMNO is a thorny issue for them because for decades they have complained of discrimination resulting from alleged UMNO policies and practices. For them, working with UMNO or doing anything that will help that party win is simply unfathomable. If PAS at the federal level were to forge a partnership with UMNO, or become too close to UMNO, many more may leave the party.[51]

Nevertheless, the current PAS leadership in Johor insist that the party will eventually emerge from this trial stronger than before. To understand this confidence, it is important to firstly appreciate the nature of PAS. While many observers have focused on PAS as an Islamist political party, PAS sees itself primarily as an Islamic movement. For PAS, their actual roles are divided into three: propagating Islam (*dakwah*), educating members (*tarbiyah*) and taking part in politics (*siyasah*).[52] Hence being a political party is only one-third of their activities and it should not be prioritized over and above the other two. Winning elections is not their end game. Their ultimate aim is to obtain God's blessings in the hereafter, and this is obtained by the work done to win, and their attitude after the win, not the win itself (Safina Ramli 2017). This concept is not easily grasped by those analysing the party through a purely secular lens. To PAS, even though the splintering of the party is a problem that must be tackled organizationally, it is also God's way of removing, or "cleansing", insincere actors from their movement and therefore it is a positive process despite its potential negative electoral consequences.[53] When PAS leaders declare that the formation of Amanah is a cleansing process, they are stating a key component of their belief system and they hold strongly to the idea that the exodus is God's way of helping them strengthen the party by ensuring that only the committed ones remain.[54]

Be that as it may, in the immediate term and from the electoral context, it is very likely that PAS Johor will be the biggest loser if they decide to go ahead with its plans to contest in forty state seats and eight parliamentary seats without working with any other party. Of course, PAS has the option of working with UMNO. But while a partnership with UMNO may be rewarding in other states, the party in Johor will suffer. They will not just lose the seats they have today because there is no reason for UMNO Johor to give way to them when they have never been strong in the state, but they are likely to continue losing members, supporters and trust from Pakatan supporters too.

APPENDIX 11.1

Slides Presented by Aminolhuda Hassan at the Meeting in Bakri on 16 July 2015, Which Culminated with the Bakri Declaration.

PAS MENUJU PERUBAHAN

16 JUN 2015
HOTEL MUAR TRADERS
BAKRI, JOHOR

ALUAN TUAN HJ AMINOL HUDA HASSAN

o **AGENDA**

1. **STAND JOHOR**

   TERUS ISTIQAMAH BERSAMA PAS DENGAN ORGANISASI TERATUR

   ATAU

   SEBAHAGIAN BERSAMA PARTI BARU DAN SEBAHAGIAN KEKAL BERSAMA PAS MENGIKUT STRATEGI-STRATEGI TERTENTU

ORGANISASI BAYANGAN

JAWATAN	PENYANDANG
AMIR	TN HJ AMINOL HUDA HASSAN
TIMB AMIR 1	TN HJ DZULKIFLI AHMAD
TIMB AMIR 2	TN MAZLAN ALIMAN
TIMB AMIR 3	TN SUHAIZAN KAYAT
SETIAUSAHA	TN HJ KHAIRUDDIN A. RAHIM
KETUA PEMUDA	TN FAIZUL SALLEH
KETUA MUSLIMAT	PN NORHAYATI BACHOK
KETUA ULAMA'	USTAZ ZULHELMI MOHD ROHANI
PENOLONG SETIAUSAHA 1	TN MAHADHIR MAT ZILI
PENOLONG SETIAUSAHA 2	TN MOHAMMAD NAJIB DAUD
BENDAHARI	TN FIRDAUS MASOD
KETUA PENERANGAN	TN ONN JAAFAR
PENGARAH PILIHAN RAYA	TN HAMID JAMAH
PENGARAH STRATEGIK	TN ISHAK MD SALLEH
PENGARAH WAR ROOM	YM UNGKU MD NOOR U. MAHMOD

JAWATAN	PENYANDANG
AHLI JAWATAN KUASA	DR SHEIKH IBRAHIM SALLEH
AHLI JAWATAN KUASA	TN HJ HISYAM MD ZIN
AHLI JAWATAN KUASA	TN HJ MOHZIT MOHID
AHLI JAWATAN KUASA	TN ZAKI ABD KADIR
AHLI JAWATAN KUASA	TN NORKHALIM SAKIB
AHLI JAWATAN KUASA	TN SYED OTHMAN ABDULLAH
AHLI JAWATAN KUASA	TN HJ MUSTAPHA ABD RAHMAN
AHLI JAWATAN KUASA	TN HJ GHAZALEY AYUIB
AHLI JAWATAN KUASA	USTAZ BAHARUN RASYID
AHLI JAWATAN KUASA	TN NAJIB ASSADOK
AHLI JAWATAN KUASA	USTAZ RUHAIZAM ABD HAMID
AHLI JAWATAN KUASA	PN NORHAYATI BIDIN
AHLI JAWATAN KUASA	CIK ANIS AFIDA AZLI

KETUA KAWASAN

KAWASAN	PENYANDANG
SEGAMAT	TN HASBI NORDIN
SEKIJANG	TN HJ KHALID KAMIRAN
LABIS	TN HJ MD ZIN
PAGOH	TN ISA ABD KARIM
LEDANG	
BAKRI	DR SHEIKH IBRAHIM SALLEH
MUAR	TN HJ MALIK MD DIAH
PARIT SULONG	TN HJ KHAIRUDDIN A RAHIM
AYER HITAM	TN JAHID
SRI GADING	TN HJ SALLEH ABD SAMAD
BATU PAHAT	IMAM KAILANI KOSNIN
SIMPANG RENGGAM	USTAZ RUHAIZAM ABD HAMID
KLUANG	TN MD SAID JONIT

KAWASAN	PENYANDANG
SEMBRONG	TN ZUHAN MD ZIN
MERSING	USTAZ AZAM RAZAK
TENGGARA	TN HJ MOHZIT MOHID
KOTA TINGGI	TN HJ KAMALDIN
PENGERANG	TN SYAWALUDIN
TEBRAU	PN NORHAYATI BIDIN
PASIR GUDANG	TN SYED OTHMAN ABDULLAH
JOHOR BAHRU	TN HJ HUSIN SAMEON
PULAI	TN SUHAIZAN KAYAT
GELANG PATAH	TN HJ DZULKIFLI AHMAD
KULAI	TN HJ HISYAM MD ZIN
PONTIAN	DR MUMAZAINI
TANJONG PIAI	USTAZ AHMAD SANI KEMAT

Q & A

PERBINCANGAAN HINGGA JAYA

DEKLARASI BAKRI 16 JUN 2015
MUAR TRADERS JAM 5.00 PETANG

○ JAWATAN KUASA BERTINDAK DI BENTUK

DI PERINGKAT PUSAT HARI INI DENGAN DI KETUAI YANG BERBAHAGIA TUAN HAJI MOHAMAD BIN SABU SEBAGAI PENGERUSI DAN TUAN HJ SALAHUDDIN AYUB SEBAGAI TIMBALAN

○ WADAH BARU DI BENTUK MELIBATKAN KEBANGKITAN RAKYAT, NGO DAN PERTUBUHAN MASYARAKAT DENGAN SEGERA. PEMBENTUKAN JAWATAN KUASA BAGI WADAH BARU INI AKAN DI BENTUK HARI INI JUGA DI BAKRI

○ DEKLARASI INI DISAKSIKAN OLEH 118 ORANG AHLI YANG HADIR PADA PETANG INI. KEPADA ALLAH KITA BERSERAH, SEMOGA SEMUA KITA DIRAHMATI ALLAH

○ DI BENTANG PADA JAM 6.45 PETANG DI DEWAN SEMINAR MUAR TRADERS, MUAR JOHOR. IN SHA ALLAH WUJUD SATU PARTI BARU DI MALAYSIA DALAM MASA TERDEKAT. AMIN

ASAS KEPADA PEMBENTUKAN WADAH
BARU INI ADALAH :

○ Memelihara dan Menjaga nama baik Islam yang tercalar
oleh Fitnah kepartian dan politik terdahulu.

○ Mengambil alih peranan dakwah Pas dan Mengembalikan
kepercayaan rakyat terutama Non Muslim kepada
keindahan Islam sebagai cara hidup seluruh Umat.
Mengambil pendekatan Islam Rahmatan Lil Alamin.

○ Menggunapakai kaedah demokrasi yang ada di Malaysia
dengan memasuki Pilihan Raya untuk menang dan
mendapat kuasa bagi melaksanakan pemerintahan yang
paling hampir menurut Islam serta menghapuskan segala
bentuk kezaliman kerajaan yang ada sekarang

Notes

1. This chapter was previously published as *Parti Amanah Negara in Johor: Birth, Challenges and Prospects*, Trends in Southeast Asia, no. 9/2017 (Singapore: ISEAS – Yusof Ishak Institute, 2017).
2. In English: National Trust Party.
3. A lengthier treatment is available in 2017 essay by this author namely, "Evolution of Islamism in Malaysian Politics: The Splintering of the Islamic Party of Malaysia and the Spread of Progressive Ideas".
4. Factionalism is a widely studied topic in the analysis of political parties. Instructive work on the topic includes those produced by Francoise Boucek, especially her 2009 essay "Rethinking Factionalism: Typologies, Intra-Party Dynamics and Three Faces of Factionalism" (*Party Politics* 15, no. 4, pp. 455–85), which provides a good summary of major works in this area.
5. Interview with Mujahid Yusof, Vice-President of Amanah, 16 April 2017. See also Mujahid Yusof, *Menuju PAS Baru: Krisis, Peluang dan Dinamisme*, 2nd ed. (Kuala Lumpur: The Malaysian Insider, 2011).
6. See, for example, the speech by PAS President Abdul Hadi Awang in parliament on 6 April 2017, http://bit.ly/bukan-islam-menganggu
7. The Malaysian Federal Constitution makes a legal link between being a Malay and a Muslim by defining a Malay, among others, as "a person who professes the religion of Islam …" (Article 160).
8. Interview with Dr Dzulkefly Ahmad, current Director of Strategy for Amanah, 16 April 2017.
9. Email conversation with Dr Muhammad Takiyuddin Ismail, 21 May 2017. For a further discussion on neoconservatism in Malay politics, see Muhammad Takiyuddin Ismail, *Saga Neokonservatif: Abdullah Badawi, UMNO dan Konservatisme* (Bangi: UKM Press, 2014). Nevertheless, the term "progressives" will be used to refer to this group. Introducing a new terminology at this stage will create a different debate altogether and that is not the purpose of this chapter.
10. "*Reformasi* era" is the oft-used label for the period following the sacking of Anwar Ibrahim from the post of Deputy Prime Minister and Deputy President of UMNO, and his subsequent imprisonment. The actions against Anwar sparked a mass movement calling for change, and many Islamists who were active in civil society organizations at that time chose to join PAS to pursue their campaign.
11. Partnering with other parties has been a long-standing strategy for PAS. In the past, they had formed coalitions with various opposition parties, and they had also joined the ruling BN.
12. Interview with Dr Dzulkefly Ahmad.
13. Interview with Mujahid Yusof.
14. PAS' internal party election takes place every two years at their annual conference or Muktamar.
15. The conservatives in PAS publicly called the routing of the progressives in 2015 as a "cleansing" process. See, for example, the statement by PAS President Abdul Hadi Awang on 13 August 2015, http://www.mstar.com.my/berita/berita-semasa/2015/08/13/tindakan-keluar-parti-pembersihan-pas/ (accessed 29 March 2017).
16. Pakatan Rakyat consisted of PAS, DAP and PKR and it dissolved in 2015. Its successor was formed in 2017, using the name Pakatan Harapan, consisting of DAP, PKR, Amanah

and Parti Pribumi Bersatu Malaysia. In this chapter, the word "Pakatan" is used to refer to the opposition's formal coalition in both forms, and should be taken to mean Pakatan Rakyat prior to its dissolution, and Pakatan Harapan after that.

17. Interview with Salahuddin Ayub, former PAS Vice President and current Amanah Deputy President, 16 April 2017.
18. Presentation by Maszlee Malik entitled "The Democrat Muslim: Rashid Ghannouchi and His Influence on Malaysia's Parti Amanah Negara", at a seminar organized by the ISEAS – Yusof Ishak Institute, Singapore, 14 October 2016, https://www.iseas.edu.sg/events/past-events/item/4069-seminar-the-democrat-muslim-rashid-ghannouchi-and-his-influence-on-malaysias-parti-amanah-negara
19. Federal Land Development Authority (FELDA), a federal statutory body tasked with resettling poor Malays into new areas. The significance of FELDA areas will be discussed later in this chapter.
20. Interview with Mazlan Aliman, 25 July 2017.
21. Interview with Haji Mohd Ashaari Sidon, Head of PAS Sri Gading Division, 11 May 2017. One of the said meetings was hosted in his house just prior to the 2015 party conference, and he objected to the idea mooted by Aminolhuda Hassan.
22. The name of this event was proposed by Mazlan Aliman.
23. Suhaizan Kayat was Head of PAS Youth, 2013–15.
24. Hu Pang Chow was the first Head of PAS' non-Muslim wing, the Dewan Himpunan Penyokong PAS (DHPP). In 2013, he became PAS' first ever non-Muslim parliamentary candidate, contesting against Wee Ka Siong from the Malaysian Chinese Association (MCA), in Ayer Hitam, Johor. Hu lost by 7,310 votes.
25. Interview with Aminolhuda Hassan, Amanah Johor State Chairman, 29 May 2017.
26. Interviews with Noh Sitam, Ayub Sheraman, Abdul Hamid Ahmad, and Abdullah Sani, all committee members of Amanah Kota Tinggi Division, 11 May 2017, and Head of Amanah Pengerang Division Sawaluddin Saleh, 12 May 2017.
27. Interview with Dr Dzulkefly Ahmad; and Amanah Johor State Chairman Aminolhuda Hassan, 10 May 2017.
28. Speech delivered at the ISEAS – Yusof Ishak Institute, 9 May 2017. Reproduced with permission.
29. Interview with Aminolhuda Hassan.
30. Interviews with Salahuddin Ayub, Aminolhuda Hassan, and Onn Jaafar, Amanah Johor Information Chief, 10 May 2017.
31. Interview with a FELDA settler during the event. The settler requested to remain anonymous.
32. Interview with six attendees of the event, all claiming to be members of PAS, and requested anonymity.
33. Interview with Sawaludin Saleh, Head of Amanah Pengerang Division, 14 May 2017.
34. Interviews with Salahuddin Ayub, Aminolhuda Hassan, and Onn Jaafar, Amanah Johor Information Chief, 10 May 2017.
35. Interviews with Aminolhuda Hassan, and Juwahir Amin, PAS Johor Youth Chief, 14 May 2017.
36. Names are not disclosed here upon request by the organizer.
37. Interview with Aminolhuda Hassan.
38. In GE-13, PAS contested thirty-one state seats, DAP fourteen, and PKR eleven in Johor.
39. P143 Pagoh, P147 Parit Sulong, P148 Ayer Hitam, P151 Simpang Renggam, P154 Mersing, P155 Tenggara, P156 Kota Tinggi, P161 Pulai.

40. The 1978 general election is chosen as the starting point here because that was the year PAS withdrew from the BN ruling coalition and contested as an opposition party.
41. N06 Bekok, N10 Tangkak, N21 Parit Yaani, N42 Johor Jaya, N46 Pengkalan Rinting.
42. N02 Jementah, N13 Sungai Abong, N15 Maharani, N19 Yong Peng, N41 Puteri Wangsa, N45 Stulang, N51 Bukit Batu, N55 Pekan Nanas.
43. Interview with Gan Ping Sieu, former Vice President of the MCA and former state legislative assembly member (2004 to 2008) for Mengkibol, Johor.
44. N02 Jementah, N06 Bekok, N10 Tangkak, N12 Bentayan, N19 Yong Peng, N42 Johor Jaya, N45 Stulang, N46 Pengkalan Rinting, N55 Pekan Nanas.
45. Interview with Aminolhuda Hassan.
46. Interviews with Aminolhuda Hassan, and Suhaizan Kayat, Amanah National Organizing Secretary, 14 May 2017.
47. General elections data 1959 to 2013, obtained from Dr Ong Kian Ming, member of parliament for Serdang.
48. Interview with Haji Mohd Ashaari Sidon.
49. Speech at the annual party conference by Shamsudin Jaafar as an official delegate representing Johor, 2 June 2016.
50. Interview with six attendees of a PAS event in Kampung Bindu, in the parliamentary constituency of Sri Gading, all claiming to be members of PAS, plus four in FELDA Pasak (Kota Tinggi parliamentary constituency) and three in FELDA Taib Andak (Kulai parliamentary constituency). All requested anonymity.
51. Interview with Kumutha Raman, head of PAS Johor non-Muslim wing Dewan Himpunan Penyokong PAS, 15 May 2017.
52. Speech by PAS Vice-President Idris Ahmad, 10 May 2017.
53. Speech by Johor PAS state commissioner Abdullah Hussin, 10 May 2017.
54. For further elaboration on how Islamic movements see those who depart from their cause, see Fati Yakan, *Al-Mutasaqitun 'Ala Tariqid-Da'wah* [Those Who Fall Astray from the Path of Da'wah] (Beirut: Muassasat ar-Risalah, 1984).

References

Azlina Othman. 2017. "Kisah Sekolah Agama Johor". *Sinar Harian*, 11 July 2017.

Department of Statistics, Malaysia. 2011. *Population and Housing Census of Malaysia, 2010.* Putrajaya: Department of Statistics.

Faiz Zainudin. 2014. "PasMa Ingin Bantu PAS Kukuhkan Hubungan Dengan PR". *Free Malaysia Today*, 9 September 2014. http://www.freemalaysiatoday.com/category/bahasa/2014/09/09/pasma-ingin-bantu-pas-kukuhkan-hubungan-dengan-pr/ (accessed 21 June 2017).

Khor Yu Leng. 2015. "The Political Economy of FELDA Seats: UMNO's Rural Fortress in GE-13". In *Coalitions in Collision: Malaysia's 13th General Elections*, edited by Johan Saravanamuttu, Lee Hock Guan, and Mohamed Nawab Mohamed Osman. Singapore: Institute of Southeast Asian Studies.

Maznah Mohamed, "Fragmented but Captured: Malay Voters and the FELDA Factor in GE-13". In *Coalitions in Collision: Malaysia's 13th General Elections*, edited by Johan Saravanamuttu, Lee Hock Guan, and Mohamed Nawab Mohamed Osman. Singapore: Institute of Southeast Asian Studies.

Safina Ramli. 2017. "Pilih Politik Matang". *Utusan Malaysia*, 17 March 2017. https://www.utusan.com.my/berita/politik/pilih-politik-matang-1.458130

Saravanamuttu, Johan. 2016. *Power Sharing in a Divided Nation: Mediated Communalism and New Politics in Six Decades of Malaysia's Elections*. Singapore: ISEAS – Yusof Ishak Institute.

Star, The. 2017. "Johor PAS Plans to Contest in Over 40 Seats during GE-14". 16 April 2017. https://www.thestar.com.my/news/nation/2017/04/16/johor-pas-plans-to-contest-in-over-40-seats-during-GE-14/ (accessed 20 May 2017).

Wan Saiful Wan Jan. 2018. "Evolution of Islamism in Malaysian Politics: The Splintering of the Islamic Part of Malaysia and the Spread of Progressive Ideas". In *Islam in Southeast Asia: Negotiating Modernity*, edited by Norshahril Saat. Singapore: ISEAS – Yusof Ishak Institute.

Weiss, Meredith, ed. 2014. *Electoral Dynamics in Malaysia: Findings from the Grassroots*. Petaling Jaya: Strategic Information and Research Development Centre.

12

THE JOHOR SULTANATE
Rise or Re-emergence?

Francis E. Hutchinson and Vandana Prakash Nair[1]

PLANES, TRAINS AND AUTOMOBILES

Malaysia is a monarchy—albeit one that is *sui generis*. Rather than following a single line of succession, the kingship rotates among a group of traditional rulers—or sultans—who head nine of the country's thirteen states. Although some of the sultanates predate the arrival of Islam in the region, they are now closely associated with the religion and have been a part of the Malayan peninsula's political context for 600 years.

During the precolonial and colonial eras, the rulers had a wide scope of prerogatives but many of these were relinquished during Malaysia's transition to independence. At present, the sultans are ceremonial rulers, and executive power rests with the prime minister at the national level, and chief ministers and menteris besar at the state level. That said, they are responsible for religion and Malay culture within their respective states, while their historic and symbolic importance as well as a number of constitutional provisions allow their influence to extend significantly further.

Over the past few years, these rulers have begun to assume a more visible role in the country's political life. In some states, they have chosen to withhold their consent for the appointment of menteris besar and, in Perak in 2009, the sultan played a decisive role in toppling the coalition in power (Faruqi 2010, p. 145). Collectively, the sultans have also weighed in on national-level issues such as the quality of governance and rule of law (*Borneo Post Online*, 7 October 2015).

Of the traditional rulers, the Sultan of Johor, Ibrahim Ismail, has been arguably the most notable. Part of his public persona revolves around his extensive collection of vehicles. He recently purchased a blue and gold 737 Boeing, which will be used to "promote Johor" and allow him to travel the world like his ancestors "who once travelled around in ships" (*Star Online*, 1 March 2016). He has also given another plane to the Johor soccer team, which is owned by his eldest son, the Crown Prince (*Rakyat Post*, 2 August 2016).

The Sultan was also the first of the rulers to obtain a locomotive driving licence, and he piloted the last Malayan Railway train out of Tanjong Pagar Station in Singapore in 2011 (*Star Online*, 29 June 2010). A long-time automobile aficionado, he has a collection of some 300 units (*ABS-CBN*, 17 June 2013). In 2015, he became the owner of the world's most expensive Mack truck, outfitted with a six-camera CCTV system, two flat-screen televisions, a kitchen, as well as a bed and seats with 72,000 stitches of gold thread (*Straits Times*, 17 October 2016).

Sultan Ibrahim Ismail has also weighed in on policy matters and issues affecting public life, from religion and culture to interethnic relations, and from land management to education. He and the Crown Prince have frequently commented on the historical and cultural specificity of the state, encapsulated in the term *Bangsa Johor*, which implies an identity based on territory and local culture—as opposed to ethnicity. The Crown Prince has provocatively stated that Johor could imagine seceding from the Malaysian Federation, under certain conditions (*New Paper*, 17 October 2015).

Some of these issues fall within the strict constitutional role prescribed for traditional rulers, largely relating to Malay religion and custom. Others involve operational issues or national-level policies, and—to some—the Sultan's comments extend beyond the role currently specified for the rulers in the Constitution. According to experts in history and constitutional law, the Constitution does not allow for the withdrawal of any state from the Federation (Wan Syamsul Amly 2015; *Straits Times*, 20 October 2015).

However, even if education, health and bilateral relations are outside the remit of traditional rulers, these were matters of routine interest for them before independence. At a deeper level, this diversity in opinions means that while the traditional rulers are a central part of the political milieu, the precise contours of their role are not immutable.

This chapter examines the Sultan of Johor's recent public statements, in light of the current political context and with reference to the state's history. It argues that his actions and comments are guided by a very specific understanding of the role of a Malay ruler which is rooted in history. First, in ceremonial aspects, clear reference is made to the role of sultans in the precolonial and colonial eras, particularly their symbolic importance and how they participated in public life. Second, in areas pertaining to policy, inspiration is drawn from the sultanate of Johor during the colonial era, which had a reputation for modern and efficient administration, multi-ethnic subjects, and a significant degree of autonomy. Taken together, these references imply a more expansive role for the Sultan of Johor in particular, and traditional rulers more generally, than had been the case in the recent past. This development could rekindle a long-running competition in Malaysia between the royalty and Malay political elites, or what some have termed the rivalry between "princes and politicians".[2]

Following this introduction, the role and prerogatives of the sultans today are examined. From there, how the Sultan of Johor has participated in political life will be analysed, in particular: how his authority is displayed in the public sphere; what domains of state-level policy he has sought to influence; and how he has intervened in national-level issues. The last section will look into the future.

MALAYSIA AND ITS SULTANS

As a constitutional monarchy, Malaysia is headed by a king, with an elected parliament and prime minister. The sultans[3] are the constitutional heads of their respective states, and state governments—led by elected chief ministers and state legislative assemblies—have responsibilities that include religion and Malay custom, land management, natural resources, and local government (Fong 2008).[4]

The Constitution lays out the responsibilities and prerogatives of the Malay rulers. While these have since been subject to debate, the king and sultans had the following prerogatives at the time of independence (Lowe 1982; Raja Azlan Shah 1986; Harding 1996 & 2012; Faruqi 2008):

- Legislation passed in parliament and state legislative assemblies required their assent to be passed.
- They could block requests to dissolve parliament or state legislative assemblies.
- They had the right to name the prime minister or menteri besar that, in their judgement, commanded the confidence of the majority party in parliament or state legislative assembly.
- They (but not their families) had legal immunity in their public and personal capacities.

The king also had the following national-level responsibilities:

- the authority to declare a state of emergency, upon advice from the prime minister; and
- the authority to appoint and remove members of organisations such as the Public Services Commission, the Judicial and Legal Services Commission, Election Commission, and Police Force Commission, as well as judges of the superior courts.

Furthermore, sultans had the following prerogatives within the confines of their respective states:

- the right to name members of the State Executive Council upon the advice of the menteri besar;

- exclusive control over Islam and Malay custom, and state-level religious bureaucracies; and
- the authority to award honours and grant pardons.

Beyond their individual privileges, the sultans have also had a number of collective responsibilities. The Conference of Rulers is a policy body that brings together the rulers, their menteris besar, the governors and chief ministers of Penang, Malacca, Sabah, and Sarawak, and the king and prime minister.[5] While it has no means of compulsion, the Conference can do the following:

- discuss and deliberate on matters of national importance; and
- provide advice on any public service appointment, particularly relating to the judiciary, as well as the Auditor-General, and key organizations such as the Election Commission and Public Services Commission.

In addition, on matters pertaining to the Malay rulers, only the king and sultans are allowed to attend the Council, and have the following prerogatives:

- decide who will be king and, if necessary, remove him by majority vote;
- approve any law relating to the privileges and position of the Malay rulers; and
- intervene in determining state boundaries.

Beyond the explicit constitutional stipulations, the sultanates also enjoy enormous social and political capital. They are seen as symbols of Malay culture in general and Malay rights in particular.

Furthermore, in recognition of the Malay rulers' long history, the Constitution states that the "sovereignty, prerogatives, powers and jurisdiction of the Rulers ... as hitherto had and enjoyed shall remain unaffected" (Harding 1996, p. 65).[6] While open to interpretation, this text implies that the sultanates are pre-existing institutions whose reach goes beyond what is outlined in the Constitution (Milner 2011a, p. 18).

Beyond these prerogatives, the position of the Malay rulers in public life is sacrosanct, and protected by a range of coercive measures. The Sedition Act prohibits any action or statement that can "bring into hatred or contempt or to excite disaffection against any Ruler or against any government" (Lowe 1982, p. 79; Rawlings 1986, p. 248).

The extent of the rulers' responsibilities and prerogatives were central to negotiations held prior to independence. The nationalist elite—led by the United Malays National Organization (UMNO)—differed with the sultans on the role that the latter were to have. While recognizing the symbolic importance of the sultans, UMNO's leaders, with strong support from the Malay ground, held most of the aces in the talks with the rulers and the British (Muzaffar 1979; Amoroso 2014).

What the nationalist elite wanted was a strong central government to drive economic development, as well as an independent judiciary, and were reluctant to have strong state governments after independence. Disagreements arose over financial provisions for the states and their sultans, as well as the remit of the Conference of Rulers. In the end, UMNO was compelled to yield more financial autonomy to the states and a wider political role for the Conference than initially desired (Fernando 2002, pp. 169–74).

The role of the sultans increased further in the wake of the 1969 riots. As part of a broader move towards bolstering the position of the Malays, in 1971 the Constitution was amended to require the assent of the Conference of Rulers for any change to the provisions relating to sensitive issues such as the national language, religion, as well as the position of the Malays and indigenous Sabahans and Sarawakians (Milner 2011a, p. 17).

However, the prerogatives and responsibilities of the sultans were subsequently circumscribed, due to two structural dynamics. First, relations between Malaysia's political leadership—particularly UMNO—and the rulers came under tension in the 1970s. In Johor, Perak, and Pahang, disagreements arose over the choice of menteris besar in their respective states. In the case of Pahang, the sultan used his ability to block state-level legislation for two years in protest. In all three cases, the unwanted ministers eventually resigned. For some, the monarch's influence in these cases clearly went beyond the intention of the Constitution (Rawlings 1986, p. 245).

Second, the country's elected leadership underwent a generational change. The first prime minister, Tunku Abdul Rahman, was part of the Kedah royalty, while the second and third came from aristocratic circles in Pahang and Johor. In contrast, the fourth prime minister, Mahathir Mohamed, was a commoner firmly wedded to the notion that the sultans should retain only a ceremonial role, arguing that "in practice the King and the rulers held significant power and authority which could negate the democratic principle of government by the people" (Mahathir Mohamad 2011, p. 452).

Given the procedures governing the rotation of the kingship, the Sultan of either Johor or Perak was slated to ascend to the throne in 1984. Seeking to circumscribe their room for manoeuvre and—perhaps as some have argued, seeking to remove a check on his authority—Mahathir attempted to amend the Constitution to reduce the monarchy's prerogatives in 1983. This entailed eliminating the constitutional checks the king and sultans had on vetoing legislation and transferring the authority to declare emergency rule from the king to the prime minister (Wain 2009, p. 204).

Despite being passed in parliament, the bill also needed to be signed by the King. Although he had initially agreed, the King subsequently changed his mind. Following a prolonged stalemate, the provisions were watered down, before being passed by parliament and accepted by the Conference of Rulers. While the King was now only allowed to delay—but not block—legislation for a maximum of sixty days, he retained the ability to declare a state of emergency. In addition, sultans retained their veto of legislation at the state level, although they pledged not to use this prerogative (Rawlings 1986, pp. 251–53; Harding 2012, p. 75).

While that particular impasse may have been resolved, the rulers still sought to influence their menteris besar and acted in ways that were thought by some to constitute interference (Harding 1996, p. 76). In addition, the wider role of the sultans and their families led to public debate about a number of issues such as: the *de facto* legal immunity enjoyed by the royalty at large; the extensive business interests of some sultans; and examples of profligacy and the implied cost to public coffers (Muzaffar 1979, p. 74; Harding 1996, pp. 118–99; Mahathir Mohamad 2011, p. 453). Furthermore, in 1992, Sultan Iskandar of Johor was alleged to have physically assaulted a member of the public (Wain 2009, p. 209).

Following this, Mahathir acted to remove the rulers' legal immunity as well as their ability to block legislation. Following intensive negotiations, including a variety of enticements and threats to the sultans, a constitutional amendment was passed in 1993. The rulers were now no longer able to veto legislation at the state level; the authority to declare a state of emergency was bestowed upon the prime minister; and sultans no longer enjoyed legal immunity in their private capacities, although such trials were to take place in a special court. In addition, constraints on parliamentary discussions regarding the role of the rulers were relaxed (Wain 2009, pp. 209–10; Harding 2012, pp. 118–19; Mahathir 2011, p. 453).[7]

For the remainder of Mahathir's tenure, there were no disagreements regarding the extent of royal prerogatives (Suwannathat-Pian 2011, p. 410). However, shortly after he stepped down in late 2003, the rulers began again to play a more public role. In 2006, the Sultan of Selangor asked a state assemblyman to resign following the revelation of his involvement in a number of financial irregularities. The following year, the Conference of Rulers rejected Prime Minister Abdullah Badawi's nominated candidate for a high-ranking judicial position (Ahmad Fauzi and Muhamad Rakiyuddin 2012, pp. 931–32).

In 2008, the ruling coalition, Barisan Nasional, unprecedentedly lost five state governments. In addition to introducing more competition for office at the state level, this turn of events provided the sultans with an opportunity to exercise their discretionary powers. In Perlis and Terengganu, two states won by Barisan Nasional, the sultans passed over the nominated candidates in favour of other state assemblypersons (Ahmad Fauzi and Muhamad Rakiyuddin 2012, p. 934). The following year, with three state legislators crossing the floor, the Sultan of Perak opted to name a menteri besar from the opposing coalition, rather than calling for fresh elections (*New Straits Times*, 2 May 2009). And in 2014, the Sultan of Selangor blocked the incumbent coalition's initial nomination for menteri besar and subsequently called for a selection of names to be put forward for his consideration (Cheah and Aiezat Fadzell 2014).

Public debates ensued on the role of the rulers. On one hand, there were calls for the sultans to refrain from engaging in politics, and to remain as ceremonial leaders (Abdul Aziz Bari 2013, pp. 334–35; Muaz Omar 2009). On the other, the Sultan of Perak, Nazrin Shah, argued that beyond the aspects of unifying the nation and representing Malay culture and religion, the country's monarchy should contribute to public life through promoting good governance and the rule of law, as well as checking extremism (Raja Nazrin Shah 2004).

THE SULTANATE OF JOHOR

Johor is the country's southernmost state, bordering on Singapore. Its flat fertile land has been particularly suited to agriculture, and the state has long been a key source of capital and foreign exchange for Malaysia. In population terms, Johor is the second largest in the country and also has the second largest number of parliamentary constituencies. It occupies a central place in Malay politics, as UMNO was founded in the state and it has contributed a disproportionate number of the first generation of independence leaders (Hutchinson 2015). Even today, the state has the largest number of UMNO party members—estimated at some 400,000 people.[8]

In addition, the state has always had dynamic sultans who vowed to make Johor "the greatest Malay power, to keep her free, and to make her rich" (Thio 1967, p. 11). From the 1840s onwards, its rulers proved particularly adept at laying claim to increasing amounts of land, cultivating relations with other sultans and polities, and lobbying London for more recognition and prerogatives.[9]

Of particular note are two sultans. The first, Abu Bakar, reigned from 1862 to 1895 and is credited with developing many of Johor's unique institutions. Unlike the Federated Malay States (FMS) of Negri Sembilan, Pahang, Selangor and Perak, which came under direct British influence in the 1870s and 1880s, Johor held out against external control until the early twentieth century. Given the sultanate's proximity to Singapore and the FMS, Abu Bakar observed and adapted many British conventions to suit his particular circumstances. By the 1890s, Johor had developed an efficient and rules-based bureaucracy that provided an extensive array of social services, managed an army, navy, and postal system, and had a quasi-diplomatic body in London to lobby parliament (Hutchinson 2015; Mohd Sarim Mustajab 1985; *Singapore and Straits Directory* 1893). In 1895, the sultanate was the first to draft its own constitution, which blended elements of Malay custom with British law and governance structures (de Vere Allen, Stockwell and Wright 1981, p. 76).

The second sultan, Ibrahim, ruled from 1895 until 1959, and is remembered for his negotiations with both the British and the nationalist elite to preserve a maximum degree of autonomy for Johor. Although Johor was compelled to accept a British adviser in 1910 and assign him substantial responsibilities in 1914, the sultanate was able to secure important concessions such as: the right to dismiss undesired British officers; retaining preference in government employment for Johor Malays; and preserving Malay, along with English, as the language of government (de Vere Allen, Stockwell and Wright 1981, pp. 108–9). As a result, the Sultan was able to retain control over strategic areas of government, with many key positions and departments remaining in the hands of his subjects. In addition, he prioritized commodity production, which allowed the state to generate high revenue streams, much of which were subsequently invested in infrastructure and social services. Indeed, due to substantial fiscal prudence, the sultanate ran a budget surplus from 1918 until the Second World War (Sugimoto 2007, p. 70).

On their return after the Japanese Occupation, the British sought to replace the various Malay States and Straits Settlements with the Malayan Union in 1946. This would have vested most responsibilities and services in a strong central government, and transferred sovereignty from the rulers to the British crown. This generated such widespread resistance in the Malay community that the Union had to be replaced by the Malaysian Federation in 1948 (Stockwell 1979).

As part of this process, the British signed nine state agreements with each of the sultans to create the new Federation. Sultan Ibrahim thus signed the Johore Agreement of 1948, and a supplementary piece of legislation updated the state's Constitution to bring it in line with the Federal Constitution. The general effect this had was to reduce the Sultan's remit to Islam and Malay custom while expanding the role of the state government beyond the advisory and administrative role envisioned in Johor's 1895 Constitution.[10] This, however, did not stop Sultan Ibrahim from taking direct interest in affairs of government and promoting the state's interest through lobbying the British for increased infrastructure expenditure, more financial autonomy, and a return of Johorean civil servants that had joined the Malayan Civil Service.[11]

Yet, this same desire for autonomy led Sultan Ibrahim to oppose Johor's independence from Britain. During the celebrations for the sixtieth year of his reign in 1955—and at the height of negotiations between Malaya's nationalist elite and the British over the timetable for their withdrawal—he questioned the wisdom of seeking independence during the Emergency. In response, UMNO leaders boycotted the celebrations and passed a motion of censure in the Johor legislative assembly (*Daily Telegraph*, 14 December 1955). The Sultan also resisted the withdrawal of the British adviser from Johor, arguing that his input was necessary for affairs to "run smoothly".[12] And in late 1955, one of the Sultan's cousins established a movement to advocate for the state's secession from Malaya and a return to its status as a British protectorate. Ignored by the nationalist leaders as well as the other traditional rulers, the movement was eclipsed when the Crown Prince of Johor signed the Federal Constitution in July 1957 (Sopiee 1975, pp. 80–85).

Thus, it is with this legacy of strong leadership, hands-on policy-making, and a desire for autonomy that Sultan Ibrahim Ismail ascended to the Johor throne in 2010.

The subsequent sections look at the effects of this legacy in the following domains: the public portrayal of sultanate; the state-level issues and policies the Sultan has dealt with; and, how he has sought to intervene in national-level issues.

The Public Portrayal of the Sultanate

Taking place more than five years after he ascended to the throne, the Sultan's coronation in March 2015 was an elaborate affair. It consisted of a month-long celebration with visits to each of the state's ten districts. There were nine key events, which included open-air concerts, fireworks displays, a boat parade, a carnival and assorted sporting competitions.

The coronation itself took place in the throne room of the main palace in Johor, the Istana Besar. The Mufti of Johor, the head of the state's religious establishment, placed a 1.6-kilogram crown topped by an Islamic crescent on the Sultan's head. Crafted by a London-based jeweller, the silver and gold crown was adorned with sapphires, emeralds, rubies, and diamonds. The Sultan's wife was crowned with a diamond-studded tiara of white gold. Both wore shoulder-length capes of blue silk, with inscriptions in gold thread (Suparto 2015; *Sun Daily*, 2 March 2015).

Many aspects of this ritual are embedded in the history of the Malay rulers, particularly in the precolonial era. According to court chronicles and legal digests, sultans were the linchpin of society. They were imbued with immense ceremonial and religious power, and referred to with titles such as "God's shadow on earth" (Milner 1981, p. 52). When they assumed the throne, they were imbued with the *daulat*—majesty and sovereignty—that is the unique preserve of the royalty (Gullick 2004, p. 45; Suwannathat-Pian 2011, p. 12).

As head of religion and custom, the sultans represented, preserved and enforced laws and traditions. Indeed, his subjects defined themselves by their societal position vis-à-vis the ruler, and it was also the ruler's obligation to name and treat his subjects according to the position that they occupied within this hierarchy. The sultan's role was so pivotal in society that *"kerajaan"*, the term used for the sultanates at that time, literally signified "the condition" of having a raja or sultan (Milner 1982, pp. 94–104).

Wealth was central to the exercise of power, as it was through this medium that sultans were able to attract and retain followers. A person's rank and material wealth needed to be aligned, and the sultan, as foremost representative of his people, had to be "exceptional … in his manner of dress and accommodation". Sumptuary laws—customs governing what people wore—were extensive, with specific colours, textiles, and luxury items associated with, and reserved for, the royalty (Milner 2011b, pp. 60–65).

This also extended to means of travel. Court annals noted when the rulers went travelling, with great importance being attached to the image they portrayed and how they were received in the host destination. For example, in 1885 when the Sultan of Terengganu travelled to Pahang for his wedding, he was accompanied by 400 people in a steamship, with 1,000 more following in sail boats. Sultan Abu Bakar had an iron steamer and then a yacht for his travel, and also kept a large carriage. It is also recorded that in the sixteenth century, a "King" of Johor travelled at the head of a procession "leading all the city's people" atop an elephant (Gullick 1992, pp. 231–32; Abdul Abdul Kadir 1970, p. 302; Borschberg 2015, p. 51).[13]

Beyond the Sultan's collection of vehicles mentioned above, the annual Kembara Mahkota Johor can be seen as a modern re-enactment of this tradition. Begun in 2001, when he was still Crown Prince, this tradition sees Sultan Ibrahim Ismail visiting Johor's ten districts at the head of a convoy of various vehicles, from motorbikes to four-wheel drives, and from trains to boats—the latter to access islands off the state's coast (Jasmine Shadique 2015; Mohd Farhaan Shah 2016; *Malay Mail Online*, 14 May 2016).

Thus, the public portrayal of the Sultan of Johor is embedded in long-standing customs regarding the role that traditional rulers should play. While many of these practices date back centuries, they still resonate with substantial segments of Johorean society. In 2012, following his successful purchase of a car registration plate for RM520,000, the Sultan was criticized by a member of the Opposition for his supposed profligacy. In response to this, a crowd of an estimated 15,000 to 30,000 people marched to the Sultan's palace in a public display of support (Mohd Farhaan Shah 2012; Sim and Jasmine Shadique 2012).

State-Level Policy Matters

Beyond the ceremonial element of his reign, Sultan Ibrahim Ismail has expressed opinions on a wide range of state-level issues and, on a number of occasions, assumed an operational role. In certain cases, these measures clearly fall within the remit of traditional rulers, but, in others, they imply a more hands-on role than had been the case in the recent past.

Religion and Malay Custom

In late 2013, the Sultan reinstated the Islamic week for government with effect from 1 January 2014, with the rationale that it would allow Muslims more time for their Friday prayers. This measure came as a surprise, as the state had long been known for its outward orientation and investment-friendly policy frameworks. In particular, private sector operations worried about the economic impact that this could have (Ng 2013).

That said, during the colonial period, Johor—along with the four northern Malay states—had observed the Islamic week. Indeed, it maintained this tradition until 1993, when the Johor state government made the decision to change the rest day from Friday to Sunday (*Malaysia Today*, 28 November 2013). This measure was taken by the serving menteri besar as part of the wider push to curtail the sultans' prerogatives. In 1996, the current Sultan's father, Iskandar, urged the government to change the weekend back to Friday and Saturday, but with no success (*Straits Times*, 10 February 1996).

While the reinstatement of the Islamic week can be seen as increasing the religious tenor of public life, Sultan Ibrahim has also made numerous appeals for moderation. He has called for Johor's inhabitants to avoid "deviant" teachings, and learn from religious teachers who possess proper credentials. In particular, Muslim preachers from outside Johor must be recognized by the Johor Islamic Religious Council (MAIJ) (*New Straits Times*, 31 March 2016).

The Sultan has also made his influence felt on matters of Malay culture. He recently cautioned Malays against growing Arabization, encouraging them to retain their own culture instead of imitating outside influences, stating "If there are some of you who wish to be an Arab and practise Arab culture ... that is up to you. I also welcome you to live in Saudi Arabia" (*Malay Mail Online*, 24 March 2016).

In addition, he has sought to nuance the position of Malays in the country, relating it back to the Malay rulers. Sultan Ibrahim Ismail stated that the term "Malay sovereignty" was more appropriate than "Malay supremacy" because it reflected the sovereignty of the Malay states with the rulers at their apex. And while the concept of Malay sovereignty encompassed the position of the Malay rulers, Islam as the Federation's official religion, Malay as the national language and Malay rights, it did not regard the other races as outsiders (*Utusan* online, 9 December 2010).

As head of religion and Malay custom within the state, these declarations by the Sultan are fully within his purview, and are specified in the Johor Constitution.[14] They are also part of Johor royalty's long-established tradition of firm control over religious affairs. Sultan Abu Bakar, for example, invited renowned scholars to the state, established a religious hierarchy, and also accumulated texts of Islamic jurisprudence. Furthermore, during the colonial period, the British scrupulously avoided interference in religious matters. While many government departments came to have British heads, this was never the case where religious matters were concerned (Milner 1995, p. 198; Gray 1978, pp. 142–43).

Bangsa Johor

The declarations on religion and Malay custom have also been accompanied by references to a unique state-level identity, expressed by the concept *"Bangsa Johor"*. According to Sultan Ibrahim Ismail, the term was developed by Sultan Ibrahim in 1920, and expressed a shared commitment to the state's progress which transcends cultures and religion (A. Jalil Hamid 2016).[15]

These statements have been accompanied by a number of measures reaching out to Johor's various communities. In January 2016, the Sultan joined Hindu devotees during the Thaipusam celebration in Johor; and in February that year, he became the first Johor ruler to launch and attend the annual Chingay festival. In September 2016, he hosted a tea party in the Chinese Hall[16] (*The Star*, 7 September 2016) in Johor's main palace to acknowledge the historic contribution of the Chinese community to the state's development. And on several occasions, he stated that Johor is home to its various ethnic communities and racist practices are forbidden (*The Star*, 19 and 25 January 2016; *Malaysian Insider*, 16 September 2015).

This wider conception of citizenship or belonging has roots in the precolonial era, where the subjects of a sultan were referred to collectively as *"rakyat"* or *"people"*, as opposed to their specific ethnicity (Milner 2011a, p. 25). Furthermore, the consolidation of the rubber-based economy in the state during the early twentieth century as well as a liberal immigration policy, led to substantial inflows of people from China, India, Java, and Sumatra. After the Second World War, Johor had the second largest population among the territories in Malaya, behind Perak, and housed one of the country's largest Chinese populations (Del Tufo 1947).

Records from the mid-1870s show that Sultan Abu Bakar included non-Malays in high-level decision-making bodies. Thus, he created a State Council to debate legislation and policy issues which brought together: the aristocracy, government bureaucrats, the religious establishment, and two of the most powerful Chinese businessmen. The Johor Constitution further formalized this tradition by specifying the Council's membership. Appointed by the Sultan, the members could be ministers, government officials, or community leaders of any ethnicity, but had to be Johore subjects (de Vere Allen, Stockwell, and Wright 1981).

This tradition of consulting various ethnic groups can be seen in the discussions in 2013 between Sultan Ibrahim and the Malaysian Chinese Association (MCA) over his choice to appoint a local MCA member to the State Executive Council. The MCA leadership had declared that no party member would accept a national or state-level position, given the party's poor electoral performance in the general elections. However, Sultan Ibrahim persisted with the appointment, stating that naming members to the Executive Council was his prerogative as traditional ruler and as established in the Johor Constitution (*Sun Daily*, 1 July 2013; *Malaysian Times*, 1 July 2013).

Johor Armed Forces

In early 2016, the Sultan proposed that the duties of the Johor Military Force (JMF) be widened from guarding the palace grounds to monitoring administrative areas such as the state capital as well as district offices, stating that this use of existing resources would be better than hiring private firms who use foreign workers. Furthermore, he called for the state government to revive the Johor Volunteer Force (JVF) and encourage members of the Johor civil service to join it, in order to boost their spirit of volunteerism and help with disaster management and community service (Lim 2009, p. 23; *Free Malaysia Today*, 8 April 2016; *Malay Mail Online*, 12 May 2016).

Johor is the only state in Malaysia to have its own military force. In 1886, Sultan Abu Bakar established it to assert Johor's independence and reduce its reliance on British forces (Lim 2009, p. 122). During the British period, the JMF remained tightly under Sultan Ibrahim's control. He used it as a means of controlling the civil service—through his ability to hire and then second JMF officers to key positions in the government—and a private police force (Gray 1978, p. 56).[17] In 1905, Sultan Ibrahim further established the Johor Volunteer Force (JVF), whose ranks drew from the civil service. In 1938, the JMF reached a peak of 1,000 troops, with a further 800 members in the JVF (Gullick 1992, p. 67). Mahathir did consider disbanding the JMF in the wake of the 1993 constitutional crisis, but it still exists and numbers some 200 troops (*Straits Times*, 19 August 1993).

Public Health

Issues pertaining to religion, Malay custom, and wider issues of identity are within the current constitutional role attributed to the sultans. However, in November 2015, the Sultan ordered a ban on the sale of vaping products in Johor for health reasons. Since vaping is a public health issue, which falls under both federal and state government responsibility, questions were raised regarding the process by which the ban was declared. Experts in Malaysian constitutional law argued that the ban would need to be enacted by the State Legislative Assembly, rather than via the Sultan's decree. However, in December 2015, this issue was put to rest when the Johor State Executive Council officially banned the sale of vape products in the state (Koh 2015).[18]

Environmental and Natural Resource Management Issues

Under the Federal Constitution, natural resources are listed as a state government responsibility, and oil and timber concessions have in fact been an important source of revenue for this level of government. In his speech before the State Legislative Assembly in May 2014, Sultan Ibrahim Ismail requested that the state government allot one fourth of its land to forest reserves, and that the awarding of logging concessions be frozen. He also suggested that a state government corporation be established to handle environmental issues, and proposed passing an enactment to allow the state government to directly approve environmental impact assessments. This contrasts with standard practice where such assessments are routed through the federal government.

The Sultan specifically cited the Benalec project, a 1,400 ha reclamation project in the Johor Strait meant to house a large oil and gas complex, which had been waiting three years for an environmental impact assessment (*Sun Daily*, 9 July 2014).[19] In addition, concerns were raised during this period about Forest City, an even larger land reclamation project. Led by an established Chinese developer, Country Garden, in conjunction with the Sultan and a state government-owned commercial vehicle, the project envisages creating four artificial islands collectively measuring some 2,000 hectares. Worries were raised that land reclamation had begun without an environmental impact assessment. Initial objections were raised by the Federal Department of the Environment, but both projects were eventually approved, although only partially in the case of the Forest City project (Zhen 2016; Reme Ahmad 2014; *Malaysian Insider*, 23 June 2014; Teoh 2015).

Land Management

Land management is a central part of state government work, holding great implications for zoning and real estate development. The Housing and Property Board 2014 enactment envisaged an agency to oversee the development of real property and housing in Johor. In its original form, the enactment gave the Sultan of Johor the power to appoint board members, dissolve the board and oversee its accounts.

This led to concerns from UMNO leaders, opposition members, as well as civic organizations regarding the operational role that it imagines for the Sultan. The deputy president of the opposition party PAS stated that his party "supports the constitutional role of the Malay rulers as defined by the Federal Constitution … Efforts to give Sultan Ibrahim … executive powers should never happen"; while UMNO party member and former Cabinet member, Zainuddin Maidin, criticized the menteri besar, stating that he "should have acknowledged that the power of the people is greater than the power of the monarchy and not proceeded with the tabling". The Malaysian Bar Council cautioned the state government that granting such far-reaching administrative powers to the ruler would expose him to criticism (Yong 2014; *Malaysia Today*, 8 June 2014; Jayasankaran 2014).

The state government eventually decided to amend the enactment to limit the Sultan's power to the right to appoint only four board members, subject to the advice of the menteri besar. The language of the provisions was also changed such that the powers would be vested in the "state authorities" rather than in the Johor "Ruler". The Sultan initially gave his assurance that he would not interfere in state executive matters but he maintained that he could only endorse the bill once state authorities had travelled around the state to explain the provisions of the enactment to Johoreans (Yong 2014).

A year later, the Sultan called for a review of the enactment, stating that it "… was amended through pressure from outsiders who were narrow minded … and do not understand the power of the ruler in Johor's state constitution". While the bill was passed by the state legislative assembly in June 2014, the Sultan has not yet officially endorsed the enactment (Ahmad Fairuz Othman 2015).

National-Level Issues

Beyond the policy issues highlighted above, Sultan Ibrahim Ismail has also spoken out on a number of national-level issues. While these do not entail an operational role, they do raise important questions, not least about the role played by the monarchy itself.

English Standards

The Sultan has, on several occasions, called for the Malaysian government to improve the standard of English in the education system and suggested that Singapore be examined as a model. In addition, he has stated that the country's various language streams have resulted in non-Malays not being able to speak Malay, and in Malays being unable to speak English (*Straits Times*, 29 October 2015; Wong and Benjamin 2015; and *AsiaOne*, 12 June 2015). Beyond the issues of educational quality that this raises, rectifying this would also mean completely reconfiguring the education system at the primary level, and switching the medium of instruction at the secondary level.

Again, this statement is based on Johor's unique history and long-standing emphasis on both English and Malay education. English medium schools were established in Johor as early as in 1864, and the first Malay school was established in 1878. The education department was established five years later, and in 1884, Sultan Abu Bakar decreed that every district in the state should have a school. In 1902, Sultan Ibrahim issued a proclamation which required all households of Johore, regardless of race, to send their male children between seven and sixteen years of age to school (Lim 2009, p. 146).

Indeed, the education system constituted one of the areas of greatest conflict between the Sultan and the British, with the former in favour of widespread education in English and the latter supporting generalized Malay-medium schools with limited provision of English education for a reduced number. The Sultan finally relinquished direct control over the education system, with the exception of religious education in 1928 (Khoo 1992, p. 159). Due to its high levels of government revenue and commitment to education, Johor had one of the highest levels of literacy among the Malay States in the 1940s (Del Tufo 1947, table 52).

Relations with Singapore

In recent years, Sultan Ibrahim Ismail has advocated for the Johor state government to play a more active role in Malaysia's relationship with Singapore. His statements have revolved around a number of issues, including: replacing the Causeway to alleviate heavy traffic flowing to and from Singapore as well as increasing mobility; the status of Pedra Branca, over which conflicting claims by Singapore and Malaysia were largely resolved by the International Court of Justice; and connecting Johor Bahru and Singapore via public transport (*AsiaOne*, 23 March 2016; *Utusan Online*, 30 May 2014; *Straits Times*, 13 June 2015).[20]

The Sultan has argued that while bilateral relations are a federal responsibility, national leaders should at least consider Johor's views when they craft policies towards Singapore, due to the state's deep understanding of its neighbour, as well as its own sentiment and legal precedent on particular issues. In line with these, he has also offered to mediate on bilateral issues (*Straits Times*, 8 March 2010; *New Straits Times*, 22 March 2015).

While not fitting into the current federal allocation of responsibilities, bilateral relations between Johor and Singapore have deep historical roots. Indeed, it was the Sultanate that contributed the greatest part of the funds to build the Causeway linking Johor with Singapore in 1923. Initially intended solely to connect Singapore to the Federated Malay States by rail, Sultan Ibrahim agreed to contribute additional funds for it to be open to pedestrians and other vehicles. All in all, the Sultanate contributed more than $3.2 million of the total $4.8 million that the project cost (State of Johore 1955, p. 20).

The Sultanate also made substantial contributions to Singapore's defence in the colonial era. In February 1915, when the Indian 5th Light Infantry guarding German internees at Tanglin Barracks mutinied, Sultan Ibrahim himself led JMF reinforcements to Singapore to help quell the mutiny (Lim 2009, p. 127). In 1935, amid an atmosphere of growing Japanese aggression in the region, Sultan Ibrahim gifted the colonial government in Singapore with £500,000 to celebrate King George V's Silver Jubilee, specifying that the money should be used to accelerate work on the Singapore naval base (*Straits Times*, 5 June 1935). £400,000 of the gift was used to install two of the three 15-inch guns of the Johore battery in Changi. These were the biggest guns outside Britain during the Second World War (Kiong and Chan 2010).

Furthermore, Sultan Ibrahim signed the first water agreement between Johor and Singapore in 1927, which then formed the basis for the 1961 and 1962 water agreements between Singapore and Malaysia. The demarcation of the border between Singapore and Johor was made through negotiations between the British Crown and the Sultan in 1928. The agreement resolved the contradiction concerning the ten-mile limit around Singapore by giving the Sultan of Johor control over islets and waters within three miles of Johor. If this had not been done, all the Johor Strait and certain areas in the southwest and southeast would have remained under the control of Singapore even though they were closer to Johor (Lee 1980).[21]

The Role of the Monarchy

Earlier this year, Sultan Ibrahim Ismail stated that Malaysia should repeal the constitutional amendments of 1993 which curtailed the prerogatives of traditional rulers and removed their legal immunity. In his opinion, these have reduced the role of the sultans to that of mere rubber stampers for laws passed by Parliament or the various state legislative assemblies. He stated that "It is not proper to limit or abolish the power of the King or the Sultan in examining and giving their Royal Assent for laws", and the constitutional amendments "grabbed the powers of the King for the sake of political or individual interest" (Teoh 2016).

In light of the wide range of policy matters that the Sultan has sought to influence, these remarks further indicate that he advocates a more traditional role and a wider ranging mandate for the rulers. One constitutional expert has stated that there is legal basis for this challenge before the Federal Court, as the 1993 constitutional amendments did not have the assent of the Conference of Rulers (*Malaysian Insider*, 7 May 2015).

CONCLUSION

The Sultan of Johor has assumed a very visible local and national political role, based on a very specific understanding of what the role of a traditional ruler should be. In its ceremonial aspects, it is rooted in the precolonial era, when sultans played a very public role deeply entrenched in symbolism. In its policy-related aspects, it is inspired by the state-building achievements of two previous sultans, who developed key aspects of Johor's state apparatus and preserved its autonomy.

This more expansive role stands in contrast to the tenor of political life since the early 1980s which has seen the rulers adopt a lower public profile. However, over the last decade, the sultans have been attempting to exercise their prerogatives more frequently. This seems to be part of a continuing process where the precise contours of the sultans' roles fluctuate.

The Sultan's various policy positions and initiatives have not gone uncontested, and there has been push-back. Political heavyweights such as Musa Hitam and Mahathir Mohamad were vocal in their opposition to the operational role framed for the Sultan in the proposed Housing and Property Board. Mahathir also disagreed with the concept of Bangsa Johor, stating that it could lead to feelings of superiority among certain sectors of society and could potentially lead to the break-up of the

Malaysian Federation. This was subsequently rebutted by the Sultan (A. Jalil Hamid 2016).

Minister for Tourism and Culture Nazri Aziz pointedly advised the Crown Prince to refrain from politics following the latter's criticism of Prime Minister Najib Razak. He stated that, should the Prince get involved in politics, he would get "whacked". He then referred to the classic contest for leadership between princes and politicians, and how politicians "are the ones protecting the royalty". The Crown Prince rejected this, subsequently raising the possibility of Johor seceding, and then posting a statement on Facebook calling upon critics of Johor to ask Prime Minister Najib to expel the state from the federation (*Sunday Times*, 14 June 2015; *Straits Times*, 16 October 2015; *Asia One*, 2 June 2016).

Initiatives proposed by the Sultan of Johor for the future include establishing a Bank of Johor to provide credit to the state's residents; building a maglev train linking the eastern and western parts of Johor Bahru; and implementing a public housing scheme (A. Jalil Hamid 2016). He also called for the federal government to address the economic situation facing the country, including the falling value of the ringgit (*New Paper*, 26 August 2015). Regarding the current position of the rulers, he has lamented the passage of the constitutional amendments, advocating their repeal and stating that "Johor has a mission. The mission is to restore the 'order'" (*Malaysiakini*, 7 May 2016).

Notes

1. This chapter was first published as *The Johor Sultanate: Rise or Re-emergence?*, Trends in Southeast Asia, no. 16/2016 (Singapore: ISEAS – Yusof Ishak Institute, 2016).
2. This term was coined by Anthony Stockwell (1988, pp. 182–97).
3. Malaysia has nine Malay rulers, from the states of Perlis, Kedah, Kelantan, Terengganu, Perak, Negri Sembilan, Selangor, Pahang, and Johor. While the majority are referred to as "Sultans", the rulers of Perlis and Negri Sembilan are referred to as "Raja" and "Yang di-Pertuan", respectively. For simplicity, the terms "sultans" and "traditional" or "Malay rulers" will be used.
4. Sabah and Sarawak, due to their later incorporation into the Federation, have a more extensive list of responsibilities.
5. Penang, Malacca, Sabah and Sarawak do not have menteri besar and sultans. The elected political leaders are referred to as chief ministers, and ceremonial leadership is vested in governors, who are appointed for four-year terms by the king on advice from the respective chief minister. See Raja Azlan Shah (1986), p. 77.
6. Article 181 of Malaysian Constitution, cited in Harding (1996), p. 65.
7. A further amendment passed in 1994 reduced the amount of time the king could delay legislation from sixty to thirty days.
8. Interview with Nur Jazlan, UMNO MP for Pulai, Johor Bahru, Malaysia, 18 May 2010.
9. For a comprehensive account of the development of the Sultanate of Johor in the nineteenth century, consult Trocki (2007).
10. The Johore Agreement 1948 and Supplement to the Constitution 1367.
11. Memorandum from Sultan Ibrahim to Donald MacGillivray, British High Commissioner to Malaya, 13 June 1954.

12. Letter from Sultan Ibrahim to the British High Commissioner to Malaya, Donald MacGillivray, 1 December 1955.
13. We are grateful to Barbara Watson Andaya for her input on this point.
14. Supplement to the Constitution of the State of Johore, no. 43 A, XXB, 5 September 1957.
15. The state's anthem, *Lagu Bangsa Johor* was composed in 1897, but its lyrics were written in 1914. They request the Sultan's protection of the state, as well as his leadership to help it attain freedom and unity: https://kemahkotaan.johor.gov.my/pengenalan/lagu-bangsa-johor/ (accessed 31 October 2016).
16. The Chinese Hall or Dewan Cina was a gift from prominent Chinese businessmen in Johor, including Wong Ah Fook, who built the Istana Besar.
17. In 1915, Sultan Ibrahim used the JMF to quell a mutiny of Indian troops in Singapore, for which he was awarded a knighthood by the British.
18. Federal Constitution of Malaysia, Articles 74, 77, Ninth Schedule.
19. Speech delivered by Sultan Ibrahim Ismail before the State Legislative Assembly of Johor, 31 May 2014.
20. Speech delivered by Sultan Ibrahim Ismail before the State Legislative Assembly of Johor, 31 May 2014.
21. Straits Settlements and Johore Territorial Waters (Agreement) Act, 1928, Colony of the Straits Settlements and Sultan of the State and Territory of Johore, 19 October 1927. See Lee (1980).

References

Abdul Abdul Kadir. 1970. *The Hikayat Abdullah*. Kuala Lumpur: Oxford University Press.
Abdul Aziz Bari. 2013. *Monarchy and the Constitution in Malaysia*. Kuala Lumpur: IDEAS.
ABS-CBN. 2013. "Sultan of Johor Shows Kris His Motorcycle, Car Collection", 17 June 2013. https://www.youtube.com/watch?v=ssBJuBIL5Pc (accessed 24 October 2016).
Ahmad Fairuz Othman. 2015. "Johor Sultan Calls for the Johor Real Property and Housing Board Bill Review". *New Straits Times*, 7 May 2015.
Ahmad Fauzi Abdul Hamid and Muhamad Rakiyuddin Ismail. 2012. "The Monarchy and Party Politics in Malaysia in the Era of Abdullah Ahmad Badawi (2003–09): The Resurgence of the Role of Protector". *Asian Survey* 52, no. 5: 900–23.
Amoroso, Donna. 2014. *Traditionalism and the Ascendancy of the Malay Ruling Class in Colonial Malaya*. Singapore: NUS Press.
Annual Report for Johor 1932. 1933. Singapore: Government Printing Office.
Annual Report for Johor 1938. 1939. Singapore: Government Printing Office.
AsiaOne. 2015. "Make English a Medium of Instruction in Schools: Sultan of Johor". 12 June 2015.
———. 2016a. "Johor Sultan: Consider Replacing the Causeway". 23 March 2016.
———. 2016b. "Critics Should Ask Najib to Expel Johor from Malaysia, Says Crown Prince", 2 June 2016.
Borneo Post. 2015. "Malay Rulers Want 1MDB Issue Settled Soonest, Demand Report", 7 October 2015.
Borschberg, Peter, ed. 2015. *Jacques de Coutre's Singapore and Johor 1594–1625*. Singapore: NUS Press.
Cheah, Bernard and Aiezat Fadzell. 2014. "Azmin Is Sultan's Choice for Selangor MB". *Sun Daily*, 22 September 2014.

Daily Telegraph. "Sultan of Johore Censured". 14 December 1955.

de Vere Allen, James, Anthony John Stockwell, and Leigh R. Wright. 1981. *A Collection of Treaties and Other Documents Affecting the States of Malaysia 1761–1963*. London: Oceana Publications.

Del Tufo, M.V. 1947. *A Report on the 1947 Census of Population*. London: Crown Agents for the Colonies.

Faruqi, Shad Saleem. 2008. *Document of Destiny: The Constitution of the Federation of Malaysia*.

———. 2010. "The 2009 Constitutional Turmoil in Perak: A Look Back". In *Perak: A State of Crisis*, edited by Audrey Quay. Petaling Jaya: Loyar Burok Publications.

Fernando, Joseph. 2002. *The Making of the Malayan Constitution*. Kuala Lumpur: Malayan Branch of the Royal Asiatic Society.

Fong, Joo Chong. 2008. *Constitutional Federalism in Malaysia*. Kuala Lumpur: Sweet and Maxwell.

———. 2012. *The Constitution of Malaysia: A Contextual Analysis*. Oxford: Hart Publishing.

Free Malaysia Today. 2016. "Sultan Ibrahim Suggests Wider Scope of Duties for JMF". 8 April 2016.

Gray, Christopher Stephen. 1978. "Johore 1910–1941: Studies in the Colonial Process". PhD dissertation, Yale University.

Gullick, John Michael. 1992. *Rulers and Residents: Influence and Power in the Malay States*. Singapore: Oxford University Press.

———. 2004. *Indigenous Political Systems of Western Malaya*. Oxford: Berg.

Hamid, A. Jalil. 2016a. "Bangsa Johor Concept now More Relevant than Ever, Says Johor Ruler". *New Straits Times*, 30 August 2016.

———. 2016b. "Concord is a Blessing". *New Straits Times*, 30 August 2016.

Harding, Andrew. 1996. *Law, Government, and the Constitution in Malaysia*. The Hague: Kluwer Law International.

Hutchinson, Francis E. 2015. "Malaysia's Independence Leaders and the Legacies of State Formation under British Rule". *Journal of the Royal Asiatic Society* 25, no. 1: 123–51.

Jasmine Shadique. 2015. "Joyous Meeting of the Sultan and his Subjects". *New Straits Times*, 25 March 2015.

Jayasankaran, S. 2014. "Controversial Johor Bill Passed After Key Changes". *Business Times*, 10 June 2014.

Khoo Lay Kim. 1992. "Sultan Ibrahim's Reign (up to 1941)". In *A History of Johore (1365–1941)*, edited by R.O. Winstedt. Selangor: Malaysian Branch of the Royal Asiatic Society.

Kiong, Jenny and Chan Fook Weng. 2010. "Johore Battery". National Library Board. http://eresources.nlb.gov.sg/infopedia/articles/SIP_1073_2010-05-07 (accessed 1 November 2016).

Koh Jun Lin. 2015. "Johor Sultan Can't Just Decree Vape Ban, Law Experts Say". *Malaysiakini*, 29 November 2015.

Lee Yong Leng. 1980. *The Razor's Edge: Boundaries and Boundary Dispute in Southeast Asia*. Singapore: Institute of Southeast Asian Studies.

Lim Pui Huen. 2009. *Johor: Local History, Local Landscapes: 1855–1957*. Singapore: Straits Times Press.

Lowe, Vincent. 1982. "Symbolic Communication in Malaysian Politics: The Case of the Sultanate". *Southeast Asian Journal of Social Science* 10, no. 2: 71–89.

Mahathir Mohamad. 2011. *A Doctor in the House: The Memoirs of Tun Dr Mahathir Mohamad*. Petaling Jaya: MPH Publishing.

Malay Mail Online. 2016a. "Stop Aping Arabs, Johor Sultan Tells Malays". 24 March 2016. https://www.malaymail.com/news/malaysia/2016/03/24/stop-aping-arabs-johor-sultan-tells-malays/1086251

———. 2016b. "Sultan Ibrahim Wants Johor Government to Revive JVF". 12 May 2016. https://www.malaymail.com/news/malaysia/2016/05/12/sultan-ibrahim-wants-johor-government-to-revive-jvf/1118165

———. 2016c. "Tiga Buah Trak Mewah Berlepas, Sultan Johor Mula Kembara Negeri" [Three Trucks Depart, the Sultan of Johor Explores the State], 14 May 2016. https://www.projekmm.com/news/berita/2016/05/14/tiga-buah-trak-mewah-berlepas-sultan-johor-mula-kembara-negeri/1119827

Malaysia Today. 2013. "Johor Sultan Has Power to Change Rest Day". 28 November 2013.

———. 2014. "Bar Wants Johor Bill Amended to Avoid Opening Sultan to Attack". 8 June 2014.

Malaysiakini. 2016. "Malay Leaders Used to Defend Powers of Monarchy, Not Any More", 7 May 2016.

Malaysian Insider. 2014. "No EIA, but Johor Coastal Reclamation Projects Already Underway, Say Sources". 23 June 2014. https://malaysia.news.yahoo.com/no-eia-johor-coastal-reclamation-projects-already-underway-225834843.html

———. 2015a. "Johor Sultan Tells Racists, Haters to Get Out of His State". 16 September 2015. https://sg.news.yahoo.com/johor-sultan-tells-racists-haters-072256965.html

———. 2015b. "Johor Sultan Can Challenge 1994 Constitutional Restrictions on This Power, Says Law Expert". 7 May 2015. http://www.themalaysianinsider.com/malaysia/article/johor-sultan-can-challenge-1994-constitutional-restrictions-on-his-powers-s

Malaysian Times. 2013. "Tee Still an Exco Member, Stop Debating, Says Sultan of Johor". 1 July 2013.

Milner, Anthony Crothers. 1981. "Islam and Malay Kingship", *Journal of the Royal Asiatic Society* 113, no. 1: 46–70.

———. 1982. *Kerajaan: Malay Political Culture on the Eve of Colonial Rule*. Tucson: The University of Arizona Press.

———. 1995. *The Invention of Politics in Colonial Malaya: Contesting Nationalism and the Expansion of the Public Sphere*. Cambridge: Cambridge University Press.

———. 2011a. *The Evolution of the Malaysian Monarchy, and the Bonding of the Nation*. Bangi: Penerbit Universiti Kebangsaan Malaysia.

———. 2011b. *The Malays*. Oxford: Wiley-Blackwell.

Mohd Farhaan Shah. 2012. "Johoreans March to Istana and Pledge Loyalty to Sultan over WWW1 Issue". *Star Online*, 11 June 2012.

———. 2016. "Ruler with a Personal Touch". *Star Online*, 4 June 2016.

Mohd Sarim Mustajab. 1985. "The Impact of Colonial Rule in Johor: A Case of Social and Political Adjustment". PhD dissertation, University of Kent.

Muaz Omar. 2009. "In Defence of Monarchy … Minus the Politics". *Malaysian Insider*, 11 February 2009. http://www.malaysianbar.org.my/general_opinions/comments/in_defence_of_monarchy...minus_the_politics.html?date=2019-07-01

Muzaffar, Chandra. 1979. *Protector?: An Analysis of the Concept and Practice of Loyalty in Leader-led Relationships within Malay Society*. Penang: Aliran.

New Paper. 2015a. "Don't Make a Fool of Raykat". 26 August 2015.

———. 2015b. "Crown Prince: Johor has Right to Withdraw from M'sia". 17 October 2015.

New Straits Times. 2009. "Perak in Crisis: Sultan Tells Nizar, Exco to Resign". 2 May 2009.

———. 2015. "It Will Be Insane to Tell Investor Not to Come to Johor". 22 March 2015.

———. 2016. "Sultan Johor: Learn Islam from Those with Credentials". 31 March 2016.

Ng, Jason. 2013. "Move to Alter Weekend Days Sparks Confusion in Malaysian State". *Wall Street Journal*, 2 December 2013.

Raja Azlan Shah. 1986. "The Role of Constitutional Rulers in Malaysia". In *The Constitution in Malaysia: Further Perspectives and Developments*, edited by F.A. Trindade and H.P. Lee. Singapore: Oxford University Press.

Raja Nazrin Shah. 2004. *The Monarchy in Contemporary Malaysia*. Singapore: Institute of Southeast Asian Studies.

Rakyat Post. 2016. "JDT Football Team Gets Private Jet from Johor Sultan". 2 August 2016.

Rawlings, Hugh F. 1986. "The Malaysian Constitutional Crisis of 1983". *International and Comparative Law Quarterly* 35, no. 2: 237–54.

Reme Ahmad. 2014. "Johor Reclamation Project 'To Create Oil Storage Hub'". *Straits Times*, 27 June 2014.

Sim Bak Heng and Jasmine Shadique. 2012. "Mind Your Own Business, Johor Ruler Tells Critic". *New Straits Times*, 15 June 2012.

Singapore and Straits Directory. 1893. Singapore: The Singapore and Straits Printing Office.

Sopiee, Nordin. 1975. *From Malayan Union to Singapore Separation: Political Unification in the Malaysia Region, 1945–65*. Kuala Lumpur: Penerbit Universiti Malaya.

Star Online. 2010. "Sultan Ibrahim Is the First Ruler to Get a Train Driver's License". 29 June 2010. https://www.thestar.com.my/news/nation/2010/06/29/sultan-ibrahim-is-the-first-ruler-to-get-a-train-drivers-licence

———. 2016a. "Sultan Ibrahim the First Johor Ruler to Attend Chingay Procession". 19 January 2016. https://www.thestar.com.my/news/nation/2016/01/19/sultan-ibrahim-the-first-johor-ruler-to-attend-chingay-procession

———. 2016b. "Sultan of Johor Braves Scorching Heat to Meet Devotees during Thaipusam". 25 January 2016. https://www.thestar.com.my/news/nation/2016/01/25/ruler-joins-in-celebration-sultan-of-johor-braves-scorching-heat-to-meet-devotees-during-thaipusam

———. 2016c. "Sultan Receives His New Aircraft". 1 March 2016 https://www.thestar.com.my/news/nation/2016/03/01/sultan-receives-his-new-aircraft-medical-grads-issue-to-drag-on-the-plane-touched-down-at-senai-afte (accessed 24 October 2016).

State of Johore. 1955. *A Souvenir Commemorating the Diamond Jubilee of His Highness the Sultan of Johore*.

Stockwell, Anthony. 1979. *British Policy and Malay Politics during the Malayan Union Experiment, 1942–1948*. Kuala Lumpur: Malayan Branch of the Royal Asiatic Society.

———. 1988. "The Constitutional Crisis in Malaysia 1983–84". In *Constitutional Head and Political Crises*, edited by D.A. Low. London: Palgrave Macmillan.

Straits Times. 1935. "Prime Minister and Johore's Jubilee Gift". 5 June 1935.

———. 1993. "KL Disbands Johor Sultan's Private Army". 19 August 1993.

———. 1996. "Johor Ruler Wants Weekend Changed Back to Friday". 10 February 1996.

———. 2015a. "Learn from S'pore Education Policy, Johor Sultan Says". 13 June 2015.

———. 2015b. "Johor Crown Prince Warns that State May Secede if Putrajaya Breaches Federation's Terms". 16 October 2015.

———. 2015c. "Malaysia Charter Doesn't Provide for Secession". 20 October 2015.

———. 2015d. "Johor Sultan Slams Malaysia's Multi-stream Schools". 29 October 2015.

———. 2016. "Sultan of Johor Buys 'Palace Truck'". 17 October 2016.

Sugimoto, Ichiro. 2007. "An Analysis of the State of Johore's Finances 1910–1940". *Journal of Malaysian Branch of the Royal Asiatic Society* 80, no. 2: 67–87.

Sun Daily. 2013. "Johor Sultan Calls on All Quarters to Stop Questioning Tee's Appointment". 1 July 2013.

———. 2014. "Johor to Table State Environment Act in 2015". 9 July 2014.

———. 2015. "Johor Ruler's Coronation, A Royal Tradition with a Difference". 2 March 2015.

Sunday Express. 1955. "The Sultan Warns: If the British Leave …". 15 September 1955.

Sunday Times. 2015. "Johor Prince Posts Defiant Video after Minister's Warning". 14 June 2015.

Suparto, Idayu. 2015. "10 Things to Know about the Celebrations to Mark the Johor Sultan's Coronation". *Straits Times*, 20 March 2015.

Suwannathat-Pian, Kobkua. 2011. *Palace, Political Party, and Power: A Story of the Socio-Political Development of Malay Kingship*. Singapore: NUS Press.

Teoh, Shannon. 2015. "Malaysia Gives Nod for Johor Reclamation Project but Cuts Size". *Straits Times*, 6 January 2015.

———. 2016. "Johor Sultan Calls for Restoration of Monarchs' Powers". *Straits Times*, 9 May 2016.

Thio, Eunice. 1967. "British Policy towards Johore: From Advice to Control". *Journal of Malaysian Branch of the Royal Asiatic Society* 40, no. 1: 1–41.

Trocki, Carl A. 2007. *Prince of Pirates: Temenggongs and the Development of Johor and Singapore, 1784–1885*. Singapore: NUS Press.

Utusan. 2010. "Johor Sultan Calls for Rephrasing of 'Malay Supremacy' as 'Malay Sovereignty'". 9 December 2010.

———. 2014. "Johor Diminta Tubuh Pasukan Rayuan Keputusan Pulau Batu Putih" [Johor Requests to Form a Team to Appeal the Decision Regarding Pulau Batu Putih]. 30 May 2014.

Wain, Barry. 2009. *Malaysian Maverick: Mahathir Mohamad in Turbulent Times*. Basingstoke: Palgrave Macmillan.

Wan Syamsul Amly. 2015. "Johor Secession No Longer Possible after Merdeka". *Astro Awani*, 18 June 2015.

Wong Chun Wai and Nelson Benjamin. 2015. "English, the Universal Currency". *Star* Online, 12 June 2015. https://www.thestar.com.my/news/nation/2015/06/12/english-the-universal-currency

Yee Xiang Yun. 2016. "Johor Ruler to Host Chinese at Event Last Seen 65 Years Ago". *The Star*, 7 September 2016.

Yong Yen Nie. 2014a. "Johor Housing Bill Amended after Uproar over Sultan's Powers". *Straits Times*, 9 June 2014.

———. 2014b. "Johor Sultan 'Will Not Interfere' in Matters of State Govt". *Straits Times*, 13 June 2014.

Zhen, Summer. 2016. "Country Garden's Ambition in Malaysia Backed by Johor's Royal Family". *South China Morning Post*, 11 February 2016.

III

Social and Environmental Issues

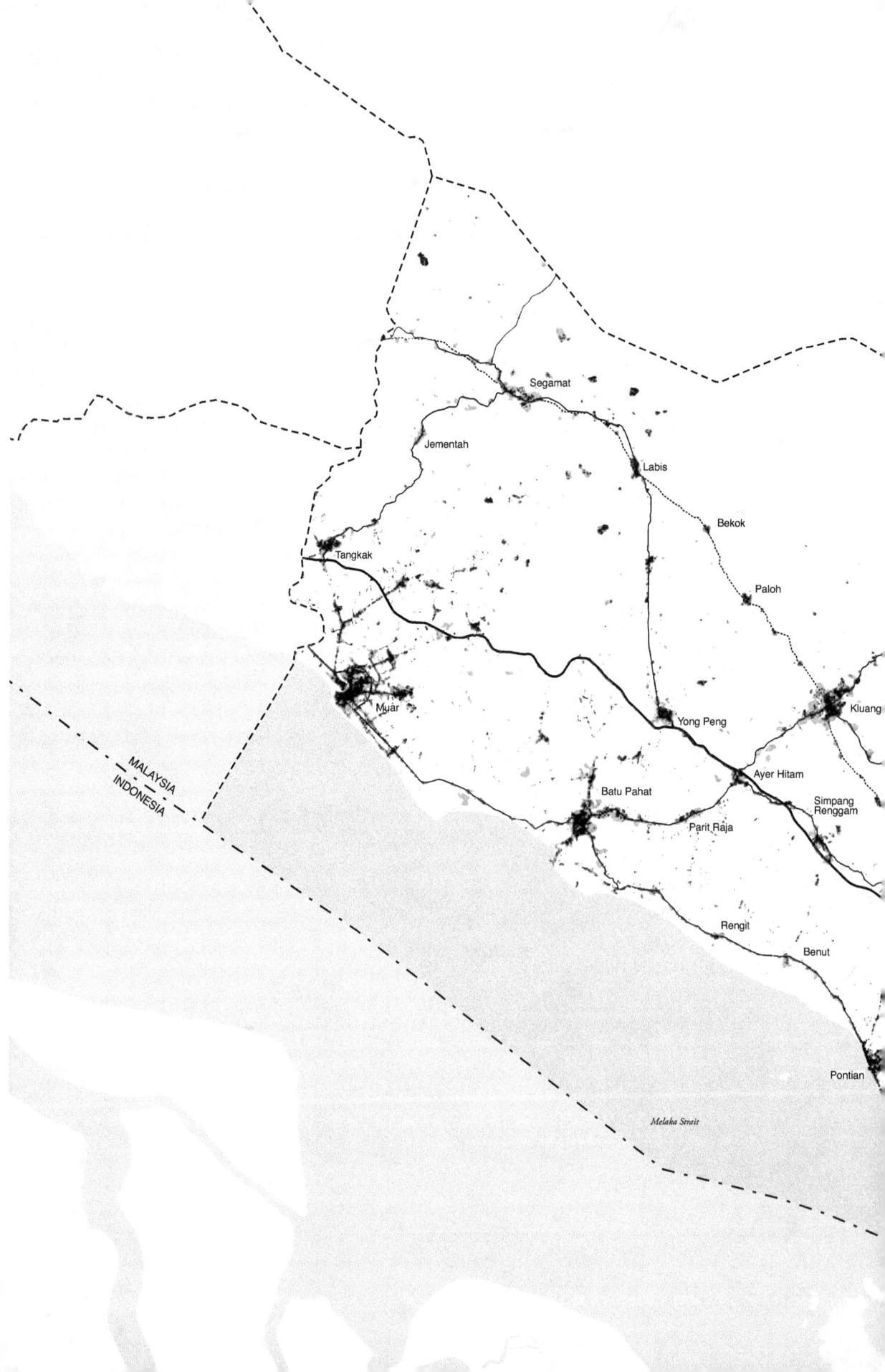

Segamat

Jementah

Labis

Bekok

Tangkak

Paloh

Muar

Yong Peng

Kluang

Batu Pahat

Ayer Hitam

Parit Raja

Simpang
Renggam

MALAYSIA

INDONESIA

Rengit

Benut

Pontian

Melaka Strait

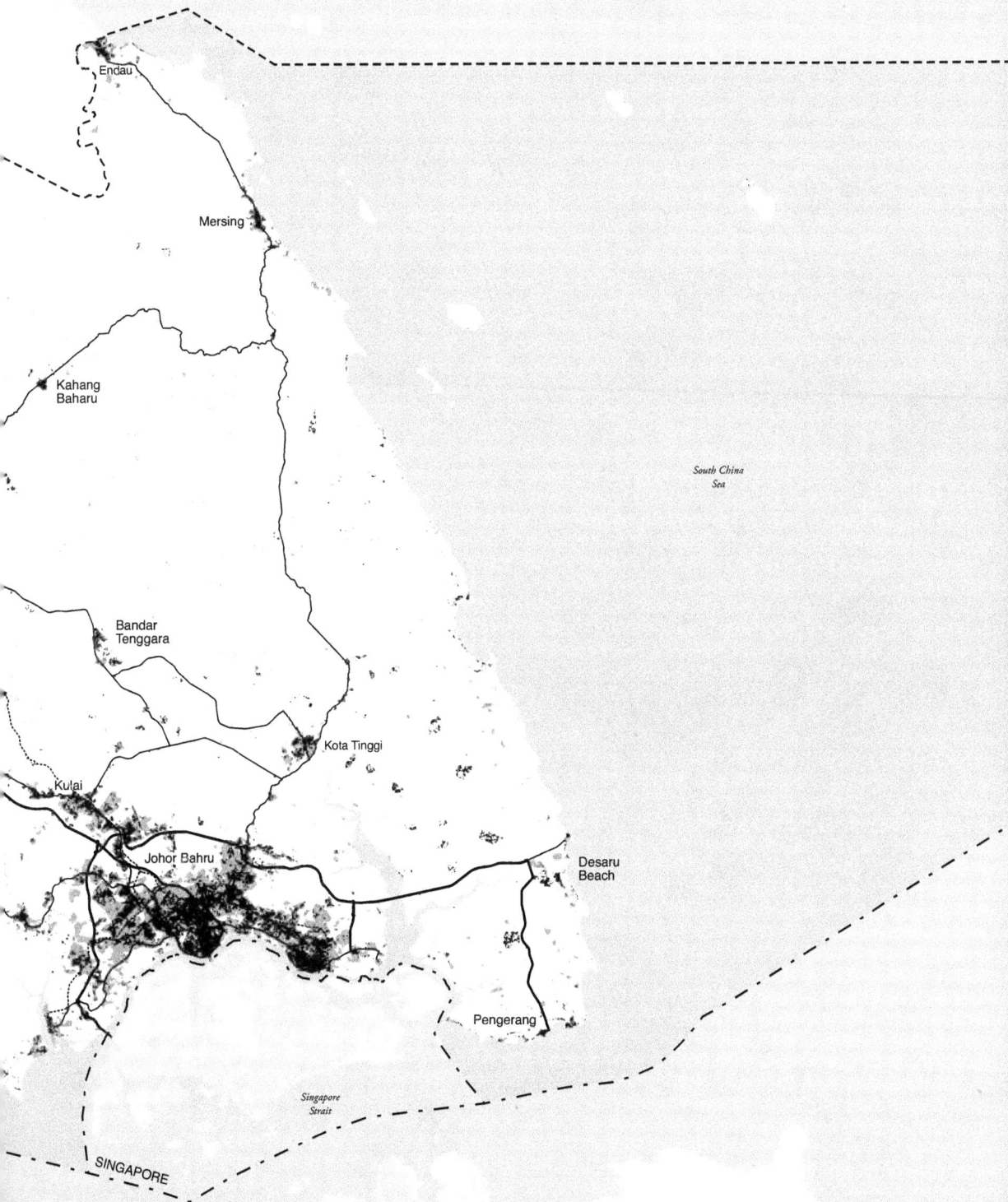

MAP 4.1
EXPANSION OF BUILT-UP AREAS

■ Built-up Area 1990
▨ Built-up Area 1990 to 2014

Endau

Mersing

Kahang
Baharu

South China
Sea

Bandar
Tenggara

Kota Tinggi

Kulai

Johor Bahru

Desaru
Beach

Pengerang

Singapore
Strait

SINGAPORE

0   10   20km

Segamat

Muar

MALAYSIA
INDONESIA

Kluang

Batu Pahat

Simpang
Renggam

Pontian

Melaka Strait

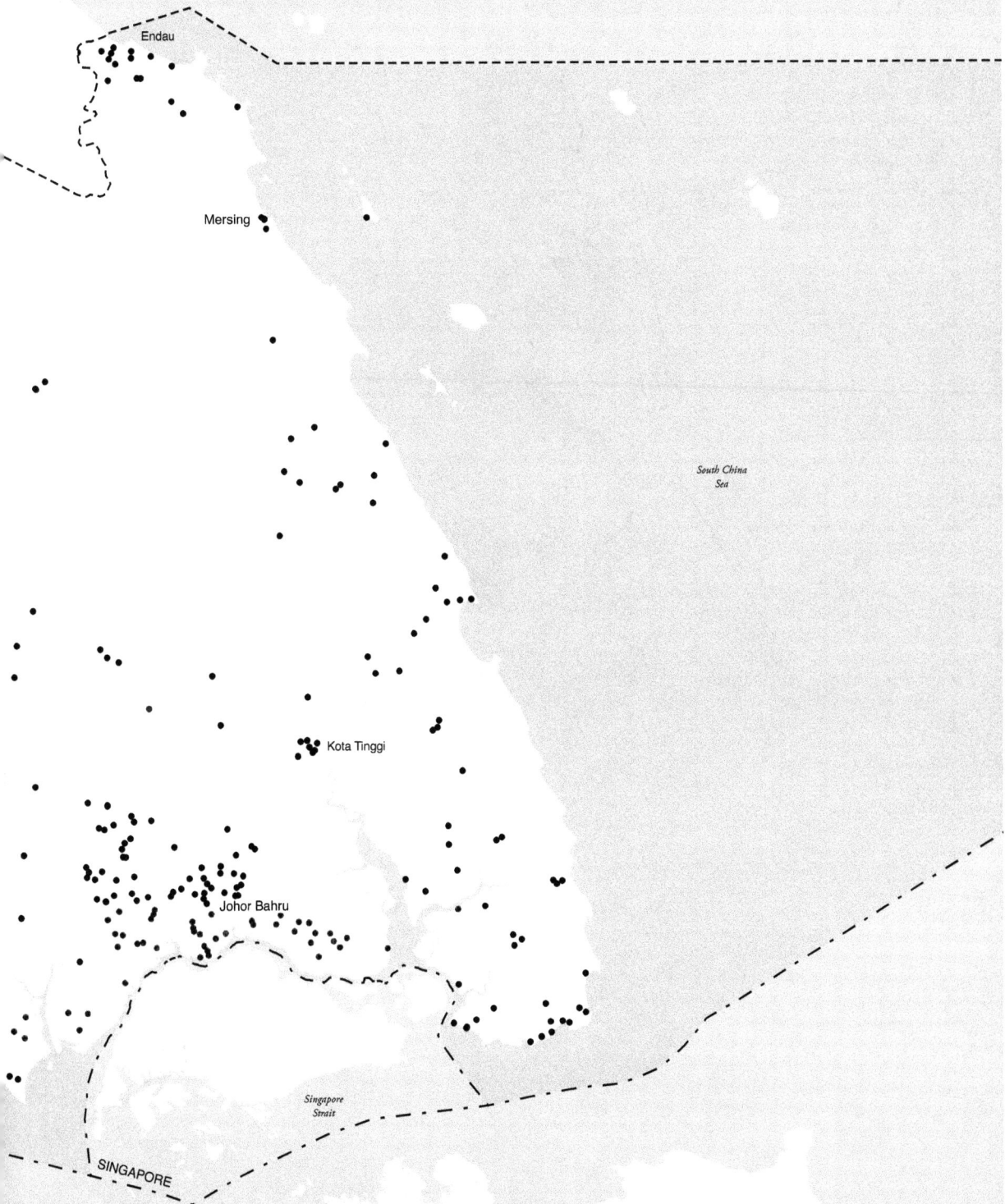

MAP 4.2
MOSQUES IN JOHOR STATE

Endau

Mersing

South China
Sea

Kota Tinggi

Johor Bahru

Singapore
Strait

SINGAPORE

0   10 20km

Gunung Ledang
1276m

▲

*Junuh
Reservoir*

Sungai Muar

*Bertam
Reservoir*

*Sembrong
Reservoir*

Gu

Sungai Batu Pahat

*Sempang
Reservoir*

Pontian
Peatland

MALAYSIA
INDONESIA

Pulau
Pisang

Melaka Strait

Mangrove Forest
Pulau Kuku

MAP 4.3
NATURAL LANDSCAPE ELEMENTS

▲ Mountain Peak
— River
Water Reservoir
Forest
Peat Soil
Mangrove Forest
Seagrass Area

Lebong Reservoir

Pulau
Pemanggil

Pulau
Rawa

Pulau
Babi Besar

Pulau
Aur

Pulau
Tinggi

Pulau
Sibu

*South China
Sea*

Sedili River

nut
Om

▲

*Linggiu
Reservoir*

Johor River

Gunung Pulai
654m

▲

Sungai Tebrau

Sungai Sedaili

Johor River

*Sultan
Iskandar
Reservoir*

*Sungai Lebam
Reservoir*

ove Forest
I Pulai

Seagrass

g Piai

*Singapore
Strait*

SINGAPORE

0   10   20km

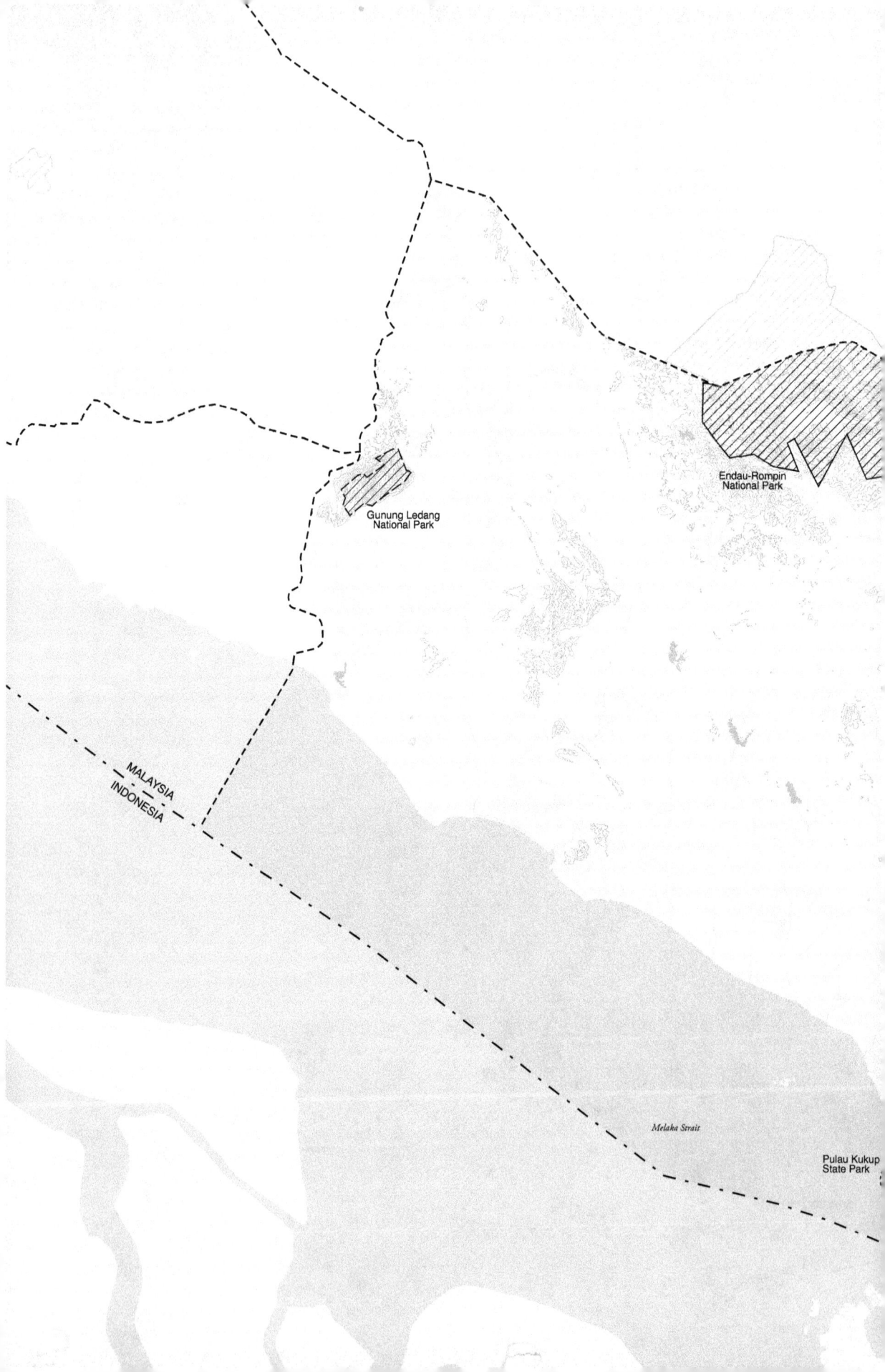

Gunung Ledang
National Park

Endau-Rompin
National Park

MALAYSIA
INDONESIA

Melaka Strait

Pulau Kukup
State Park

MAP 4.4
PROTECTED NATURE

● RAMSAR Site
Marina Park
Protected Landscape
Strict Nature Reserve
Wilderness Area

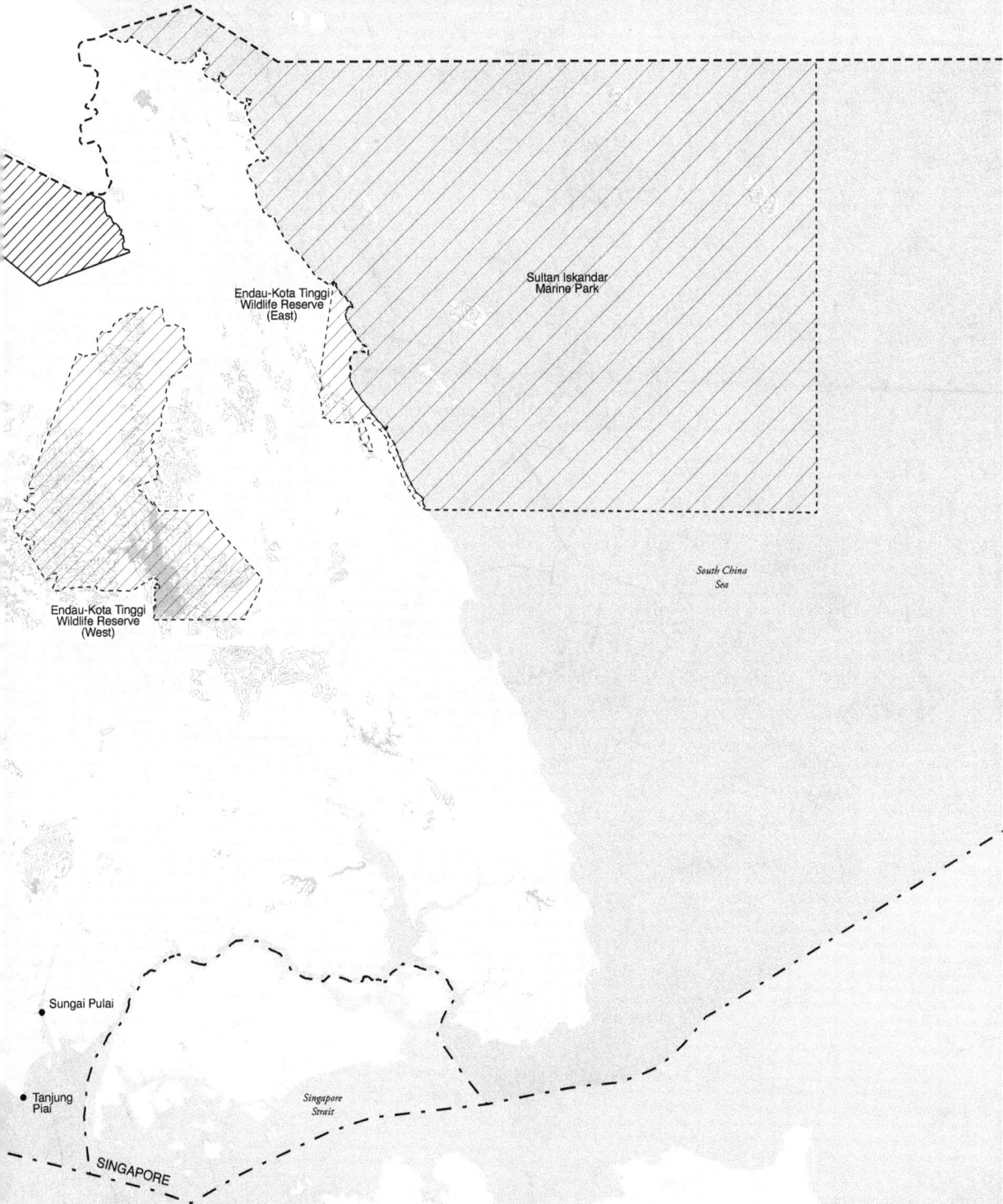

Endau-Kota Tinggi
Wildlife Reserve
(East)

Sultan Iskandar
Marine Park

Endau-Kota Tinggi
Wildlife Reserve
(West)

*South China
Sea*

● Sungai Pulai

● Tanjung
Piai

*Singapore
Strait*

SINGAPORE

0   10   20km

MAP 4.5
FOREST CITY ISKANDAR MALAYSIA
COUNTRY GARDEN

Forest City
Golf Resort
Development
Site

Sungai Pulai
Mangrove Forest
(RAMSAR)

Phoenix
International
Golf Hotel

Forest City
Golf Resort

Second Link Expressway
to Johor Bahru

Poresia Golf
Country Club

Forest City
Industrial Building
System (IBS)
Factory

Sungai Pulai

Tanjung
Pelepas
Port

Second Link to
Singapore

Island
3

Tebrau Strait

Country Gardens'
Forest City

Tanjung Bin
Power Plant

Tanjung
Kupang
Seagrass
Meadow

Island
1

Island
2

Island
4
(Projected)

MALAYSIA
SINGAPORE

0   1   2km

MAP 4.6
IBRAHIM INTERNATIONAL BUSINESS
DISTRICT JOHOR BAHRU

Jalan Seri Lang

Hilton
Hotel

Sultan Iskandar
Customs and Immigration
Complex

JB Sentral Train Station

Jalan Ayer Molek

Federal
Government
Offices

Persada Johor
International
Convention
Centre

City
Square
Mall

Merlin
Tower

The Puteri
Pan Pacific
Hotel

Jalan Tun Abdul Razak

Plaza
Kotaraya

Bangunan
Tabung Haji

Bangunan
Sultan Ibrahim

Diamond
Jubilee Hall

Tourism
Center

Malaya
High Court

Persiaran Tun Sri Lanang

R&F Princess Cove
Development Site

Causeway
to Singapore

Johor Waterfront

MALAYSIA
SINGAPORE

Tebrau Strait

0   100   200m

13

FOREIGN WORKERS IN JOHOR
The Dependency Dilemma

Benedict Weerasena

INTRODUCTION

In recent years, Johor's economic growth has been above the national average. In fact, the state's broad-based economy is the third largest contributor to Malaysia's gross domestic product (GDP) across agriculture, manufacturing and services (Maslynnawati, Weerasena, and Fawzi 2017).

However, many activities within these sectors are synonymous with high volumes of foreign workers. As these activities have grown, so too have the number of foreign workers. In turn, Malaysians have increasingly had to share facilities, such as public spaces, and services, such as public transportation, with this new and growing population. In certain towns in Johor, such as Muar, which has a booming furniture sector, and Pengerang, which is home to a new integrated petroleum complex, parks and other shared spaces are crowded with foreign workers over the weekends. This creates some uneasiness among local communities (Benjamin 2018; Soo 2018).

Moreover, in the recent review of the 11th Malaysia Plan, dependency on low-skilled foreign workers was highlighted as a crucial issue impeding human capital development.[1] Specifically, the overdependence on low-skilled foreign labour serves as a disincentive for more capital-intensive operations—resulting in many Malaysian industries remaining at the lower end of the value chain (Ministry of Economic Affairs 2018).

Hence, the 11th Malaysia Plan set a cap on foreign workers of 15 per cent of the total workforce or not more than 2.3 million people by the year 2020. In addition, a greater focus was placed on managing and screening the entry of foreign workers through the formulation of a comprehensive immigration and employment policy.

However, it is important to consider whether the cap of 15 per cent of employment of foreign workers is a sensible target to begin with. This is because Malaysia records 1,758,328 active Temporary Employment Visit Pass (PLKS[2]) holders (Ministry of Home Affairs 2018a), which constitutes 11.5 per cent of the total workforce.[3] Since the number of documented foreign workers is less than 2.3 million and the policy implies that the number of foreign workers exceeds 2.3 million; this indicates some official acknowledgement of the prevalence of undocumented workers. However, there is no credible official estimate of the number of undocumented workers, either in Malaysia or in Johor.

Various business stakeholders, especially in Johor, such as the Muar Furniture Association and Master Builders Association Malaysia, have voiced their concerns as their businesses are already facing a shortage of manpower (*Sun Daily,* 26 March 2017; Malaysian Trade Union Congress 2017). A reduction in dependence on foreign workers could almost certainly affect the country's output and revenue in the short term. In the long term, this could potentially be mitigated through automation or by hiring local workers.

This raises a few questions: Are businesses in Johor ready to mechanize their operations? Do business stakeholders prefer hiring local or foreign workers? As Johor progresses towards becoming a high-income state, is it viable to replace foreign workers with their local counterparts?

Hence, the dependency dilemma persists. Should Johor maintain or decrease its dependency on foreign workers? How will this affect the state's economic growth in the long run? Will a reduction in foreign worker dependency stifle the growth of businesses? More importantly, how many documented and undocumented foreign workers are there in Johor?

This chapter first sets out the historical background of foreign workers in Johor and Malaysia. From there, it examines the latest data available on documented foreign workers, presents estimates of the number of undocumented workers, and explores Johor's dependency on foreign workers.

FOREIGN WORKERS IN MALAYSIA: HISTORICAL BACKGROUND

Johor's economy has long benefited from Malaysia's supportive immigration policies. When the New Economic Policy (NEP) was implemented in 1971, massive urbanization and rural-urban migration led to labour shortages, especially in rural areas. Labour shortages in several key economic sectors such as agriculture and other natural resource related sectors were largely addressed by the arrival of foreign workers from Thailand, Philippines and Indonesia (Carpio, Özden, and Testaverde 2015). However, in that decade, foreign workers were employed in small numbers to meet seasonal demand.

When rapid industrialization spurred the economy in the 1980s and 1990s, rising wages and skill shortages attracted large numbers of foreign workers. Low-skilled workers were compatible with the low value-added production at that time, which alleviated production pressures (Ang, Murugasu, and Chai 2018). Although the entry of low-skilled foreign workers was initially supposed to function as a transitionary crutch to ease production constraints, this unintendedly became an entrenched feature of the Malaysian economy (Carpio, Özden, and Testaverde 2015). In addition, the initial uncontrolled entry of foreign workers had negative consequences—in particular affecting the internal and border security of Malaysia (Azizah and Zin 2011). This was especially serious in Johor due to its long coastline.

Furthermore, rapid urbanization and increased prosperity among urban populations generated demand for labour in the construction and domestic services sector, which was met with an increased supply of foreign workers. This was due to the expansion of formal education among young Malaysian workers, who preferred formal and better remunerated jobs over menial jobs especially in the construction sector (Athukorala 2006). Similarly, increasing educational opportunities for young Malaysian women resulted in greater participation in the workforce, indirectly leading to a rise in demand for foreign domestic helpers. The country's stable economy and comparatively higher living standards attracted more foreign labour to Malaysian shores.

In these decades, immigration in the Southeast Asian region was largely due to different population dynamics (Walmsley, Aguilar, and Ahmed 2013), wherein Malaysia's labour shortages were resolved by neighbouring countries with a much larger population base. Besides the pull factors, political instability in neighbouring countries, coupled with relatively lower wages and higher levels of unemployment, compelled many of their citizens to seek better economic opportunities in Malaysia.

In terms of government policy on foreign workers, the framework regulating the latter has been vague and erratic (Devadason and Chan 2014; Aziz, Ayob, and Abdulsomad 2017). Policy reversals, such as retrenchments, deportations and import bans, followed with return migration and lifting of those bans were frequent. This is attributed to various reasons including ad hoc management of in-migration, lack of long-term oversight of labour management and the lax enforcement of existing regulations.

For instance, in August 1997, the Asian Financial Crisis resulted in a temporary movement to expel unskilled and undocumented foreign workers (Shamsulbariah 2003). However, in less than a year, the intake of foreign workers was encouraged to address the decline in foreign direct investment. To alleviate labour shortages in 2004, undocumented foreign workers who were initially deported under a four-month amnesty programme were later allowed to return on official permits (Devadason and Chan 2014). Policy reversals were evident again during the 2008 Global Financial Crisis. In this case, as a result of job layoffs due to company closures in the manufacturing sector, policymakers initially froze foreign worker inflows. Yet, within six months, they reopened the intake of foreign workers in electrical and electronics and textile industries following appeals by key industry players. Most recently, the government reversed a decision on making skilled foreign workers pay 80 per cent of the annual RM10,000 levy in one day, after employers started to complain that their workers could not afford it (Dermawan 2018). Time and again, the inability of policymakers to recognize the critical long-term contribution of foreign workers resulted in policies premised on short-term solutions for labour shortfalls (Yaw 2002).

Although policies for the employment of foreign workers are under the jurisdiction of the Federal Government,[4] the government of Johor has also proposed state-level efforts regarding foreign workers. In the 2017 State Budget Speech, the Chief Minister outlined a strategy to reduce foreign worker dependency by: conducting in-depth research on the real need for foreign workers in Johor; formulating a labour rationalization plan; and working with the Federal Government to ensure there are no loopholes regarding the entry of foreign workers in Johor (Nordin 2016). Most recently, the Pakatan Harapan state government announced plans to set up a committee to control the influx of foreigners seeking employment in Johor (*The Star*, 25 May 2019). However, these plans and proposals remain as such and efforts to bring them to fruition are piecemeal.

GENERAL DATA ON FOREIGN WORKERS IN MALAYSIA

The following data from the Ministry of Home Affairs (MOHA) derives the number of foreign workers from the total registry of active PLKS holders throughout Malaysia as of 28 February 2018. These figures constitute a universe, unlike other sources such as the Labour Force Survey and Current Population Estimates by the Department of Statistics Malaysia and the National Employment Returns by the Ministry of Human Resources, which are samples. However, one downside of MOHA's data is that it only records documented foreign workers and is not able to account for undocumented foreign workers across Malaysia. Thus, it is important to note that only the approved sectors for PLKS holders are listed here, namely manufacturing, plantation, agriculture, construction, services and foreign domestic helpers.

As shown in Figure 13.1, there are 1,758,328 active PLKS holders throughout Malaysia. 36.6 per cent of them are working in the manufacturing sector, with 18.8 per cent working in construction, 15.1 per cent on plantations,[5] 13.6 per cent in services, 8.8 per cent in agriculture,[6] and finally 7.1 per cent as foreign domestic helpers (FDH) (Ministry of Home Affairs 2018a).[7]

In terms of source countries, the highest number of documented foreign workers in Malaysia are from Indonesia (40.1 per cent), followed by Nepal (21.8 per cent), Bangladesh (15.3 per cent), India (6.5 per cent) and Myanmar (6.1 per cent), as shown in Figure 13.2 (Ministry of Home Affairs 2018a).[8]

From Figure 13.2, it can be observed that the Nepalese make up the majority of foreign workers in the manufacturing sector, followed by Indonesians, Bangladeshis and Myanmarese. Meanwhile, the construction sector mostly hires Indonesians, followed by Bangladeshis and Filipinos. On the other hand, Indonesian foreign workers dominate the plantation sector, while Nepalese and Indian foreign workers

FIGURE 13.1
Number of Foreign Workers by Sector, Malaysia, 2018

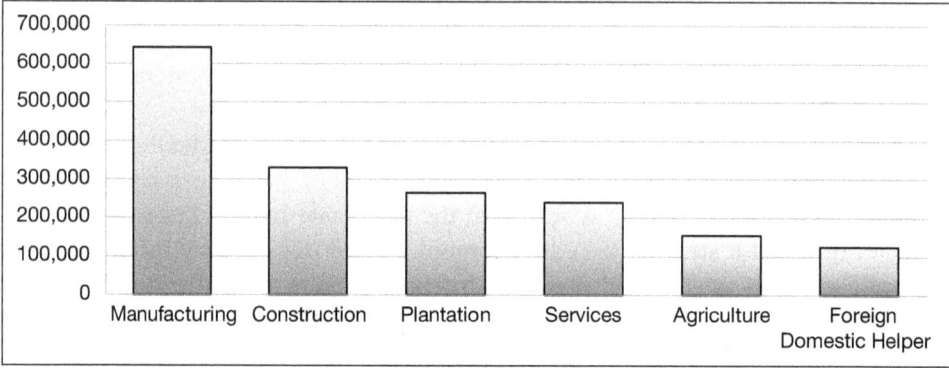

Source: Ministry of Home Affairs.

FIGURE 13.2
Number of Foreign Workers by Source Country and Sector, Malaysia, 2018

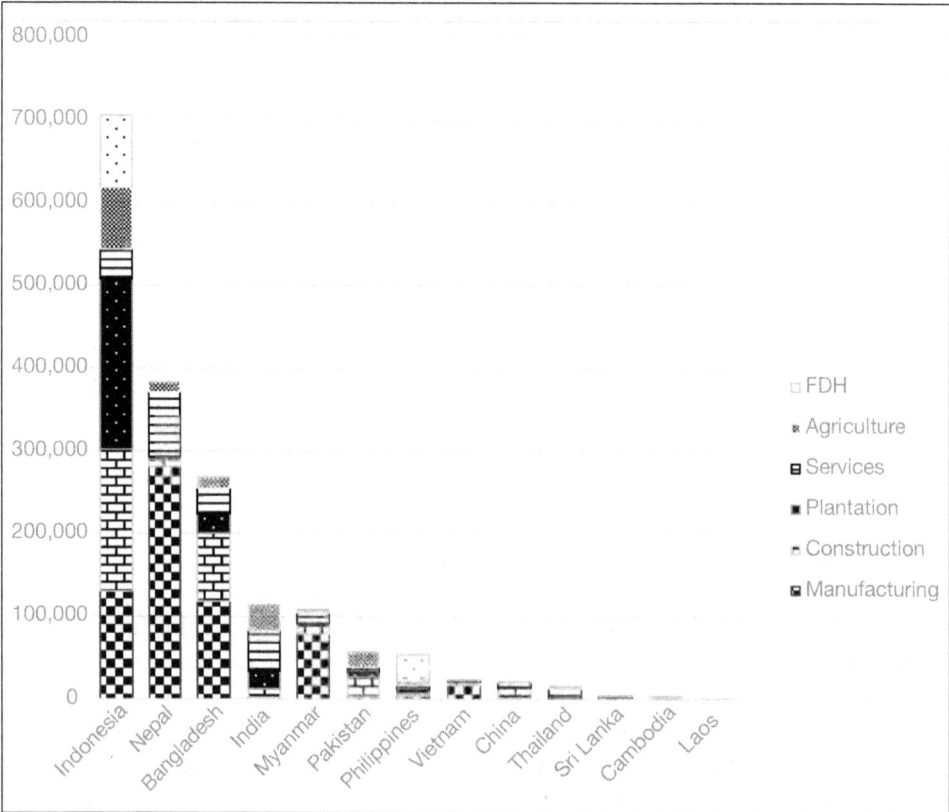

Source: Ministry of Home Affairs.

make up the majority in the services sector. The foreign domestic helper sector largely employs Indonesian and Filipino women.

The data provided can also be classified according to the state in which the PLKS was registered, which indicates the state where the foreign worker is employed—assuming they do not work in a different state. As shown in Figure 13.3, Selangor recorded the highest number of foreign workers (30 per cent), followed by Johor with 308,190 foreign workers (17.5 per cent), WP Kuala Lumpur (14.6 per cent), Penang (7.4 per cent), and then Sabah and Sarawak (Ministry of Home Affairs 2018b).[9]

Sectoral Distribution of Foreign Workers in Johor

The Ministry of Home Affairs (2018a) recorded the number of PLKS holders by sector and gender for the state of Johor, as of 28 February 2018. Overall, there is a total of 308,190 active PLKS holders or documented workers in Johor.

The manufacturing sector in Johor recorded the largest number of active PLKS holders at 170,835 or 55.4 per cent, followed by the construction sector (46,260), agriculture (32,667), services (26,312), plantations (21,431) and foreign domestic helpers (10,685) (Figure 13.4).

As seen in Figure 13.5, a large majority of the documented foreign workers in Johor are men (258,810 or 83.9 per cent) as compared to 49,380 women (16.1 per

FIGURE 13.3
Number of Foreign Workers by State, Malaysia, 2018

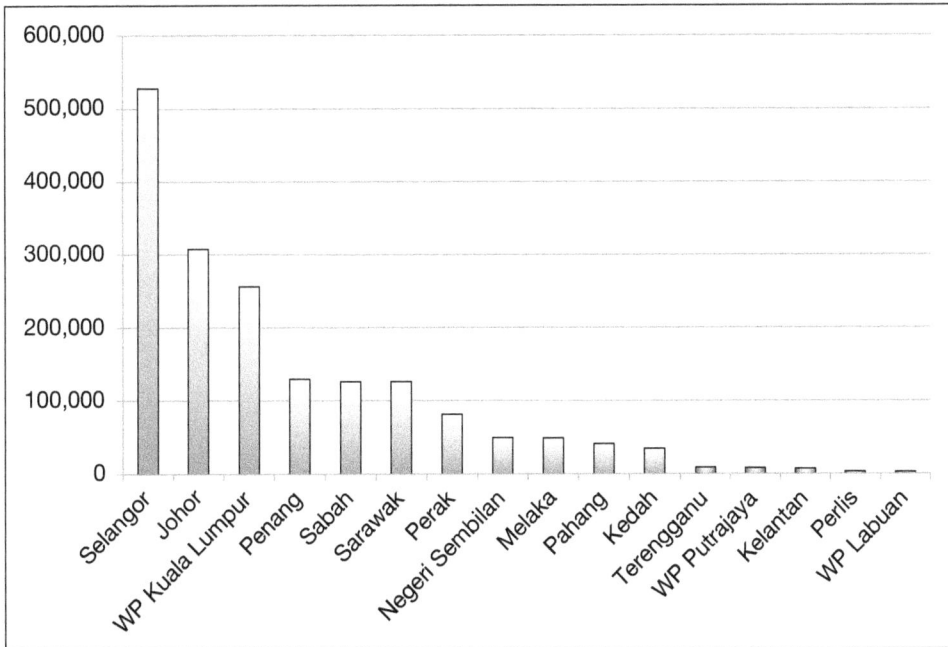

Source: Ministry of Home Affairs.

FIGURE 13.4
Percentage of Foreign Workers by Sector, Johor, 2018

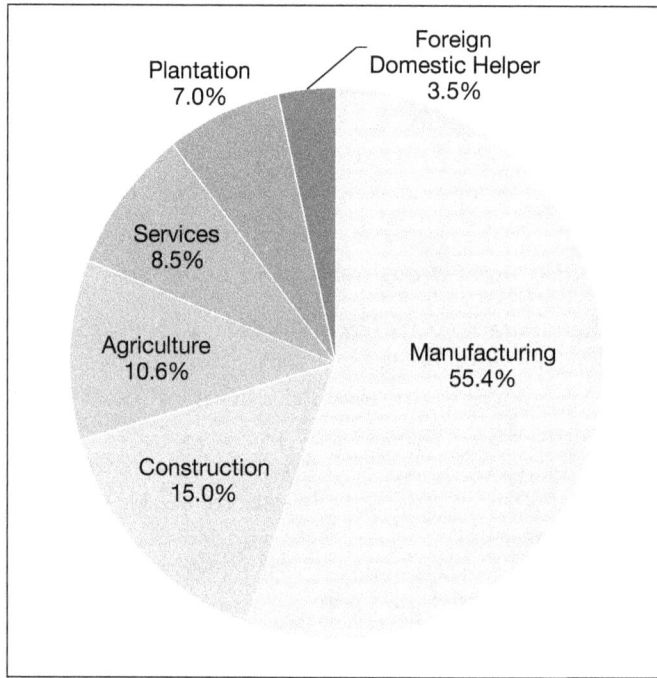

Plantation 7.0%

Foreign Domestic Helper 3.5%

Services 8.5%

Agriculture 10.6%

Manufacturing 55.4%

Construction 15.0%

Source: Ministry of Home Affairs.

FIGURE 13.5
Number of Foreign Workers by Gender and Sector, Johor, 2018

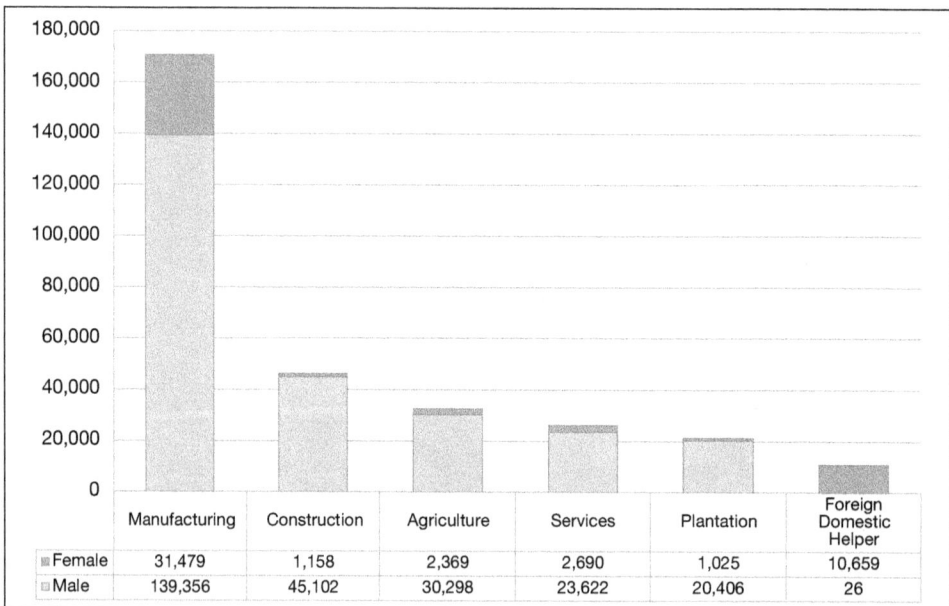

	Manufacturing	Construction	Agriculture	Services	Plantation	Foreign Domestic Helper
Female	31,479	1,158	2,369	2,690	1,025	10,659
Male	139,356	45,102	30,298	23,622	20,406	26

Source: Ministry of Home Affairs.

cent). Once again, it is important to remember that the Ministry of Home Affairs only records documented foreign workers and is not able to account for undocumented foreign workers in Johor.

The data presented above does not portray reality in terms of the total number of foreign workers in Johor, as the data does not record the number of undocumented foreign workers including those who are categorized as illegal immigrants (PATI[10]). It is challenging and difficult to ascertain the number of undocumented foreign workers as this working population is not registered with the authorities. In addition, their entry and exit in the labour market are not recorded (Lee and Khor 2018).

Several sources which act as reference material and supplementary data shed light on the estimated number of undocumented foreign workers in the country. First, the Malaysian Employers Federation estimates that for every documented foreign worker in Malaysia, there are 2.3 undocumented foreign workers (Muhamading 2018). On the other hand, the Malaysian Trades Union Congress estimates that, as of 2016, there are approximately a total of 7 million documented and undocumented foreign workers in Malaysia (MTUC Memorandum 2016). However, both these estimates are not verifiable as no official government source was provided.

According to the Ministry of Human Resources (MOHR), as of late 2014 there are an estimated 6.7 million foreign workers in Malaysia including immigrants without official documentation (*Astro Awani*, 24 April 2018)—indicating that an approximate seven out of ten foreign workers are undocumented. However, in 2016 the ministry revised the number of undocumented workers to seven out of seventeen total foreign workers, stating that an estimated 40 per cent of the labour workforce in Malaysia is undocumented (Shagar 2016). This drastic reduction suggests the possibility that reporting of undocumented foreign workers could be biased downwards.

On the other hand, the Immigration Department of Malaysia stated that there were 600,000 foreign nationals working illegally in Malaysia as of July 2017 (*Bernama*, 21 July 2018). As of yet, there has not been any statement from the Pakatan Harapan government on the number of undocumented foreign workers in Malaysia.

However, the new Johor government estimates that the average number of undocumented foreign workers in the state is approximately 750,000 as of September 2018 (H.H. Nurul 2018; Dass 2018). The Johor State Executive Chairman of Consumerism, Human Resources and Unity added that this estimate constitutes 20 per cent of the total number of undocumented foreign workers in Malaysia, which is the second highest after Selangor.

One interesting development to note is the ongoing private project entitled *Program Bancian Warga Asing*[11] or Foreign Citizen Census Programmer carried out to collect data and information on foreigners including those who enter the country illegally (*Sun Daily*, 26 March 2018), though there are no updates about the progress of this census so far.

It is thus of utmost importance that a numerical estimation is carried out to understand the scale of the foreign worker situation in Johor, especially those who work without an active PLKS. The number of undocumented foreign workers can be estimated with reference to the supplementary data presented above.[12]

Thus, the estimated number of undocumented foreign workers in Johor is between 105,180 and 126,920 (Table 13.1). If we take the average of the range of undocumented foreign workers it is estimated that, for every 10 documented workers, there are 3.8 undocumented workers.

Given data limitations, it is important to clarify that this exercise may not be completely accurate in estimating the total number of foreign workers in Johor. Johor's 400-km coastline bordering the Straits of Malacca, Straits of Johor and the South China Sea has resulted in at least twenty hotspots that are used by illegal immigrants to enter and exit the country (*The Star*, 29 August 2013). This points to the possibility that Johor might have a higher share of undocumented foreign workers than the 17.53 per cent figure cited above. Also, the rapid development of Johor's broad-based economy presents a wider range of job opportunities for foreign workers, as compared to other states that have a less broad-based economy. The factors listed here explains why the estimate of 750,000 undocumented foreign workers provided by the Johor state government is much higher than estimated through the calculations made above.

TABLE 13.1
Estimated Number of Undocumented Foreign Workers in Johor

Source and Year	Overall Estimation (Malaysia)	Number of Undocumented Foreign Workers[a] (Malaysia)	Estimated number of Undocumented Foreign Workers[b] (Johor 17.53%)	Estimated Total Documented and Undocumented Foreign Workers (Percentage of Total Labour Force[c])
Immigration Department of Malaysia (2017)	600,000 foreign workers working illegally	600,000	105,180	413,370 (21.2%)
Ministry of Human Resource (2016)[d]	7 out of 17 foreign workers are undocumented	724,017	126,920	435,110 (22.3%)

Notes and Sources:

a. The number of undocumented foreign workers is calculated by referring to Ministry of Home Affairs (2018a) statistics which records 1.758 million active PLKS holders as of February 2018. Hence, the number of documented foreign workers is deducted from the overall total estimate to calculate the number of undocumented foreign workers.

b. The estimated number of undocumented foreign workers is calculated by referring to the Ministry of Home Affairs statistics which records Johor having 17.53 per cent of all documented foreign workers in Malaysia.

c. This percentage is calculated by dividing the estimated total number of foreign workers with the State's total Labour Force (from Labour Force Survey Report Year 2017; Department of Statistics Malaysia 2018) after the number of non-Malaysians are deducted and replaced with the foreign worker estimates instead. This is because the Labour Force Survey Report only samples private living quarters, thereby excluding hostels, boarding houses, construction sites and workers' dormitories. Hence, there is a strong concern for under-sampling of foreign workers especially undocumented workers as many are excluded by design (Lee and Khor 2018).

d. The data employed here is sourced from the Ministry of Human Resource in 2016, instead of 2014 because the former gives a more current and realistic picture of the number of undocumented foreign workers, especially after efforts have been carried out to reduce undocumented foreign workers.

At the same time, undercounting undocumented foreign workers is possibly cancelled out by the Pakatan Harapan government's 2019 initiatives to: regularize the labour market; implement a foreign worker rehiring scheme; crackdown on undocumented foreign workers; and dismantle questionable monopolies involved in foreign worker recruitment. Further research and analysis on the number of undocumented foreign workers is crucial once the impact of these new initiatives is observed through the labour market.

Taking the earlier discussion a step further, the estimated total number of foreign workers (documented and undocumented) is between 413,370 and 435,110—which gives an average of 424,240 or 21.8 per cent of the total Johor labour force.[13] This is because the total number of Johor's labour force[14] (after the number of non-Malaysians are dropped and replaced with foreign worker estimates above[15]) totals up to 1,947,055 workers (Department of Statistics Malaysia 2018; Ministry of Home Affairs 2018b). This dependency percentage of 21.8 per cent in Johor is higher than the 15 per cent cap proposed in the 11th Malaysia Plan.

With data from the Ministry of Home Affairs and the Labour Force Survey Report 2017, the percentage of foreign workers in Johor's total labour force can be calculated according to their respective sectors,[16] with reference to Figure 13.6.[17] The three sectors of agriculture, manufacturing and construction show a substantially high dependency on foreign workers, as compared to services.

FIGURE 13.6
Percentage of Foreign Workers of Labour Force by Sector, Johor, 2018

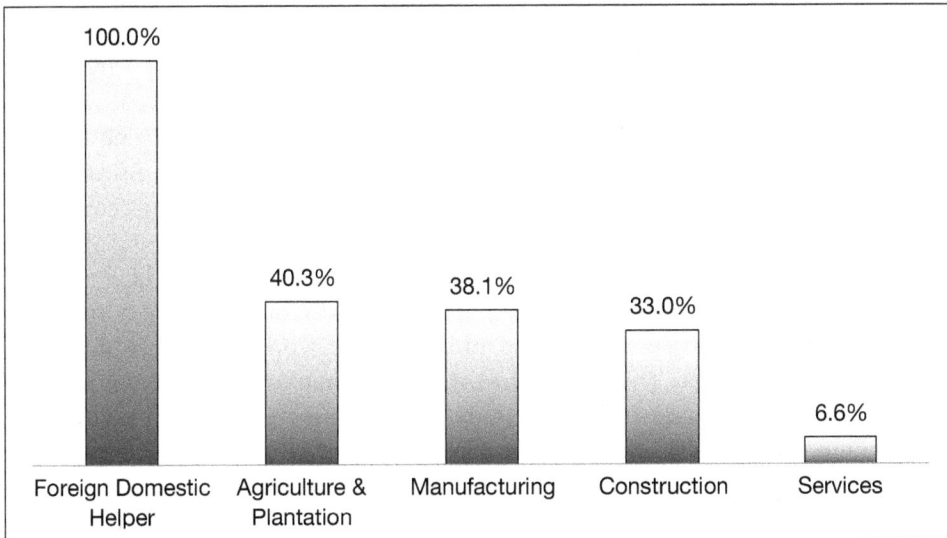

Source: Ministry of Home Affairs, Department of Statistics Malaysia.

Dependency on Foreign Workers

With an understanding that both documented and undocumented foreign workers substantially make up over one-fifth of the total labour force, it is certain that the growth of various economic sectors in Johor, especially those that are labour intensive, is dependent on foreign workers. In other words, it is an uphill challenge for the government to reduce its dependency on foreign workers as they are almost indispensable for the economic development of the state. In fact, various stakeholders have voiced their concern regarding recent efforts to reduce foreign worker dependency, stating that many companies in Johor Bahru in particular bear the brunt of insufficient manpower as many locals prefer to take up jobs in Singapore (*The Star*, 26 July 2018).

To understand and analyse the reliance of various industries on foreign workers in Johor, a Study on Foreign Worker Dependency was carried out in March 2018. This study employed the simple random sampling method to survey 338 manufacturing companies across Johor Bahru, Kulai, Muar, Batu Pahat, Pontian, Kluang and Kota Tinggi.[18] The companies surveyed were of varying size, from less than 50 employees to over 500 employees, with a substantial number (37.3 per cent) employing more foreign workers than local workers.[19]

In terms of skill level, a large majority (83.8 per cent) of the foreign workers employed are low-skilled workers while only 3.9 per cent are high-skilled. The rest of the 12.3 per cent are semi-skilled (Intelligent Johor 2018). This finding is consistent with the understanding that most low-skilled foreign workers are concentrated in the manufacturing sector in Malaysia (Kaur 2010).

From this study on foreign worker dependency, many employers attest to the better attitude and quality of work of foreign workers as compared to local workers. A majority of the respondents (93.5 per cent) either agreed or strongly agreed that foreign workers were willing to work longer hours as compared to local workers, giving a composite score of 1.41[20] (Figure 13.7). This finding supports the notion that foreign workers contribute a greater number of working hours more efficiently as they are obedient, productive and, thus, have higher economic value as compared to local workers (Hanoomanjee, Jaunky, and Ramesh 2017).

Several manufacturers commented that local workers tend to arrive later at work, in addition to being absent during working hours. Furthermore, many of them are unable to work for a long period of time, unlike foreign workers who are more than willing to work overtime. The neoclassical microeconomics model of labour markets in which the utility function expresses trade-offs in preference between leisure time and income from time used for labour can be applied here. Foreign workers are more likely and willing to trade off more of their leisure hours and work harder to receive higher wages, unlike most local workers who value leisure hours more in comparison.

The study also revealed that 89.4 per cent of the respondents agreed that foreign workers are willing to work under any conditions, while 75.2 per cent agreed that foreign workers are willing to carry out jobs that locals will not do (Intelligent Johor

FIGURE 13.7
Factors for Hiring Foreign Workers

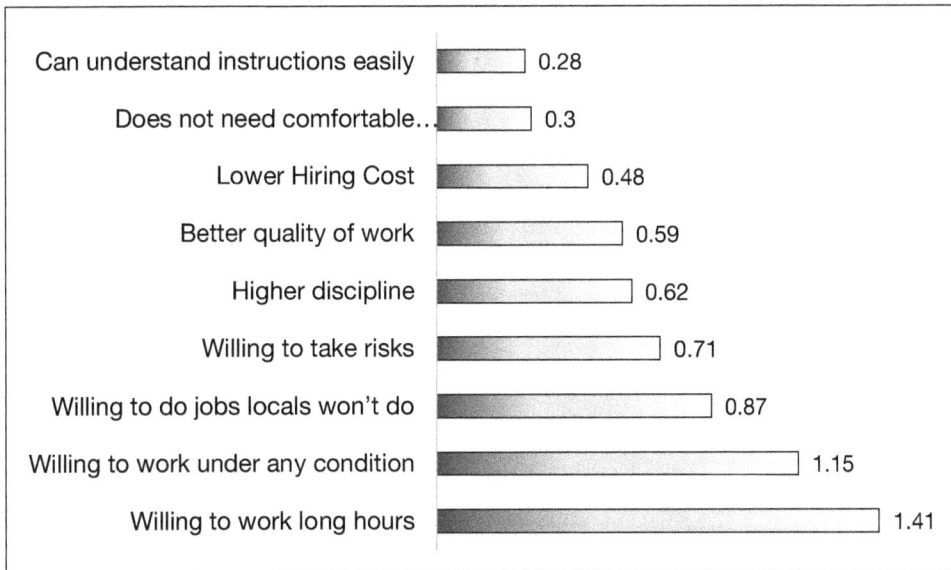

Factor	Value
Can understand instructions easily	0.28
Does not need comfortable...	0.3
Lower Hiring Cost	0.48
Better quality of work	0.59
Higher discipline	0.62
Willing to take risks	0.71
Willing to do jobs locals won't do	0.87
Willing to work under any condition	1.15
Willing to work long hours	1.41

Source: Intelligent Johor (2018).

2018). This is in line with the observation made by the Federation of Malaysian Manufacturers (FMM) that locals are not keen to carry out dirty, dangerous and difficult (3D) jobs and that the demand for foreign workers will remain even though minimum wages improve (Ong 2018).

However, the new Minister of Human Resources recently pointed out that many Malaysians are willing to take on 3D jobs in other countries such as Singapore and Australia as the higher wages are seen as adequate compensation for the social stigma (A.A. Nurul 2018). Hence, the question remains as to whether higher wages in the local job market can lessen Johor's dependence on foreign workers. Unfortunately, it is almost impossible to match the wages offered overseas given the Malaysian ringgit's weaker exchange rate.

Meanwhile, 70.7 per cent of Johor's manufacturers agree that foreign workers have better discipline compared to local workers while 68 per cent attested to the better quality of work by the former, as compared to local workers (Intelligent Johor 2018). As stated above, 83.8 per cent of all the foreign workers employed by the 338 companies are in fact low-skilled workers, indicating that these workers are able to contribute higher quality work than locals, including local graduates. There is thus very little reason for an employer to hire a local worker who might be a fresh graduate and would demand a higher wage to do the same tasks as their less expensive and less certified foreign counterparts. This highlights the conundrum faced by the government in their efforts to reduce the reliance on foreign workers.

In the long run, foreign worker dependency might continue until and unless drastic measures are taken. Referring to the same study, 50 per cent of the companies stated that the percentage of foreign workers they hire is expected to remain the same in the next five years, with the largest group of respondents coming from the companies with 30 per cent or less foreign workers (Figure 13.8). The rest of the respondents are almost equally split between raising and lowering their dependency by 5–10 per cent (Intelligent Johor 2018). This does not bode well for the direction that the new government is taking.

What is even more interesting is that 29.5 per cent of companies with over 70 per cent of foreign workers among all employees foresee that they will increase their proportion of foreign workers in five years' time. In other words, companies who mostly hire foreign workers instead of local workers intend to increasingly pursue the same trend.

It is important to note that government policies are more likely to influence long-term foreign worker dependency compared to social factors. According to the study on Foreign Worker Dependency, 35 per cent of all respondents stated that legal barriers would pressure employers to reduce their dependency on foreign workers as shown in Figure 13.9. Legal barriers here include regulatory measures by the Malaysian government and the suspension or banning of foreign workers by foreign source country governments, among others.

FIGURE 13.8
Trend in Hiring of Foreign Workers in Five Years, across Proportion of Foreign Workers

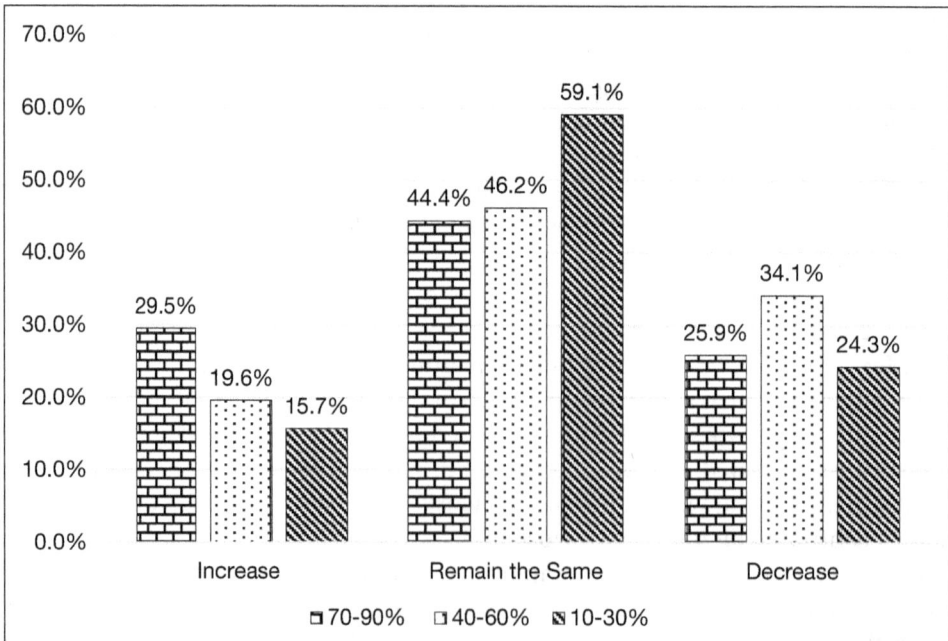

Source: Intelligent Johor (2018).

FIGURE 13.9
Factors to Reduce Dependency on Foreign Workers in Five Years

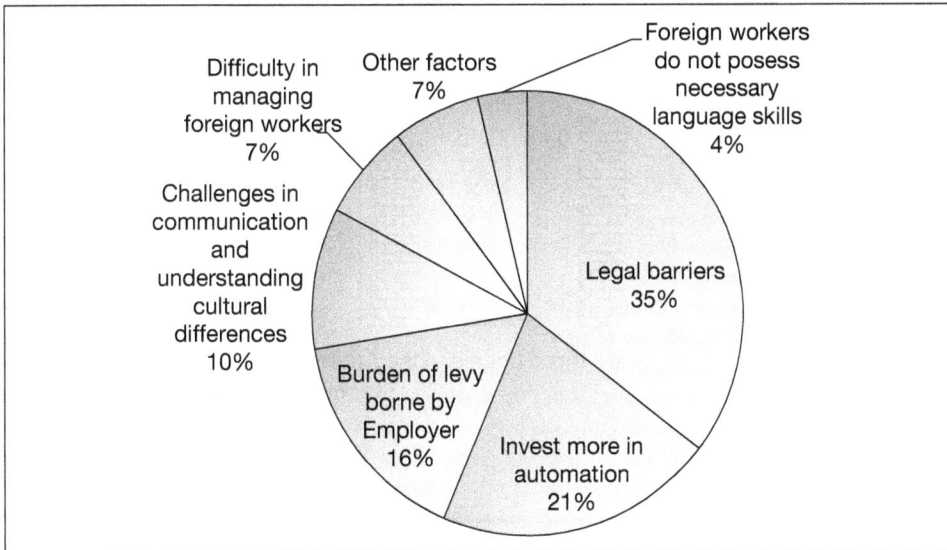

Source: Intelligent Johor 2018.

Figure 13.9 also demonstrates that 21 per cent of the employers agree that investing in automation will help reduce foreign worker dependency. This result is in line with the finding whereby 56.8 per cent agree that technological advancements will enable manufacturers to reduce their dependency on foreign workers (Intelligent Johor 2018). Hence, relevant government policies are needed to incentivize this transition to automation and higher technology, especially for small and medium enterprises (SMEs) in the move from labour-intensive to capital-intensive production.

The third main factor to reduce dependency in five years is the burden of foreign worker levy borne by the employer (Intelligent Johor 2018). In fact, 42.3 per cent of the 338 companies agree that the levy on foreign workers imposed since January 2018 (RM1,850 for manufacturing) will reduce the company's dependency on foreign workers. As shown in Figure 13.10, the lower the proportion of foreign workers, the lower the impact of the levy in reducing foreign workers.

In general, companies agree that they will hire more local workers, with the strongest response (composite score of 0.57) coming from companies with over 70 per cent of foreign workers (Figure 13.10). Similarly, the latter will revert to using automation and machinery in manufacturing processes to mitigate the impact of the foreign worker levy. On the flip side, companies in general disagree with hiring undocumented workers to avoid paying the levy, with the strongest refusal (composite score of –1.03) coming from companies with 30 per cent of foreign workers or less.

FIGURE 13.10
Impact of Levy on Foreign Workers, across Proportion of Foreign Workers

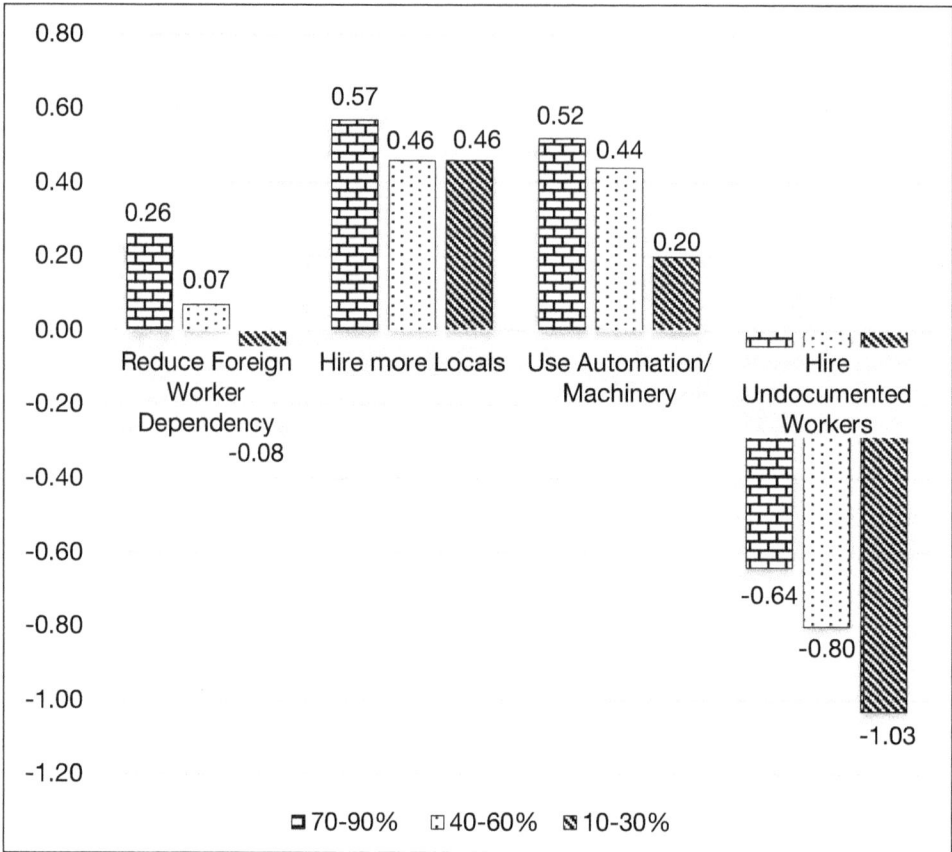

Source: Intelligent Johor (2018).

This is a very interesting finding as the Human Resource Minister recently announced that a multi-tiered levy system for the hiring of foreign workers will be implemented (Zainul 2018). This system, based on the Singaporean model, employs the principle that the more foreign workers are hired, the higher is the levy imposed. This indicates that companies with a significantly higher number of foreign workers will consequently be compelled to reduce their dependency on foreign workers as a cost-cutting measure, once the burden of the multi-tiered levy system is borne by the former.

FINAL THOUGHTS

While data is available for the number of documented foreign workers in Johor and Malaysia, there is still missing information on the number of undocumented workers. This chapter has estimated that for every 10 documented workers in Johor, there are 3.8 undocumented workers. The estimated number of undocumented foreign workers thus amounts to 116,050 with a total of 424,240 foreign workers or 21.8 per cent of the total labour force in Johor. This level of dependency is above the specified target of 15 per cent cap set in the 11th Malaysia Plan, highlighting the dependency dilemma.

The Ministry of Home Affairs and Ministry of Human Resources are marching ahead with their quest to reduce Malaysia's dependency on foreign workers, even as there are calls by employers for the cap to be reconsidered. What remains to be seen is how the new initiatives proposed will bear fruit and whether they are able to reduce the number of foreign workers without adversely affecting economic growth in Johor and Malaysia. These new initiatives include: a study analysing the socio-economic impact of employing low-skilled foreign workers; a multi-tiered levy system to strictly reduce and regulate the number of foreign workers; an Employer Undertaking initiative to enable better management and safeguard the welfare of foreign workers; the proposed amendment of the Employment Act 1955 to impose a mandatory requirement for employers to credit salaries of foreign workers through the banking system to prevent exploitation; as well as to monitor remittances by foreign workers. The impact of these proposed initiatives opens future opportunities for research.

Having presented the number of documented and undocumented foreign workers in Johor coupled with the strong dependency and consequent challenges, I would like to point out some limitations of this paper. Due to constraints in time and access to research data, this chapter largely focuses on the dependency of foreign workers in the manufacturing sector in Johor. This is also because the manufacturing sector in Johor records the largest number of documented foreign workers across sectors which can be most easily replaced with local workers, unlike the agriculture and construction sector which involves more 3D job scopes. These sectors are nonetheless significant and should be explored through future research.

APPENDIX

TABLE 13.2
Number of Foreign Workers by Sectors, Malaysia, 2018

Sectors	Number of Foreign Workers	Percentage
Manufacturing	643,122	36.6%
Construction	330,521	18.8%
Plantation	265,027	15.1%
Services	239,661	13.6%
Agriculture	154,718	8.8%
Foreign Domestic Helper	125,189	7.1%
All Sectors	1,758,328	100.0%

Source: Ministry of Home Affairs.

TABLE 13.3
Number of Foreign Workers by State, Malaysia, 2018

All States	Number of Foreign Workers	Percentage
Selangor	527,448	30.0%
Johor	308,190	17.5%
WP Kuala Lumpur	256,126	14.6%
Penang	130,076	7.4%
Sabah	126,533	7.2%
Sarawak	126,389	7.2%
Perak	81,448	4.6%
Negeri Sembilan	49,299	2.8%
Melaka	48,784	2.8%
Pahang	40,899	2.3%
Kedah	34,629	2.0%
Terengganu	8,435	0.5%
WP Putrajaya	7,874	0.4%
Kelantan	6,869	0.4%
Perlis	2,956	0.2%
WP Labuan	2,283	0.1%
All States	1,758,238	100.0%

Source: Ministry of Home Affairs.

TABLE 13.4
Number of Foreign Workers by Source Country and Sector, Malaysia, 2018

Countries	Manufacturing	Construction	Plantation	Services	Agriculture	FDH[a]	All Sectors	Percentage
Indonesia	131,040	170,980	206,008	35,967	73,484	87,675	705,154	40.1%
Nepal	280,820	9,093	2,988	78,769	10,923	58	382,651	21.8%
Bangladesh	118,388	82,794	22,613	31,505	12,626	124	268,050	15.2%
India	2,513	10,100	21,481	48,926	29,953	918	113,891	6.5%
Myanmar	78,711	12,056	1,077	12,215	3,415	81	107,555	6.1%
Pakistan	3,473	23,817	5,711	6,131	17,547	40	56,719	3.2%
Philippines	4,282	3,577	4,073	5,113	4,016	33,341	54,402	3.1%
Vietnam	17,807	3,959	33	1,338	367	398	23,902	1.4%
China	1,323	12,793	14	6,978	80	77	21,265	1.2%
Thailand	224	1,075	721	11,252	1,951	292	15,515	0.9%
Sri Lanka	3,147	166	213	816	155	632	5,129	0.3%
Cambodia	1,387	110	94	644	200	1,537	3,972	0.2%
Laos	7	1	1	7	1	16	33	0.0%
All Countries	643,122	330,521	265,027	239,661	154,718	125,189	1,758,238	100.0%

Note: a. FDH refers to Foreign Domestic Helper.
Source: Ministry of Home Affairs.

TABLE 13.5

Calculation on Percentage of Documented and Undocumented Foreign Workers of Total Labour Force, Malaysia, 2018

Sector	A	B	C = A+B	D	E	F = C+E	G = C/F x 100%
	Documented[a]	Undocumented[b]	Total Foreign Workers	Labour Force[c]	Malaysian Labour Force	New Total Labour Force	Percentage[d]
Manufacturing	170,835	64,329	235,164	418,800	381,501	616,664	38.1%
Construction	46,260	17,419	63,679	141,700	129,080	192,759	33.0%
Agriculture & Plantation	54,098	20,371	74,469	121,200	110,406	184,874	40.3%
Services	26,312	9,908	36,220	565,800	515,409	551,628	6.6%
Foreign domestic helper[e]	10,685	4,023	14,708	—	—	14,708	100.0%
Approved sectors[f]	308,190	116,050	424,240	1,247,500	1,136,395	1,560,635	27.2%
Total[g]				1,671,700	1,522,815	1,947,055	21.8%

Notes:

a. Data for Documented Foreign Workers by sectors sources from Ministry of Home Affairs (2018b).

b. Undocumented Foreign Workers by sector estimated by using the ratio of 3.8 undocumented workers for every 10 documented foreign workers, as calculated in Table 13.1.

c. Data for Labour Force sourced from Labour Force Survey Report Year 2017 (Department of Statistics Malaysia 2018).

d. This percentage is calculated by dividing the estimated total number of foreign workers with the State's total Labour Force (from Labour Force Survey Report Year 2017; Department of Statistics Malaysia, 2018) after the number of non-Malaysians are deducted and replaced with the foreign worker estimates instead, giving the new Total Labour Force. This is because the Labour Force Survey Report only samples private living quarters, thereby excluding hostels, boarding houses, construction sites and workers' dormitories. Hence, there is a strong concern for under-sampling of foreign workers especially undocumented workers as many are excluded by design (Lee and Khor 2018).

e. Foreign Domestic Helpers are unaccounted for in the Labour Force Survey Report.

f. Approved sectors here account for the working population which excludes sectors prohibited for foreign workers such as education services, information and communications, financial and insurance activities.

g. The Total here refers to all labour force including sectors in which foreign workers are prohibited from working.

Source: Ministry of Home Affairs, Department of Statistics Malaysia.

TABLE 13.6
Percentage Share of 338 Companies Surveyed, by Industrial Sector

Industrial Categories[a]	Percentage Share (%)
Plastics and packaging	13.6
Manufacture of Furniture	13.0
Food based products	11.2
Metal products	10.1
Electrical and electronics (E&E)	8.6
Textiles	6.2
Chemical products	6.2
Manufacture of machines	5.3
Non-metallic mineral based products	5.3
Rubber based products	4.1
Automotive	2.8
Paper products	2.5
Timber based products	2.5
Oil and gas based products	2.2
Precision instruments (including optical instruments, laboratory equipment and measuring tools	1.5
Recycling	1.5
Others	3.8

Note: a. The 338 companies were classified according to industry types by adapting the Malaysian Standard Industrial Classification (MSIC 2008) which is the latest industrial classification based on the International Standard Industrial Classification of All Economic Activities (ISIC) Revision 4.
Source: Intelligent Johor (2018).

FIGURE 13.11
Number of Total Employees (Local and Foreign) in the 338 Companies

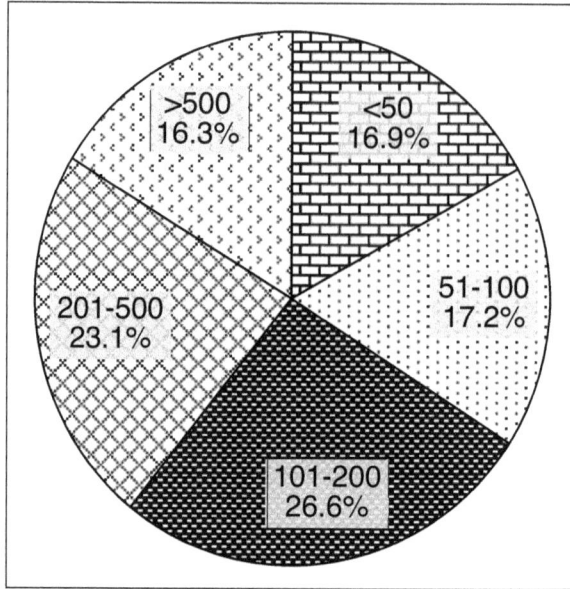

Source: Intelligent Johor (2018).

FIGURE 13.12
Number of Foreign Workers in the Company

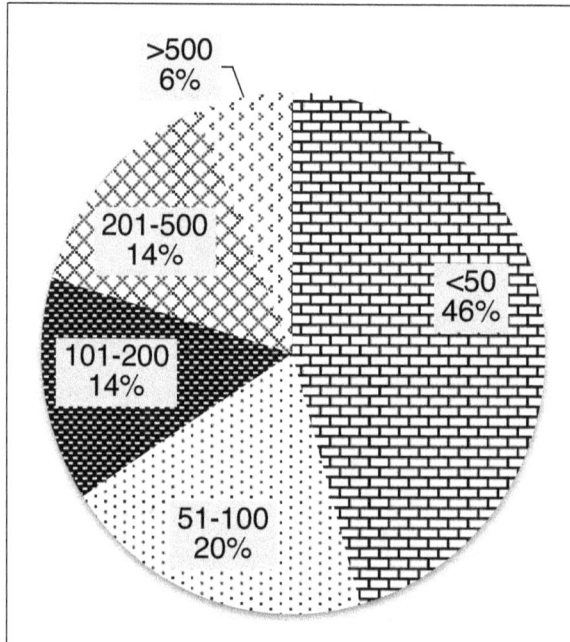

Source: Intelligent Johor (2018).

FIGURE 13.13
Percentage of Foreign Workers (FW) in the Company

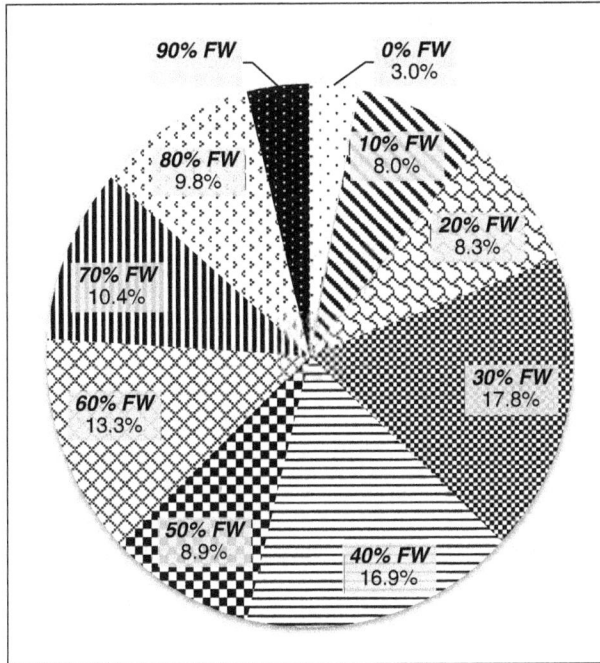

Source: Intelligent Johor 2018.

Notes

1. The 11th Malaysia Plan is the country's five-year social and economic development plan. The Mid-Term Review essentially takes stock of the progress made half-way through the implementation period and highlights the new Pakatan Harapan administration's reform agenda.
2. The Temporary Employment Visit Pass (PLKS) or otherwise known as Visit Pass (Temporary Employment) is a work permit issued by the Ministry of Home Affairs to skilled and unskilled foreign workers in Malaysia.
3. The percentage of foreign workers is calculated using labour force statistics (Department of Statistics Malaysia 2018) as of February 2018. This is because the latest available data on documented foreign workers is only available up to February 2018.
4. For Sabah and Sarawak, the approval of foreign workers' employment permits is governed by the State Government accordingly.
5. Plantation (*Perladangan*) refers to a large farm, estate or area of land that is cultivated by unskilled or semiskilled labour under central direction.
6. Agriculture (*Pertanian*), on the contrary, refers to the science of cultivating the ground which includes harvesting crops, raising livestock, tillage and the preparation and marketing of resulting products.
7. See Table 13.2 in the Appendix for the detailed number and percentage of foreign workers by sector.
8. See Table 13.4 in the Appendix for the detailed number and percentage of foreign workers by source country and sector.
9. See Table 13.3 in the Appendix for the detailed number and percentage of foreign workers by state.
10. *Pendatang Asing Tanpa Izin* (PATI) are undocumented immigrations who do not have Entry Permits. Section 55B of the Immigration Act 1959/63 criminalizes the act of employing one or more persons other than citizens or Entry Permit holders who do not have a valid pass. Moreover, Section 56(1)(d) of the Immigration Act 1959/63 states that a person shall not knowingly harbour any person whom he knows or has reasonable grounds for supposing to have contravened the Immigration Act 1959/63.
11. The *Program Bancian Warga Asing* is independent research carried out by the *Sekretariat Khidmat Imigran* (SKI) or Immigration Services Secretariat in collaboration with Pertubuhan Penyatuan Pembelaan Melayu Malaysia (PPPMM), a non-governmental organization. Announced in March 2018, the project was slated to be carried out after the 14th General Elections.
12. A few caveats for this estimation include the following assumptions:
    - trends in the number of documented foreign workers move in tandem with the number of undocumented foreign workers across Malaysia;
    - there is no substantial change in the number of documented and undocumented foreign workers over the last five years and, thus, the sources of supplementary data are comparable though recorded in different years;
    - the percentage share of undocumented foreign workers in Johor out of the whole of Malaysia is similar to the percentage share of documented foreign workers which is 17.53 per cent.
13. See Table 13.5 in the Appendix for detailed calculation on percentage of foreign workers of total labour force.

14. Based on the Labour Force Survey Report 2017 (Department of Statistics Malaysia 2018), labour force refers to both Malaysian citizens and non-Malaysian citizens who are part of the working age population who may be employed or unemployed.
15. See note 12 for detailed explanation.
16. See Table 13.5 in the Appendix for a detailed calculation.
17. The sector for Foreign Domestic Helpers specifically refers to foreign workers who are hired for domestic chores, which does not include local helpers. Agriculture and Plantation are combined under one sector here because the Labour Force Survey Report 2017 does not present labour force data separately for the two sectors. Hence, it is not possible to divide the classification as presented by the Ministry of Home Affairs.
18. The sample size of 338 business meets the 90 per cent confidence level with a ±5 per cent margin of error, determined based on the number of business entities in Johor, which totals up to 99,770.
19. Refer to Table 13.6 and Figures 13.11 to 13.13 in the Appendix for more information on the general profile of the dataset.
20. The composite index of the level of consent is calculated by obtaining the overall average score of the respondents, whereby strongly agree is given a score of 2, agree (1), disagree (–1), strongly disagree (–1), not applicable (0), not sure (0). In other words, a composite index of 2 indicates that all respondents strongly agree with the statement, while the composite index –2 indicates that all respondents strongly disagree with the statement.

References

Ajis, M.N., M.F. Keling, Z. Othman, and M.S. Shu. 2014. "The Dilemma of Managing Foreign Workers in Malaysia: Opportunities and Challenges". *Global Journal of Human-Social Science* 14, no. 4: 42–53.

Ang, J.W., A. Murugasu, and Y.W. Chai. 2018. "Low-Skilled Foreign Workers' Distortions to the Economy". *Annual Report 2017*. Kuala Lumpur: Bank Negara Malaysia.

Astro Awani. 2018. "Warga Kuala Lumpur Mahu Polisi Pengurusan Warga Asing Yang Cekap". 24 April 2018. http://www.astroawani.com/berita-malaysia/warga-kuala-lumpur-mahu-polisi-pengurusan-warga-asing-yang-cekap-173650 (accessed 2 January 2019).

Athukorala, P. 2006. "International Labour Migration in East Asia: Trends, Patterns and Policy Issues". *Asian Pacific Economic Literature* 20, no. 1: 18–39.

Aziz, M.A., N.H. Ayob, and K. Abdulsomad. 2017. "Restructuring Foreign Worker Policy and Community Transformation in Malaysia". *Historical Social Research* 42, no. 3: 348–68.

Azizah, K., and R.H.M. Zin. 2011. "Policy on Irregular Migrants in Malaysia: An Analysis of Its Implementation and Effectiveness". *Philippine Institute for Development Studies Discussion Paper Series* no. 2011-34.

Benjamin, N. 2018. "Johor Shops Run by Foreigners Mushrooming". *Star Newspaper*, 27 October 2018. https://www.thestar.com.my/news/nation/2018/10/27/johor-shops-run-by-foreigners-mushrooming-some-of-them-have-become-suppliers/ (accessed 5 January 2019).

Bernama. "Malaysia's Immigration Department Pledges to Rid Country of Illegal Immigrants". *Straits Times*, 21 July 2018. https://www.straitstimes.com/asia/se-asia/malaysias-immigration-department-pledges-to-rid-country-of-illegal-immigrants (accessed 6 March 2019).

Carpio, X., Ç. Özden and M. Testaverde. 2015. "Foreign Workers in Malaysia: Labour Market and Firm-Level Analysis". *Malaysian Journal of Economic Studies* 52, no. 1: 1–19.

Dass, M.V. 2018. "Ramainya PATI di Johor". *Harian Metro*, 6 September 2018. https://www.hmetro.com.my/mutakhir/2018/09/374817/ramainya-pati-di-johor (accessed 6 March 2019).

Department of Statistics Malaysia. 2018a. *Labour Force Survey Report Malaysia 2017*. Published April 2018.

———. 2018b. *Key Statistics of Labour Force in Malaysia, March 2018*. Published 10 May 2018. https://www.dosm.gov.my/v1/index.php?r=column/pdfPrev&id=NHZ3QmE0c UhkcllqRlY4RXRpbWtIUT09 (accessed 4 January 2019).

Dermawan, A. 2018. "No 'U-turn', Guan Eng Says on Skilled Foreign Workers' Levy". *New Straits Times*, 27 September 2018. https://www.nst.com.my/news/nation/2018/09/415440/no-u-turn-guan-eng-says-skilled-foreign-workers-levy (accessed 4 March 2019).

Devadason, E.S. and W.M. Chan. 2014. "A Critical Appraisal of Policies and Laws Regulating Migrant Workers in Malaysia". *Journal of Contemporary Asia* 44, no. 1: 19–35.

Hanoomanjee, E., V.C. Jaunky, and V. Ramesh. 2017. "The Impact of Foreign Workers on Economic Growth: Evidence from the Mauritian Manufacturing Industry". *International Journal of Management and Applied Science* 3, no. 5: 87–91.

Intelligent Johor. 2018. "Study on Foreign Worker Dependency in Johor 2018". *Johor Human Capital Unit*.

Kaur, A. 2010. "Labour Migration Trends and Policy Challenges in Southeast Asia". *Policy and Society* 29: 385–97.

Lee, H.A. and Y.L. Khor. 2018. "Counting Migrant Workers in Malaysia: A Needlessly Persisting Conundrum". *ISEAS Perspective*, no. 25/2018, 25 April 2018.

Malaysian Trades Union Congress. 2017. "Labour Woes in Furniture Industry to Be Resolved Soon". 15 June 2017. http://www.mtuc.org.my/labour-woes-in-furniture-industry-to-be-resolved-soon/ (accessed 3 January 2019).

Maslynnawati, A., B. Weerasena, and Z. Fawzi. 2017. *Johor Development Report 2016*. Kuala Lumpur: Bait Al-Amanah.

Memorandum MTUC. 2016. "Cabaran bagi Pekerja dan Kesatuan Sekerja". *Malaysian Trades Union Congress*. http://www.mtuc.org.my/memorandum-mtuc-2016/?lang=MS (accessed 2 January 2019).

Ministry of Economic Affairs. 2018. *Mid-term Review of the 11th Malaysia Plan 2016–2020: New Priorities and Emphases*. Kuala Lumpur: Percetakan Nasional Malaysia Bhd, 2018.

Ministry of Home Affairs. 2018a. "Latest Foreign Worker Statistics According to Nationality and Sector as of 28 February 2018". *Malaysian Administrative Modernisation and Management Planning Unit (MAMPU)*. http://www.data.gov.my/data/ms_MY/dataset/statistik-pekerja-asing-terkini-mengikut-warganegara-dan-sektor (accessed 28 December 2018).

———. 2018b. "Latest Foreign Worker Statistics According to State and Sector as of 28 February 2018". *Malaysian Administrative Modernisation and Management Planning Unit (MAMPU)*. http://www.data.gov.my/data/ms_MY/dataset/statistik-pekerja-asing-terkini-mengikut-negeri-dan-sektor (accessed 28 December 2018).

Muhamading, M. 2018. "Send Illegal Workers Home Fast". *New Straits Times*, 8 June 2018. http://www.mef.org.my/news/mefitn_article.aspx?ID=691&article=NST180608a (accessed 2 January 2019).

Nordin, M.K. 2016. "Johor Berkemajuan, Rakyat Sejahtera". Ucapan Bajet Negeri Johor Darul Ta'zim Tahun 2017. Portal Rasmi Kerajaan Negeri Johor. Persidangan Dewan Negeri

Johor, 17 November 2016. https://www.johor.gov.my/kerajaan/bajet-johor/tahun-2017 (accessed 4 March 2019).

Nurul, A.A. 2018. "Why Malaysians Will Do 3D Jobs Overseas but Not at Home". *Free Malaysia Today*, 26 November 2018. https://www.freemalaysiatoday.com/category/nation/2018/11/26/why-malaysians-will-do-3d-jobs-overseas-but-not-at-home/ (accessed 25 February 2019).

Nurul, H.H. 2018. "750,000 Pekerja Haram di Johor". *Utusan Online*, 7 September 2018. https://www.utusan.com.my/berita/wilayah/johor/750-000-pekerja-haram-di-johor-1.743174 (accessed 6 March 2019).

Ong, S. 2018. "Foreign Worker Sector Braces for a Tough 2019". *Malaysian Reserve*, 24 December 2018. https://themalaysianreserve.com/2018/12/24/foreign-worker-sector-braces-for-a-tough-2019/ (accessed 27 February 2019).

Shagar, L.K. 2016. "More than 40% of Foreign Workers Undocumented, Says Richard Riot". *The Star*, 18 October 2016. https://www.thestar.com.my/news/nation/2016/10/18/richard-riot-parliament-foreign-workers-numbers/#RPL5rhvPMKJ4MjQH.99 (accessed 2 January 2019).

Shamsulbahriah, K.A. 2003. "Malaysia after the Asian Crisis: An Overview of Labour Market Issues". In *Malaysian Economics and Politics in the New Century*, edited by C. Barlow and F.K.W. Loh, pp. 46–61. Cheltenham: Edward Elgar.

Soo, W.J. 2018. "PPBM: Why Is Muar so Backward?". *Free Malaysia Today*, 9 March 2018. https://www.freemalaysiatoday.com/category/highlight/2018/03/09/ppbm-why-is-muar-so-backward/ (accessed 26 February 2019).

Star, The. 2013. "MMEA Monitoring 20 Hotspots". 29 August 2013. https://www.thestar.com.my/news/nation/2013/08/29/mmea-monitoring-20-hotspots/ (accessed 27 February 2019).

———. 2018. "Long-Term Solution Needed on Foreign Labour". 26 July 2018. https://www.thestar.com.my/news/nation/2018/07/26/longterm-solution-needed-on-foreign-labour-smes-forced-to-look-elsewhere-as-msians-arent-keen-to-wor/ (accessed 27 February 2019).

———. 2019. "Johor State Govt Plans to Control Foreign Worker Influx". 25 May 2019. https://www.thestar.com.my/news/nation/2019/05/25/johor-state-govt-plans-to-control-foreign-worker-influx/ (accessed 20 May 2019).

Sun Daily, The. 2017. "Immigration Crackdown Causes Labour Shortage". 11 July 2017. https://www.thesundaily.my/archive/immigration-crackdown-causes-labour-shortage-BTARCH460317 (accessed 3 January 2019).

———. 2019. "PPPMM, SKI to Conduct Census on Foreigners in Malaysia". 26 March 2018. https://www.thesundaily.my/archive/pppmm-ski-conduct-census-foreigners-malaysia-DUARCH535416 (accessed 16 January 2019).

Walmsley, T., A. Aguilar, and S.A. Ahmed. 2013. "Labour Migration and Economic Growth in East and Southeast Asia". *World Bank Policy Research Working Paper* No. WPS 6643.

Yaw, A.D. 2002. "Introduction: Migrant Workers in Pacific Asia". In *Migrant Workers in Pacific Asia*, edited by A.D. Yan, pp. 1–18. London: Frank Cass Publishers.

Zainul, E. 2018. "Multi-tier Levy System for Hiring of Foreign Workers Gets Green Light". *The Edge Markets*, 24 October 2018. http://www.theedgemarkets.com/article/multitier-levy-system-hiring-foreign-workers-gets-green-light (accessed 26 February 2019).

14

JOHOR REMAINS AS THE BASTION OF *KAUM TUA*

Norshahril Saat[1]

INTRODUCTION

In 1916, Haji Abdul Karim Amrullah,[2] an Islamic religious scholar (*ulama*) from Sumatra, made a sneering remark about the Mufti of Johor.

> To become a Government Mufti in Malaya is a great glory. You have an official uniform, with a whole banana-comb of epaulettes on the shoulder, a *jubbah* [Arabic-style garment] embroidered with gold thread, a silk turban, and your own car. The *ra'ayat* [people] fear and obey you, eat the scraps from your table, your spat of *sireh* [betel leaf]. And if you want to get married … *Bismillah* [anytime with God's consent]. (Roff 1994, p. 67)

Muftis are religious scholars whose role is to provide guidance to the Muslim community and issue *fatwa* (religious rulings). In Malaysia, Muftis are appointed by the Malay Rulers. Ideally, an *alim* (singular for *ulama*) must not blindly serve the interest of ruling elites; instead, they must be pious individuals who protect the interests of the religious community. Haji Abdul Karim's harsh words showed that he must have felt strongly that the Johor Mufti of his time had been falling far short of those ideals.

To be sure, Haji Abdul Karim and the then Johor Mufti came from rival schools of thought.[3] Haji Abdul Karim was a key player in the reformist/modernist movement in Sumatra, which called for Indonesian Muslims to return to the fundamentals of the Quran and the hadith (sayings and deeds of the Prophet Muhammad). The movement appealed for "pure" Islam in Indonesia, one that was erased of local beliefs coloured with mysticism and irrationalism.

The reformists' position on theology, rituals and cultural practices was in fact quite similar to that held by Salafi-Wahhabi scholars. Salafism is a Sunni orientation that can be traced back to the theologian Ibn Taimiyyah (b.1263–d.1328). It urges Muslims to return to Islam's pristine past, and considers the first three generations after Prophet Muhammad's death as the ideal period for Islamic societies to copy. Salafis believe that ideas and scholarship generated by savants of these three generations should therefore be applied in contemporary social and political life. One of the main tenets of Salafism is its rejection of Islamic innovations. Its followers can however be either progressive or regressive in their religious outlook. For progressive Salafis, reliving the system of the first three generations after the Prophet means the upholding of its values and principles. They embrace modern social life and scientific knowledge, but promote ideals such as justice, gender equality, and human rights. Some Salafis are even tolerant of Sufism, a religious order that promotes spirituality and metaphysics.

On the other hand, the Wahhabi interpretation of Salafism is a traditionalist one. This article uses the term Salafi-Wahhabi to describe this puritanical orientation. Founded in eighteenth century Arabia by Muhammad Ibn Abdul Al-Wahab (Delong-Bas 2004), Salafi-Wahhabism has been seeking to cleanse Islamic beliefs of "innovations", a teaching that when applied to the Malay world means the forbidding of rituals such as: the *slametan* (mass prayers and communal feasting); participation in *tariqah* groups (Sufi groups engaging in devotional rituals such as rhythmic repetition of Allah's virtues); *ziarah kubur* (visit to graves of pious Muslims); and *maulid Nabi* (celebration of Prophet Muhammad's birthday). The Wahhabis considered these practices alien to the Prophet and his companions, and to be without basis in the Quran and Hadith. Ibn Abdul Al-Wahab and his followers destroyed many tombs including those of key Muslim personalities and heroes (Delong-Bas 2004, p. 26). Following in the footsteps of their ideologue, Salafi-Wahhabism in Southeast Asia has sought to end practices such as visits to tombs of pious Muslims and Sufi saints, which are common in the Malay world. The tenacity of Salafi-Wahhabis in Malaysia and Singapore has alarmed some academics in Malaysia and Southeast Asia, who believe that the ideology contributes to extremism and even terrorism (See Alatas 2014; Ahmad Fauzi Abdul Hamid 2016).

The Johor Muftis, however, have always adopted what is known in the region as the *kaum tua* tradition. They condone Sufi practices and rituals which Salafi-Wahhabis condemn. Historically, their role has always been tied to the royal house and to Malay aristocracy. Today, Johor still houses traditional *pondok* or *maahad* schools (boarding schools) which train religious teachers and *hafidz* (those who memorize the thirty chapters of the Quran by heart), and most are shaped by the Sufi tradition. The Islamic Religious Council of Johor today continues to allow many *tariqah* networks to practise.

Given the perceived rise of Salafi-Wahhabi ideas in Malaysia, one needs to ask if Johor has managed to remain the bastion of *kaum tua*. I argue that Johor's religious discourse, at the least, remains strongly *kaum tua*. The Johor Muftis seem crucial players in preventing Salafi-Wahhabi-oriented clerics from proselytizing in the state. Moreover, the overt intervention of the Sultan Ibrahim Sultan Iskandar in the state's religious affairs means that its religious institutions are protected from encroachment by federal Islamic institutions, especially JAKIM (Department of Islamic Development). However, this Sultan-Mufti alliance does not necessarily mean that only progressive *fatwa* are passed in Johor. On many aspects, including women's role in society, religious minority rights, and intrafaith diversity, many of the *fatwas* or opinions passed by the Johor Muftis are traditionalist in nature.

The Johor case does contribute fruitfully to the ongoing debate about countering extremism in Islam. Some analysts equate Salafism-Wahhabism to intolerance (see El-Fadl 2005), and Sufism to progress and as the remedy for terrorism (see Webster 2016; *Times of India*, 15 October 2016). The reality, however, is much more complex.

The Johor religious bureaucracy makes an important case study, especially for those interested in understanding the impact of Malaysian religious discourse in Singapore. Johor is the Lion City's closest neighbour and historically, many members of Singapore's religious elite studied in religious schools in Johor. Moreover, the Johor religious elite, including the Muftis, often go over to Singapore to preach, and speak at forums organized by Singapore NGOs and mosques.

The Johor Islamic institution is also unique in Malaysia in portraying itself as the bastion of Sufism at a time when scholars are associating Malaysia with Arabization and Salafi-Wahhabism. Johor is also seen as a state that retains its Malay character effectively, led by a strong royal institution.

THE JOHOR ISLAMIC RELIGIOUS BUREAUCRACY

As a rule, the Malay Rulers appoint all key positions in the Islamic institutions in their states (in contrast from the federal religious institution, JAKIM). This is in accordance with the Federal Constitution. The constitution of each state also maintains that the Ruler must be a person of Islamic faith, and that Islam is the official religion of all the states except Sarawak (Faruqi 2005, p. 274). The Malaysian King (Yang di-Pertuan Agong) is the head of Islam for states that do not have a sultan—Malacca, Penang, Sabah, Sarawak, and the Federal Territories.[4] The key appointments in the religious bureaucracy include members of the Islamic Religious Council (Majlis Agama Islam Negeri) and the Mufti, who is the ex-officio of the Council, which has the important role of issuing *fatwas* (Islamic rulings). In many Muslim countries, *fatwas* are not legally binding, but in Malaysia, once a *fatwa* is published in the state gazette, it is enforceable. The Ruler has the final say on whether a *fatwa* gets published or not. A fatwa applies only to Muslims, and the maximum punishment for a sharia offence is a fine of RM5,000 (S$1,660), six strokes of the cane, and three years' imprisonment. In late 2016, plans have been presented by the federal government, taking the lead from PAS (Islamic Party of Malaysia) president Abdul Hadi Awang, to harden sharia punishments by amending Act 355 or Syariah Courts (Criminal Jurisdiction) Act 1965.

The federal Fatwa Committee of the National Islamic Council (JKF-MKI) consists of all the Muftis, and some other ulama. This body discusses issues of national concern, after which in some cases leads to a collective *fatwa*.

The state of Johor was in fact one of the earliest to delineate the powers of the Ruler, the Islamic Religious Council, and the Mufti. In 1895, the Undang-undang Tubuh Kerajaan Negeri Johor (Johor State Constitution 1895) introduced new laws and departments into the administrative service. It spelt out the authority of the Sultan of Johor as the Head of Islam in the state, and his right to appoint members of the Majlis Agama Islam Negeri Johor (Johor Islamic Religious Council) and the Mufti. The law declared Islam the religion of the state, and also introduced the Jabatan Agama Islam Johor (Islamic Department of Johor). It also specifies that all religious queries should be directed to the Mufti, while the *qadi* (meaning either a judge, administrator, or mediator) and his assistants will run the religious affairs of the state (Hasnan Kasan 2008, p. 26). Most of these provisions remain to this day. Under section 4 of Enactment No. 16/2003, it is stated that "There shall be a body known as the 'Majlis Agama Islam Negeri Johor' to aid and advise His Majesty the Sultan in matters relating to the religion of Islam" (Enactment No. 16 of 2003, Johor). According to section 6 of the Enactment, the Council shall aid and advise the Sultan on all matters relating to the religion of Islam in the state of Johor, except on matters of *Hukum Syarak* (jurisprudence) and administration of justice. It is the Mufti who has *authority over hukum syarak* while the administration of justice falls under the sharia courts.

The Majlis Agama Islam is presided over by eight members: the Chairman; the Vice-Chairman; the state legal advisor; the state finance officer; the Mufti (ex-officio); deputy Mufti; Qadi Besar Johor (sharia court judge), and Chief Assistant Director of Religious Education. On matters relating to Islamic legal opinions, a separate *fatwa* body, chaired by the Mufti, plays an important role.[5] According to section 48, a *fatwa* is prepared by the committee before it is presented by the Mufti to the Council, which will then discuss and make recommendations to the Sultan. If royal assent is given, the Council then instructs the state government to publish the *fatwa* in the gazette in *Jawi* (Malay written with Arabic alphabets). This procedure means that a *fatwa* can become law without going to the state assembly.

In general, the Muslim community looks to the Mufti for religious guidance. For queries on religious rulings, members of the religious community may call, email, or write to the Mufti department directly. The Muftis also attend state and palace functions to recite prayers. Table 14.1 lists Johor Muftis from the colonial period to the present.

JOHOR MUFTIS SINCE THE NINETEENTH CENTURY

Table 14.1 reveals several aspects of the religious and political orientation of the Muftis. First, the earlier Muftis were mostly involved in the administrative service. Apart from being judges, they were members of the state's Executive Committee (equivalent to Ministers of the State government). Interestingly, the fifth Mufti,

TABLE 14.1
Johor Muftis since the Nineteenth Century

Year	Mufti	Highlights
Before 1873	Tuan Syed Salim Ahmad Al-Attas[a]	In 1873, he was appointed a member of the State Council.[b] The role of the Mufti then was different from today. Back then, the Mufti assisted the judge in trials.
1899–1907	Dato' Haji Abdullah Bin Musa	He was a former judge and Executive Committee member in the Johor state government.
1907–33	Datuk Syed Abdul Kadir Bin Mohsin Al-Attas	Like his predecessor, he was a former judge and Executive Committee member in the Johor state government.
1934–41	Dato' Syed Alwi Bin Tahir Al-Haddad	Of Hadrami (Yemen) descent, he left the position of Mufti during the Japanese occupation and resumed the position in 1947.
1941–47	Tan Sri Datuk Haji Hassan Bin Yunus	Studied in Mecca and Egypt (Al-Azhar). In 1957, he ventured into politics and was elected member of parliament for Bukit Serampang. Between 1959 and 1967, he was Johor Chief Minister.
1947–61	Dato' Syed Alwi Bin Tahir Al-Haddad	He resumed the Mufti position after the Japanese occupation.
1961–64	Tan Sri Dato' Abd. Jalil Hassan	His was the shortest stint. He then ventured into academia, and served as Chairman of National *Fatwa* Committee at the Federal Level.
1965–77	Dato' Haji Rahim Bin Yunus	He is the brother of Hassan Yunus, and a graduate of Al-Azhar University (Egypt).
1977–81	Datuk Syed Alwee Bin Abdullah Al-Hadad	He studied mainly in Johor Islamic schools before heading to Al-Azhar University (Egypt).
1981–99	Dato' Haji Ahmad Bin Awang	He studied at Al-Azhar University. Upon his retirement in 1999, he was appointed Advisor to the Islamic Religious Council of Johor.
1999–2008	Dato' Haji Nooh Bin Gadot	He served in several key institutions at the state and federal levels. Upon his retirement, he served as Advisor to the Islamic Religious Council of Johor.
2008–2018	Dato' Haji M. Tahrir Bin Dato' Kiyai Hj Samsudin	Retired as Mufti in 2018.
2018–present	Dato' Yahya Ahmad	Served as Deputy Mufti under the previous Mufti.

Sources:
a. Abdul Jalil Borham (2002).
b. Hasnan Kasan (2008), p. 26.

Hassan Yunus, ran for office and became Chief Minister of Johor from 1959 to 1967. Second, the earlier Muftis showed how the Arabs, particularly the "Syeds", played an important role shaping the religious discourse in Johor. The "Syeds" are well respected by the populace in the Malay world and in the Middle East for being descendants of Prophet Muhammad. Interestingly, the fourth Mufti, an Arab, went into hiding during the Japanese occupation, suggesting that he had worked closely with the colonial government. The dominance of Arabs in Johor religious affairs also demonstrates the entrenchment of Sufi-oriented *kaum tua* ideology. Historically, the Hadrami Sufis (who came from the region that is today's Yemen) played a significant role in spreading Islam to the region.

Finally, most of the Muftis received their early education in religious schools in the state, and later moved to Al-Azhar University in Cairo. Al-Azhar is the most prestigious institute of higher learning in the Islamic world. Though Al-Azhar is a traditionalist institution, its graduates are less sympathetic to Salafi-Wahhabi when compared to their counterparts in Saudi Arabia. To this day, Al-Azhar continues to discuss the different Islamic sects with its students, including schools that many Malaysian ulama consider deviant, such as Shiism and Mu'tazilite (rationalists) (Jainal Shihab 2007, p. 3).

MAHATHIR'S STRENGTHENING OF FEDERAL ISLAMIC INSTITUTIONS

Although the Constitution declares that Islam is a state matter, federal Islamic institutions underwent massive upgrading in terms of infrastructure and powers under the first Mahathir administration (1981–2003). In 1984, the Federal Territory Administration of Islamic Laws Enactment was passed to streamline the administration of Islamic laws in all states. The shariah courts were strengthened, and in the federal territory, they were expanded into three levels: the lower court, high court and appeal court. In 1991, the shariah courts in the other thirteen states followed suit.

One of the key federal institutions that Mahathir upgraded was the Islamic Affairs Unit in the Prime Minister's Office, BAHEIS (Bahagian Hal Ehwal Agama Islam, Jabatan Perdana Menteri, Malaysia). In 1997, this became JAKIM. The body continues to serve as the secretariat of the National Islamic Council (Majlis Kebangsaan Bagi Hal Ehwal Ugama Islam Malaysia or MKI) and handles inter alia research, *fatwa* management, the coordination of Islamic legal matters across all Malaysian states, and publishing. The MKI also hosts the aforementioned JKF-MKI. JAKIM also determines what constitutes the correct interpretation of Islam, censorship of publications, and halal certification. There have been instances when JAKIM prevented scholars from speaking in public events. JAKIM officials are known to be intolerant of those spreading pluralism, liberalism, feminism and Shiism. In October 2014, JAKIM forbids a roundtable discussion featuring Indonesian scholar Ulil Abshar Abdalla because he was seen as promoting liberal Islamic thinking. In another instance, JAKIM was proactive in banning books by laureate Faizal Musa (or Faizal Tehrani) for promoting Shiism. The extent of JAKIM's powers is in fact significant to such an extent that the Constitutional provision that Islam is a state-level matter is called into question.

In October 2016, JAKIM asked for its annual budget to be increased to RM1 billion (S$328 million), something it claimed was needed to reflect its expanded role. The Deputy Minister in the Prime Ministers Department, Datuk

Dr Asyraf Wajdi Dusuki, argued that JAKIM needed the extra amount in order to combat ISIS (Islamic State in Iraq and Syria), liberalism, pluralism, and LGBT (lesbian, gay, bisexual, and transgender) issues. JAKIM Director-General Datuk Othman Mustapha further stated that part of the increment will be distributed to state Islamic religious departments (Aizyl Azlee 2016). This request was strongly criticized, also by the Sultan of Johor.

JOHOR MUFTIS AND THE *KAUM TUA* ORIENTATION

The official reason for expanding the power of the federal Islamic institutions has been the need for uniformity between state religious institutions. Mahathir was, however, also suspected of aiming to dilute the authority of the Malay Rulers.

In truth, to make Islamic laws uniform across all states would be futile because the Muftis do not speak with one voice. They are factionalized between the *kaum tua* and *kaum muda* (modernists) orientations. States in the southern part of the peninsula such as Johor, Negeri Sembilan, Melaka, Pahang, and also northerly Perak, are more at home with *kaum tua* thinking, while others, especially Perlis, are oriented towards reform (both liberal and at times, Wahhabi). In fact, some states with *kaum tua* orientation have prevented Dr Mohd Asri Zainul Abidin, the Mufti of Perlis, from speaking in their states. In 2010, he was detained for speaking without a permit in Selangor, and in February 2016, he was listed as one of sixteen speakers banned in Johor (*Malay Mail* Online, 2 February 2016). Another individual who is banned is UMNO politician, Dr Fathul Bari Mat Jahaya, who is seen to hold Salafi-Wahhabi views.

Datuk Tahrir Samsudin, the former Johor Mufti, exhibits *kaum tua* thinking in many ways, and as with his predecessors, he is also sympathetic to Sufism. During my interview with him, Datuk Tahrir defended the *tariqah* groups in Johor, even though the religious department is keeping a close eye on them for departing from "true" Islamic teachings.[6] In fact, the Mufti emphasizes his commitment to promoting *tariqah* groups in the state. He does not deny that Salafi-Wahhabi ideas are gaining traction in Malaysia, especially when these are propagated through the social media, but considers Johor the bastion of the Sunni tradition. He admits though, that the arrival of Salafism-Wahhabism has led to some disunity in Johor.

The Mufti also says that Johor ulama feel that since they inherited their religious traditions from pious Muslim scholars, they can never be misguided in upholding Sufism.[7] In April 2016, he presented a paper pointing out that Johor ulama should follow the methods of the earlier Johor Mufti, Datuk Syed Alwi Tahir al-Haddad when issuing a *fatwa*, although this did not mean that the new *fatwa* should not differ from al-Haddad's.[8] Syed Alwi was Mufti between 1941 to 1934 and 1947 to 1961, and wrote many *fatwa*s condemning Wahhabism and the modernists.

The dominance of the *kaum tua* orientation is also seen in the publications of Johor's Islamic Religious Council. The Mufti Department of Johor runs an e-book series that is downloaded by the public. These contain anti-Salafi-Wahhabi ideas, as the discussion below on two of these publications demonstrates.[9]

The first e-book is entitled *Sambutan Maulidur Rasul Bidáh Dhalalah?* (Celebration of the Prophet Muhammad's Birthday: A Forbidden Innovation?), written by Haji Jainal Al-Jauhari, Chief Executive of the Islamic Religious Council of Johor. The book was vetted by Nooh Gadot, the former Mufti (Al-Jauhari 2008). In essence, it attacks the Salafi-Wahhabi position that celebrating Prophet Muhammad's birthday is an innovation and un-Islamic. Jainal argues that the practice is allowed by the Sunni school of jurisprudence (Ahli Sunnah wal Jamaah), which is the only school allowed in Malaysia. He underscores how such celebrations could bring the religious community closer to the teachings of the Prophet. He claims that the celebration is an expression of happiness over the birth of the Prophet, and it has been practised by savants of the past, for example, under the rule of Salahuddin Al-Ayubi between 1171 and 1193. The celebration normally includes reciting verses from the Quran and singing praises to the Prophet, and would often end with a feast. The common practice in Malaysia is for a *maulid* to be accompanied by a procession. The book also points out that the celebration is Islamic and should be encouraged because it can unite Muslims and strengthen their faith.

Another e-book that reflects the Mufti's Sufist thinking is written by Muhammad Fuad, entitled *Kepentingan Tariqah dan Tasawwuf* (The Importance of *Tariqah* and Islamic Spirituality) (Al-Maliki 2008). The *tariqah* is a Sufi order that mainly teaches spirituality (*tasawwuf*) through *zikr* (chanting verses from the Quran or repeating praises to the Prophet). There are many such Sufi orders in Malaysia, including the Naqshabandiyah and Ahmadiyah Idrisiah. These are headed by *murshid*s (spiritual leaders) and their followers pledge allegiance to their masters before becoming part of the group (*bai'ah*). Some *tariqah* groups promote mysticism, spirituality and metaphysics, practices that are also frowned upon by the Salafis-Wahhabis for the same reasons they are against the celebrating of the Prophet's birthday, i.e., that they are not found in the Quran and that these groups therefore practice innovations. The book mainly supports the existence of *tariqah* groups in Johor because these are within the spirit of the religion and are in accordance with the teachings of the Prophet.

Some scholars, including some from the West, posit that Sufism is a more tolerant orientation than Salafism-Wahhabism, and this has become an ever more dominant view after September 11. Sufism is considered by them to be the solution to terrorism. But what we see is that the embracing of Sufism by the Johor Muftis has not made them more progressive. In fact, they are basically traditionalists. Sociologist Robert Towler (1986, pp. 90–91) defines traditionalism as a mode of thinking that holds on to old ways, and resists change and is marked by an unquestioning celebration of its own certainty.

Many views expressed by the previous Mufti Nooh Gadot are traditionalist in essence. In 2006, Nooh Gadot published an article suggesting that the state come up with guidelines for how women should dress in public. He also said that although women can join the workforce, they have to prioritize their role as mothers (Nooh Gadut 2006, pp. 34–35).

The Johor religious elite's traditionalism also leads to exclusivist thinking, especially on relations with non-Muslims. In 2014, Nooh Gadot was quoted in *Berita Harian* condemning opposition leader Anwar Ibrahim for allowing non-Muslims to use the term "Allah". Malaysia has since the 1980s been debating whether the term Allah is exclusive to Muslims. Malay-speaking Christians, especially from Sarawak have traditionally been using the term in their Bible. According to Nooh Gadot, Anwar was disrespectful of the *fatwa* issued by fourteen Malaysian Muftis in 1986 which claimed the term for exclusive use by Muslims (*Berita Harian*, 19 February 2014). Nooh Gadot continues to play an important religious role in Johor, and is a trusted ally of the Sultan. Upon his retirement, he was made Advisor to the Islamic Religious Council of Johor and to the Sultan.

Two other e-books warn Johor Muslims of the Shia and the liberal Islam "threat", and mirrors the general trend among Malaysian religious elite that Shiism is a deviant ideology and that liberalism is a threat to Islam (Wan Adli Wan Ramli 2012; Jainal Sakiban 2012). They call on those who harbour these trends of thought to repent. In truth, Sunni Muslims in many parts of the world have lived peacefully alongside the Shias. Moreover, many ulama around the world, including those in Indonesia, have pointed out that Shiism should be seen as part of mainstream Islam (Norshahril Saat 2014).

THE SULTAN OF JOHOR: RESISTING FEDERAL INTRUSION

Johor Muftis tend to participate in royal events. In March 2015, the Mufti played an important role during the Sultan's coronation ceremony. He placed a 1.6-kilogram crown—capped with sapphires, emeralds, rubies, and diamonds which included an Islamic crescent—on the Sultan's head, performing a role similar to that played by the Archbishop of Canterbury, who would normally do the same during the coronation of a British Monarch (Hutchinson and Nair 2016, pp. 15–16). The same was done for Princess Raja Zarith Sofiah (*Bernama*, 23 March 2015).

In March 2016, the Mufti was also present at the Sultan's birthday celebrations (*myMetro*, 24 March 2016). On 4 August 2016, he read the opening prayers for the Sultan's grandson birth rituals (*Berita Harian*, 4 August 2016), and in September 2016, allowed Muslims to join mass prayers for *Bangsa Johor* (the Johor Nation), which involved non-Muslims. At the end of the ceremony, participants went to the palace Istana Bukit Serene to release 100 birds in accordance with Chinese customs (*Berita Minggu*, 18 September 2016).

There have been instances when the Sultan has publicly made a stand on religious issues. In late 2013, he was instrumental in reinstating the Islamic week starting from 1 January 2014. This means that working days for the state are now between Sunday and Thursday. The rationale for this is to allow Muslims more time to complete their Friday prayers. Johor had in fact been practising this Islamic week since the colonial period, until it was reversed in 1993 by Chief Minister of the state (Hutchinson and Nair 2016, p. 18). The Sultan's reinstatement of the Friday and Saturday off-days boosted his image as a protector of Islam. In an exclusive interview with *The Star* in 2015, he iterated that it was he who was the authority of Islam in the state and that JAKIM could only advise the religious councils. He explained that he had the final authority to appoint members to the religious council, and that only he could approve *fatwas*. To be sure, he had occasionally questioned *fatwas* and sought further clarification, and emphasized that JAKIM had no authority to meddle in the state's religious affairs. He has also questioned JAKIM's request for a bigger budget and has asked for the breakdown of their spending at the Conference of Ruler's meeting (Wong and Benjamin 2015).

Recently, the Sultan also publicly criticized Malays for mimicking the Arabs in their religious orientation. He urged them to stick to their culture: "If there are some of you who wish to be an Arab and practise Arab culture and do not wish to follow our Malay customs and traditions, that is up to you. I also welcome you to live in Saudi Arabia" (*Straits Times*, 25 March 2016). It has also been noted that the Sultan prefers to use Malay words such as "Hari Raya" (a day of celebration upon the completion of the fasting month) and *"buka puasa"* (breaking fast) instead of the recently popularized Arabic equivalents of "Eid al-fitr" and *"iftar"* respectively (*Malay Mail Online*, 24 March 2016).

In February 2016, while opening the Majlis Tilawah Al-Quran (Quran Recitation Competition), the Sultan emphasized that members of the religious elite preaching in the state must obtain accreditation from the Islamic Religious Council of Johor. He added that even speakers who are popular and credible must respect this because that has been the law since 1895, when the Ruler was established as the Head of Islam in the state (Badrul Kamal Zakaria 2016). Indeed, in May 2016, a popular preacher from Singapore, Ustaz Rasul Dahri, was fined for RM5,000 (S$1,690) and jailed by the Islamic Religious Department of Johor for teaching there without proper accreditation (*Berita Harian*, 7 May 2016). He was also accused of spreading views that are not in line with the Sunni school of thought.

The Sultan emphasized that Johoreans must be proactive in tackling both extremism and deviant teachings, and should therefore study religion from teachers recognized by the state. Interestingly, he positioned Salafi-Wahhabi teachings alongside Shia, liberalism and pluralism as deviant ideologies (Ahmad Fairuz Othman 2016).

CONCLUSION

Overall, there has been continuity in the religious and political behaviour of the Johor Muftis. They remain committed to upholding Sufism, and are active in stopping Salafi-Wahhabi ideas from entering the state. Sufi values are promoted in the *fatwas* passed by the Islamic Religious Council, and through publications.

The Sultan's interventions in religious affairs also ensure that the Johor Mufti and the religious institutions under his charge are protected from federal encroachment. The Ruler acts as the gatekeeper for Johor Islamic identity, preventing Salafi-Wahhabi thinking from penetrating the state's religious discourse.

Nevertheless, being close to Sufism does not mean that Johor Muftis have not expressed exclusivist tendencies. This is evident in their views towards women and to alternative discourses.

What becomes clear in Johor is that the contestation between *kaum tua* and Salafi-Wahhabi has not ended despite many decades of debate. In fact, it remains in the interest of the Johor Mufti to maintain the state's reputation as the bastion of *kaum tua*.

Notes

1. This chapter was previously published as *Johor Remains as the Bastion of Kaum Tua*, Trends in Southeast Asia, no. 1/2017 (Singapore: ISEAS – Yusof Ishak Institute, 2017). The author would like to thank the former Mufti of Johor, Sahibus Samahah Datuk Hj Mohd Tahrir Bin Dato' Kiyai Hj Samsuddin for sharing his thoughts, the Mufti Department of Johor and the Johor Archives for facilitating his research.
2. Haji Abdul Karim Amrullah is the father of the well-known Indonesian religious scholar Hamka.
3. This rivalry between the *kaum tua* and the reformists extended to name-calling. Haji Abdul Karim's son, Hamka, also criticized the Johor Mufti for wrongly representing modernists (*kaum muda*) as "communists" and "stooges" of Christian missionaries in Indonesia. See Hamka (2009).
4. The position of the Yang di-Pertuan Agong rotates among the nine Malay Rulers once every five years.
5. Before 1978, the power for issuing religious opinion rested only with the Mufti. The Islamic Religious Council only acted as a rubber stamp. After 1978, the Johor government formed a *fatwa*-making body to assist the Mufti, called Lujnah Fatwa. At any one time, the body consists of not more than four clerics, and is chaired by the Mufti (Kasan 2008, p. 26).
6. Interview with Sahibus Samahah Datuk Hj Mohd Tahrir Bin Dato' Kiyai Hj Samsuddin, 23 October 2016.
7. Ibid.
8. Ibid. Datuk Tahrir disagrees with al-Haddad's *fatwa* on some issues.
9. See Jabatan Mufti Negeri Johor website: http://Mufti.johor.gov.my/v3/muatturun

References

Abdul Jalil Borham. 2002. *Majalah Ahkam Johor: Latar Belakang, Perlaksanaan dan Komentar*. Johor Darul Ta'zim: Universiti Teknologi Malaysia Skudai.

Ahmad Fairuz Othman. 2016. "Sultan Johor: Learn Islam from Those with Credentials". *New Straits Times*, 31 March 2016.

Ahmad Fauzi Abdul Hamid. 2016. "ISIS in Southeast Asia: Internalized Wahhabism is a Major Factor". *ISEAS Perspectives*, no. 24/2016, 16 May 2016. https://www.iseas.edu.sg/images/pdf/ISEAS_Perspective_2016_24.pdf

Aizyl Azlee. 2015. "JAKIM Says Will Comply with Johor Sultan's Demand for It to Explain RM1b Funding". *Malay Mail Online*, 28 December 2015. http://www.themalaymailonline.com/malaysia/article/jakim-says-will-comply-with-johor-sultans-demand-for-it-to-explain-rm1b-fun (accessed 18 October 2016).

Alatas, Syed Farid. 2014. "Battle Against Extremism Within Islam". *Straits Times*, 5 April 2014.

Al-Jauhari, Haji Jainal. 2008. *Sambutan Maulidur Rasul Bidáh Dhalalah?* Johor: Majlis Agama Islam Negeri Johor.

Al-Maliki, Muhammad Fuad Kamaludin. 2008. *Kepentingan Tariqah dan Tasawwuf.* Johor: Majlis Agama Islam Negeri Johor.

Badrul Kamal Zakaria. 2016. "Pendakwah ke Johor Perlu Tauliah MAIJ". *Berita Harian*, 24 February 2016.

Berita Harian (Singapore). 2014. "Dua Mufti Lagi Kecam Anwar". 19 February 2014.

———. 2016a. "Pendakwah S'pura Dipenjara di Johor". 7 May 2016.

———. 2016b. "Sultan Johor Hadiri Majlis Akikah Cucunda". 4 August 2016.

Berita Minggu. 2016. "Ribuan Rakyat Jayakan Program Gabungan Doa Bangsa Johor". 18 September 2016.

Bernama. 2015. "Istiadat Kemahkotaan Berlangsung Gilang Gemilang". 23 March 2015.

Delong-Bas, Natana J. 2004. *Wahhabi Islam: From Revival and Reform to Global Jihad*. New York: Oxford University Press.

El-Fadl, Khaled Abou. 2005. *The Great Theft: Wrestling Islam from the Extremists*. New York: HarperOne.

Faruqi, Shad Saleem. 2005. "The Malaysian Constitution, The Islamic State and Hudud Laws". In *Islam in Southeast Asia: Political, Social and Strategic Challenges for the 21st Century*, edited by K.S. Nathan and M.H. Kamali. Singapore: Institute of Southeast Asian Studies.

Hamka. 2009. *Teguran Suci dan Jujur Terhadap Mufti Johor*. Shah Alam: Pustaka Dini.

Hasnan Kasan. 2008. *Institusi Fatwa di Malaysia*. Bangi: Universiti Kebangsaan Malaysia.

Hutchinson, Francis E. and Vandana Prakash Nair. 2016. *The Johor Sultanate: Rise or Re-Emergence?* Trends in Southeast Asia, no. 16/2016. Singapore: ISEAS – Yusof Ishak Institute.

Jabatan Mufti Negeri Johor website. http://Mufti.johor.gov.my/v3/muatturun

Jainal Sakiban. 2012. *Kebatilan Akidah Syi'ah*. Johor: Majlis Agama Islam Johor.

Johor State Government. 2003. Enactment No. 16 of 2003 in Administration of the Religion of Islam (State of Johor). http://www2.esharia.gov.my/esharia/mal/portalv1/enakmen2011/Eng_enactment_Ori_lib.nsf/100ae747c72508e748256faa00188094/a079fdb33f522cdf482576c000093a03?OpenDocument (accessed 19 September 2016).

Mufti Perlis. 2016. "Exco Pemuda Umno dilarang ceramah di Johor". *Malay Mail Online*, 2 February 2016. http://www.themalaymailonline.com/projekmmo/berita/article/Mufti-perlis-exco-pemuda-umno-dilarang-ceramah-di-johor (accessed 25 October 2016).

myMetro. 2016. "Tanda Taat Setia". 24 March 2016.

Nooh Gadut. 2006. "Pandangan Islam Terhadap Pencapaian Wanita". In *Memahami Kedudukan Wanita dari Perspektif Islam*, edited by S.F. Rahman. Kuala Lumpur: MPH and IKIM.

Norshahril Saat. 2014. "'Deviant' Muslims: The Plight of Shias in Contemporary Malaysia". In *Religious Diversity in Muslim-Majority States in Southeast Asia: Areas of Toleration and Conflict*, edited by B. Platzdasch and J. Saravanamuttu. Singapore: Institute of Southeast Asian Studies.

———. 2016. "Exclusivist Attitudes in Malaysian Islam Have Multifarious Roots". *ISEAS Perspectives*, no. 39/2016, 5 July 2016. https://www.iseas.edu.sg/images/pdf/ISEAS_Perspective_2016_39.pdf

Roff, William R. 1994. *The Origins of Malay Nationalism*. 2nd ed. Kuala Lumpur: Oxford University Press.

Shihab, Quraish M. 2007. *Sunnah-Syrah: Bergandengan Tangan Mungkinkah?* Iputat: Lentera Hati.

Straits Times. 2016. "Johor Sultan to Malays: Stick to Your Own Culture". 25 March 2016.

Times of India. 2016. "Sufism Can Act as Antidote to Terrorism: Arjun Meghwal". 15 October 2016. http://timesofindia.indiatimes.com/city/jaipur/Sufism-can-act-as-antidote-to-terrorism-Arjun-Meghwal/articleshow/54862205.cms (accessed 8 December 2016).

Towler, Robert. 1986. *The Need For Certainty: A Sociological Study of Conventional Religion.* London: Routledge and Kegan Paul.

Wan Adli Wan Ramli. 2012. *Bahaya Liberalisme dan Pluralisme Agamana Terhadap Akidah Belia Muslim.* Johor: Majlis Agama Islam Johor.

Webster, Jason. 2014. "Sufism: A Natural Antidote to Fanaticism". *The Guardian*, 23 October 2014. https://www.theguardian.com/books/2014/oct/23/sufism-natural-antidote-fanaticism-the-sufis-idries-shah (accessed 8 December 2016).

Wong Chun Wai and Nelson Benjamin. 2015. "Johor Ruler: I'm Above Politics". *The Star*, 27 December 2015. http://www.thestar.com.my/news/nation/2015/12/27/johor-ruler-im-above-politics-the-interest-of-the-rakyat-always-comes-first/ (accessed 27 December 2015).

Zahari Azman, Nur Salida and Adel. 2008. *Biografi Mufti-Mufti Malaysia.* Negeri Sembilan: Universiti Sains Islam Malaysia.

15

JOHOR BAHRU'S URBAN TRANSFORMATION
Authority and Agency Revisited

Keng Khoon Ng

INTRODUCTION

Johor, West Malaysia's southernmost state, has undergone a tremendous urban transformation over the last decade. Its strategic location, adjacent to Singapore, has contributed to escalating development and rising land values. The state offers many opportunities for investors; its rapid urban transformation is closely associated with the establishment of Iskandar Malaysia, a special economic zone (SEZ) that was officially launched in 2006. Initially 2,217 square kilometres in area, Iskandar Malaysia was singled out as the highest-impact development project in the Ninth Malaysia Plan (2006–10). Modelled ostensibly after the Pearl River Delta Economic Zone, Iskandar Malaysia seeks to maximize spillover effects for business and industry from land-scarce Singapore as well as other destinations. In its wake, the SEZ brought an unprecedented building boom and speculation in the international property sector.

Malaysia has a long-standing history of land reform and redistribution. From independence, land reform was deemed critical for poverty reduction, as seen through large-scale initiatives such as the Federal Land Development Authority (FELDA), which sought to create livelihoods for poor rural families with little or no assets (Henley 2015).

However, while land management is, according to the Constitution, a state government responsibility, national-level needs and initiatives have led to federal government encroachment in these and many other areas (Hutchinson 2014). As land remains a premium asset for the both levels of government, the process of sourcing for and developing land can become contested.

Johor's land redistribution policy and property development practices have undergone profound changes over the last ten years. The state government has opened up Johor Bahru's high-end residential market to both local non-bumiputra enterprises and foreign developers. There are about forty ongoing or recently completed property projects in Johor. These projects attributed to 42 per cent of the stock of 702,101 new houses in the state. From 2007 to 2016, Johor recorded a total sale of investment properties of more than US$8.1 billion. In 2013, over 76.4 per cent of investment properties (mostly residential) were purchased by foreign investors (Savills World Research Malaysia 2015).

This chapter aims to understand and reflect on Johor Bahru's fast-changing urban environment. It intends to broaden the study of land reform by considering how government-linked companies, bureaucratic elite and foreign developers have acted together to reshape land development practices in contemporary Johor. Through a critical reading of land policies, development actors and mega-projects, this chapter provides a more nuanced understanding of Johor's Iskandar Malaysia in relation to changing federal and state government priorities.

This chapter comprises four sections. Following this introduction, the second section begins with an overview of Johor Bahru's urban specifics and its emerging regional significance. The section examines Johor's growth-oriented entrepreneurial strategies that have affected development in its cities. The third section is an appraisal of Iskandar Malaysia that traces its origins and development history from the mid-2000s. This section will expound on land politics, in essence the Johor government's dependence on land revenue and conversion versus the federal government's desire to rein in real estate investment and reclamation. This analysis is a case study of Nusajaya (later renamed Iskandar Puteri), a large-scale mixed development purporting to be the crown jewel of Iskandar Malaysia. Against this backdrop, the fourth section then explains how Johor-based interests began to assert a higher degree of agency over land stocks and international real estate development in the Johor Bahru City Centre. The chapter concludes by reflecting on changing centre-state relations in Malaysia, especially in the face of increasing exertions of power by the local government.

JOHOR BAHRU'S EMERGING REGIONAL SIGNIFICANCE

With a total land area of 19,016 square kilometres, Johor is the fifth largest state in Malaysia and is also the third most populated state, boasting a 3.8 million-strong population (DoS 2019). Developing briskly over the past three decades, Johor Bahru has emerged the de facto commercial hub of southern Malaysia, and is the second largest city in the country after Kuala Lumpur. With better employment opportunities in neighbouring Singapore, Johor Bahru has benefited from migration both from within Johor and other parts of the country.

One of Southeast Asia's most populous urban centres, Johor Bahru is the nucleus of the southern economic corridor, Iskandar Malaysia. With a population of approximately 1.73 million in Johor Bahru alone, and 7.23 million in the Singapore-South Johor transborder region, the population and economic growth rate is among the highest in Southeast Asia. With this backdrop, the concept of the "Straits Mega-City Region" (Rizzo and Khan 2013) was proposed to position Johor Bahru in a new sphere of transnational urbanism by coupling it with Kuala Lumpur and Singapore. Johor's large population, strategic location and links with Singapore—which suffers high land costs—offer great opportunities for real estate development. According to Mercer's 19th Annual Quality of Living Survey, Johor Bahru was ranked the third best city in Southeast Asia, 14th in a range of Asian cities and 103rd globally (Brown 2017).

Johor Bahru (formerly known as Tanjung Puteri/Iskandar Puteri) was founded as the state capital in 1855 by Temenggong Daing Ibrahim, and marked the beginning of the modernization of Johor. The city prospered under his son, Sultan Abu Bakar. In 1866, the designated capital of Johor at the Temenggong's residence in Teluk Blangah was relocated to this new administrative town. At the time, Tanjung Puteri was only a small village located on the edge of the Tebrau Strait (also known as the Johor Strait) (Lim 2009).

In 1858, Sultan Abu Bakar planned on building a palace to reflect the state's power and sovereignty. The Istana Besar (Grand Palace) was completed on the first day of January 1866. On the same day Iskandar Puteri was renamed Johor Bahru ("*bahru*" meaning "new") to signify the opening of a new Johor capital. Construction of the Johor-Singapore Causeway (JSC) began in 1919 and was completed in 1923; a 1.05-kilometre bridge linking Johor Bahru across the Tebrau Strait to the town of Woodlands in Singapore. Johor Bahru's city limits continued to expand from 12.12 square kilometres in 1933 to 119.50 square kilometres in 1971, and eventually covering an area of about 373.18 square kilometres in 2016 (MBJB 2018).

The Federation of Malaya achieved independence in 1957. Between independence and the recent 14th General Elections, Johor was ruled by the UMNO-led Barisan Nasional federal government. Johor's economy was profoundly influenced by the New Economic Policy (NEP 1971–90), an overarching redistributive policy announced in the 1970s (Government of Malaysia 1971).

Between 1970 and 1990, 300,000 hectares of land under the Johor Tenggara Scheme were opened up for settlement and turned over to the cultivation of rubber and oil palm. Johor's rapid development was further boosted by growing industrialization and diversification of its economic base (Vatikiotis 1992, 1993). The FELDA controlled a large proportion of oil palm production in Johor under the scheme. However, its business model changed in the 1990s, when new settlement activities were stopped. Following a greater emphasis on privatization, the organization's remit began to stress commercial profitability to a greater degree (Sutton and Buang, 1995).

When industrialization picked up in the 1980s, foreign investments began to pour in, especially from Singapore and Japan. Industrial parks and infrastructural projects began to emerge on Johor Bahru's outskirts, especially in Pasir Gudang.

The state's first international port for trading, Johor Port, was built in 1977. The port helped Johor's economic transition from away agriculture towards becoming a regional hub for industry and logistics. Johor Port and Pasir Gudang Industrial Estate were set up by the state investment arm Johor State Economic Development Corporation (now known as Johor Corporation or JCorp) (Guiness 1992). The state capital, with many state-affiliated companies, was also essential to the establishment of major manufacturing firms in palm oil refining, ship engineering and steel and tin manufacturing.

In the 1990s, Johor set its sights on becoming a new technopolis after a fall in commodity prices revealed the limitations of its dependence on agriculture. However, the Malaysian Constitution allocates the bulk of revenue-generating responsibilities to the federal government, thereby constraining the bargaining power of state governments.

Despite this, state governments retain control over land and natural resources, both of which Johor is abundantly endowed with. Consequently, since the 1970s, the Johor state government has sought to use these revenue sources (Hutchinson 2015). However, since the 1960s, the federal government has sought to centralize power at the expense of state governments. This has been achieved through a variety of tactics, including appropriation, altering incentives for state governments, privatisation, and organizational duplication (Hutchinson 2014).

Thus, attempts to attract investment and develop new sectors at the state level are not always supported by the federal government. Indeed, during the 1980s and 1990s, the two levels of government clashed over different strategies for attracting foreign investment (Hutchinson 2015).

The section that follows will describe Iskandar Malaysia's background, as well as the organizational goals of the various government agencies involved.

GLOBALIZING JOHOR: THE LAUNCH OF ISKANDAR MALAYSIA

On 4 November 2006, Prime Minister Datuk Seri Abdullah Badawi launched the Iskandar Development Region, which was then renamed as Iskandar Malaysia. As one of the four economic corridors that make up the bulk of the Ninth Malaysia Plan (2006–10), Iskandar Malaysia covers 2,217 square kilometres in South Johor and was designated as a special economic zone. Iskandar Malaysia's ambitious vision hinges on its ties and "strategic proximity" to Singapore. At the launch of the project, Abdullah Badawi announced that Iskandar Malaysia would be to Singapore, as "Shenzhen is to Hong Kong". It is poised to attract an influx of foreign and high-level public-private investments as discerning investors look to benefit from the freeing of borders in South Johor. In line with the National Physical Plan 2005–20, Iskandar Malaysia was to adhere to the concept of "national spatial planning" and "promote balanced regional development for national unity" (Khazanah Nasional 2006).

Khazanah Nasional Berhad (Khazanah) was assigned to conduct a feasibility study for the development of a special economic zone in South Johor, modelled after the successful Shenzhen-Hong Kong economic zone. Khazanah is the Malaysian government's strategic investment fund, entrusted to hold national assets and undertake investments (Lai 2012). Iskandar Malaysia was established as a joint endeavour between the federal government and Johor's state government.[1]

Iskandar Malaysia was designed to capture the spillover from Singapore. It is interesting to note that Iskandar Malaysia did not strongly emphasize pro-bumiputra policies, which meant that unlike other SEZs, Iskandar Malaysia's economic activities are open equally to other races and international investors (Tey 2011). In a comparative analysis of Iskandar Malaysia and MSC Malaysia/Putrajaya, Rizzo and Glasson (2012) opine that the similarities between these two mega-regional projects are their "top-down national policies":

> Putrajaya and Nusajaya are both the result of strong individual, political commitment, rather than multinational companies' interests in exploiting cheap labour as the global city theory suggests, which at times may not match with market volatility (Rizzo and Glasson 2012, p. 32).

Iskandar Malaysia is one of the major catalysts and high-impact developments for the country under the Ninth Malaysia Plan. Iskandar Malaysia was clearly a deliberate strategy pursued by visionary political leaders; a top-down rather than grassroots-led initiative as civil society did not participate in the planning process. For example, more than 2,900 households living in traditional villages and squatter settlements were cleared and made way to realize the 8.1-kilometre Eastern Dispersal Link (EDL), connecting the North-South Expressway interchange to the Sultan Iskandar Customs, Immigration and Quarantine building at the Causeway. Land required for infrastructure projects was undertaken by state-private sector partnerships was acquired by the government and local people displaced in the name of national progress. This led to social segregation and profits going only to developers and certain income groups (Nasongkhla and Sintusingha 2013; Nadalutti 2015; Sultan 2016).[2]

The development of Iskandar Malaysia is based on Comprehensive Development Plans (CDP I and II), which are strategic planning frameworks and development strategies drafted by Khazanah. The CDPs encompass a broad spectrum of objectives from economic, legal and statutory, physical planning, socio-culture to environment and sustainability. The implementation of the CDP is undertaken by the Iskandar Regional Development Authority (IRDA), which is co-chaired by the Prime Minister of Malaysia and the Chief Minister of Johor (Figure 15.1).

The physical planning of Iskandar Malaysia comprises five strategic flagship zones. UEM Sunrise's focus has been on developing Nusajaya (Flagship Zone B) in Iskandar Malaysia. Nusajaya was designated the prime development zone (Map 3.3) and had the lofty ambition of becoming the largest integrated urban development in Southeast Asia by the time it is fully completed in 2025. Nusajaya is majority-owned and developed by UEM Sunrise, a wholly owned subsidiary of Khazanah. Many joint-venture deals have been sealed with local and foreign partners to build developments and amenities in the 24,000-acre township (Figure 15.2).

FIGURE 15.1
Iskandar Malaysia, Flagship Zones A-E

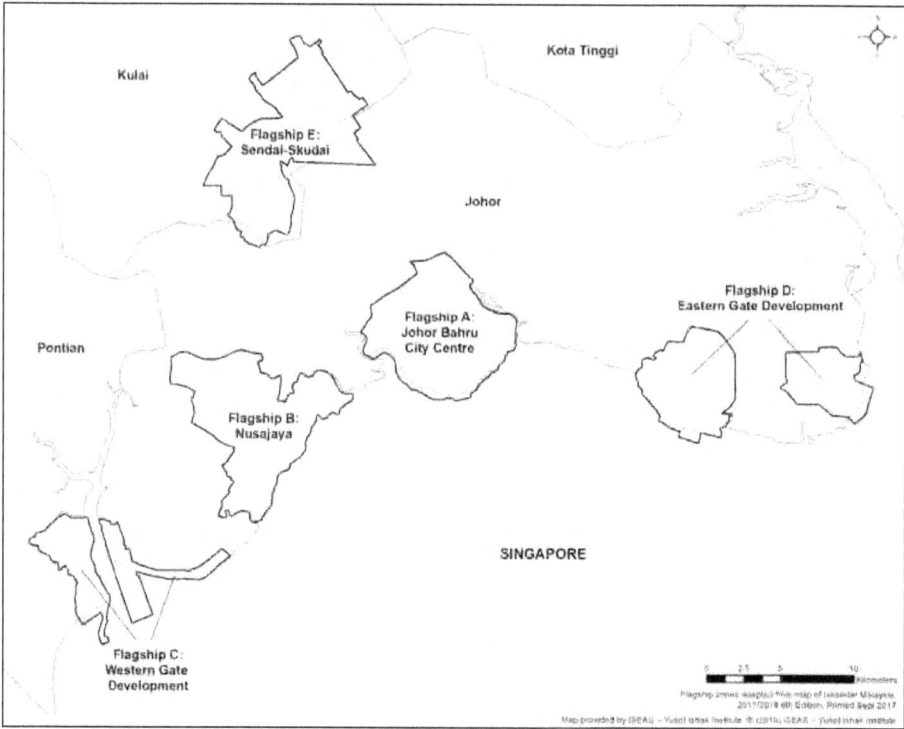

FIGURE 15.2
Medini Iskandar Malaysia in Flagship Zone B

As a new city, it was founded on two major premises: in accordance with the federal government's top-down plans; and to generate profits for government-linked enterprises. Consequently, its aims were to expand and speculate on Johor's widening market of luxury property that leverages on its proximity to Singapore.

In the 1990s, Prolink Development Sdn Bhd (Prolink) was the titleholder of the sprawling 25,000-acre plot of agricultural land in South Johor that became Nusajaya. Prolink was a 64-per-cent-owned subsidiary of Renong Berhad (Renong), one of the biggest Malaysian private conglomerates with close ties to the government. Renong was established in 1982 and owned by a new class of bumiputra elites.[3] Haggard (2000, p. 168) commented that "Renong was one of the most successful stories of the Mahathir strategy of privatization".

Prolink's land bank came about as part of the construction of the Malaysia-Singapore Second Link connecting the North South Expressway to Singapore. Renong benefited tremendously from newly established policies on infrastructure privatization and government-linked enterprises. Renong became financially and politically powerful in Johor, not merely because of its prized land assets in Nusajaya and the Tuas Second Link, but presumably also because of its close relationship with federal government agencies.

Nusajaya's lustre (and the group's fortunes) began to fade when the Asian Financial Crisis hit in 1997 and the federal government had to step in to bail out ailing corporations. The rescue of the Renong-UEM group was undertaken by Khazanah because the group's outstanding debts were too high and posed a risk to the national banking system.[4] The attempts at "nationalizing" Renong-UEM illustrate the change in policy from a private sector-led economy towards one with a greater degree of state control. As a result of the financial crisis and the restructuring of government policy, Khazanah inherited large tracts of land in Nusajaya from former landowners Renong and Prolink.

After the consolidation exercise, Renong was renamed UEM Land Holdings Berhad in 2003 (and subsequently renamed UEM Sunrise Berhad). Prolink Development was renamed Bandar Nusajaya Development (BND). Both UEM Sunrise and BND then became flagship companies for the real estate investment arm of UEM Group, which is wholly owned by Khazanah. Ultimately, Nusajaya moved away from private ownership to publicly controlled assets.[5]

The shift demonstrated how the federal government and government-linked companies were taking on an even more central role in the planning of the entire Nusajaya region. The 1997 financial crisis took its toll and set Nusajaya back by several years. In 2003, a new proposal for Nusajaya was submitted to the Johor government, seeking planning approval at the state level. Most notably, "Node 1" was an integrated city launched under a joint-venture between Khazanah and Middle Eastern investors (IRDA 2008).

The entry of Middle Eastern investors marked a new milestone for Nusajaya. Sentiments, however, plunged during the 2008 Global Financial Crisis. The unexpected withdrawal of Middle Eastern monies forced the federal government to look for alternative business partners to sustain developments in Nusajaya (Khor 2011).

Even with the withdrawal of Middle Eastern monies, Nusajaya continued to function on the basis of federal plans to ensure profits for government-linked enterprises. UEM Sunrise and Iskandar Investment Berhad (IIB) become the two master developers responsible for the development of Nusajaya, and this enabled the federal government to oversee investments on the ground. Nusajaya continued to rely heavily on capital investments, achieving this through an array of tax and fiscal incentives enabled by Putrajaya. An array of tax incentives was available for six qualifying sectors: creative, education, financial advisory and consulting, healthcare, logistics and tourism (Khazanah Nasional 2007). This attempt at pairing tax policies with key projects secured Nusajaya's position as the most attractive site for investment in Iskandar Malaysia. Other flagship zones did not enjoy the same privileges.

According to an investment report published by Khazanah and IRDA in 2013, real estate was the most influential sector in Iskandar Malaysia, constituting 33.25 per cent of total investments (IRDA 2013). Although real estate was not initially considered as a key sector in Nusajaya, it surpassed the other six catalytic sectors in its proportional economic impact. This explains why real estate was reserved as full-right and priority for the government-linked developers. The managing director and CEO of UEM Sunrise Wan Abdullah opined "We aspire to be a global property development outfit like CapitaLand. We hope to one day play a similar role in Khazanah—be what CapitaLand is to Temasek … Our strategy is concurrent development by working in collaboration or partnership with other reputable developers to catalyse Nusajaya's development" (Thean 2010). The transformation of low-priced farm land into high-priced luxury residences was the ultimate goal for the Khazanah-backed UEM Sunrise to extract most of its revenue from Nusajaya.

Land prices have skyrocketed in Nusajaya. The land was priced between RM3.50 to RM6.00 per sq. foot in 2001. A tipping point was reached in 2012, when residences in Nusajaya were priced between RM600 to RM1,000 psf (Loh 2012). For example, semi-detached houses at Nusajaya were RM800,000 and RM1.2 million per unit, a price almost comparable to property prices in some areas within the Klang Valley (*The EdgeProperty*, 2011). To date, UEM Sunrise has developed more than 22,000 residential, office and retail units (over fifteen projects) comprising large-scale townships and luxury high-rise apartments (as shown in Table 15.1). About 26 per cent of property buyers in Nusajaya were foreigners, with 73 per cent of that figure being Singaporeans (Whang 2016). Property developers benefited greatly because there were no other incentives as attractive as those available in Nusajaya. Investing in areas beyond Nusajaya would entitle investors to only the Flagship Incentive, which is a relatively less attractive package of tax rebates.

This section has shown how Nusajaya was developed and transformed under the purview of the federal government and government-linked developers. Nusajaya was shaped mostly by commercial needs and real estate investments. It is planned as a globally competitive destination for investment and relocation, in which UEM Sunrise, Khazanah, and IIB are the major forces behind the grand vision. Given such enormous support from Putrajaya, Khazanah can arbitrarily influence decisions

TABLE 15.1
List of Residences Developed by UEM Sunrise in Nusajaya, Flagship Zone B

Townships	No. of Units	Apartments	No. of Units
Horizon Hills (joint venture)	4,035	Somerset (joint venture)	168
Emerald Bay (joint venture)	1,649	Imperia	246
East Ledang	3,677	Encorp Marina	538
Nusa Bayu	2,877	Almas	1,513
Nusa Idaman	2,897	Teega	1,371
Estuari	350	Southern Marina (joint venture)	456
Melia Residences	625	Impiana	488
Denai Nusantara	1,217	Afiniti Residences (joint venture)	147

Source: UEM Sunrise—compiled by author.

over investments and policies because Khazanah is the largest shareholder and land owner in Nusajaya. Furthermore, in acquiring land for its own projects, the federal government is decreasing the available land bank under the control of the Johor state government.

THE JOHOR BAHRU TRANSFORMATION PLAN: RECONFIGURING LAND AND AUTHORITY

The previous section has shown how Nusajaya's achievements between 2006 and 2015 were built on a mandate from the federal government. However, the rising role of the state government and local authorities cannot be dismissed. In reviewing the decade-old Iskandar Malaysia, Hutchinson (2015, p. 102) wrote:

> The 2004–13 period was the most turbulent in relations between the federal and Johor state governments. These tensions arose precisely because federal interest was accompanied by far-reaching encroachment into areas formerly of the state government's exclusive purview. While the Menteri Besar (Chief Minister) was able to preserve some modicum of relevance for the state government by securing joint control of the Iskandar Malaysia regulatory agency, the whole initiative's design seriously reduced the autonomous revenue-earning potential of the Johor government.

Hutchinson's analysis indicates that Iskandar Malaysia is an arena where both federal and state government goals are articulated and operationalized. At times, these goals compete with one another. After a decade of federal-driven development, Iskandar Malaysia now faces changes attributed, in part, to the growing autonomy of the Johor state government. It is now more apt to describe the relationship between the two levels of government as a dynamic one entwined in negotiation and competition.

Since 2012, the Johor state government and state-owned investment entities have adopted strategies to consolidate their control over land management in the state. These include the promotion of new housing policies and the establishment of a new international zone (Ng and Lim 2017).

Nusajaya, Flagship Zone B is where most of the land and developments are held by Khazanah. The Johor government has now established its own master plan and land bank in Flagship Zone A to attract foreign investments. This is seen by the establishment of new public-private partnerships promoted by the state government to streamline land reclamation and large-scale property projects in Danga Bay, Tebrau Bay and downtown Johor Bahru.

The projects located in Flagship Zone A are developed under the purview of Johor-based authorities through the state-owned company Iskandar Waterfront Holdings (IWH). In response to the rise of developments in Flagship Zone A, the chief executive officer of UEM Group Datuk Izzadin Idris pointed that "Khazanah (Nasional Bhd), our parent company, has its plans and we know what the future demand is going to be and we are planning in that context. Some of the development we will do and others Khazanah will do. What we don't know is what is going to happen beyond Nusajaya. What happens in Danga Bay and so on is beyond our control but the board is taking a cautious view of that" (Thean 2014).

Operating on behalf of the state government, IWH's leading role is to uphold planning controls and policies for new property projects in Flagship Zone A and developing Danga Bay and Tebrau Bay into an integrated waterfront city, as well as transform Johor Bahru into an international destination. IWH is 60 per cent owned by Tan Sri Lim Kang Hoo through his private company Credence Resources Sdn Bhd, while 40 per cent of its shares are held by the Johor state equity firm— Kumpulan Prasarana Rakyat Johor (KPRJ). Unlike Nusajaya, IWH is a public-private development driven primarily by the Johor government in Iskandar Malaysia's Flagship Zone A. IWH owns 3,900 acres of land in Johor. IWH and KPRJ each have a 47.16 per cent and 6.5 per cent stake respectively in IWC, which has 1,200 acres located mainly in Tebrau, near Johor Bahru.

Land reclamation commenced in Danga Bay in the late 1990s. However, major works in Danga Bay were halted when the economic crisis hit the country in 2007. The development of Danga Bay was resumed in 2012 when the first China-based developer, Country Garden Holdings bought 55 acres of land there in a RM900 million deal from IWH. Country Garden is a Guangdong-based developer from China established in 1992. In the following year, Country Garden launched Johor's first Chinese invested project—Country Garden Danga Bay, the 9,500-unit mega residential project. Conceived as an RM18 billion project, the ambitious Danga Bay project was expected to expand Johor's international property market to both Singaporean and Chinese investors. This project marked the inception of IWH's land-banking activities in Flagship Zone A. Taking Country Garden Danga Bay as a successful model of a Johor-Chinese joint venture, several more projects were launched based on this development model. To date, some thirteen companies have committed investments to develop properties in joint-ventures with IWH with a cumulative GDV of RM125 billion. See Table 15.2.

Majlis Bandaraya Johor Bahru (MBJB), the Johor Bahru city council is responsible for the redevelopment planning of JBCC. MBJB has taken a proactive role in restructuring JBCC under a series of special area plans—often in partnership with

TABLE 15.2
Some Key Property Developments in Danga Bay and Tebrau Coast

Companies (Country)	Land (ha)	Land Value	Project Name
Greenland Group (China)	14	RM600 million	Jade Palace
Greenland Group (China)	51.80	RM2.4 billion	Helios Bay
Country Garden Holdings (China)	22.26	RM900 million	Country Garden Danga Bay
Temasek Holdings (Singapore)	28.33	RM800 million	A2 Island
Walker Group	81.75	JV—RM3.8 billion	Senibong Cove
DiJaya Group (Malaysia)	99.15	JV—RM3.8 billion	Tropicana Danga Bay
Hao Yuan Investment (China)	15	JV	—
Brunsfield Group (Malaysia)	10.12	JV	—

Source: News release composed by author.

state-linked companies. To date, several major projects have been launched in response to the call for a Johor Bahru Transformation Plan. KPRJ, Johor Corporation (JCorp) and Johor Land are among the key forces behind the Johor Bahru Transformation Plan, providing the local government with a new arena for the financing and redevelopment of Johor Bahru.

The Ibrahim International Business District (IIBD) announced by Sultan Ibrahim in conjunction with his birthday in November 2015 marks the overall vision of the JBCC Transformation Plan. IIBD is spearheaded by the state government, MBJB and the state government's corporate arm, the Johor Corporation (JCorp). IIBD's purpose is to boost the state's economic activities and to transform Johor Bahru's old city core into an international business district. Despite the fact that IIBD will not be designated as a special zone, the state government can offer incentives for businesses, as well as tax breaks for the owners of existing buildings that need refurbishment.

The IIBD's masterplan covers a 250-acre transformation zone (as shown in Map 4.6) that will reinvigorate the city's economic outlook by injecting new commercial activities and services into the city: 51 per cent of the area is classified for commercial use; 24 per cent open space; and 14 and 9 per cent for institutional and residential use, respectively. IIDB is partially supported by the federal government through a RM250 million facilitation fund allocated for the construction of a 268-metre link bridge between JB Sentral and Persada Annexe and an elevated viaduct.

The first IIBD project, Coronation Square, is seen to be the jewel of the district and was so named in honour of Sultan Ibrahim's coronation in 2015. This 6.32-acre mixed use development is expected to be a catalyst "for the other components in the CBD" stated the JCorp president and CEO Datuk Kamaruzzaman Abu Kassim (Wong 2015). The developer of Coronation Square is JCorp's Coronade Properties Sdn Bhd. This project plans to contain: the Persada Annex; a high-rise medical suite; two blocks of serviced apartments; an office tower; and a hotel. The medical suites will be managed by JCorp's healthcare arm, KPJ Healthcare Bhd.

In contrast to the greenfield-based developments in Nusajaya which are adjacent to the Second Link, IIBD's potential lies in its location in a mature downtown area close to the Causeway. IIBD needs to compete against the recent raft of mega-projects launched in Nusajaya-Medini and the upcoming CBD close to the Tuas Second Link. From a business perspective, having two CBDs within the same city is preferred by investors because it helps to create competition.

Thus, if Medini Iskandar Malaysia is the crown jewel of Nusajaya (Flagship Zone B), then IIBD can be seen as the crown jewel of Johor Bahru (Flagship Zone A). In other words, the competition between Nusajaya and JBCC also can be seen as attempts by the federal and state governments to extend their influence over the development of iconic projects and land management in Johor.

The Johor Bahru Transformation Plan centres on restyling the city with iconic architecture. Launched in December 2013, The Astaka at One Bukit Senyum (OBS) is being developed on an 11.8-acre site. The freehold tract where OBS is situated was the site of the former Johor indoor stadium and hockey stadium. The developer acquired the plot of land from the state government by agreeing to build a new headquarters for the Johor Bahru City Council. OBS is a signature project built upon public-private initiatives between Astaka Padu Sdn Bhd and the Johor Bahru City Council. Astaka Padu is the developer and land proprietor of OBS. Astaka Padu Bhd is a fully owned subsidiary of Astaka Holdings Limited. Daing A. Malek is the founder of Astaka Padu Sdn Bhd and the largest shareholder of Astaka Holdings (Astaka Holdings 2016). Daing A. Malek is also one of the key business partners of the Johor-linked enterprise. Damansara Realty Bhd's (DRealty) largest stakeholder is Daing A. Malek with 51 per cent, while the Johor government entity JCorp owns 14.2 per cent. This project shows another joint venture initiated and controlled by the Johor government.

The two-phased development is expected to generate an estimated RM6 billion in gross development value. Phase 1 comprises two residential towers named "The Astaka". Sitting on 2.42 acres, the project offers 438 spacious units in two towers that soar 64 and 70 storeys high. Phase 2 is divided into two smaller phases, 2A and 2B. The RM300 million Johor Bahru City Council headquarters will occupy 2.42 acres in phase 2A and is slated for completion in 2019. Phase 2B consists of an 8.05-acre integrated development with a gross development value of RM4.6 million. It consists of a 62-storey five-star hotel and branded residences, a 46-storey "Grade A" office tower and a 10-storey high-end retail mall. Upon completion, The Astaka will be an imposing ultra-luxury condominium standing at 1,020 feet. It will be the tallest residence in Southeast Asia and one of Malaysia's top ten tallest buildings.

On the same site of OBS, Astaka Padu will construct and then sell the new MBJB headquarters with a price tag of RM308 million. Approximately 800 government staff will relocate to this new office complex. The public-private partnerships have received support from the state government. For example, the 2 per cent foreign state consent levy and 0.5 per cent stamp duty are exempted.

The planned Rapid Transit System (RTS) between downtown Johor Bahru and Singapore is located within the core of Johor Bahru that is being redeveloped. The Astaka and OBS will have unrivalled access to Singapore. Their strategic location adjacent to the proposed RTS station site promises long-term benefits. Planning decisions were made to protect both the future of OBS and its right to land and development matters. The building of a two-way tunnel linking OBS with other major sites, especially the upcoming RTS, is a prime example of this intention. IIBD and OBS will accelerate growth in downtown Johor Bahru and contribute to the state's economic and infrastructural development. To this end, both IIBD and OBS (The Astaka) should be seen as part of the Johor government's internationalization attempts. Placing these two iconic structures at the forefront of the Johor Bahru Transformation Plan will legitimize investment opportunities for the Johor-linked developers and provide the local government with a new arena to finance Johor Bahru.

This section has reviewed some of the major projects and land transactions in Flagship Zone A. Most of the state government-driven projects were initiated after 2012, some six years after the establishment of Iskandar Malaysia under the aegis of the federal government-owned Khazanah. While investment into Flagship Zone B is of benefit to the state government, as it receives tax revenue from property transactions, it is ultimately less financially interesting than real estate development led by its own stable of government-linked corporations. There are two potential reasons underlying the Johor state government's heightened involvement in the real estate sector in Flagship Zone A. First, the transactions carried out with participation from state government-owned GLCs yield additional revenue. Second, unlike in Flagship Zone B, where the state government must contend with other actors, in Flagship Zone A, it is entirely at liberty to articulate its own desired image of an international city. In short, the Johor Bahru Transformation Plan reaffirms the role of Johor-based authorities over urban spaces, particularly in the state's capital, in contrast to the federal government-led planning seen in Nusajaya.

CONCLUSION

Land is now the main concern of urban politics in contemporary Johor. The opening section of this chapter showed the evolution of land ownership since the early days of Nusajaya's development. The analysis demonstrated the concern evoked regarding the top-down practices implemented by the federal government. Nusajaya's inception constrained the revenue-raising potential of the Johor government. Seen as a globally competitive destination for investment and relocation, UEM Sunrise, Khazanah, and IIB act on behalf of Putrajaya in Johor and are major forces behind the grand vision. Nusajaya's emergence has opened the market to more participants linked to the federal government, disrupting the state government's near-monopoly over land.

While the federal government has ownership rights over land in Nusajaya, the Johor state government, with the collaboration of IWH, has expanded its land bank through reclamation and international real estate projects. The case studies in this chapter further show how IIBD and OBS are of paramount importance to redeveloping downtown Johor Bahru and, by extension, have become an iconic means to articulate the vision of the Johor state government. To encapsulate the complex state-developer relations discussed in this chapter, Figure 15.3 illustrates parallel governance structures: one comprised of the Johor government and state-

FIGURE 15.3

Parallel Governance Structures of Land Development in Iskandar Malaysia

The Johor state government — The federal government

Flagship Zone—Johor Bahru — Flagship Zone B—Nusajaya (Iskandar Puteri)

Master developers: Kumpulan Prasarana Rakyat Johor, IWH, Johor Land & MBJB — Master developers: Khazanah Nasional Berhad, UEM Sunrise Berhad

Sub-developers: Country Garden Holdings; Greenland Group, CapitaLand; Brunsfield Tropicana; Walker; Astaka Padu. — Sub-developers: Gamuda Land; BCB; Mah Sing; Sunway; UM Land; WCT; E&O; Zhuoyuan; B&G Property

---

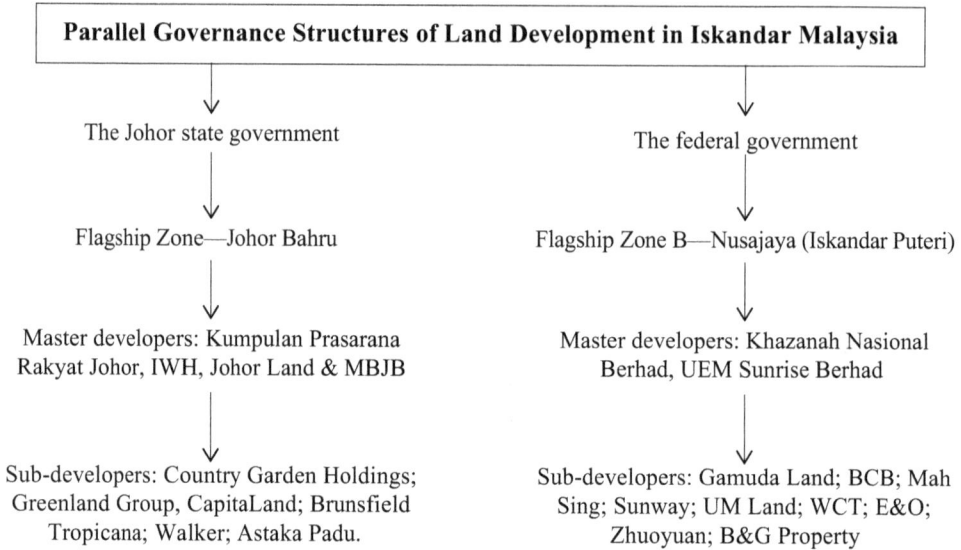

linked master developers; and another one consisting of the federal government, along with Khazanah-UEM Sunrise and its strategic partners.

This chapter has examined the complex relationship that exists in Johor Bahru's urban transformation. It used the case studies of Nusajaya and Johor Bahru City Centre within the Iskandar Malaysia region to illustrate the competition for influence between the federal and state governments. Iskandar Malaysia has been a venue of negotiation and contestation between the two levels of government. The various political and economic roles assigned to land and property projects—and the changes in the ways that land was governed and to whom legitimacy was given—emerged as part of the political process of urban transformation in Johor. The practice of collective deliberation reveals the networks of power comprising government agencies, government-linked companies and government-backed developers.

Notes

1. It is important to note that there was conflict between the two levels of government during Iskandar Malaysia's early days. In particular, the state government wanted a greater degree of involvement in the initiative as well as say in selecting its leadership. For more details, consult Khor (2011).

2. The opposition had warned that only UMNO's "cronies and companies" will benefit (Chua 2013). For example, the Islamic political party (PAS) distributed 100,000 booklets warning that the project would degrade the economic status of Malays. The political noise, however, did not affect the overall progress of Iskandar Malaysia. In defiance of the critics, the federal government injected billions of Malaysian ringgit into new infrastructure and key catalytic projects to stimulate more investment opportunities.

3. Tan Sri Halim Saad was the main player in Renong from 1985 to 2001. He is a protégé of former Finance Minister Tun Daim Zainuddin, Tun Dr Mahathir Mohamad's economic adviser during his first tenure. His vision was to create a bumiputra capitalist class through the overarching policy of state-guided economy (see Gomez 1990).

4. Renong's former chairman, Halim Saad, claimed that PLUS Expressways Bhd, which was then a subsidiary of UEM, had issued bonds to the tune of RM8.4 billion, then lent them the money to settle their debts. He also revealed that he was not allowed to sell Renong's assets (including the land in Nusajaya) to reduce debts. The dispute continued as Halim filed a legal case against Khazanah and Nor Mohamed Yakcop, Mahathir's adviser in the re-engineering of corporate Malaysia after the 1997 Asian Financial Crisis. For the news reports on the controversy of Renong, see Hanes (1998); Ranawana (2000); McMillan, (2001); Shanmugam (2015).

5. "Land Grab Malaysian-Style" a news report criticizing Nusajaya in relation to the controversy of Land Acquisition Act A804 that was amended in 1991 (see Fann 2012).

References

Astaka Holdings. 2016. *Annual Report 2016*. http://astaka.com.my/wp-content/themes/astaka-full-site/img/sgx/Astakapercent20Annualpercent20Reportpercent202016.pdf (accessed 7 March 2017).

Brown, Victoria. 2017. "KL and JB Ranked Second and Third in South-East Asia". *The Star Online*, 15 March 2017.

Bunnell, T., and A.M. Nah. 2004. "Counter-global Cases for Place: Contesting Displacement in Globalising Kuala Lumpur Metropolitan Area". *Urban Studies* 41, no. 12: 2447–67.

Chua, J.M. 2013. "Peanuts for Landowners, Millions for Cronies". *Free Malaysia Today*, 18 January 2013.

Department of Statistics. 2019. *Pocket Stats Quarter 4 2018*. Putrajaya: Department of Statistics of Malaysia.

EdgeProperty, The. 2011. "Iskandar Malaysia Making Progress". 9 September 2011.

Fann, T. 2012. "Land Grab Malaysian-Style". *Malaysiakini*, 14 October 2012.

Gomez, E.T., and K.S. Jomo. 2007. *Malaysia's Political Economy: Politics, Patronage and Profits*. New York: Cambridge University Press.

Government of Malaysia. 1971. *Second Malaysia Plan 1971–1975*. Kuala Lumpur: Government Press.

Guiness, P. 1992. *On the Margin of Capitalism: People and Development in Mukim Plentong, Johor, Malaysia*. Singapore: Oxford University Press.

Haggard, S. 2000. *The Political Economy of the Asian Financial Crisis*. Washington: Peterson Institute for International Economics.

Hammim, R. 2017. "Fed Govt Should Review IRDA Role, Says Sultan". *New Straits Times*, 23 February 2017.

Hanes, K. 1998. "The Rescue of Renong". *Global Finance* 12, no. 1 (January).

Henley, D. 2015. *Asia-Africa Development Divergence: A Question of Intent*. London: Zed Books.

Hutchinson, F.E. 2014. "Malaysia's Federal System: Overt and Covert Centralisation". *Journal of Contemporary Asia* 44, no. 3: 422.

———. 2015. *Mirror Images in Different Frames? Johor, the Riau Islands, and Competition for Investment from Singapore*. Singapore: ISEAS – Yusof Ishak Institute, 2015.

———. 2017. "(De)centralization and the Missing Middle in Indonesia and Malaysia". *Sojourn: Journal of Social Issues in Southeast Asia* 32, no. 2: 291–335.

Iskandar Regional Development Authority (IRDA). 2008. *Flagship B: Important Facts and Details on Nusajaya*. Johor and Kuala Lumpur: Khazanah Nasional Berhad.

———. 2013. *Annual Report 2013*. Johor and Kuala Lumpur: Khazanah Nasional Berhad.

Kamarulnizam Abdullah. 2009. "Johor in Malaysia-Singapore Relations". In *Across the Causeway: A Multi-Dimensional Study of Malaysia-Singapore Relations*, edited by T. Shiraishi, pp. 125–38. ingapore: Institute of Southeast Asian Studies.

Khazanah Nasional. 2006. *Comprehensive Development Plan for South Johor Economic Region, 2006–2025*. Kuala Lumpur: Khazanah Nasional Berhad.

———. 2007. *Iskandar Development Region: Initial Incentive and Support Package*. 22 March 2007. http://www.khazanah.com.my/Media-Downloads/News-Press-Releases/2007/Khazanah-announces-CEO-designate-of-MAS-NewCo-(9) (accessed 28 September 2018).

Khoo, B.T. 2012. *Policy Regimes and the Political Economy of Poverty Reduction in Malaysia*. Basingstoke: Palgrave Macmillan.

Khor, Y.L. 2011. "Iskandar Malaysia: Policy, Progress and Bottlenecks". RSIS Malaysia Programme, Malaysia Update: September 2011. Singapore: Nanyang Technological University.

Lai, J. 2012. "Khazanah Nasional: Malaysia's Treasure Trove". *Journal of the Asia Pacific Economy* 17, no. 2: 236–52.

Lim, Patricia. 2009. *Johor: Local History, Local Landscapes 1855–1957*. Singapore: Straits Times Press.

Loh, J. 2012. "UEM Land's Nusajaya to be Driven by New Projects". *The Star Online*, 7 June 2012.

Lunkapis, G.J. 2013. "Confusion Over Land Rights and Development Opportunities Through Communal Titles in Sabah, Malaysia". *Asia Pacific Viewpoint* 54, no. 2: 198–205.

MBJB (Majlis Bandaraya Johor Bahru). n.d. "Info Majlis Bandaraya Johor Bahru". http://www.mbjb.gov.my/sites/default/files/buku_info_mbjb/isi_info_mbjb_malay_color1.pdf

McMillan, A.F. 2001. "Renong Bullish on Bid for UEM". *CNN Cable News Network*, 5 August 2001.

Nadalutti, E. 2015. "Regional Integration and Migration in Southeast Asia: The Rise of 'Iskandar Malaysia' ". In *Handbook of the International Political Economy of Migration*, edited by L.S. Talani and S. McMahon, pp. 399–420. Cheltenham, Massachusetts: Edward Elgar Publishing Limited.

Nasongkhla, S., and S. Sintusingha. 2013. "Social Production of Space in Johor Bahru". *Urban Studies* 50, no. 9: 1836–53.

Ng, K.K. and G. Lim. 2017. *Beneath the Veneer: The Political Economy of Housing in Iskandar Malaysia, Johor*. Trends in Southeast Asia, no. 12/2017. Singapore: ISEAS – Yusof Ishak Institute.

Ranawana, A. 2000. "The $1.3-billion Man: Halim Looks for Cash to Buy Most of the Renong". *Asiaweek* 26, no. 43.

Rizzo, A. and J. Glasson. 2012. "Iskandar Malaysia". *Cities* 29, no. 6: 32.

———, and S. Khan. 2013. "Johor Bahru's Response to Transnational and National Influences in the Emerging Straits Mega-City Region". *Habitat International* 40: 154–62.

Savills World Research Malaysia. 2015. *Asian Cities Report: Iskandar Malaysia Investment, Hong Kong: Asia Pacific Headquarters*. http://pdf.savills.asia/asia-pacific-research/asia-pacific-research/asian-cities---my-is-investment-2h-2015.pdf (accessed 20 January 2017).

Shanmugam, M. 2015. "Halim: Don't Compare Renong with 1MDB". *The Star Online*, 30 May 2015.

Sidhu. 2012. "Johor in RM80bil Joint Venture with Lim to Build Waterfront City". *The Star Online*, 10 February 2012.

Star Online, The. 2015. "Sultan Ibrahim: I Have a Vision for Johor". 28 December 2015.

Sultan, Z., et al. 2016. "Between Land and People: A Review of Socioeconomic Issues Within the Context of Rapid Development in Iskandar Malaysia". *International Journal of Built Environment and Sustainability* 3, no. 3: 191–98.

Sutton, K., and A. Buang. 1995 "A New Role for Malaysia's FELDA: From Land Settlement Agency to Plantation Company". *Geography* 80, no. 2: 125–37.

Tey, T.H. 2011. "Iskandar Malaysia and Malaysia's Dualistic". In *Special Economic Zones in Asian Market Economies*, edited by C. Carter and A. Harding. Oxon and New York: Routledge.

Thean, L.C. 2010. "UEM Land's Aspirations for Iskandar". 23 January 2010.

Vatikiotis, M. 1992. "Ambitious Johor". *Far Eastern Economic Review* 155, no. 15.

———. 1993. "Malaysia: The Pride of Johor". *Far Eastern Economic Review* 156, no. 3.

Whang, Rennie. 2016. "Forest City Developer Presses Ahead Amid Reclamation Issues". *Straits Times*, 8 March 2016.

Wong and Benjamin. 2016. "Make JB the Second Biggest City". *The Star Online*, 23 March 2016.

Wong, K.W. 2015. "JB: Will the Malaysian Border Town Grow Up to Usurp Singapore?". *The Edge Property*, 30 November 2015.

16

HOUSING POLICY IN JOHOR
Trends and Prospects[1]

Guanie Lim and Keng Khoon Ng

INTRODUCTION

Housing development in Johor has undergone profound transformation over the last few decades. High-rise apartments are now a common sight in downtown Johor Bahru. Luxury enclaves, complete with gated security and leisure facilities, encroach on waterfront land along the Tebrau Strait. Foreign developers have built new townships on reclaimed land, exhorting international buyers to invest their future in the project as well as the rest of Johor. This chapter will examine housing policies and development strategies in Johor, especially those related to the establishment of Iskandar Malaysia (IM). The history of Johor's housing trends and its prospects in the near and medium term will also be analysed. This chapter argues that the launch of IM had a far-reaching impact not only on housing stock, but also on property ownership practices in Johor.

There are three main sections in the chapter. The first section focuses on housing provision and policy in Johor with an analysis of statistical data such as housing stock and distribution of income. The section will ascertain the manner in which the state government manages Johor's housing blueprint. It also discusses associated opportunities and challenges faced by the state government and housing developers, both private and government-linked corporations (GLCs).

The following section illustrates overall practices of housing development in Malaysia since independence. This section considers how housing is managed under national development plans, by-laws, and policies. We examine the major agendas and aspirations for housing in Malaysia and how housing provisions is carried out at both federal and state levels. We also look at the roles of the different layers of government and private developers in housing provision and how these roles evolved in tandem with global trends of economic liberalization. We then take a closer look at housing trends in southern Johor over the last decade, especially those related to the implementation of Iskandar Malaysia.

Acknowledging the rise of Iskandar Malaysia as a regional business hub and its profound impact on Johor, the third section adopts a grounded approach in presenting two case studies to make sense of the housing situation in the state. These projects are Medini Iskandar Malaysia (Medini) and Forest City, two of the largest housing projects within Iskandar Malaysia. It will also reflect on the rather different business models, architectural concepts, and development strategies of both projects. The two case studies will discuss the socio-economic implications of luxury and foreigner-oriented housing in the region. The chapter concludes by considering near- to medium-term prospects, especially the challenges of housing development in Johor. The overall prognosis is derived by analysing the situation in tandem with the growing influence of Iskandar Malaysia. Amongst other things, the conclusion raises some uneasy questions regarding issues such as the appropriate degree of competition amongst developers, housing for the less wealthy, and the need to preserve the wellbeing of local communities. Some policy recommendations are then put forward.

OVERVIEW OF HOUSING POLICY AND DEVELOPMENT IN JOHOR

Housing Stock Analysis

Johor is a state located in the southern end of Peninsular Malaysia. With a total land area of 19,016 km^2, Johor is the fifth largest state in Malaysia. It is also the third-most populated state in the country, boasting a population of 3.8 million (Department of Statistics 2019). According to the Town and Country Planning Department of Johor (2017), the state's population is projected to reach 6.06 million by 2030. The median income level of Johor is RM3,650, while its unemployment rate is 3.6 per cent (Department of Statistics 2017). The state's capital is Johor Bahru, which generates almost 70 per cent of the entire state's economic output while housing just over half its population.

Johor consists of ten districts—Kota Tinggi, Ledang, Mersing, Segamat, Batu Pahat, Muar, Pontian, Kulai Jaya, Johor Bahru and Kluang. Johor Bahru, the capital, occupies prime position for it hosts the highest number of living quarters and households within the state (42.7 per cent on both metrics) (see Table 16.1). Due to better employment opportunities in Johor Bahru as well as its proximity to wealthy Singapore, the city has benefited from internal migration both from within and outside Johor. As a result, Johor Bahru has become the de facto commercial hub of

TABLE 16.1
Living Quarters and Households in Johor by District

District	Number of Living Quarters			Number of Households		
	1991	2000	2010	1991	2000	2010
Johor Bahru	159,371	258,835	390,406	131,101	214,177	331,095
Batu Pahat	66,985	87,306	109,263	59,369	72,573	90,548
Kluang	58,483	72,640	80,421	46,703	57,825	70,018
Kulai	26,089	45,106	65,647	26,089	45,106	65,647
Others	192,558	232,872	269,277	159,868	182,972	218,030

Source: Department of Statistics.

TABLE 16.2
Housing Stock in 2016

State	Residential Units				Serviced Apartments			
	Existing Stock	Incoming Supply	Planned Supply	Total	Existing Stock	Incoming Supply	Planned Supply	Total
Johor	731,633	138,369	147,296	1,017,298	12,623	61,961	41,522	116,106
Kuala Lumpur	424,434	42,773	50,588	517,795	35,862	38,168	42,326	116,356
Pulau Pinang	407,107	94,124	48,120	549,321	1,625	1,719	2,848	6,192
Selangor	1,389,220	164,848	92,785	1,646,853	30,254	38,400	14,728	83,382

Source: National Property Information Centre.

southern Malaysia. Batu Pahat and Kluang are the other more populated districts in Johor, ranked in second and third place respectively. That said, the number of living quarters and households in both districts trail those of Johor Bahru.

Table 16.2 illustrates housing stock in the four most populated and urbanized states in Malaysia. With a total of 1,017,298 residential units, Johor holds the second largest stock in the country, trailing only Selangor. Johor also has a very high supply of incoming and planned residential units. In the serviced apartment category, the southern state will soon outpace Selangor when its incoming and planned supplies are fulfilled. With a total of 116,106 units, Johor's stock in serviced apartments will closely resemble that of Kuala Lumpur (116,356). Taken together, these two observations are somewhat odd as Johor's total population of under 4 million trails that of Selangor (5.8 million). While Kuala Lumpur houses only 1.8 million people, it is a far smaller (and denser) territory compared to Johor. Like most of the highly urbanized cities within Asia, Kuala Lumpur suffers from land scarcity, so the proliferation of high-rise buildings such as serviced apartments is logical. The same cannot be said for land-abundant Johor.

Johor's seemingly lopsided housing stock is similarly reflected in its property transaction. Table 16.3 displays the residential property transactions in Johor for the

TABLE 16.3
Residential Property Transaction (Quarter 3, 2016)

Property Type	Johor Bahru	Batu Pahat	Kluang	Kulai	Others
1–1.5 storey terrace	622	197	131	203	356
2–2.5 storey terrace	1,084	249	120	120	250
2–2.5 storey semi-detached	124	41	15	9	96
Detached	78	22	38	7	91
Condo/apartment	376	4	0	4	11
Low-cost house	142	67	61	28	97
Low-cost flat	64	2	0	7	0

Source: National Property Information Centre.

TABLE 16.4
Distribution of Newly Launched Houses in Johor Bahru, 2008–13

Price Range (RM)	2008	2009	2010	2011	2012	2013	Total
100,000–150,000	1,522	1,621	320	1,485	84	0	5,032
150,001–200,000	1,120	1,130	1,071	1,081	810	528	5,740
200,001–250,000	953	956	937	954	2,293	10	6,103
250,001–500,000	1,877	3,814	2,602	6,053	3,775	3,785	21,906
500,001–1,000,000	496	697	693	2,653	5,078	2,186	11,803
1,000,001–above	87	10	109	388	2,129	1,089	3,812
Total	6,055	8,228	5,732	12,614	14,169	7,598	54,396

Source: National Property Information Centre.

third quarter of 2016. Terrace houses are by far the most popular residential types, while Johor Bahru is the most active market in the entire state. Low-cost houses and low-cost flats were collectively the second most transacted properties. This suggests that there is an inherent demand for low-cost housing in Johor, a point further elaborated in subsequent paragraphs.

Table 16.4 shows the distribution of newly launched houses in Johor Bahru from 2008 to 2013. Overall, houses within the price range of RM250,001 to RM500,000 were the most launched in Johor Bahru. Comprising about 40 per cent of total houses launched, this price range serves as a yardstick for home affordability for the majority. At the lower end of the spectrum, the launch of houses priced between RM100,000 and RM150,000 has greatly declined. This is also observable for housing stock priced between RM150,001 and RM200,000, although the figures have shrunk at a less drastic pace. At the higher end of the market, the launch of luxury houses (RM500,001 to exceeding RM1,000,001) has increased drastically since 2010. While such launches moderated in 2013, the long-term upward trend is undeniable.

Table 16.5 shows varying degrees of housing affordability across Malaysian states. Johor, with a median multiple affordability score of 4.2, ranks amongst the

TABLE 16.5
Housing Affordability across States

	Monthly Median Income (RM)	Annual Median Income (RM)	Median House Price (RM)	Median Multiple Affordability	Affordability
Terengganu	3,777	45,324	250,000	5.5	5.1 and Over
Kuala Lumpur	7,620	91,440	490,000	5.4	(Severely
Pulau Pinang	4,702	56,424	295,000	5.2	Unaffordable)
Sabah	3,745	44,940	230,000	5.1	
Pahang	3,389	40,668	200,000	4.9	4.1 to 5.0
Kelantan	2,716	32,592	157,740	4.8	(Seriously
Malaysia	4,585	55,020	242,000	4.4	Unaffordable)
Perak	3,451	41,412	180,000	4.3	
Perlis	3,500	42,000	181,000	4.3	
Johor	5,197	62,364	260,000	4.2	
Selangor	6,214	74,568	300,000	4.0	3.1 to 4.0
Negeri Sembilan	4,128	49,536	188,888	3.8	(Moderately
Sarawak	3,778	45,336	164,667	3.6	Unaffordable)
Kedah	3,451	41,412	140,000	3.4	
Melaka	5,029	60,348	180,000	3.0	3.0 and Under (Affordable)

Source: Khazanah Research Institute (2015).

"seriously unaffordable" category. With about 40 per cent of house launches priced from RM250,001 to RM500,000 in Johor Bahru, private housing in southern Johor has most certainly exceeded Johor's housing affordability cut off point (i.e., median housing price) of RM260,000 (see Tables 16.4 and 16.5). This issue will likely worsen as Johor is relatively less urbanized than Pulau Pinang, Selangor or Kuala Lumpur. As it develops and urbanizes further in the near to medium term, housing demand—especially in urban areas such as Iskandar Malaysia—is likely to intensify. This will in turn jack up housing prices if the supply remains constant. The pressing issue of housing affordability, indeed, can be understood as one of the outcomes arising from the launch of Iskandar Malaysia. The opening up of this special economic zone (SEZ) is highly associated with the booming trend of luxury properties in Johor (Hutchinson 2015).

Iskandar Malaysia: Johor's Latest Crown Jewel

In 2005, the Malaysian federal government, under the new administration of Prime Minister Abdullah Ahmad Badawi, acknowledged the need to refocus development efforts into southern Johor. Learning from the successful model of Shenzhen-Hong Kong, the federal government assigned Khazanah Nasional Bhd (KNB) to conduct a feasibility study for the development of an SEZ in southern Johor. In the following year, this South Johor Economic Region was subsequently rebranded as "Iskandar Malaysia" and launched as a high-impact project under the Ninth Malaysia Plan (2006–10). Guided by a Comprehensive Development Plan (CDP) spanning 2006 to 2025, Iskandar Malaysia can be interpreted as a federal government effort to promote investment and economic liberalization in southern Johor (Khazanah Nasional 2006). Due to its close proximity to Singapore, Iskandar Malaysia is designed to capture spillover effects from its tiny neighbour, in a manner similar to Shenzhen-Hong Kong. It is also interesting to note that this 2,217 km^2-wide SEZ does not strongly emphasize pro-bumiputra policies. In other words, most economic activities are open to non-bumiputra and international investors.

The CDP maps out five flagship zones as catalysts for several forms of economic activities. Out of the five flagship zones, Flagship Zone A (Johor Bahru City Centre) and Flagship Zone B (Iskandar Puteri; formerly known as Nusajaya) have attracted the most attention from real estate developers because of their more urbanized outlook and connectivity to Singapore. From 2006 to 2012, real estate investment amounted to RM35.1 billion, representing 33.1 per cent of total investment capital in Iskandar Malaysia (IRDA 2014, 2016). To date, there are about sixty real estate development projects across Iskandar Malaysia, adding a pipeline of more than 380,000 private homes (planned or under construction) to Johor's housing stock. Real estate growth is further stoked by a series of ambitious projects driven by prominent players from both federal and state levels, often in collaboration with foreign companies.

Hosting Kota Iskandar (the new administrative centre for the state government of Johor) and various high-end industrial estates, Iskandar Puteri (formerly known as Nusajaya) is often touted as the "heart" of the entire SEZ (Hutchinson 2015). Indeed, since the 2006 inception of Iskandar Malaysia, Iskandar Puteri has transformed into an integrated hub where international schools, private universities, high-end properties, and medical centres agglomerate, serving the domestic as well as international populace (with Singaporean and Singapore-based expatriates forming the majority). GLC developers have been quick to react to the business opportunities opened up in Iskandar Puteri. Acting as the master developer and land proprietor, UEM Sunrise (a subsidiary of KNB-owned UEM Group) has developed a number of townships in the area. Some of the more popular ones include Puteri Harbour (an international ferry terminal and luxury waterfront township) and a series of medium- to high-end residential projects (e.g., Horizon Hills, Estuari, and East Ledang). Medini, the focus of the next section, is another noteworthy urban mega project undertaken mainly by the federal government through GLC developers.

Iskandar Malaysia's growth has attracted investment dollars from foreign developers. There are currently ten projects driven by Chinese companies per se in IM. Among the highest profile ones are Princess Cove (R&F Properties) and Forest City (Country Garden Group) (Lim, 2015). These two projects are notable for the expected injection of substantial housing supply into the market, in addition to expanding the land area of Johor as they are constructed on sites reclaimed from the sea. Forest City's experience shall be detailed in a subsequent section.

OVERVIEW OF HOUSING POLICY AND DEVELOPMENT IN MALAYSIA

The Role of the Federal Government

Malaysian housing policy is regulated through two institutional platforms. Firstly, it is based on the New Economic Policy (NEP) and Malaysian Five-Year Plans. The eradication of poverty and restructuring of society through integration of diverse ethnic communities has been the prime focus of the country's housing programme for many years. In practical terms, two basic rules are worth highlighting here: (1) Under the low-cost housing programme, developers must allocate at least 30 per cent of their project to low-cost housing; (2) Developers must allocate at least 30 per cent of total units to bumiputra buyers with discounted prices under the Bumiputra Lot Quota Regulation (the indigenous policy). These two requirements have underpinned the development of all housing projects in Peninsular Malaysia since 1982.

Secondly, housing development in Malaysia is enforced by a series of legal acts authorized under the Ministry of Housing and Local Government (MHLG). There are two legislative acts that directly influence housing development. The Housing Development Act 1966 (Control and Licensing) [Act 118] provides guidelines for housing developers in terms of duties and responsibilities, which in turn safeguards the rights of home purchasers. Another important legal reference is the Town and Country Planning Act 1976 [Act 172]. The Act aims to control and regulate matters on town and country planning, e.g., land and building use, planning permission, and acquisition of land. Together, these two legislative frameworks allow the government to monitor housing delivery and the business conduct of housing developers.

In 2012, two new housing policies were introduced and implemented at the national level. The National Housing Policy (NHP) was launched by MHLG under the Tenth Malaysia Plan. This policy serves as a stand-alone policy, but is essentially in line with the overall housing directive. The NHP detailed by the National Housing Department (2012) is especially noteworthy for its ambition to strengthen coordination between the relevant government departments (at the federal, state, and local levels) and the private sector in housing provision. While this newly enacted policy will undergo periodic revision, what is certain is the increased tendency for the government to intervene in the sector, including regarding house prices (Chan 2016). The other policy is Act 739—Perumahan Rakyat 1Malaysia Act 2012 (PR1MA). This Act regulates matters pertaining to the development of housing accommodation, infrastructure, and facilities under the direct purview of the Prime Minister's Office (PMO) and the Economic Planning Unit (EPU).[2] A statutory body, PR1MA Corporation Malaysia, is formed under this new act, and the Prime Minister serves as the chairman of the PR1MA Advisory Council. Unlike conventional housing acts, PR1MA operates as a legal housing programme or corporation that aims to produce affordable houses for the medium income group (a monthly household income between RM2,500 to RM15,000) across Malaysian states (National Housing Department 2012).

Overall, the establishment of NHP 2012 and PR1MA can be interpreted as a combined move to provide more rigorous housing requirements on developers. They are also policy measures to address the housing needs of middle-income earners, a vital vote bank (especially in urban areas). In terms of state-market relationship, these two recent items of legislation serve to complicate the situation as the federal government is now participating directly in housing provision (i.e., it has become a de facto housing developer) (*Daily Express*, 30 November 2015). In addition, housing policy is no longer under the sole purview of the MHLG as PR1MA is also empowered to draft its own plans and regulations for its own housing schemes. Such a development might cause inconsistencies in housing policy and governance in the future.

The Role of State Governments

The federal government's role in housing policy is complemented by that of the various state governments and local authorities. In general, the MHLG is accountable for the issuance of housing development licences, advertisement, and sale permits after the developer has obtained a development order and building plan approvals from the local authority. The state government and local authority in turn provide physical planning in conjunction with industrial, education, religion, leisure, and infrastructure needs. Under local government requirements, all housing developments need to apply for land development approval as well as approvals for building plans and the prescribed utilities. As specified by the National Housing Department (2012):

- NHP 1.3: State Governments are given flexibility in determining the quota of low-cost houses to be built in mixed-development areas based on the suitability of the location and local demand (p. 83).
- NHP 3.5: Public housing programmes at the federal level are placed under the responsibility of a single federal agency which plans, implements, sells/rents and maintains them. State governments are still responsible for public housing programmes at the state level through their subsidiary agencies (p. 87).

The above clauses underline the autonomy of the state government in housing planning. The state's power is further explained by planning and development procedures.[3] In Malaysia, physical planning and development of housing occurs at four major levels: (1) National Physical Plan (NPP);[4] (2) Structure Plan; (3) Local Plan; and (4) Special Area Plan. The Structure Plan consists of policies and proposals for physical development and land use within the state. It is a comprehensive planning tool that outlines development policies and strategies for ten to fifteen years. A Local Plan is then prepared by local councils to materialize the policies and proposals set out in the Structure Plan. This plan will set out the detailed planning and undertaking within a local planning authority area. A Special Area Plan is undertaken by the local planning authority to provide special treatment such as heritage conservation or tourism promotion plans. This brief discussion of development protocol shows us the importance of state and local governments in housing development.

While housing is a matter managed by both federal and state governments, the latter enjoys more executive power where actual implementation is concerned. In practical terms, housing developers are more likely to conform to local government planning blueprints and building requirements, instead of those at the national level. On balance, it is safe to conclude that the state and local governments function as the de facto gatekeepers of housing policy in the country.

The Role of Housing Developers

In Malaysia, housing is planned and constructed by developers from either the public or private sectors. Under Malaysian laws, no housing project can be undertaken without a licensed developer. As enacted in Act 118, housing developers are defined as any person, body of persons, company, firm or society that engages in or carries on a housing development. A developer acts as the chief proprietor and coordinator of the whole development team that consists of architects, engineers, surveys, contractors and other building professionals. Housing developers must obtain a licence from the MHLG. They are also encouraged to register as members of the Real Estate and Housing Developers' Association Malaysia (REHDA). REHDA is the sole national representative body for housing developers. It plays a central role in ensuring that developers' voices are heard by the relevant authorities and government agencies.

Courtesy of a stable macroeconomic structure and a relatively functional bureaucracy, Malaysia's housing developers have been provided with a favourable business environment to expand their businesses. Indeed, many of them have grown in size and stature over the decades. Some of the more reputable and well-capitalized housing developers are SP Setia Bhd, IJM Land Bhd, Sunway Group, Sime Darby Property, Mah Sing Group, Eco World Development Group, Gamuda Land, UEM Sunrise Bhd, IOI Properties Group, and Eastern and Oriental Bhd.

Among these companies, some are GLCs or private companies that are partially owned by the GLCs (Lim 2014). These companies have gradually moved to high-end and large-scale housing developments in search of a bigger profit margin. Instead of giving priority to low-cost housing (as was habitually done in the past), these GLCs are increasingly competing with private developers in the luxury housing market (Jayaseelan and Intan Farhana 2017). This new trend is a manifestation of the government's intention to more fully liberalize the economy, which has taken place most noticeably since the 1980s. As a small and open economy, Malaysia has found it expedient to conform to the liberalization wave taking place in most of the industrialized world.

In recent years, several foreign developers, mainly from Singapore and China, have ventured into the Malaysian private housing sector. Under the recent amendment exercise affecting the National Land Code in 2015, foreign developers must now secure consent from relevant state governments to acquire land and development rights in Peninsular Malaysia. This reaffirms the autonomy given to the state government in handling any land-related matters within the subnational territory. However, there is a lack of standardized policy to oversee issues and practices of foreign acquisitions of land across the different Malaysian states (Salleh 2017). Nevertheless, this has not halted the developers' growth. Indeed, many of them have learnt to collaborate with the relevant authorities to advance their business goals.[5] As a result, the housing developers have transformed a formerly rudimentary sector into one which is increasingly high-end and international in outlook.

JOHOR'S HOUSING POLICY: CHANGES AND DEVIATIONS

Constitutionally, the Housing Division under the State Secretary of Johor is responsible for the implementation of housing policies and programmes. In line with the national policy, the core objective of Johor's housing policy is to provide sufficient houses that are affordable for all of its citizens, especially the lower income group. Allocation of low-cost housing and bumiputra quotas are the two most direct housing policy tools available to the state government.

In 2013, a study of Johor's housing policy was undertaken by the state government and the Iskandar Regional Development Authority (IRDA), a federal statutory body tasked to develop Iskandar Malaysia. To this end, "Dasar Perumahan Rakyat Johor—Di Iskandar Malaysia— (DPRJ) or "Housing Policy for Johoreans—in Iskandar Malaysia" was officially introduced in January 2014. This policy applies to all parts of Johor, barring some exceptions such as Iskandar Malaysia. Another statutory board, the Johor Housing and Real Property Board, was soon established for its role in planning and managing the state's housing in accordance to the new policy.[6]

· In principle, DPRJ is a revision of current housing policies in Johor. Similar to the previous policy (spanning 1997 to March 2013), housing developers are required to allocate 40 per cent (the highest rate in all Malaysian states) of total houses as affordable housing in projects exceeding 5 acres. There are four types of affordable houses that cater to the needs of different income groups. PKJ Type A and PKJ Type B are the two basic house types that fall directly under the provision of low-cost housing in the new policy. "Rumah Mampu Milik Johor" (RMMJ) is a newer generation of affordable housing that caters to the middle-income earners. The state government aims to deliver 46,000 units of RMMJ houses by 2018. Of the total, 19,600 units will be allocated in Johor Bahru (Office of Chief Minister of Johor 2015). There are also medium-cost units that target slightly more affluent middle-income earners, but this category is relatively small vis-à-vis the other three categories.

Notably, there is a deviation of policy in that the percentages for affordable houses are slightly different within and outside of Iskandar Malaysia. The deviation is allowed to ensure more flexibility, especially in Iskandar Malaysia (see Table 16.6). For the provision of RMMJ, 20 per cent is required for housing development within Iskandar Malaysia. For areas outside of it, only 10 per cent of RMMJ is needed, but

TABLE 16.6
Affordable Housing Schemes Inside and Outside of Iskandar Malaysia

Type	Percentage	Built up Area (sq ft)	Plot Size	Type	Maximum Selling Price (RM)	Proposed Eligibility (RM)
Within Iskandar Malaysia						
PKJ Type A	5 per cent	720	N/A	Strata	42,000	3,000
PKJ Type B	10 per cent	850	N/A	Strata	80,000	4,500
			16' x 55'	Landed		
RMMJ	20 per cent	1,000	18' x 60'	Landed (Terrace House)	150,000	6,000
			20' x 70'	Town House		
			N/A	Strata		
Medium-Cost Shop	5 per cent	1,200	N/A	Landed	200,000	7,000
Total	40 per cent	of total development				
Outside Iskandar Malaysia						
PKJ Type A	10 per cent	720	16' x 60'	Landed/Strata	42,000	3,000
PKJ Type B	15 per cent	850	18' x 60'	Landed/Strata	80,000	4,500
RMMJ	10 per cent	1,000	20' x 70'	Landed (Terrace House)	140,000 to 150,000	6,000
Medium-Cost Shop	5 per cent	1,200	N/A	Landed	150,000 to 170,000	7,000
Total	40 per cent	of total development				

Source: State Secretary of Johor (2014).

a higher percentage of PKJ Type A and PKJ Type B is required. If developers do not adhere to the policy, in principle RM40,000 for each exempted unit will need to be paid to the state as a form of compensation (State Secretary of Johor 2014). However, developers cannot get exemptions from building RMMJ housing as it is determined to be the most required type of abode in Johor. Moreover, a ten-year moratorium against any transfer of ownership of RMMJ housing has been set aside to minimize illegal ownership transfers.

In addition, the Johor government imposes the highest percentage of bumiputra lot quotas and bumiputra discounts in Malaysia (Office of Chief Minister of Johor 2015; State Secretary of Johor 2014). For landed properties priced above RM250,000, there is a need for developers to market 20 per cent of the housing as bumiputra units (only for bumiputra buyers), with a special discount of 15 per cent on their selling price. For high-rise apartments, there is also a need to allocate 40 per cent of the total housing as bumiputra units, and a discount of 15 per cent on their selling price. For unsold bumiputra units, the developers can appeal to the local authority for a release consent. In this new release mechanism, 7.5 per cent of the selling price will need to be paid to the state government for each unit released as a penalty. Prior to 2014, no fees were required for discharging the unsold bumiputra lots. The new release mechanism enables developers to transfer ownership of unsold bumiputra units to non-bumiputra buyers through land status conversion.

Taken together, these two policies have enabled the state government to strengthen its capability, especially its coffers. Property taxes, stamp duties, penalty payments, and other administration charges, have generated a sizeable revenue stream for the state government, allowing it to fulfil the undersupply of affordable housing. To date, the state government has collected RM600 million from developers for the conversion of bumiputra lot status, which was then used to build more than 6,000 units of housing under the RMMJ housing programme (Azlan 2017). Nevertheless, there is still a mismatch of supply and demand as there are 90,000 registered applicants for affordable housing in Johor, with only 60,000 affordable units to be completed by the end of 2019 (Low 2015).

For certain projects within Iskandar Malaysia, the state government adopts a more flexible management mechanism. By legislating new zoning policies for selected projects such as Tebrau, Danga Bay, Medini, Tanjung Puteri, and Forest City, foreign buyers are allowed to purchase properties without being subjected to price, nationality, and ethnicity (i.e., bumiputra) restrictions.[7] In return, such "International Zones" are subjected to higher than usual land assessment rates and property taxes (Benjamin 2017; *Borneo Post*, 12 July 2014; Reme 2015). By attracting and keeping the international population within the zones, the state government claims that it can protect locals from being priced out of the market. Nevertheless, this is a relatively new policy. As such, there is a paucity of details on how the zoning policies actually operate.

The implementation of the abovementioned policies has not been smooth or easy. In particular, the practice of converting bumiputra lots requires a transparent managerial system to ensure its integrity. Although this practice is not new to

Malaysian states, the case of Johor stands out because it is quite unprecedented for a state government to manage such a large amount of conversion cases—especially for relatively new projects in southern Johor. The power of officialdom, unfortunately, also opens up opportunities for ill-intentioned parties to collude and seek rent in some cases. As recently as June 2017, former state executive councillor Abdul Latif Bandi, his eldest son, and a property consultant were charged with twenty-one counts of money laundering amounting to RM35.78 million in connection to a land scandal in Johor. The case pertains to the conversion of bumiputra lots to non-bumiputra lots in projects in Kota Masai, Tebrau, Kulai, Kempas, Iskandar Puteri and Johor Bahru, the earliest of which stretched back to just six months after Abdul Latif assumed office. More specifically, Abdul Latif Bandi—the former state Housing and Local Government committee chairman—was charged with thirteen counts of money laundering amounting to RM17.59 million (Kili 2017).

CASE STUDIES

Medini: A Singapore-Themed Enclave

Medini Iskandar Malaysia (Medini) is one of the largest projects within Iskandar Malaysia. Sitting on a land bank of 2,230 acres (9.0 km²), Medini is a new mixed-use township within Iskandar Puteri (Flagship Zone B under the Iskandar Malaysia development blueprint). It is envisioned to be the new central business district of Iskandar Malaysia, with sustainability and innovation among its key features. Medini is also conveniently located beside the new administrative centre for the state government of Johor (Kota Iskandar). Medini is surrounded by newly established entities such as Pinewood Iskandar Malaysia Studios and EduCity. The master developer of this project is Medini Iskandar Malaysia Sdn Bhd (MIM). It was established in 2007 and is co-owned by Jasmine Acres Sdn Bhd (60 per cent; Malaysia), United World Infrastructure (20 per cent; US), and Mitsui and Co Ltd (20 per cent; Japan). MIM is also a private-public partnership as Jasmine Acres is jointly owned by two GLCs—KNB and Iskandar Investment Bhd (IIB) (Medini Iskandar Malaysia 2017a; *The Edge,* 23 September 2016).

Medini is split into six different zones, with each of them performing particular functions (see Figure 16.1). For instance, Zone B is a planned business and media district. It is expected to house commercial centres (including a small and medium enterprise business park) and hotels (Medini Iskandar Malaysia 2017b). Zone C, on the other hand, is envisioned as the trade and logistics zone. It offers world-class integrated services including warehousing, distribution (transport and freight services), packaging, and business process outsourcing. The total development duration of Medini is earmarked at twenty years.

As the master developer, MIM undertakes two key roles. Firstly, it functions as a comprehensive master planner to ensure proper connectivity with Medini's adjacent areas and to monitor the development of individual projects as well as the overall progress of Medini. MIM's two main GLC shareholders—KNB and IIB—also facilitate

FIGURE 16.1
Six Different Zones of Medini

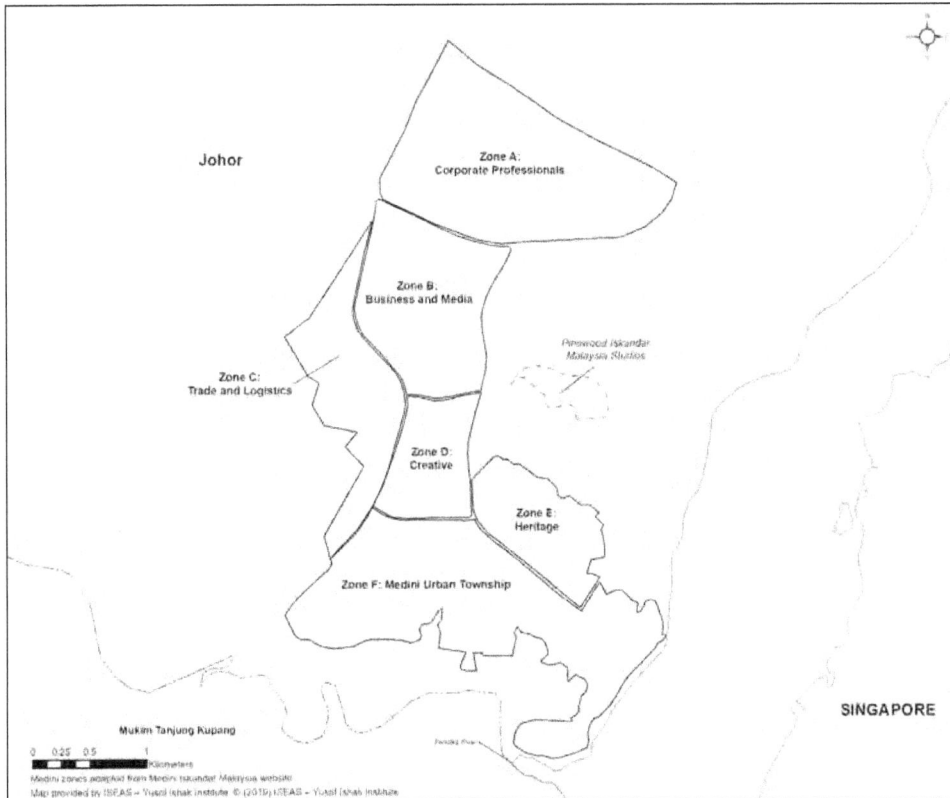

Johor

Zone A:
Corporate Professionals

Zone B:
Business and Media

Pinewood Iskandar
Malaysia Studios

Zone C:
Trade and Logistics

Zone D:
Creative

Zone E:
Heritage

Zone F: Medini Urban Township

SINGAPORE

Mukim Tanjuog Kupang

0   0.25   0.5   1
Kilometers
Medini zones adapted from Medini Iskandar Malaysia website
Map provided by ISEAS – Yusof Ishak Institute © (2019) ISEAS – Yusof Ishak Institute

Source: Medini Iskandar Malaysia (2017b).

dialogue between the relevant government departments and other GLCs. Secondly, MIM develops some plots by itself although it more commonly auctions off plots to other developers such as the Sunway Group and WCT Holdings Bhd (*The Edge Property*, 20 December 2015). In certain projects, MIM has entered into joint ventures with other investors (e.g., collaborating with China's Zhuoda Group in developing the Paradiso Nuova project in Medini's Zone A). It also coordinates investment and construction decisions with respective investors to prevent duplication and under-delivery of buildings and other forms of amenities.

As property developers in Iskandar Malaysia are not legally required to disclose sales or rental updates, it is next to impossible to determine the profile of homebuyers in Medini. Nevertheless, anecdotal surveys suggest that a sizeable portion of homebuyers are non-Malaysians, with Singaporeans amongst the most represented buyers (Lim 2015). Certain projects within Medini are especially popular with Singaporeans. For instance, Mah Sing released 495 units in The Meridin, a high-rise project in Zone A of Medini in May 2013. Mah Sing's chief executive officer disclosed that 75 per cent of these units were taken up within two months (Yahya 2013). He also noted that about half of these buyers were Singaporeans. Another project that is well received by Singaporean homebuyers is Paradiso Nuova, a 382-unit condominium. According to the project's sales and marketing director, about half of the people who registered interest in this project are Singaporeans (Yahya 2013).

For Singaporeans, Medini is an attractive proposition in large part because of its affordability. Table 16.7 displays the prices of some of the more popular projects in Medini vis-à-vis those in Singapore. With prices starting from RM650 per square foot (psf), residential properties in Medini are considerably cheaper than those in Jurong East, Jurong West, and Woodlands, three housing areas closest to Iskandar Malaysia. Moreover, Medini is appealing because of several other factors such as its proximity to Singapore and a less congested environment. While these factors are just as applicable to other projects within Iskandar Malaysia, Medini stands out because of an extra set of exemptions encouraging foreign buyers. Unlike most projects in Johor (and the rest of the country), Medini has no restrictions on foreign as well as non-bumiputra ownership. There is also no minimum price threshold for foreign property buyers, and foreign property purchases are exempted from real property gains tax until 2025 (*The Edge Property*, 23 January 2017*)*.

The socio-political impacts of Medini have been generally positive. For one, it has raised the profile of Iskandar Malaysia as well as the entire state of Johor, both as a business address and a residential setting (see IRDA 2016). To this end, several projects within Medini have won prizes at the national, regional, and international stages. Some of the more notable winners include UMLand Bhd and MIM. The former's UMCity Office Tower—part of the UMCity Medini Lakeside development—bagged the Best Office Development Asia Pacific and Best International Office Development titles at the International Property Awards Grand Finals 2015 (J. Lim 2016). In 2016, Medini 10 by MIM earned the Best Commercial Development and Best Commercial Development (Malaysia) awards respectively at the South East Asia Property Awards (Malaysia) (*Borneo Post*, 13 August 2016).

TABLE 16.7
A Price Comparison between Key Residential Properties in Medini and Singapore

	Pricing (RM per sq ft)
Medini Signature (Medini)	Tower 1: 650 (Average)
	Tower 2: 680 (Average)
Iskandar Residences (Medini)	767 (Average)
Afiniti Medini (Medini)	850–1,000
Jurong East (Singapore)	1,797–5,322
Jurong West (Singapore)	1,677–4,302
Woodlands (Singapore)	1,782–4,077

Note: S$1.00 = RM3.00.
Source: HSR (2013).

Nevertheless, as far as domestic homebuyers are concerned, Medini has exhibited a Janus-faced outcome. While it has drawn in homebuyers from abroad (especially Singapore) and other domestic locations largely because of its housing affordability (relative to international standards), the properties sold by the developers within Medini are out of reach for the majority of Johoreans (and by extension, Malaysians). With prices ranging from RM650 to RM1,000 psf, housing in Medini has already exceeded Johor's housing affordability cut off point (i.e., median housing price) of RM260,000 (see Tables 16.5 and 16.7). If anything, one can even make the claim that the launch of Medini is strongly correlated with the rise of luxury housing in Iskandar Malaysia. In other words, the issue of a mismatch in supply and demand of affordable housing has been almost entirely bypassed by the corporate players driving Medini as well as the planning authorities.

Forest City: A Heavy Chinese Presence

Forest City is an ambitious project that purports to be Southeast Asia's largest smart city. It is to be built on four reclaimed islands, spanning an area of 1,370 hectares, which will accommodate a total of 700,000 residents upon completion (*Malay Mail*, 6 March 2016). It is also scheduled to draw in RM170 billion worth of investment over twenty to thirty years. Located near the Malaysia-Singapore Second Link, Forest City is arguably the project that is closest in distance to Singapore (see Map 4.5). While the entire Iskandar Malaysia is designed to function as a localized version of Shenzhen (with Singapore mirroring Hong Kong), Forest City is deepening this model by packaging itself as a 'mini Shenzhen' within Iskandar Malaysia (Nylander 2017).

Country Garden Pacificview Sdn Bhd (CGPV) is the master developer of Forest City. It is a joint venture company between Country Garden Group and Esplanade Danga 88 Sdn Bhd. The project is 66 per cent controlled by the former with the remaining 34 per cent owned by Esplanade Danga 88. Country Garden is a Guangdong-based developer from China, established in 1992 and listed on the Hong Kong Stock Exchange in 2007. Its first development in Johor was the 9,500-unit Country Garden Danga Bay residential project. For Esplanade Danga 88, its largest shareholder is the Johor Sultan (64.4 per cent). Another 20 per cent and 15.6 per cent of this company is held respectively by Kumpulan Prasarana Rakyat Johor (KPRJ) (the investment arm of Johor state) and Daing Malek Daing Rahaman (a member of the Royal Court of Advisers to the Johor Sultan) (Aw 2014). Such a tie-up essentially makes Forest City a collaboration between Chinese and Johorean capital (largely driven by the monarch) (Lim 2014).

Given the large number of properties in Forest City, the project is a significant source of tax revenue for the state government. The Johor state government is expected to earn about RM72 million (based on a RM3,000 payment for each of the 24,227 lots) from land ownership in the first phase of projects on the first reclaimed island. Furthermore, the state government will earn another RM2.58 million of quit rent from the 24,227 lots in the first phase of the project (Ahmad Fairuz 2017). However,

Forest City's direct contribution to the provision of affordable and low-cost houses in Johor Bahru is undisclosed as no official data can be found on this subject. There is also no provision of bumiputra quotas in this project as it falls under the category of the newly established international zone.

More crucially, houses in Forest City belong to the high-end segment, with an average price of RM1,200 psf (Whang 2016). Such a steep price tag has caused some unease in the broader Iskandar Malaysia market for it is even more costly than other more mature housing projects such as those in Medini (see Table 16.7). Forest City's exorbitant home prices imply that CGPV is not targeting domestic buyers. To this end, it has focused most of its marketing efforts towards the Chinese market. According to *FreeMalaysiaToday* (14 March 2017), 17,000 units of high-rise apartments have been sold in Forest City, with 90 per cent of the buyers originating from China. This marketing direction, whether intentional or otherwise, has led to some severe criticism of issues of land and sovereignty, especially from Mahathir Mohamad and his political allies prior to the 14th Malaysian General Election (*Today*, 17 January 2017).[8] These incidents not only hurt the profile of Forest City, but also the stature of the Johor Sultan and state government. The Sultan, in an interview, responded: "Mahathir has gone too far with his twisting of the issue … creating fear, using race, just to fulfil his political motives" (Wong and Benjamin 2017). In another move to distance Johor from Mahathir's criticism, the Sultan claimed that: "As custodian of my people, I know what is best for Johoreans" (*The Star*, 16 January 2017).

While Mahathir's public criticism of Forest City is driven by his own political leanings and the urge to do well as the leader of the Pakatan Harapan coalition, there is still some truth to his grievances. Like Medini, Forest City does not address the issue of low-cost housing which disproportionately affects the bumiputra community. If anything, its emergence merely exacerbates the lopsided nature of Johor's housing situation, as documented in the earlier sections. For example, the marketing of houses with an average price of RM1,200 psf will most definitely add to Johor's already burgeoning supply of luxury houses (see Tables 16.3 and 16.4). It will also put housing further out of reach for the majority of Johoreans (see Table 16.5). There is also the issue of the proper management of new revenue (land ownerships and quit rent) brought about by Forest City. In theory, this new revenue stream can be utilized to help both the poor as well as the bumiputra community. However, the arrest of Abdul Latif Bandi, a former key member of the Johor state government, has dimmed optimism on this issue, at least for the near term.

In March 2017, the project was hit by a fresh round of capital controls instituted by the Chinese government on its citizens. This latest round of capital controls was invoked to more directly curb the outflow of funds and to stabilize the Chinese yuan (CNY) exchange rate. As most of its customers are from China, Forest City suffered a double blow. Firstly, Country Garden was forced to suspend the marketing of Forest City in China as indicated by the shuttering of all its sales centres in the country. Secondly, Country Garden had to refund buyers who made down payments on properties at Forest City but were no longer able to transfer remaining payments out of China (Zhen 2017). However, because Country Garden salespeople earn high commissions for selling units, they may have been reluctant to let buyers off the hook despite the official stance on refunds by the senior management. As of May 2017, it was not certain whether buyers who were unable to continue with their purchases had finally received their rightful refunds.

Forest City's sustainability is challenged further if one takes a longer term perspective. For instance, there was already some disquiet concerning Forest City prior to Mahathir's attacks as well as Beijing's move to curb capital outflows. As early as March 2015, the impact of land reclamation on the livelihood of the fishermen in the vicinity was raised in the Malaysian parliament, with the Ministry of Agriculture and Agro-based Industry explaining that the project will affect 1,023 of Johor's registered 6,354 fishermen, who earn an average of RM2,660. The ministry also estimated that the income of these fishermen will be reduced by 50 per cent because they are forced to fish elsewhere (Palansamy 2015). In addition, the Singaporean government also conveyed its concerns about the project on a number of occasions to the Malaysian government, asking for more information on the reclamation and construction (Chong 2016; Lee 2015).

CONCLUSION

This chapter has set out some noticeable shifts in Johor's housing trends, especially since the emergence of Iskandar Malaysia. Firstly, there is a housing boom within the region following the entrance of prominent developers from Malaysia and beyond. Notwithstanding this housing boom, southern Johor (and the rest of the state) still does not provide enough affordable houses as a considerable proportion of this boom is based on high-end homes. While the provision of low-cost and affordable homes in Johor remains a core objective in the state government's housing policy, it offers options for exemptions via fine payments and land surrenders as opposed to more vigorously pressing developers to build social housing. The collection of such monies paves the way for the state government to provide affordable homes through its own in-house schemes such as the RMMJ. Nevertheless, the state government has encountered criticisms over the integrity of the RMMJ scheme (Low 2017). The increase in tax revenue is definitely an advantage for the state government, but it will need to establish a more effective and transparent mechanism for the utilization of funds collected from developers. This will not only manage the expectations of the public and the opposition, but also minimize possible rent-seeking activities from less than honest quarters.

Secondly, the fine payment system complicates the relationship between developers and the state government. To be specific, the practice of paying penalties to minimize affordable housing is not new to Malaysia as the national housing system is hinged on the importance of tax revenue. However, the creeping increase in the scale and scope of licensing and penalty fees in recent years is a major put-off for developers. As a result, many local and small development companies have struggled under the new policy (see Azlan Raofuddin, Syed Putra, and Mastura 2015). At the same time, well-capitalized developers have begun to assert their dominance in the market. This is especially noticeable in Iskandar Malaysia where big developers such as Sunway Group and Gamuda Land have come to account for more than 50 per cent of the housing market. Their increasing stranglehold of the housing market has shifted the attitude of homebuyers towards them and their branding appeal. Consequently, it reduces opportunities for the local and small developers. This situation, if left unchecked, could defeat healthy competition and equality in the Johor housing sector. It will also jeopardize the interest of homebuyers as they are denied access to wider offerings. To this end, a fair competition commission cum watchdog at the regional level, covering the entire Iskandar Malaysia, is a useful option to consider.

Medini and Forest City share some common characteristics. They are essentially private-public partnerships with substantial involvement from foreign investors, although the "public" portion of Forest City is rather diluted with KPRJ being a relatively small shareholder in the venture. In addition, both projects are well received by foreign buyers. For Forest City in particular, its popularity amongst the Chinese is a by-product of China's increasingly wealthy consumer market as well as corporate China's internationalization drive in recent years. Yet, the reliance on Chinese homebuyers is not a feasible option, at least in the short to medium term, following the recent round of capital controls. More prosaically, there is the uncomfortable observation that Medini and Forest City are likely to become enclaves populated by the rich (Malaysians and foreigners)—although Medini seems to have taken a less aggressive posture in attracting foreign buyers. These two projects produce almost exclusively luxury homes as they do not need to fulfil conventional affordability and bumiputra requirements set by the authorities. This situation, if left unattended, can generate disenchantment with the projects and the rest of Iskandar Malaysia.

This finding raises some uneasy questions regarding the long-term socio-economic implications of these mega projects. While both Medini and Forest City have broader economic objectives such as stimulating high value-added industries, the sustainability of these industries and the associated ecosystem is bound to be threatened if the locals who work in the vicinity struggle to afford homes. There is also some political economic risk involved if the homebuyers originate largely from a certain region, as currently seen in Forest City. Therefore, the Johor state government would do well to impose greater monitoring and control over these projects to ensure a better alignment with its overall housing policy goals. The Johor state government must also pay attention to the longer term socio-political effects of such mega projects. For instance, the establishment of international zones should not be understood from a purely economic dimension; it must be examined in a more balanced manner. To this end, the issues of housing affordability and social gentrification, especially in city centre areas, must be pondered seriously by the state government, in addition to grievances such as environmental pollution (e.g., in the coastal areas adjacent to Forest City). By examining housing matters from a macro perspective, the dynamic, if not the conflicting, impacts of urban development in Iskandar Malaysia can be seen.

Notes

1. This chapter draws some of its content from *Beneath the Veneer: The Political Economy of Housing in Iskandar Malaysia, Johor*, Trends in Southeast Asia, no. 12/2017 (Singapore: ISEAS – Yusof Ishak Institute, 2017). Updated information has since been added.
2. To date, 265,033 units of homes have been approved by PR1MA. Of that total, 139,419 units are currently under construction (Eusoff 2017).
3. See Azlan Raofuddin, Syed Putra, and Mastura (2015) for a detailed elaboration on housing planning and development procedures in Malaysia.
4. The NPP is a written statement that summarizes the strategic direction for physical development and conservation for all of Peninsular Malaysia. NPP has been approved by the National Physical Planning Council (NPPC) on 26 April 2015.
5. The Ninth Malaysia Plan (2006–10) determines that "private sector as the engine of growth while public sector takes up the roles of facilitator and regulator and civil society and others as partners in development" (Economic Planning Unit 2006, p. 23).
6. The new housing board came under fire from critics who claim that it contradicted Malaysia's constitutional monarchy. Subsequently, former Johor Menteri Besar Mohamed Khaled Nordin went on to clarify that the Sultan of Johor will not have direct executive control under the proposed Johor Housing and Property Board Bill (*Malay Mail*, 7 June 2014).
7. In Johor, the minimum threshold for all types of property purchased by foreigners is set at RM1 million, effective from 1 May 2014. Prior to this, the minimum threshold was RM500,000. In addition to this minimum threshold, 2 per cent of the purchase price or a lump sum of RM20,000 (whichever is higher) has to be duty stamped and paid to the government.
8. Mahathir harps on two interrelated issues—the outflow of capital and jobs to Chinese companies and the influx of Chinese people. The latter has quickly become a nationwide political issue as Mahathir claims that the Chinese citizens brought in through Forest City would be given identity cards, enabling them to vote in general elections. In addition, he suggests that Forest City will become a foreign enclave owned and settled by the Chinese. These allegations, if proven true, will likely unsettle Malaysia's current political scenario.

References

Ahmad Fairuz, Othman. 2017. "Johor to Earn RM72m in Revenue from Forest City First Phase". *New Straits Times*, 15 May 2017. https://www.nst.com.my/news/nation/2017/05/239450/johor-earn-rm72m-revenue-forest-city-first-phase

Aw, Nigel. 2014. "Royal Businesses—Who Is Daing A Malek?". *Malaysiakini*, 18 July 2014. http://www.malaysiakini.com/news/269133

Azlan Raofuddin, Nuruddin, Syed Abu Bakar Syed Putra, and Jaafar Mastura. 2015. "Unveiling the Challenges Faced by Malaysian Housing Developers through Government Policy Changes". *Journal of Construction in Developing Countries* 20, no. 2: 37–52.

Azlan, Zamhari. 2017. "MB: 3,000 Units of Bumi Quota in Johor Converted since 2013". *Malaysiakini*, 4 March 2017. http://www.malaysiakini.com/news/374521

Benjamin, Nelson. 2017. "Not Affected by New Ruling on Foreign Ownership". *The Star*, 24 February 2017. http://www.thestar.com.my/metro/community/2017/02/24/not-affected-by-new-ruling-on-foreign-ownership/

Borneo Post. 2014. "International Zone to Limit Foreign Ownership in Johor". 12 July 2014. http://www.theborneopost.com/2014/07/12/international-zone-to-limit-foreign-ownership-in-johor/

———. 2016. "Southeast Asia Property Awards Names Winners". 13 August 2016.

Chan, Dawn. 2016. "Ministry to Review Housing Policy, Says Noh". *New Straits Times*, 11 September 2016. https://www.nst.com.my/news/2016/09/172362/ministry-review-housing-policy-says-noh

Chong, Zi Liang. 2016. "Singapore Concerned over Johor Strait Projects". *Straits Times*, 18 February 2016. http://www.straitstimes.com/singapore/singapore-concerned-over-johor-strait-projects

Country Garden Pacific View. 2017. "Forest City Johor". http://forestcityjohor.com/

Daily Express. 2015. "PR1MA—Malaysia's Top Housing Developer". 30 November 2015. http://www.dailyexpress.com.my/news.cfm?NewsID=104890

Department of Statistics. 2017. "Johor". https://www.dosm.gov.my/v1/index.php?r=column/cone&menu_id=d1dTR0JMK2hUUUFnTnp5WUR2d3VBQT09

———. 2019. *Pocket Stats Quarter 4 2018*. Putrajaya: Department of Statistics of Malaysia, 2019.

Economic Planning Unit. 2006. *The Ninth Malaysia Plan, 2006–2010*. Putrajaya: Economic Planning Unit, 2006.

Edge, The. 2016. "Medini: Poised for Success". 23 September 2016.

Edge Property, The. 2015. "Sunway-Khazanah JV Acquires Land in Medini Iskandar for RM745m". http://www.theedgeproperty.com.my/content/sunway-khazanah-jv-acquires-land-medini-iskandar-rm745m

———. 2017. "Minimum Property Purchase Prices for Foreign Buyers". https://theedgeproperty.wordpress.com/2017/01/23/minimum-property-purchase-prices-for-foreign-buyers/

Eusoff, Neily. 2017. "PR1MA to Put 21,672 Homes on the Market in 2017". *The Edge*, 11 May 2017. http://www.theedgemarkets.com/article/pr1ma-put-21672-homes-market-2017

FreeMalaysiaToday. 2017. "Will Johor Bail Out Forest City if It Falters?". 14 March 2017. http://www.freemalaysiatoday.com/category/nation/2017/03/14/will-johor-bail-out-forest-city-if-it-falters-2/

HSR. 2013. *Property Take: Singapore and Iskandar Malaysia*. [Author: incomplete info?]

Hutchinson, Francis. 2015. *Mirror Images in Different Frames? Johor, the Riau Islands, and Competition for Investment from Singapore*. Singapore: Institute of Southeast Asian Studies.

IRDA. 2014. *Annual Report 2014: Ensuring a Sustainable Environment*. Johor Bahru: IRDA.

———. 2016. *Iskandar Malaysia 2006–2016: 10 Year Progress Report*. Johor Bahru: IRDA.

Jayaseelan, Risen, and Intan Farhana Zainul. 2017. "Property Investments by Government Funds". *The Star*, 8 April 2017. http://www.thestar.com.my/business/business-news/2017/04/08/property-investments-by-government-funds/

Khazanah Nasional. 2006. *Comprehensive Development Plan for South Johor Economic Region, 2006–2025*. Kuala Lumpur: Khazanah Nasional.

Khazanah Research Institute. 2015. *Making Housing Affordable*. Kuala Lumpur: Khazanah Research Institute.

Kili, Kathleen. 2017. "Ex-Johor Exco Latif Bandi, Two Others Charged with Laundering RM35.7mil". *The Star*, 14 June 2017. http://www.thestar.com.my/news/nation/2017/06/14/exjohor-exco-latif-bandi-two-others-charged-with-laundering-rm35dot7mil/.

Lee, Marissa. 2015. "Controversial Johor Strait Land Reclamation Project Forest City Gets the Go-Ahead". *Straits Times*, 14 January 2015. http://www.straitstimes.com/business/controversial-johor-strait-land-reclamation-project-forest-city-gets-the-go-ahead

Lim, Guanie. 2014. "The Internationalisation of Mainland Chinese Firms into Malaysia: From Obligated Embeddedness to Active Embeddedness". *Journal of Current Southeast Asian Affairs* 33, no. 2: 59–90.

———. 2015. "China's Investments in Malaysia: Choosing the 'Right' Partners". *International Journal of China Studies* 6, no. 1: 1–30.

Lim, Jessie. 2016. "Striving for Greater Success". *The Star*, 30 January 2016. http://www.thestar.com.my/metro/smebiz/news/2016/01/30/striving-for-greater-success-developer-bags-international-recognition-for-its-innovative-architectur/.

Lim, Yvonne. 2015. The Big Read: Iskandar's Lure is a Strong Pull for S'poreans. Retrieved from http://www.todayonline.com/singapore/big-read-iskanders-lure-strong-pull-sporeans-0

Low, Sock Ken. 2015. "Johor Stands Firm on Housing Policy". *The Sun Daily*, 13 December 2015. http://www.thesundaily.my/news/1635998

———. 2017. "Johor DAP Seek Transparency over RM600m Housing Fund". *The Sun Daily*, 7 March 2017. http://www.thesundaily.my/news/2185724

Malay Mail. 2014. "MB: No Executive Powers for Sultan under New Johor Housing Board Bill". 7 June 2014. http://www.themalaymailonline.com/malaysia/article/mb-no-executive-powers-for-sultan-under-new-johor-housing-board-bill#xcuqK9I87M86ktia.97

———. 2016. "Johor's Forest City Accorded Duty-Free Status, PM Says". 6 March 2016. http://www.themalaymailonline.com/money/article/johors-forest-city-accorded-duty-free-status-pm-says

Medini Iskandar Malaysia. 2017a. "Catalyst to the Pulse of Iskandar Puteri". http://www.medini.com.my/

———. 2017b. "Masterplan". http://www.medini.com.my/master-plan/

National Housing Department. 2012. *National Housing Policy*. Kuala Lumpur: Ministry of Housing and Local Government.

Ng, Keng Khoon and Guanie Lim. *Beneath the Veneer: The Political Economy of Housing in Iskandar Malaysia, Johor*. Trends in Southeast Asia, no. 12/2017. Singapore: ISEAS – Yusof Ishak Institute.

Nylander, Johan. 2017. "Troubles in Malaysia's Forest City 'Paradise'". *Asia Times*, 6 May 2017. http://www.atimes.com/article/troubles-malaysias-forest-city-paradise/

Office of Chief Minister of Johor. 2015. *Makluman Status Pelaksanaan Pembangunan Rumah Mampu Milik Johor (2014–2018)* [Status Update of Affordable Housing in Johor (2014–2018)]. Kota Iskandar: Office of Chief Minister of Johor.

Palansamy, Yiswaree. 2015. "Ministry: Forest City, Tanjung Piai Reclamation to Cut Fisherman Income by Half". *Malay Mail*, 25 March 2015. http://www.themalaymailonline.com/malaysia/article/ministry-forest-city-tanjung-piai-reclamation-to-cut-fisherman-income-by-ha

Reme, Ahmad. 2015. "Johor to Earmark Zones for Foreign Home Buyers". *AsiaOne*, 16 May 2015. http://www.asiaone.com/malaysia/johor-earmark-zones-foreign-home-buyers

Salleh, Buang. 2017. "Foreign Ownership of Land, Clear Policy Needed". *New Straits Times*, 12 January 2017. https://www.nst.com.my/news/2017/01/203696/foreign-ownership-land-clear-policy-needed

Star, The. 2017. "Sultan Ibrahim Throws Former Premier a Challenge". 16 January 2017. http://www.thestar.com.my/news/nation/2017/01/16/sultan-ibrahim-throws-former-premier-a-challenge/

State Secretary of Johor. 2014. *SUKJ-100-1/7/1: Dasar Perumahan Rakyat Johor* [SUKJ-100-1/7/1: Housing Policy for Johorean]. Kota Iskandar: Johor Housing Division.

Today. 2017. "Malaysia Gains Nothing but Trouble from Forest City: Dr M". 17 January 2017. http://www.todayonline.com/world/asia/look-east-policy-not-about-selling-land-foreigners-dr-mahathir-tells-sultan

Town and Country Planning Department of Johor State. 2017. *Laporan Tinjauan Rancangan Struktur Negeri Johor 2030 (Kajian Semula)* [A Review Report for the Planning Structure of Johor 2030 (Revision)]. Kota Iskandar: http://epublisiti.townplan.gov.my/rsn/RSN_Johor2030/FlyersJohor2030.pdf

Whang, Rennie. 2016. "Forest City Developer Presses Ahead amid Reclamation Issues". *Straits Times*, 8 March 2016. http://www.straitstimes.com/business/property/forest-city-developer-presses-ahead-amid-reclamation-issues

Wong Chun Wai and Nelson Benjamin. 2017. "Johor Ruler Slams Dr M over Chinese Investment Comments". *The Star*, 16 January 2017. http://www.thestar.com.my/news/nation/2017/01/16/political-spin-angers-sultan-johor-ruler-slams-dr-m-over-chinese-investment-comments/

Yahya, Yasmine. 2013. "S'pore Buyers Flock to Johor's Medini Project". *Straits Times*, 20 July 2013. http://www.stproperty.sg/articles-property/foreign-property-news/spore-buyers-flock-to-johors-medini-project/a/129130

Zhen, Summer. 2017. "Country Garden Pledges Refund for Forest City Buyers Caught in Beijing Crackdown". *The Star*, 5 April 2017. http://www.thestar.com.my/business/business-news/2017/04/05/country-garden-pledges-refund-for-forest-city-buyers-caught-in-beijing-crackdown/

17

JOHOR'S FOREST CITY FACES CRITICAL CHALLENGES

Serina Rahman[1]

INTRODUCTION

Forest City, the multimillion dollar mixed development project rising out of four artificial islands in the Tebrau Straits off the southwestern coast of Johor appears by most accounts to be a bundle of contradictions. While potentially injecting millions of ringgit into, and spurring great infrastructural development in, the surrounding areas, it has jarred the local property market. New foreign exchange regulations in China add further questions to its financial viability.

While Forest City is portrayed as a role model for future cities, especially in its application of green technology and environmental sustainability, the land reclamation that underpins its existence is doing serious damage to local seagrass, mangroves and fishery habitats. Claims that the project has the potential to create thousands of jobs for the local population have been countered by those who question the wisdom of allowing such a huge influx of foreigners, both as contract workers and as residents, as well as its implications for the racial status quo.

To the general public, the saga of Forest City began in early 2014 when sand barges seemed to appear overnight to begin round-the-clock reclamation work without public notice or signage on the project. Those caught unaware included the Singapore government. It eventually lodged an official complaint with the Federal government, and Malaysia's Department of the Environment issued a stop-work order. The Detailed Environmental Impact Assessment (DEIA) process revealed that some local regulations had been sidestepped. While most local leaders had already known about the project in 2013, the information and RM3 million in compensation from the developer had not yet been passed on to the affected villages.

Controversy continues to surround the project till this day and the development swings between being the victim of political positioning for the upcoming elections and the bogeyman of choice for the media and local community; obliterating all mention of other developers and developments in the area which could have as much environmental, economic and social impact as Forest City.

In contrast to the typical tale in developed nations of project instigation, endorsement and financial support, Forest City was envisioned by a Malaysian person of prominence and modelled on the success of Shenzhen and its evolution from Hong Kong backwater to thriving metropolis. That a Chinese developer became the main actor in the project is a nod to China's re-emergence as a global player and to its strategic interests in Southeast Asia. The adaptation of sustainable development principles as one of the project's main marketing pillars incorporates the developed world's enchantment with balancing environmental and community needs with larger national political and economic goals. Issues arise when the implementation of the vision is hampered by political manoeuvring, and by discrepancy between top-down economic agendas on one hand and the everyday lives of the people most affected by the development on the other.

This chapter will take a closer look at the sustainability of the Forest City project—both economic and environmental, and explore the market for the final product on offer, the political entanglements that have emerged, and the actual economic costs of the project as a whole. It also provides an update to the DEIA report that was ordered in January 2015.

It argues that the economic value of the project might be overstated, given its actual environmental and social costs. While the initial motivation was based on a clear vision and on worthy goals, the implementation has elicited many questions due to some lack of clarity, and the consequences of divergent objectives at lower levels of the project hierarchy and among its stakeholders. The socio-cultural implications of the Forest City project, while numerous, will be discussed in a subsequent publication.

This chapter is the result of more than eight years of extended fieldwork and total immersion in the community living around the Forest City project.

PROJECT BACKGROUND

The Forest City development is a joint venture between Country Garden Group, a Guangdong-based company listed in Hong Kong since 2007, and Iskandar Esplanade Danga 88 Sdn Bhd (EDSB), which is partially owned by Kumpulan Prasarana Rakyat Johor (KPRJ), a Johor state-owned company (CGPV Official Website). The partnership gave birth to Country Gardens PacificView Sdn Bhd (CGPV). According to Sultan Ibrahim Ibni Almarhum Sultan Iskandar, Johor's monarch, Forest City was his idea and he was the one who brought in the developers and investors; through the development, opportunities would abound for local employment, retailers, infrastructure improvements and state government revenues (*New Straits Times*, 22 March 2015).

According to CGPV executive director Md Othman Yusof, the Sultan "wanted to see balanced development", and existing plans under Iskandar Malaysia focussed too much on the southeastern side of the state while the "south-western side appeared to be left out" (*Malaysiakini*, 19 March 2014). Sultan Ibrahim himself stated that "ordinary Johoreans must see the spillover effects" and he wanted "the people to benefit from all these changes" (*The Star*, 19 March 2015).

A report by *Malaysiakini* (14 July 2014) in 2014 revealed that Country Garden has a 66 per cent stake in Country Garden PacificView Sdn Bhd through Country Garden Waterfront Sdn Bhd, Country Garden Danga Bay Sdn Bhd and Country Garden Real Estate Sdn Bhd, all Malaysia-registered subsidiaries. EDSB holds the remaining 34 per cent stake as the representative of the state government. In turn, EDSB itself is 64.4 per cent owned by Sultan Ibrahim, 15.6 per cent owned by Daing A. Malek, who is also a director in EDSB, and 20 per cent by KPRJ, or the Johor state government (*Malaysiakini*, 18 July 2014). Daing A. Malek is also the executive director of Country Garden PacificView Sdn Bhd (*The Edge Singapore*, 16 February 2016). One of Johor's biggest sand extraction companies is Mados Sdn Bhd, which as at 17 July 2014 according to *Malaysiakini* was 99.95 per cent owned by the late Johor sultan, Sultan Iskandar Sultan Ismail, while the remaining shareholders were his second wife and their children. Mados Sdn Bhd has the sand extraction rights to a shoal in Teluk Ramunia, which is the source of the sand used in the Forest City reclamation (Forest City DEIA, pp. 5–27).

On the Country Garden website, Forest City is positioned as being "adjacent to Singapore" and is highlighted as the showcase of a "Liveable Eco-City" concept with 20 sq. km of parks and recreational spaces. Forest City is not Country Garden's only Malaysian endeavour. It is also behind the Country Garden Danga Bay project, a "5-Star Integrated Seaview Development" in Johor Bahru, and is in a joint venture with the Malaysian Mayland Group of Companies for the Mountain View Villa Township development in Rawang, Selangor and Diamond City, a landed housing development in Semenyih, also in Selangor (*The Edge Singapore*, 16 February 2016).

Forest City is Country Garden's largest project worldwide; a complete metropolis on four islands comprising apartment and villa housing, office buildings, parks, hotels, shopping malls and an international school. Its proximity to Iskandar Puteri (formerly known as Nusajaya, Johor's government centre) also gives it quick access to EduCity, an education hub that boasts a number of international schools, colleges and universities. The sheer size of this development is often cited as the justification for reclamation. While Iskandar Malaysia still has 2,217 sq. km of available undeveloped land (three times the size of Singapore), it lies inland unfortunately; Md Othman Yusof, CGPV's Executive Director, explained that inland sites simply cannot match the appeal of a waterfront city (ibid.).

This metropolis is projected to house 700,000 people, initially expected to be mostly from China. It opened its second international sales office in a high-end neighbourhood of Kuala Lumpur at the end of 2016, and more sales galleries are planned for Taiwan, Myanmar, Dubai and Indonesia. Middle-class Chinese who are unable to afford housing in expensive Chinese urban centres such as Beijing and Shanghai have been the main targeted clients for this development (*City Lab*, 30 December 2016). However, since new regulations on foreign exchange were announced in China in January 2017, this strategy may have to quickly adapt to focus on international markets.

Although no final figures have been released by CGPV, a *Straits Times* report (13 May 2015) estimated that 116,666 new homes will be built (under the assumption that each unit would accommodate six people). The units currently on offer on the Forest City website range from 1 bedroom/1 bathroom/1 balcony apartments of 59 sq. m to 4 bedroom/3 bathroom/1 balcony units of 173 square metres. While the sales gallery scale model features villas on the island, current sales seem to be focussed on the apartments, with no additional information on the website of potential bungalows or semi-detached houses. The property website mysgprop.com indicates that as of November 2016, 1,252 1-bedroom units, 542 2-bedroom units and 268 3-bedroom units were available for sale.[2] Units with 2 or more bedrooms are eligible for at least one parking space. Half of the apartment blocks and the individual villa units on the scale model in the Forest City Show Gallery display "sold" tags.

The development is pitched as a "3D multi-layered urban planning concept" that ensures that there are parks, activity spaces and railways to lessen pollution at pedestrian-friendly levels. Vehicles will be parked in a transportation hub or in lower levels of the islands. Forest City properties are sold under "freehold property rights" with "zero inheritance tax" and "no economic environmental constraints" to property ownership on the islands (CGPV Official Website).

Property in Forest City is priced to begin at US$170,000; about a third as compared to those available on the Chinese mainland and a quarter of property prices in Singapore. The common use of Mandarin and other Chinese dialects in the region and myriad incentives provided by the Malaysian government make ownership highly attractive to Chinese nationals. The Forest City website projects a 6–9 per cent rental yield for its properties. Potential buyers from China are bussed to the Forest City show gallery as part of subsidized Singapore-Malaysia tours organized by Country Garden, and are met by sales agents who reportedly achieve an immediate 50 per cent sales success from the groups (*Today* Online, 22 November 2016).

A Liveable Eco-City

Forest City prides itself on being a "Prime Model of Future City" (*sic*) and much of its website showcases innovations for sustainable development. Among these offerings are its position as a car-free city, where vehicles are docked in either underground parking or in a breathable transport hub, and a free monorail service, for lower carbon emissions and a safer neighbourhood, which transports people throughout the development. Vertical greening includes building façades covered in plants and roof-top gardens.

Vincent Woon, CGPV's Strategy Manager also explained the company's interest in nurturing urban and rooftop farming, and its work with Sasaki Associates to ensure the recreation of critical marine habitats, a walkable urban environment and a contiguous rooftop landscape that links all parts of the development yet accommodates the need for stormwater run-off and native habitats. The green approach can also be seen in the details; green technology is widely applied in this development, from a smart metering system to control energy consumption and leakage to numerous electric car charging stations and recycled materials in its speed humps and parking blocks.[3]

Sasaki's US$40.9 billion masterplan depicts a "symbiotic relationship" between built and natural environments in which a 250-hectare seagrass preserve will be recreated, and more than 9 km of mangroves and 10 km of shallow coves and mudflats will be re-established. All of this, it claims, will maintain the area's ecological sustainability and provide resilience against sea-level rise. In an interview with *The Star* (19 March 2015), Sultan Ibrahim discussed his interest in the environment of Johor, citing Forest City as an example of a development that emphasizes environmental protection and greenery.

Forest City is also applying for GreenRE certification, a green rating standard driven by Real Estate and Housing Development Association Malaysia (REHDA), which promotes the development of more sustainable and liveable built environments. The Forest City website thus extolls its incorporation of natural elements; its natural lighting and ventilation; its optimized heat and energy conservation and rainwater harvesting systems; water-efficient devices; and recycled water use.

Location, Location, Location

While much of the Forest City website discusses its green innovations in urban planning and development, access to Singapore seems to be one of its core marketing pillars. The website notes that it is only 2 km away from Singapore, just 39 km away from Singapore's main shopping strip Orchard Road, and that it plans to have a 24-hour shuttle bus to and from the island city-state. There is also mention of recent approval for the establishment of new entry points and independent customs facilities by sea and by land, through Forest City.

Much of the Forest City promotional material in Hong Kong and other parts of China also emphasizes the project's proximity to Singapore.[4] Marketing paraphernalia highlighted, for example, the ability to "enjoy the prosperity of Singapore and the affordability of Malaysia", as well as the duty-free benefits of the newly reclaimed islands and the ease of attaining long-term residency through the Malaysia My Second Home programme. In its show gallery and on its website, location maps point out the ease of access to both Singapore and other parts of Malaysia by highways, the planned High-Speed Railway line between Singapore and Malaysia, and Singapore's Mass Rapid Transit (MRT) system.

Iskandar Malaysia

Launched by former Prime Minister Abdullah Badawi in 2006, this economic corridor was created to reignite investor interest in Malaysia. Managed by the Iskandar Regional Development Authority (IRDA), Iskandar Malaysia (IM) was always seen as the potentially most successful of the five promoted corridors because of its proximity to Singapore. The Forest City project is located in the Western Gate of the Iskandar Development Region (see Figure 17.1 for map) which had initially been designated as a completely industrial area, centred around the Port of Tanjung Pelepas (PTP), the Tanjung Bin Power Plant and the Tanjung Bin International Maritime Centre (IRDA 2008).

Early critics of Forest City declared that it would "block the growth of PTP and threaten the development of Iskandar Malaysia as it was not part of the master plan". Datuk Zamani Kassim, CGPV Project Director at the time, stated that Forest City would be integrated into the overall plan of Iskandar Malaysia (*The Edge*, 22 September 2014). Forest City now leverages on its proximity to EduCity, Iskandar Malaysia's centre for international educational institutions, and collaborates with Iskandar Malaysia to establish research centres and technical training institutions (CGPV Official Website). An MOU on its smart city initiatives was signed between IRDA and Forest City in December 2015 (IM Media Release 2016). IRDA also serves as facilitator and consultant for CGPV, providing relevant expertise and acting as a neutral platform for agencies and stakeholders to discuss priorities and concerns (Williams 2016).

ECONOMIC VIABILITY

In its Statement of Need, the DEIA report states that investments of RM700 million (S$233.9 million) will be made to upgrade infrastructure around the Forest City site (Forest City DEIA, pp. 4–5), and that the no-build option would mean that the state government will lose potential revenue in fees, taxes and premiums of RM30 million (S$9.6 million) a year. The local population would also "not be able to benefit from an estimated 62,200 new employment opportunities" (Forest City DEIA, pp. 2–6). A minimum 30 per cent quota of local employment was recommended by the DEIA Report (Forest City DEIA, pp. 3–14).

Prime Minister Najib Razak has stated that the project will not only improve the local economy through job opportunities, but also help boost tourism and spur the development of manufacturing, high-tech services and the financial sectors (*The Star*, 7 December 2016). Sultan Ibrahim confirmed that the investment will add to the state government's surplus budget (*The Star*, 18 March 2015); it will receive fees such as annual assessments and quit rent from the developers (*New Straits Times*, 22 March 2015). With projected tax revenues of RM66 billion (S$21.11 billion) over the next twenty years and an expected contribution of RM1.98 trillion (S$630 billion) to the nation's GDP, CGPV executive director Datuk Md Othman Yusof is confident that the total investment of about US$100 billion will attract good returns (*The Star*,

FIGURE 17.1
Forest City Land Plots (A to F) Alienated to CGPV, Set Within the Western Gate of the Iskandar Development Region

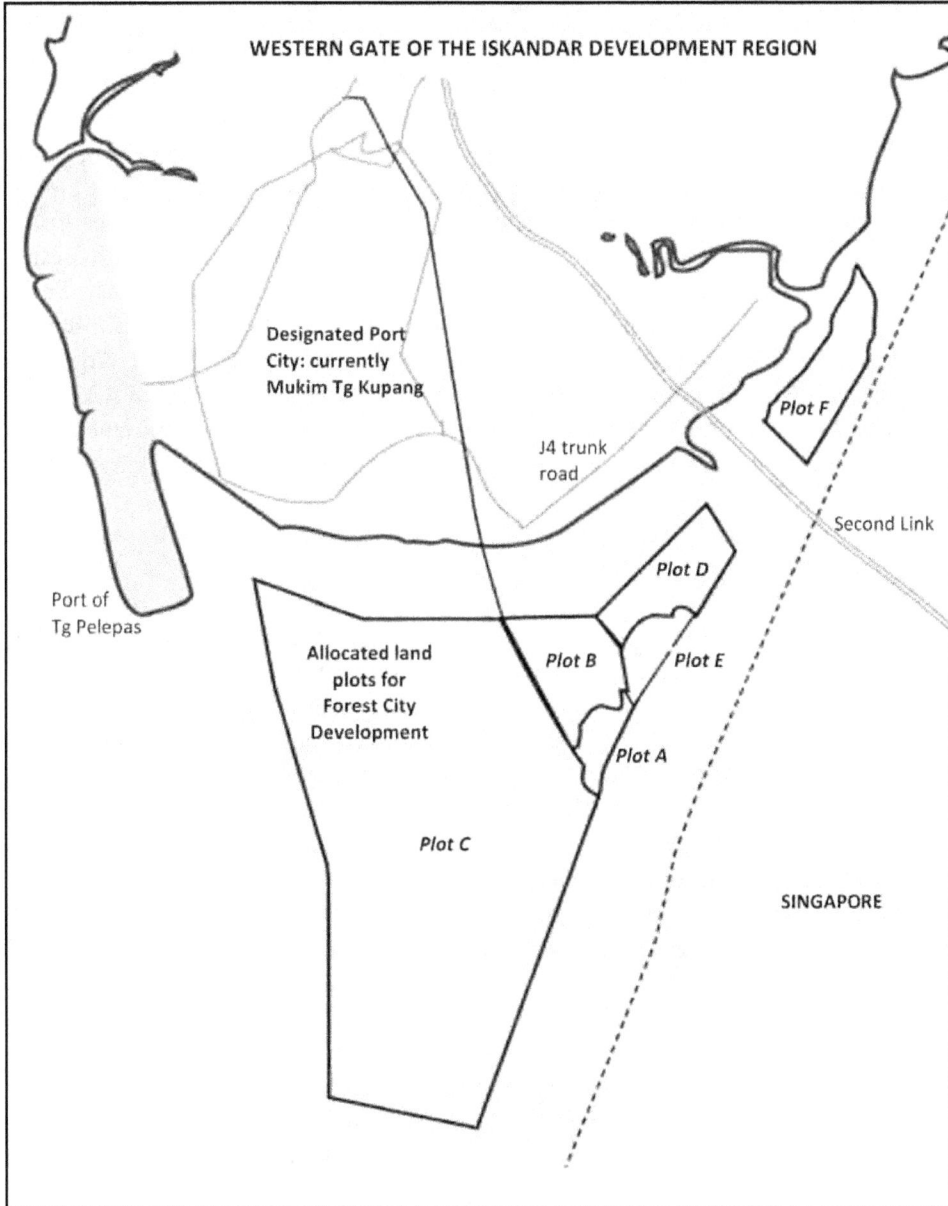

WESTERN GATE OF THE ISKANDAR DEVELOPMENT REGION

Designated Port City: currently Mukim Tg Kupang

Plot F

J4 trunk road

Second Link

Plot D

Port of Tg Pelepas

Allocated land plots for Forest City Development

Plot B

Plot E

Plot A

Plot C

SINGAPORE

Note: Plot A was to be the first island reclaimed beginning January 2014.
Source: Reproduced with kind permission of Benjamin Cheh Ming Hann.

7 December 2016). Forest City is visited by 300 to 800 visitors daily (ibid.), and had a total of about 100,000 visitors in 2016[5] with at least 11,000 units already sold (*The Star*, 7 December 2016). PM Najib projects that Forest City will turn Johor into the next Dubai (*Straits Times*, 21 January 2017).

In an interview with *The Star* (18 March 2015), Sultan Ibrahim of Johor pointed out that for every square foot of land reclaimed by CGPV for the Forest City project, RM0.30 (S$0.10) is placed in a fund to help affected fishermen, bringing in more than RM104 million (S$33.26 million). The Sultan was most likely referring to the Johor Fisherman's Foundation announced by Azli Mohamad Aziz, the South Johor Fisherman's Association Chairman (*The Star*, 13 October 2014). The monies in the foundation will be used for oil palm and other business ventures, with profits being channelled back to fishermen affected by development in both Gelang Patah and Pengerang. To launch the foundation at the time, a start-up contribution of RM10 million (S$3.2 million) was requested from the state government. Added to that was the RM3 million (S$1 million) in compensation disbursed by CGPV to the community in 2013.[6] All these funds would provide substantial financial and other support to fishing communities, especially in light of declining catch numbers worldwide.

Is There a Market?

The CGPV website highlights the stable property market in Johor as being characterized by "high transparency" and a "commonwealth legal and banking system" that will protect the interests and privacy of the buyers. It also declares that there will be "asset value preservation". However, soon after the public became aware of the scale of this mixed development, pundits began to predict a glut in the Iskandar property market. The Forest City properties will add to the existing 336,000 homes already planned for Johor. As at end 2014, there were 719,421 homes already in existence in the state (*Straits Times*, 13 May 2015).

With financial struggles in China, many suggest that large ventures like Forest City will be the final nail in the real estate coffin. The *Wall Street Journal* reported that the CGPV attitude towards these naysayers was, "we will create the market and the customers will arrive" (*Wall Street Journal*, 1 March 2016). Sultan Ibrahim in turn interjected that the developers were not building all the units at once, and that the middle class in China and elsewhere (including Malaysia) would in any case need to find a place to stay given rising costs in many capital cities worldwide (*The Star*, 18 March 2015). The Sultan has been very firm in his drive to develop Johor and his vision is to move his state capital from the infamy of being the "sleepy backyard of Singapore" (*New Straits Times*, 22 March 2015) towards becoming the second biggest city in Malaysia after Kuala Lumpur (*The Star*, 23 March 2016).

Chinese visitors to Forest City have tended to marvel more at how beautiful the scenery is and how much they enjoyed the view from the Forest City beachfront, than be bothered by Singapore's industrial skyline.[7] Bo Wang explained the oblivion as a comparative lack of pollution to China where smog is the order of the day.

Forest City being promoted as a planned city with all manners of environmental protection, safety and energy reduction has apparently enchanted the Mainland Chinese as being a novel and remarkable concept.[8] Interviews by the *South China Morning Post* (26 March 2017) indicate that indeed, middle-class buyers are taken in by the seductive package of clean tropical surroundings, access to good schooling, easy long-term residency options and proximity to Singapore when they commit to purchasing Forest City units.

However, the recently announced regulations on individual foreign exchange and restrictions on currency use have thrown a spanner in the works. Not only will this reduce the ability of average middle-class Chinese nationals to buy up the available lots, it has put an immediate halt to installation payments by those who have already made the initial down payment. Property agents will now have to focus on Chinese nationals who already have funds overseas, or they will have to substantially broaden their clientele to other countries.

Researchers have noted growing optimism in the Malaysian property sector and overall warming of perceptions since the MH370 disaster. But they warn that maintenance of these glitzy properties will need to be improved if international investor confidence is to be maintained. More efficient commuting options between Singapore and Malaysia would also help to sustain investor interest (Khor and Mavroeidi 2014).

In essence, for markets beyond China, CGPV will have to find selling points that appeal to the non-Chinese buyer. As it stands, Forest City properties generate little interest among Malaysians as apartment prices there are comparable to those in the Kuala Lumpur city centre, which is by far a more desirable location; and furthermore, local buyers tend to focus on landed property.[9] Table 17.1 shows a comparison between condominium property prices in Forest City with those from a number of other locations. Individual bungalow or semi-detached houses on the Forest City islands are reported to be more expensive and Chinese nationals looking for landed property for their retirement have settled on those in nearby gated communities such as Leisurefarm Resort.[10]

While it was often posited that Singaporeans would be the main buyers in the Iskandar Development Region given the higher cost of living and of homes in Singapore, the response has in fact been lukewarm, partly due to Johor's minimum purchase price regulation: Foreigners can only buy properties worth more than RM1 million and there is a capital gains tax of 30 per cent for units sold within five years of purchase (*Straits Times*, 14 May 2015). Should the property be put on the resale market, the price tag would be far beyond the reach of the average local budget. In addition, Malaysia's reputation for lack of certainty and of transparency in business and investment transactions—although improving—is another stigma that Singaporean buyers do not easily forget. Recent media coverage of the predicament faced by Chinese nationals who committed to Forest City units but who are now unable to follow through with payments given capital controls regulations adds to the negative perceptions that need to be overcome (*Today Online*, 3 April 2017).

TABLE 17.1
Comparison of Average Condominium Property Prices per square foot

Location	Property	Average price per square foot (RM)	Average price per square foot (S$)
Johor Bahru	Forest City[a]	RM1,280	S$409
	Horizon Residences, Bukit Indah[a]	RM623	S$199
	Fairway Suites, Bukit Indah[b]	RM497	S$159
Kuala Lumpur	The Binjai, KLCC[b]	RM3,208	S$1,025
	K-Residence, Avenue K[b]	RM1,387	S$443
	Lakeview Homes, Mt Kiara[b]	RM550	S$175
	Mount Kiara Banyan[b]	RM682	S$218
	Nadi Bangsar[c]	RM1,270	S$406
Singapore	Siglap Seaside[c]	RM5,321	S$1,700
	Clement Canopy[d]	RM4,382	S$1,400

Sources:
a. "Forest City's Chinese Buyers in Limbo Over Developer's Penalty Claims", *Today Online*, 3 April 2017.
b. "Property Snapshot 3: What Are Prices Like in Johor Bahru?", *The Edge Property*, 3 February 2016.
c. Survey of current prices on www.propertyguru.com.my, 5 April 2017.
d. Personal communication with Janette Woo, Singaporean property agent on 3 April 2017.

Questions of Safety

Yet another reservation that potential buyers have concerns safety. CGPV takes pride in the speed with which they are able to reclaim land and build their properties. The Forest City Show Gallery has an exhibition area that depicts the method with which "new land is created from the sea"; one month after sand dumping begins an island is formed, and eight months after that, foundation work begins. Chinese building contractors have a reputation for carelessness and for having little regard for safety (*New York Times*, 26 November 2015). This can also be seen at the Forest City project site as there is free access by anyone to the CG Causeway through the construction entrance, where large heavy vehicles travel at speed, some while packed full of workers. Interviews with people who work onsite reveal that little heed is paid to health and safety standards and several local and foreign workers' lives have already been lost since construction began.

It is also clear that in spite of the technological innovations used to reclaim and build, sand dumped on (mud) seabed needs more than the publicised time to settle. Cracks are clearly visible in both the Show Gallery and hotel buildings and sections of the new road and dispersal link show signs of settlement and ground-level sinking. These are quickly covered over, and a contractor has been hired to constantly monitor ground levels.[11] Staff of a food outlet within Forest City reported that they faced many wiring and other problems; large chunks of the ceiling once fell just before they opened and a glass door pane shattered without warning during operating hours.[12] An interview with a development consultant who declined to be named revealed that the ground is indeed clearly sinking and that the Show Gallery roof has leaks, both due to the haste in which it was built, as well as to the desire to keep costs to a minimum.[13]

According to the consultant, however, because piling has been cast in clusters deep in the rock base (beyond the seabed depth) and further strengthened with walls of concrete encircling both reclaimed land and piling clusters, the buildings are stable. The visible cracks occur at the prefabricated material joints, a common surface-only occurrence in this type of construction method. But according to the consultant, land settlement will continue, leaving the building suspended on the piling showing a gap between the building floor and the actual ground level. Some parts of the settlement cannot be refilled with sand or other substrate as they have already been sealed off with the enclosing concrete. There could then be a hollow piling structure under the building. Externally visible areas of settlement will have to be either refilled or steps built for smooth access to the building from the actual ground levels.

The questions that arise from the physical reliability of the islands and their infrastructure are difficult to dismiss. This is even more so for potential buyers from Singapore where reclamation has been the norm and where residents are used to seeing reclaimed land left to settle and rehabilitate naturally for years before any form of construction begins on it.

Political Entanglements

Adding to the controversy surrounding Forest City is the political furore that has emerged around the project—especially as Malaysia moves towards its national elections. The recent tiff between Tun Dr Mahathir Mohamad and Sultan Ibrahim reignites long-standing tensions between the royal houses and the former premier. The friction began when the former curtailed royal powers during his term as Prime Minister (Norshahril Saat 2017) and removed royal immunity from persecution. The Johor Sultan, in particular, has often accused Tun Dr Mahathir of stoking racial and religious discord for political gain (*The Star*, 16 January 2017), which he says goes against the state practice of *Bangsa Johor*. The former Prime Minister's apparent attempts to invoke xenophobic fears of Chinese investors are believed to be an attempt to pull away rural Malay votes in the UMNO stronghold to his new opposition party, Parti Pribumi Bersatu Malaysia (PPBM). The Forest City project has thus become the unwitting pawn in this political positioning.

Yet another theory put forward to explain the vilification of Forest City is the battle between the business interests of Mahathir and the Sultan. The affiliations are simple; Forest City is a state project sanctioned by Sultan Ibrahim. The placement of the Forest City project obstructs some of the initial development plans of the Port of Tanjung Pelepas (PTP) (IRDA 2008), which is a federal project launched during Mahathir's term as Prime Minister and helmed by his close associate Syed Mokhtar Al-Bukhary (*KiniBiz Online*, 12 November 2013). Add to that are Mahathir's current animosity with Prime Minister Najib Razak and the latter's recent embrace of China and Chinese investors. Together, these elements result in public relations problems for CGPV and the Forest City project.

In defence of Sultan Ibrahim's decision to reclaim Forest City in the Tebrau Straits is his demand that there not be "too much interruption to the lives of the people in the vicinity" (*New Straits Times*, 22 March 2015). This too could be a veiled reference to the long-term plan in the IRDA Blueprint to transform much of Mukim Tanjung Kupang into a Port City, with possible displacement of the villagers into "resettlement areas" (IRDA 2008).

While most buyers, especially those from overseas, will leave the political parlance in the background, the negative publicity does have some effect on Forest City's branding. These issues may not have a direct impact on the financial success of the project but they are a neat reflection of development and political economy concerns. Furthermore, this battle between the elder statesman and the Johor Sultan which was publicly played out in the press is one between two giants, both of whom inhabit totally different spheres from those who live in the immediate vicinity of the Forest City projects.

The great disparity between the three levels of society participating in this development illustrates the political economy realities involved. Those who will potentially benefit financially from Forest City hold much power over the project's future. These are the privileged few. Those who are able to participate through their purchasing power stand to benefit in terms of lifestyle choices and well-being. Thirdly, the people whose lives and future livelihoods are directly affected by the project's impact on the environment, have little to no opportunity to participate in the project or to enjoy its benefits.

Accurate Economic Costs of Project

The economic valuation of the project took into account potential investment, fees, taxes and other returns. In a valuation of costs and benefits, the DEIA calculated that over a period of fifty years, with an 8 per cent discounted loss of environmental services, the total present value of the streamed annual loss will be RM116 million (S$37.10 million) (Forest City DEIA, pp. 13–16). In coming to this figure, the following items were taken into consideration:

    i.   direct use values of mudflats lost to reclamation (through potential income from the sales of cockles, bivalves, gastropods, shrimps/prawn and fish;

   ii.   direct use values of muddy seabed lost to dredging (calculated as above);

  iii.   costs to fishermen (through loss of fishing ground and increased costs of fuel consumption);

  iv.   loss of seagrass habitat productivity (through direct use values of fisheries, tourism, education and research and indirect use values of nutrient cycling and carbon sequestration).

No details were provided on the components considered under fisheries, tourism, education and research. But then even those figures would be insufficient since the following habitats and/or ecosystem services values have not been included in the calculation (adapted from WWF Malaysia 2013; Sidik, Harah, and Ashad 2014, pp. 1–19; writer's field book):

1. Ecosystem connectivity values;
2. Nutrient and pollutant sequestration;
3. Coastal protection from sea level rise, wave action and erosion;
4. Sediment trapping and stabilization.
5. Ecological engineering values;
6. Food chain and sediment community biodiversity values for nearshore and coastal productivity;
7. Fisheries species nursery, feeding and breeding grounds;
8. Aquaculture and recreational fishing values;
9. Ecotourism and aesthetic values;
10. Food chain value (through benthic invertebrates);
11. Fisheries value (i.e., gleaning);
12. Biodiversity and structural complexity values;
13. Medicinal values;
14. Non-use and existence values;
15. Socio-cultural heritage and identity values.

Assessing the habitat alone, however, is not enough. In order to accurately determine the proper economic value (or opportunity costs) of the development, the following variables also need to be taken into account:

1. Economic contribution of fisheries input (e.g., materials and supplies, production factors);
2. Economic output values of fisheries industry and fisheries-related manufacturing industries (e.g., downstream fish processing, packaging, ice manufacturing);
3. Costs of damages incurred from accidents or net damage related to the development or its contractors;
4. Subsidies values;
5. Increasing market prices for fish given scarce resources;
6. Fisheries option values (opportunities for fishing at a later date);
7. Recreational fishing;
8. Socio-cultural heritage and identity values;
9. Bequest values (fishing by the next generation).

In addition, fishing-dependent communities who make up the majority of the people living around the Forest City project are among the most vulnerable of socio-economic working groups. They have a high dependence on fisheries for cash income, whereby the ability to earn cash, such as through the immediate sales of fish, translates into access to essential services, goods and food. Thus, the actual value of the sale of a day's harvest at sea is far higher than the monetary value assigned to it (Béné 2006). Should all these variables be taken into consideration, the actual costs of the project would be far higher than its projection in the DEIA. While there are ways to mitigate and offset these costs, the fact remains that the prices tagged to the properties for sale should be far higher, with more taxation or other fees being needed to ensure that some financial benefits are channelled to those immediately affected by the physical and environmental effects of the development.

ENVRONMENTAL SUSTAINABILITY

The environmental sustainability of the Forest City project has been an issue that has dogged it since its inception. Given the great emphasis on its green qualifications, a higher benchmark is at stake. But with the controversy that has erupted around it however, the project's environmental credibility has been harder to establish.

In Forest City's immediate vicinity is Mukim Tg Kupang, a subdistrict of Gelang Patah inhabited by a population of about 10,972 people settled in nine villages (Forest City DEIA, pp. 7–11). Many of these are artisanal nearshore and estuary fishermen, while others work in the port or its surrounding factories and facilities. The fishermen in this area fall under the South Johor Fishermen's Association and comprise both Malay and Chinese locals who have been dependent on the area's natural habitats for generations. While Orang Seletar indigenous people also fish within the Forest City development area, they are not residents there and often come from Kampung Simpang Arang near Gelang Patah or the Danga Bay area.

Controversy

To the fishermen and many others in the Mukim Tg Kupang community, the start of reclamation came as a surprise. Photo evidence taken by a local community organization, Kelab Alami, showed marker buoys put in place by 1 January 2014. Then sand barges arrived to offload tons of sand around the clock. The Forest City DEIA document states that reclamation for Phase 1 of the project began on 22 January 2014, with seventeen sand barges working continuously twenty-four hours a day with at least seventeen trips to shuttle sand between Teluk Ramunia and the Forest City reclamation site (Forest City DEIA, pp. 110–13). The project had an immediate goal of dumping 25,406,201 m^3 of fill material to create the first island. The entire project would require a total of 161,891,980 m^3 of fill material (Forest City DEIA, pp. 5–20). By the end of February 2014, a small island of sand was already visible.[14]

During this period there was still little information about the project available to the average community member. Sand dumping continued and fishermen at most jetties were only able to grumble amongst themselves about the potential impact to their livelihoods. Democratic Action Party (DAP) politicians Cheo Yee How and Liew Chin Tong raised the matter but it was not until Singapore had sent a diplomatic note to the Federal government in May 2014 that action was taken (*Malaysiakini*, 14 July 2014).

Singapore's Concerns

According to the Singapore Ministry of Foreign Affairs (MFA) press release (9 July 2014), Singapore's concerns about the Forest City project revolved around the lack of information provided to them by the Malaysian government. Diplomatic notes were sent by various parties in Singapore, including the Prime Minister, to their counterparts in the Malaysian government. The matter was also raised during the Malaysia-Singapore Joint Committee on the Environment Working Group meeting in Malaysia in May 2014. The issues on which Singapore requested clarification included the following: potential changes in water current speeds and the subsequent impact on navigational safety; possible erosion that might affect shoreline and Second Link infrastructure; and changes in water quality and morphology that might affect the coastal and marine environment and local fish farms. Singapore requested that all reclamation work be put on hold until these issues were investigated and the DEIA report was shared.

Initially the Chief Minister of Johor, Khaled Nordin reassured Singapore that the Forest City development would have no environmental impacts. At the same time, the state government asked CGPV to prepare an action plan to resolve the issue of sediment plumes resulting from the reclamation work (Williams 2016). The order for mitigation work to be carried out onsite was issued on 2 June 2014, a request for a DEIA was sent to CGPV on 6 June 2014, and on 17 June 2014 the stop work order was issued by the Johor Department of Environment (DOE Johor) (Forest City DEIA, pp. 2–6). DAP spokesperson on environmental issues, Cheo Yee How (22 September 2014), reported however that work continued on the ground despite the stop-work order. This claim was corroborated by Kelab Alami photo documentation of trucks transporting sand to the reclamation site via the CG Causeway, which could now be reached from the main J4 trunk road through Mukim Tg Kupang after mangrove and secondary forests were cleared for this thoroughfare.

The Question of the DEIA

Thus, it was revealed that this almost 2,000-hectare project was approved and launched without a DEIA. According to the Malaysian Department of Irrigation and Drainage (DID) Guidelines, for any coastal reclamation involving an area of 50 hectares or more, it is mandatory that an EIA be carried out. All reclamation projects of any size require impact evaluation studies that include hydrodynamics and morphological change modelling reports (Department of Irrigation and Drainage Guidelines Malaysia). Following this, the project allegedly broke up into islands of 49.3 hectares each, to avoid the DEIA process (Williams 2016).

According to the National Policy Plan-2 (NPP2), sensitive coastal and marine ecosystems such as wetlands (mangrove) and seagrass areas, especially those critical to marine fisheries should be gazetted as protected areas. Any proposal involving reclamation needs to be referred to the National Physical Planning Council. The actual area within which Forest City was proposed is labelled Management Unit (MU) 3-9: Merambong under the Iskandar Malaysia Shoreline Management Plan (IRDA 2011). This area is deemed an Environmentally Sensitive Area (ESA) Rank 1, where no development is allowed save low-impact nature tourism, research and education. In order to begin work on Forest City, this protected area had to be de-gazetted. The Forest City DEIA mentions that DOE Johor issued a Preliminary Site Approval on 13 January 2014 for the reclamation of Phase 1. It was with this document that CGPV began reclamation work. The Johor State Economic Planning Unit, in a letter dated 3 September 2014, waived the need for the reclamation to be referred to the National Physical Planning Council (Forest City DEIA, pp. 1–12).

In community stakeholder meetings, CGPV representatives insisted that they had no idea that the reclamation area held such a rich diversity of wildlife and fisheries species. They implied that they were given the go-ahead to begin work and to carry on as necessary.[15] A local advisor to CGPV who declined to be named[16] mentioned that he had warned them not to break up the project to avoid the DEIA process, but the plan went ahead nevertheless.

In its original plans, the Forest City development was to be a single geometrically shaped block of land wedged between Singapore and Malaysia. The map in Figure 17.1 (adapted from Forest City DEIA, p. 2; IRDA 2008, p. 13) depicts the land plots alienated to CGPV, amounting to about 1,900 hectares. Little public mention is made of Plot F on the northern side of the Second Link Bridge. Reclamation in this area would have an immediate impact on several floating fish farms there.

As part of the DEIA requirements, CGPV's environmental consultant, DHI Malaysia, carried out more than fifty modelling simulations to revise the shape of their islands to take into consideration the issues highlighted by Singapore and to ensure minimal impacts on the natural habitats in the vicinity.[17] Among the concerns taken care of were: the stipulation of a buffer of at least 1 km between the development and Singapore, the Second Link and PTP's future expansion area; a maximum change of current velocities of 10 per cent; buffers of between 200 m to 500 m between the development and the Tg Kupang seagrass meadow, 600 m from Merambong Island and 200–300 m from the mainland to allow for the movement of local fishing boats; sea level rise due to global warming; the prevention of possible flooding and erosion; and the ensuring of shoreline protection and vegetation (Forest City DEIA, pp. 3–6).

The revised layout of the development thus evolved into four separate islands around the Tg Kupang seagrass meadow with specifications as listed in Table 17.2. With all mitigating tools and factors in place, this would help to reduce the impact of reclamation and construction on the Tg Kupang seagrass meadow. The revised island plan is shown in Figure 17.2 (adapted from Forest City DEIA, pp. 5–14). This revision reduced the project's total acreage by about 30 per cent to 1,380 hectares. Its

TABLE 17.2
Specifications of Revised Forest City Island Plan

Island	Acreage	Purpose
1	979	High-tech industrial zone, CBD, residential, shopping mall, IT industrial park, playgrounds, transportation hub
2	1,895	CBD, tourism, residential, central park, sports park, hospital, ferry terminal
3	405	Customs, duty-free shopping, convention centre, luxury hotel,
4	164	international exchange centre

Source: www.mysgprop.com/forest-city-country-garden-johor/.

gross development value was thus also reduced from RM600 billion (S$191.91 billion) to RM450 billion (S$143.93 billion) (*The Edge*, 16 February 2016). The development thus leaves the Tg Kupang seagrass meadow intact, albeit surrounded by the new artificial islands.

Is This Greenwashing?

Singapore's concerns about the Forest City project stemmed mainly from its environmental impacts. While the habitat descriptions and details in both the IM Blueprint and the DEIA may be inaccurate and/or incomplete, they do highlight some resident species of seagrass and marine fauna and acknowledge the importance of the habitat. According to the Blueprint (published in 2011), the biggest threat to these habitats was the Port of Tg Pelepas. At the time of publication of this Blueprint, the Forest City plan had not yet materialized; thus, there was no expectation of other potential threats to the environment.

Copious publications have highlighted the importance of the area in terms of its biodiversity and significance to local fisheries and the ecosystems services that it provides. The intertidal seagrass meadow that the CG Causeway divides is the largest in Peninsular Malaysia and harbours at least eight species of seagrass and thirty species of seaweed which in turn supports the existence of numerous fisheries and other vital marine species. These include large endangered species such as dugongs and two types of turtles. The mangrove areas that line the coasts here are also known to harbour endemic (found only in this area) and endangered species, as well as enigmatic fauna such as the Estuary Crocodile, Smooth Otter and Leopard Cat, among others.

Beyond individual habitat and biodiversity importance is the value of these areas' habitat connectivity. The link between mangroves, intertidal mudflats, seagrass meadows and the nearby island rocky shore and soft coral areas facilitate and support the breeding, nursery and feeding grounds of a substantial web of marine species that provide for local community protein needs as well as the region's fisheries output. The Forest City project encompasses much of this area and if mitigating measures are not taken, it could possibly damage the links between these vital components of a

FIGURE 17.2
The Revised Layout of What Are Now Four Forest City Islands after the DEIA

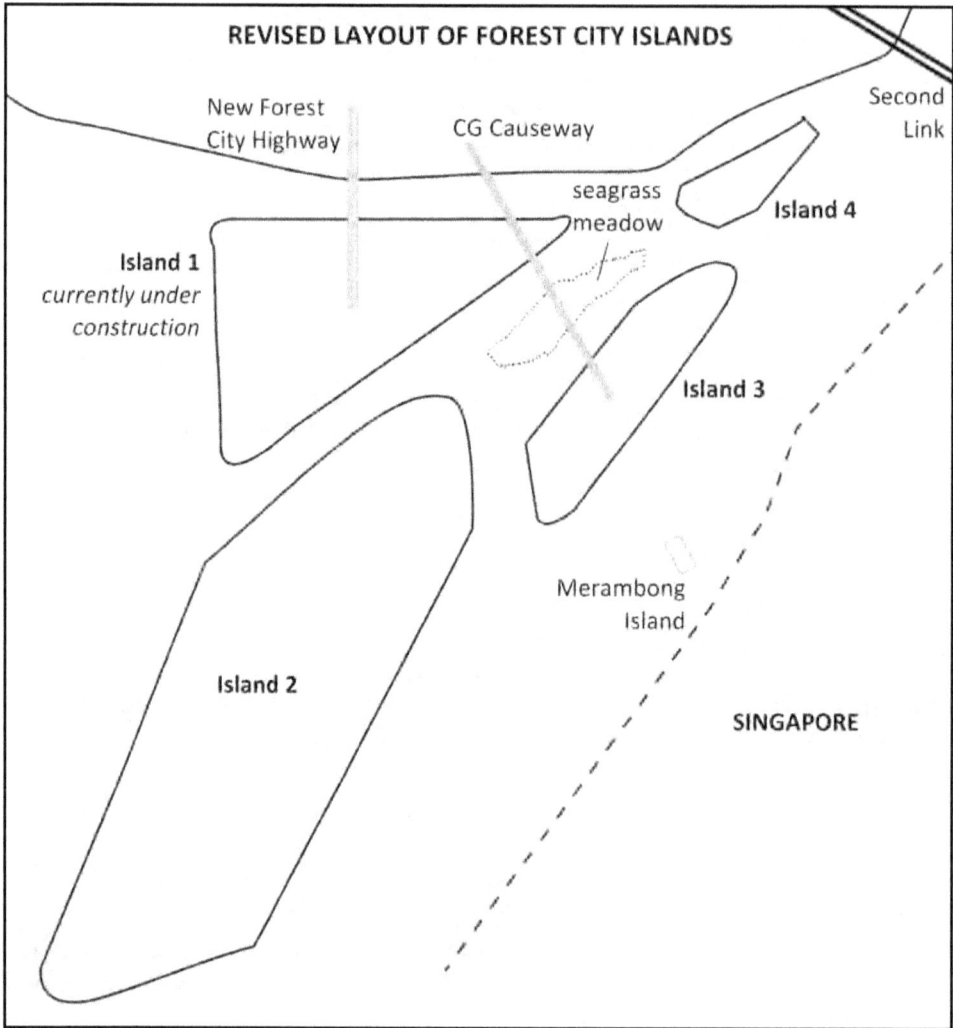

Source: Reproduced with kind permission of Benjamin Cheh Ming Hann.

larger ecosystem, thereafter severely affecting local fisheries supplies and community access to subsistence food sources.

An Update to the Environmental Assessment

While the DEIA took note of some of the issues that will result from the development and that had already occurred at the time of publication, an update of the environmental status and the accuracy of the DEIA report is in order. The biggest impact of a reclamation project is assumed to be that of sedimentation plumes on surrounding habitats. The DEIA report states that a double layer of silt curtains would be installed around the reclamation site to prevent sedimentation (Forest City DEIA, pp. 5–19). However, photographic evidence taken by Kelab Alami showed that at least some of the silt curtains were not unrolled throughout the project reclamation period and were therefore not functional.

Research by seagrass specialists from University Putra Malaya (UPM) hired to monitor and eventually rehabilitate the local seagrass habitat indicated that there did not seem to be any sedimentation impact on Singapore, not only because CGPV was very careful when it came to the transboundary impact of their development, but also because of deeper waters and strong currents between the project site and Merambong Island, as well as between Merambong Island and Singapore. The research showed that the reclamation has had little impact on Merambong Island's fauna and flora thus far, because of these channels. This then means that there will be little subsequent impact on Singapore.

On the other hand, the presence of the CG Causeway had direct impact on the Tg Kupang seagrass meadow. Not only did it effectively smother 3.96 hectares of seagrass beneath it (Forest City DEIA, pp. 5–16), the reclamation left a "thick glutinous [layer of] silt, often many centimetres deep" on the northern half of the remaining seagrass meadow. Coupled with increased suspended solids in the water, the anoxic nature of the settled silt resulted in localized losses of fauna and seagrass death (Sidik, Harah, and Arshad 2014). Dr Leena Wong of UPM reported that the positioning of the silt curtains made a difference, and that relocating them could improve conditions on the seagrass bed.[18] However, they would have to be properly installed (unrolled) and maintained in order to be effective.

The placement of both the CG Causeway and the silt curtains have led to the fishermen having to take a long detour around the project site instead of hugging the coast to get to their usual fishing sites. This has added to their fuel costs as accounted for in the DEIA report. In addition, because of construction in their regular fishing grounds, including the complete reclamation over some of their most prolific prawn-catching locations, they have had to find alternative fishing locations. To make up for decreasing catches, fishermen are not only going out more often than they used to but they are also diversifying in terms of target species and fishing methods. Fishermen who only used to fish for high-value species such as pomfret and prawns now supplement their incomes with crab fishing for which incomes are comparatively stable.[19] While this is understandable given the desperation that subsistence fishermen are driven to, it adds pressure to already limited and decreasing resources.

The DEIA describes the use of a perimeter bund to contain reclamation fill material. UPM's Dr Leena Wong noted that this bund was made of sand; and that the sand from the bund itself could also be washed off in the tides or a storm, resulting in further sedimentation and negative habitat impacts.[20] Norashekin Baharin, Kelab Alami's scientific officer and resident mangrove expert noted that the accumulation of silt and clay sediments resulting from the reclamation could transform the seagrass meadow into a mudflat and change the texture and substrate of the natural shoreline.[21]

The key factor behind this is water hydrology. Long-term satellite mapping of the Tg Kupang seagrass meadow shows that the presence of the CG Causeway has had a visible impact on the habitat (Misbari and Hashim 2015). While changes in meadow composition have occurred since the expansion of PTP in 2003, drastic one were clearly seen in 2014 only after reclamation began. The study showed that the meadow which comprised mostly seagrass, transformed into a largely macroalgae and mud area, with the seagrass reduced to mere patches. Kelab Alami photo documentation corroborates this and shows that areas with minimal water movement (such as the northern half of the Tg Kupang seagrass meadow) are overgrown with macroalgae (*Ulva* sp.,[22] *Gracillaria fisherii* and *Amphiroa fragilissima* (Sidik, Harah, and Arshad 2014)) which adds further stress to the seagrass ecosystem and has resulted in low levels of oxygen. Dr Wong confirmed that the reduction in water flow has led to the death of most filter feeders such as sponges, tunicates and anemones. In their place is an increase of snails and clams; species usually found in mangroves.

The overabundance of macroalgae is detrimental to fishermen's gillnets, with some having to be destroyed; this results in additional replacement costs to the fishermen of between RM500 and RM2,000 (S$160–S$640). Local fishermen, especially those who depend on gleaning in the seagrass meadow report smaller numbers of dog conch. While this fisheries species are known to be seasonal, they have also been reported to move to deeper waters when stressed (i.e., when water quality deteriorates) (Che Cob et al. 2014, pp. 503–11). Easy access to the seagrass meadow at low tide through the construction entrance to the CG Causeway from the J4 trunk road has also resulted in greater numbers of local folk as well as the construction site workers collecting food. This has resulted in clearly unsustainable harvesting of local resources such as pen shells, dog conch and sea cucumbers.[23]

Increased turbidity from dredging and reclamation work is directly linked to a reduction in fish stocks. The DEIA (pp. 5–16) report states that the total dredging area for the project will be 259.42 hectares. This will have a direct impact on coastal mudflats that serve as a key source of food for fisheries species and fish stocks, which is further compounded by input from runoff and direct discharge of wastes from land to the estuary (Sidik, Harah, and Arshad 2014). Fishermen reported that after new dredging or reclamation work began, there has been a spike in prawn catch around the dredged area. However, this only lasted for a short period as large numbers of fishermen then descended on the vicinity to earn the most that they possibly could. Conversely, crab numbers have decreased with reclamation and dredging, even after seasonal variations are taken into consideration.[24]

The World Wildlife Fund (WWF) Malaysia reported that the productivity of fishermen on the west coast of Peninsular Malaysia has been in decline since 2000. While landings figures may have increased in some locations, this is due to increased effort to land a catch (such as fishermen heading out to sea more often than usual), resulting in overfishing and unsustainable resource exploitation (WWF Malaysia 2013). This assessment can be seen in Mukim Tg Kupang.

The UPM team maintains that the CG Causeway needs to be removed to allow the sediment to be washed away naturally by the currents; this has also been stated in the DEIA. Thus far, the 2.25-km CG Causeway has been narrowed and shortened, but not yet completely removed (Misbari and Hashim 2015). Dr Vincent Woon of CGPV stated that the complete removal of the causeway will be completed by March 2017.[25] At the time of publication, the CG Causeway still remains. Sand that is removed from the causeway is meant to be transferred for use on the new islands, but reports by fishermen and Kelab Alami documentation have shown contractors pushing the sand back out to sea so that it is not visible at low tide, instead of transferring it onto trucks. The CGPV management was apparently unaware of this practice by their sub-contractors.[26] This deceptive displacement of sand added to the problems of the local fishermen as it created many new shallow areas around the project site. Several fishermen unaware of the changes in depth or travelling at night have been caught and grounded on these barely visible shallows, resulting in costly boat and propeller damage.

Dr Leena Wong reported that given even the minimal shortening of the causeway that has been done to date, noticeable changes are evident on the northern half of the Tg Kupang seagrass meadow. Their last monitoring visit in December 2016 revealed clearer waters, less macroalgae and some visible increase in fauna.[27] CGPV has repeatedly expressed their intention to support the replanting of seagrass and replenishment of fisheries species once the causeway is removed.

The DEIA report stated that while coastal mangroves might suffer from erosion due to hydrological changes in the area, they would not be affected by sedimentation. The report claims that the presence of larger reclaimed landmasses will in fact stabilize the mangrove habitats and that no mitigating measures are required (Forest City DEIA, pp. 13–122).

On the contrary, Kelab Alami's Scientific Officer Norashekin Baharin notes that slower currents or less water movements do not bode well for mangrove forests as the influx of silt and clay affects both mudflat and mangrove benthos (animals that live in the substrate), as well as destroy mangrove roots.[28] Of greater concern is the clearing of coastal mangroves that has taken place in Kg Pok to allow for the new Forest City dispersal link, as well as the still ongoing clearing of mangroves in the Shahbandar area (between Kg Pekajang and Kg Tiram Duku) to create factory space for the prefabricated panels for infrastructure in Forest City.[29] It has also been mentioned that a substantial plot of RAMSAR mangroves has been excised for use by Forest City for a golf course. Managed by a separate subsidiary of Country Garden, there is little awareness and/or publicity about the habitat damage and possible environmental repercussions in this area.[30]

Evaluating Forest City's Environmental Practices

The language on the CGPV website leans more towards green marketing than environmental substance. Some of its habitat information is clearly incorrect. That said, however, there seems to be substantial effort behind the scenes to look into the application of green technology wherever possible. CGPV also constantly seeks the advice of UPM scientists and DHI Malaysia, their environment-modelling consultants, in planning their next steps.

The biggest obstacle that CGPV might face is a lack of understanding of conditions on the ground because work is entrusted to contractors who might not necessarily convey the right information and/or who might choose to cut corners. This has already been seen in contractor reports of successful silt curtain implementation when fishermen's reports and Kelab Alami documentation indicate otherwise. UPM researchers have also reported that the CGPV management might insist that the buffer zone between their development and the environmentally sensitive areas is 300 m but they are not aware that the actual buffer zone on the ground is barely 100 m. Again, this contradicts reports by their contractors.[31] The DEIA Report and Dr Woon stated that sand for the reclamation is sourced from Teluk Ramunia, but unverified reports from the village claim that sand from local hills is also being used at the project site. This then increases the negative environmental impact on the community with hill-razing for sand leading to floods and inland erosion.

While CGPV has the support of very qualified seagrass scientists, there seems to be a lack of authentic mangrove expertise in their midst. Representatives from their project site have previously asked Kelab Alami for advice on mangrove transplanting. Their questions indicated a clear lack of understanding of the mangrove habitat and its sensitivities.[32] It is unclear whether the Sasaki masterplan can be achieved if an expert on such matters is not engaged.

Also unexplored are the implications of a dense population on four small islands. While the DEIA report lists its future sources of water and plans for sewage treatment, as well as local authorities' confirmation of sufficient water supplies, the reliability of these declarations is in doubt. Local residents in the area already face regular unannounced water shortages and Johor is known for its water scarcity. There is a credible fear that water will be diverted from the local villages to serve the needs of luxury property owners. With doubts over quality standards in a Chinese development and the very real matter of land settlement, it is possible that sewage pipes will be damaged, thereafter leading to contamination of the surrounding areas. These issues and the measures taken to alleviate them do not seem to be thoroughly examined.

It is plausible that the habitats around Forest City will be able to recover once development is completed. That the completely smothered Tg Adang seagrass meadow managed to recover after the port expansion is an indication of the ability of the natural environment to survive stresses that are not sustained. However, the Forest City Project will take thirty years to complete. Scientists have expressed worries over whether an ecosystem can withstand such a prolonged period of stress. Add to that the stress of other long-term projects in the immediate vicinity such as the Tanjung Piai Maritime Industrial Park by Benelac Holdings Berhad, the Tanjung Agas Oil and Gas Maritime Industrial Park within the Pulai River, the Port of Tanjung Pelepas planned expansion, Singapore's mega-port development in Tuas and the Sunway Iskandar project around the Pendas River, and the impact on the seagrass meadows and coastal mangroves in the Tebrau Straits will be heavy indeed.

CONCLUSION

The Forest City project is one of many initiatives intended to improve Johor's economic standing and increase contributions to its coffers. However, in calculating the costs and benefits of this development, some parameters were excluded. As a result, the financial valuation may be inaccurate. The economic viability of this project is compounded by complications that arose from foreign exchange restrictions in China. After all, the entire design, sales and marketing pitch of the development seems geared towards the Chinese buyer. All this then will have to be transformed into a package that can overcome prevailing negative perceptions of Chinese development safety and quality and appeal to buyers from other parts of Asia and Europe. As it stands, Forest City has limited appeal to the local Malaysian and Singaporean buyer.

The environmental sustainability of the project can only be possible if enough mitigating measures are taken—especially the complete removal of the CG Causeway and the maintenance of the buffers between the artificial islands and natural habitats as stipulated in the DEIA report. The different departments and entities within CGPV also need to work more closely to ensure that all those involved in the development are on the same page. If a mutual understanding of the importance of preserving the environment—for whatever reason—is not achieved across the developer's staff hierarchy and between its divisions, it will be very difficult for the lofty standards that it has set for itself through its marketing and publicity material to be met.

Authentic environmental awareness and action by a developer is difficult to achieve but the value of that authenticity is priceless. Should CGPV be able to attain this, there is a possibility that the project's economic and environmental sustainability can be achieved.

Notes

1. This chapter was previously published as *Johor's Forest City Faces Critical Challenges*, Trends in Southeast Asia, no. 3/2017 (Singapore: ISEAS – Yusof Ishak Institute, 2017).
2. www.mysgprop.com/forest-city-country-garden-johor/ (accessed 13 January 2017).
3. Interview with Vincent Woon, CGPV Strategy Manager 14 December 2016.
4. Personal communication with Bo Wang, a New York-based Chinese artist and filmmaker who was Artist-in-Residence at the Nanyang Technological University, Singapore, 4 October 2016.
5. Interview with Vincent Woon, CGPV Strategy Manager, 11 January 2017.
6. Interviews with former advisors to Forest City who declined to be named, 14 December 2016.
7. Personal communication with Nick Allen (MIT researcher), 6 June 2016.
8. Personal communication with Bo Wang (NTU Artist in Residence), 4 October 2016.
9. Talk by Loong Chee Wei on PRC Investment in the Real Estate and Construction Sectors in Malaysia at the ISEAS – Yusof Ishak Institute on 20 March 2017.
10. Personal communication with Ernest Goh, Resident of Leisurefarm Resort currently engaged in discussions with property agents and potential buyers of his landed property, 2 March 2017.

11. Personal communication with an employee of the contractor who declined to be named, 7 January 2017.
12. Personal communication with a former employee of the food outlet who declined to be named, 2 April 2017.
13. Interview with former development consultant who declined to be named, 14 December 2016.
14. Kelab Alami photo documentation.
15. Personal observation, CGPV stakeholder engagement, 1 October 2014.
16. Interviews with former advisors to Forest City who declined to be named, 14 December 2016.
17. Interview with Vincent Woon, CGPV Strategy Manager, 14 December 2016.
18. Interview with Dr Leena Wong, University Putra Malaysia, 21 December 2016.
19. Personal observation/interviews from fieldwork, 2008–17.
20. Interview with Dr Leena Wong, University Putra Malaysia, 21 December 2016.
21. Interview with Norashekin Kamal Baharin, Kelab Alami Scientific Officer, 21 December 2016.
22. Kelab Alami photo documentation.
23. Personal observation, fieldwork 2008–17.
24. Interviews with fishermen/personal observation, fieldwork 2008–17.
25. Interview with Vincent Woon, CGPV Strategy Manager, 14 December 2016.
26. Interview with Dr Leena Wong, University Putra Malaysia, 21 December 2016.
27. Ibid.
28. Interview with Norashekin Kamal Baharin, Kelab Alami Scientific Officer, 21 December 2016.
29. Kelab Alami photo documentation.
30. Personal communication with several staff of different local government agencies who declined to be named. Interviews between December 2016 and February 2017.
31. Interview with Dr Leena Wong, University Putra Malaysia, 21 December 2016.
32. Interview with Norashekin Kamal Baharin, Kelab Alami Scientific Officer, 21 December 2016.

References

Béné, Christophe. 2006. "Small-Scale Fisheries: Assessing Their Contribution to Rural Livelihoods in Developing Countries". Circular No. 1008. Rome: Food and Agriculture Organisation of the United Nations.

Che Cob, Zaidi, Aziz Arshad, Japar Sidik Bujang, and Mazlan Abd Ghaffar. 2014. "Spatial and Temporal Variations in *Strombus canarium* (Gastropoda: Stromidae) Abundance at Merambong Seagrass Bed, Malaysia". *Sains Malaysiana* 43, no. 4: 503–11.

City Lab. 2016. "Is China Building a Ghost City on Malaysian Islands?". 30 December 2016. http://www.citylab.com/housing/2016/12/is-china-building-a-ghost-city-abroad/511757/

Country Garden Pacific View Sdn. Bhd. 2014. *Detailed Environmental Impact Assessment for the Proposed Forest City Reclamation and Mixed Developments*. Kuala Lumpur: Dr Nik and Associates Sdn Bhd.

———. 2017. Official Website. 13 January 2017. https://cgpvforestcity.wordpress.com/about/

Democratic Action Party. 2014. "Disagreement with the Proposed Forest City Project". Media statement, 22 September 2014. https://dapmalaysia.org/statements/2014/09/22/19174/

Department of Irrigation and Drainage Malaysia. 1997. "Guidelines on Erosion Control for Development Projects in the Coastal Zone 1/97". http://extwprlegs1.fao.org/docs/pdf/mal33709.pdf

Edge, The. 2104. "Johor Residents Object to Forest City at Dialogue". 22 September 2014. http://www.theedgeproperty.com.my/content/johor-residents-object-forest-city-dialogue

———. 2016a. "Property Snapshot 3: What Are Prices Like in Johor Bahru?". 3 February 2016. https://www.edgeprop.my/content/property-snapshot-3-what-are-prices-johor-bahru

———. 2016b. "Country Garden's Big Sell". 16 February 2016. http://www.theedgeproperty.com.sg/content/country-garden%E2%80%99s-big-sell

Iskandar Malaysia. 2016. "Iskandar Malaysia and UKTI sign MOU to Promote Collaboration on Smartcity Initiatives". Media Release, 15 March 2016. http://iskandarmalaysia.com.my/iskandar-malaysia-ukti-sign-mou-promote-collaboration-smartcity-initiatives/

Iskandar Regional Development Authority. 2008. "Iskandar Malaysia Flagship C: Important Facts and Details on the Western Gate Development". http://www.worldwidepropertyinvestment.com/uploads/1/1/0/2/11028993/flagship-c-en.pdf

———. 2011. "Shoreline Management Plan: Blueprint for Iskandar Malaysia".

Khor Yu Leng, and Vasiliki Mavroeidi. 2014. "Iskandar Malaysia Labours to Develop". *ISEAS Perspective*, no. 2014/58/, 4 November 2014.

KiniBiz Online. 2013. "The Sprawling Empire of Syed Mokhtar Albukhary". 12 November 2013. http://www.kinibiz.com/story/issues/58876/the-sprawling-empire-of-syed-mokhtar-albukhary.html

Malaysiakini. 2014a. "Johor Sultan 'Initiated' Forest City Mega Project". 19 March 2014. http://www.malaysiakini.com/news/292541

———. 2014b. "The Case of Forest City and the Johor Sultan". 14 July 2014. http://www.malaysiakini.com/news/268649

———. 2014c. "Of Reclamation, Sand And The Royal Company". 18 July 2014. http://www.malaysiakini.com/news/268962

Ministry of Foreign Affairs, Singapore. 2014. Transcript of Senior Minister of State for Foreign Affairs Masagos Zulkifli's reply to Parliamentary Questions, 9 July 2014. https://www.mfa.gov.sg/content/mfa/media_centre/press_room/pr/2014/201407/press_20140709.html

Misbari, Syarifuddin, and Mazlan Hashim, 2015. "Temporal and Spatial Dynamics of Submerged Seagrass at Merambong, Johor using Landsat Data". Paper presented at the 36th Asian Association on Remote Sensing, Quezon City, Metro Manila, 24–28 October 2015.

Mysgprop. 3 January 2019, <www.mysgprop.com/forest-city-country-garden-johor/>.

New Straits Times. 2015. "It Will Be Insane to Tell Investors Not to Come to Johor". 22 March 2015. http://www.nst.com.my/news/2015/09/%E2%80%98it-will-be-insane-tell-investors-not-come-johor%E2%80%99

New York Times. 2015. "Beware of China's Safety Record". 26 November 2015. https://www.nytimes.com/2015/11/26/opinion/beware-of-chinas-safety-record.html?_r=0

Norshahril Saat. 2017. *Johor Remains the Bastion of Kaum Tua*. Trends in Southeast Asia, no. 1/2017. Singapore: ISEAS – Yusof Ishak Institute.

Sidik, B. Japar, Z. Muta Harah, and A. Arshad, 2014. "Seagrass Shoals of Sungai Pulai Estuary, Johor". *Malaysian Nature Journal* 66, no. 1 and 2: 1–19.

South China Morning Post. 2017. "How China's Overseas Property Dream Turned Into a Nightmare". 26 March 2017. http://www.scmp.com/news/china/policies-politics/article/2080433/how-chinas-overseas-property-dream-turned-nightmare

Star, The. 2014. "New Foundation Set Up to Care for Fishermen". 13 October 2014. http://www.thestar.com.my/news/community/2014/10/13/help-for-fishermen-new-foundation-set-up-to-care-for-fishermen/

———. 2015a. "Sultan of Johor Speaks His Mind". 18 March 2015. http://www.thestar.com.my/news/nation/2015/03/18/sultan-of-johor-speaks-his-mind-ruler-gives-a-special-no-holds-barred-interview-on-a-wide-range-of-t/

———. 2015b. "Sultan Ibrahim Also Wants a Balanced Development Where the People Will Benefit". 19 March 2015. http://www.thestar.com.my/news/nation/2015/03/19/ruler-is-strict-when-conferring-awards/

———. 2016a. "Make JB the Second Biggest City". 23 March 2016. http://www.thestar.com.my/news/nation/2016/03/23/make-jb-the-second-biggest-city-johor-ruler-strategic-location-a-prime-catalyst-for-realising-its-fu/

———. 2016b. "Forest City Has Great Potential". 7 December 2016. http://www.thestar.com.my/news/nation/2016/12/07/forest-city-has-great-potential-najib-mega-project-has-already-attracted-investments-worth-rm10bil/

———. 2017. "Johor Ruler Slams Dr M Over Chinese Investment Comments". 16 January 2017. http://www.thestar.com.my/news/nation/2017/01/16/political-spin-angers-sultan-johor-ruler-slams-dr-m-over-chinese-investment-comments/

Straits Times. 2015a. "Johor's Forest City Could House up to 700,000: Developer". 13 May 2015. http://www.straitstimes.com/business/johors-forest-city-could-house-up-to-700000-developer

———. 2015b. "5 Reasons to Be Careful When Buying Property in Johor and Iskandar". 14 May 2015. http://www.straitstimes.com/business/5-reasons-to-be-careful-when-buying-residential-property-in-johor-and-iskandar

———. 2017. "Forest City Project Can Turn Johor Into Next Dubai: Najib". 21 January 2017. http://www.straitstimes.com/asia/se-asia/forest-city-project-can-turn-johor-into-next-dubai-najib

Today Online. 2016. "This S$143b Chinese-Made City in Johor 'Scares the Hell out of Everybody'". 22 November 2016. http://www.todayonline.com/business/chinese-property-investors-gamble-s143b-jb-be-next-shenzhen

———. 2017. "Forest City's Chinese Buyers in Limbo Over Developer's Penalty Claims". 3 April 2017. http://www.todayonline.com/singapore/penalty-clause-adds-to-woes-of-forest-city-chinese-buyers

Wall Street Journal. 2016. "Ambitious Chinese Developers Plan Cities Abroad from Ground Up". 1 March 2016. https://www.wsj.com/articles/ambitious-chinese-developers-plan-cities-abroad-from-ground-up-1456815602

Williams, Joseph Marcel R. 2016. "Evaluating the Diverse Impacts of Megaprojects: The Case of Forest City in Johor, Malaysia". Masters dissertation, Department of Urban Studies and Planning. https://dspace.mit.edu/handle/1721.1/105036

World Wildlife Fund Malaysia. 2013. "An Assessment of Fisheries and Marine Ecosystem in Peninsular Malaysia".

18

THE STRUGGLE FOR BALANCE
Johor's Environmental Issues, Overlaps and Future

Serina Rahman

INTRODUCTION

Johor has a multitude of natural treasures within its boundaries. The only state in Peninsular Malaysia that has a coastline on three sides of about 400 km, it faces the South China Sea in the east, the Melaka Strait in the west and the Tebrau Strait in the south. Johor's marine habitats run the gamut of intertidal mud flats to white-sand beaches and coral-fringed islands. Seagrass meadows and mangrove forests that host large megafauna such as dugongs and turtles can be found all along its shoreline. Within these marine borders, Johor's terrestrial habitats comprise peatlands, forests, hills and mountains, of which 12.4 per cent are protected as national parks or wildlife and forest reserves (UPEN Johor 2017, p. 3). These landscapes are host to myriad endangered and endemic species, including the Malayan tiger, Asian elephant and Malayan tapir.

Gunung Ledang (also known as Mount Ophir) is Johor's highest point at 1,276 metres and is the source for thirteen rivers and a key water catchment area for both Johor and neighbouring Melaka. Johor's ten main river basins are the mainstay of the state's water security as 97 per cent of its raw water supplies come from surface water sources. The Johor River alone provides 60 per cent of the state's water supply.

These natural habitats and features are not the only components to be considered in a discussion of Johor's environment. In studying Johor's environmental policies, other issues that need to be explored include: matters of energy sources and use; carbon creation and sequestration; environmental and carrying capacities; traffic congestion and urbanization impacts; land-use; pollution; resource optimization; waste management; and air quality (IRDA 2014). Technologies or infrastructural innovations that mitigate development impacts or enhance sustainability should also be considered (UPEN Johor 2017, p. 52).

This chapter discusses the main environmental issues faced by Johor and the action taken to mitigate some of the problems. It also examines the policies that govern environmental management and action in Johor, as well as complications that arise from overlapping legislation and jurisdictions at the federal level, and its effects, if any, on Singapore and the Riau Archipelago. The chapter also briefly discusses environmental decision-making under the past and current state government and ends with a look forward in terms of Johor's efforts for the environment and sustainability.

JOHOR'S ENVIRONMENTAL ISSUES

While Johor has bountiful natural resources and assets, protecting and preserving them has been difficult. The state faces a number of issues that threaten myriad habitats and natural areas. Many of the problems arise as a result of the unbridled development that contributed to the state's recent economic growth spurt and success. Johor is slowly but surely working towards a sustainable balance between economic gain and environmental preservation but the journey is long and littered with obstacles.

Water is a limited and highly sought-after resource all over the world, but it seems to be even more so in this southernmost state, where a portion of its resources are consigned in an agreement to supply Singapore with raw water from the Linggiu Reservoir and the Johor River.[1] Water shortages have occurred more frequently over recent years in Johor, at times caused by drought (*The Star Online*, 16 May 2016), at other times caused by source river pollution (Kili 2017). Water rationing for Johor residents can occur during dry spells (*Channel NewsAsia*, 13 March 2019) or as a result of large development projects (Pau 2013) or oil palm plantations (*New Straits Times*, 12 August 2014).

Johor's water scarcity issues comes about notwithstanding its average annual rainfall of 1,778 mm per year (Jackson and Domondon 2016, p. 3), and regular incidences of flash flooding (*Channel NewsAsia*, 12 December 2018) due to heavy rains coinciding with a high tide. These problems are amplified by logging and loss of forest lands (Butler 2015) or due to the quarrying of earth for reclamation projects (Rahman 2017, p. 36). Johor has the highest number of golf courses in Malaysia (Shah 2017), which are popular tourism assets known to deplete water resources and add to chemical run-off (Adler 2007).

Reclamation is another environmentally sensitive issue in Johor. There has been extensive coverage of large-scale reclamation projects along Johor's coastline. These include (but are not limited to) the Forest City mixed development (Rahman 2017,

p. 21), the Pengerang Integrated Petroleum Complex (PIPC) (Rahman 2018, p. 31) and the Tanjung Piai Maritime Industrial Park.[2] While reclamation results in high-value coastal or island properties that can generate good economic outcomes for the state, it comes at a high cost. Not only are valuable fishing grounds and marine ecosystems smothered by these new lands, but coastal mangroves are often also cleared in the development process.

Figure 18.1 projects the future of the western Tebrau Strait (within twenty to thirty years) when ongoing development is complete. The Pulai River estuary within which these developments are planned are the traditional fishing grounds of artisanal fishermen from Mukim Tanjung Kupang, Pontian, the Pulai River and Danga Bay. There is also word of new reclamation projects planned within the narrowest parts of the Tebrau Strait, between the northern tip of Puteri Harbour to Danga Bay.[3] Once the planned developments are complete, the original meeting point of the Tebrau and Melaka Straits, as well as the Pulai River estuary will be

FIGURE 18.1
Projected Developments in the Western End of the Tebrau Strait (by 2045)

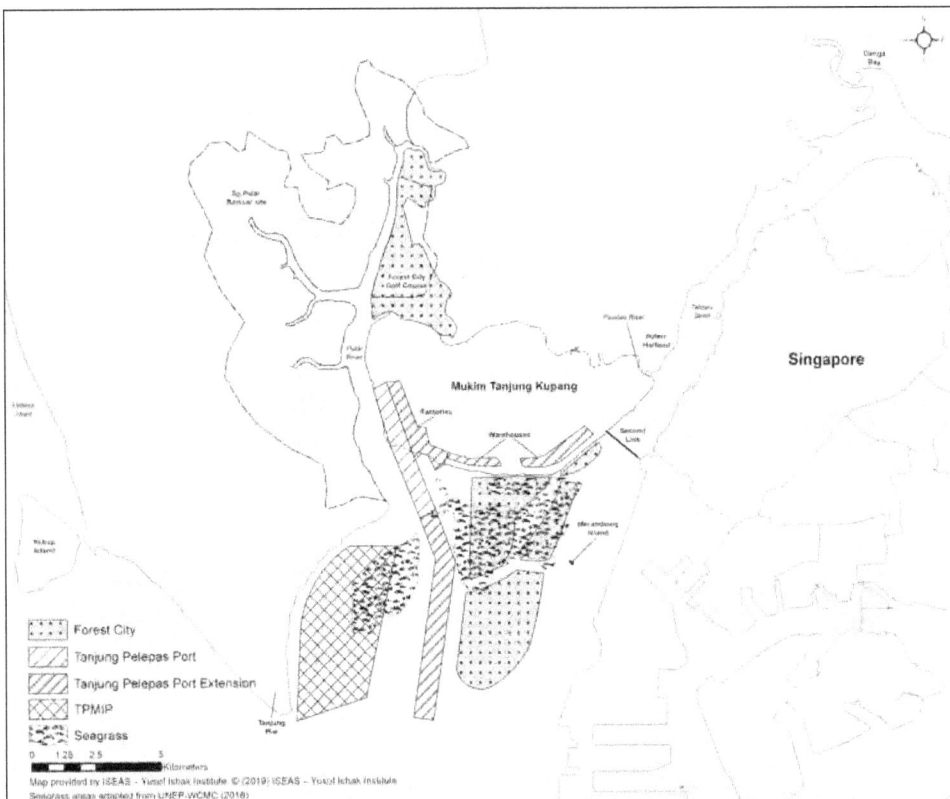

Note: This map is not to scale, and is estimated based on individual development projections collated from corporate publicity material and presentations. Seagrass meadows shown here are based on areas mapped in 2003; some have already been lost to reclamation.

reduced to narrow channels between the new plots of land. Fishing will no longer be a viable endeavour.

Given the fluidity of coastal waters, habitats adjacent to reclamation project sites are also negatively affected by sedimentation that travels with the tides. Source areas for the sand used in these reclamation projects are also severely affected when sand is dredged and removed. Not only do fishermen lose livelihoods at both ends of the process, but erosion at the source location can occur as land is literally taken away from under their feet. Dredging for sand in Johor is known to occur in Teluk Ramunia (Rahman 2017, p. 36), Parit Jawa, Muar (Chua 2017) and the Linggiu and Sayong Rivers (*Today Online*, 14 March 2019), with dire consequences to those who depend on the area to survive.

With global fisheries resources already under great pressure from climate change, rising temperatures, extreme weather phenomenon and changes in water currents, added pressure comes from reduced water quality from coastal development, industrial waste and agricultural run-off, as well as habitat destruction. This damage can negatively affect a number of key marine species that exist in Johor waters such as the dugong, green and hawksbill turtles, three species of seahorses and countless marine fisheries species. At times, there is a complete loss of traditional fishing grounds, severely affecting coastal communities. As the fisheries sector in Johor supports some of its poorest communities, continued environmental degradation has severe socio-economic impacts beyond just natural asset and resource loss.

Waste and its disposal is a constant issue for Johor. Most recently, toxic waste dumped into the Kim Kim River in Pasir Gudang, Johor led to the closure of all schools in the vicinity and resulted in more than 500 ill and several in the intensive care unit, including emergency services personnel; all affected by methane fumes from the dumpsite (*New Straits Times*, 13 March 2019). While industrial and factory wastes have on several occasions in the past had detrimental effects, including the temporary shut-down of water supplies (Kannan 2018), illegal plastic recycling plants have also been an issue (Chan 2019). The incident at the Kim Kim River was the result of illegal dumping by a tyre recycling company.

Much has already been written on pollution and waste issues in the Johor Bahru city centre, where the Segget River revitalization project is an effort to clean up the city's main artery.[4] But observations of traditional villages indicate that sewage treatment and waste collection are serious and widespread problems on the rural outskirts. With no municipal entity collecting waste, rubbish is often dumped into streams and rivers or burnt in the open. Household greywater and wastes from food stalls and restaurants also flow straight into streams and rivers. Sewage is often stored in a septic tank next to homes (if this facility is built when the house is raised), but there is no tank clearing or treatment carried out. The content is just left to settle and "clear" liquids overflow into nearby drains and streams, possibly contaminating water tables as well.[5]

Land use and conversion in Johor generates substantial income for the state economy, but can also have dire consequences on the environment. Figure 18.2 depicts the current land use in Johor. The map illustrates how developed areas are

FIGURE 18.2
Current Land Use in Johor

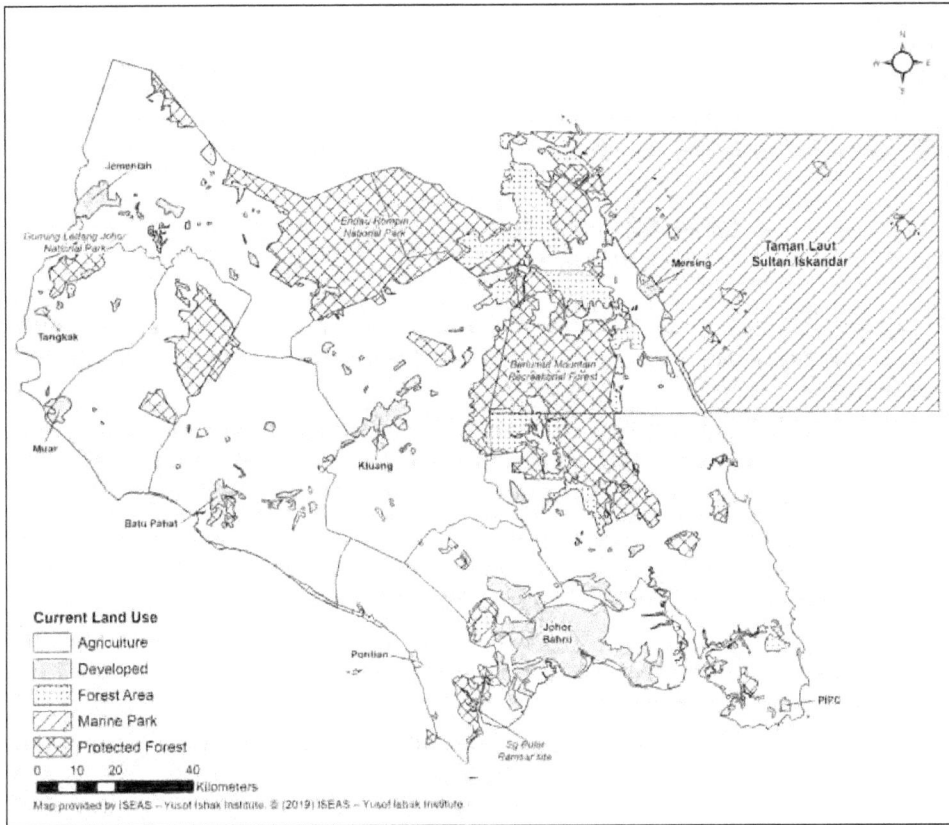

Source: Adapted from the Majlis Perbandaran Batu Pahat (Batu Pahat City Council) website: http://www.mpbp.gov. my/sites/default/files/draf_rsnj_2030.pdf and the GeoJohor website (Draf Gambarajah Utama Rancangan Struktur Negeri Johor 2030): http://geoportal.johor.gov.my/petaawam/rsnj2030

largely concentrated in the south, with agricultural land making up the main form of land use in the state.

Industrial waste issues have already been discussed, as have the problems of agricultural pesticide and other chemical run-off into waterways (especially from oil palm plantations). Oil palm plantations can also deplete water resources and drain adjacent peat swamps, which are also vital ecosystems. Johor has been known to be a source of haze when drained peat swamps catch fire, either by accident or intentionally (Zakaria 2016). This adds to any other air pollution issues that arise from industrialization. The clearing and logging of forest, mangrove and peat swamps in Johor can severely impact its megafauna population, known to include species such as the Malayan tiger, rare spotted leopard, barking and sambar deer and the Asian elephant.

Johor has seven oil- and gas-related facilities (including the PIPC) and two main ports (Johor Port in Pasir Gudang and the Port of Tanjung Pelepas in Mukim Tanjung Kupang), as well as several ferry terminals and numerous fishing and recreational boat harbours. Economic growth has also increased vessel traffic around Johor's extensive coast, resulting in a number of vessel, port and construction related accidents. These incidents can have severe environmental impacts and negatively affect coastal community livelihoods.[6]

EFFORTS TO MITIGATE NEGATIVE ENVIRONMENTAL IMPACTS

While Johor has numerous environmental issues, the state has taken steps to mitigate damage and find a balance between economic growth and long-term environmental sustainability.

The Johor National Park Corporation (JNPC) was established in 1989 to develop, manage and supervise national parks in Johor. These include Endau Rompin, Gunung Ledang and the internationally recognized Ramsar wetlands sites of Tanjung Piai, Kukup Island and the Pulai River. Today JNPC also helps to market and promote these sites as well as the recently established Sultan Iskandar Marine Park which is under the purview of the federal Department of Marine Parks Malaysia (DMPM) which has been moved to the Ministry of Agriculture and Agro-based Industry under the new Pakatan Harapan (PH) government.[7] While Johor state does not have an environmental office of its own, there is an officer assigned specifically to environmental matters within the State Economic Planning Unit (UPEN Johor); an indication of the issue's importance to the state government.

Johor's royal house has taken steps to demonstrate its commitment to environmental preservation in a number of ways, including the launch of the Sultan Iskandar Marine Park, within which there are dugongs, a highly endangered and charismatic marine mammal, healthy coral reefs and vital seagrass meadows (*Malay Mail*, 7 August 2017). Sultan Ibrahim Iskandar has also announced his desire to see the Malaysian Nature Society take an active role in wildlife and forest preservation in the state (*The Star Online*, 24 January 2019). Johor is one of the few states in Malaysia that has banned all commercial hunting (Big Cat Rescue 2018).

Johor's efforts in preserving the environment came to the forefront recently when it was revealed that Kukup Island had been converted to Sultanate Land without consultation with local stakeholders (*Today Online*, 11 December 2018). The island is the world's second largest uninhabited mangrove island and is recognized as a Ramsar wetlands area of international importance under the United Nations' Convention on Wetlands. Managed by JNPC since 2003, its status as a state park was revoked and its redesignation as Sultanate Land was published in October 2018. Following the online and civil society furore in response to the announcement, the Crown Prince assured the public that the Sultan's intention was merely to ensure that it is better protected (Tan 2018). The Sultan published a letter that reinforced this point and stated his intention for the island to remain under JNPC management (Tay 2018) and thereafter it was reported that the island has now regained its national park status (*Free Malaysia Today*, 13 December 2018). Not long after that incident, the Sultan demonstrated his commitment to forest preservation by announcing that he had instructed the state government to stop issuing logging quotas in 2014, and that he too had surrendered his quota at the time (*Malaysiakini*, 20 February 2019).

Of late, the Johor government has taken steps to ensure that potentially dangerous industries are not allowed to set up business in the state (Hammim 2019), and a relatively new effort spearheaded by the Johor's Tunku Temenggong (second prince) will process waste water in the state (Othman 2017). The Iskandar Regional Development Authority (IRDA), which supports investments and development within the Iskandar Malaysia economic corridor (IM) also has a slew of incentives to support green technology and low-carbon initiatives by investors and industries.

IRDA has a range of environmental initiatives that have shown considerable success. This includes its Partnership for Interdisciplinary Studies for Shoreline Ecosystems (PESISIR) programme, its Low Carbon Society initiatives which were showcased at the 23rd Conference of Parties (COP23) in Bonn, Germany and its United Nations University (UNU) Regional Centre of Excellence (RCE Iskandar) that focuses on advocating education for sustainable development, especially in terms of a low carbon society. IRDA's support for community cooperative efforts in low-impact tourism (through the Friends of Iskandar Malaysia programme (KIM)) has also driven efforts to protect natural areas on the basis of their importance to local livelihoods and economies.

POLICIES AND PLANS THAT GOVERN ENVIRONMENTAL MANAGEMENT

While there are both environmental problems and efforts to resolve them, there are also a number of grey areas and overlapping jurisdictions and roles that compound the issues at hand. This section illustrates some of these complications and provides examples of predicaments that have arisen as a result of the lack of clarity.

The power to govern environmental matters in Malaysia rests largely at the federal level, but there are several caveats that allow the state to have the last word, as the following sections will illustrate. With a new government in place since the 2018 elections, environmental matters have been reorganized into two federal ministries, with the Department of Marine Parks Malaysia moved to the Ministry of Agriculture and Agro-based Industry.[8] Figure 18.3 depicts the new arrangements.

Environmental and other related policies for the entire nation are made at this ministerial level, and are expected to be translated into action and implemented at the state level. In practice, however, this execution may not necessarily occur. In spite of the wide-ranging federal legislation available, environmental matters are still sometimes insufficiently regulated. Numerous loopholes exist in the institutional infrastructure for the environment, with one of the factors contributing to this

FIGURE 18.3

Restructuring of Environmental Components in the New Pakatan Harapan Ministries

Ministry of Energy, Science, Technology, Environment and Climate Change (MESTECC)	Ministry of Water, Land and Natural Resources (KATS)	Ministry of Agriculture and Agro - based Industry (MOA)
Ministry of Energy, Green Technology and Water (KeTTHA)	Forestry Department (*Jabatan Perhutanan*)	Fisheries Development Authority of Malaysia (*Jabatan Perikanan M'sia*)
Ministry of Science, Technology and Innovation (MoSTI)	Department of Wildlife and National Parks (*Perhilitan*)	Department of Marine Parks Malaysia (*Jabatan Taman Laut M'sia*)
Department of the Environment (DOE)	All remaining departments under MNRE	
Environmental legislation (formerly under the Ministry of Natural Resources and the Environment (MNRE))		

complication being the State List (Constitution of Malaysia 1957, Ninth Schedule, List II), of which an extract is shown in Table 18.1.

The State List entails exceptions to federal legislation for which the state is able to legislate, govern and rule. Table 18.1 lists the items on the State List which may prevent wholesale enforcement of federal laws and statutes on environmental matters. The exceptions apply to all states in Malaysia except the Federal Territories of Kuala Lumpur, Putrajaya and Labuan.

The most important items to note from the list, and that have the most implications on environmental preservation are: clause numbers 2—all matters related to land; 3—agriculture and forests; and 12—turtles and riparian fishing. The state can also make laws on matters in the Federal List, subject to conditions or restrictions imposed by Parliament (Article 76A, Constitution of Malaysia, 1957). In the event that state laws are inconsistent with federal law, however, the federal law will prevail and the state law will be void (up to the extent of the inconsistency: Article 75, Constitution of Malaysia, 1957). The state can also make laws on any matter that does not fall under the Federal List (Article 77, Constitution of Malaysia, 1957). The Concurrent List details items over which both federal and state authorities can legislate.

In Johor, a number of state departments and organizations have a direct impact on environmental policy, legislation and governance as shown in Appendix 18.1. The table lists some of these entities which may have an influence on environmental management as a result of their scope of work or investment interests. In Johor, some of these responsibilities have been assigned to "corporations" which are created by state enactments, but can be privately or publicly owned. The overarching objectives

TABLE 18.1
Items on the State List That May Affect Wholesale Implementation of Federally Constituted Environmental Laws

Constitution of Malaysia 1957, Ninth Schedule, List II – State List	
List No.	Caveat
2a	Land tenure, registration of titles and deeds relating to land, colonization, land improvement and soil conservation;
2b	Malay reservations or, in the States of Sabah and Sarawak, native reservations;
2c	Permits and licences for prospecting for mines; mining leases and certificates;
2d	Compulsory acquisition of land;
2e	Transfer of land, mortgages, leases and charges in respect of land;
3a	Agriculture and agricultural loans;
3b	Forests
4a	Local administration; municipal corporation; local town and rural board and other local authorities;
4c	Housing and provision for housing accommodation;
5b	Boarding houses and lodging houses;
5c	Burial and cremation grounds;
5d	Pounds and cattle trespass;
5e	Markets and fairs;
6a	Public work for State purposes
6b	Roads, bridges and ferries other than those in Federal List,
6c	Subject to the Federal List, water (including water supplies, rivers and canals); … riparian rights
12	Turtles and riparian fishing
Constitution of Malaysia 1957, Ninth Schedule, List III – Concurrent List	
3	Protection of wild animals and wild birds; National Parks
5	Town and country planning, except in the federal capital
8	Drainage and irrigation
9	Rehabilitation of mining land and land which has suffered soil erosion

Source: Extracted and adapted from the Constitution of Malaysia 1957, Ninth Schedule: Legislative Lists. Downloaded from http://www.commonlii.org/my/legis/const/1957/24.html on 11 Jan 2019.

of these entities may therefore not focus solely on the greater public good as expected of a state or federal government department.

Aside from these state entities, there are also local branches of federal ministries or departments that oversee matters provided for in the Federal List. Not only are there grey areas between federal and state entities, but the above organizations sometimes also overlap each other at the state level. For example, mangrove areas are deemed forests that lie under the state branch of the Forestry Department's jurisdiction, however those that lie within national park boundaries are regulated and managed by the Johor National Parks Corporation (JNPC) (Goh 2016). Catalytic developers and other large organizations like ports also have direct impacts on environmental management and policies within their property boundaries.

The Johor State Executive Committee (ExCo; state assembly members given additional duties as an advisory cabinet) and his or her immediate staff may oversee and influence some aspects of environmental management and policy, even if there are no specific state departments allocated to the area in question. The State ExCo is the highest administrative authority on land administration in Johor, reporting to the State Legislative Assembly and is able to decide on any land matter as long as it does not contravene federal or state laws or policies agreed upon by the National Land Council (Forestry Department/DANCED 1999, p. 5). Appendix 18.2 highlights the various areas given to these committee members at the time of writing. The list indicates that while there is an ExCo member specifically assigned to an environment portfolio, decision-making and implementation of laws and legislation could be affected by overlaps in scope between matters of natural resources and tourism.

OVERLAPPING ROLES AND GREY AREAS

Overlapping roles between federal and state authorities are further illustrated in Table 18.2, which highlights some of the federal and state entities that oversee similar areas. The wide range of fields that that fall under the banner of "the environment" result in many influences on the labyrinth of environmental policy and management.

Added to the tangle that governs the environment in Malaysia are the specific laws, acts and statutes that legislate environmental matters at both state and federal level. In Johor, there are a number of additional policies, frameworks and blueprints that guide environmental matters in Iskandar Malaysia alone. This is shown in Table 18.3.

Tables 18.2 and 18.3 demonstrate the extent of the web that governs environmental matters and how it may be possible to find loopholes to move around environmental regulation. For example, while the Department of the Environment (DOE) is tasked with regulating pollution and has regulations pertaining to land development, there is no state entity that specifically oversees the environment and the DOE serves only as a technical advisor (Goh 2016). Effective implementation of the Environmental Quality Act hence requires good working relations between federal and state agencies (Jamaludin 1996). At the same time, while urban planning is a joint responsibility under the Concurrent List and there is a National Physical Plan that provides a broad land-use planning concept drawn up at the federal level, the final decision pertaining to land matters lies with the local authority and state land office, with no stipulated need to refer to or defer to federal plans or guidelines (Goh 2016).

Sand mining is another area in which overlaps in jurisdiction can compound enforcement on the ground. The seabed and waters beyond the 4.8 km limit to the waters of the continental shelf are under federal jurisdiction, but some permits approved by the state fall within this periphery. State-issued leases for land (including the seabed) under federal jurisdiction are not legally enforceable. However, mining continues given the state approval in hand. These problems may arise as a result of a lack of understanding, coordination and consultation between state and federal departments, coupled with a lack of monitoring and manpower to enforce laws on the ground. Given that sand mining is conducted in a fluid habitat (the sea), the effects of mining sand in one area will have negative impacts on other areas which

TABLE 18.2

Comparison between Federal and State Entities that Govern or Manage the Environment

Federal	State	Others
Ministry of Energy, Science, Technology, Environment and Climate Change(MESTECC) / Department of the Environment (DOE)	Johor Biotechnology and Biodiversity Corporation (JBiotech)	National Biodiversity Committee
Ministry of Water, Land and Natural Resources (KATS)		National Technical Committee on Biological Diversity
Department of Forestry	Johor State Forestry Department (state branch of federal entity)	National Forestry Council
		National Committee on Sustainable Forest Management
		National Mangrove Committee
		Coastal Zone Management Committee
Department of Fisheries	Johor National Parks Corporation	
	Johor Fisheries Department (state branch of federal entity)	
Department of Town & Country Planning	Jabatan Landscape Negeri Johor	National Development Council
	Pejabat Tanah Johor	National Land Council
Ministry of Tourism & Culture / Tourism Malaysia	Johor Tourism	
Department of Wildlife	Jabatan Perhutanan Negeri Johor (state branch of federal entity)	
Dept of Irrigation and Drainage (JPS)	Badan Kawal Selia Air Negeri Johor (BAKAJ)	
	Pejabat Tanah & Galian Johor	
	SAJ Ranhill (water supply GLC)	
Indigenous People's Development Department (JAKOA)		
Ministry of Agriculture and Agro-based Industry	Johor State Department of Agriculture	
Ministry of Rural Development	Johor State Housing Department	
Economic Planning Unit	Unit Perancangan Ekonomi Negeri (UPEN)	National Economic Action Council

Source: Collated and adapted from Management Plan for Mangroves of Johor (Forestry Department/DANCED, 1999); Official website of the Johor state government: https://www.johor.gov.my/

TABLE 18.3

Selected Federal and State Laws and Regional Blueprints that Legislate and Guide Environmental Matters in Johor

Federal	State	Regional
Environmental Legislation		
Environmental Quality (Act 127/1974)	Johor Sustainability Policy (2017–2021)	Environmental Planning Blueprint for Iskandar Malaysia (IRDA)
EQA: EIA order 1987		
EQA gives MOSTE (now MESTECC) power to regulate pollution problems with assistance from state departments		
Street, Drainage and Building Act (Act 133/1974)	Irrigation Areas Ordinance (Ord 31/1953)	Drainage Stormwater Management Blueprint for Iskandar Malaysia (IRDA)
		Renewable Energy and Energy Efficiency Blueprint for Iskandar Malaysia (IRDA)
Natural Resources		
Fisheries Act (Act 317/1985)	Fisheries (Riverine) Rules of 1984	
	Fisheries (Turtle and Turtle Eggs) Rules of 1984	
State rules give power to Federal Department of Fisheries to issue licences and impose conditions to protect and conserve fish and turtles		
National Forestry Act (Act 313/1984)	Forest Enactment, 1984 (En No 58)	
National Park Act (Act 226/1980)	State Park Enactment (1986)	
	National Parks (Johor) Corporation Enactment 1989	

Pesticide Act (Act 149/1974)		
Protection of Wildlife (Act 76/1972)		
Waters Enactment (Chap 146/1920)	Water Enactment, 1926 (Rivers) / Johor En No 66	
Mining Enactment (Chap 147/1929)	Mining Enactment (Chap 147/ Johor En No 58)	
Mineral Development Act (Act 525/1994)		

Land Planning

National Physical Plan		Comprehensive Development Plan II for Iskandar Malaysia (IRDA)
National Land Code (Act 56 & 474/1965)	State Structure Plan 2030	Integrated Land Use Blueprint for Iskandar Malaysia (IRDA)
Town & Country Planning Act (Act 172/1976)	Local Government Act (Act 171/1976)	Johor Tenggara Regional Development Act (KEJORA)
Land Conservation Act, 1960 (state land & mines)	Land Conservation Act (ordinance 3/1960 Johore)	
	Land Acquisition Act (Act 34/1960)	
	The Sultanate Lands Enactment, 1934 (EN. 5/1934)	
	Coastal Resources Management Plan for South Johor (1992)	Shoreline Management Plan Blueprint for Iskandar Malaysia (IRDA)

Source: Collated and adapted from Jamaludin, M.J., 1996; Iskandar Malaysia website: iskandarmalaysia.com.my; Management Plan for Mangroves of Johor (Forestry Department/ DANCED, 1999); The Coastal Environmental Profile of South Johor, Malaysia (ASEAN, 1991).

may not be within the state jurisdiction and contravene environmental quality regulations (ASEAN 1991).

Even as KATS may have national regulations and responsibility for the development of mineral resources, marine and estuarine habitats and water supplies, the final decision on land, agriculture, forestry, state works and water, riverine fisheries, and especially the use of these resources for economic benefit, lies with the state (Jamaludin 1996; Mohideen and Shahridan 1996). Fisheries and marine park matters fall within the jurisdiction of the Ministry of Agriculture and Agro-based Industry. One of the key differences between federal and state regulation on the environment is the manner in which natural assets are viewed. While federal regulation may deem them common goods that need to be preserved and protected for the long-term benefit of all, the state may view them as resources to be exploited for economic benefit.[9]

In Johor, this is especially salient as land and land-related matters generate a large portion of the state's revenue. In the 1990s, land taxes, the granting of mining and quarrying licences and interest income contributed up to 20 per cent of Johor's revenue. Johor Corporation, the state's economic development corporation further increased this land-based revenue by managing oil palm plantations and selling land for industrial use (Hutchinson 2015, p. 44).

In 2016, Johor was the fourth largest contributor to the national GDP at 9.4 per cent (after Selangor, Kuala Lumpur and Sarawak). However, it outpaced overall national growth at 5.7 per cent (compared to the national figure of 4.2 per cent growth). Of this, Johor's construction sector logged the highest growth at 24.0 per cent, followed by the mining and quarrying sector at 19.4 per cent (Department of Statistics, Malaysia 2017). According to the Johor State Budget 2019, land taxes and fees contributed RM404.81 million to state revenue (26.07 per cent of the overall revenue collected) in 2018. While the services sector contributed RM56 billion (48 per cent) to the state's GDP, the industrial sector contributed RM43 billion (37 per cent). These figures indicate a continued boom in land-related development contributing to the state economy and highlights the importance of land as a resource to be used and developed for the state.

The Management Plan for the Mangroves of Johor State noted that the biggest threat to forested areas in Johor is its elimination as part of urbanization and the expansion of industrial areas, as well as for large infrastructure projects. The report noted that economic and physical development are constantly emphasized in Johor policy and planning documents, but there is no coherent planning for the management and conservation of natural resources (Forestry Department/DANCED 1999, p. 23). Figure 18.4 depicts the land area that can be built up in future. The map indicates that development is planned to expand beyond the Iskandar Malaysia region, even after having taken into account recent announcements on IM's expansion (*Straits Times*, 23 February 2019).

Iskandar Malaysia's Comprehensive Development Plan II (IRDA 2014, p. 4.1.) counters the stand made by the plan above in that it attempts to provide guidelines for wealth generation that is in balance with social and environmental needs, as

FIGURE 18.4
Potential Land Use: Areas That Can Be Built Up in Johor

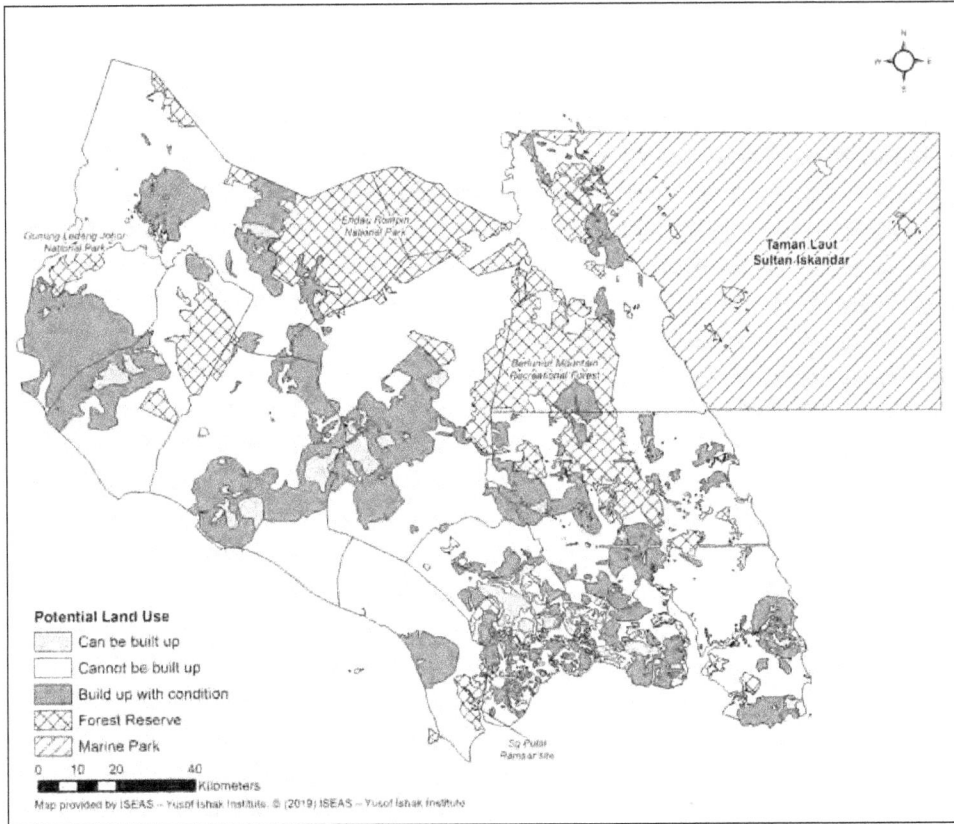

Source: Adapted from the Majlis Perbandaran Batu Pahat (Batu Pahat City Council) website: http://www.mpbp.gov.
my/sites/default/files/draf_rsnj_2030.pdf; and the GeoJohor website (Draf Gambarajah Utama Rancangan Struktur
Negeri Johor 2030): http://geoportal.johor.gov.my/petaawam/rsnj2030

well as encourage the mainstreaming of a green economy. The release of the Johor
Sustainable Policy 2017–21 also reinforces the state's commitment to protecting
natural assets and controlling pollution while ensuring economic growth and
social well-being. The policy is founded on a multi-stakeholder approach to
environmental responsibility, inculcating sustainable action and decision-making
through responsible lifestyles, a green economy, improved governance and the
empowerment of Johor's people.

Forest City is an extensive mixed-development project that requires the reclamation
of four islands in the western half of the Johor Strait. Elaborated in Chapter 17 in this
volume, Forest City is an example of how overlapping jurisdictions and conflicts in
legislation can lead to loopholes. IRDA's initial development plans designated this
part of the Johor Strait as an industrial development zone, anchored by the Port of
Tanjung Pelepas and the Tanjung Bin Power Plant. An executive decision and the

allure of a multimillion international investment led to the contravention of the area's original plan.

The presence of a foreign developer meant that myriad approvals have to go through the federal government, but because land and coastal resources come under state jurisdiction, the developer was able to quickly push through its reclamation work and land clearing. Only an official complaint by Singapore about the development taking place without any prior warning resulted in a stop-work order and the enforcement of a Detailed Environmental Impact Assessment (DEIA). But as approvals for land and sand mining (for reclamation material) were issued by the state, the project was quickly approved by DOE and allowed to continue.

Legislative overlaps in the issues surrounding Kukup Island occurred because the island falls under state jurisdiction, but its value to the environment, tourism and the country's larger natural heritage meant that it is of federal concern. National parks fall under the Concurrent List in Schedule Nine of the Malaysian Constitution. However, even though the cabinet released a statement on its hope that the island remains a forest reserve, the absolute power to decide on the use of the island remains with the state. It is interesting to note that there was no mention of any allocation to Kukup Island in the 2019 state budget, even though tourism, ecotourism and improvements to the infrastructure at nearby Tanjung Piai (also a Ramsar site) were included in the allocations.

Even as the extensive plans and guidelines for environmental considerations in development and governance (as devised by the federal government and their agencies) are disregarded by executive decisions at the state level, the importance of land development to the state continues to be highlighted. The Review of the Johor 2030 State Structural Plan (Rancangan Struktur Negeri Johor 2030 (Kajian Semula)) conducted in mid-2018 notes that there is still a need for 64,420 hectares of land to be developed by 2030. The 2019 state budget, announced soon after the recent elections and change of government noted the need to strengthen the state mining industry and increase earnings from land-related taxes and other fees.

INFLUENCE AND IMPACT OF SIJORI

Environmental Relations with Singapore

There are a number of platforms for Singapore and Johor to share knowledge and engage with each other. At the ministerial level, there is a Joint Ministerial Committee for Iskandar Malaysia (JMCIM) that has (among others) an Environment Work Group (EWG) and a Tourism Work Group (TWG) that share experiences, strengthen environmental cooperation and explore opportunities for collaboration between Singapore and Iskandar Malaysia. This platform has thus far enabled groups from Johor to learn from Singapore's experiences in river revitalization and nature tourism. This has triggered ideas that helped with the Segget River rehabilitation project in Johor Bahru city centre, as well as the "Passport 2 Nature" initiative between Singapore's Sungai Buloh Wetland Reserve and Johor's Kukup Island.

At the federal level, there is a Malaysia-Singapore Joint Committee on the Environment (MSJCE) which has Annual Exchange of Visits (AEV) between the two nations' environment ministries. These meetings discuss matters related to water quality, including chemical and oil spills, land reclamation and biodiversity protection. There are also joint training activities and programmes and an agreement to share information pursuant to the Settlement Agreement of 2005 and matters that affect the environment in the Straits of Johor.

In spite of these efforts to bring the two neighbours together for sharing, mutual benefit and learning, there is some hesitation on both sides as to how much can be shared in case it is used against either party in national negotiations or in competition for tourism or business.[10] There has been a history of some tension between Malaysia and Singapore at the federal level, such as over reclamation areas, maritime boundaries, water supply and pricing, flight paths and noise pollution. While these matters are expected to directly affect Johor, it seems that the state is intent on cultivating a positive relationship with Singapore.[11]

Environmental Collaboration with the Riau Islands

Between Johor and the nearby Riau Province, the SOSEK MALINDO Socio-Economic Cooperation (Jawatankuasa/Kumpulan Kerja Sosial Ekonomi Malaysia-Indonesia) creates a platform for Johor, Melaka and the Riau Province and archipelago to discuss issues pertaining to economy and business, society and culture, safety and border area management. The priority of this group is to ensure border area safety and management, but one of its objectives mentions the preservation of the shared environment. While Johor state agency staff interviewed mentioned that there has been some interaction with the Riau Province on environmental matters, this collaboration seems to be far less prominent than engagement with Singapore.[12] Online reports of SOSEK MALINDO's activities seem to indicate that the grouping now encompasses far more than just the Riau Province,[13] and envelops all engagements between Indonesia and Malaysia. The most prominent environmental issue that arises between the Riau Islands and Johor is that of haze, but this is often dealt with at the federal level, with direct negotiations between the two governments, or at the ASEAN level (Varkkey 2017).

ENVIRONMENTAL MANAGEMENT AND POLICY UNDER THE FORMER BN STATE GOVERNMENT

Informant interviews and observations of the former state government's efforts for the environment were generally seen as positive. The former Chief Minister, Khaled Nordin, was viewed as being open to ideas on environmental management and the State Executive Councillor of Health and the Environment, Ayub Rahmat, was proactive and willing to take action for better environmental policies in Johor.[14] The Johor Sustainability Policy was one outcome of their top-down support for better approaches to environmental management in the state. Key to ExCo Ayub's initiatives for the environment was a circle of capable advisors, including genuine experts from environmental consultancies such as Dr G. Balamurugan from ERE Consulting Group and other individuals from IRDA, UPEN, JNPC and other agencies who were brought together through joint committees and other engagement platforms. This coterie of advisors comprising people whose priority was environmental protection was able to ensure that he fully understood the issues at hand and what needed to be done.[15]

Added to that was the state's commitment to frequent multilevel stakeholder meetings on the environment and other related matters. The Johor Sustainability Policy alone canvassed views from 200 stakeholders from myriad sectors through focus group sessions, phone calls, interviews and workshops over a period of more than a year (UPEN Johor 2017, p. 119). Many other matters related to environmental education, community empowerment for natural area conservation, use of natural areas for tourism, environmental research needs and direction in the state have also been advised by wide-reaching feedback (workshops, interviews, consultations and meetings) through multiple means before being locked into policy.[16]

The Johor Sustainability Policy illustrates the past state government's commitment to both top-down direction and interest in environmental policy, as well as support for grassroots and ground-up community efforts for environmental conservation. The policy emphasizes the need for community empowerment and involvement as the basis of the success of its plans, (UPEN Johor 2017, p. 69) while at the same time pointing out the need for a shift in governance approaches to a greener economy (ibid., p. 51). The policy is the direct outcome of and a tribute to the ability of staff from myriad sectors and agencies to come together beyond their traditional silos and overcome territorial distrust to put forward a new direction for Johor.

While there is clear evidence of positive state support and action for better environmental management, there were issues in terms of implementation. Even with top-down directives and mandates, policy implementation was hampered by lethargy at the level of local authorities.[17] While there are some driven, inspired and passionate individuals, some state government staff were either not willing or unable to take on the extra work necessary to fully enforce and implement environmental laws and initiatives. At other times, a lack of funding and capable manpower hampered proper implementation of environmental initiatives. Because mid-to-high level civil servant heads of departments are frequently rotated, many staff opt to achieve simpler short-term goals that produce immediate results.[18]

This tendency to reach for low-hanging fruit instead of persisting with projects that require more long-term behavioural and attitude change results in superficial efforts that only skim the surface of what needs to be done for better environmental action on the ground. At the same time, the overwhelming array of policies, guidelines and plans that need to be corroborated and integrated tends to frighten away attempts to consolidate and strengthen efforts. IRDA's blueprints and plans are only guidelines; it is not actually mandatory for state agencies to abide by their recommendations.[19]

ENVIRONMENTAL MANAGEMENT AND POLICY UNDER A NEW PAKATAN HARAPAN GOVERNMENT

With a new PH government in power for only a fraction of its term, its approach to environmental policy and management is still unclear. The 14th General Election has, however, led to a more vocal and assertive civil society movement. Since the change in government, several non-governmental organizations (NGOs) have come together to form the Johor People's Forum (Forum Masyarakat Johor, or FMJ) with a view to seeking partnership with the new government so as to advise and provide input into state decisions. Environmental groups have recently revived questions about the Forest City development, especially about its new golf resort complex that was built within the Pulai River Ramsar site (*Malaysiakini*, 14 February 2019). However, a new government in power also means that grassroots organizations that had, in the past, worked out a network to reach out to for support and access to opportunities now have to start all over again to demonstrate their worth to the new regime.

While past policies such as the Johor Sustainability Policy are technically still valid, the new government has taken many steps to demonstrate that it wants to change the way Johor is governed. Informant interviews revealed that there is little hope for environmental protection per se, as the emphasis is far more focused on wealth generation than sustainable balance.[20] Of the Sustainability Policy components, several felt that the low carbon and green technology initiatives may be continued as they are easy to market internationally, generate good investments and do not get in the way of land sales, purchase and development. The 2019 budget released by the PH government concur with these views.

A comparison of Johor's 2019 budget core components is shown in Table 18.4. These calculations are based on the available figures released to the public in the online Johor Budget 2019 documents. Not all budget points have Malaysian ringgit values allocated to them, hence the figures derived are not completely representative of actual (undisclosed) budget allocations. However, the calculations can still be used as a rough benchmark to indicate the importance given to environmental components in comparison to other core focuses.

Several insights can be gleaned from the above breakdown. Guaranteeing Citizens' Prosperity (Core Focus I) is of utmost priority, making up 77.3 per cent of the declared budget. In comparison, Sustainable Development and Resource Conservation (Core Focus II), while placed as second in importance, only makes up 3.5 per cent of the total declared budget, far less than the third Core Focus (Infrastructural Development, Activation of Digital Trade Zone & Community) which makes up 16.7 per cent of the budget. Notwithstanding differences in actual costs of these varied components, the great difference in actual figures allocated to the environmental component is telling. At the same time, not all components within Core Focus II can be directly attributed to the environment; some of these include agricultural incentives and expenses. Budgeted expenses directly linked to the environment make up only 10.9 per cent of this section's subtotal.

TABLE 18.4
Breakdown of Announced Components of 2019 Johor Budget 2019

	Core Focus	RM (%)	Environmental Component (RM)	Environmental Component of each Core Focus (%)
I	Guaranteeing Citizens' Prosperity	RM7,776,650,000 (77.3%)	0	
II	Sustainable Development & Resource Conservation	RM348,110,000 (3.5%)	RM37,760,000	10.9%
III	Infrastructural Development, Activation of Digital Trade Zone & Community	RM1,679,640,000 (16.7%)	RM155,000,000	9.2%
IV	Dynamic Democracy & Fair Society	RM180,850,000 (1.8%)	RM11,800,000	6.5%
V	Modernising Islamic Studies Systems, Human Capital and Cultural Heritage	RM32,950,000 (0.3%)	0	
VI	Ensuring an Efficient and Democratic Government Administration of Integrity	RM279,760,000 (2.9%)	No figures given	
	Total	RM10,054,700,000	RM204,560,000	2.03% of total budget

Source: Based on Titik Fokus Belanjawan Johor 2019 from https://www.johor.gov.my/kerajaan/bajet-johor/tahun-2019#tab-id-4 (accessed 6 January 2019).

All the environmental components from all Core Focuses combined make up only 2 per cent of the total declared budget. This figure comes about even after including components that contribute to water security such as water tanks and ensuring water supply in rural areas (Core Focus V) and other water-related infrastructural development (Core Focus III). Water infrastructure are big ticket items, with total expenses in this budget expected to go up to RM166.8 million.

It is also interesting to note that land matters are mentioned several times in the budget. In Core Focus I, land purchases to build affordable homes by a state-linked GLC is budgeted to take up RM87 million (1.1 per cent of the section's subtotal). Land matters are also mentioned in Core Focus VI. Adjustments to land-related administrative fees, service delivery taxes and other land-related administration matters are expected to raise at least RM2 million for the state and require some (undisclosed) budget expense.

THE WAY FORWARD

This chapter has attempted to sketch the complex web of legislation, jurisdictions and prerogatives that oversee environmental policy, management and decision-making in Johor. For a state that places high value on land as a resource to be exploited and developed, as well as a major contributor to state revenue and GDP, there is little hope that land preservation for purely environmental purposes will be a priority.

Even as the new government tries to find its way in a state that has always been ruled by the BN regime and struggles between balancing executive decisions with the need to meet demands by the populace, one of the best ways forward is to continue the multi-level stakeholder engagement on environmental matters that the past regime often executed. For even though executive decisions may at times be made remotely, at least consulted and collaborating parties can work out how to make the best of available opportunities within the given constraints.

With IRDA being one of many federal agencies and GLCs linked to the former government being reviewed for its relevance to the new regime, its ability to continue supporting environmental and grassroots initiatives hangs in the balance. For the most part, Johor's approach to environmental matters under the new government will require some time to play itself out. Recent incidents indicate that civil society's strengthened voice will continue to monitor and consistently have an impact on actions taken by the state. Since the Kim Kim River disaster, myriad social media reports have been posted on other waste dumping locations all over the country, forcing Department of Environment officials to take action.

In the meantime, initiatives by responsible private and catalytic developers might be the only way forward to ensure effective implementation of environmental policies. Some examples of this already taking place are plans by Iskandar Investment Berhad (IIB) to protect a vast tract of its mangrove forest and create a nature education centre. Medini City has taken the initiative to include many parks and lakes within its development at Iskandar Puteri, with its Edible Park and Heritage Forest being its prime natural attractions. Sunway Iskandar, whose property includes some of the healthiest remaining riverine mangroves in South Johor has also pledged to develop on a 1 to 1 ratio (development to preservation) and is in the midst of finalizing the details of its support for a community-led environmental and ecotourism organization to use its property as its base.

It is important that both state and federal agencies recognize the connection between community livelihoods and environmental protection. The implications of environmental damage go beyond merely the loss of natural habitats, but have severe consequences on rural communities that have depended on those habitats for generations. While some of the damage is inevitable and unavoidable, the state needs to take concrete action to enable these communities to cope with the changes in the environments that are intrinsic to their lives, and survive. Only then can development be said to be sustainable; when it can balance the economy, the environment and the communities who tend to fall by the wayside.

With Johor's economy projected to grow by 5.5 per cent in 2019, hinging largely on continued development, land revenue, mining and the like, the new Johor government needs to quickly catch up with the efforts by private developers and citizens to ensure better environmental decision-making, policies and management by the state.

APPENDIX 18.1
Selected Johor State or State-Linked Entities That May Influence Environmental Policy

Entity or Organization	Scope of Work
State Government Departments	
State Economic Planning Unit (UPEN)	State economic planning: land, resources and development are dealt with under separate policy committees. Environmental policy objective is to maintain a clean and green environment.
Local Authorities (District Land Office)	Management of forest habitat (including mangroves) on state land. Has the most detailed information on land ownership.
Johor Landscape Office (JLNJ)	Ensure that state surroundings and developed areas are comfortable, clean and cheerful, with landscaping for recreational and functional uses.
Department of Land & Mines (PTG)	Land allocation for all state lands (including mangroves and forest areas). Coordinates application of land for development—proposals are finally forwarded to State National Resource Committee.
Johor Tourism	Promote Johor to international visitors, support local tourism efforts by providing access to markets and marketing
State Government-Linked Corporations	
Johor National Parks Corporation (JNPC)	Conservation of fauna and flora, nature education and research, ecotourism.
Kumpulan Prasana Rakyat Johor (KPRJ) (kprj.com.my)	Private company wholly owned by Johor state government. Developer for social and infrastructural projects. Johor's investment arm, especially real estate and infrastructure development.
Johor Corporation (JCorp) (www.jcorp.com.my)	Public enterprise and statutory body (via Johor Enactment No. 4, 1968 with amendments under Enactment No. 5, 1995). Core business that includes palm oil, property, port services and oil and gas.
Johor Biotechnology and Biodiversity Corporation (J-Biotech) (jbiotech.gov.my)	Johor state government agency focusing on spearheading the bioeconomic growth of Johor.
Federal Agencies	
Iskandar Regional Development Authority (IRDA) (www.irda.com.my)	Federal agency created to develop, market and manage Iskandar Malaysia as the first choice to invest, work, live and play.

Source: Collated and adapted from Management Plan for Mangroves of Johor (Forestry Department/DANCED, 1999); Official website of the Johor state government: https://www.johor.gov.my/ and individual organization websites (listed above).

APPENDIX 18.2
Johor State Executive Committee Members and Their Relevant Environmental Domains, 2017

State Executive Committee Member	Scope of Work
Osman Sapian (Chief Minister)	Executive Chairman of Natural Resources, Administration, Finance and Economic Planning and Development
Dzulkefly Ahmad	Housing and Rural Development
Tan Hong Pin	Local Government, Science and Technology
Mazlan Bujang	Public Works, Infrastructure and Transportation
Jimmy Puah Wee Tse	Investment and Utilities
Liow Cai Tung	Women, Development and Tourism
Dr Sahruddin Jamal	Health, Environment and Agriculture

Notes

1. The agreements that govern this arrangement have recently been raised in recent media sparring between Singapore and the Malaysian federal government. Throughout the exchanges, however, Johor's Crown Prince has maintained that water is a state resource and that the state has the power to decide on the details of its management and sale. Refer to this link for more information on his comments: Amir Yusof, "Exclusive: Johor Crown Prince claims 'sovereignty' over water in the state, prefers no 'federal interference' on the issue" and this link for background information on the water agreements: Ministry of Foreign Affairs, Government of Singapore, https://www1.mfa.gov.sg/SINGAPORES-FOREIGN-POLICY/Key-Issues/Water-Agreements (accessed 14 March 2019).

2. Tg Piai Maritime Industrial Park, website: http://tgpiaimaritime.com.my/ (accessed 14 March 2019).

3. Mentioned by several informants from developers and other development-related consultancies during conversations and interviews in November 2018. All who mentioned it reported that they had seen the plans and were aware of the source of the plan but the details cannot be revealed. The project was described to be a narrow strip of island to be reclaimed (less than 1 km wide in parts), leaving a narrow buffer between Singapore and the Johor shore. This purported development was not included in the map as it was not verified at the land office.

4. Refer to the following articles on issues in the Johor Bahru city centre: H.L. Koh, P.E. Lim, and Z. Midun, "Management and Control of Pollution in Inner Johor Strait", *Environmental Monitoring and Assessment* 19, iss. 1–3 (1991): 349–59; and Z.Z. Noor, "Towards Sustainable Household Waste Management in Urban Areas: Determinants the Hindered the Recycling Activities in the city of Johor Bahru, Malaysia", Malaysia Sustainable Cities Program Working Paper, Massachusetts Institute of Technology, 2016, https://malaysiacities.mit.edu/papernoor (accessed 14 March 2019), and the following link for a media article on the Segget River revitalization project: M.F. Shah, "Rejuvenating Sungai Segget", *The Star Online*, 15 April 2017, https://www.thestar.com.my/metro/community/2017/04/15/rejuvenating-sungai-segget-the-rm120mil-vertical-sewerage-plant-is-expected-to-restore-river-quality/ (accessed 14 March 2019).

5. Personal observation from eleven years of immersion in Johor rural villages.

6. The following media articles provide information on vessel accidents in east and west Johor: *Channel NewsAsia*, "300 tonnes of Oil Spilled after Singapore-Registered Ship Collides with Vessel off Johor", 4 January 2017, https://www.channelnewsasia.com/news/singapore/300-tonnes-of-oil-spilled-after-singapore-registered-ship-collid-7537142 (accessed 14 March 2019); and M.H. Mahpar, "Port of Tg Pelepas Files RM31.9 mil Oil Spill Damage Suit", *The Star Online*, 20 July 2017, https://www.thestar.com.my/business/business-news/2017/07/20/port-of-tg-pelepas-files-rm31pt9mil-oil-spill-damage-suit/ (accessed 14 March 2019). The author has observed and documented a chemical spill that allegedly occurred in the Port of Tg Pelepas in 2009 which led to the death of many marine species in the area and a complete loss of fish catch and incomes for local fishermen for the next three months. This event was not publicized or reported and samples taken from the incident could not be processed for verification of the claims.

7. That the duty of JNPC is now one of marketing and promotion of the Sultan Iskandar Marine Park was conveyed to me in a personal conversation with a JNPC officer who declined to be named (19 February 2019). In the past there was some overlap in

jurisdiction and roles between JNPC and DMPM, but this has since been clarified (personal communication, Dr Goh Hong Ching, University Malaya, 10 February 2019).

8. There has been some dissatisfaction with the move of the DMPM to the resource extraction focussed Agricultural and Agro-based Industry Ministry and concern that environmental preservation will come second to economic benefit (refer to: M.M. Chu, and R.S. Bedi, "Moving Marine Parks Dept to Ministry that Maximises Fisheries is Wrong say Conservationists", *The Star Online*, 25 October 2018, https://www.thestar.com.my/news/nation/2018/10/25/moving-marine-parks-dept-to-ministry-that-maximises-fisheries-is-wrong-say-conservationists/ (accessed 14 March 2019).

9. Refer to Chapter 7 "Tourism in Johor and Its Potential" in this volume.

10. Information provided by interviews with state and agency officers between 19 November 2018 and 30 November 2018, names withheld.

11. Johor's royal house and state government has often maintained close and positive relations in spite of any wayward conditions at the federal level. In the past this has proven to agitate the federal government (refer to Hutchinson 2015, p. 46). In recently revived discussions about the sale of raw and treated water between Johor and Singapore, Johor's Crown Prince made it a point to express his thanks to Singapore and confirm his desire for continued positive relations between Johor and Singapore (*Straits Times*, "Johor Prince Thanks Singapore During Droughts", 30 June 2018, https://www.straitstimes.com/asia/se-asia/johor-prince-thanks-spore-for-help-during-droughts (accessed 14 March 2019).)

12. Information conveyed in interview with UPEN Johor officer on 27 November 2018, name withheld.

13. Laman Web Rasmi Majlis Keselamatan Negara [Official Website of the National Safety Council], Federal Government of Malaysia] https://www.mkn.gov.my/page/latar-belakang-ringkas-penubuhan-jawatankuasa-kerja-sosial-ekonomi-malaysia-indonesia-sosek-malindo (accessed 9 December 2018).

14. Interview with IRDA officer on 29 November 2018, name withheld.

15. Information provided by interviews with state and agency officers between 19 November 2018 and 30 November 2018, names withheld.

16. Author's personal observation and participation in state and agency programmes and processes between 2015 and 2019.

17. Information provided by interviews with state and agency officers between 19 November 2018 and 30 November 2018, names withheld.

18. Author's personal observation and participation in state and agency programmes and processes between 2015 and 2019.

19. Interview with IRDA officer on 29 November 2018, name withheld.

20. Information provided by interviews with state and agency officers between 19 November 2018 and 30 November 2018, names withheld (Hutchinson 2015).

References

Adler, B. 2007. "The Case Against Golf". *The Guardian*, 14 June 2007. https://www.theguardian.com/commentisfree/2007/jun/14/thecaseagainstgolf (accessed 14 March 2019).

ASEAN. 1991. *The Coastal Environmental Profile of South Johor, Malaysia*. Manila: Association of Southeast Asian Nations/United States Coastal Resources Management Project Technical Publications Series 6.

Big Cat Rescue. 2018. "Johor Bans Hunting of Wildlife". *BigCatRescue.org*, 22 November 2018. https://bigcatrescue.org/johor-bans-hunting-of-wildlife/ (accessed 14 March 2019).

Butler, R.A. 2015."High Deforestation Rates in Malaysian States Hit by Flooding". *Mongabay*, 19 January 2015. https://news.mongabay.com/2015/01/high-deforestation-rates-in-malaysian-states-hit-by-flooding/ (accessed 14 March 2019).

Chan, D. 2019. "Illegal Plastic Recycling Plants—'Operators Shifted to other States'". *New Straits Times*, 24 February 2019. https://www.nst.com.my/news/nation/2019/02/463130/illegal-plastic-recycling-plants-operators-shifted-other-states (accessed 14 March 2019).

Channel NewsAsia. 2018. "More Than 600 Residents of Johor Town Evacuated Due to Flash Floods". 12 December 2018. https://www.channelnewsasia.com/news/asia/605-residents-johor-town-kota-tinggi-evacuated-flash-floods-11024168 (accessed 14 March 2019).

Chua, W.B. 2017. "The Impact of Marine Sand Mining in Johor". *Malaysiakini*, 28 November 2017. https://www.malaysiakini.com/letters/403574?fbclid=IwAR06YDRAPeuXK lQAHKNcGMZVdtrt2sEJwWACS-Q8wEtoMBPPw2GNF4i_vu0 (accessed 14 March 2019).

CLJ Legal Network Sdn Bhd. 1934. *The Sultanate Lands Enactment*. En. 5/1934. www.cljlaw. com/Members/PrintActSection.aspx?ActSectionId=3154159617&ActType=JOHORE (accessed 6 December 2018).

Federal Government of Malaysia. 1957. "Constitution of Malaysia, 1957". Ninth Schedule. www.commonili.org/my/legis/const/1957/24.html (accessed 6 December 2018).

Department of Statistics, Federal Government of Malaysia. 2016. "GDP by State 2016". 6 September 2016. https://www.dosm.gov.my/v1/index.php?r=column/cthemeByCat&cat= 102&bul_id=VS9Gckp1UUpKQUFWS1JHUnJZS2xzdz09&menu_id=TE5CRUZCblh4 ZTZMODZIbmk2aWRRQT09 (accessed 6 December 2018).

Forestry Department/DANCED. 1999. *Management Plan for the Mangroves of Johor 2000–2009*. Johor: Forestry Department Peninsular Malaysia/Danish Cooperation for Environment and Development, 1999.

Free Malaysia Today. 2018. "Sultanate Land Can't Have National Park Status, Lawyer Tells Johor". 13 December 2018. https://www.freemalaysiatoday.com/category/nation/2018/12/13/sultanate-land-cant-have-national-park-status-lawyer-tells-johor/ (accessed 14 March 2019).

Goh H.C. 2016. "Assessing Mangrove Conservation Efforts in Iskandar Malaysia". *Malaysia Sustainable Cities Program, Working Paper Series*. Hong Ching Goh & Massachusetts Institute of Technology.

Hammim, R. 2018. "Johor Says No to Non-environmentally Friendly Investments". *New Straits Times*, 29 June 2018. https://www.nst.com.my/news/nation/2018/06/385556/johor-says-no-non-environmentally-friendly-investments (accessed 14 March 2019).

Hangzo, P.K.K. 2013. "Will Rapid Development in Johor Impact Water Access, Quality or Price in Singapore?". *NTS Insight* 13-06. https://www.rsis.edu.sg/rsis-publication/nts/2512-will-rapid-development-in-joho/#.XIm_3SgzZPY (accessed 14 March 2019).

Hutchinson, F.E. 2015. *Mirror Images in Different Frames? Johor, the Riau Islands, and Competition for Investment from Singapore*. Singapore: Institute of Southeast Asian Studies.

Iskandar Regional Development Authority (IRDA). 2011. *Integrated Land Use Blueprint for Iskandar Malaysia*. Johor Bahru: Iskandar Regional Development Authority.

———. 2014. *Iskandar Malaysia Comprehensive Development Plan II 2014–2025*. Johor Bahru: Iskandar Regional Development Authority.

Jackson, E., and K. Domondon. 2016. "Drought, Pollution and Johor's Growing Water Needs". *ISEAS Perspective*, no. 2016/47, 26 August 2016, pp. 1–10.

Jamaluddin M.J. 1996. "Environmental Policies, Laws and Institutional Arrangements: A Critique and Suggestions". In *State of the Environment Malaysia*, pp. 457–63. Penang: Consumers Association of Penang.

Kannan, H.V. 2019. "Ammonia Pollution: Johor Poultry Farm Gets 6 months Grace to Sort out Operations". *New Straits Times*, 5 February 2019. https://www.nst.com.my/news/nation/2018/02/332274/ammonia-pollution-johor-poultry-farm-gets-6-months-grace-period-sort-out (accessed 14 March 2019).

Kerajaan Negeri Johor. 2019a. "Belanjawan Johor 2019: Slide Pebentangan". https://www.johor.gov.my/kerajaan/bajet-johor/tahun-2019#tab-id-3 (accessed 6 January 2019).

———. 2019b. "Belanjawan Johor 2019: Titik Fokus". https://www.johor.gov.my/kerajaan/bajet-johor/tahun-2019#tab-id-4 (accessed 6 January 2019).

———. 2019c. "Johor 2030—Rancangan Struktur Negeri Johor 2030 (Kajian Semula)". http://www.mdsrenggam.gov.my/ms/mdsr/pusat-media/berita/johor-2023-rancangan-struktur-negeri-johor-2030-kajian-semula (accessed 6 January 2019).

Kili, Kathleen Ann. 2017. "Taps in 1.8 million South Johor Households Run Dry". *The Star Online*, 28 October 2017. https://www.thestar.com.my/news/nation/2017/10/28/taps-in-1_8-million-southern-johor-households-run-dry/ (accessed 14 March 2019).

Malay Mail. 2017. "Get Prior Approval Before Diving in Sultan Ismail Marine Park, Says Sultan Ibrahim". 7 August 2017. https://www.malaymail.com/news/malaysia/2017/08/07/get-prior-approval-before-diving-in-sultan-ismail-marine-park-says-sultan-i/1437753 (accessed 14 March 2019).

Malaysiakini. 2019a. "Gov't Must Review Development at Sg Pulai Reserve—Peka". 14 February 2019. https://www.malaysiakini.com/news/463974 (accessed 14 March 2019).

———. 2019b. "Johor Ruler Surrenders 'Logging Quota', Wants to Keep State Green". 20 February 2019. https://www.malaysiakini.com/news/464857 (accessed 14 March 2019).

Mohideen, A.K., and F. Shahridan. 1996. "Landuse Laws and Policies and Environmental Degradation". In *State of the Environment Malaysia*, pp. 457–43. Penang: Consumers Association of Penang.

New Straits Times. 2014. "Johor Rivers Face Water Shortage". 12 August 2014. https://www.nst.com.my/news/2015/09/johor-rivers-face-water-shortage (accessed 14 March 2019).

———. 2019. "34 Schools Ordered to Close following Pasir Gudang Toxic Waste Disaster". 13 March 2019. https://www.nst.com.my/news/nation/2019/03/468815/34-schools-ordered-close-following-pasir-gudang-toxic-waste-disaster (accessed 14 March 2019).

Othman, A.F. 2017. "Johor Prince Spearheads Effort to Recycle Waste Water to Boost State's Water Reserves". *New Straits Times*, 28 February 2017. https://www.nst.com.my/news/2017/02/216201/johor-prince-spearheads-effort-recycle-waste-water-boost-states-water-reserves (accessed 14 March 2019).

Rahman, S. 2017. *Johor's Forest City Faces Critical Challenges*. Trends in Southeast Asia, no. 3/2017. Singapore: ISEAS – Yusof Ishak Institute.

———. 2018. *Developing Eastern Johor: The Pengerang Integrated Petroleum Complex*. Trends in Southeast Asia, no. 16/2018. Singapore: ISEAS – Yusof Ishak Institute.

Shah, M.F. 2017. "Johor to Promote its Golf Courses to Attract More Tourists". *The Star Online*, 17 May 2017. https://www.thestar.com.my/metro/community/2017/05/17/johor-to-promote-its-golf-courses-to-attract-more-tourists/ (accessed 14 March 2019).

Star Online, The. 2016. "Act on Water Shortage Woes, Johor Urged". 16 May 2016. https://

www.thestar.com.my/news/nation/2016/05/16/act-on-water-shortage-woes-johor-urged/ (accessed 14 March 2019).

————. 2019. "Take the Lead, MNS Told". 24 January 2019. https://www.thestar.com.my/metro/metro-news/2019/01/24/take-the-lead-mns-told/ (accessed 14 March 2019).

Straits Times, The. 2019. "Malaysia Doubles Size of Iskandar Corridor". 23 February 2019. https://www.straitstimes.com/asia/se-asia/malaysia-doubles-size-of-johors-iskandar-corridor (accessed 14 March 2019).

Tan, B. 2018. "TMJ: Pulau Kukup will Be Under Sultanate Land to Better Protect It". *Malay Mail*, 5 December 2018. https://www.malaymail.com/news/malaysia/2018/12/05/tmj-pulau-kukup-will-be-under-sultanate-land-to-better-protect-it/1700311 (accessed 14 March 2019).

Tay, T.Y. 2018. "Kukup". *Sin Chew Daily*, 13 December 2018. http://www.mysinchew.com/node/120681 (accessed 14 March 2019).

Today Online. 2019a. "Two Rivers Dry Up in Johor, Allegedly from Sand Mining".14 March 2019 https://www.todayonline.com/world/two-rivers-dry-johor-allegedly-sand-mining (accessed 14 March 2019).

————. 2019b. "Green Groups Question Pulau Kukup's Status from National Park to Crown Land". 11 December 2019. https://www.todayonline.com/world/green-groups-question-pulau-kukups-status-national-park-crown-land (accessed 14 March 2019).

UPEN Johor. 2017. *Johor Sustainability Policy 2017–2021*. Iskandar Puteri, Malaysia.

Varkkey, H. 2017. "The Politics of Fires and Haze in Southeast Asia". Politics, Oxford Research Encyclopedias, January 2017. https://doi.org/10.1093/acrefore/9780190228637.013.262 (accessed 9 December 2018).

Zakaria, R. 2016. "Protect Our Peat Swamps". *New Straits Times*, 24 September 2016. https://www.nst.com.my/news/2016/09/175651/protect-our-peat-swamps (accessed 14 March 2019).

Conclusion

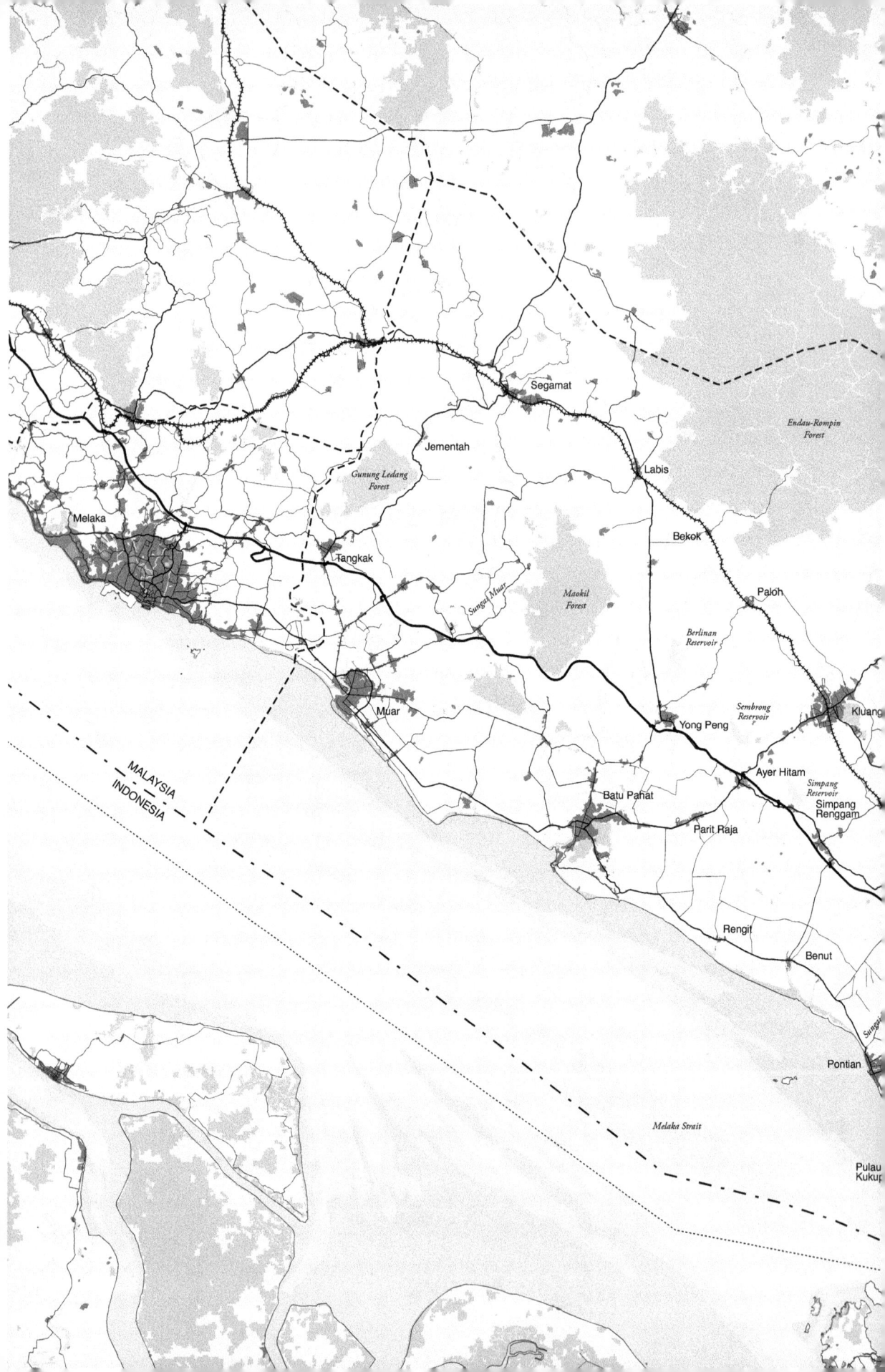

Endau-Rompin
Forest

Segamat

Jementah

Gunung Ledang
Forest

Labis

Melaka

Bekok

Tangkak

Paloh

Sungai Muar

Maokil
Forest

Berlinan
Reservoir

Sembrong
Reservoir

Muar

Yong Peng

Kluang

MALAYSIA

INDONESIA

Ayer Hitam

Simpang
Reservoir

Simpang
Renggam

Batu Pahat

Parit Raja

Rengit

Benut

Pontian

Melaka Strait

Pulau
Kukup

MAP 5.1
JOHOR STATE

- Built-up Area
- Industrial Area
- Agriculture
- Forest
- Water
- Road Network

Pulau Tioman

Endau

Labong Reservoir

Pulau Rawa

Pulau Babi Besar

Pulau Aur

Mersing

Endau River

Sibu-Tinggi Achipelago

South China Sea

Endau-Kota Tinggi Forest

Linggiu Reservoir

Bandar Tenggara

Johor River

Kulai

Kota Tinggi

Johor River

Desaru

Johor Bahru

Pengerang

Sungai Pulai

Singapore Strait

SINGAPORE

0 10 20km

19

JOHOR
Abode of Development?

Serina Rahman and Francis E. Hutchinson

INTRODUCTION

This volume has evaluated myriad aspects of Johor's current reality, setting out many of the key issues facing Peninsular Malaysia's southernmost state. It has illustrated in maps and words the workings of different sectors of Johor's economy, its unique political context, and the myriad social and environmental challenges it is facing.

This publication is the second in a series that focuses on the Singapore-Johor-Riau Islands or SIJORI Cross-Border Region (CBR). Unlike the first of the series, *The SIJORI Cross-Border Region: Transnational Politics, Economics, and Culture*, which takes Singapore as the anchor-point for the geo-economic entity, this volume on Johor and the third volume on the Riau Islands focus on the other two territories in the Cross-Border Region. They explore how these territories are influenced by their belonging to a larger political entity—Malaysia and Indonesia, respectively—yet are also shaped by their connections to their neighbouring territories.

While analysis on the SIJORI CBR may tend to be overly shaped by Singapore's influence, so, too, work on Malaysia and Indonesia can focus overmuch on the Klang Valley and Java, respectively. Consequently, these two tomes also seek to redress the geographic imbalance in the study of these two countries by deepening our knowledge of two economically vital but physically non-central territories.

One key date that both Johor and the Riau Islands share is 1990, when both territories sought to market their economies through the Growth Triangle, comprised of these two entities plus Singapore. The benefits of this partnership have been deep and far-reaching, as the economies of both the Malaysian and Indonesian territories underwent structural change on the back of heightened investment flows and the construction of cross-border production networks (Hutchinson 2015).

With this as a backdrop, the guiding questions for these two books are:

- Is the manufacture for export model put in place by Johor and the Riau Islands still valid, and what effect have measures to catalyse new sectors had?
- What have been the political, social, and environmental impacts on these territories of the rapid economic development set in motion since the early 1990s?
- How are these two territories evolving in response to developments within their respective countries on one hand, and the SIJORI Cross-Border Region on the other?

The structure of this book mirrors the conceptual order of the questions. Thus, the first section looks at the workings of the state's economy, through analysing key sectors and policy measures to develop existing or new activities. The second and third sections proceed to explore Johor's political context and current social and environmental challenges, many of them directly linked to the state's economic model. The three sections collectively provide an assessment of Johor's place within Malaysia, as well as the manner within which it is influenced by its location within the Cross-Border Region.

This final chapter will briefly review each of the three sections of the book to: provide an overall picture of what has happened in the state during the period under study; identify areas for continuing and future research; and then conclude by relating the themes back to the Cross-Border Region.

ECONOMICS

In 2018, Johor's state revenue was RM1.6 billion, a decrease from RM1.7 billion the previous year; its 2018 GDP per capita value was RM36,394. The state recorded a 9.6 per cent contribution to Malaysia's national GDP in 2018, fourth behind Selangor (23.7 per cent), the Federal Territory of Kuala Lumpur (16.1 per cent) and Sarawak (9.7 per cent). Bolstered not only by Iskandar Malaysia (the nation's southern economic corridor, with its nexus at Iskandar Puteri), but also by extensive development in the Johor Bahru city centre, the state is evolving quickly, recording a GDP growth rate of 5.6 per cent (Department of Statistics, Malaysia 2019).

Chapters 2 and 3 outline the little-known history of agriculture in Johor and how it evolved from pepper and gambier to other cash crops and oil palm today. In addition to that, the state is home to one of Malaysia's more successful home-grown poultry operations, Leong Hup, which now controls a quarter of the local poultry market and owns entities in Singapore, Indonesia, Philippines and Vietnam. Map 2.5

illustrates how much of the state is dedicated to agriculture, while Map 2.6 shows how much of this is now dedicated to oil palm cultivation. Johor's strategic location next to Singapore, with easy access to its highly efficient Changi Cargo Terminal also facilitates the export of products such as cut flowers and ornamental fish; both highly lucrative markets.

In addition to greater access to world markets through Singapore's transport infrastructure, Johor can also leverage on offshoring opportunities offered by the city-state's burgeoning economy. The oil and gas sector is one of Johor's core economic drivers, and the state's position at the centre of the region's oil and gas tradelines, as shown in Map 2.7, reinforces the high expectations of the Pengerang Integrated Petroleum Complex. Chapter 4 examines both local and regional views and responses to the project, as well as the community and environmental impacts of a development that is slated to catalyse the development of the southeastern corner of Johor.

Of all of Johor's economic sectors, construction was the highest contributor to state GDP in 2018 (9.6 per cent), with services in second place at 7.3 per cent (an increase from 6.6 per cent in 2017) (Department of Statistics, Malaysia 2019). This growth pattern has been part of the state's economic transformation over the past decade and a half, as manufacturing has given way to the tertiary sector. One key driver of this process has been the Iskandar Malaysia region, which has sought to catalyse the emergence and subsequent development of service activities. This process has had some setbacks, notably the financial services as well as the creative industries sectors (Khor 2011; *The Edgeprop,* 12 July 2019). However, promising new areas include healthcare and education, both of which are identified as key thrusts of the state's economy.

To this end, Chapters 5 and 6 examine the extent to which Johor has begun to exploit these areas, as well as the challenges the state may need to overcome to maximize their potential. With regard to healthcare, in 2015, Johor's gross output value of health services was RM1.55 billion, the outcome of a growth in new health service establishments resulting in a 60.7 per cent increase in gross output value from 2011 (Chapter 5). Johor has had a steady increase in public health clinics, private medical and dental clinics, but a decrease in the development of private hospitals. However, public and private hospital bed capacity has increased between 2008 and 2016.

Map 2.3 illustrates the location of existing healthcare facilities in the state; many in convenient proximity to Singapore. The city-state's market is one that can be tapped given the benefits of the currency exchange; the ability to use Singapore's Medisave Funds in some hospitals; and that service quality can be kept at high standards. With a steady rise in Johor's population over the years, local demand for health services is also increasing, especially with growing urbanization in the state, higher expectations of healthcare and a high concentration of seniors in Iskandar Malaysia.

As an integrated learning hub in Iskandar Malaysia, EduCity (shown in Map 2.9) has contributed to the growth of private higher education in Johor. The Newcastle

University of Medicine Malaysia (NUMed) is already contributing to research and development related to the health services sector. There are a number of other institutes in EduCity that contribute to this growing centre of academia within Iskandar Puteri, such as the University of Reading Malaysia and the Multimedia University, the latter gaining recognition in film and creative industry studies. Beyond providing the physical infrastructure for multiple campuses within a 305-acre integrated learning hub, EduCity Iskandar Sdn Bhd works to market and support the institutes, as well as to create a conducive and holistic environment and community space for the students and staff on its grounds (Chapter 6). EduCity's proximity to both Singapore and Johor Bahru enables it to offer quality education within a refined neighbourhood (for those who choose to live and study or work there) and easy access to the amenities of both Singapore and Johor's capital city. EduCity also enhances opportunities for local youth, having within it government primary and secondary schools that enjoy greater infrastructural support and opportunities.

Johor's position as the southernmost point in Peninsular Malaysia means that its doors are open to vast tourism opportunities for visitors from Singapore and beyond. Johor's tourism earnings have improved recently, with the state ranking third highest of those contributing to national tourism industry incomes in 2016 (Chapter 7), with much of this growth attributed to large-scale, high-end attractions such as the Johor Premium Outlets, Legoland, Puteri Harbour and Desaru Coast. Leveraging on both Singapore and Senai airports' access to the wider region, the state can be the first Malaysian stopover on international tourists' itinerary. Should the state be able to overcome the issues of high congestion and long waiting times at its two main land entry points (the Causeway and the Second Link Bridges), there is great scope to enhance its tourism potential through new sectors such as experiential packages (traditional and cultural tourism and homestays) and halal tourism. The state is also popular as a domestic tourism destination.

Map 2.4 illustrates some of the main tourism attractions available in the state, but there are many smaller local offerings which have yet to be mapped and effectively highlighted. With the development of the Iskandar International Business District (refer to Map 4.6), more high-end hotels and improved infrastructure and other amenities in Johor Bahru, MICE tourism could yield much potential.

POLITICS

The second section of the book sets out the key pillars of the state's political context, in particular through exploring the relationship between Malaysia's key national political parties and the state's historical and political context. Map 3.3 depicts Johor's seat of government, Maps 3.4 and 3.5 cartographically set out the state's parliamentary and state legislative assembly constituencies, and Maps 3.6 to 3.8 lay out the results of the 2018 general election (GE-14) in Johor.

Once an independent nation-state, with its own constitution before the Federation of Malaya came into being, Johor held its own in engagements with colonial powers and was one of the first sultanates to include its people (of all ethnicities) in its drive to develop (Trocki 2007). It was among the first to capitalize on the potential of commodity exports, and used these proceeds to develop its government and social services. By 1893, the Johor government had its own armed forces, coast guard, postal service, as well as network of schools and hospitals (Government Press, 1893).

Despite its distance from the Klang Valley, Johor has played a central role in the country's political life, as two of Malaysia's oldest political parties have close connections to the state. Thus, Chapter 8 traces the history of Johor's support for Barisan Nasional (BN) and its largest component member, the United Malays National Organization (UMNO), and Chapter 9 looks at the local level development of the Malaysian Chinese Association (MCA), itself another BN component.

Notwithstanding these deep connections, Johor also proved a key battlefield during GE-14, and was treated as such by Pakatan Harapan. In Chapters 10 and 11, Wan Saiful Wan Jan examines the launch and growth of two of Malaysia's newest political parties, Parti Pribumi Bersatu Malaysia (PPBM) and Parti Amanah Negara (Amanah) in Johor, and explores the reasons underlying their ability to draw some of the state's Malay voters away from UMNO.

Collectively, the chapters argue that Johor's historical importance as the birthplace of UMNO and the consistent bulwark of Barisan Nasional's support was not sufficient to preserve the status quo. As part of a contiguous belt of states beginning with Johor in the south and extending up until Kedah in the north, BN was swept from power. Yet, in spite of the urban and semi-urban tip towards Pakatan Harapan, much of Malay-majority rural Johor (as shown in Map 3.7) still stands firmly behind UMNO and its ethnocentric focus. For its part, MCA was almost demolished with unprecedented losses across Johor in 2018.

Much of Johor's early development was due to its lineage of dynamic traditional rulers—the sultans. The first map in this section (3.1) was commissioned by one of Johor's most influential sultans, Abu Bakar, in 1893. Taking a full two years to complete, it was done in order to conclusively establish the physical contours of the sultanate. Map 3.4 sets out the grounds of the Istana Besar, Johor's oldest palace, constructed on the orders of Abu Bakar in 1866 (Lim 2011).

Today, although Johor's royalty continually declare their position above politics, the royal family has always loomed large in the state and the country. Hutchinson and Nair (Chapter 12) examine the rise and re-emergence of Sultan Ibrahim Ismail and his family in recent years, exploring continuities between the present and the pre-independence period, as well as the relationship between the royal family and Malaysia's political elite.

SOCIAL AND ENVIRONMENTAL ISSUES

Section 3 of this volume examines the gamut of social and environmental issues facing Johor, ranging from matters related to foreign workers, religion, the political economy of development projects, including that of Johor Bahru and Forest City (shown in Map 4.5), as well as issues related to housing and environmental policies in the state. Weerasena's chapter (Chapter 13) on foreign workers takes the discussion beyond just Johor citizens to the conditions of its many foreign residents who work in sectors such as services, agriculture and manufacturing, examining the issues surrounding their documentation and legality. Even as businesses in Johor (especially in manufacturing) bear the brunt of short-term policy changes on the acceptance or rejection of foreign workers, this study estimates that for every ten documented workers in Johor, there are 3.8 undocumented workers.

Islam is central to Johor's social, cultural, and political life. In Chapter 14, Norshahril Saat examines Johor's approach to religion; referred to as the *kaum tua* tradition, allowing for Sufi rituals that are usually condemned by the growing Salafi-Wahhabi movement. Key to this is Johor's strong royal institution and its ability to retain a Malay character in religious practice, as opposed to the "Arabization" that is often adopted by those leaning towards Salafi-Wahhabi interpretations. Norshahril posits, however, that while some see Sufism as a solution to increasing Islamic radicalism, Johor's religious institution remains strongly traditionalist even as they embrace Sufi customs. The state continues to practise approaches handed down from past religious leaders, some of which are exclusivist and sexist.

Change is a persistent constant in Johor, with infrastructural construction and project development occurring all across the state, as depicted in Map 4.1, which sets out the expansion of built-up areas from 1990 to 2014. As mentioned earlier, in 2018 Johor's construction sector logged the highest growth of all the state's sectors at 9.6 per cent (Department of Statistics, Malaysia 2019). In Chapter 15, Ng examines Johor's urban development processes, through a comparison of federal government-led and state government-led projects in the state's west and central portions, respectively. One of these, the state government-led Ibrahim International Business District is set out in Map 3.4.

Johor's housing policy has also recently been under scrutiny, with reports of 51,459 units of unsold property worth RM36.75 billion as of the first quarter of 2019 (*The Star Online*, 2 July 2019), comprising residential and commercial units, as well as industrial buildings that are either completed or under construction. Many of the unsold residential units are those pitched to the luxury or foreign market. Ng and Lim (Chapter 16) examine the political economy of housing development in Johor and explore the issues surrounding the oversupply and continued construction both within and beyond Iskandar Malaysia in spite of this surplus.

Chapter 17 analyses the case of Forest City, a joint venture that promises a sustainable mixed development on four reclaimed islands rising out of the Tebrau Strait (Map 4.5). The author examines the balance (or otherwise) of federal and state authority in these projects and the manner in which they were developed. The implications of the projects in terms of community and environmental impacts and potential economic benefits are also discussed.

Given the implications of rampant development on the environment, Chapter 18 then examines environmental policy in Johor, outlining the overlaps and loopholes between the federal and state governments in environmental jurisdiction and legislation. Map 4.3 illustrates the vast range of Johor's natural assets, while Map 4.4 indicates the (limited) extent to which those areas are recognized and protected. The chapter outlines how the current structure and Johor's reliance on land transactions for a substantial percentage of the state's economic earnings lend themselves to a highly complex scenario that does not necessarily place the protection of the environment as a priority.

AREAS FOR CONTINUING AND FUTURE RESEARCH

In addressing the guiding questions set out above, this volume has sought to be as comprehensive as possible. Nonetheless, many topics have been omitted, and the rapid pace of change in Johor means that even those subjects covered will require consistent updating. The paragraphs ahead will briefly set out some of the persisting gaps in knowledge and will highlight key trends to follow in the coming years.

With regard to economics, agriculture will continue to be a key motor of the state's economy, and an employer of note. Dating back to the early 1900s, agricultural exports have been a key driver of the state's economy. The state's vast expanses of flat, fertile land have been repeatedly harnessed over the decades, and the reservoirs of managerial talent run deep. Looking forward, planned increases in oil palm acreage and a renewed focus on the agricultural sector since the change in government in May 2018 bode well for the sector. On the positive side, Johor's oil palm industry's unique composition of more smallholders than plantations promises a more equitable distribution of oil palm wealth, and the state's long history of agriculture and reuse of old plantation land negates anti-oil palm conservationists' accusations of deforestation.

The oil and gas industry also offers new promise for the state's manufacturing sector which has been shrinking for the past fifteen years. Much of this attrition has been concentrated in the electrical and electronics sector, which has faced considerable competition from low-cost locations, as well as the relocation of certain subsectors away from Singapore (van Grunsven and Hutchinson 2016). However, despite this new sector's promise, simple proximity to Singapore is not sufficient, and sufficient policy attention needs to be placed on capabilities to attract and retain activities across the oil and gas value chain.

Turning to services, Iskandar Malaysia has been successful in catalysing the development of a number of new sectors, including healthcare and education, as well as deepening the state's tourism assets. Looking forward, the government will need to ensure constant attention to these sectors as they grow, as requirements for follow-up and facilitation increase, requiring agility and responsiveness. The duplication of functions between the state and federal governments in certain areas will need to be addressed (Hutchinson 2015).

Logistics is also a key sector for the state's future development. The gradual accumulation of ports, from Johor Port in 1977 to Port Tanjung Pelepas in 1999 has diversified Johor's logistical capabilities. Not only is the state a gateway from Singapore to Peninsular Malaysia, but it is an increasingly important transhipment hub. Given existing government plans such as the National Physical Plan 3 and the Logistics and Trade Facilitation Masterplan, the role for the Port of Tanjung Pelepas will only increase in future.

With regard to Johor's political context, GE-14 has ushered in a new era. The state merits close study for a number of reasons. First, due to its ethnic composition, as well as its degree of urbanization, the state is a key bell-wether for prevailing national trends. Second, a significant proportion of the rural Malay population has remained steadfast in its loyalty to UMNO, and the party's grassroots network have remained intact. Yet, Johor is also one of the country's centres for Parti Pribumi Bersatu Malaysia, particularly in the state's northwest. Thus, Johor will constitute a vital "window" through which to study evolving national trends.

There are also a number of other political dynamics that warrant monitoring. In 2018, the Johor state government was led by a non-BN administration for the first time since independence. A new crop of state legislative assembly-people has assumed office and beyond the need to master their portfolios, this process has also entailed reaching an understanding with the Johor civil service as well as local government employees. This change-over will require some time, and will certainly influence the degree to which reforms can be implemented successfully.

Second, the constitutional amendment to lower the voting age from twenty-one to eighteen will have a very significant impact on the state's political life. Like much of Malaysia, Johor has a young population and its high level of urbanization means that the state possesses a sizeable digitally literate and youthful voting base with age-specific concerns regarding education, job opportunities and amenities.

Third, the Johor royal family has very clear ideas about the role that it should play in the state, and the prerogatives that the monarchy should have in Malaysia. Regardless of whether Barisan Nasional, Pakatan Rakyat, or any other coalition is in power, the relationship between the royalty and the state's political elite will be fluid.

With regard to Johor's social, cultural and environmental context, there are also many dynamics that will require consistent monitoring.

As highlighted in Chapter 16, housing is a significant issue and one that will take substantial time and resources to address. The mismatch between supply and demand continues. While public housing schemes have been rolled out, if the distribution and access to those homes are not transparent, those who are unable to benefit from the policy will question the ability of the state to provide for their needs. At the same time, if rules are relaxed to encourage more foreign ownership, the cost of living in Johor, already seen to be equivalent to that of Kuala Lumpur, will continue to rise. This will also have adverse impacts on the bottom 40 per cent struggling to survive and afford homes. All of this may have an impact in the 15th General Elections.

Second, the state's growing population and the scale of many of the projects has put pressure on the environment, as highlighted by many of this volume's chapters. In coming years, some of Johor's priorities may conflict with each other, such as the push to develop the oil and gas industry, and the drive to increase tourism attractions and revenues.

While legislative and jurisdictional overlaps between the federal government and Johor state occur in many sectors ranging from tourism to development and environmental policies, the state needs to work within the constraints to establish policies and laws that benefit its citizens. Just as Selangor has implemented stricter legislation for water pollution and Sabah abides by higher standards for oil palm production, Johor too needs to establish its own legislative requirements within the limits of the Ninth Schedule of the Constitution. At the very least, this may prevent further environmental disasters such as those that have occurred in Pasir Gudang in 2019 as a result of industrial pollution and decades of inadequate environmental oversight.

Even as Sultan Ibrahim remains fiercely protective of his state's inclusive and Sufi-based approach to religion, creeping Salafi-Wahhabism in Malaysia and popular acceptance of literal Islam and its Arabized form may threaten the state's existing racial and religious harmony. Even as the concept of Bangsa Johor bridges ethnic gaps, the divisiveness of exclusivist Islam may jeopardize social relations within the state.

JOHOR WITHIN THE SIJORI CROSS-BORDER REGION

This last section will 're-embed' Johor within the SIJORI Cross-Border Region.

Turning directly south, Johor continues to have a deep, multi-levelled, and vital relationship with Singapore. Hundreds of thousands of people cross the border every day from Johor to Singapore to work—including one of the authors of this volume (Rahman). Pipelines carrying raw water south and treated water north also link the two territories. And, Johor-grown produce from poultry to fresh vegetables is a key staple of Singaporean diets.

Yet, while many look to these visible indications of economic interdependence, the links run deeper. Malaysia and Singapore are each other's second most important trading partner. This relationship has remained unchanged over the last decades, in spite of the trade relationships of both countries reconfiguring away from linkages with the United States and Europe towards China (Hutchinson and Bhattacharya 2019).

Looking under the "bonnet" of this trade relationship, it consists of an exceptionally diverse range of products, including goods as diverse as watches, glue, and liquor. Yet, the pillars of the relationship centre on petroleum and related by-products, electronic microcircuits and electrical and electronic components, as well as chemical products (Hutchinson and Bhattacharya 2019). This trade axis between the two countries is a link in a wider chain of global production networks. And, while not all of these activities are located in Johor, the state is the gateway through which many of these production links must pass.

Following the political change in Malaysia in the wake of the 2018 elections, certain projects have been put on hold, and tensions between the two countries—albeit temporary—have surfaced. Many of these, perforce, have an impact on the linkages between Singapore and Johor.

Due in part to the need to contain substantial debt, the incoming Pakatan Harapan administration has re-examined a number of large infrastructure projects. Key among them was the High-Speed Rail, which would have linked Singapore with Kuala Lumpur, and also connected a number of urban centres along the peninsular west coast—including three in Johor. The construction date for this project has been deferred until 2020 (*Marketline*, 7 September 2020). This has also affected the Rapid Transit System, which was slated to link northern Singapore and downtown Johor Bahru and ease traffic congestion by ferrying up to 10,000 passengers per hour in each direction (*Straits Times*, 23 August 2018). At the time of writing, the decision whether to proceed with the construction of the RTS had been postponed until late October 2019 at Malaysia's request (*Channel NewsAsia*, 29 September 2019).

In addition, a number of bilateral issues surfaced in the early months of the Pakatan Harapan administration, including: the price of water supplied by Malaysia to Singapore; the replacement of the Causeway by a "crooked" bridge; and the construction of a third road link between eastern Singapore and Johor (*Straits Times*, 28 October 2018; Liu 2018). Two additional issues surfaced, including the management of south Johor's airspace, which has been managed by Singapore; and the specific delineation of the maritime border between the two countries in the Straits of Johor (*Straits Times*, 14 December 2018).

Thus, despite the deep linkages, trends toward greater and deeper integration are not always constant. Notwithstanding this, the proximity between Malaysia and Singapore, and their symbiotic existence across a number of key axes acts as a strong incentive to make progress across a number of these dimensions.

Johor and the Riau Islands also have a relationship that is independent of Singapore. Deep cultural ties link the two territories, which are rooted in the precolonial period. For example, for many Johor Malays, the Riau Islands are the site of "genuine" Malay culture, as they house heritage sites from the Johor-Riau Sultanate and were the home of pioneers of the Malay language (Hutchinson 2020; Carruthers 2018).

Recent developments have deepened these connections, as different cost structures and a porous border regime have resulted in lively cross-border flows of formal and informal trade, as well as labourers from the Riau Islands and elsewhere in Malaysia seeking work in Johor and contiguous states. Current policy frameworks also heighten flows of tourists in both directions, supplemented by a growing market of mid-priced health services in Johor targeted at Riau Islanders. And, in recent years, inhabitants from the Riau Islands have increasingly sought to study in Johor's public universities (Hutchinson 2020).

The third and final volume in this series, *The Riau Islands: Setting Sail*, will deepen our understanding of the constituent parts and sum total of the three territories by looking at the southernmost component territory of the SIJORI Cross-Border Region.

References

Azhar K. 2018. "GE-14: Johor Launches BN Manifesto, Aims to 'Chase the Lion'". *The Edge Markets*, 14 April 2018. https://www.theedgemarkets.com/article/GE-14-johor-bn-launches-manifesto-aims-%E2%80%9Cchase-lion%E2%80%9D (accessed 1 September 2019).

Carruthers, Andrew. 2018. *Living on the Edge: Being Malays (and Bugis) in the Riau Islands*. Trends in Southeast Asia, no. 12/2018. Singapore: ISEAS – Yusof Ishak Institute.

Channel NewsAsia. 2019. "Singapore, Malaysia Agree to Extend RTS Link Deadline by Another Month: Malaysia's Transport Ministry", 29 September 2019. https://www.channelnewsasia.com/news/singapore/rts-link-singapore-malaysia-agree-extend-deadline-another-month-11953516 (accessed 10 October 2019).

Department of Statistics, Malaysia. 2019. "State Socioeconomic Report 2019". https://www.dosm.gov.my/v1/index.php?r=column/cthemeByCat&cat=102&bul_id=a0c3UGM3MzRHK1N1WGU5T3pQNTB3Zz09&menu_id=TE5CRUZCblh4ZTZMODZIbmk2aWRRQT09 (accessed 10 October 2019).

Edgeprop, The. 2019. "Pinewood Group Pulls Out of Iskandar Malaysia Studio, Says Report". 12 July 2019. https://www.edgeprop.my/content/1561286/pinewood-group-pulls-out-iskandar-malaysia-studios-says-report (accessed 10 October 2019).

Government Press. 1893. *The Singapore and Straits Directory for 1893*. Singapore: Government Press.

Hamid, A.J. 2016. "Bangsa Johor Concept Now More Relevant Than Ever Says Johor Ruler". *New Straits Times*, 30 August 2016. https://www.nst.com.my/news/2016/08/169238/bangsa-johor-concept-now-more-relevant-ever-says-johor-ruler (accessed 1 September 2019).

Hutchinson, Francis E. 2015. *Mirror Images in Different Frames: Johor, the Riau Islands, and Competition for Investment from Singapore*. Singapore: Institute of Southeast Asian Studies.

———. 2020. "In the Shadow of the Gateway: Interactions between Singapore's Hinterlands". *Growth and Change: A Journal of Urban and Regional Policy*.

———, and Pritish Bhattacharya. 2019. "Singapore-Malaysia Economic Relations: Deep Interdependence". *ISEAS Perspective*, no. 2019/2, 11 January 2019.

Khor Yu Leng. 2011. "Iskandar Malaysia: Policy, Progress, and Bottlenecks". RSIS Malaysia Programme, Malaysia Update, Nanyang Technological University, September 2011.

Lim, Patricia. 2011. *Johor: Local History, Local Landscapes, 1855–1957*. Singapore: Straits Times Press.

Liu, Sebastian. 2018. "Deep Waters, Close Quarters: Malaysia and Singapore's Cross-Strait Disputes". *The Diplomat*, 20 December 2018.

Marketline. 2018. "Singapore Defers HRS Project Until 2020 as Malaysia Cites High Costs", 7 September 2018.

Oh Su-Ann, and Reema B. Jagtiani. 2016. "Singaporeans Living in Johor and Batam: Next-Door Transnational Living and Border Anxiety". In *The SIJORI Cross-Border Region: Transnational Politics, Economics, and Culture*, edited by Francis E. Hutchinson and Terence Chong. Singapore: ISEAS – Yusof Ishak Institute.

Star Online. The. 2019. "More than 51,000 units of property in Johor unsold as of Q1 2019." 2 July 2019. www.thestar.com.my/business/business-news/2019/07/02/more-than-51000-units-of-property-in-johor-unsold-as-of-q1-2019 (accessed 2 Sept 2019).

Straits Times. 2018a. "Singapore, Malaysia Look Forward to Bringing RTS Link to Fruition: Ministry of Transport". 23 August 2018.

———. 2018b. "Do Singapore and Johor Need a Third Link?". 28 October 2018.

———. 2018c. "Key Questions on Settling Maritime Disputes". 14 December 2018.

Trocki, Carl. 2012. *Prince of Pirates: the Temenggongs and the Development of Johore and Singapore: 1784–1885.* Singapore: NUS Press.

van Grunsven, Leo, and Francis E. Hutchinson. 2016. "The Evolution of the Electronics Industry in Johor (Malaysia): Strategic Coupling, Adaptiveness, Adaptation, and the Role of Agency". Geoforum 74: 74–87.

Appendix

SOURCES FOR THE JOHOR MAPS

Hans Hortig and Karoline Kostka

The maps presented in this book are based on site-specific field studies, official datasets and online resources compiled by Karoline Kostka and Hans Hortig between October 2018 and April 2019. They are uniquely produced for this publication.

The authors gathered additional insights into the Singapore-Johor-Riau region during their work at the Chair of Architecture of Territory at the Singapore ETH-Centre, Future Cities Laboratory (FCL), from 2013 to 2015. Further discussions and feedback from the editors Francis Hutchinson and Serina Rahman helped to shape the final version of the map sections.

The most significant sources for creating the base map that was used in the various sections are:

- Open Street Map (OSM), Open source geo-referenced information, data retrieved in the period of October 2018 to April 2019.
- Natural Earth, free vector and raster map data, https://www.naturalearthdata.com/downloads/ (accessed December 2018).
- Johor State Structural Plan 2030 (Draft), Draf Gambarajah Utama Rancangan Struktur Negeri Johor 2030, http://geoportal.johor.gov.my/petaawam/rsnj2030 (accessed February 2019).
- University of California San Diego, Institute of Oceanography, "Measured and Estimated Seafloor Topography", https://topex.ucsd.edu/WWW_html/mar_topo.html (accessed November 2018).

The maps in each section are based on these sources, and then respectively adapted by data from the following sources.

Introduction
Malaysia and Johor

Global Administrative Areas. "GADM dataset of Global Administrative Areas". https://gadm.org/index.html (accessed November 2018).

Marineregions. "Maritime Boundaries—Exclusive Economic Zones". http://www.
    marineregions.org/eezmapper.php (accessed January 2019).
Malaysian Maritime Enforcement Agency. "Malaysia Maritime Zone". https://www.
    mmea.gov.my/eng/index.php/en/citizens-and-public/36-malaysian-maritime-zone
    (accessed November 2018).

Section 1: Economics
Mobility and Transport

Open Sea Maps. "Ferry Connections". http://www.openseamap.org/index.php?id=
    openseamap&no_cache=1 (accessed November 2018).

Industries and Trade Regimes

Malaysian Investment Development Authority. "Infrastructure Support". http://www.
    mida.gov.my/home/infrastructure-support/posts/?lg=EN (accessed November
    2018).
Royal Malaysian Customs Department, "Zon Bebas". http://www.customs.gov.my/ms/
    pg/Pages/pg_fz.aspx (accessed November 2018).
Kostka, K., and H. Hortig. Mapping via Google Maps, Wikimapia, Bing Maps, October
    2018 to April 2019.

Healthcare Facilities

Peta Kemudahan Kesihatan. Map of Health Facilities, GeoJohor Land Use Portal, http://
    geoportal.johor.gov.my/en/petaawam/kesihatan (accessed November 2018).
Ormond, M., and C. Lim, C. 2018. *The Private Healthcare Sector in Johor: Trends and Prospects.*
    Trends in Southeast Asia, no. 17/2018. Singapore: ISEAS – Yusof Ishak Institute.

Tourism

Kostka, K., and H. Hortig. Mapping via Google Maps, Wikimapia, Google Earth, October
    2018 to April 2019.
Topalovic, M., H. Hortig, and K. Kostka. 2016. "Sources for the SIJORI Maps". In *The
    SIJORI Cross-Border Region: Transnational Politics, Economics, and Culture*, edited by
    F. Hutchinson and T. Chong, pp. 465–70. Singapore: ISEAS – Yusof Ishak Institute.

Land under Cultivation

Transparent World and Global Forest Watch. "Tree Plantations". http://data.
    globalforestwatch.org/datasets/baae47df61ed4a73a6f54f00cb4207e0_5 (accessed
    November 2018).
ESA Climate Change Initiative. Land Cover—led by UCLouvain. "2015 Global Land
    Cover". http://maps.elie.ucl.ac.be/CCI/viewer/download.php (accessed November
    2018).

Palm Oil Territories

Transparent World and Global Forest Watch. "Palm Oil Plantations". http://data.
    globalforestwatch.org/datasets/baae47df61ed4a73a6f54f00cb4207e0_5 (accessed
    November 2018).

FoodReg, WRI, and Global Forest Watch. "Palm Oil Mills". http://data.globalforestwatch.org/datasets/palm-oil-mills (accessed November 2018).

World Resources Institute. "RSPO Palm Oil Mills". http://datasets.wri.org/dataset/683f1bb1d88e4fe99df38e3e60b1d0d8_6 (accessed November 2018).

Kostka, K., and H. Hortig. Mapping via Google Maps, Wikimapia, Google Earth, October 2018 to April 2019.

Oil and Gas Networks

Open Street Map (OSM). Open source geo-referenced information, data retrieved in January 2019.

Revilla Diez, Javier, Moritz Breul, and Jana Moneke. 2018. "Territorial Complementarities and Competition for Oil and Gas FDI in the SIJORI Growth Triangle". ISEAS Economics Working Papers no. 2018/2. Singapore: ISEAS – Yusof Ishak Institute.

Pengerang Oil and Gas Complex

Open Street Map (OSM). Open source geo-referenced information, data retrieved in January 2019.

Rahman, S. 2018. *Developing Eastern Johor: The Pengerang Integrated Petroleum Complex.* Trends in Southeast Asia, no. 16/2018. Singapore: ISEAS – Yusof Ishak Institute.

Kostka, K., and H. Hortig. Mapping via Google Maps, Wikimapia, Google Earth, February 2019.

EduCity@Iskandar Malaysia Education Hub

Open Street Map (OSM). Open source geo-referenced information, data retrieved in February 2019.

Nusajaya Malaysia. "Educity". https://www.nusajayacity.com/education/educity.html (accessed February 2019).

Kostka, K., and H. Hortig. Mapping via Google Maps, Wikimapia, Google Earth, February 2019.

Section 2: Politics
Johor Territory 1893

Lake, Harry. 1894. "Johore". *The Geographical Journal* 3, no. 4: 298–300.

Istana Besar and the Grand Palace Park

Open Street Map (OSM). Open source geo-referenced information, data retrieved in February 2019.

Kostka, K., and H. Hortig. Mapping via Google Maps, Wikimapia, Google Earth, February 2019.

Kota Iskandar, Nusajaya—Johor's New Governmental Seat

Open Street Map (OSM). Open source geo-referenced information, data retrieved in February 2019.

Nusajaya Malaysia. "Kota Iskandar". https://www.nusajayacity.com/government/gv_kota.html (accessed February 2019).

Kostka, K., and H. Hortig. Mapping via Google Maps, Wikimapia, Google Earth, February 2019.

Parliamentary Constituency Boundaries in Johor
The Star. The 14th General Election. "Johor". https://election.thestar.com.my/johor.html#cN49 (accessed March 2019).

ESRI GIS Server. "Comparing GE13 and GE14 Parliamentary Boundaries". http://tindakmalaysia.maps.arcgis.com/apps/StorytellingSwipe/index.html?appid=bc4d7c82af2e4b618bce487a4ad650e9# (accessed March 2019).

State Legislative Constituencies in Johor
The Star. The 14th General Election. "Johor". https://election.thestar.com.my/johor.html#cN49 (accessed March 2019).

Redelineated Parliamentary Constituencies in Johor (2018)
The Star. The 14th General Election. "Johor". https://election.thestar.com.my/johor.html#cN49 (accessed March 2019).

Election Commission of Malaysia. "Statistics Johor". http://www.spr.gov.my (accessed March 2019).

Section 3: Social and Environmental Issues
Expansion of Built-Up Areas
JRC Earth Observation Data and Processing Platform (JEODPP). "Global Human Settlement Layer". http://cidportal.jrc.ec.europa.eu/ftp/jrc-opendata/GHSL/GHS_BUILT_LDSMT_GLOBE_R2018A/GHS_BUILT_LDSMT_GLOBE_R2018A_3857_30/V2-0/ (accessed February 2019).

Mosques in Johor State
Kostka, K., and H. Hortig. Mapping via Google Maps, Wikimapia, Google Earth, March 2019.

Natural Landscape Elements
Global Forest Watch. "Malaysian Peat Land". http://data.globalforestwatch.org/datasets/8d8462fca7b74b298598490b85d3bd44_9?geometry=85.922%2C0.353%2C133.427%2C8.018 (accessed November 2018).

UN Environment World Conservation Monitoring Centre. "Global Mangroves Watch", 2010. http://data.unep-wcmc.org/datasets/45 (accessed January 2019).

UN Environment World Conservation Monitoring Centre. "Global Distribution of Seagrasses". 2018. http://data.unep-wcmc.org/datasets/7 (accessed January 2019).

Protected Nature
Protected Planet. "World Database on Protected Areas (WDPA)". https://www.protectedplanet.net (accessed January 2019).

Ramsar Site Information Service. "Malaysia". https://rsis.ramsar.org/ris-search/?f%5B0%5D=regionCountry_en_ss%3AAsia&f%5B1%5D=regionCountry_en_ss%3AMalaysia&pagetab=0 (accessed January 2019).

Johor State Structural Plan 2030 (Draft) [*Draf Gambarajah Utama Rancangan Struktur Negeri Johor 2030*]. Johor State Urban and Urban Planning Department. http://www.mpbp. gov.my/sites/default/files/draf_rsnj_2030.pdf (accessed February 2019).

Forest City, Iskandar Malaysia and Country Garden

Open Street Map (OSM). Open source geo-referenced information, data retrieved in March 2019.

Forest City Johor by Country Garden Pacific View (CGPV) in Iskandar Malaysia. http:// forestcityjohor.com (accessed March 2019).

Country Garden Pacificview Sdn Bhd, Malaysia Sales Gallery, Sales Brochure, 2019. http:// forestcityindonesia.id/forestcity-golf-resort/ (accessed March 2019).

Kostka, K., and H. Hortig. Mapping via Google Maps, Wikimapia, Google Earth, March 2019.

Ibrahim International Business District, Johor Bahru

Open Street Map (OSM). Open source geo-referenced information, data retrieved in March 2019.

Menara JLand. "The Future of Johor Bahru City Centre". http://www.menarajland.com. my/about-us/why-menara-jland/ (accessed March 2019).

Kostka, K., and H. Hortig. Mapping via Google Maps, Wikimapia, Google Earth, March 2019.

Conclusion
Johor State

For information on sources, please consult the information detailed for the previous chapters.

INDEX

Note: Page numbers followed by "n" refer to notes.

www.ingramcontent.com/pod-product-compliance
Lightning Source LLC
Chambersburg PA
CBHW060947210326
41598CB00031B/4751